WISDOM

BIBLE

Books by Sanderson Beck:

Living In God's Holy Thoughts (LIGHT)

CONFUCIUS AND SOCRATES: The Teaching of Wisdom

THE WAY TO PEACE: The Great Peacemakers,
Philosophers of Peace and Efforts toward World Peace

LIFE AS A WHOLE: Principles of Education
Based on a Spiritual Philosophy of Love

THE FUTURE AND HOW: A Philosopher's Vision

ETHICS OF CIVILIZATION:

Volume 1: To 30 BC
ANCIENT WISDOM AND FOLLY

Volume 2: 30 BC - 1300
AGE OF BELIEF

These and other writings by Sanderson Beck can be found at:
san.beck.org

WISDOM

BIBLE

From Ancient China, India, Greece, the Middle East, and Rome

Way Power Book (Dao De Jing) by Lao-zi
Two Confucian Classics
Seven *Upanishads*
The Lord's Song (Bhagavad-Gita)
Union Threads (Yoga Sutras) by **Patanjali**
Buddha's First Sermon
Path of Truth (Dhammapada)

Plato's *Alcibiades,*
Defense of Socrates, Crito, **and** *Phaedo*
Epicurus
Wisdom of Solomon
Good Message of Jesus the Christ
Manual of Epictetus
Consolation of Philosophy **by Boethius**
Qur'an **Selections**

English Versions and Translations
by Sanderson Beck

World Peace Communications

Ojai, California

World Peace Communications was founded September 1, 2001 as a non-profit corporation for educational, literary, and charitable purposes.

For more information or to order books or audio CDs, please contact:

World Peace Communications
P. O. Box 495
Ojai, CA 93024
USA
worldpeacebooks.org
san@beck.org

Publishers Cataloging-in-Publication Data

Wisdom Bible: From Ancient China, India, Greece, the Middle East, and Rome / translated by Sanderson Beck;
Includes complete texts of *Way Power Book (Dao De Jing)* by Lao-zi; *Center of Harmony (Zhong Yong)* by Zi-si; *7Upanishads; The Lord's Song (Bhagavad-Gita); Yoga Sutras* by Patanjali; *Path of Truth (Dhammapada); Alcibiades, Defense of Socrates, Crito,* and *Phaedo* by Plato; *Wisdom of Solomon; Good Message of Jesus the Christ; Manual of Epictetus; Consolation of Philosophy* by Boethius.
— 1st ed.
Ojai, California: World Peace Communications, 2002
xxii, 920 p. 22 cm.
ISBN 0-9717823-0-X (hardcover)
ISBN 0-9717823-1-8 (paperback)
1. Wisdom. 2. Sacred Books. 3. Philosophy, Ancient. 4. Wisdom Literature. 5. Philosophy, Asian. I. Beck, Sanderson, 1947-
BL70.W58 2002   291.8'2—dc21   LCCN: 2002101110

Contents

Topics

Introduction

Everyone would like more wisdom and could benefit from becoming wiser, which is supposed to come with age and experience. Yet we can enhance and awaken our inner spiritual wisdom by studying and learning from the wisdom of others. In fact the wise are able to avoid mistakes and find a more direct path to enlightenment by learning from the experiences of others as well as their own. Only fools burn their fingers on a hot stove after having been warned.

Today there seems to be less understanding of wisdom than in the ancient times and with all our modern complexities an even greater need for it. T. S. Eliot lamented, "Where is the wisdom we have lost in knowledge? Where is the knowledge we have lost in information?"

Wisdom transcends the knowledge of science, because it concerns not only knowledge but also spiritual and human values. Knowledge and science alone cannot tell us what to do but only how to do something. All our choices are based on values; our values are what we love. We may conceptualize these as good and bad, loving what we consider good and avoiding what we consider bad. Wisdom helps us to understand what is truly good, giving us the ability to love well.

Ancient philosophy often placed great importance on knowing what is good and how we can learn to choose what is good. The ancients endeavored to discover and realize human virtues in order to avoid the pain and misery which come from vices. They also sought the higher spiritual truths found in the enlightenment which comes from experiencing the divine or the soul or the source of truth and goodness. In many of these texts realization of eternal spiritual reality obviates the fear of death.

The *Wisdom Bible* combines together some of the greatest wisdom ever put in literary form from the great philosophical and religious traditions of ancient China, India, Greece, the Middle East, and Rome. Having examined the recorded history of human civilization I would say that five great philosophical traditions stand out for the depth, power, and spirituality of their knowledge: from the ancient times China, India, Greco-

Roman, and the Middle East, and in recent centuries Europe and America.

This collection brings together under one cover the greatest texts of spiritual wisdom from the four ancient traditions so that their lasting value can contribute to our modern world. They are drawn from the richest period of philosophy and extend from the eighth century BC to 632 CE. Their influence and ideas have continued to this day.

These texts are some of the best writings from Daoism (Taoism), Confucianism, Hinduism, Buddhism, Platonism, Epicureanism, Judaism, Christianity, Stoicism, and Islam. They contain wisdom from such great philosophers and spiritual teachers as Lao-zi, Confucius, Krishna, Buddha, Socrates, Epicurus, Jesus, Epictetus, Boethius, and Muhammad.

In most cases I have included whole texts. I have selected the brief portion by Confucius from the *Da Xue*, usually titled *The Great Learning* and which I call *Higher Education*, and have not included the bulk of the text which is a commentary on the words of Confucius by Zeng-zi. Included complete are seven of the shorter principal *Upanishads*. I did select the first sermon of the Buddha, because I think it encapsulates his main teachings. The selections from Epicurus focus on his ethical teachings. I have taken selections from the *Qur'an*, because it is very long and repetitive.

The main exception is what I call *The Good Message of Jesus the Christ*. This is a synthesis of the four traditional *Gospels* of *Mark, Matthew, Luke,* and *John,* with some highlights from the recently discovered Gnostic *Gospel of Thomas*. Of course the four *Gospels* have been widely available for a long time in the *New Testament*. However, this synthesis combines together the various elements from the four different versions into one continuous narrative so that readers can get the whole story as we have it from these sources in a unified comprehensive account. I hope this will make the life and teachings of Jesus as presented in the *Gospels* even more available to people who seek this wisdom in a single, clear and readable narrative.

The *Wisdom Bible* is not an attempt to replace the *Holy Bible* of the Judeo-Christian tradition, but I do hope that it will supplement that collection of ancient texts with a wider collection of the spiritual wisdom of humanity. The *Wisdom*

Bible does not duplicate the *Bible*, because *The Good Message of Jesus the Christ* synthesis is a new contribution beyond the four *Gospels*, and the one text from the tradition of Judaism, the *Wisdom of Solomon*, is taken from the *Old Testament Apocrypha*, which is not included in most Bibles.

The *Wisdom Bible* also supplements the Great Books of the Western World which were gathered together and published in 1952. In 1976 I asked Mortimer Adler when they were going to put out a collection of the great books of the Eastern world, but he said that it was very far off in the future. The *Wisdom Bible* gathers a few of the greatest texts from Eastern civilization along with some of the best spiritual wisdom of Western culture. The only overlap with the Great Books of the Western World is in Plato. I have included *Defense of Socrates (Apology)*, *Crito*, and *Phaedo* because of their great importance and concise wisdom. In addition I have selected the first *Alcibiades*, which is not included in the Great Books edition of Plato, because I believe it offers a marvelous introduction to Socratic method and wisdom on the important theme of self-knowledge.

As we move into a global age in which we encounter many more peoples and cultures than ever before, I believe that a good liberal education will expose individuals to a wide variety of spiritual teachings such as are contained in this book. As our understanding evolves and our spiritual wisdom awakens, we will begin to see the universal principles of human life which can be found in various traditions.

I believe the age of parochial religion will be passing away as we grow and expand our awareness of universal truths and delight in the diverse cultural history of our world civilization. Instead of the closed and dogmatic attitude that "my religion" is the only one that is any good, we can learn from many different philosophies and wise teachers who have lived and shared their insights. This does not mean that we must give up our own tradition, whether it is the religion we were born into and brought up in by our family or whether it is the set of teachings we have chosen to follow as our personal path of enlightenment or salvation. Nevertheless we can gain knowledge and insight into other cultures and wisdom for our own lives through the study of great teachings.

I believe that in the future more people will be searching
for the truth anywhere they can find it. Tolerance of ideas and
beliefs different from our own is essential to understanding
and respecting the people of other cultures. Without this
tolerance misunderstanding and conflict can cause much
human misery that might be avoided. It seems to me that as we
become more aware and enlightened we become more
universal in our interests and knowledge.

Having studied the great world religions and philosophies
for many years, I am offering here what I consider to be the
most helpful of ancient texts in the development of wisdom. It
is difficult for one person to be an expert in everything; yet
after many lifetimes of spiritual endeavor and thirty-five years
of spiritual searching, work, teaching and writing in this life, I
believe that I can bring an intuitive understanding to the
concepts expressed in these various texts. Thus these English
versions are in some respects unified by my consciousness. I
have attempted to select the best modern English words to
describe the original spiritual meaning of the texts so that
similar concepts from the different books can be understood
more easily.

Nevertheless I must admit to my limitations. I have translated the Plato, Epicurus, the *Wisdom of Solomon*, the *Gospels*,
and Epictetus from the Greek originals, and I translated
Boethius from the Latin. In the case of the *Bhagavad-Gita*, the
edition annotated by Winthrop Sargeant is so detailed in giving
the grammatical form and various meanings of every word
that by using these tools I could almost call my English version
a translation.

In regard to the other texts originally written in ancient
Chinese, Sanskrit and Pali, I compared several English translations and used my intuition to select what I considered to be
the most spiritually accurate words after having read the
various choices of other translators. Having studied and taught
the philosophies of China and India, I understand many of the
terms and concepts. On the Chinese texts I have been assisted
by the useful advice of Ken Tsang, who compared my English
versions to the original Chinese and made useful suggestions.
With the *Upanishads*, Patanjali's *Yoga Sutras*, the Buddha's first

sermon, the *Dhammapada,* and the *Qur'an* I cannot call my work
translations but only English versions.

In all the translations and English versions in this collection
I have attempted to be as accurate to the original as I could be,
trying to find the comparable or nearest English expressions. I
often found that other translations rather freely paraphrased or
summarized what is in the original. I have avoided doing this
even at the risk of making the text seem a little more difficult or
awkward, although I have avoided awkwardness as much as I
could. I want the readers to have the best chance they can to
understand what was originally written even though it might
be a slightly different way of saying something than we would
today.

I often found that if I gave myself enough time to understand the author's use of words that suddenly, as though a
light had come on, the sentence began to make sense as it was
written in a different way than it had been translated by others.
I could only do this, of course, in the translations. Since this is
the first edition of this book, I would be grateful for any corrections or suggestions individuals might like to offer for
improving these versions and the translations.

I have attempted to avoid sexist language as much as
possible but not so much as to change the original meaning of
the texts. Some translators have used sexist language when it is
unnecessary to do so. In referring to God or Spirit I might use
the impersonal pronoun "it" unless the male pronoun was
more clearly indicated in the original. For example, Jesus often
refers to God as Father and himself as the son; I left these this
way. Instead of putting "kingdom" I have used "sovereignty."
In some cases in referring to the earth or other personifications
the female pronoun was used, and of course I translated them
that way. Often in the Chinese texts there is no indication in the
original of gender, number, or even the tense of verbs. Thus
problems could be avoided by using the plural, for example.

Perhaps another major contribution of this *Wisdom Bible* is
the way the words are phrased line by line like free verse so
that they are easier to read and understand. Ancient texts were
often written and copied in this manner, but the only one I
found to be entirely in this form is the *Wisdom of Solomon.* In the
case of that text almost every line of my translation matches a

line of the original. The other example of this is with the poetry
in Boethius' *Consolation of Philosophy*. I do believe that by
putting all of these English versions in "phrase-form," as I call
it, the readers will find them much easier to read and understand. It also makes them easier to read aloud to a congregation.

Almost every text is broken up into numbered divisions.
The only texts that included titles to these sections within the
texts themselves are the *Yoga Sutras*, the *Dhammapada*, and the
Qur'an. I have included those titles in the text also. However, to
help readers find different subjects in the various texts I have
given topical titles to each of the numbered sections in the
Topics listed at the beginning of this book. Other than the very
shortest of these texts the only one that did not have any
numbered divisions in the original is Plato's *Alcibiades*; I have
made numbered divisions for this text myself. Also I have
divided *The Good Message of Jesus the Christ* into one hundred
chapters.

Each text contains a brief introduction to the historical
background and gives biographical facts for contextual understanding. At the end of these introductions I have provided a
few notes to clarify some of the references in the text by using
the chapter numbers, but there are no footnotes nor any
detailed scholarly apparatus.

Perhaps the main purpose of this book is to popularize the
ancient wisdom teachings by making them more available to
people in a single, easy-to-read edition. I believe that the
universality of these teachings can be understood by anyone
who cares to study them. I hope that someday the *Wisdom Bible*
might be found on almost everyone's bedside table if not in
every motel room. I feel that churches and other religious and
social groups could benefit by reading aloud and studying
these texts. Of course the *Wisdom Bible* could also be used as a
source-book for high school or college courses in the human-
ities or philosophy or world religions.

My greatest hope is that more people will apply these
teachings of wisdom, love, and justice in their actions so that
we can all live more in freedom, harmony and peace with each
other on this planet. I trust that the readers will be able to find
their own personal and spiritual interpretations of the meaning

of these writings for themselves and that they will be inspired by them to live a better life for the benefit of everyone.

Introduction to Lao-zi

Very little is known about the author of the *Dao De Jing*, which is attributed to Lao-zi. According to the historian Sima Qian who wrote about 100 BC, Lao-zi lived during the sixth century BC in the state of Chu in China and in the imperial capital Luoyang held the office of *shi* which in ancient China meant a keeper of the archives and sacred books who also may have been skilled in astrology and divination.

Sima Qian wrote how Lao-zi once met with Confucius, whom he criticized for pride and ambition. However, Confucius told his disciples, "I know how birds can fly, how fish can swim, how animals can run. Yet the runner may be trapped; the swimmer may be hooked; and the flyer may be shot by an arrow. But who knows how dragons ride on winds through clouds into heaven? Today I have seen Lao-zi and can compare him only to a dragon."

According to legend, when in old age Lao-zi was leaving Chu, he was stopped by the guardian of the pass into the state of Chin and asked to write down his wisdom. After three days he produced the book of about 5,250 characters known as the *Dao De Jing*. *Dao* means way or path; *de* means virtue or power; and *jing* means book or classic.

Note to:

50: The thirteen organs of life may refer to the nine openings in the body and the four limbs.

Way Power Book
(Dao De Jing)
by Lao-zi

1

The Way that can be described is not the absolute Way;
the name that can be given is not the absolute name.
Nameless it is the source of heaven and earth;
named it is the mother of all things.
  Whoever is desireless, sees the essence of life.
Whoever desires, sees its manifestations.
These two are the same,
but what is produced has different names.
They both may be called the cosmic mystery:
from the cosmic to the mystical
is the door to the essence of all life.

2

When the people of the world all know beauty as beauty,
there arises the recognition of ugliness.
When they all know the good as good,
there arises the recognition of bad.
  Therefore being and non-being produce each other;
difficult and easy complete each other;
long and short contrast each other;
high and low distinguish each other;
sound and voice harmonize with each other;
beginning and end follow each other.
  Therefore the wise manage affairs without interfering
and teach beyond the words.
  All things rise, and they do not turn away from them.
They give them life, but do not take possession of them.
They act, but do not rely on their own ability.
They accomplish, but claim no credit.
Because they claim no credit,
their accomplishment remains with them.

3

Do not exalt the worthy,
so that people will not compete.
Do not value rare treasure,
so that people will not steal.
Do not display objects of desire,
so that people's hearts will not be disturbed.
  Therefore the wise lead by keeping
their hearts pure, their bellies full,
their ambitions weak, and their bones strong,
so that the people may be purified
of their thoughts and desires;
and the cunning ones will not interfere.
By acting without interfering, all may live in peace.

4

The Way is infinite; its use is never exhausted.
It is bottomless, like the fountainhead of all things.
It smoothes its roughness; it unties its tangles.
It softens its light; it calms its turmoil.
Deep and still, ever present.
I do not know its source.
It seems to have existed before the Lord.

5

Nature is not humane.
It treats all things like straw dogs.
The wise are not humane.
They regard people like straw dogs.
  How the universe is like a bellows!
While empty, it is never exhausted.
The more it is worked, the more it produces.
Much talk brings exhaustion.
It is better to keep to the center.

6

The spirit of the valley never dies.
It is called the mystical female.
The door of the mystical female
is the root of heaven and earth.

It seems to be continuously within us.
Use it, and it will never be exhausted.

7
Heaven is eternal, and the earth is very old.
They can be eternal and long lasting,
because they do not exist for themselves,
and for this reason can long endure.
Therefore the wise put themselves last,
but find themselves foremost.
They exclude themselves,
and yet they always remain.
Is it not because they do not live for themselves
that they find themselves fulfilled?

8
The best are like water.
Water benefits all things and does not compete with them.
It flows to the lowest level that people disdain.
In this it comes near to the Way.
In their dwellings, they love the earth.
In their hearts, they love what is profound.
In their friendship, they love humanity.
In their words, they love sincerity.
In government, they love peace.
In business, they love ability.
In their actions, they love timeliness.
It is because they do not compete
that there is no resentment.

9
Stretch a bow to the very full,
and you will wish you had stopped in time.
Temper a sword-edge to its very sharpest,
and the edge will not last long.
When gold and jade fill your hall,
you will not be able to keep them safe.
To be proud with honor and wealth
is to cause one's own downfall.

Withdraw as soon as your work is done.
Such is heaven's way.

10
  Can you embrace the One with your soul,
and never depart from the Way?
Can you concentrate your vital force
to achieve the gentleness of a new-born baby?
Can you cleanse and purify your mystic vision
until it is clear?
Can you love the people and govern the state
without interfering?
Can you play the role of the female
in opening and closing the doors of heaven?
Can you understand all and penetrate all
without using the mind?
  To give birth and to nourish,
to give birth without taking possession,
to act without obligation,
to lead without dominating—
this is mystical power.

11
  Thirty spokes are united around the hub of a wheel,
but the usefulness of the wheel
depends on the space where nothing exists.
Clay is molded into a vessel,
but the usefulness of the vessel
depends on the space where nothing exists.
Doors and windows are cut out of the walls of a house,
and the usefulness of the house
depends on the space where nothing exists.
  Therefore take advantage of what exists,
and use what does not exist.

12
  The five colors blind the eyes;
the five musical tones deafen the ears;
the five flavors dull the taste.
Racing and hunting madden the mind.

Precious goods keep their owners on guard.
Therefore the wise satisfy the inner self
rather than external senses.
They accept the one and reject the other.

13

Good fortune and misfortune cause apprehension.
Regard great trouble as you regard your self.
What is meant by
"Good fortune and misfortune cause apprehension?"
Those with good fortune are apprehensive of their gain.
Those with misfortune are apprehensive of their loss.
What is meant by
"Regard great trouble as you regard your self?"
Great trouble comes from being selfish.
Being selfless, what trouble is there?
Therefore those who value the world as themselves
may be entrusted to govern the world.
Those who love the world as themselves
may be entrusted to care for the world.

14

We look at it, and do not see it; it is invisible.
We listen to it, and do not hear it; it is inaudible.
We touch it, and do not feel it; it is intangible.
These three elude our inquiries, and hence merge into one.
Not by its rising, is it bright,
nor by its sinking, is it dark.
Infinite and eternal, it cannot be defined.
It returns to nothingness.
This is the form of the formless, being in non-being.
It is nebulous and elusive.
Meet it, and you do not see its beginning.
Follow it, and you do not see its end.
Stay with the ancient Way
in order to master what is present.
Knowing the primeval beginning is the essence of the Way.

15

The wise have ancient mystic wisdom
and profound understanding, too deep to comprehend.
Because they can not be comprehended,
they can only be described by analogy:
cautious, like crossing a stream in winter;
alert, like one aware of danger on all sides;
courteous, like a visiting guest;
self-effacing, like ice beginning to melt;
genuine, like a piece of uncarved wood;
open and receptive, like a valley;
freely mixing, like muddy water.

Who can make sense of a muddy world?
Let it be still, and it becomes clear.
Who can remain calm,
and through activity come back to life?
Those who embrace this Way do not over-extend themselves.
Because they do not over-extend themselves,
they do not wear out and are not replaced.

16

Empty yourself of everything.
Maintain a steady serenity.
All things take shape and become active,
but I see them return to their source,
like vegetation that grows and flourishes,
but returns to the root from which it springs.

Returning to the source is serenity;
it is to realize one's destiny.
To realize one's destiny is to know the eternal.
To know the eternal is to be enlightened.
Not to know the eternal
is to act blindly and court disaster.

Whoever knows the eternal is open to everything.
Whoever is open to everything is impartial.
To be impartial is to be universal.
To be universal is to be in accord with heaven.
To be in accord with heaven is to be in accord with the Way.
To be in accord with the Way is to be eternal

and to live free from harm even though the body dies.

17
The best leaders the people barely know.
The next best they love and praise.
The next they fear.
And the next they hate.
Those who lack trust will not be trusted.
Then they resort to promises.
But when they accomplish their task and complete their work,
the people say, "We did it ourselves."

18
When the great Way is forgotten,
the doctrines of humanity and morality arise.
When knowledge and cleverness appear,
there emerges great hypocrisy.
When family relationships are not in harmony,
filial piety and parental love are advocated.
When a country falls into chaos and disorder,
there is praise of loyal patriots.

19
Abandon wisdom and discard cleverness,
and people will benefit a hundredfold.
Abandon humanity and discard morality,
and people will rediscover love and duty.
Abandon skill and discard profit,
and there will be no thieves or robbers.
These three things relate to externals and are inadequate.
People need what they can depend on:
reveal simplicity; embrace the natural;
control selfishness; reduce desires.

20
Abandon memorizing, and vexations end.
How much difference is there between yes and no?
How much difference is there between good and evil?
Is what people fear really to be feared?
How very remote the actual occurrence!

The people of the world make merry
as though at a holiday feast or a spring carnival.
I alone am inactive and desireless,
like a new-born baby who cannot yet smile,
unattached, as though homeless.
   The people of the world possess more than enough.
I alone seem to have lost all.
I must be a fool, so indiscriminate and nebulous.
   Most people seem knowledgeable and bright.
I alone am simple and dull.
   Most people see differences and are sharp.
I alone make no distinctions,
seeming aimless, drifting as the sea,
like the wind blowing about, seemingly without destination.
   People of the world all have a purpose.
I alone seem impractical and out of place.
I am different from others,
and value drawing sustenance from the Mother.

21
   All-embracing power proceeds only through the Way.
What is called the Way is elusive and intangible.
Intangible and elusive, yet within it are thought-images.
Elusive and intangible, yet within it are objects.
Deep and obscure, yet within it is the life-force.
The life-force is very real, and within it is certainty.
   From the ancient times till now
its manifestations have never ceased,
by which we may see the beginning of all things.
How do I know that the beginnings of all things are so?
Through this certainty.

22
   To yield is to preserve unity.
To bend is to become straight.
To empty oneself is to become full.
To wear oneself out is to be renewed.
To have little is to be content.
To have abundance is to be troubled.

Therefore the wise embrace the One
and become examples for the world.
They do not display themselves and are therefore illumined.
They do not justify themselves and are distinguished.
They do not make claims and are therefore given credit.
They do not seek glory and therefore are leaders.

Because they do not compete,
the world cannot compete with them.
Is not the ancient saying true,
"To yield is to preserve unity?"
for true wholeness comes from turning within.

23

Nature says few words.
A whirlwind does not last all morning,
nor does a rainstorm last a whole day.
What causes them? Nature.
If even Nature's utterances do not last long,
how much less should human beings'?
Those who follow the Way are one with the Way.
Those who follow power are one with power.
Those who abandon it are one with abandonment.
Those one with the Way are welcomed by the Way.
Those one with power are welcomed by power.
Those one with abandonment are welcomed by abandonment.
Those who lack trust will not be trusted.

24

Those who stand on tiptoe are not steady.
Those who strain their strides cannot long keep up the pace.
Those who display themselves do not illuminate.
Those who justify themselves are not distinguished.
Those who make claims are not given credit.
Those who seek glory are not leaders.
According to the Way these are like extra food and waste,
which all creatures detest.
Therefore followers of the Way avoid them.

25

There is something mysterious and whole
which existed before heaven and earth,
silent, formless, complete, and never changing.
Living eternally everywhere in perfection,
it is the mother of all things.

I do not know its name; I call it the Way.
If forced to define it, I shall call it supreme.
Supreme means absolute.
Absolute means extending everywhere.
Extending everywhere means returning to itself.

Thus the Way is supreme.
Heaven is supreme.
Earth is supreme.
And the person is supreme.

There are four supremes in the universe,
and the person is one of them.
The person reflects the earth.
The earth reflects heaven.
Heaven reflects the Way.
And the Way reflects its own nature.

26

Gravity is the foundation of levity.
Serenity masters hastiness.
Therefore the wise travel all day
without leaving their baggage.
In the midst of honor and glory
they remain leisurely and calm.

How can a leader of a great country
behave lightheartedly and frivolously?
In frivolity, the foundation is lost.
In hasty action, self-mastery is lost.

27

A good traveler leaves no trace.
A good speaker makes no slips.
A good accountant uses no devices.
A good door needs no bolts to remain shut.

A good fastener needs no rope to hold its bond.
  Therefore the wise are good at helping people,
and consequently no one is rejected.
They are good at saving things,
and consequently nothing is wasted.
This is called using the Light.
  Therefore the good teach the bad,
and the bad are lessons for the good.
Those who neither value the teacher nor care for the lesson
are greatly deluded, though they may be learned.
Such is the essential mystery.

28
  Know the male and keep to the female.
Become the valley of the world.
Being the valley of the world is eternal power
and returning to the innocence of a baby.
  Know the bright and keep to the obscure.
Become an example for the world.
Being an example for the world is eternal power
and returning to the infinite.
  Know glory and keep to humility.
Become the valley of the world.
Being the valley of the world is eternal power
and returning to the natural.
Breaking up the natural makes instruments.
The wise use them and become leaders.
Therefore a leader does not break.

29
  Those who take over the world and act upon it,
I notice, do not succeed.
The world is a sacred vessel, not to be tampered with.
Those who tamper with it, spoil it.
Those who seize it, lose it.
  Some lead, and some follow.
Some blow hot, and some blow cold.
Some are strong, and some are weak.
Some are up, and some are down.

Therefore the wise avoid excess, extravagance, and pride.

30
  Whoever advises a leader according to the Way
opposes conquest by force of arms.
The use of force tends to rebound.
Where armies march, thorns and brambles grow.
Whenever a great army is formed, scarcity and famine follow.
  The skillful achieve their purposes and stop.
They dare not rely on force.
They achieve their purposes, but do not glory in them.
They achieve their purposes, but do not celebrate them.
They achieve their purposes, but do not take pride in them.
They achieve their purposes, but without violence.
  Things reach their prime and then decline.
Violence is contrary to the Way.
Whatever is contrary to the Way will soon perish.

31
  Weapons are tools of destruction hated by people.
Therefore followers of the Way never use them.
In peace leaders favor the creative left.
In war they favor the destructive right.
  Weapons are tools of destruction,
not used by good leaders.
When their use cannot be avoided,
the best policy is calm restraint.
  Even in victory there is no glory.
Those who celebrate victory delight in slaughter.
Those who delight in slaughter
will not be successful leaders.
Fortune is on the left;
Misfortune is on the right.
That is to regard it as a funeral.
The killing of many should be mourned with sorrow.
A victory should be celebrated with funeral ceremonies.

32

The Way is absolute and undefined.
Like natural uncarved wood in simplicity,
even though it is insignificant,
none in the world can overcome it.
If leaders would hold to it,
the whole world would serve them spontaneously.
  Heaven and earth join, and gentle rain falls,
beyond the command of anyone, evenly upon all.
When civilization arose, names began.
With names, one should know when to stop.
Knowing when to stop, frees one from danger.
The Way in the world is like
rivers and streams flowing into the sea.

33

Those who know others are wise.
Those who know themselves are enlightened.
Those who overcome others require force.
Those who overcome themselves need strength.
Those who are content are wealthy.
Those who persevere have will power.
Those who do not lose their center endure.
Those who die but maintain their power live eternally.

34

The great Way flows everywhere, both left and right.
All things derive their life from it,
and it does not turn away from them.
It accomplishes its work, but does not take possession.
It provides for and nourishes everything,
but does not control them.
  Always without desires, it may be considered small.
The destination of all things, yet claiming nothing,
it may be considered great.
Because it never claims greatness,
its greatness is achieved.

35

Hold to the great form, and all the world follows,
following without meeting harm,
in health, peace, and happiness.
Music and delicacies to eat induce travelers to stay.
But the Way is mild to the taste.
Looked at, it is invisible.
Listened to, it is inaudible.
Applied, it is inexhaustible.

36

In order to contract, it is necessary first to expand.
In order to weaken, it is necessary first to strengthen.
In order to reduce, it is necessary first to build up.
In order to receive, it is necessary first to give.
This is called the mystic Light.
The soft and gentle overcome the hard and strong.
As fish stay in the deep water,
so sharp weapons of the state should not be displayed.

37

The Way never interferes,
yet through it everything is done.
If leaders would follow the Way,
the world would be reformed of its own accord.
When reformed and desiring to act,
let them be restrained by what is simply natural.
Undefined simplicity is free of desires.
Being free of desires, it is serene;
and the world finds peace of its own accord.

38

Superior power does not emphasize its power,
and thus is powerful.
Inferior power never forgets its power,
and thus is powerless.
Superior power never interferes nor has an ulterior motive.
Inferior power interferes and has an ulterior motive.
Superior humanity takes action but has no ulterior motive.
Superior morality takes action and has an ulterior motive.

Superior custom takes action, and finding no response,
stretches out arms to force it on them.
　Therefore when the Way is lost, power arises.
When power is lost, humanity arises.
When humanity is lost, morality arises.
When morality is lost, custom arises.
Now custom is a superficial expression
of loyalty and faithfulness, and the beginning of disorder.
　Foreknowledge is the flowering of the Way
and the beginning of folly.
Therefore the mature dwell in the depth, not in the thin,
in the fruit and not in the flowering.
They reject one and accept the other.

39
　The ancients attained oneness.
Heaven attained oneness and became clear.
Earth attained oneness and became stable.
Spirits attained oneness and became divine.
The valleys attained oneness and became fertile.
Creatures attained oneness and lived and grew.
Kings and nobles attained oneness and became leaders.
What made them so is oneness.
　Without clarity, heaven would crack.
Without stability, the earth would quake.
Without divinity, spirits would dissipate.
Without fertility, the valleys would be barren.
Without life and growth, creatures would die off.
Without leadership, kings and nobles would fall.
　Therefore humility is the basis for nobility,
and the low is the basis for the high.
Thus kings and nobles call themselves
orphans, lonely, and unworthy.
Do they not depend upon the common people for support?
Dismantle the parts of a chariot, and there is no chariot.
Rather than tinkle like jade, rumble like rocks.

40
  Returning is the movement of the Way.
Gentleness is the method of the Way.
All things in the world come from being,
and being comes from non-being.

41
  When the wise hear the Way, they practice it diligently.
When the mediocre hear of the Way, they doubt it.
When the foolish hear of the Way, they laugh out loud.
If it were not laughed at, it would not be the Way.
  Therefore it is said,
"The enlightenment of the Way seems like dullness;
progression in the Way seem like regression;
the even path of the Way seems to go up and down."
  Great power appears like a valley.
Great purity appears tarnished.
Great character appears insufficient.
Solid character appears weak.
True integrity appears changeable.
Great space has no corners.
Great ability takes time to mature.
Great music has the subtlest sound.
Great form has no shape.
  The Way is hidden and indescribable.
Yet the Way alone is adept
at providing for all and bringing fulfillment.

42
  The Way produced the One;
the One produced two;
two produced three;
and three produced all things.
  All things have the receptivity of the female
and the activity of the male.
Through union with the life force they blend in harmony.
  People hate being orphaned, lonely, and unworthy.
Yet kings and nobles call themselves such.
Often gain can be a loss, and loss can be a gain.

What others teach, I teach also:
"The violent die a violent death."
I shall make this primary in my teaching.

43

The softest things in the world overcome the hardest.
Non-being penetrates even where there is no space.
Through this I know the value of non-action.
Teaching without words and the value of non-action
are understood by few in the world.

44

Fame or your life, which do you love more?
Life or material wealth, which is more valuable?
Loss or gain, which is worse?
Therefore those who desire most spend most.
Those who hoard most lose most.
Those who are contented are not disappointed.
Those who know when to stop prevent danger.
Thus they can long endure.

45

The greatest perfection seems incomplete,
but its utility is never impaired.
The greatest fullness seems empty,
but its use cannot be exhausted.
What is most direct seems devious.
The greatest skill seems awkward.
The greatest eloquence seems like stuttering.
Movement overcomes cold.
Stillness overcomes heat.
The serene and calm are guides for all.

46

When the world lives in accord with the Way,
horses work on farms.
When the world does not live in accord with the Way,
the cavalry practices on battlefields.
The greatest temptation to crime is desire.
The greatest curse is discontent.

The greatest calamity is greed.
Whoever is content with contentment is always content.

47
  One can know the world without going outside.
One can see the Way of heaven
without looking out the window.
The further one goes the less one knows.
Therefore the wise know without going about,
understand without seeing,
and accomplish without acting.
48
  The pursuit of learning is to increase day by day.
The practice of the Way is to decrease day by day.
Less and less is done until one reaches non-action.
When nothing is done, nothing is left undone.
The world is led by not interfering.
Those who interfere cannot lead the world.

49
  The wise have no mind-set.
They regard the people's minds as their own.
They are good to people who are good.
They are also good to people who are not good.
This is the power of goodness.
They are honest to those who are honest.
They are also honest to those who are dishonest.
This is the power of honesty.
The wise live in the world peacefully and harmoniously.
The people share a common heart,
and the wise treat them as their own children.

50
  Coming into life and going out at death,
the organs of life are thirteen;
the organs of death are thirteen;
and these thirteen make life vulnerable to death.
  Why is this so?
Because they feed life too grossly.

It is said that those who preserve life
walk the earth without fearing tigers and wild buffalo,
and in battle they are not touched by weapons of war.
The wild buffalo's horns find nothing to gore;
the tiger's claws find nothing to tear;
and weapons' points find nothing to pierce.
   Why is this so?
Because they have nothing for death to enter.

51
   The Way produces all things.
Power nourishes them.
Matter gives them physical form.
Environment shapes their abilities.
Therefore all things respect the Way and honor power.
The Way is respected, and power is honored
without anyone's order and always naturally.
   Therefore the Way produces all things,
and power nourishes them,
caring for them and developing them,
sheltering them and comforting them,
nurturing them and protecting them,
producing them but not possessing them,
helping them but not obligating them,
guiding them but not controlling them.
This is mystical power.

52
   The beginning of the universe is the mother of all things.
Those who discover the mother understand the children.
Understanding the children and returning to the mother,
they live always free from harm.
   Close the mouth, shut the doors,
and all of life is without strain.
Open the mouth, meddle with affairs,
and all of life is beyond help.
   Seeing the small is insight;
to stay with the gentle is strength.
Use the Light, return to insight,

and thereby be preserved from harm.
This is practicing the eternal.

53

  Those with even a scrap of sense
walk on the main way and fear only straying from the path.
The main way is smooth and easy,
but people like to be side-tracked.
  While the courts are arrayed in splendor,
the fields are full of weeds,
and the granaries are empty.
Yet some wear embroidered clothes, carry sharp swords,
over-indulge themselves with food and drink,
and have more possessions than they can use.
They are leaders in robbery.
This is not the Way.

54

  What is well established cannot be uprooted.
What is firmly held cannot slip away.
The power of sacrifice continues on
from generation to generation.
  Cultivated in the person, power becomes real.
Cultivated in the family, power becomes abundant.
Cultivated in the community, power endures.
Cultivated in the nation, power flourishes.
Cultivated in the world, power becomes universal.
  Therefore see the person as a person,
the family as a family, the community as a community,
the nation as a nation, and the world as universal.
How do I know that the world is like this?
By this.

55

  Those filled with power are like new-born children.
Poisonous insects will not sting them;
ferocious beasts will not pounce upon them;
predatory birds will not swoop down on them.
Their bones are pliable, their muscles tender,

but their grip is firm.
They have never known the union of man and woman,
but the organ is fully formed,
meaning that the vital essence is strong.
They may cry all day without getting hoarse,
meaning that the harmony is perfect.
To know harmony is to be in accord with the eternal.
To know the eternal is to be enlightened.
  To try to force life is ominous.
To force the vital essence with the mind is violence.
The prime is past, and decay follows,
meaning that it is contrary to the Way.
Whatever is contrary to the Way will soon perish.

56
  Those who know do not speak.
Those who speak do not know.
Close the mouth; shut the doors.
Smooth the sharpness; untie the tangles.
Dim the glare; calm the turmoil.
This is mystical unity.
Those achieving it are detached from friends and enemies,
from benefit and harm, from honor and disgrace.
Therefore they are the most valuable people in the world.

57
  States are governed by justice.
Wars are waged by violations.
The world is mastered by nonintervention.
How do I know this? By this:
the more restrictions there are, the poorer the people;
the more sharp weapons, the more trouble in the state;
the more clever cunning, the more contrivances;
the more rules and regulations, the more thieves and robbers.
  Therefore the wise say,
"Do not interfere, and people transform themselves.
Love peace, and people do what is right.
Do not intervene, and people prosper.
Have no desires, and people live simply."

58

When the government is relaxed, people are happy.
When the government is strict, people are anxious.
Good fortune leans on bad fortune;
bad fortune hides behind good fortune.
Who knows the results of process?
Is there no justice?
When the just become unjust, goodness becomes evil.
People have been deluded for a long time.
Therefore the wise are square but not cornered,
sharp but not cutting, straight but not strained,
brilliant but not dazzling.

59

In leading people and serving heaven
it is best to be frugal.
Being frugal is to be prepared from the start.
Being prepared from the start is to build up power.
By building up power nothing is impossible.
If nothing is impossible, then there are no limits.
Those without limits are capable of leading a country.
Those with maternal leadership can long endure.
This is to be deeply rooted in a firm foundation,
the way of long life and eternal vision.

60

Leading a large country is like cooking a small fish.
When the world is led in accord with the Way,
spirits lose their powers.
It is not that they lose their powers,
but that their powers no longer harm people.
Not only do the spirits not harm people,
but the wise also do not harm people.
Not harming each other, spiritual power grows.

61

A large country is like low land where rivers flow,
a place where everything comes together, the female of all.
The female overcomes the male with tranquillity.
Tranquillity is underneath.

A large country wins over a small country
by placing itself below the small country.
A small country wins over a large country
by placing itself below the large country.
  Thus some win by placing themselves below,
and others win by being below.
A large country wants to protect people,
and a small country wants to join and serve.
Thus both get what they want.
It is best for the large country to place itself below.

62
  The Way is sacred to all things.
It is treasure for the good and sanctuary for the bad.
Fine words can buy honor.
Good deeds can gain respect.
Though there be bad people, why reject them?
  Therefore at the crowning of the emperor
or at the installation of the three ministers,
instead of sending gifts of jade and a team of four horses,
remain still and send the Way.
  Why did the ancients prize this Way?
Did they not say, "Seek, and you will find;
let go, and you will be forgiven."
Therefore the Way is valued by the world.

63
  Act without interfering.
Work without doing.
Taste the tasteless.
Large or small, many or few, repay injury with goodness.
  Handle the difficult while it is still easy.
Handle the big while it is still small.
Difficult tasks begin with what is easy.
Great accomplishments begin with what is small.
  Therefore the wise never strive for the great
and thus achieve greatness.
Rash promises inspire little trust.
Taking things too lightly results in much difficulty.

Thus the wise always confront difficulties
and therefore have no difficulty.

64

  What stays still is easy to hold.
Without omens it is easy to plan.
The brittle is easy to shatter.
The minute is easy to scatter.
Handle things before they appear.
Organize things before there is confusion.
A tree as big as a person's embrace grows from a tiny shoot.
A tower nine stories high begins with a mound of earth.
A journey of a thousand miles begins under one's feet.
  To act is to fail.
To grab is to lose.
Therefore the wise do not act and do not fail.
They do not grab and do not lose.
In handling things people usually fail
when they are about to succeed.
Be as careful at the end as at the beginning,
and there will be no failure.
  Therefore the wise desire to have no desires.
They do not value rare treasures.
They learn what is unknown,
returning to what many have missed
so that all things may be natural without interference.

65

  The ancients who ruled skillfully
did not try to enlighten people but kept them in the dark.
People are hard to lead when they are too clever.
Those who lead with cleverness rob the country.
Those who lead without cleverness bless the country.
Understanding these two is to know the eternal standard.
Knowing the eternal standard is mystical power.
Mystical power is deep and far-reaching,
leading all things to return to perfect harmony.

66

Great rivers and seas are lords of all mountain streams,
because they are good at staying below them.
Therefore they are lords of the streams.
Thus the wise in watching over the people
speak humbly from below the people,
and in leading the people get behind them.
In this way the wise watch over the people
but do not oppress them;
they lead the people but do not block them.
Thus everyone happily goes along without getting tired.
Because they do not compete,
the world cannot compete with them.

67

Everyone says the Way is great and beyond comparison.
Because it is great, it cannot be compared.
If it were compared, it already would have seemed small.
I have three treasures to be maintained and cherished:
the first is love;
the second is frugality;
the third is not pushing oneself ahead of others.
From love comes courage;
from frugality comes generosity;
from not pushing oneself ahead of others comes leadership.
Now courage without love, generosity without frugality,
and leadership by pushing oneself ahead of others are fatal.
For love wins all battles and is the strongest defense.
Heaven gives love to save and protect.

68

The best soldier is not violent.
The best fighter is not angry.
The best winner is not contentious.
The best employer is humble.
This is known as the power of not striving,
as ability in human relations,
and as being in accord with heaven.

69

The strategists say,
"Do not be the aggressor but the defender.
Do not advance an inch, but retreat a foot instead."
This is movement without moving,
stretching the arm without showing it,
confronting enemies with the idea there is no enemy,
holding in the hand no weapons.
No disaster is greater than underestimating the enemy.
Underestimating the enemy will destroy my treasures.
Thus when the battle is joined,
it is the kind who will win.

70

My ideas are easy to understand and easy to practice.
Yet no one understands them or practices them.
My ideas have a source; my actions have a master.
Because people do not understand this, they do not know me.
Since few know me, I am very precious.
Therefore the wise wear coarse clothes
and keep the jewel inside.

71

To know that you do not know is the best.
To think you know when you do not is a disease.
Recognizing this disease as a disease is to be free of it.
The wise are free of disease,
because they recognize the disease as a disease.
Therefore they are free of disease.

72

When people lack a sense of awe,
then something awful will happen.
Do not constrict people's living space.
Do not suppress their livelihoods.
If you do not harass them, they will not harass you.
 Therefore the wise know themselves
but do not display themselves.
They love themselves but do not exalt themselves.
They let go of one and accept the other.

73

Those brave in killing will be killed.
Those brave in not killing will live.
Of these two, one is beneficial, and one is harmful.
Some are not favored by heaven. Who knows why?
Even the wise consider it a difficult question.

The Way of heaven does not strive; yet it wins easily.
It does not speak; yet it gets a good response.
It does not demand; yet all needs are met.
It is not anxious; yet it plans well.
The net of heaven is vast;
its meshes are wide, but nothing slips through.

74

If people are not afraid to die,
then why threaten them with death?
If people were afraid of death,
and lawbreakers could be caught and put to death,
who would dare to do so?
There is the Lord of Death who executes.
Trying to do his job
is like trying to cut wood for the Master Carpenter.
Those who try to cut wood for the Master Carpenter
rarely escape injuring their own hands.

75

People are hungry,
because rulers eat too much tax-grain.
That is why people are starving.

People are hard to govern,
because rulers interfere too much.
That is why they are hard to govern.

People do not care about death,
because rulers demand too much of life.
That is why they do not care about death.
Only those who do not interfere with living
are best at valuing life.

76
When people are born, they are tender and supple.
At death they are stiff and hard.
All things, like plants and trees,
are tender and pliant while alive.
At death they are dried and withered.
Therefore the stiff and hard are companions of death.
The tender and supple are companions of life.
Thus strong arms do not win.
A stiff tree will break.
The hard and strong will fall.
The tender and supple will rise.

77
The Way of heaven is like bending a bow.
The high is lowered; the low is raised.
The excessive is reduced; the deficient is increased.
The Way of heaven takes from those who have too much
and gives to those who do not have enough.
The human way is different.
It takes from those who do not have enough
and gives to those who have too much.
Who has more than enough to give to the world?
Only the person of the Way.
Therefore the wise act but do not rely on their own ability.
They accomplish the task but claim no credit.
They have no desire to seem superior.

78
Nothing in the world is softer and weaker than water.
Yet nothing is better at attacking the hard and strong.
There is no substitute for it.
The weak overcomes the strong; the soft overcomes the hard.
Everyone knows this, but no one puts it into practice.
Therefore the wise say,
"Those who bear the humiliation of the people
are able to minister to them.
Those who take upon themselves the sins of the society
are able to lead the world."

Words of truth seem paradoxical.

79
  Compromising with great hatred surely leaves some hatred.
How can this be considered good?
Therefore the wise keep their part of an agreement
and do not blame the other party.
The good fulfill their obligations;
the bad exact obligations from others.
The Way of heaven is impartial.
It always stays with the good.

80
  In a small country with few people
machines that can work ten or a hundred times faster
are not needed.
People who care about death do not travel far.
Even if there are ships and carriages, no one takes them.
Even if there are armor and weapons, no one displays them.
People return to knotted rope for records.
Food is tasty; clothes are beautiful;
home is comfortable; customs are delightful.
Though neighboring communities see each other
and hear each other's cocks crowing and dogs barking,
they may grow old and die without going there.

81
  True words are not beautiful.
Beautiful words are not truthful.
The good do not argue.
Those who argue are not good.
Those who know are not scholarly.
The scholarly do not know.
  The wise do not hoard.
The more they give to others, the more they have.
The Way of heaven benefits and does not harm.
The Way of the wise accomplishes without striving.

Introduction to Confucius

Kong Fu-zi (Latinized as Confucius) was born in the state of Lu in 551 BC. and died in 479 BC. He was born into a family of impoverished lower aristocrats. Confucius studied the classics and music. According to Mencius he was at one time a keeper of stores and at another in charge of pastures. Confucius had a life-long devotion to learning and summarized his development this way: "At fifteen my mind was set on learning. At thirty my character had been formed. At forty I had no more perplexities. At fifty I knew the will of heaven. At sixty I was at ease with whatever I heard. At seventy I could follow my heart's desire without transgressing moral principles." He thought if he had fifty years to study the *Yi Jing* (*Book of Changes*) he might be free of great mistakes. He married, and had a son and a daughter. Confucius accepted gifts or money for teaching adults and is considered the first professional teacher of higher education in Chinese history.

In his late fifties he left the state of Lu to travel in order to see if he could advise other rulers to put his principles into practice. In the state of Wei Confucius was not afraid to talk with the infamous Nan-zi, a woman who had been involved in incest, adultery, and political intrigue. When the Duke of Wei asked his advice on military strategy, Confucius replied that he had not studied warfare; the next day he left Wei to go to Chen. While he was traveling through Song, Huan Tui, the Song Minister of War, attempted to intercept and assassinate him. Confucius responded calmly, "Heaven produced the virtue that is in me. What do I have to fear from such a one as Huan Tui?" Nevertheless Confucius still accepted Huan Tui's brother Sima Niu as one of his regular students.

Although eager to give political advice, twice he renounced invitations by rulers, because they were involved in civil wars. Confucius was also trapped at Kuang, and for a while thought that his favorite disciple Yen Hui was dead. By the time they got to Chen they were weak and short of supplies. After talking with the Minister of Crime about propriety, Confucius decided to go back to Lu, because his disciples were becoming "headstrong and careless."

Again in Wei he advised the Minister Kong Yu for a while; but when Kong asked Confucius how he should attack a man who had married his daughter but was still seeing a concubine, Confucius advised against it and prepared to leave. When the minister apologized, Confucius was ready to stay; but then messengers from Lu arrived inviting him to return to his own state.

In his last years Confucius worked on editing such classics as the *Book of Odes, Spring and Autumn Annals,* and the *Book of Changes.* The wisdom of Confucius is best known to us through the *Lun-Yu* or *Analects,* which contains numerous conversations of Confucius and his students. The *Analects* was combined with the *Da Xue (Higher Education), Zhong Yong (Center of Harmony),* and the *Book of Mencius* to form the four great Confucian classics studied for centuries by the Chinese for civil service examinations.

The following text is the portion of the *Da Xue* which is supposed to be the words of Confucius handed down by Zeng-zi. The remainder of the *Da Xue,* which is a commentary by Zeng-zi on this text, has not been included in this collection.

Higher Education
(Da Xue)
by Confucius

The Way of higher education is cultivated and practiced by
manifesting the enlightening character of spiritual power,
loving the people,
and holding to the highest good.
  By knowing how to hold to the highest good,
purpose is directed.
When purpose is directed, calm clarity results.
Calm clarity leads to peaceful poise.
Peaceful poise leads to careful deliberation.
Careful deliberation leads to success.
Living things have their roots and branches;
human events have their beginnings and endings.
To understand what is first and last
will lead one near the Way.
  The ancients who wished to manifest
the enlightening character of spiritual power to the world
would first bring order to their government.
Wishing to bring order to their government,
they would first bring harmony to their families.
Wishing to bring harmony to their families,
they would first cultivate their personal lives.
Wishing to cultivate their personal lives,
they would first set their hearts right.
Wishing to set their hearts right,
they would first make their wills sincere.
Wishing to make their wills sincere,
they would first extend their knowledge to the utmost.
Such extension of knowledge comes from investigating things.
  When things are investigated, knowledge is extended.
When knowledge is extended, the will becomes sincere.
When the will is sincere, the heart is set right.
When the heart is right, the personal life is cultivated.
When personal lives are cultivated,
families become harmonious.

When families are harmonious,
government becomes orderly.
And when government is orderly,
there will be peace in the world.

From the Son of Heaven down to the common people,
all must regard cultivation of the personal life as the root.
A disordered root cannot grow into ordered branches.
If what is near is neglected,
how can one take care of what is far away?
This is the root and foundation of knowledge.

Center of Harmony
(Zhong Yong)
by Zi-si

The *Center of Harmony* (*Zhong Yong*), like *Higher Education* (*Da Xue*), also became one of the *Four Books* of Confucianism. According to the historian Sima Qian it was written by Zi-si (492-431 BC), who was the grandson of Confucius and possibly the teacher of Mencius.

Notes to:

6, 17, and 30: Shun was a legendary sage-emperor of the third millennium BC.

18, 19, 20, and 30: King Wen was the founder of the Zhou dynasty and ruled from 1171 to 1122 BC, and King Wu was his successor and ruled from 1121 to 1116 BC; Duke Zhou was King Wu's brother and died in 1094 BC.

20: Lord Ai ruled Lu from 494-465 BC.

28: The Xia dynasty lasted from 2183 to perhaps 1752 BC. The Shang dynasty lasted from 1751 to 1123 BC. The Western Zhou dynasty lasted from 1122 to 770 BC.

29: The three emperors are the founders of the Xia, Shang, and Zhou dynasties.

30: Yao was also a legendary sage-emperor of the third millennium BC.

1

What heaven gives to people is called human nature.
Following our nature is called the Way.
Cultivating the Way is called education.
The Way cannot be separated from us for a moment.
What can be separated is not the Way.
Therefore the best people are careful when they are unseen
and apprehensive when they are unheard.
Nothing is more visible than what is hidden,
and nothing more manifest than what is subtle.
Therefore the best people look into their hearts
when they are alone.
   Before the feelings of pleasure, anger,
sorrow, and joy are aroused,
one is in what is called the center.
When these feelings are aroused,
and they each attain due measure and degree,
it is called harmony.
The center is the supreme foundation of the universe,
and harmony is its universal expression.
When the center and harmony are realized fully,
then order and happiness abound
throughout heaven and earth,
and all things are nourished and flourish.

2

   Confucius said,
"The best people live in the center of harmony.
The worst people act contrary to the center of harmony.
The best people live harmoniously,
because they always maintain the center.
The worst people act contrary to harmony,
because they are not aware of the center."

3

   Confucius said, "The center of harmony is perfect;
for a long time few people have been able to follow it."

4

Confucius said, "I know why the Way is not pursued.
The smart ones go beyond it,
and the stupid ones do not come up to it.
I know why the Way is not understood.
The worthy go beyond it,
and the unworthy do not come up to it.
There is nobody who does not eat and drink,
but there are few who really appreciate flavors."

5

Confucius said, "Alas, how the Way is not being pursued!"

6

Confucius said, "Shun was indeed a man of great wisdom!
He loved to question people
and examine their simple answers.
He passed over the bad in them and displayed the good.
He shunned their extremes, found the center,
and applied it in his dealing with the people.
In this way he became Shun."

7

Confucius said, "Everyone says, 'I am wise,'
but they are driven forward into nets,
caught in traps or pitfalls,
and they do not know how to escape.
Everyone says, 'I am wise,'
but choosing to pursue the center
they are not able to keep to it for a full month."

8

Confucius said,
"Hui was a man who chose to pursue the center,
and when he found something that was good,
he embraced it as if wearing it on his breast,
and he never lost it."

9

Confucius said,
"The world, states, and families can be put in order.
honors and rewards can be declined,
bare, naked weapons can be trampled upon,
but still the center of harmony is not being followed."

10

Zi-lu asked about energy.
Confucius said, "Do you mean the energy of the south,
the energy of the north,
or the energy you should cultivate yourself?
To be kind and gentle in teaching others
and not to revenge unreasonable conduct
is the energy of southern people.
The best people practice it.
To lie under arms and meet death without regret
is the energy of northern people.
The brave people practice it.
Thus the best people maintain harmony and strength.
How firm are they in their energy!
They stand in the middle without leaning to either side.
How firm are they in their energy!
When the Way prevails in the government
they do not change their private life.
How firm are they in their energy!
When the Way does not prevail in the government
they do not change even though they may die.
How firm are they in their energy!"

11

Confucius said,
"There are people who seek mysteries and practice wonders
in order to be remembered in future ages,
but this is what I will not do.
There are good people who proceed in accord with the Way,
but abandon it when they have gone half-way.
However, I could never give it up.
There are good people in accord with the center of harmony
who retire from the world,

are unknown to their age, and have no regret.
It is only the wise who can do this.

12
"The Way of the best people functions everywhere,
yet it is hidden.
Men and women of simple intelligence
can find this knowledge.
Yet in its ultimate extent,
even the wise do not know it all.
Men and women of simple intelligence can practice it.
Yet in its ultimate extent,
even the wise do not practice it all.
Great as heaven and earth are,
people still find something in them to criticize.
Thus when the best people speak of the greatness of the Way,
nothing in the world could contain it.
When they speak of its minuteness,
nothing in the world could split it.
The Book of Odes says,

> 'The hawk flies up to heaven;
> The fish dive down to the deep.'

This means it is clearly seen above and below.
The Way of the best people finds its simple beginnings
in the relationship between a man and a woman,
but in its ultimate extent
it can be clearly seen illuminating heaven and earth."

13
Confucius said, "The Way is not far from people.
If a person pursues a way which removes him from people,
this course cannot be considered the Way.
The Book of Odes says,

> 'When hewing an ax handle,
> Hew an ax handle;
> The pattern is not far off.'

If we grasp an ax handle to hew another ax handle,
and look skeptically from one to the other,
we may still think the pattern is far away.
Thus the best people govern people

according to human nature,
and as soon as they become correct, they stop.
Conscientiousness and reciprocity are not far from the Way.
What you do not wish others to do to you, do not do to them.
  "There are four things in the Way of the best people,
none of which have I as yet attained.
To serve my father as I would have my son serve me:
that I have not attained.
To serve my ruler as I would have my minister serve me:
that I have not attained.
To serve my older brother
as I would have my younger brother serve me:
that I have not attained.
To be first to treat friends as I would have them treat me:
that I have not attained.
Earnest in practicing the virtues in everyday life
and in being careful in ordinary conversation,
when there is excess
they do not allow themselves license.
Their words correspond to their actions,
and their actions correspond to their words.
Are not the best people genuine?"

14
  The best people do what is proper in their position;
they do not desire to go beyond this.
In a position of wealth and honor
they do what is proper to a position of wealth and honor.
In a poor and humble position
they do what is proper to a poor and humble position.
Situated among barbarous tribes
they do what is proper among barbarous tribes.
In a position of difficulty and danger
they do what is proper in difficulty and danger.
There is no situation in which they are not themselves.
In a high position
they do not treat their inferiors with contempt.
In a low position
they do not court the favor of their superiors.
They correct themselves and seek nothing from others.

They do not complain and do not resent heaven or people.
Thus the best people live peacefully and calmly,
waiting for their destiny,
while the worst people walk in dangerous paths,
hoping for good luck.

Confucius said, "In archery we have something
like the Way of the best people.
When archers miss the center of the target, they turn around
and seek for the cause of their failure in themselves."

15

The Way of the best people is like a long journey.
We must begin with what is near.
It is like ascending a height;
we must begin from the lower ground.
The Book of Odes says,

"Happy union with wife and children
Is like the music of lutes and harps.
When brothers live in concord and peace,
The harmony is sweet and delightful.
Let your family live in concord
And enjoy your wife and children."

Confucius said, "How happy will their parents be!"

16

Confucius said, "How abundantly do spiritual beings
display the power that belongs to them!
We look for them, but do not see them.
We listen to them, but do not hear them.
They are in all things, and there is nothing without them.
They cause all people in the world
to fast and purify themselves
and put on robes in order to sacrifice to them.
Like the rush of overflowing water
they seem to be above and on the left and right.
The Book of Odes says,

'The approaches of the spirits
Cannot be surmised.
Yet they cannot be disregarded.'

Such are the manifestations of the subtle.
Such is the impossibility of hiding the real."

17
Confucius said, "How great was the filial piety of Shun!
In virtue he was a sage;
in honor he was the Son of Heaven;
and in wealth he owned all within the four seas.
Temple sacrifices were made to him,
and his descendants preserved the sacrifices to him.
Thus whoever has great virtue will certainly attain
high position, great wealth, fame, and lasting life.
For heaven in the production of things
is sure to be bountiful to them according to their qualities.
Thus the tree that is well taken care of is nourished,
while that which is about to fall is overthrown.
The Book of Odes says,

'The admirable, amiable prince
Displayed conspicuously his excellent virtue.
He put his people and his officers in concord,
And he received his compensation from heaven.
It protected him, assisted him, and appointed him king.
Heaven gave its blessings to him again and again.'

Therefore whoever has great virtue
will certainly receive a mandate from heaven."

18
Confucius said, "Only King Wen was without sorrow.
He had King Ji for a father and King Wu for a son.
His father laid the foundation, and his son carried it on.
King Wu continued the enterprise
of King Tai, King Ji, and King Wen.
Once he buckled on his armor, the world became his.
He did not lose his personal reputation in the world.
In honor he was the Son of Heaven;
and in wealth he owned all within the four seas.
Temple sacrifices were made to him,
and his descendants preserved the sacrifices to him.

"King Wu received heaven's mandate to rule in his old age.
Duke Zhou completed the virtuous course

of King Wen and King Wu.
He carried up the title of king to Tai and Ji,
and sacrificed to all the former dukes with royal ceremonies.
He extended this rule
to the princes, officers, and common people.
If the father was a great officer
and the son a minor officer,
when the father died,
he was buried with the rite of a great officer,
but afterward sacrificed to with the rite of a minor officer.
If the father was a minor officer
and the son a great officer,
then the father was buried with the rite of a minor officer,
but afterward sacrificed to with the rite of a great officer.
The rule for one year of mourning for relatives
was extended to include great officers,
but the rule for three years of mourning
was extended to include the Son of Heaven.
In the mourning for a father or a mother
there was no difference for the noble or the commoner.
The practice was the same."

19
  Confucius said, "How influential
was the filial piety of King Wu and Duke Zhou!
  "Filial piety is
the skillful carrying out of the wishes of forefathers,
and the skillful carrying forward of their undertakings.
  "In spring and autumn they
repaired their ancestral temple,
displayed their ancestral vessels,
exhibited the ancestral robes,
and presented the appropriate offerings of the season.
By means of the ritual of the ancestral temple
they distinguished the descent of the royal kindred.
By ordering those present according to their rank,
they distinguished the more noble and the less.
By the arrangement of the services
they distinguished the talented and worthy.
In the pledging ritual the inferiors

presented the cup to their superiors
so that the humble would have something to do.
At the feast honored places were given
to people with white hair
so that the differences in age were observed.

"To occupy places of their forefathers,
to practice their rites,
to perform their music,
to reverence those whom they honored,
to love those who are dear to them,
to serve the dead as they were served while alive,
and to serve the departed
as they were served while still with us:
this is the height of filial piety.

"By the ceremonies of sacrifices to heaven and earth
they served the Most High Lord,
and by the ceremonies of the ancestral temple
they served the ancestors.
Whoever understands the ceremonies
of sacrifices to heaven and earth
and the meaning of the seasonal sacrifices to the ancestors
will govern a kingdom as easily as looking at one's palm."

20
Lord Ai of Lu asked about the way to govern.
Confucius said, "The government of King Wen and King Wu
is revealed in the historical records.
With their kind of people government will flourish,
but without their kind of people government decays and dies.

"With the right people government is prompt,
just as in the right soil vegetation grows rapidly.
Indeed, good government is like a fast-growing plant.
Therefore the conduct of government depends on the people.
The right people are obtained by the ruler's character.
The character is cultivated by following the Way.
Following the Way is cultivated by goodness.

"Goodness is human,
and the greatest expression of it is in loving relations.
Justice is the principle of setting things right and proper,

and the greatest expression of it is in honoring the worthy.
The relative love to relations
and the degrees of honoring the worthy
give rise to the rules of propriety.

"If those in inferior positions
do not have the confidence of their superiors,
they will not be able to govern the people.
Thus rulers must not fail to cultivate their personal lives.
Wishing to cultivate their personal lives,
they must not fail to serve their parents.
Wishing to serve their parents,
they must not fail to know people.
Wishing to know people,
they must not fail to know heaven.

"The duties of universal obligation are five,
and the virtues by which they are practiced are three.
The duties are between the ruler and the minister,
between father and son, between husband and wife,
between older and younger brothers,
and those in the intercourse between friends.
These are the five duties of universal obligation.

"Wisdom, love, and courage
are the three universal virtues.
The way by which they are practiced is one.

"Some are born knowing these things;
some learn them through study;
some learn them through hard experience;
but when the knowledge is acquired,
it comes to the same thing.

"Some practice them naturally and easily;
some practice them for their own advantage;
some practice them with effort and difficulty;
but when the achievement is made,
it comes to the same thing."

Confucius said, "Love of learning is akin to wisdom.
To practice vigorously is akin to goodness.
A sense of shame is akin to courage.
Those who know these three things
know how to cultivate their personal lives.

Knowing how to cultivate their personal lives
they know how to govern other people.
And knowing how to govern other people
they know how to govern the world, its states, and families.

   "To govern the world, its states, and families,
there are nine rules:
cultivating the personal life,
honoring the worthy,
loving the relatives,
respecting the great ministers,
identifying oneself with the welfare of all the officers,
treating the common people as one's own children,
promoting all the useful arts and crafts,
being kind to strangers from far countries,
and taking interest in the princes of the world.

   "If rulers cultivate their personal lives,
the Way will be established.
If they honor the worthy, mistakes will not occur.
If they love their relatives,
their uncles and brothers will not grumble.
If they respect the great ministers,
they will not be deceived.
If they identify themselves
with the welfare of all the officers,
then the officers will gratefully return this courtesy.
If they treat the common people as their own children,
then they will exhort one another to do good.
If they promote all the useful arts and crafts,
then there will be sufficient wealth and resources.
If they are kind to strangers from far countries,
then people from all over the world will flock to them.
And if they take an interest in the princes of the world,
then the world will respect their authority.

   "By cleanliness, purification, dressing correctly,
and not doing anything contrary to the rules of propriety—
this is the way to cultivate the personal life.

   "By discarding flatterers,
keeping away from seductive women,
regarding riches lightly, and honoring virtue—

this is the way to encourage the worthy.

"By giving them honorable positions
and ample compensation,
and sharing their likes and dislikes—
this is the way to encourage love among relatives.

"By allowing them many officers
to carry out their functions—
this is the way to encourage the great ministers.

"By dealing with them loyally and faithfully
with generous compensation—
this is the way to encourage the officers.

"By requiring their services only at the proper time
and taxing them lightly—
this is the way to encourage the common people.

"By inspecting them daily and examining them monthly
and rewarding them according to their workmanship—
this is the way to encourage the various artisans.

"By welcoming them when they come
and escorting them when they go
and commending the good among them
while showing compassion to the incompetent—
this is the way to be kind to strangers from far countries.

"By restoring broken family lines,
reviving extinguished states,
bringing order to chaotic states,
supporting states in danger,
having set times for receptions at court,
and presenting generous gifts
after expecting little when they come—
this is the way
to take an interest in the princes of the world.

"To govern the world, its states, and families,
there are nine rules,
but the way by which they are practiced is one.
In all matters success depends on preparation;
without preparation there will be failure.

"If what is to be said is planned well,
there will be no stumbling.

"If the business to be done is planned well,
there will be no difficulty.

"If the action to be taken is planned well,
there will be no trouble.

"If the Way to be pursued is planned well,
there will be no limits.

"If those in inferior positions
do not have the confidence of their superiors,
they will not be able to govern the people.

"There is a way to gain the confidence of the superiors:
if you are not trusted by your friends,
you will not gain the confidence of your superiors.

"There is a way to be trusted by your friends:
if you are not obedient to your parents,
you will not be trusted by your friends.

"There is a way to obey your parents:
if you examine yourself and find yourself to be insincere,
you will not be obedient to your parents.

"There is a way to be sincere with yourself:
if you do not understand what is good,
you will not be sincere with yourself.

"Sincerity is the Way of heaven.
To think how to be sincere is the way of humans.
Those who are sincere hit on what is right without effort
and understand without thinking.
They are naturally and easily in harmony with the Way.
Such people are wise.
Those who think how to be sincere
choose the good and hold to it.

"Study the way to be sincere extensively,
inquire into it accurately, think it over carefully,
clearly discern it, and practice it thoroughly.
When there is anything not yet studied,
or studied, but not yet understood, do not give up.
When there is any question not yet asked,
or asked, but its answer not yet known, do not give up.
When there is anything not yet thought over,
or thought over, but not yet assimilated, do not give up.
When there is anything not yet discerned,

or discerned, but not clearly, do not give up.
When there is anything not yet practiced,
or practiced, but not thoroughly, do not give up.
If another succeeded by one effort, use a hundred efforts.
If another succeeded by ten efforts, use a thousand efforts.
Let people really follow this course,
and though stupid, they will surely become intelligent,
and though weak, they will surely become strong."

21

Enlightenment resulting from sincerity is ascribed to nature.
Sincerity resulting from enlightenment is ascribed to education.
Given sincerity, there will be enlightenment,
and given enlightenment, there will be sincerity.

22

Only those who are absolutely sincere
can fully develop their nature.
By fully developing their nature
they can fully develop the nature of others.
By fully developing the nature of others
they can fully develop the nature of things.
Those who fully develop the nature of things
are worthy to assist in the transforming
and nourishing process of heaven and earth.
Those worthy to assist in the transforming
and nourishing process of heaven and earth
can thus form a trinity with heaven and earth.

23

Next in order are those
who cultivate themselves to the utmost.
From this they can attain to the possession of sincerity.
As there is sincerity, there will be its expression.
As it is expressed, it will become manifest.
As it becomes manifest, it will be full of light.
As it is full of light, it will move others.
As it moves others, it changes them.
As it changes them, they are transformed.
Only those who are absolutely sincere can transform others.

24

It is characteristic of absolute sincerity
to be able to foreknow.
When a nation or family is about to flourish,
there are sure to be good omens.
When a nation or family is about to perish,
there are sure to be bad omens.
These omens are revealed in divination
and in the movement of the body's four limbs.
When disaster or blessing is about to come,
it can surely be known ahead if it is evil.
Therefore whoever has absolute sincerity is like a spirit.

25

Sincerity means the completion of self,
and the Way of it is self-directing.
Sincerity is the end and beginning of things.
Without sincerity there would be nothing.
Therefore the best people value sincerity above everything.
Sincerity is not only the completion of one's own self,
it is that by which all things are completed.
The completion of the self means goodness.
The completion of all things means wisdom.
These are the virtues of our being,
and the Way in which the internal and external are united.
Thus whenever they are employed, everything done is right.

26

Thus absolute sincerity is ceaseless.
Being ceaseless, it is eternal.
Being eternal, it is manifest.
Being manifest, it is infinite.
Being infinite, it is extensive and deep.
Being extensive and deep, it is transcendental and brilliant.
Because it is extensive and deep, it contains all things.
Because it is transcendental and brilliant,
it illuminates all things.
Because it is infinite and eternal, it perfects all things.
In being extensive and deep, it is like earth.
In being transcendental and brilliant, it is like heaven.

In being infinite and eternal, it is unlimited.
Such being its nature,
it manifests itself without being seen,
produces changes without motion,
and accomplishes its ends without acting.
   The Way of heaven and earth
may be described in one sentence:
They are without doubleness
and produce things in a way that is unfathomable.
The Way of heaven and earth is extensive, deep,
transcendental, brilliant, infinite, and eternal.
   The heaven now before us is only this bright shining mass,
but when viewed in its immeasurable extent,
the sun, moon, stars, and constellations are suspended in it,
and all things are illuminated by it.
   The earth before us is only a handful of soil,
but in its breadth and depth,
it sustains the great mountains without feeling their weight,
and contains the rivers and seas without letting them leak;
everything is supported by it.
   The mountain before us is only a pebble,
but in all the vastness of its size,
grass and trees grow upon it,
birds and beasts dwell on it,
and precious minerals are found in it.
   The waters before us are only a spoonful of liquid,
but in all their unfathomable depth,
the monsters, dragons, fish, and turtles
are produced in them,
and many useful articles abound in them.
   The Book of Odes says,
   "The destiny of heaven,
   How beautiful and unceasing!"
That is to say, this is what makes heaven to be heaven.
   "How bright it is,
   The purity of King Wen's virtue!"
That is to say, this is what makes King Wen what he was.
Purity is also unceasing.

27
How great is the Way of the wise!
Overflowing, it produces and nourishes all things
and rises up to the height of heaven.
How magnificent it is!
It embraces the three hundred rules of ceremony
and the three thousand rules of conduct.
It waits for the proper person to put it into practice.
Thus it is said, "Unless there is perfect virtue
the perfect Way cannot be realized."
   Therefore the best people honor their virtuous nature
and apply themselves to study and inquiry.
They broaden and deepen their knowledge,
and pursue the refined and subtle.
While seeking to attain the highest and most brilliant,
they maintain the center of harmony.
They make the old come alive again to find out what is new.
They are devoted and honest
and respect the rules of propriety.
Thus when occupying a high position, they are not proud,
and when serving in a low position,
they are not insubordinate.
When the Way prevails in the country,
their words bring prosperity.
When the Way does not prevail in the country,
their silence assures their preservation.
The Book of Odes says,
   "Intelligent and wise,
   They protect themselves."
This is what it means.

28
Confucius said,
"To be stupid and want to use one's own judgment,
to be in a low position and want to give orders,
to live in the present age
and go back to the ways of the past—
people like this bring calamity on themselves.
Only the Son of Heaven is to decide on ceremonies,
set the weights and measures,

and determine the written characters.
In the world today, carriage wheels are the same size;
all writing is with the same characters;
and conduct is governed by the same principles.
One may occupy the throne;
but if he does not have the proper virtue,
he dare not institute ceremonies or music.
One may have the proper virtue;
but if he does not occupy the throne,
he also dare not institute ceremonies or music."

　Confucius said,
"I could describe the ceremonies of the Xia dynasty,
but what remains in the state of Qi
does not provide sufficient evidence.
I have studied the ceremonies of the Shang dynasty,
and in the state of Song they are still preserved.
I have studied the ceremonies of the Zhou dynasty,
which are in use today. I follow the Zhou."

29

　If whoever attains to the sovereignty of the world
has these three important things, there will be few mistakes.
However excellent may have been the regulations
of former times, there is no evidence for them.
Without evidence, they cannot command credence,
and not being credited, the people would not follow them.
　However excellent might be the regulations
made by one in a low position, his position is not honored.
Not being honored, he cannot command credence,
and not being credited, the people would not follow them.
　Thus the Way of good rulers
is rooted in their personal lives
and is evidenced by the cooperation of the people.
It is examined according to the three emperors
and found to be without error.
It is applied before heaven and earth
and found to be without contradiction in its operation.
It is presented before spiritual beings
without question or fear,

and can wait a hundred generations for a sage
without doubting.
  Being presented before spiritual beings
without question or fear
shows that they know heaven.
Waiting a hundred generations for a sage without doubting
shows that they know people.
  Thus every move such rulers make
is an example to the world for ages;
every action becomes a guide to the world for ages;
those who are far away look longingly to them,
and those who are near never tire of them.
The Book of Odes says,

"There they do not dislike them;
Here they do not get tired of them.
From day to day and night to night
They will perpetuate their praise."

There never has been a ruler
who did not fit this description
and yet could obtain early renown throughout the world.

30
  Confucius transmitted the ancient doctrines
of Yao and Shun as if they had been his ancestors,
and he adopted and perfected the systems of Wen and Wu.
These harmonized with the divine order
governing the revolutions of the seasons in heaven above,
and with the principles governing land and water below.
  They may be compared
to earth in its supporting and containing,
and to heaven in its overshadowing and embracing all things.
They may be compared to the four seasons in their succession,
and to the sun and the moon in their alternate shining.
  All things are nourished together
without injuring one another.
Their courses are pursued without conflict.
The lesser energies flow continuously like river currents,
while the greater energies silently and deeply transform.
This is what makes heaven and earth so great.

31

It is only the perfectly wise in the world who have
the quick apprehension, intelligence, insight, and wisdom
to be able to rule all people;
the greatness, generosity, kindness, and tender heart
to be able to embrace all people;
the energy, strength, steadiness, and resolution
to be able to maintain everything;
the balance, seriousness, centeredness, and correctness
to be able to command reverence;
the order, refinement, concentration, and penetration
to be able to exercise discernment.

All-embracing and vast, deep and active as a fountain,
these virtues always spring forth from them.
All-embracing and vast like heaven
and deep and active as a fountain like an abyss,
they appear, and all people respect them;
they speak, and all people believe them;
they act, and all people are pleased with them.

As a result their fame spreads out over China
and extends to the barbarous tribes.
Wherever ships and carriages travel,
wherever the work of people penetrates,
wherever the heavens overshadow and the earth sustains,
wherever the sun and moon shine,
and wherever frosts and dews fall,
all who have blood and breath honor and love them.
Thus it is said, "They are the counterparts of heaven."

32

Only those who are absolutely sincere
can adjust the great relations of mankind,
establish the great foundations of humanity,
and know the transforming
and nourishing process of heaven and earth.
Do they depend on anything except themselves?

How devoted and sincere is their goodness!
How profound and unfathomable is their depth!
How vast and great is their divinity!

Who can know them except those who have
quick apprehension, intelligence, insight, wisdom,
and understanding of heavenly virtue?

33
 The Book of Odes says,
  "Over her embroidered robe
  She wore a plain and simple dress,"
implying she disliked to display its elegance.

 Thus the way of the best people is hidden,
while it becomes more illustrious every day;
whereas the way of the worst people is conspicuous,
but it gradually goes to ruin.

 The best people appear plain,
but people do not get tired of them.
They are simple, but gracefully accomplish.
They are easy, yet thorough.
They know what is distant begins with what is near.
They know where the winds come from.
And they know how the subtle becomes manifest.
Such people enter into virtue.

 The Book of Odes says,
  "Although the fish dive down to the bottom,
  It is still quite clearly seen."
Therefore the best people examine their own hearts
that there may be nothing wrong there,
and that they may have no cause to be dissatisfied.
The best people are better at observing things
other people do not see.

 The Book of Odes says,
  "While the ceiling looks down upon you,
  Be free from shame in your own house
  As though exposed to the light of heaven."
Therefore the best people are reverent without moving
and truthful without speaking.

 The Book of Odes says,
  "Throughout the ritual not a word is spoken.
  In the presence there is not the slightest contention."

Therefore the best people do not use rewards,
and people are encouraged to be good.
They do not show anger,
and people are awed more than by hatchets and axes.
The Book of Odes says,
>"What needs no display is virtue;
>yet all the princes emulate it."

Therefore when the best people are sincere and reverent,
the world will be in order and at peace.
The Book of Odes says,
>"I cherish your brilliant virtue,
>Which makes no great noise or show."

Confucius said, "Among the means to regenerate mankind,
noise and show are of little importance."
The Book of Odes says,
>"His virtue is as light as a hair."

Still, a hair has weight to compare.
"The workings of heaven have neither sound nor smell."
That is perfect virtue.

Introduction to the Upanishads

The *Upanishads* were written by sages of India between the eighth and fourth centuries BC. They are the final part of the *Vedas* and the basis for the philosophy of Vedanta, which means the end of the *Vedas*. The *Vedas* are the most ancient and sacred scripture of India; the name signifies wisdom. The *Rig Veda* gives the verses or hymns. The *Yajur Veda* has sacrificial formulas. The *Sama Veda* contains the melodies of the chants. The *Atharva Veda* is magic formulas. The four parts of the *Vedas* are the following: *Samhita* is the main part and has hymns, prayers, and litanies; the *Brahmanas* discuss the meaning of the sacrificial rites and ceremonies; the *Aranyakas* are forest-texts; and the *Upanishads* are the teachings of the sages on mystical experience. As part of the *Vedas* the *Upanishads* are considered revealed scripture.

The word *Upanishad* literally means "sitting down near" and implies studying with a spiritual teacher. The seven *Upanishads* presented complete in this collection are drawn from the twelve principal *Upanishads* and appear in what is considered their chronological order, the *Kena, Katha,* and *Isha,* being considered pre-Buddhistic and thus from the eighth or seventh centuries BC. The name *Kena* comes from the first word which means "By whom." *Isha* comes from the first word meaning "Lord." *Prashna* comes from the word for "question."

The gods referred to in these *Upanishads* are Agni the god of fire, Vayu the god of air or wind, Indra the god of heroic power and storms, Rudra a god of destruction and of healing, Savitri a sun god or goddess, Brahma the creator, and Vishnu the preserver. In the *Katha Upanishad* 5 the city of eleven gates refers to the nine openings in the body, the navel, and the sagittal suture on top of the head, and in the *Shvetashvatara Upanishad* 3 the nine-gated city refers merely to the body's nine openings. The triad in *Mundaka* 1 refers to the first three *Vedas,* while the triad in *Shvetashvatara* 1 seems to refer to three aspects of God. In *Mundaka* 3 Vedanta means the end of the *Vedas.*

Kena Upanishad

1

By whom directed does the mind project to its objects?
By whom commanded does the first life breath move?
By whom impelled are these words spoken?
What god is behind the eye and ear?

That which is the hearing of the ear,
the thought of the mind, the voice of the speech,
the life of the breath, and the sight of the eye.
Passing beyond, the wise leaving this world become immortal.

There the eye does not go, nor speech, nor the mind.
We do not know,
we do not understand how one can teach this.
Different, indeed, is it from the known,
and also it is above the unknown.
Thus have we heard from the ancients who explained it to us.

That which is not expressed by speech,
but that by which speech is expressed:
know that to be God, not what people here adore.

That which is not thought by the mind,
but that by which the mind thinks:
know that to be God, not what people here adore.

That which is not seen by the eye,
but that by which the eye sees:
know that to be God, not what people here adore.

That which is not heard by the ear,
but that by which the ear hears:
know that to be God, not what people here adore.

That which is not breathed by the breath,
but that by which the breath breathes:
know that to be God, not what people here adore.

2

If you think you know it well,
only slightly do you know the form of God.
What refers to you and what refers to the gods
then is to be investigated by you.

I think it is known.
I do not think that I know it well,
nor do I think that I do not know it.
Those of us who know this know it,
and not those of us who think they do not know it.
  The one who has not thought it out has the thought of it.
The one who has thought it out does not know it.
It is not understood by those who understand it;
it is understood by those who do not understand it.
  When it is known by an awakening, it is correctly known,
for then one finds immortality.
By the soul one finds ability;
by knowledge one finds immortality.
  If here one knows it, then there is truth;
if here one does not know it, then there is great loss.
Seeing it in all beings,
the wise on leaving this world become immortal.

3
  God won a victory for the gods,
and in this victory the gods were proud,
saying, "Ours is the victory, ours the greatness."
It knew this and appeared before them,
and they did not know what this spirit was.
  They said to Agni, "O all-knowing one,
find this out, what this spirit is."
  "So be it."
He hurried toward it, and it asked him, "Who are you?"
  "I am Agni," he said. "I am the all-knowing one."
  "What power is in you?"
  "I can burn all things on earth."
  It placed a straw before him. "Burn this."
He went at it with all speed, but could not burn it.
  Then he returned and said,
"I have not been able to find out what this spirit is."
  Then they said to Vayu, "O Vayu,
find this out, what this spirit is."

"So be it."
He hurried toward it, and it asked him, "Who are you?"
"I am Vayu," he said. "I am air expanding in space."
"What power is in you?"
"I can blow away all there is on earth."
It placed a straw before him. "Blow away this."
He went at it with all speed, but could not blow it away.
  Then he returned and said,
"I have not been able to find out what this spirit is."
  Then they said to Indra, "O giver of wealth,
find this out, what this spirit is."
  "So be it."
He hurried toward it. It disappeared from before him.
In the same region of the sky,
he came across a very beautiful woman,
Uma, the daughter of the snowy mountains.
He asked her, "What is this spirit?"

4
  She replied, "This is God,
and in the victory of God you glory."
Then he knew it was God.
  Therefore these gods, Agni, Vayu, and Indra,
surpassed the other gods, for they came nearest to its touch
and first knew that it was God.
Therefore Indra surpassed the other gods,
for he came nearest to its touch
and first knew that it was God.
  Of it there is this teaching:
this is like the lightning which flashes forth
or the blinking of the eye,
this teaching referring to the divine.
  Now the teaching referring to the self:
toward this the mind appears to move,
and by it the will remembers constantly.
It is called "that prize."
As that prize it should be revered.
Whoever knows it thus is sought by all beings.

You asked me to explain the mystic doctrine.
The mystic doctrine has been explained to you.
We have told you the mystic doctrine of God.
Discipline, restraint, and work are its foundation.
The Vedas are all its limbs.
Truth is its home.
Whoever knows this, overcoming sin,
is firmly established in infinite heaven—
yes, firmly established.

Katha Upanishad

1
  Zealously Vajashrava gave away all his possessions.
He had a son named Nachiketas.
As the gifts were being offered,
faith entered him, although he was merely a boy.
He thought, "Their water drunk, their grass eaten,
their milk milked, their organs worn out—
joyless surely are the worlds to which he goes
who gives such."
  He said to his father, "Papa, to whom will you give me?"
A second and third time he asked.
  To him then he said, "To Death I give you."
  "Of many I go as the first; of many I go in the middle.
What has Death to do with me today?
Consider how it was with those of old;
look how it will be with those to come.
Like grain a mortal ripens; like grain one is born again."
  "Like a fire a priest enters a house as a guest.
Make a peace offering; bring water, son of the sun.
Hope and expectation, friendship and joy,
sacrifices and good works, sons and cattle,
all are taken away from a person of little understanding
in whose house a priest remains unfed."
  "Since you have stayed in my house as a sacred guest
for three nights without food, I salute you, priest.
May it be well with me.
Therefore in return choose three gifts."
  "May Gautama with anxiety allayed and anger gone
be kind to me, O Death, and recognizing me,
welcome me when I am released by you;
this I choose as the first gift of the three."
  "As before will Auddalaki, son of Aruna, recognize you,
and by my power his sleep will be sweet at night
without anger, seeing you released from the jaws of death."
  "In the heavenly world is no fear whatever.
You are not there, nor does anyone fear old age.

Having crossed over both hunger and thirst,
leaving sorrow behind one rejoices in the heavenly world.
Death, you know that sacred fire that leads to heaven.
Explain it to me who has faith
how those in heaven gain immortality.
This I choose as my second gift."

   "Knowing well that sacred fire which leads to heaven
I will explain it to you.
Listen and learn from me.
Attainment of the infinite world and also its support,
know this to be in the secret place."
He told him of the fire of creation,
what bricks, how many, and how laid.
And he repeated it just as it was told.

   Then pleased with him, Death spoke again.
Delighted the great soul said to him,
"I give you here today another gift.
By your name will this fire be called.
Receive also this garland of many figures.
Whoever has lit the triple Nachiketas fire,
having attained union with the three,
performing the triple work, crosses over birth and death.
By knowing the knower born of God, the god to be praised,
by revering one goes to eternal peace.
Whoever has lit the triple Nachiketas fire,
having known this triad,
and so knowing builds up the Nachiketas fire,
throwing off first the bonds of death and overcoming sorrow,
rejoices in the heavenly world.
This is the heavenly fire, Nachiketas,
which you chose as your second gift.
This fire people will call by your name.
Choose now, Nachiketas, the third gift."

   "There is doubt concerning people who are deceased.
Some say they exist, and others say they do not exist.
Being taught by you, I would know this.
Of the gifts, this is the third gift."

   "Even the gods of old had doubt as to this.
It is not easy to understand, so subtle is this law.

Choose another gift, Nachiketas.
Do not press me; release me from this one."
   "Even the gods had doubt as to this,
and you, Death, say it is not easy to understand.
And another teacher of it like you is not to be found.
No other gift is comparable to this at all."
   "Choose sons and grandsons who shall live a century,
many cattle, elephants, gold, and horses.
Choose a great estate of land
and live as many years as you want.
If you think this is an equal gift,
choose wealth and long life.
Nachiketas, be the ruler of a great country;
I will make you the enjoyer of your desires.
Whatever desires are hard to get in the mortal world,
request all those desires at your pleasure.
Here are lovely maidens with chariots and music;
these are not to be attained by anyone.
Be served by these whom I give you.
Nachiketas, do not ask about death."
   "Transient are the things of mortals, Ender,
wearing away all the vigor of their senses.
Even a full life is short.
Yours be the chariots; yours be the dance and song.
A person cannot be satisfied with wealth.
Shall we enjoy wealth when we have seen you?
Shall we live so long as you are in power?
This is the gift to be chosen by me.
Having approached undecaying immortality,
what decaying mortal on this earth below that understands,
that contemplates the pleasures of beauty and enjoyment,
would delight in an over-long life?
This about which they doubt, Death,
what there is in the great passing-on—tell us that.
This gift that penetrates the mystery,
no other than that does Nachiketas choose."

2

"The good is one thing, and the pleasant quite another.
Both of these with different purposes bind a person.
Of these two, well is it for the one who takes the good;
failure of aim is it for the one who chooses the pleasant.
The good and the pleasant come to a person.
The thoughtful mind looking all around them discriminates.
The wise chooses the good in preference to the pleasant.
The fool out of getting and having prefers the pleasant.
You, Nachiketas, having examined desires that are pleasant
and that seem to be pleasing, have rejected them.
You have not taken that chain of wealth
in which many mortals sink down.

"Opposite and widely divergent are these two:
ignorance and what is known as knowledge.
I think Nachiketas desires knowledge,
for many desires do not distract you.
Those who are in ignorance,
thinking themselves wise and learned,
running here and there, go around deluded
like the blind led by one who is blind.

"The passing-on is not clear to the childish or careless
or those deluded by the glamour of wealth.
Thinking 'This is the world; there is no other;'
they fall again and again into my power.
This which cannot even be heard of by many,
that many even hearing do not know,
wonderful is the one who can teach this,
and skillful the one who can learn it,
wonderful the one who knows even when proficiently taught.
This taught by an inferior person is not well understood,
being considered in many ways.
Unless taught by another, there is no going to it,
for it is inconceivably more subtle than the subtle.
Not by reasoning is this thought to be attained.
Taught by another, it is well understood, dear friend.
You have obtained it, holding fast to the truth.
May we find an inquirer like you, Nachiketas."

"I know that riches are impermanent,
and that stability is not attained by the unstable.
Therefore the Nachiketas fire has been laid by me,
and by sacrificing the impermanent
I have reached the eternal."

"The obtaining of desire, the foundation of the world,
the endlessness of power, the other shore of fearlessness,
the greatness of fame, the wide expanses, the foundation,
you, wise Nachiketas, have steadily let them go.
That which is hard to see, entering the hidden,
set in the secret place, dwelling in the primal depth,
by meditating on this as God through the uniting of the soul,
the wise person leaves joy and sorrow behind.
Hearing this and comprehending,
a mortal extracting what is concerned with virtue,
and subtly taking this, rejoices,
having attained the source of joy.
I know that such a home is open to Nachiketas."

"Aside from virtue and aside from vice,
aside from what is done and what is not done here,
aside from what has been and what is to be,
what you see as that, tell me that."

"The word which all the Vedas glorify,
and which all austerities proclaim,
desiring which people live as holy students—
that word I tell you briefly is AUM.
This word truly is God; this word is supreme.
Knowing this very word, whatever one desires is gained.
This support is the best; this support is the highest.
Knowing this support, one becomes great in the world of God.

"The wise soul is not born nor does it die.
This one has not come from anywhere
nor has it become anyone.
Unborn, eternal, constant, primal,
this one is not killed when the body is killed.
If the killer thinks to kill,
if the killed thinks oneself killed,
both of these do not understand.
This does not kill nor is it killed.

"Smaller than the small, greater than the great,
is the soul set in the heart of every creature.
The one who is not impulsive sees it, freed from sorrow.
Through the grace of the creator
one sees the greatness of the soul.
Sitting one travels far; lying one goes everywhere.
Who else but myself can know the god of joy and sorrow.
The one who is bodiless among bodies,
stable among the unstable, the great all-pervading soul—
on realizing this, the wise grieve no longer.

"This soul cannot be attained by instruction
nor by intellectual ability nor by much learning.
It is to be attained only by the one this one chooses.
To such a one the soul reveals its own self.
Not those who have not ceased from bad conduct,
not those who are not tranquil,
not those who are not composed,
not those who are not of a peaceful mind,
can attain this by intelligence.
The one for whom the priesthood and the nobility are as food,
and death is as a sauce, who knows where this one is?

3

"There are two who drink of justice
in the world of good works.
Both are lodged in the secret place and in the highest plane.
Knowers of God speak of them as light and shade,
as do those who maintain the five sacrificial fires,
as those also who perform the triple Nachiketas fire.
That bridge for those who sacrifice,
and which is the highest imperishable God
for those who wish to cross over
to the fearless farther shore,
that Nachiketas fire may we master.

"Know the soul as lord of a chariot,
the body as the chariot.
Know the intuition as the chariot driver,
and the mind as the reins.
The senses, they say, are the horses;
the objects of sense the paths.

This associated with the body, the senses and the mind,
the wise call 'the enjoyer.'

"Those who do not have understanding,
whose minds are always undisciplined,
their senses are out of control,
like the wild horses of a chariot driver.

"Those, however, who have understanding,
whose minds are always disciplined,
their senses are under control,
like the good horses of a chariot driver.

"Those, however, who have no understanding,
who are unmindful and always impure,
do not reach the goal but go on to reincarnation.

"Those, however, who have understanding,
who are mindful and always pure,
reach the goal from which they are not born again.
Those who have the understanding of a chariot driver,
controlling the reins of the mind,
they reach the end of the journey,
the supreme home of Vishnu.

"Beyond the senses are the objects of sense.
Beyond the objects of sense is the mind.
Beyond the mind is the intuition.
Beyond the intuition is the great soul.
Beyond the great is the unmanifest.
Beyond the unmanifest is Spirit.
Beyond the Spirit there is nothing at all.
That is the end; that is the final goal.

"Though hidden in all beings the soul is invisible.
It is seen by the subtle seers
through their sharp and subtle intelligence.
An intelligent person should restrain speech in mind,
and mind should be restrained in the knowing soul.
The knowing soul should be restrained in the intuitive soul.
That should be restrained in the peaceful soul.

"Arise! Awake!
Having attained your gifts, understand them.
Sharp as the edge of a razor and hard to cross,
difficult is this path, say the sages.

What has no sound nor touch nor form nor decay,
likewise is tasteless, eternal, odorless,
without beginning or end, beyond the great, stable,
by discerning that, one is liberated from the mouth of death.
   "The Nachiketas story, Death's ancient teaching—
by telling and hearing it,
the wise become great in the world of God.
Whoever recites this supreme secret
before an assembly of priests,
or devoutly at the time of the ceremonies for the dead,
this prepares one for immortality.
This prepares one for immortality.

4
   "The self-existent pierced the openings outward;
therefore one looks outward, not inside the soul.
A certain wise person, however, seeking immortality,
looking within saw the soul.
   "The childish go after outward pleasures;
they walk into the net of widespread death.
But the wise, aware of immortality,
do not seek the stable among things which are unstable here.
That by which form, taste, smell, sound, and caressing
are discerned is with that.
What is there that remains?
This truly is that.
   "By recognizing as the great, omnipresent soul
that by which one perceives
both the dream state and the waking state,
the wise person does not grieve.
Whoever knows this honey-eater as the living soul close-by,
Lord of what has been and what will be,
one does not shrink away from it.
This truly is that.
   "The ancient one born from discipline,
the ancient one born from the waters,
who stands having entered the secret place
and looked forth through beings—
this truly is that.

"She who arises with life, infinity, the soul of the gods,
who stands having entered into the secret place,
who was born with the beings.
This truly is that.

"Agni, the all-knower hidden in the fire-sticks
like the embryo well born by pregnant women,
worthy to be worshipped day by day
by watchful people with oblations.
This truly is that.

"From where the sun rises and where it goes to rest;
in it are all gods founded,
and no one ever goes beyond it.
This truly is that.

"Whatever is here, that is there.
Whatever is there, that also is here.
Whoever seems to see a difference here
goes from death to death.

"By the mind is this to be attained:
there is no difference here at all.
Whoever seems to see a difference here
goes from death to death.

"Spirit, the size of a thumb,
lives in the middle of one's soul,
Lord of what has been and what will be.
One does not shrink away from it.
This truly is that.

"Spirit, the size of a thumb,
like a flame without smoke,
Lord of what has been and what will be.
It is the same today and tomorrow.

"As water raining upon the mountains
runs down the hills on many sides,
so whoever views virtues separately
runs to waste after them.
As pure water poured into pure water stays the same,
so is the soul, Gautama, of the seer who has understanding.

5
"By ruling over the city of eleven gates,
the unborn who is not devious-minded does not grieve,
but when set free is truly free.
This truly is that.

"The swan in the sky, the god in the atmosphere,
the priest at the altar, the guest in the house,
in people, in gods, in justice, in the sky,
born in water, born in cattle, born in justice,
born in rock, is justice, the great one.
Upwards it leads the out-breath,
downwards it casts the in-breath.
The dwarf who sits in the center all the gods reverence.
When this incorporate one that is in the body
slips off and is released from the body,
what is there that remains?
This truly is that.

"Not by the out-breath and the in-breath
does any mortal live.
But by another do they live
on which these both depend.

"Look, I shall explain to you
the mystery of God, the eternal,
and how the soul fares after reaching death, Gautama.
Some enter a womb for embodiment;
others enter stationary objects
according to their actions and according to their thoughts.

"Whoever is awake in those that sleep,
the Spirit who shapes desire after desire,
that they call the bright one.
That is God; that indeed is called the immortal.
On it all the worlds rest, and no one ever goes beyond it.
This truly is that.

"As one fire has entered the world
and becomes varied in shape
according to the form of every object,
so the one inner soul in all beings
becomes varied according to whatever form
and also exists outside.

"As one air has entered the world
and becomes varied in shape
according to the form of every object,
so the one inner soul in all beings
becomes varied according to whatever form
and also exists outside.

"As the sun, the eye of the world,
is not defiled by the external faults of the eyes,
so the inner soul in all beings
is not defiled by the evil in the world, being outside it.

"The inner soul in all beings, the one controller,
who makes this one form manifold,
the wise who perceive this standing in oneself,
they and no others have eternal happiness.

"The one eternal among the transient,
the conscious among the conscious,
the one among the many, who grants desires,
the wise who perceive this standing in oneself
they and no others have eternal happiness.

"This is it.
Thus they recognize the ineffable supreme happiness.
How then may I understand this?
Does it shine or does it reflect?
The sun does not shine there, nor the moon and the stars;
lightning does not shine there, much less this fire.
After that shines does everything else shine.
The whole world is illuminated by its light.

6
"Its root is above, its branches below—
this eternal fig tree.
That is the bright one. That is God.
That is called immortal.
On it all the worlds rest,
and no one ever goes beyond it.
This truly is that.

"The whole world, whatever here exists,
was created from and moves in life.
The great awe, the upraised thunderbolt—

they who know that become immortal.

  "From awe of it fire burns;
from awe the sun gives heat;
from awe both Indra and wind and death, the fifth,
speed on their way.

  "If one is able to perceive here on earth
before the body falls away,
according to that
one becomes fit for embodiment in the world-creations.

  "As in a mirror, so is it seen in the soul;
as in a dream, so in the world of the parents;
as is seen in water, so in the world of the spirits;
as light and shade in the world of God.

  "Recognizing the separate nature of the senses
and their rising and setting apart,
the wise does not grieve.
Beyond the senses is the mind;
above the mind is true being;
over true being is the great soul;
above the great is the unmanifest.
Higher than the unmanifest is Spirit,
all-pervading and without any mark whatever.
Knowing this a mortal is liberated and reaches immortality.

  "This form is not to be observed.
No one ever sees it with the eye.
It is apprehended by the heart, by the thought, by the mind.
They who know that become immortal.

  "When the five sense perceptions
together with the mind cease,
and the intuition does not stir,
that, they say, is the highest state.
This they consider to be uniting,
the steady control of the senses.
Then one becomes undistracted,
for uniting is the arising and the passing away.

  "Not by speech, not by mind, not by sight,
can this be apprehended.
How can this be comprehended
except by the one who says, 'It is.'

It can be comprehended only as existent
and by the real nature in both ways.
When it is comprehended as existent,
its real nature becomes clear.

"When every desire found in the human heart is liberated,
then a mortal becomes immortal and here one attains to God.
When all the knots of the heart here on earth are cut,
then a mortal becomes immortal.
So far is the teaching.

"There are a hundred and one channels of the heart.
One of them rises up to the crown of the head.
Going upward through that, one becomes immortal.
The others are for going in various directions.

"Spirit, the size of a thumb, is the inner soul,
always seated in the heart of creatures.
This one should draw out from one's own body,
like an arrow-shaft out from a reed, steadily.
This one should know as the bright one, the immortal.
Yes, this one should know as the bright one, the immortal."

Then Nachiketas gaining this knowledge taught by Death
and the whole discipline of uniting,
attained God and became free from emotion and from death;
and so may any other who knows this concerning the soul.

Isha Upanishad

By the Lord is enveloped
all that moves in the moving world.
By renouncing this, find your enjoyment.
Do not covet the possessions of others.
Working here one may wish to live for a hundred years.
Thus it is up to you—there is no other way than this—
the work does not adhere to you.
Demonic are those worlds named,
covered in blinding darkness;
there after death go those people who kill the soul.

Unmoving the one is faster than the mind.
The angels do not reach it, as it is always beyond them.
Standing still it passes beyond those who run.
In it the Mother establishes the waters.
It moves, and it does not move.
It is far, and it is near.
It is within all this, and it is also outside all this.

Whoever sees all beings in the soul
and the soul in all beings
does not shrink away from this.
In whom all beings have become one with the knowing soul
what delusion or sorrow is there for the one who sees unity?
It has filled all.

It is radiant, incorporeal, invulnerable,
without tendons, pure, untouched by evil.
Wise, intelligent, encompassing, self-existent,
it organizes objects throughout eternity.

Into blind darkness enter those who follow ignorance;
into even greater darkness go those who follow knowledge.
It is distinct, they say, from knowledge.
It is distinct, they say, from ignorance.
So have we heard from the wise who explained it to us.
Knowledge and ignorance, whoever knows the two together
with ignorance passes over death,
with knowledge attains immortality.

Into blind darkness enter those who follow non-becoming;
into greater darkness enter those who follow becoming.

It is distinct, they say, from becoming.
It is distinct, they say, from non-becoming.
So have we heard from the wise who explained it to us.
Becoming and destruction, whoever knows the two together
with destruction passes over death,
with becoming attains immortality.
  The face of truth is covered with a golden disc.
Unveil it, nourisher,
for one whose duty is to see the truth.
Nourisher, one seer, controller, sun, child of the creator,
spread your light and gather your brilliance
that I may see your loveliest form.
Whatever is that Spirit, that also am I.
May this life enter into the immortal breath!
This body then ends in ashes. Aum.
Purpose, remember! Action, remember!
Purpose, remember! Action, remember!
  Agni, lead us by a good path to success,
you god who knows all ways.
Keep us away from deceitful sins.
We offer ample prayer to you.

Mundaka Upanishad

1

God originated before the gods,
the creator of all, the protector of the world.
It taught the knowledge of God, the basis of all knowledge,
to Atharvan the eldest son.
What God taught to Atharvan, the knowledge of God,
Atharvan in the ancient times told to Angir.
He taught it to Bharadvaja Satyavaha,
and Bharadvaja to Angiras—both the higher and the lower.

Saunaka, a great householder, duly approached Angiras
and asked, "By understanding what, venerable sir,
does all this become understood?"

To him he said, "Two kinds of knowledge are to be known.
which the knowers of God speak of, the higher and lower.
Of these the lower is the Vedas: Rig, Yajur, Sama, Atharva,
phonetics, ritual, grammar, definition, metrics, astrology.
The higher is that by which the imperishable is apprehended.

"That which is invisible, intangible,
without family, without class,
without sight or hearing, without hands or feet,
eternal, all-pervading, omnipresent, most subtle,
that is the imperishable
which the wise perceive as the source of creation.

"As the spider puts out and gathers in,
as plants grow on the earth,
as hair on the head and body of a living person,
so from the imperishable arises everything here.

"By discipline God expands.
From that, matter is produced;
from matter, life, mind, reality,
the worlds, and in works immortality.
Whoever is all-knowing and all-wise,
whose discipline consists of knowledge,
from this is produced what is God here,
name and form and matter.
This is that truth.

"The works which the sages saw in the hymns
were variously expressed in the triad.
Perform them constantly, lovers of truth.
This is your path to the world of good works.

"When the flame moves after the fire has been kindled,
then between the two pourings of melted butter
one should throw with faith the offering.
If one's altar fires are empty of the offerings
for the new moon, the full moon, the rains, the harvest,
or without guests or offerings or ceremonies to the gods
or contrary to rule, one loses hope of all the seven worlds.
The black, the terrible, the swift as thought,
the blood-red, the smoke-colored,
the spark-scattering, the all-shaped goddess,
are the seven flickering tongues of fire.

"Whoever performs sacrifices,
making offerings at the proper time when these are shining,
these as rays of the sun lead one
to where the one Lord of the gods lives.
Saying, 'Come, come,' the radiant offerings
carry the sacrificer by the rays of the sun,
praising and honoring one with pleasant words:
'This is your holy world of God attained by good works.'

"Unsafe are the boats of the eighteen sacrificial forms
in which are expressed the lower work.
The deluded who approve them as leading to good
fall again into old age and death.
Remaining in ignorance,
thinking themselves learned and wise,
the deluded afflicted with troubles
go about like the blind led by the blind.
Remaining in various forms of ignorance,
thinking immaturely, 'We have accomplished our aim.'
Since those who perform rituals
do not understand because of attachment,
therefore when their rewards are exhausted,
they sink down, wretched.
Thinking sacrifices and works of merit are most important,
the deluded know nothing better.

Having enjoyed the high heaven won by good works,
They enter again this world or even a lower one.
  "Those who practice discipline and faith in the forest,
the peaceful knowers who live on charity,
depart without attachment through the door of the sun,
to where lives the immortal Spirit, the imperishable soul.
Having tested the worlds won by works,
let the seeker of God arrive at detachment.
What is not made is not attained by what is done.
  "For this knowledge,
let one go with fuel in hand to a teacher
who is learned in the scriptures and established in God.
To the one who has approached properly,
whose mind is calm, who has attained peace,
let the one knowing teach in the truth of reality
that knowledge of God
by which one knows the imperishable Spirit, the true.

2
  "This is the truth:
as from a blazing fire
thousands of flaming sparks come forth,
so from the imperishable, my friend,
various beings come forth and return there also.
Divine and formless is the Spirit,
which is outside and inside, unborn, not breath, not mind,
pure, higher than the high imperishable.
  "From this is produced breath, mind, and all the senses,
space, air, light, water, and earth supporting all.
Fire is its head, its eyes the sun and moon,
the regions of space its ears, the revealed Vedas its speech,
air its breath, its heart the world.
The earth is its footstool.
  "It is the inner soul of all beings.
From it comes fire whose fuel is the sun,
from the moon, rain, plants on the earth;
the male pours seed in the female;
thus creatures are produced from the Spirit.

"From it come the hymns, the chants,
the formulas, the rites of initiation,
and all the sacrifices, ceremonies, and offerings,
the year too, and the sacrificer,
and the worlds where the moon shines and the sun.

"From it also are born various gods, the celestials,
people, cattle, birds, the in-breath and the out-breath,
rice and barley, discipline,
faith, truth, chastity, and the law.

"From it come forth the seven life-breaths,
the seven flames, their fuel, the seven oblations,
these seven worlds in which move the life-breaths
set within the secret place, seven and seven.

"From it the seas and mountains all;
from it flow the rivers of all kinds;
from it come all plants and the essence
by which the inner soul lives in the elements.

"The Spirit itself is all this here:
works and discipline and God, beyond death.
Whoever knows that which is set in the secret place,
that one here on earth, my friend,
cuts apart the knot of ignorance.
Manifest, hidden, moving in the secret place, the great home.
In it lives all that moves and breathes and sees.

"Know that as being, as non-being, as most to be desired,
beyond understanding, as what is best of all.
That which is luminous, subtler than the subtle,
in which are set all the worlds and their inhabitants—
that is the imperishable God.
It is life; it is speech and mind.
That is the real; it is immortal.

"It is to be known, my friend; know it.
Taking as a bow the great weapons of the *Upanishads*,
place on it an arrow sharpened by meditation.
Stretching it with thought directed to that,
know that imperishable as the target, my friend.

"The word AUM is the bow; the soul is the arrow.
God is said to be the target.
By the unfaltering it is to be known.

One becomes united with it as the arrow.
"In whom sky, earth, and atmosphere are interwoven,
and also the mind together with all the life breaths,
this alone know as the one soul.
Other words dismiss. This is the bridge to immortality.
"Where the channels are brought together
like the spokes in the hub of a wheel
there it moves and becomes manifold.
"AUM. Thus meditate on the soul.
May you be successful in crossing over
to the farther shore beyond darkness.
"Whoever is all-knowing, all-wise,
whose is this greatness on the earth,
in the divine city of God
and established in heaven is the soul.
"Using the mind, leading the life-breaths and the body,
established in matter one finds peace in the heart.
By this knowledge the wise perceive
the light of blissful immortality.
The knot of the heart is loosened, all doubts vanish,
and one's works cease when it is seen, the lower and higher.
"In the highest golden sheath is God,
without stain or parts.
Radiant is it, the light of lights,
that which the knowers of the soul know.
The sun does not shine there nor the moon nor the stars;
lightning does not shine; how then could this fire?
The whole world is illuminated by its light.
God truly is this immortal.
God in front, God behind, to the right and the left.
Spread out below and above, God is all this great universe.

3
"Two birds, close companions, cling to the same tree.
Of these two, one eats the sweet fruit,
and the other looks on without eating.
The soul is the one sitting immersed on the same tree,
deluded and sad because helpless.
But seeing the other who is the Lord and beloved,

it realizes its greatness and overcomes the sadness.

"When a seer sees the brilliant creator,
Lord, Spirit, God-source,
then being a knower, shaking off good and evil,
stainless one reaches supreme identity.
Truly it is life that shines forth in all beings.
Understanding this one knows there is nothing else to say.

"Delighting in the soul,
enjoying the soul, doing holy works,
such a one is the best of the knowers of God.
The soul can be attained by truth, by discipline,
by correct knowledge, by studying God.
Within the body, made of light, pure is this
which the ascetics, their faults removed, view.

"Truth alone conquers, not falsehood.
By truth is laid out the path leading to the gods
by which the sages whose desires are satisfied
ascend to where the supreme home of truth is.
Vast, divine, its form unthinkable, subtler than the subtle,
it shines out, farther than the far, yet close-by.
resting in the secret place,
even here it is seen by those with vision.

"It is not grasped by sight nor even by speech
nor by other angels, nor by austerity nor by work.
By the grace of wisdom and mental purity
by meditating one does see the indivisible.
The subtle is to be known by consciousness
in which the five different breaths have centered.
All of human thought is interwoven with the life-breath.
When that is purified, the soul manifests its power.

"Whatever world a person of pure heart
holds clearly in mind,
and whatever desires that one desires,
that world is obtained and those desires.
Therefore whoever desires success
should honor the knower of the self.
That one knows the supreme home of God,
founded on which the whole world shines radiantly.

"The wise who, free from desires, worship the Spirit,
pass beyond the sperm.
Whoever entertains desires, dwelling on them,
is born here and there on account of these desires;
but one whose desire is satisfied, whose soul is perfected,
all desires here on earth vanish away.

"This soul can not be attained by instruction
nor by intellect nor by much learning.
It can be attained only by the one whom it chooses.
To such a one this soul reveals its own nature.

"This soul can not be attained by one lacking strength
nor by carelessness nor by misdirected discipline;
but the one striving by these means who knows,
this soul enters into the home of God.

"Attaining this, the seers, happy with knowledge,
souls perfected, free from emotion, tranquil,
attaining the one who is universally omnipresent,
those wise, united souls enter into the all itself.

"Those who have ascertained
the meaning of the Vedanta knowledge,
ascetics with natures purified by the way of renunciation,
they in the God-worlds at the end of time,
transcending death are all liberated.
The fifteen parts return to their foundations,
and all the angels to their divinities.

"One's actions and the soul composed of wisdom
all become one in the supreme imperishable.
As rivers flowing into the ocean disappear
losing name and form,
so the knower liberated from name and form
reaches the divine Spirit, higher than the highest.

"Whoever knows that supreme God becomes God.
In that family no one is born who does not know God.
This one crosses over sorrow, crosses over sins,
liberated from the knots of the heart, becomes immortal.
This has been declared in the verse:

'Doers of the works, learned in scriptures,
absorbed in God, having faith
make offerings to the one seer,
to those one should declare this knowledge of God,

by whom the rite of the head
has been performed according to rule.'"
 This is the truth.
The seer Angiras declared it long ago.
Let no one who has not performed the rite read this.
Salutation to the highest seers!
Salutation to the highest seers!

Prashna Upanishad

First Question
 Sukesha Bharadvaja, Shaibya Satyakama,
Sauryayani Gargya, Kaushalya Ashvalayana,
Bhargava Vaidarbhi, and Kabandhi Katyayana
were devoted to God, intent on God,
in search of the highest God.
Thinking, "He can tell us all,"
bringing fuel they approached the revered Pippalada.

 The seer said to them, "Live with me one more year
in discipline, holiness, and faith.
Then ask what you want.
If I know, I will tell you all."

 Then Kabandhi Katyayana came to him and asked,
"Sir, from where are all these creatures born?"

 The seer answered him, "The creator desired creatures.
Gathering energy, with this energy
it produced a pair, matter and life,
thinking, 'These two will produce various creatures.'
The sun is life, and the moon is matter.
Matter really is everything here,
both what is formed and what is formless;
thus form is matter.

 "When the rising sun enters the east
it absorbs the eastern life-breaths into its rays.
When it illumines the south and west and north,
below and above and all space, it illumines everything;
then it takes all the life-breaths in its rays.
That fire rises as universal life in all its forms.
This has been declared in the *Rig Veda*:

> 'This has all forms, the golden one, all-knowing,
> the final goal, the one light, heat-giving,
> with a thousand rays, a hundred existences;
> this sun arises as the life of all creatures.'

 "The year is the creator.
This has two paths: the southern and the northern.
Those who worship thinking,
'Sacrifice and merit have perfected us,'

attain only the lunar world;
these return to be born again.
Thus the seers desiring children take the southern course,
which is the path to the ancestors.
This is matter that leads to the ancestors.
Those seeking the soul by discipline,
holiness, faith, and knowledge
by the northern course attain the world of the sun.
There is the resting place of the life-breaths.
There immortality is without fear.
That is the final goal.
From there they do not return; that is the stopping.
As to that a verse states:

> 'They mention a father five-footed and twelve-formed,
> rich in moisture, as in the upper half of heaven,
> but others mention a sage
> in a chariot of seven wheels and six spokes.'

"The month is the creator.
Its dark period is matter; its bright period life.
Thus these seers perform sacrifice in the bright period,
others in the dark.

"Day and night are the creator.
The day is life, and the night is matter.
They waste their life who join in sexual enjoyment by day;
holy are those who join in sexual enjoyment by night.

"Food is the creator.
From this seeds are produced,
and from them are creatures born.

"Those who follow the rule of the creator produce a pair.
Those have that God-world who have discipline and holiness,
in whom truth is established.
Theirs is the stainless God-world,
in whom there is no deceit nor lying nor illusion."

Second Question
  Then Bhargava Vaidarbhi asked him,
"How many angels support a creature?
How many illumine it? And which of them is supreme?"

The seer answered him, "Space is such an angel,
also air, fire, water, earth, speech, mind, sight, hearing.
These, having illumined the creature,
said, 'We support and preserve this being.'
  To them the supreme life-breath said, 'Do not be deluded.
I dividing soul fivefold support and preserve this union.'
They did not believe it.
Offended it rose up out.
When it rises up, then all the others rise up;
and when he settles down, they settle down.
As all the bees rise up after the king bee rises,
and all settle down when it settles down,
thus did speech, mind, sight, and hearing.
  "They being satisfied praised the life-breath.
'As fire, it burns; it is the sun,
the bountiful rain, the air, the earth, matter,
angels, being and non-being, and immortality.
Like spokes on the hub of a wheel,
so everything is established on the life-breath—
the hymns, the formulas, the chants,
the sacrifice, the nobility, and the priesthood.
As the creator you move in the womb and are born again.
  "'To you, life, creatures bring offerings,
who by the breath live.
You are the chief bearer of gifts to the gods.
You are the first offering to the ancestors.
You are the truth of the seers,
the descendants of Atharvan and Angiras.
You are Indra, life, with your brilliance.
You are Rudra for protection.
You move in the atmosphere as the sun, the Lord of lights.
When you rain upon them, life,
then all your creatures are happy,
because there will be food for all desires.
  "'You are uninitiated, life, the only seer,
a consumer of all, and Lord of reality.
We are the givers for your consuming.
You are the parent of the wind.
Your form which is established in speech, sight, and hearing,

and is extended in the mind, make favorable; do not go away.
All this universe is in your power,
even what is established in the third heaven.
As a mother her child, protect us,
give us prosperity and wisdom.'"

Third Question
   Then Kaushalya Ashvalayana asked him, "Sir,
from where is this life-breath born?
How does it come into this body?
How does it dividing the soul become established?
By what does it depart?
How does it relate to the external and to the soul inside?"

   The seer answered him, "You are asking much,
but because you are very holy, I will tell you.
The life-breath is born from the soul.
As a shadow is cast by a person,
so is this life-breath extended by the soul,
and for the perfection of the mind it comes into this body.
As a ruler commands the officials,
saying, 'Govern these villages,'
so this life-breath rules the other breaths.
The out-breath is in the organs of excretion and generation;
the life-breath itself is in the eyes, ears, mouth and nose;
while the equalizing breath is in the middle,
for it equally distributes the offering of food.
From this arise the seven flames.
   "The soul lives in the heart.
Here there are one hundred and one channels.
Each of these has one hundred smaller channels.
Each of these has seventy-two thousand branching channels.
Within these moves the diffused breath.
Rising upward through one of these,
the up-breath leads by virtue to the heaven of virtue,
by sin to the hell of sin,
and by both back to the human world.
   "The sun rises externally as the life-breath,
for it helps the life-breath in the eye.
The goddess of the earth supports a person's outbreath.

What is between, namely space, is the equalizing breath.
Air is the diffused breath.
Heat is the up-breath.
Therefore one whose heat has ceased goes to rebirth
with the senses sunk in the mind.
  "Whatever is one's consciousness,
with that one enters into the life-breath.
The life-breath joined to the heat together with the soul
lead to whatever world has been imagined.
The wise who know the life-breath thus
do not lose their offspring and become immortal.
As to this there is this verse:

> 'The source, its coming, its staying,
> its fivefold division,
> and the relation of the soul to the life-breath—
> by knowing these one enjoys immortality.
> By knowing these one enjoys immortality.'"

Fourth Question
  Then Sauryayani Gargya asked him, "Sir,
what are those that sleep in a person here?
What are those that remain awake?
What is the angel who sees dreams and who enjoys them?
In whom are all these things resolved?"
  The seer answered him, "Gargya,
as the rays of the setting sun
all become one in a circle of brilliance,
and again when it rises,
so all the human becomes one in the mind, the highest god.
In that condition people do not see, hear, smell, taste,
touch, speak, take, give, nor move.
It is said, 'They sleep.'
  "The fires of the life-breath remain awake in this city.
The out-breath is the householder's fire.
The diffused breath is the southern fire.
The life-breath is the sacrifice fire,
and as the eastern fire takes its fuel from the western,
so in sleep the life-breath takes from the lower.
The equalizing breath is called this,
because it equalizes the two offerings:

the in-breath and the out-breath.
The mind is the sacrificer;
the upper breath is the fruit of the sacrifice,
for it leads the sacrificer day by day to God.

"The mind in sleep experiences its greatness.
Whatever it has seen it sees again.
Whatever it has heard it hears again.
Whatever it has felt and thought and known
in many regions and various places
it experiences these again.
What has been seen and not seen, heard and not heard,
experienced and not experienced, both real and unreal,
one sees it all, for the mind is all.

"When one is overcome with light,
then the god dreams no longer.
Then in this body arises happiness.
As birds return to their nesting tree, friend,
so do all these return to the supreme soul.
Earth and elements of earth, water and elements of water,
light and elements of light, air and elements of air,
space and elements of space,
sight and what is seen, hearing and what is heard,
smell and what is smelled, taste and what is tasted,
the skin and what is touched, speech and what is spoken,
the hands and what is taken,
the genitals and what is enjoyed,
the anus and what is excreted,
the feet and what is walked on,
mind and what is thought,
intuition and what is understood,
ego and what is identified with,
consciousness and what it is aware of,
light and what is enlightened,
life-breath and what is sustained;
for the seer, toucher, hearer, smeller, taster,
thinker, understander, actor, knowing soul—
this human soul returns to the supreme imperishable soul.

"Whoever knows that shadowless, bodiless, colorless,
bright imperishable, friend, attains the imperishable.

Knowing all, one becomes all.
On this there is the verse:

'Friend, whoever knows the imperishable
wherein the consciousness with all its angels
and the life-breaths and the elements do rest,
knowing the all has entered the all.'"

Fifth Question

Then Shaibya Satyakama asked him, "Sir,
if someone here should meditate on the word AUM
until the end of one's life, then which world is won?"

The seer answered him, "Satyakama,
the word AUM is the higher God and also the lower.
Thus with this support the wise attain one or the other.

"Whoever meditates on one letter,
quickly returns to earth.
The *Rig Veda* leads one to the human world.
There endowed with discipline, holiness, and faith
one experiences greatness.

"Whoever is united in mind with two letters
is led by the *Yajur Veda* to the regions of the moon,
then returns here again.

"Whoever meditates on the supreme Spirit
with the three letters of AUM
is united in brilliance with the sun.
As a snake is freed from its skin, so is one freed from sin,
and is led by the *Sama Veda* to the world of God,
where one can see the Spirit
that lives in the city of the human body
and is above the highest life.
As to this there are these two verses:

'Using the three letters separately leads to death.
When they are used correctly
for outward, inward, and intermediate actions,
the wise do not fear.
With the *Rig* hymns leading to this world,
the *Yajur* formulas to the intermediate world,
and the *Sama* chants to the heaven of the wise,
with the support of the word AUM
the wise attain to that which is

peaceful, unaging, immortal, fearless, and supreme.'"

Sixth Question
  Then Sukesha Bharadvaja asked him, "Sir,
Hiranyanabha, a prince of Koshala, came to me
and asked this question, 'Bharadvaja,
do you know the Spirit with the sixteen parts?'
I answered the youth, 'I do not.
If I knew it, how could I say I did not know it?
Whoever lies dries up to the roots. Thus I will not lie.'
In silence he mounted his chariot and departed.
Now I ask you. Where is that Spirit?"

  The seer answered him, "Even here in the body, friend,
is that Spirit in whom they say arise the sixteen parts.
It thought to itself, 'In whose departure shall I depart,
and in whose staying shall I stay?'
It created the life-breath, from the life-breath faith,
space, air, light, water, earth, senses, mind, food;
from food, virility, discipline, affirmations, actions,
the world; and in the worlds, naming.

  "As these flowing rivers move toward the ocean,
and on reaching the ocean are lost,
their name and form destroyed,
and all are called merely ocean,
so all the sixteen parts of the witness move towards Spirit,
and reaching the Spirit are lost,
their name and form destroyed,
and all are called merely the Spirit.
That one continues without parts, immortal.
As to this there is the verse:
  'In whom the parts rest
  as the spokes in the hub of a wheel,
  know that as the Spirit to be known
  so that death shall not disturb you.'"

  Then he said to them, "Thus far I know the supreme God.
There is nothing higher than it."

  They praised him saying, "You are our father
who has carried us over to the shore beyond ignorance.
Salutation to the supreme seers!
Salutation to the supreme seers!"

Mandukya Upanishad

AUM. This imperishable word is the universe.
It is explained as the past, the present, the future;
everything is the word AUM.
Also whatever transcends threefold time is AUM.
All here is God; this soul is God.
This same soul is fourfold.

The waking state outwardly conscious,
having seven limbs and nineteen doors,
enjoying gross objects common to all, is the first.

The dreaming state inwardly conscious,
having seven limbs and nineteen doors,
enjoying subtle objects that are bright, is the second.

When one sleeps without yearning for any desires,
seeing no dreams, that is deep sleep.
The deep-sleep state unified in wisdom gathered,
consisting of bliss, enjoying bliss,
whose door is conscious wisdom, is the third.

This is the Lord of all; this is the omniscient;
this is the inner controller; this is the universal womb,
for this is the origin and end of beings.
Not inwardly wise nor outwardly wise nor both ways wise
nor gathered wisdom, nor wise nor unwise,
unseen, incommunicable, intangible,
featureless, unthinkable, indefinable,
whose essence is the security of being one with the soul,
the end of evolution, peaceful, good, non-dual—
this they deem the fourth.

It is the soul; it should be discerned.
This is the soul in regard to the word AUM and its parts.
The parts are the letters,
and the letters are its parts: A U M.

The waking state common to all is the letter A,
the first part, from "attaining" or from being first.
Whoever knows this attains all desires and becomes first.

The sleeping state, the bright, is the letter U,
the second part, from "uprising" or from being in between.

Whoever knows this rises up in knowledge and is balanced;
no one ignorant of God is born in that family.

The deep-sleep state, the wise, is the letter M,
the third part, from "measure" or from being the end.
Whoever knows this measures everything and reaches the end.

The fourth is without a letter, the incommunicable,
the end of evolution, good, non-dual.

Thus AUM is the soul.
Whoever knows this enters by one's soul into the soul;
this one knows this.

Shvetashvatara Upanishad

1
  Lovers of God ask, "What is the cause? God?
Where do we come from? By what power do we live?
On what are we established?
Who rules over our various pains and pleasures,
God-knowers?"
  Time or its own nature or necessity or chance
or the elements or a womb or Spirit are to be considered,
not a combination of these, because of the soul's existence.
The soul cannot be the cause of pleasure and pain.
  Those who practiced meditation and union
saw the divine soul power hidden in their own qualities.
It is the one who rules over all these causes,
from time to the soul.
  It is understood as one wheel with three layers,
sixteen parts, fifty spokes, twenty counter-spokes,
six groups of eight, whose one rope is diverse,
which has three different paths,
whose single illusion has two conditioning causes.
  It is understood as an impetuous and crooked river
of five streams from five sources,
whose waves are the five vital breaths,
whose origin is fivefold understanding,
with five whirlpools, a violent flood of fivefold misery,
divided into five disturbances with five branches.
  In this which vitalizes all things,
which appears in all things, the supreme—
in this God-wheel the human spirit wanders around
thinking that the soul and the causer are different.
  When favored by this, one attains immortality.
This has been sung as the supreme God.
In it there is a triad.
It is the firm support, the imperishable.
By knowing what is in there, God-knowers merge in God,
intent on it, liberated from the womb.

What is joined together as perishable and imperishable,
as manifest and unmanifest—the Lord supports it all.
Without the Lord, the soul is bound because of enjoying;
by knowing the divine, one is released from all restriction.

There are two unborn ones: the wise and the unwise,
the powerful and the powerless.
She too is unborn who is connected
with the enjoyer and objects of enjoyment.

The soul is infinite, universal, detached.
When one discovers this triad, that is God.
What is perishable is the material.
What is immortal and imperishable is the bearer.
Over both the perishable and the soul the divine one rules.

By meditating on this, by union with this,
and by entering into this being more and more
there finally occurs the cessation of every illusion.
By knowing the divine, every restriction passes away;
with disturbances ended, birth and death cease.

By meditating on this,
there is a third stage at the dissolution of the body,
universal lordship;
being absolute, one's desire is satisfied.
That eternal should be known as present in the soul.
Nothing higher than that can be known.

When one recognizes the enjoyer, the object of enjoyment,
and the universal causer, all has been said.
This is the threefold God.

As the form of fire when latent in its material
is not perceived—
and yet there is no disappearance of its potential—
but it may be sparked again by a drill in its material,
so both are found in the body by the use of AUM.
By making one's body the lower friction-stick
and the word AUM the upper friction-stick,
by practicing the friction of meditation,
one may see the divine which is hidden come to light.

As oil in sesame seeds, as butter in cream,
as water in springs, and as fire in the friction-sticks,
so is the soul found in one's own self,

if one looks for it with real discipline.
 The soul which pervades all things,
as butter is contained in cream,
which is rooted in self-knowledge and discipline—
this is God, the highest mystic doctrine!
This is God, the highest mystic doctrine!

2
 Savitri, first controlling the mind and thought for truth,
discerned the light of fire and brought it out of the earth.
With mind controlled, we are inspired by the god Savitri,
for heaven and strength.
With mind having controlled the powers
that go into heaven through thought,
may Savitri inspire them to become great light!
 The seers of the great god
control their mind and thoughts.
The one who knows the rules has arranged the rituals.
The chorus sings the glory of the god Savitri.
I join your prayer to God with adoration.
May my verses go forth like the sun on its path.
May all the children of immortality listen,
even those who have ascended to heaven.
 Where the fire burns, where the wind blows,
where the juice overflows, there mind is born.
Inspired by Savitri one should delight in the prayer to God.
If you make this your foundation,
the past will not tarnish you.
 Holding the body steady with the three parts erect,
and causing the senses with the mind to enter into the heart,
the wise with the God-boat cross over the rivers of fear.
Having restrained one's breath here in the body,
and having one's movements checked,
one should breathe through the nostrils with lessened breath.
Like the chariot yoked with wild horses,
the wise should restrain the mind attentively.
 In a clean, level spot,
without rubbish, fire, and blemishes,
where the sound of water and other surroundings

are favorable to thought, not offensive to the eye,
in a hidden retreat protected from the wind,
one should practice union.

   Fog, smoke, sun, fire, wind, fire-flies,
lightning, crystal, and a moon—
these are the preliminary appearances
before the manifestation of God in union.

   When the fivefold quality of union has been produced,
arising from earth, water, fire, air, and space,
no sickness nor old age nor death
has the one who obtains a body made from the fire of union.

   Lightness, health, steadiness, a clear countenance,
a pleasant voice, a sweet odor, and scant excretions—
these are the first stage in the progress of union.

   Just as a mirror covered by dust
shines brilliantly when it has been cleaned,
so the embodied one on seeing the nature of the soul,
becomes one, the goal attained, free from sorrow.

   When with the nature of the self, as with a lamp,
a practicer of union sees here the nature of God,
unborn, firm, from every nature free—
by knowing the divine, one is released from all restriction.

   That God faces all the quarters of heaven.
It was born, is in the womb, is born, and will be born.
It stands opposite creatures facing all directions.
The God who is in fire, who is in water,
who has entered into the whole universe,
who is in plants, who is in trees—
to that God be the glory—yes, the glory!

3
   The one spreader of the net, who rules with power,
who rules all the worlds with power,
the one who stands alone
in their rising and continuing existence—
those who know that one become immortal.

   For Rudra is the one, others notwithstanding for a moment,
who rules all the worlds with power,
watching over creatures as their protector,

after creating them all, merging them together at the end.
Having eyes and mouths everywhere,
arms and feet everywhere,
the one God making hands and wings,
creates the heaven and the earth.

The source and origin of the gods,
ruler of all, may Rudra,
the great seer, who anciently created the golden germ,
endow us with clear intellect.
Your form, Rudra, which is kind, free from fear and evil,
with that most loving form, appear to us,
resident of the mountains.
Resident of the mountains, make kind the arrow
which you hold in your hand to throw, mountain protector.
Do not injure human nor animal.

Higher than this is God, the supreme, the infinite,
hidden in all things, body by body,
the one embracing the universe—
by knowing this as Lord, humans become immortal.

I know this great Spirit,
radiant as the sun, beyond darkness.
Only by knowing this does one pass over death;
there is no other path for going there.
Nothing else is higher; nothing else is smaller,
nothing greater than the one
that stands like a tree established in heaven.

The whole world is filled by this, the Spirit.
That which is beyond this world
is without form and without ill.
Those who know that become immortal,
but others go only to sorrow.

The face, the head, the neck of all,
living in the hearts of all, all-pervading is this,
and generous, thus omnipresent and kind.
A great Lord is the Spirit, the initiator of goodness
to its purest attainment, the glory of imperishable light.

Spirit, the size of a thumb, is the inner soul,
always seated in the hearts of beings,
it is reached by the heart, by understanding, by the mind.

Those who know that become immortal.
  The Spirit has innumerable heads, eyes, and feet.
It surrounds the earth on all sides
and stands ten inches beyond.
The Spirit in truth is the whole universe,
whatever has been and whatever will be,
also sovereign of immortality and whatever grows by food.
Its hands and feet are everywhere,
everywhere its eyes and head and face;
its ears are everywhere. It stands encompassing all.
  Seeming to have the quality of all the senses,
it is empty of all the senses,
the sovereign Lord of all, the great shelter of all.
Though embodied in the nine-gated city,
back and forth to the external flies the human spirit,
the master of the universe, both the moving and non-moving.
  Without foot or hand, it is swift and a grabber.
It sees without eyes and hears without ears.
It knows whatever can be known, but no one knows it.
People call it the supreme primal Spirit.
  Subtler than the subtle, greater than the great,
is the soul that is set in the heart of a being here.
One sees it as being without active will
and becomes liberated from sorrow,
when through the grace of the creator
one sees the Lord and its greatness.
  I know this undecaying, primal soul of all,
always present in everything,
exempt from birth, as they say,
for the God-knowers speak of it as eternal.

4
  The one who is without color,
diversified by its union power,
distributes many colors in its hidden purpose,
and into this, its end and beginning, the universe dissolves.
  It is divine.
May it endow us with clear intellect.
It is fire; it is the sun; it is air, and it is the moon.

It is the seed; it is God;
it is the waters; it is the creator.

  You are woman; you are man;
you are the boy and the maiden.
You are that old person who walks supported by a staff.
Being born, you face every direction.
You are the blue bird and the green one with scarlet eyes.
You give birth to lightning and are the seasons and the seas.

  Without beginning you are inherently present
in all beings which are born.
With the one unborn female, red, white, and black,
who gives birth to many creatures like herself,
there lies the one unborn male enjoying her.
The other unborn male leaves after enjoying her.

  They are two birds, close companions,
clasping the same tree.
Of the two, one eats sweet fruit;
the other looks on without eating.
On this same tree a person,
sunk and grieving in slavery, is deluded,
but upon observing the Lord happy and great,
becomes free of sorrow.

  What good are the sacred verses,
in the highest heaven where all the gods are seated,
to the one who does not know this?
Those who know this are assembled here.

  Sacred poetry, sacrifices, ceremonies, vows,
the past, the future, and what the scriptures declare,
all this the illusion-maker projects out of this,
and in it by illusion the other is confined.

  Thus know that nature is illusion
and that the great Lord is the illusion-maker.
The whole world is filled
with beings who are parts of this.

  The one who rules over every source,
in whom the universe comes together and dissolves,
the Lord, giver of blessings, divinely loving,
by revering this, one finds peace.

That which is the source and origin of the gods,
sovereign of all, may Rudra, the great seer,
who saw the golden germ when it was born,
endow us with clear intellect.

Who is the master of the gods on whom the worlds rest?
Who is the Lord of the two-footed and four-footed here?
To what god shall we reverently give offerings?

Subtler than the subtle in the middle of confusion,
the creator of all in various forms,
the one embracer of the universe,
by knowing this as kind one attains eternal peace.

It is the protector of the world in time,
the master of the universe, hidden in all creatures,
with whom the seers of God and the gods are joined in union.
By knowing this, one cuts the ties of death.

By knowing as kind the one who is hidden in all things,
very fine like clarified butter, richer than butter,
the one who encompasses the whole universe—
by knowing the divine you may be released from bondage.

This God, the world-builder, the great soul,
always seated in the heart of creatures,
is reached by the heart, by understanding, by the mind.
Those who know that become immortal.

When there is no darkness, then there is no day or night,
no being or non-being, only the kind one alone.
That is the imperishable, the splendor of Savitri;
from that came primal wisdom.

Not above nor across
nor in the middle has one grasped this.
There is no comparison to that whose name is great glory.
Its form cannot be seen; no one ever sees it with eyes.
Those who know it in heart and mind
as living in the heart become immortal.

Knowing you are unborn, one approaches in fear.
Rudra, with your smiling face protect me forever.
Do not hurt our children nor our grandchildren,
nor our lives nor our cattle nor our horses.
Do not kill our heroes in anger, Rudra.
With offerings we always call upon you.

5

In the imperishable, infinite, supreme God
two things are hidden: knowledge and ignorance.
Ignorance dies, but knowledge is immortal.

That which is master of both is something else,
the one who rules over every source of creation,
all forms and all sources,
who holds in thought and sees when born
that red seer who was born at the beginning.

That God spreads out every net diversely
and draws it together in this field.
Thus having created the exercisers,
the Lord, the great soul, exercises universal sovereignty.

As the radiant sun shines
upon all regions above, below, and across,
so does this glorious one God of love
rule over whatever creatures are born from a womb.

The source of all who develops its own nature,
who brings to maturity whatever can be ripened,
that one distributes all qualities
and rules over this whole world.

What is hidden in the secret of the *Vedas*,
that is, in the *Upanishads*—
God knows that as the source of the sacred.
The gods and ancient seers who knew that
have become by its nature immortal.

Whoever has qualities performs works that bring results;
of such actions one experiences the consequences.
Undergoing all forms, characterized by the three qualities,
walking the three paths, the ruler of the vital breaths
wanders around according to one's actions.

It is the size of a thumb, bright as the sun,
when coupled with conception and ego.
But with only the qualities of understanding and soul,
it appears the size of the point of an awl.
This life is the hundredth part
of the point of a hair divided a hundred times,
and yet in it is infinity.

Not female nor male nor is it neuter.
Whatever body it takes to itself, with that it is connected.
By the delusions of imagination, touch, and sight,
and by eating, drinking, and impregnating
there is birth and development of the soul.
According to its actions the embodied one
successively assumes forms in various conditions.
Gross or refined, the embodied one chooses many forms
according to its own qualities.
Subsequently the cause of its union with them can be seen
because of the quality of its actions and of itself.
The one who is without beginning and without end,
in the middle of confusion, the creator of all,
of diverse form, is the one embracer of the universe.
By knowing the divine, one is released from all restriction.
The incorporeal is to be apprehended by the heart,
the master of existence and non-existence, the kind one,
the divine maker of all creation and its parts.
Those who know this, leave the body behind.

6
Some seers say it is self-existence,
others time; they are deluded.
It is the greatness of God in the world
by which this wheel of God revolves.
It envelopes the whole universe, is intelligent,
the creator of time, possessing the qualities, omniscient.
Ruled over by this, the cycle of works revolves,
earth, water, fire, air, and space.
It creates this work and rests again.
It joins itself with principle after principle,
with one, two, three, or eight,
with time and the subtleties of soul.
It begins with works subject to the qualities
and distributes all existences.
In the absence of these
the work that has been done disappears.
In the destruction of the work it continues,
because it is essentially different.

The beginning, the efficient cause of what is combined,
it is to be seen as beyond the three times and timeless.
Revere this as infinite, the origin of all being,
the God of love who lives in one's own thoughts, the primal.
Higher and different than the cosmic tree, time, and forms
is this from whom proceeds all phenomena.

Bringer of justice, remover of evil, Lord of prosperity—
know this as in one's own soul, as the immortal home of all.
This who is the supreme Lord of Lords, supreme God of gods,
supreme ruler of rulers, paramount,
this let us know as the God of love, the Lord of the world.

No action or organ of it can be found.
There is not seen its equal nor a superior.
Its high power is revealed to be diverse,
and innate is the working of its intelligence and strength.
It has no ruler in the world nor Lord, nor is there any mark.
It is the cause, sovereign over the Lord of sense-organs.
It has no parent nor ruler.

The one God which covers itself like a spider,
with a web produced from primal matter of its own existence,
may this grant us entrance into God.

The one God hidden in all things, all-pervading,
the inner soul of all beings, the master of action,
living in all things, the witness, the thinker,
without qualities, the one controller of the passive many,
who makes the one seed manifold—
the wise who perceive this as standing in one's soul,
they and no one else have eternal bliss.

That which is constant among the changing,
the intelligence in all consciousness,
the one among the many, who fulfills desires,
that cause, attainable by discernment and spiritual union—
by knowing God, one is released from all restriction.

There the sun does not shine, nor the moon and stars;
lightning does not shine, much less this fire.
As it shines, so does everything else shine.
This whole world is illuminated by its light.

The one swan of being in the heart of this universe,
this is the fire that has entered into the ocean.

Only by knowing this does one transcend death.
There is no other path for going there.
   That which is the creator of all, all-knowing,
originating from itself, intelligent, creator of time,
possessor of qualities, omniscient,
is the ruler of primal matter and the field of understanding,
Lord of the qualities, cause of reincarnation and liberation,
of continuance and of bondage.
   This is the immortal, existing as the Lord,
intelligent, omnipresent, protector of the universe,
who constantly rules this world.
Is there any other ruler than this?
   That which anciently created Brahma
and gave him the *Vedas*,
to that God who is the light of self-knowledge,
do I, questing for liberation, go for refuge,
to that which is without parts, without activity, peaceful,
faultless, stainless, the supreme bridge to immortality,
like a fire without smoke.
   When people roll up space like a skin,
then there will be an end of evil without knowing God.
   By the efficacy of his discipline and by the grace of God,
the wise Shvetashvatara correctly declared God
to the students of the most advanced stage of discipline,
which is well pleasing to the company of seers.
   The supreme mystery in the end of the *Vedas*,
which has been declared in former times,
should not be given to one who is not peaceful,
nor to anyone who is not a son or a pupil.
   If one has supreme devotion to God,
and for one's teacher as much as for God,
to this one these teachings which have been declared
may become manifest in a great soul,
yes, may become manifest in a great soul.

Introduction to the Bhagavad-Gita

The Lord's Song (Bhagavad-Gita) is contained in Book 6 of the great Hindu epic, *Mahabharata*, probably the longest poem in all of literature. The *Gita* was written between the fifth century BC and the second century CE and is attributed to Vyasa. According to Aurobindo, who studied Vyasa's writings, nothing disproves his authorship.

The *Mahabharata* tells the story of a civil war in ancient India between the sons of Kuru (Kauruvas) and the sons of Pandu (Pandavas) over a kingdom the Pandavas believe was stolen from them by the cheating of the Kauruvas. Every attempt by the Pandava brothers to regain their kingdom without war has failed.

The *Bhagavad-Gita* is primarily a dialog between Arjuna, the third Pandava brother, and his charioteer, Krishna. Remaining neutral, Krishna allowed one side to use his vassals in battle, while the other side could have him as a charioteer although he would not fight himself. The old blind King Dhritarashtra declined a great sage's offer to give him sight for the battle, because he did not want to see the bloodshed. Instead the great sage gave Sanjaya the ability to perceive at a distance everything that was going on, and he describes the events for the King.

In the *Gita* Krishna, who is the uncle and friend of the Pandavas, gives Arjuna teachings on yoga, which means union and implies union with God. Krishna is considered by Hindus to be an incarnation of the god Vishnu, the preserver.

In the first chapter of the *Gita*, some of the heroes of the two armies are mentioned by King Duryodhana, the oldest Kaurava brother, first the Pandavas: the son of Drupada, Bhima, Arjuna, Yuyudhana, Virata, Drupada, Dhrishtaketu, Chekitana, the King of Kashi, Purujit, Kuntibhoja, Shaibya, Yudhamanyu, Uttamauja, the son of Subhadra, and the sons of Draupadi; then the Kauravas: Bhishma, Karna, Kripa, Ashvatthaman, Vikarna, Saumadatti, and Drona. When they blow their conch-horns, Arjuna's brothers are named: Bhima, Yudhishthira, Nakula, and Sahadeva.

Throughout the text various epithets or nicknames are used for Krishna and Arjuna. Krishna is called: Madhava

(descendant of Madhu), Hrishikesha (bristling-haired),
Keshava (handsome-haired), Govinda (chief of herdsmen),
slayer of Madhu (a demon), Janardana (agitator of humans),
Varshneya (clansman of the Vrishnis), Vasudeva (son of
Vasudeva), Hari, and slayer of Keshin (a demon). Arjuna is
called: son of Pandu, Gudakesha (thick-haired), Partha (son of
Pritha, Kunti's original name), Kaunteya (son of Kunti),
Bharata (ancient name of India, used for other characters as
well), Bharata bull, wealth winner, foe scorcher, great-armed
one, blameless one, tiger spirit, and Kuru's joy or best of Kurus
(Kuru being a common ancestor of both the Pandavas and the
Kauravas). Gandiva is the name of Arjuna's bow.

Notes to:

2: *Kshatriya* is the ruling warrior caste, and a *brahman* is of the
priest caste.
2, 3, 5, and 18: Sankhya is one of the six orthodox schools of
   Hindu philosophy emphasizing the difference between
   Spirit and Nature, the knower and the field of knowledge.
3: Janaka was an ancient philosopher-king.
4: Vivasvat is a sun god, Manu his son, and Ikshvaku the son of
   Manu.
10: The four Manus are ancestors of the human race.
   Adityas are supreme gods.
   Marici was the chief of the Maruts or storm gods.
   Vasava is another name for the chief god Indra.
   Rudras are storm gods of destruction, and their chief is
      Shiva, here called Shankara.
   Vittesha is a Lord of wealth.
   Yakshas and Rakshasas are spirits.
   Vasus are bright gods.
   Meru is the most sacred mountain.
   Brihaspati is a priest of the gods.
   Skanda is a god of war.
   Bhrigu was an ancient seer who mediated quarrels among
      the gods.
   Narada was a seer, son of Brahma and goddess of learning.
   Chitraratha is the chief of the Gandharvas, the heavenly
      musicians.
   Kapila was the founder of the Sankhya philosophy.

Uchchaihshravas is the name of Indra's horse.

Airavata is Indra's elephant.

Vasuki is king of the snakes.

Ananta means unending and is a snake which encircles the earth.

Varuna is god of the sea.

Aryaman is the chief of the ancestors.

Yama is the god of death.

Prahlada defected from the Daityas, who are the enemies of the gods.

Vainateya is a bird known as Garuda, who was used as a vehicle by Vishnu.

Rama is the warrior hero of the *Ramayana*.

Makara is a sea monster identified with Capricorn in the Hindu zodiac, also a vehicle for Varuna.

The daughter of Jahnu is the river Ganges, so called because the sage Jahnu drank up the river before allowing it to flow from his ear.

The Brihat Saman is a chant to Indra in the *Sama Veda*.

The gayatri is a *Rig Veda* meter with three lines of eight syllables each, suitable for the priests.

The Vrishnis are the clan from which Vasudeva (Krishna) descended.

Vyasa, the legendary sage, was to said to have composed *Vedas* and the *Mahabharata*.

Ushanas was an ancient seer and poet.

11: The Ashvins are celestial twin gods of healing.

Sadhyas are celestial beings.

Vishvas are devas or spirits.

Ushmapas are steam drinkers or ancestors.

Asuras are demons or enemies of the gods.

Siddhas are perfected ones.

15: The ashvattha tree is sacred in India.

17: "AUM" or "OM" is the sacred mantra; "tat" means that; and "sat" means reality, truth, being.

18: The word "karma" usually is translated action, but in one instance it is translated as karma, because it implies the karmic pattern of one's actions.

The Lord's Song
(Bhagavad-Gita)

1

Dhritarashtra said,
"In the field of duty in the field of Kuru,
gathered together to fight,
what did mine and Pandu's sons do, Sanjaya?"

Sanjaya said,
"Seeing the Pandava army arrayed,
King Duryodhana then approaching his teacher
said this speech:

'Look, master, at the Pandava's great army
arrayed by the son of Drupada, your intelligent student.
Here are heroes, great archers
equal in battle to Bhima and Arjuna;
Yuyudhana and Virata and Drupada of the great chariot;
Dhrishtaketu, Chekitana and the valiant King of Kashi,
Purujit and Kuntibhoja and Shaibya, a human bull;
bold Yudhamanyu and valiant Uttamauja;
the son of Subhadra and the sons of Draupadi;
all having great chariots.

"'Ours who are distinguished know them,
best of the twice-born,
the leaders of my army,
by proper names I tell them to you:
yourself and Bhishma and Karna
and Kripa, victorious in battle,
Ashvatthaman and Vikarna and Saumadatti also;
and many other heroes risking lives for my sake,
armed with various weapons, all skilled in battle.

"'Inadequate is that force of ours guarded by Bhishma,
but adequate is this force of theirs guarded by Bhima.
So in all designated formations
make sure you all protect Bhishma.'

"Cheering him up, the aged Kuru grandsire,
roaring loudly like a lion,
blew his conch horn powerfully.
Then conch horns and kettledrums, tabors, drums, horns

suddenly sounded this tumultuous uproar.
Then standing in the great chariot yoked with white horses,
Madhava and the son of Pandu blew their divine conch horns:
Hrishikesha his Panchajanya, wealth winner his Devadatta;
wolf-bellied Bhima blew Paundra, his great conch horn;
King Yudhishthira blew Anantavijaya;
Nakula and Sahadeva blew Sughosha and Manipushpaka;
and Kashya, top archer, and Shikhandi, of the great chariot,
Dhrishtadyumna and Virata and invincible Satyaki,
Drupada and the sons of Draupadi,
all together, O Lord of the earth,
and strong-armed Saubhadra,
each blew their own conch horns.
This noise burst the hearts of the sons of Dhritarashtra,
and the tumult caused the sky and earth to resound.

"Then seeing the sons of Dhritarashtra in battle order,
in the ensuing clash of weapons
the monkey-bannered son of Pandu raising his bow
then said this speech to Hrishikesha, Lord of the earth:
'Position my chariot between the two armies, changeless one,
so that I may see these who are formed and eager to fight.
With whom must I fight in undertaking this bash?
I see these who are ready to fight
wishing to serve in war
the evil-minded son of Dhritarashtra.'

"Thus Hrishikesha addressed by Gudakesha, O Bharata,
having positioned the best chariot between the two armies,
in front of Bhishma, Drona, and all the rulers of the earth,
said, 'Partha, look at these Kurus assembled here.'

"There Partha saw positioned fathers and grandfathers,
teachers, uncles, brothers, sons, grandsons, friends as well,
fathers-in-law and even companions in both armies also.
Regarding all these relatives arrayed, this Kaunteya,
filled with deep pity despondently said this:
'Seeing this, my own people, Krishna, approaching to fight,
my limbs sink, and my mouth dries up,
and trembling in my body and bristling hair occur.
Gandiva slips from my hand, and my skin burns;
and I am not able to stand, and my mind wanders;

and I see contrary omens, Keshava;
and I do not foresee good fortune
in killing my own people in battle.

  "'I do not want victory, Krishna,
nor kingdom nor pleasures.
What is kingdom to us, Govinda?
What is enjoyment or life?
Those for whose sake
we want kingdom, enjoyment and pleasure
are these positioned for battle, abandoning life and riches,
teachers, fathers, sons, and also grandfathers, uncles,
fathers-in-law, grandsons, brothers-in-law, and other kin.

  "'These I do not wish to kill,
even though they are killing, slayer of Madhu,
even for the sovereignty of the three worlds,
how then for the earth?
Striking down the sons of Dhritarashtra,
what joy could be ours, Janardana?
Evil should cling to us for killing these attackers.
Therefore we should not kill
the sons of Dhritarashtra, our relatives.
How could we ever be happy
killing our own people, Madhava?

  "'Even if these whose thoughts are overpowered by greed
see no wrong in causing the destruction of family,
injury to friends and crime,
why is it not understood by us to turn away from this evil,
the family-destruction wrong, by discernment, Janardana?
In family destruction the ancient family duties vanish;
in losing duty lawlessness also overcomes the whole family.
From the overcoming of lawlessness, Krishna,
the women of the family are corrupted;
in the spoiling of the women, Varshneya,
is born the intermixture of caste.
The intermixture of the family destroyers and the family
leads to hell;
their ancestors fall, deprived of rice-ball and water rites.
By wrongs of the family destroyers
producing caste intermixture

race duties and eternal family duties are abolished.
Of family-duty-abolishing men dwelling indefinitely in hell
we have often heard.
   "'Oh alas! What great evil are we resolved to do,
which through greed for royal pleasures
we are prepared to kill our own people.
If the sons of Dhritarashtra should kill in battle,
unresisting, unarmed, that would be greater happiness to me.'
   "Thus speaking on the battlefield,
Arjuna sat down on the chariot seat,
throwing down bow and arrow,
his mind overcome by sorrow."

2

  Sanjaya said,
"To him thus overcome by pity,
whose eyes were filled with tears and downcast, despairing,
the slayer of Madhu said this speech:
   "The blessed Lord said,
'How has this timidity in difficulty come upon you,
not proper for an Aryan, not leading to heaven,
causing disgrace, Arjuna?
You should never be a coward, Partha!
this is not fitting in you.
Abandon base faintheartedness, stand up, foe scorcher!'
   "Arjuna said,
'How shall I in battle, slayer of Madhu,
with arrows fight against Bhishma and Drona,
the two venerable enemies, slayer of foes?
Instead of killing noble gurus
it is better to live by begging in this world;
having killed gurus desiring gain here on earth
I should enjoy pleasures smeared with blood.
Nor do we know which of these two is more important for us,
whether we should conquer or if they should conquer us,
those standing before us, the sons of Dhritarashtra,
whom having killed, we should not want to live.

"'Weak pity discouraging my being,
I, uncertain in thought as to duty, ask you
which should be better for certain, tell it to me.
I am your student fallen at your feet; correct me!
I do not see what would remove this sorrow of mine,
which dries up the senses,
even if obtaining unrivaled prosperity on earth,
royal power or even the sovereignty of the gods.'"
  Sanjaya said,
"Thus having spoken to Hrishikesha,
Gudakesha, foe scorcher, saying,
'I shall not fight' to Govinda, became silent.

  "Hrishikesha smiling, so to speak, Bharata,
between the two armies said to the dejected this speech:
  "The blessed Lord said,
'You grieve for those who should not be grieved for;
yet you speak wise words.
Neither for the dead nor those not dead do the wise grieve.
Never was there a time when I did not exist
nor you nor these lords of men.
Neither will there be a time when we shall not exist;
we all exist from now on.
As the soul experiences in this body
childhood, youth, and old age,
so also it acquires another body;
the sage in this is not deluded.

  "'Material sensations, Kaunteya,
causing cold, heat, pleasure, pain,
coming and going are impermanent;
you must endure them, Bharata.
The person whom these do not trouble, powerful person,
pain and pleasure being equal to the sage,
he is ready for immortality.

  "'The existence of the unreal is not found;
the non-existence of the real is not found.
The certainty of both of these has been seen
by the seers of essence.
Know that indestructible essence
by which all this is pervaded.

No one is able to cause the destruction of the imperishable.
These bodies have an end;
it is said of the indestructible, infinite soul
that it is eternal.
Therefore, fight, Bharata!
   "'Whoever believes this the killer
and whoever thinks this the killed,
they both do not understand;
this does not kill and is not killed.
Neither is it born nor does it die at any time,
nor having been, will this again not be.
Unborn, eternal, perpetual this ancient being
is not killed with the killing of the body.
   "'Whoever knows this, the indestructible,
the eternal, the unborn, the imperishable,
how does this person, Partha, cause the killing of anyone?
Whom does one kill?
As a person abandoning worn-out clothes takes new ones,
so abandoning worn-out bodies the soul enters new ones.
Weapons do not cut this nor does fire burn this,
and waters cannot wet this nor can wind dry it.
Not pierced this, not burned this, not wetted nor dried,
eternal, all-pervading, stable,
immovable is this everlasting.
Unmanifest this, it is said.
   "'Therefore knowing this you should not mourn.
And if you think this is eternally born or eternally dying,
even then, you mighty armed, you should not mourn this.
Death is certain for the born,
and birth is certain for the dead.
Therefore you should not mourn over the inevitable.
   "'Beings have unmanifest beginnings,
manifest middles, Bharata, unmanifest ends again.
What complaint is there?
Marvelously someone sees this,
and marvelously another thus tells,
and marvelously another hears this,
but even having heard no one knows this.
This embodied soul is eternally inviolable

in the body of all, Bharata.
Therefore you should not mourn for any being.

   "'So looking at your duty you should not waver,
for there is no greater duty than battle for the *kshatriya*.
And by good fortune gaining the open door of heaven,
happy *kshatriyas*, Partha, encounter such a battle.
Now if you will not undertake this combat duty,
then having avoided your duty and glory, you will incur evil.
And also people will relate your perpetual dishonor,
and for the esteemed, dishonor is worse than dying.
The great warriors will think
you withdraw from battle out of fear,
and having been thought much of
among those you will be held lightly.
And enemies will say of you many words not to be spoken,
deriding your strength.
What is more painful than that?

   "'Either killed you will attain heaven,
or conquering you will enjoy the earth.
Therefore stand up, Kaunteya, resolved to the battle.
Making pleasure and pain the same,
gain and loss, victory and defeat,
then engage in battle.
Thus you will not incur evil.

   "'This intuition described for you in Sankhya philosophy,
learn this in yoga;
unified by intuition, Partha,
you shall avoid the bondage of action.
There is no lost effort here; no setback occurs.
Even a little of this discipline protects from great fear.

   "'Self-determined intuition is one here, Kuru's joy,
but intuitions of the irresolute many-branched, so endless.
This flowery speech which the ignorant proclaim,
delighting in the letter of the scripture, Partha,
saying there is nothing else,
minds desiring the highest heaven,
offering birth as the fruit of action,
performing many special rituals,
aimed toward enjoyment and power,

attached to enjoyment and power,
whose thoughts are stolen away by this,
to those,
self-determined intuition in meditation is not granted.
   "'The scriptures categorize three qualities.
Be without the three qualities, Arjuna,
without opposites, eternally staying in goodness,
without possessiveness, soul-established.
As much use as in a well in water overflowing everywhere,
so much are all the scriptures to an enlightened *brahman*.
   "'In action alone is your claim,
never to its fruits at all.
Never should the fruit of action be your motive;
never let there be attachment in your inactivity.
Staying in yoga do your actions,
letting go of attachment, wealth-winner.
Seek refuge in intuition.
Pitiful are those motivated by fruit.
Unified intuition here lets go of both good and bad deeds.
   "'Therefore unify yourself with yoga;
yoga is skilled in actions.
Letting go of the fruit of action,
the intelligent of unified intuition,
liberated from the bondage of birth,
go the way free from misery.
When your intuition passes beyond the confusion of delusion,
you will become indifferent to what you hear
and to what has been heard in scripture.
Disregarding scripture, when in meditation
your immovable intuition will stand unmoving,
then you will attain union.'
   "Arjuna said,
'What is the definition of one who is
steady in wisdom, steady in meditation, Keshava?
How should one steady in thought speak?
How should one sit? How should one move?'
   "The blessed Lord said,
'When one gives up all desires emerging in the mind, Partha,
satisfied in the soul by the soul,

then one is said to be steady in wisdom.

"'Whoever in pain is free of mental anxiety,
in pleasure is free of desire,
departing from passion, fear, and anger,
steady in thought, is called a sage.

"'Whoever is without attachment in all things,
accepting this or that, pleasant or unpleasant,
neither liking nor disliking,
the wisdom of this one is established.

"'And when this one withdraws,
like a tortoise all its limbs,
the senses from the objects of sense,
the wisdom of this one is established.

"'Objects turn away from the embodied one who is fasting,
except flavor;
even flavor turns away from the one seeing the supreme.
Kaunteya, tormenting senses forcibly carry away the mind
even of the striving person of learning.
Restraining all these,
one should sit unified with me in the supreme;
whose senses are in control,
the wisdom of this one is established.

"'From a person's contemplating objects
is born attachment to them;
from attachment is born desire;
from desire is born anger;
from anger comes delusion;
from delusion, memory wandering;
from memory wandering, loss of intuition;
from loss of intuition, one perishes.

"'Lust and aversion eliminated,
but engaging objects with the senses,
the self-governing by self-control attains tranquillity.
In tranquillity is born cessation of all one's pains.
Having clear thoughts, quickly the intuition becomes steady.

"'There is no intuition for the undisciplined,
and for the undisciplined no concentration,
and without concentration no peace.
Without peace, where is happiness?

When the mind is led by the wandering of the senses,
then it carries away wisdom
like the wind a ship on the water.
   "'Therefore, mighty-armed, the one whose senses
are completely withdrawn from the objects of sense,
the wisdom of this one is established.
What is night to all beings
in this the restrained is awake;
what beings are awake in
that is the night of the seeing sage.
Just as waters dissolve in the ocean, filled, unmoved, still,
so too all desires dissolve in the one who attains peace,
not in the desirer of desires.
The person who, giving up all desires,
lives free from longing, without possessiveness,
without egotism, this one attains peace.
This is a holy state, Partha.
No one attaining this is deluded.
Steady in this even at the time of death,
one reaches holy nirvana.'

3
   "Arjuna said,
'If your intuition idea is better than action, Janardana,
then why do you urge me into this terrible action, Keshava?
With equivocal speech you confuse my intuition.
This one thing tell me without doubt:
by which I should attain what is better.'
   "The blessed Lord said,
'In this world a two-fold basis
was previously taught by me, blameless one:
the knowledge yoga of the *Sankhyas*
and the action yoga of the yogis.
Not by abstention from actions
does a person attain freedom from action,
and not by renunciation alone
does one approach perfection.
No one even for an instant can ever stay actionless.
Everyone must perform action unwillingly
by the qualities born of nature.

"'Whoever sits, restraining the powers of action
with the mind remembering sense objects,
this deluded self is called a hypocrite.
But whoever, controlling the senses with the mind, Arjuna,
engages by the powers of action in action yoga,
unattached, this one is distinguished.

"'You do controlled action.
Action is better than inaction.
Even your body maintenance
could not be accomplished without action.
Aside from action for the purpose of sacrifice
this world is bound by action.
Perform action for this purpose, Kaunteya,
free from attachment.

"'Having sent forth creatures along with sacrifices,
the Creator anciently said, "By this bring forth;
may this be the milk of your desires."
May you cherish by this the gods;
may the gods cherish you;
cherishing each other, you will attain the supreme good.
Cherished by sacrifice,
the gods will give to you wished-for enjoyments.

"'Whoever enjoys these without offering gifts to them
is just a thief.
The good who partake of the rest of the sacrifice
are released from all evils,
but the wicked who cook for their own sake enjoy impurity.

"'Creatures come from food;
food is produced from rain;
rain comes from sacrifice;
sacrifice is produced by action.
Know that God-produced action
originates in imperishable God.
Therefore all-pervading God
eternally remains in the sacrifice.

"'Thus whoever does not turn the revolving wheel here,
who is malicious, sense-delighted,
this one lives vainly, Partha.
The person who is self-pleased and self-satisfied

and self-content, this one's task is not found.
Whoever has no purpose in what is done or not done,
has no need of purpose in anyone.

  "'Therefore without being attached
always perform the action to be done.
Practicing action without being attached,
a person attains the supreme.
By action Janaka and others attained perfection.
You also observing what the world needs should act.

  "'Whatever the best do, that others do also.
This sets a standard that the world follows.
Partha, there is nothing for me to do in the three worlds,
nothing unattained to be attained;
yet I engage in action.
If I should not engage in tireless action at all,
people everywhere would follow my path, Partha.
If I should not perform action,
these worlds would be ruined;
I should be a maker of confusion,
and I should destroy these creatures.

  "'As the unwise act attached to action, Bharata,
so the wise should act unattached,
intending to maintain the world.
One should not cause the mental breakdown
of the action-attached ignorant.
The wise, practicing union, should encourage all actions.

  "'All actions being performed by the qualities of nature,
the ego-deluded self thinks that the "I" is the doer.
But knowing the truth, great-armed one,
of the two roles of quality and action,
"qualities work in qualities,"
thus thinking one is not attached.
Those deluded by the qualities of nature
are attached to qualified actions.
The knower of the whole should not disturb
fools who are ignorant of the whole.

  "'Entrusting all actions to me,
meditating on the supreme soul,
being free from desire, free from possession,

fight, cured of fever.
People who constantly practice this doctrine of mine,
trusting, not complaining,
they also are liberated from actions.

"'But those who, complaining about this,
do not practice my doctrine,
confusing all knowledge,
know them to be lost, thoughtless.

"'Even the wise act according to their own nature.
Creatures follow nature.
What will constraint accomplish?
Like-dislike situated in sense and the object of sense,
one should not come under the power of these two adversaries.
Better one's own imperfect duty
than another's duty well performed.
Death in one's own duty is better.
Another's duty brings fear.'

"Arjuna said,
'Then by what compulsion does a person commit harm,
even unwillingly, Varshneya,
as if commanded by force?'

"The blessed Lord said,
'This is desire, this is anger,
born of the emotional quality.
Voracious and greatly injurious,
know this to be the enemy here.
As fire is obscured by smoke, and a mirror by dust,
as the embryo is enveloped by the amnion,
so this is covered by it.
Knowledge is covered by this eternal enemy of knowers,
in the form of desire, Kaunteya,
which is an insatiable fire.
The senses, mind, and intuition are said to be its seat.
With these it confuses knowledge, covering the embodied.
Therefore you, at first restraining the senses,
Bharata bull, kill this harmful thing
that destroys intelligent knowledge.

"'The senses, they say, are high.
Higher than the senses is the mind,

but higher than the mind is the intuition,
but higher than the intuition is this.
Thus intuiting what is higher than the intuition,
sustaining the soul with the soul,
kill the adversary, great-armed one,
the desire-form difficult to approach.'

4
   "The blessed Lord said,
'This imperishable yoga I declared to Vivasvat.
Vivasvat communicated it to Manu,
and Manu told it to Ikshvaku.
Thus received by royal succession,
the royal sages knew this.
In the long time here this yoga was lost, foe scorcher.
This same ancient yoga is declared by me to you today,
since you are my devoted friend.
This is the supreme mystery.'
   "Arjuna said,
'Later was your birth, earlier the birth of Vivasvat.
How should I understand
that you declared this so in the beginning?'
   "The blessed Lord said,
'Many of my births have passed away,
and yours too, Arjuna.
I know them all; you do not know, foe scorcher.
Though being a birthless imperishable soul,
though being Lord of beings,
controlling my own nature,
I come into being by the magic of my soul.
   "'Whenever a decrease of justice occurs, Bharata,
and an uprising of injustice,
then I give forth my soul.
For the protection of the good
and for the destruction of the evil-doers,
for the purpose of establishing justice
I am born from age to age.
   "'Whoever truly knows my divine birth and action,
having left the body does not go to rebirth;

this one comes to me, Arjuna.
Passion, fear, and anger gone,
absorbed in me, relying on me,
many purified by disciplined knowledge
have attained my existence.
Whoever approaches me, I love them.
People everywhere follow my path, Partha.

　　"'Wanting successful actions, they worship gods here.
Quickly in the human world successful action comes.
Four castes were brought forth by me
according to the distribution of the action qualities.
Although I did this,
know me as the imperishable non-doer.
Actions do not affect me, not desiring their fruit.
Thus whoever understands me is not bound by actions.
Thus knowing, action done by the ancients
was also for the seeking of liberation.
Therefore you do actions
as they were done earlier by the ancients.

　　"'What is action? What is inaction?
Even the poets were confused about this.
I shall explain to you this action,
which knowing you will be liberated from evil.
Being enlightened about action and also wrong action,
and being enlightened about inaction,
the way of action is profound.
Whoever perceives inaction in action and action in inaction
is enlightened among people;
this one does all action united.
The one whose every undertaking
is without desirous intention
has consumed actions in the fire of knowledge;
this one the enlightened call learned.

　　"'Having abandoned attachment to the fruit of action,
always satisfied, independent even while engaging in action,
one does not do anything.
Hoping for nothing with soul-controlled consciousness,
abandoning every possession,
performing action with the body alone,

one incurs no guilt.
Content with spontaneous gain, transcending duality,
free from envy, indifferent to success and failure,
even when acting one is not bound.

"'With attachment gone, liberated,
thought established in knowledge,
action undertaken as a sacrifice is completely dissolved.
God is the offering; God is the gift
poured out into the fire of God by God.
God is attained by one who contemplates the action of God.

"'Some yogis practice sacrifice to the divine;
others offer sacrifice in the fire of God by sacrifice.
Some offer hearing and other senses
in the fires of restraint;
others offer sound and other sense objects
in the fires of the senses.
Others offer all sense actions and all breath actions
in the yoga fire of self-restraint kindled by knowledge.
Material sacrifices, discipline sacrifices,
yoga sacrifices are thus some;
self-study of knowledge sacrifices
and ascetics are of sharpened vows.

"'Some offer inhalation into exhalation,
also exhalation into inhalation,
restraining the breathing paths
intent on controlling the breath.
Others regulating food offer inhalations into inhalations.
All these knowing sacrifice by sacrifice destroy wrongs.
Those eating the sacred food left from the sacrifice
go to God eternal.

"'Not even this world is for those not sacrificing,
how then the other, best of Kurus?
Thus sacrifices of many kinds
are spread out in the mouth of God.
Know them all to come from action;
knowing this you shall be released.

"'Better than the sacrifice of material possessions
is the knowledge sacrifice, foe scorcher.
All action, without exception, Partha,

is completely comprehended in knowledge.
Know this: by respect, inquiry, service,
knowers who perceive the truth will teach you knowledge,
which knowing you shall not fall again into delusion,
son of Pandu; by this you shall see
every being in the soul, then in me.
    "'Even if you are the most evil of all the evil-doers,
by the boat of knowledge you shall cross over all wickedness.
As wood kindled by fire is burned to ashes, Arjuna,
the fire of knowledge burns all actions to ashes also.
No purifier equal to knowledge is found in the world.
The self perfected in union in time finds that in the soul.
    "'The trusting gains that knowledge which is supreme;
controlling the senses, gaining knowledge,
one attains supreme peace without delay.
The ignorant and untrusting and self-doubting are lost.
Neither this world nor that beyond nor happiness
is for the self-doubting.
    "'Union renouncing action, knowledge severing doubt,
soul composed, no actions bind, wealth winner.
Therefore severing ignorance-produced doubt in the heart
with the knowledge sword of the soul,
establish union and rise, Bharata.'

5
    "Arjuna said,
'Krishna, you praise renunciation of actions and also yoga.
Which one of these two is better?
Tell me this definitely.'
    "The blessed Lord said,
'Both renunciation and action yoga lead to the best,
but of the two, action yoga surpasses renunciation of action.
Whoever is indifferent to dualities, great-armed one,
is easily released from bondage.
Sankhya and yoga are separate,
maintain the foolish, not the wise.
Whoever practices even one correctly
finds the fruit of both.
That state attained by the Sankhyas

is also reached by the yogis.
Whoever sees Sankhya and yoga as one, sees.
But renunciation, great-armed one,
is difficult to attain without union.
The wise united in yoga quickly attain God.

"'United in yoga the purified soul
self-controlled, controlling senses,
the soul being the soul of all beings,
even while acting is not affected.
"I am doing nothing at all," thinks the united truth knower,
seeing, hearing, touching, smelling,
eating, walking, sleeping, breathing,
talking, releasing, holding, opening eyes and closing eyes,
believing that the senses operate in the sense objects.

"'Whoever acts putting actions in God,
abandoning attachment, is not affected by evil,
like a lotus leaf by water.
With the body, mind, intuition, and even the senses alone,
yogis perform action, abandoning attachment,
for self-purification.
United, abandoning the fruit of action,
one attains complete peace.
Disunited by desirous action,
attached to the fruit, one is bound.

"'Renouncing all actions with the mind,
the embodied sits happily, master in the city of nine gates,
neither acting nor causing action.
The Lord creates neither agency nor actions of the world
nor the union of action with fruit,
but nature proceeds.
The omnipresent does not take anyone's evil or goodness.

"'Knowledge being concealed by ignorance,
people are deluded by this.
But those whose ignorance is destroyed by knowledge of soul,
like the sun, their knowledge illuminates this supreme.
Those intuiting that, thinking that, established in that,
devoted to that, go not again to rebirth,
knowledge shaking off wrongs.

"'The wise look equally on a *brahman*
endowed with cultivated learning,
on a cow, an elephant, a dog, or an outcaste.
Here birth is conquered by those
whose mind is established in equanimity.
Guiltless and impartial is God;
therefore they are established in God.
    "'One should not rejoice obtaining the pleasant
nor be sad obtaining the unpleasant.
Firm intuition unconfused knowing God
is established in God.
The soul unattached to external contacts
finds happiness in the soul.
This soul united to God by yoga
enjoys imperishable happiness.
Delights born of contact are wombs of pain,
having a beginning and an end, Kaunteya.
The enlightened one is not content in them.
    "'Whoever is able to endure here
before release from the body
the agitation originating from desire and anger
is united; this is a happy person.
Whoever has inner happiness, inner joy,
and thus inner light,
this yogi attains the nirvana of God, oneness with God.
Seers attain the nirvana of God, sins wiped out,
dualities dissolved, self-controlled,
rejoicing in the welfare of all beings.
Rid of desire and anger, thoughts restrained, souls known,
the ascetics' nirvana of God lies near.
    "'Making external contacts excluded
and the gaze in between the two eyebrows,
making inhalation and exhalation equal,
moving within the nose,
with controlled senses, mind, and intuition,
the sage seeking ultimate liberation,
rid of desire, fear, and anger is forever liberated.
Knowing me, the enjoyer of sacrifice disciplines,
great Lord of all the world, friend of all beings,

one reaches peace.'

6
"The blessed Lord said,
'Not depending on the fruit of action to be done
whoever performs action is the renouncer and yogi,
not the one without the fire and without action.
Thus what they call renunciation
know this to be yoga, son of Pandu.
Without renouncing motive, no one becomes a yogi.

"'It is said that action is the method
of the sage wishing to ascend to union;
it is said that serenity is the method
of the one who has ascended to union.
When he is not attached to sense objects nor to actions,
renouncing all motivation,
then he is said to have ascended to union.

"'One should uplift the self by the soul;
one should not lower the soul.
The self is the friend of the soul;
the self is the enemy of the soul.
The self is a friend of the soul
whose self is mastered by the soul,
but the self of the non-soul
might become hostile like an enemy.

"'The highest self of the self-mastered, the peaceful,
is steadfast in cold, heat, pleasure, or pain,
as well as in honor or dishonor.
Content in the wisdom of self-knowledge, immutable,
having mastered sense, united thus,
one is said to be a yogi,
to whom a clod, a stone, and gold are the same.
Detached from companions, allies, foes,
neutral toward enemies and friends, also the good and evil,
impartial intuition is distinguished.

"'The yogi should unite constantly with the soul,
situated in solitude, one self-controlled consciousness
without wanting, without possessing.
In a clear place establishing the firm seat of the soul,

neither too high nor too low,
covered with cloth, antelope skin, and kusha grass,
there making the mind single,
consciousness and sense activity controlled,
sitting on the seat
one should practice union for self-purification.
Keeping even the unmoving body, head, and neck steady,
concentrating the eyes on the tip of the nose,
and not looking around,
the self calmed, fear banished, staying in chastity,
controlling the mind, conscious of me,
united, one should sit devoted to me.
Thus always united with the soul,
the yogi of disciplined mind
attains peace, supreme nirvana, founded with me.
    "'Yoga is neither eating too much nor not eating at all,
and neither the habit of sleeping too much
nor that of keeping awake, Arjuna.
Food and recreation disciplined,
disciplined in the actions of behavior,
disciplined in sleep and waking,
yoga becomes the ending of sorrow.
    "'When conscious control is established in the soul,
free from the longing of all desire,
then one is said to be thus united.
As a lamp in a windless state does not flicker,
the analogy is remembered of the yogi
of conscious control united in the yoga of the soul.
Where consciousness rests curbed by the practice of yoga,
and where by the soul seeing the soul
in the soul one is content.
One knows this perpetual happiness,
which is intuitively perceived beyond the senses,
and established there does not deviate from that truth;
and which having gained, one thinks no other gain
better than this in which is established
one who is not disturbed even by heavy sorrow.
Let it be known that
this dissolution of union with sorrow is called yoga.

"'This yoga is to be practiced
with determination without discouraged thought.
Abandoning without exception all desires born of motivation,
completely mastering the senses with the mind,
one should gradually with firm intuitive perception
quiet the mind, the soul making it stand still.
One should not think of anything at all.
Whenever the unsteady moving mind wanders here and there,
mastering this, one should direct the will in the soul.
Supreme happiness comes to this peaceful mind of the yogi,
emotion pacified, God-realized, sinless.
Thus always uniting the soul, the yogi freed from evil
easily reaches the endless happiness of God-contact.

"'The soul united in yoga observes the soul in all beings
and all beings in the soul, everywhere the same revelation.
Whoever sees me everywhere and sees everything in me,
I am not lost to this one, and this one is not lost to me.
Whoever is established in oneness honors me in all beings;
moving in any way also this yogi lives in me.
Whoever sees by soul analogy everywhere the same, Arjuna,
whether happiness or sorrow,
this one is thought a supreme yogi.'

"Arjuna said,
'This yoga which is explained by you with equanimity,
slayer of Madhu, I do not see standing steady
because of instability.
Unstable is the mind, Krishna, impetuous, strong, rigid;
I think holding it back, like the wind, is difficult.'

"The blessed Lord said,
'Without doubt, great-armed one,
the restless mind is hard to control,
but by practice, Kaunteya, and by detachment
it is controlled.
Undisciplined by the self, union is hard to achieve,
thus is my opinion;
but by self-controlled effort
one is able to reach it by this means.'

"Arjuna said,
'The uncontrolled one, endowed with faith,

the mind straying from union, not attaining perfect union,
walks what road, Krishna?
Failing both is one not lost like a disappearing cloud,
unsupported, great-armed one, confused on the path of God?
Krishna, you can resolve entirely this doubt of mine;
other than you there exists no solver of this doubt.'
   "The blessed Lord said,
'Partha, neither here nor above is found the ruin of this;
dear son, no one doing good goes to misfortune.
Reaching the worlds of the good doers,
staying endless years in the house of the radiant glorious
the one fallen from union is born again.
Or one may be born in a family of wise yogis;
such a birth is difficult to obtain in this world.
There this same intuitive union
one receives from a previous embodiment,
and one strives from there again toward perfection, Kuru joy.
By this previous practice one is irresistibly carried on;
wishing to know also of union one transcends divine sound.
But through persevering mental control
the yogi cleansed of guilt, perfected through many births,
then goes to the supreme goal.
   "'The yogi is superior to the ascetics,
is also thought to be superior to the knowledgeable,
and the yogi is superior to the active.
Therefore, be a yogi, Arjuna.
Of all these yogis, the one going to me
with inner soul full of faith, who loves me,
this one is thought by me to be most united.'

7
   "The blessed Lord said,
'The mind absorbed in me, Partha,
practicing union relying on me,
without doubt how you shall know me completely: hear that.
I shall tell you without omission
this knowledge with discrimination, which having understood
nothing more remains here to be known.
Of thousands of people hardly anyone strives for perfection;
of those striving, even of the perfected,

hardly anyone knows me truly.

"'Earth, waters, fire, wind,
space, mind, intuition, and ego,
thus is this divided nature of mine eightfold.
This here is the lower, but know my other highest nature,
the life-being, great-armed one,
by which this universe is sustained.
Understand this to be the womb of all beings.
I am the origin of the entire universe, also its dissolution.
There is nothing whatever higher than me, wealth winner.
On me all this is strung like pearls on a thread.

"'I am the flavor in the waters, Kaunteya;
I am the radiance of the moon and sun,
the sacred word in all the Vedas,
the sound in the air, the virility in men,
and the pure fragrance on the earth;
and I am the brilliance in flame,
the life in all beings,
and I am the austerity in ascetics.

"'Know me as the primeval seed of all beings, Partha.
I am the intuition of the intelligent;
the brilliance of the brilliant am I.
And I am the strength of the strong,
freed from desire and passion;
I am the desire in beings
that is not contrary to duty, Bharata bull.

"'And the good states, the active and the slow
which come from me, know them thus:
I am not in them, but they are in me.
Because of these states formed by the three qualities
all this deluded universe does not recognize me
as higher than these and eternal.

"'Divine indeed is this quality-produced illusion
that is difficult to penetrate;
they attain me who transcend this illusion.
Deluded evil doers, the lowest people, do not attain me,
their knowledge robbed by illusion,
attached to demonic existence.

"'Four kinds of benevolent people worship me, Arjuna:
the suffering, those wanting knowledge,
those wanting success, and the wise, Bharata bull.
Of them the wise, eternally united,
devoted to the One, is the best.
I am extremely fond of the wise, and this one is fond of me.
All these are noble, but the wise is considered my soul.
Staying in this soul union with me is the supreme goal.

"'At the end of many births the wise attains me.
Vasudeva is thus all to this great soul who is hard to find.
Those whose knowledge is taken away by various desires
attain other gods, practicing various disciplines,
constrained by their own nature.
Whoever wants to worship with faith
any form one is devoted to,
on that one I bestow this unswerving faith.
United by this faith one is eager for this propitiation,
and receives from there the desires ordained by me.
But this fault of the short-sighted is temporary.

"'Those unenlightened think of me, the unmanifest,
as fallen into manifestation,
unaware of my highest being, eternal and supreme.
I am not visible to all; enveloped in yoga illusion,
this deluded world does not recognize me, unborn and eternal.
I know the past and present and future beings, Arjuna,
but no one knows me.
By the duality delusion arising from like-dislike, Bharata,
all beings fall into confusion at birth, scorcher of foes.

"'But of those in whom evil has come to an end,
whose actions are pure, they liberated from duality delusion
are devoted to me with firm vows.
Those who strive for release from old age and death,
taking refuge in me, know this God fully,
the oversoul, and action without exception.
They who know me as Lord of being, divine Lord
as well as Lord of sacrifice, and also at the time of death,
know me with united consciousness.'

8

   "Arjuna said,
'What is this God? What is this oversoul?
What is action, best person?
And what is Lord of being declared to be?
What is divine Lord said to be?
How and who is the Lord of sacrifice
here in this body, slayer of Madhu?
And how at the time of death
are you known by the self-controlled?'

   "The blessed Lord said,
'Imperishable God is supreme;
the oversoul is said to be its own essence,
which originates the essence of being;
action is known as creative power.
The realm of being is the perishable essence,
and the divine realm is Spirit.
I am Lord of sacrifice here in the body, best embodied one.
And at the last hour whoever dies remembering me,
releasing the body, goes to my essence.
There is no doubt about this.
Moreover whatever essence is remembered at the end
when one abandons the body, one goes to that, Kaunteya,
always becoming that essence.
Therefore at all times remember me and fight.
The intuitive mind fixed on me, you will surely come to me.

   "'Practicing yoga by uniting, by consciousness,
by not going toward anything else,
one goes to supreme divine Spirit, Partha, meditating.
Whoever meditates on the ancient poet, the ruler,
smaller than an atom, supporter of all,
unimaginable form, the color of the sun beyond darkness,
at the time of death with unmoving mind,
with devotion and united with the strength of yoga,
causing the breath to enter correctly between the eyebrows,
one approaches this supreme divine Spirit,
which the knowers of the *Vedas* call imperishable,
which the ascetics free of passion enter,
which wanting they follow the way to chastity;
this path I shall explain to you briefly.

"'Controlling all doors
and shutting up the mind in the heart,
placing in the head the breath of the soul,
established in yoga concentration,
chanting thus AUM, the one syllable, God, remembering me,
whoever dies, abandoning the body, goes to the supreme goal.
Having undivided consciousness perpetually,
whoever remembers me always,
for this one I am easy to reach,
Partha, for the yogi who is always united.
Coming to me, the great souls gone to supreme perfection
do not incur rebirth, the impermanent home of suffering.
Up to the God realm, worlds are successive rebirths, Arjuna;
but approaching me, Kaunteya, rebirth is not found.

"'As extending a thousand ages they know a day of God,
a night ending a thousand ages, those knowing day and night.
From the unmanifest all manifestations originate at daybreak;
at nightfall they are dissolved there
into what is known as unmanifest.
This multitude of beings becoming, existing, is dissolved
at nightfall without will, Partha;
it comes into existence at daybreak.

"'But higher than this unmanifest
is another ancient unmanifest essence
which in the perishing of all beings does not perish.
Thus the eternal unmanifest is called the supreme goal,
which attaining they do not return.
This is my supreme abode.
This supreme Spirit, Partha, is to be attained
by undivided devotion, within which beings exist,
by which all this universe is pervaded.

"'But where in time
dying yogis go to non-return and return,
of this time I shall speak, Bharata bull.
Fire, light, day, waxing moon,
six months of spring and summer:
dying then the God-knowers go to God.
Smoke, night, thus the waning moon,
six months of autumn and winter:

there attaining moonlight, the yogi returns.
These two light and dark paths
are thought to be eternal for the universe.
By one one goes to non-return;
by the other one returns again.
Knowing these two paths, Partha,
the yogi is not confused at all.
    "'Therefore at all times be united in yoga, Arjuna.
The meritorious fruit which is ordained in the *Vedas*,
in sacrifices, in austerities, and in charity,
the yogi transcends this; knowing all this
he attains the supreme state and realm.'

9
    "The blessed Lord said,
'Now I shall explain the greatest secret
to you, the uncomplaining:
knowledge combined with wisdom,
knowing which you will be liberated from evil.
Ruling knowledge, a ruling secret is this highest purifier,
directly intelligible, correct,
easy to practice, imperishable.
Persons without faith in this doctrine, scorcher of foes,
not attaining me are born again
into the path of death and reincarnation.
    "'By my unmanifest form this whole universe is pervaded.
All beings are situated in me, and not I situated in them.
And beings are not situated in me.
Look at my majestic yoga, sustaining beings
and not staying in beings, my soul becoming beings.
As the great omnipresent wind is eternally staying in space,
so all beings stay in me.
Consider this.
    "'All beings, Kaunteya,
go to my nature at the end of an era;
at the beginning of an era I send them forth again.
Embracing my own nature I send forth again and again
this whole powerless multitude of beings
by the power of nature.

And these actions do not bind me, wealth winner,
sitting indifferently unattached to these actions.
With me as supervisor nature produces
the animate and inanimate;
by this cause, Kaunteya, the universe revolves.

"'The deluded despise me, the assumed human form,
not knowing my higher essence, the great Lord of beings.
Vain hopes, vain actions, vain thoughtless knowledge
resort to fiendish and demonic deluded nature.

"'But great souls resorting to me, the divine nature,
their undivided minds are devoted to knowing
the imperishable source of being.
Always glorifying me and striving with firm resolve
and honoring me with devotion, they worship ever united.

"'And by the knowledge sacrifice also
others sacrificing worship me,
by oneness, by multiplicity, diversely, omnisciently.
I am the ritual; I am the sacrifice; offering am I;
I am the medicinal herb; the mantra am I;
I am clarified butter; I am fire; I am the oblation.

"'I am the father of this universe, mother, supporter,
grandfather, what is to be known, purifier, sacred AUM,
the *Rig, Sama*, and *Yajur Vedas*,
the goal, sustainer, Lord, witness, home, refuge, friend,
the origin, dissolution, state, treasury, seed eternal.
I radiate heat; I withhold and send forth rain;
immortality and death, and truth and untruth am I, Arjuna.

"'Knowers of the three *Vedas*,
soma drinkers cleansed of evil,
worshipping me with sacrifices seek the way to heaven.
They, attaining the pure world of the gods,
enjoy the heavenly divine pleasures in heaven.
They, enjoying this vast heaven world,
in exhausted merit enter the mortal world.
Thus following the triple duty
desiring desires they obtain the going and coming.
The people of undivided contemplation who worship me,
I lead their constant uniting to security.

"'Even those devoted to other gods
who sacrifice accompanied by faith
they also sacrifice to me, Kaunteya, outside the rules.
For I am the enjoyer and Lord of all sacrifices,
but they do not recognize me in truth;
therefore they fall.
Those devoted to the gods go to the gods;
to the ancestors go those devoted to the ancestors.
To the spirits go those sacrificing to the spirits;
those sacrificing to me go also to me.

"'Whoever offers to me with devotion
a leaf, flower, fruit, water,
that devotion offered from a pure soul I accept.
Whatever you do, whatever you eat, whatever you offer,
whatever you give, whatever austerity you practice, Kaunteya,
do it as an offering to me.
Thus you will be released from good and evil fruits,
from the bonds of action;
the soul united in the yoga of renunciation,
liberated, you shall come to me.

"'I am the same in all beings;
there is none disliked or favored by me.
But whoever loves me with devotion,
they are in me, and I am also in them.
Even if an evil doer loves me with undivided devotion,
this one is to be considered good;
for this one is correctly resolved.
Quickly the soul becomes right; it enters perpetual peace.

"'Kaunteya, be aware.
No devotee of mine is lost.
Relying on me, Partha, even if they should be
women of evil wombs, merchants, even servants,
they also reach the supreme goal.
How much more then holy teachers, devoted ruling seers!
Having obtained this impermanent unhappy world, love me.
With the mind on me, be devoted to me;
sacrificing to me, honor me;
thus uniting the soul with me as the supreme aim
you will come to me.'

10
"The blessed Lord said,
'Again, great-armed one, hear my supreme word,
which I shall tell to you, the beloved,
with desire for your welfare.
Neither the many gods nor the great seers know my origin,
for I am the source of the divine ones
and the great seers in every way.
Whoever knows me, unborn and without beginning,
the great Lord of the world,
this one undeluded among mortals is released from all evils.
    "'Intuition, knowledge, non-delusion, patience, truth,
control, equanimity, happiness, sorrow,
being, non-being, and fear and fearlessness,
nonviolence, impartiality, contentment, austerity, charity,
fame, disrepute, the manifold essences of being
come to be from me alone.
The seven great seers of old, the four Manus also,
are my mental essences,
whose creatures are born in the world.
    "'Whoever knows in truth this manifest power and my union,
by unwavering yoga is united; of this there is no doubt.
I am the origin of everything; from me everything proceeds.
Thinking thus, the wise honor me endowed with essence.
Those conscious of me, their vitality focused on me,
enlightening each other and always speaking of me,
they are content and pleased.
To those worshippers constantly united affectionately,
I give this intuitive union by which they come to me.
Out of compassion for them,
I staying in the soul essence,
destroy the darkness born of ignorance
with the illuminating lamp of knowledge.'
    "Arjuna said,
'Supreme God, supreme domain, purifier supreme, Lord,
eternal divine Spirit, primal God, unborn, omnipresent,
thus all seers call you,
the divine seer Narada, Asita Devala, Vyasa,
and yourself, you tell me.

I think all this is right which you say to me, Keshava,
for neither the gods nor the demons
know your manifestation, blessed one.
You know the soul by your soul alone, highest Spirit,
essence of being, Lord of beings,
God of gods, ruler of the universe.
You can tell completely the divine soul manifestations
by which manifestation you stay pervading these worlds.
    "'How may I know you, yogi, always meditating?
And in what various essences
are you conceived by me, blessed one?
Explain further in detail
the union and manifestation of the soul, Janardana,
for to me there is no satiation of hearing immortality.'
    "The blessed Lord said,
'Listen, for I shall explain to you
the main soul manifestations, best of Kurus;
there is no end to my expansion.
    "'I am the soul, Gudakesha,
staying in the heart of all beings,
and I am the beginning and the middle and the end of beings.
Of the Adityas, I am Vishnu;
of the lights, the radiant sun;
I am Marici of the Maruts;
of the mighty ones, I am the moon.
Of the *Vedas*, I am the *Sama Veda*;
of the gods, I am Vasava;
and of the senses, I am the mind;
of beings, I am the consciousness.
And of the Rudras, I am Shankara,
Vittesha of the Yakshas and Rakshasas;
and of the Vasus, I am fire;
I am Meru of the mountains.
And of the household priests, Partha,
know me to be the chief, Brihaspati;
of the army commanders, I am Skanda;
of the lakes, I am the ocean.
Of the great seers, I am Bhrigu;
of words, I am the one syllable;

of sacrifices, I am the prayer,
of immovable things, the Himalaya,
the sacred fig tree of all trees
and of the divine seers, Narada,
of the Gandharvas, Chitraratha,
of the perfected, the sage Kapila.
Uchchaihshravas of the horses,
know me to be born of nectar,
Airavata of the lordly elephants,
and of people, the Lord of people.
Of weapons, I am the thunderbolt;
of cows, I am the cow of plenty;
and I am the generating desire god;
of snakes, I am Vasuki,
and I am Ananta of the cobras;
I am Varuna of the water creatures,
and of the ancestors, I am Aryaman.
I am Yama of the governors,
and I am Prahlada of the Daityas;
I am time of the calculators,
and of the beasts I am king of beasts;
and I am Vainateya of the birds.
I am the wind of the purifiers;
I am Rama of the warriors,
and of sea monsters, I am Makara;
of rivers, I am the daughter of Jahnu.
   "'Of creations, I am the beginning
and the end and also the middle, Arjuna;
oversoul science of the sciences,
I am the dialectic of those who debate.
Of letters, I am the letter A
and the dual of the compounds;
I am imperishable time;
I am the establisher facing all directions,
and I am all-destroying death
and the origin of things that come to be.
Fame, prosperity, and speech of the feminine words,
memory, intelligence, courage, patience,
also the Brihat Saman of the chants,
I am the *gayatri* of the meters;

of months, I am Sagittarius, of seasons, the spring.
I am gambling of the cheats;
I am the splendor of the splendid ones;
I am victory; I am determination;
I am the goodness of the good ones.
Of the Vishnis, I am Vasudeva,
of the sons of Pandu, wealth winner,
of the sages, I am also Vyasa,
of the poets, the poet Ushanas.
I am the clout of the rulers;
I am the guidance of those seeking victory;
and I am also the silence of secrets;
I am the knowledge of those that know.
And that which is the seed of all beings, I am that, Arjuna;
there is no being, animate or inanimate,
that could exist without me.
There is no end to my divine manifestations, foe scorcher;
but this extent of the manifestation
declared by me is illustrative.
   "'Whatever manifest goodness, glorious and powerful,
you understand that
that originates from a fraction of my splendor.
However, what is this extensive knowledge to you, Arjuna?
I support this whole stable universe with one fraction.'

11
   "Arjuna said,
'As a favor to me, the word has been spoken by you
which is the supreme secret known as the oversoul.
By this my delusion has departed,
for the origin and dissolution of beings
have been heard in detail by me from you,
lotus-petal-eyed, and also imperishable greatness.
So this, as you say, is the soul, supreme Lord.
I wish to see your lordly form, highest Spirit.
If you think that it is possible for me to see this, Lord,
then, yoga Lord, reveal to me your imperishable soul.'
   "The blessed Lord said,
'Look, Partha, at my hundreds of forms, or thousands,
diverse, divine, of various colors and shapes.

Look at the Adityas, the Vasus, the Rudras,
the two Asvins, the Maruts, also;
look at many wonders previously unseen, Bharata.
Look at the whole universe standing as one here now
everything animate and inanimate in my body, Gudakesha,
and whatever else you wish to see.
But you are not able to see me with your own eye.
I give you a divine eye; look at my majestic union.'"
  Sanjaya said,
"Saying this then, king, the great yoga Lord, Hari,
revealed to Partha the supreme majestic form,
many faces, many marvelous aspects,
many divine ornaments, many raised divine weapons,
wearing divine garlands and garments,
divine perfumed ointment, made of all marvels,
the divine, infinite, omniscient.
If there should be in the sky a thousand suns risen at once,
such brightness as this
would be like the brilliance of this great soul.
There standing as one the whole universe,
divided in many ways,
the son of Pandu then was seeing
in the body of the god of gods.
Then the amazed wealth winner, his hair standing on end,
bowing with the head to the god reverently, spoke.
  "Arjuna said,
'I see divinities in your body, divine one,
also all kinds of beings assembled,
the Lord God on the lotus seat
and all seers and divine serpents,
many arms, bellies, faces, eyes;
I see you everywhere, infinite form;
not the end nor the middle nor yet the beginning of you
do I see, cosmic Lord, cosmic form.
With crown, mace, and disk,
a massive radiance shining everywhere I see you,
though it is hard to look completely at
the blazing fire of shining sun immeasurable.

"'You are the supreme imperishable to be known;
you are the supreme haven of all;
you are the immortal protector of eternal justice;
you are the ancient Spirit of my thought.
Without beginning, middle, or end, infinite power,
innumerable arms, eyes of moon and sun,
I see you, a face of blazing fire
burning all this universe with its brilliance,
for here between heaven and earth is pervaded
by you alone and all directions.

"'Seeing this marvelous mighty form of yours
the three worlds trembled, great soul,
for yonder companies of gods enter you,
some terrified they praise reverently.
Thus saying, "Hail!" the companies of perfected great seers
praise you with resounding hymns.
The Rudras, Adityas, Vasus, and the Sadhyas,
Vishvas, the two Asvins, the Maruts, and Ushmapas,
the companies of Gandharvas, Yakshas, Asuras, Siddhas
see you and are all amazed.
Seeing your great form of many faces, great-armed one,
many arms, thighs, feet, many bellies, many terrible teeth,
the worlds are trembling, and so am I.

"'For seeing you touching the sky,
a blazing many-colored open mouth, fiery enormous eyes,
my inner self trembling I find no courage nor calm, Vishnu.
And seeing your mouths of terrible teeth
like the fires of destructive time,
I do not know directions, and I do not find refuge.

"'Have mercy, divine Lord, universal home!
And yonder to you all the sons of Dhritarashtra,
along with the ruling companies, Bhishma, Drona, Suta's son,
thus there together with our chief warriors also,
enter speedily your faces of fearful terrible teeth,
some are seen clinging in between teeth with crushed heads.
As the many rushing waters of rivers flow toward the sea,
so those heroes of the human world enter your flaming faces.
As moths accelerating to destruction enter a blazing flame,
so too worlds accelerating to destruction enter your faces.

You lick swallowing from every side all the worlds
with flaming mouths, filling all the universe with splendor,
your fierce radiance consumes it, Vishnu.
   "'Tell me who you are, the terrible form.
Honor be to you, most divine one! Have mercy!
I wish to understand you, the primal one.
I do not comprehend your work.'
   "The blessed Lord said,
'I am time, powerful destroyer of worlds
working here to annihilate worlds.
Even without you, all the warriors
who are deployed in the opposing armies will not exist.
Therefore stand up, obtain glory!
Conquering the enemies, enjoy prosperous kingship.
By me these have already been struck down;
Be the mere instrument, left-handed one.
Drona and Bhishma and Jayadratha and Karna
as also other warrior heroes killed by me, slay.
Do not hesitate; fight!
You will conquer the adversaries in battle.'"
   Sanjaya said,
"Hearing this speech of Keshava,
the crowned one, trembling reverently, bowing again,
spoke to Krishna falteringly, bowing low, frightened.
   "Arjuna said,
'Properly, Hrishikesha, the universe rejoices
and is delighted by your fame.
Frightened demons flee in all directions,
and companies of perfected ones will give homage.
And why should they not give homage to you, great soul?
to the original creator, a greater teacher even than God,
the infinite divine Lord, universal home,
you, the imperishable, being, nonbeing, which is beyond that.
You are the ancient primal divine Spirit,
supreme heaven of this universe;
you are the knower to be known and the supreme state.
The universe is pervaded by you, infinite form.
You are Vayu, Yama, Agni, Varuna, the moon,
the Lord of creatures, and the great grandfather.

"'Hail, hail to you; may it be a thousand times!
Further and also again hail, hail to you!
Hail from in front, moreover hail to you from behind!
May it be to you on all sides, the all.
Infinite valor, boundless strength,
you fulfill all; therefore you are all.
    "'Thinking, impetuously thus a friend who said,
"Oh Krishna, oh Yadava, oh friend,"
out of ignorance of your greatness this was said by me
from negligence or even with affection,
and as if for a jest you are not respected at play,
while in bed, seated, dining, alone, or even before others,
unshaken one, I ask your pardon for this, boundless one.
    "'You are father of the world,
of the animate and inanimate,
and you are its revered and venerable teacher.
There is nothing like you, how then any even greater
in the three worlds, incomparable power?
    "'Therefore bowing, prostrating the body,
I ask your mercy, honored Lord;
as a father of a son, as a friend of a friend,
a lover to a lover, you are able to be patient, Lord.
I am excited seeing what was unseen before,
and my mind trembled with fear.
    "'Reveal to me that form, Lord;
have mercy, divine Lord, universal home!
I wish to see you with crown, mace, and disk;
become the four-armed form, thousand-armed one of all
forms.'
    "The blessed Lord said,
'By my grace to you, Arjuna,
this supreme form is revealed from soul union,
made of universal, infinite, original brilliance of mine
which no one other than you has seen before.
Not by Vedic sacrifice study nor by gifts
and not by ritual acts nor by severe austerities
can I be seen in such a form in the human world
except by you, Kuru hero.
You should not tremble nor be confused,

seeing this so awful form of mine;
fear gone away, your mind is cheerful again;
look at this form of mine.'"

  Sanjaya said,
"Saying this to Arjuna,
Vasudeva thus revealed his own form once more
and consoled this frightened one,
becoming again the gentle, handsome great soul.

  "Arjuna said,
'Seeing this human form of yours, gentle Janardana,
now I am composed with thoughts returned to normal.'

  "The blessed Lord said,
'Hard to see is this form which you have seen;
even gods are always wishing for the revelation of this form.
Not by the *Vedas*, not by discipline, not by charity,
and not by ritual can I be seen in such a way
as you have seen me,
but by unswerving love I can in such a way, Arjuna,
be known, seen, and truly reached, foe scorcher.
Whoever does my work, intent on me, loving me,
attachment let go, free from hostility to any being,
comes to me, son of Pandu.'

12
  "Arjuna said,
'Of the constantly united who worship you with love
and those with the imperishable unmanifest,
which has the best knowledge of union?'

  "The blessed Lord said,
'The mind focused on me, those who worship me
eternally united, endowed with supreme faith,
they are thought to be most united with me.

  "'But those who worship the imperishable, ineffable,
unmanifest, omnipresent and inconceivable,
unchanging, immovable, constant,
controlling the senses, the same intuition everywhere,
they attain me, rejoicing in the welfare of all beings.
The exertion is great for those whose consciousness
is set on the unmanifest, for the goal of the unmanifest

is reached with difficulty by the embodied.

"'But those renouncing in me all actions,
intent on me with undistracted union,
who meditating worship me,
I soon become their deliverer
from the ocean of the death cycle, Partha,
whose consciousness has entered into me.

"'Keep the mind on me; let the intuition enter into me;
then no doubt you will live in me hereafter.
If you are not able to keep consciousness steadily on me,
then by yoga practice seek to attain me, wealth winner.
If you are unable even in practice,
become intent on my work;
doing actions for my sake also, you will attain perfection.
If you are even unable to do this,
then resorting to my union,
renouncing all the fruits of action, act self-restrained.
For knowledge is better than practice;
meditation is superior to knowledge;
renunciation of the fruit of action
is better than meditation;
from renunciation peace follows.

"'A non hater of all beings, friendly and compassionate,
free of "mine," free of ego,
indifferent to pain and pleasure, patient,
the yogi who is always satisfied, self-restrained,
firmly resolved with mind and intuition focused on me,
who is devoted to me, this one is my beloved.

"'Whomever the world does not trouble
and who does not trouble the world,
who is liberated from the anxieties of joy, anger, and fear,
this one also is my beloved.

"'Whoever is impartial, pure,
capable, detached, untroubled,
who renouncing all undertakings is devoted to me,
this one is my beloved.

"'Whoever does not rejoice nor hate nor grieve nor crave,
renouncing good and bad, who is full of love,
this one is my beloved.

"'The same toward enemy and friend
and thus in honor and disgrace,
the same in cold, heat, pleasure, pain,
freed from attachment,
alike in blame or praise, quiet,
satisfied with anything whatever,
homeless, steady-minded,
the person full of love is my beloved.
Those who worship this immortal justice previously spoken
endowed with faith, intent on me, devoted,
they transcendentally are my beloved.'

13

"Arjuna said,
'Nature and Spirit, the field and the knower of the field,
this I wish to know: knowledge and what is known, Keshava.'
    "The blessed Lord said,
'This body, Kaunteya, is called the field;
this one who knows it,
the knowers of that declare the knower of the field.
And also know me as the field knower in all fields, Bharata,
knowledge of the field and the field knower,
which is thought by me to be true knowledge.
    "'What that field is and of what kind
and of what modifications and from where
and who this one is and what its power is,
hear that briefly from me.
Chanted many times by the seers in various sacred hymns
and distinctly in God's scriptures,
with undeniable reasons,
the great elements, ego, intuition, and the unmanifest,
the senses ten and one, and the five objects of the senses,
desire, aversion, pleasure, pain,
combination, consciousness, firmness,
this in brief is the field described with modifications.
    "'Non-pride, non-deceit, nonviolence, patience, honesty,
service of the teacher, integrity, stability, self-control,
in the objects of sense detached, and non-ego;
insight into the pain and evil

of birth, death, old age, disease;
non-attachment, non-clinging to son, wife, home, et cetera,
and constant equanimity in wanted and unwanted events;
and unswerving love to me by exclusive union,
resorting to a secluded place, dissatisfied in a crowd,
constant oversoul knowledge,
observing the purpose of true knowledge:
this knowledge is explained thus;
ignorance is what is contrary to this.

"'What is to be known that I shall explain,
knowing which, one attains immortality;
this beginningless supreme God
is said to be neither being nor non-being.
Everywhere having hands and feet,
everywhere eyes, heads, faces,
everywhere in the world ears,
this stands all pervading,
the appearance of all sense qualities, freed from all senses,
unattached and yet all supporting,
free of the qualities and enjoyer of the qualities.

"'Outside and inside of beings inanimate and animate,
because of its subtlety this is unknown;
also far away and nearby is this
Also undivided and as if staying divided in beings,
also supporting beings this is to be known,
the devourer and the creator.
This is even the light of lights,
said to be beyond darkness—
the knowledge to be known, the goal of knowledge
situated in the heart of all.
Thus the field and the knowledge to be known are described.

"'My devotee, understanding this, approaches my essence.
Know nature and Spirit, both also beginningless,
and know the modifications and qualities coming from nature.
Concerning the doer, the doing, and the instrument,
nature is said to be the cause.
Spirit is said to be the cause
in the experiencing of pleasure and pain,
for Spirit situated in nature

experiences the qualities born of nature.
Attachment to the qualities is the instrument
of its birth in good and evil wombs.

"'The supreme Spirit in this body is also said to be
the observer, allower, supporter, experiencer,
the great Lord and the supreme soul.
Whoever thus knows Spirit and nature
together with the qualities,
even in any stage of existence,
this one is not born again.

"'Some perceive the soul through meditation
by the soul in the soul,
others by Sankhya yoga, and others by action yoga;
yet others, not knowing this, worship hearing it from others,
and they also transcend death following the scripture.
Since any being, stable or moving,
is born from the union of the field and the field knower,
know that, Bharata bull.

"'Whoever perceives the same supreme Lord
situated in all beings, not perishing in their perishings,
this one perceives;
for perceiving the same Lord established everywhere,
one does not hurt the soul with the soul.
Then one goes to the supreme goal.

"'And whoever perceives actions
completely performed by nature,
the soul thus the non-doer, this one perceives.
When one discerns various states of being situated in one
and spreading out from that, then one attains God.

"'Because this imperishable supreme soul
dwelling in the body
is beginningless and free of qualities also, Kaunteya,
it does not act nor is it stained.
As omnipresent space from its subtlety is not stained,
so the soul situated in the body is not ever stained.

"'As the one sun illumines this entire world,
so the Lord of the field illumines the entire field, Bharata.
Those who know by the eye of knowledge
this distinction between the field and the field knower

and the liberation of being from nature
go to the supreme.'

14
"The blessed Lord said,
'I shall explain the supreme knowledge,
best of the sciences, knowing which
all the sages have gone from here to supreme perfection.
Having recourse to this knowledge,
arrived at my state of identity,
even at creation they are not born
and at dissolution they do not tremble.

"'My womb is great God; in it I put the seed.
The origin of all beings comes from there, Bharata.
In all wombs, Kaunteya, forms come to be
of which God is the great womb.
I am the seed-sowing father.

"'Goodness, emotion, darkness—
thus the qualities born of nature
bind, great-armed one, in the body
the imperishable embodied one.

"'Of these, goodness, free from impurity, illuminating,
healthy, binds by attachment to happiness
and by attachment to knowledge, sinless one.

"'Know that emotion whose soul is passion
is born of thirsty attachment.
This binds down the embodied one, Kaunteya,
by attachment to action.

"'But know that darkness is born of ignorance,
confusing all embodied ones.
This binds down by negligence, laziness, sleep, Bharata.

"'Goodness causes attachment to happiness,
emotion to action, Bharata,
but obscuring knowledge, darkness
even in negligence causes attachment.
Prevailing over emotion and darkness,
goodness comes to be, Bharata,
emotion over goodness and darkness,
likewise darkness over goodness and emotion.

"'When the light of knowledge is born
in all the doors in this body,
then it may be known
that goodness has thus grown powerful indeed.
Greed, exertion, undertaking of actions, unrest, lust,
these are produced when emotion is in power, Bharata bull.
Lack of light and lack of exertion, negligence and confusion,
these are produced when darkness is in power, Kuru joy.

"'But with goodness in power,
when the embodied one goes at dissolution,
then one arrives at the stainless worlds
of the knowers of the highest.
Going to dissolution in emotion,
one is born among those attached to action;
likewise dissolving in darkness,
one is born in wombs of the deluded.

"'Of action well done they say
the fruit is good without impurity,
but the fruit of emotion is pain,
the fruit of darkness ignorance.

"'From goodness springs knowledge
and from emotion greed;
negligent confusion comes from darkness, as does ignorance.

"'Those staying good go upward;
the emotional remain in the middle;
the lowest quality state, the dark, go downward.

"'When the observer perceives
no doer other than the qualities
and knows the highest, this one attains my essence.
Transcending these three qualities coming to be in the body,
the embodied, released from birth, death, old age, pain,
attains immortality.'

"Arjuna said,
'By what characteristics does the one transcending
these three qualities come to be, Lord?
What is the conduct?
And how does one transcend these three qualities?'

"The blessed Lord said,
'Illumination and progress and delusion, son of Pandu,

one neither hates their occurrence
nor longs for their absence.
Whoever is seated impartially
is not disturbed by the qualities;
the qualities operate thus;
whoever stands firm does not waver;
the same in pain and pleasure, self-reliant,
the same to a clod, a stone, gold,
equal to the loved and the unloved, constant,
equal to blame and praise,
in honor and dishonor equal,
equal toward friend and enemy,
renouncing all undertakings,
this one is said to be quality-transcending.
And whoever serves me with unswerving devotional union,
transcending these qualities
this one is fit for God realization.
For I am the foundation of God,
of the immortal and of the imperishable
and of everlasting justice and of absolute happiness.'

15
   "The blessed Lord said,
'High the root, low the branch,
they say the ashvattha tree is eternal;
its leaves are sacred hymns.
Whoever knows this is a *Veda* knower.
Below and above its branches spread,
nourished by qualities sprouting sense objects,
and below the roots stretch forth
engendering action in the human world.
Its form is not perceived here in this way
nor the end nor the beginning nor the maintenance.
This ashvattha tree with fully grown root
being cut down by the strong ax of detachment,
then that place is to be sought,
having gone to which they do not return again;
and I take refuge in that primal Spirit
from where ancient progress flowed.

"'Without arrogant delusions,
with evil attachments conquered,
the eternal oversouls, with desires turned away,
released from dualities known as pleasure-pain,
go unconfused to that imperishable place.
The sun does not illumine nor the moon nor fire
that place going to which they do not return;
that is my supreme home.
My primeval part becoming alive in the world of the living
draws existing in nature the senses,
of which the mind is the sixth.

"'When the Lord acquires a body,
and also when the Lord departs,
taking these the wind blows scents as if from the source.
Presiding over hearing, sight, touch, taste and smell,
and mind, this one enjoys the objects of the senses.

"'Whether it is departing, staying, or enjoying,
those confused by the accompanying qualities do not perceive;
those with the eye of knowledge do perceive.
And striving yogis perceive this one existing in the soul,
while striving undisciplined thoughtless souls
do not perceive this one.

"'That brilliant sunshine which lights the entire universe,
the brilliance which is in the moon and in fire,
know that to be mine.
And entering the earth I maintain creatures with energy,
and I nourish all plants becoming the flavor-souled nectar.
Becoming digestive fire entering the body of the breathing
uniting with the breath I digest the fourfold food.
And I am seated in the hearts of all;
from me are memory, knowledge, and reasoning;
and I am recognized by all the *Vedas*;
I am the Vedanta maker and the *Veda* knower.

"'There are these two spirits in the world,
perishable and imperishable,
and all creatures are perishable;
the imperishable is called unchanging.

"'But the highest spirit is another,
called the supreme soul, who,

entering the three worlds as the undying Lord,
supports them.
Since I transcend the perishable
and am higher than the imperishable,
therefore I am celebrated in the world and in the *Veda*
as the highest spirit.
Whoever thus unconfused knows me as the highest spirit,
this omniscient one worships me
with the whole being, Bharata.
So this most secret doctrine explained by me, blameless one,
intuiting this, one should be enlightened
and accomplished, Bharata.'

16
"The blessed Lord said,
'Fearlessness, purity of heart,
perseverance in knowledge of union,
charity and restraint and sacrifice,
spiritual study, austerity, straightforwardness,
nonviolence, truth, no anger, renunciation, peace,
no slander, compassion for creatures, no greed,
kindness, modesty, no fickleness,
vigor, patience, courage, purity,
no hatred, and no excessive pride
are the endowment of the one born to the divine, Bharata.
"'Hypocrisy, arrogance and conceit,
anger and harshness, and ignorance
are the endowment of the one born to the demonic, Partha.
"'The divine endowment is for liberation,
for bondage the demonic, it is thought.
Do not grieve.
To the divine endowment you are born, son of Pandu.
Two created beings are in this world,
the divine and the demonic.
"'The divine has been described in detail;
hear from me about the demonic, Partha.
Progress and cessation demonic people do not understand;
neither purity nor good conduct nor truth is found in them.
Untruthful, they are unstable.

The universe, they say, is godless,
not by a succession created.
What else but desire caused it?
Holding this view lost souls of little intelligence
and evil actions come forth as enemies
for the destruction of the world.

   "'Attached to insatiable desire,
accompanied by hypocrisy, arrogance, and lust,
out of confusion accepting false notions,
they proceed with impure purposes,
and clinging to immeasurable anxiety ending in death,
with gratification of desire their highest aim,
convinced that this is all,
bound by a hundred expectations,
devoted to desire and anger,
they wish for the gratification of desires
by the unjust means of hoards of wealth.

    ""'This today was acquired by me;
this wish I shall obtain;
this is it; and this shall be my property also.
That enemy was slain by me;
and I shall kill others also.
I am the Lord; I am the enjoyer;
I am perfect, powerful, happy.
I am wealthy, aristocratic.
Who else is there like me?
I shall sacrifice, give, be merry."

Thus are those deluded by ignorance.
Led astray by more than one thought,
wrapped in a net of delusion,
attached to the gratification of desires,
they fall into an unclean hell.

   "'Conceited souls, stubborn,
full of the pride and intoxication of wealth,
they sacrifice in the name of sacrifices with hypocrisy,
not in the sacred manner.
Clinging to the ego, force, insolence, desire, and anger,
the envious hate me in the soul of others' bodies.
Those hating, cruel, vicious wretches I throw continually
into the cycles of reincarnation in demonic wombs.

Entering a demonic womb, the deluded in birth after birth
not attaining me, Kaunteya, go then to the worst path.
"'This threefold gate of hell is destructive of the soul:
desire, anger, and greed.
Therefore one should renounce this threesome.
Released from these three dark gates, Kaunteya,
the best person practices for the soul,
then goes to the supreme goal.
"'Whoever, discarding scriptural knowledge,
follows willful desire does not attain perfection
nor happiness nor the supreme goal.
Therefore scripture is your authority
for determining what is to be done or not to be done.
Knowing what is said in scripture you should do work here.'

17
"Arjuna said,
'Those who, discarding scriptural knowledge,
sacrifice filled with faith,
what is their position, Krishna?
Is it goodness, emotion, or darkness?'
"The blessed Lord said,
'Triple is the faith of the embodied;
it is essentially goodness, emotion, and darkness.
"'Thus hear of this.
The faith of each becomes according to the form of goodness.
This Spirit is made of faith.
Whoever has the faith which this is is this.
The good sacrifice to the gods,
the emotional to spirits and demons,
and others, the men of darkness,
sacrifice to the dead and ghosts.
"'People who undergo terrible austerities
not ordained by scripture,
joined with egotistical hypocrisy
along with desire, rage, and force,
torturing the organs within the body,
and unconscious of me inside within their body,
know them to be demonic in their resolves.

"'But food also preferred by each becomes triple,
as sacrifice, austerity, and charity.
Hear this distinction of these.
Promoting life, goodness, strength, health,
happiness, and satisfaction,
flavorful, juicy, substantial, and hearty foods
are liked by the good.
Pungent, sour, salty, hot, spicy, dry, burnt foods
are wanted by the emotional,
causing pain, misery, and sickness.
Spoiled, tasteless, putrid, stale,
and what is rejected as well as the unclean
is the food liked by the ignorant.

"'Scripture-ordained sacrifice which is offered
by those not desiring the fruit,
offering thus with the mind focused, this is good.
But having in view the fruit and also hypocritical purpose,
Bharata, know this sacrifice which is offered is emotional.
Scripture discarded, food unoffered, sacred words discarded,
no price paid, devoid of faith,
they regard as ignorant sacrifice.

"'Revering the divine,
the twice-born, the teacher, the wise,
purity, virtue, continence, and nonviolence
is called the austerity of the body.
Non-disturbing speech, true, pleasant, beneficial,
and which practices reciting sacred texts
is called speech-making austerity.
Mental clarity, kindness, silence, self-control,
purity of being, this is called mental austerity.

"'This triple austerity practiced with the highest faith
by people united by not desiring fruit, they regard as good.
And austerity which is done with hypocrisy
for the sake of honor, respect, and reverence here on earth,
this is said to be emotional, insecure, impermanent.
Austerity which is done with torture of self
with a deluded notion
or for the purpose of destroying another,
this is said to be dark.

"'The gift which is given as being given,
to one who does no favor,
at the proper place and time and to a worthy person,
this gift is considered good.
But that which is given for the sake of reward
or again with a view to the fruit or unwillingly,
that gift is considered emotional.
That gift which is given
in the wrong place and time to the unworthy
disrespectfully and with contempt is said to be dark.
 ""AUM tat sat" is considered the triple symbol of God.
By this the priests and the Vedas and the sacrifices
were anciently ordained.
Therefore acts of sacrifice, charity, and austerity
always begin by uttering AUM
as proclaimed in the precepts of the expounders of God.
Saying tat without interest in the fruit,
acts of sacrifice, austerity, and various charities
are done by those desirous of liberation.
In meaning truth and in meaning goodness this sat is used.
In praise, also in action the sound sat is used, Partha.
In sacrifice, austerity and charity
steadiness is also called sat,
and action related to this is likewise designated sat.
 "'An offering given or an austerity practiced and done
which is without faith is said to be false, Partha,
and that is nothing to us here or hereafter.'

18
 "Arjuna said,
'Great-armed one, I wish to know the truth
of renunciation and of relinquishment, Hrishikesha,
individually, slayer of Keshin.
 "'The blessed Lord said,
'The renouncing of desired actions
the sages know as renunciation;
relinquishment of the fruit of all action
the clear-sighted say is relinquishment.
Some thinkers say that action is to be relinquished as wrong,

and others that action by sacrifice, charity, and austerity
is not to be thus relinquished.

"'Hear my conclusion in this matter of relinquishment,
best Bharata, for relinquishment, tiger spirit,
is described as threefold.
Action by sacrifice, charity, and austerity
is not to be relinquished;
that sacrifice, charity, and austerity
are the purifiers of the thinkers.
But these actions are to be done
relinquishing attachment and the fruits.
This, Partha, is definitely my final opinion,
for renunciation of required action is not proper;
the confused relinquishing of this is declared dark.
Whoever relinquishes action which is troublesome
out of fear of physical suffering,
doing emotional relinquishment
would not obtain the fruit of that relinquishment.
Action which is to be done is done in a disciplined way,
Arjuna, relinquishing attachment and the fruit;
this relinquishment is thought of as good.

"'Filled with goodness, intelligent, doubt eliminated,
the relinquisher, does not hate disagreeable action
nor is attached to the agreeable,
for embodied beings can not relinquish actions entirely.
But whoever is a relinquisher of the fruit of action,
this one is called thus a relinquisher.
Triple is the fruit of action for the dying relinquishers:
unwanted, wanted, and mixed;
but for the renouncers there is none whatever.

"'Great-armed one, learn from me these five factors
proclaimed in Sankhya doctrine for success in all actions:
the basis, also the actor,
and the instrument of various kinds,
and many separate movements,
and the divine as the fifth.
Whatever action a person undertakes
with body, speech, and mind,
whether right or wrong, these are its five factors.

"'But in this reality,
whoever sees the soul as the only actor
out of incomplete understanding, this fool does not see.
The one whose condition is not egoistic,
whose intuition is not affected,
even though killing these people,
this one does not kill and is not bound.

"'Knowledge, the known, and the knower
are the threefold action incentives;
the instrument, the action, and the actor
are the threefold constituents of action.
Knowledge, action, and the actor are said to be threefold,
determined by the qualities in the qualities-doctrine.

"'Hear about these also.
Learn that good knowledge by which one sees in all creatures
one imperishable essence undivided in the divided.
But the knowledge which regards as separate
the different beings of various kinds in all creatures
learn that knowledge is emotional.
But that which is attached
to one thing to be done as if it were all,
without reason, without true purpose, and insignificant,
is said to be dark.

"'Action which is controlled, free of attachment,
done without liking or disliking, wishing to obtain no fruit,
that is called good.
But action which is done wishing to obtain desire
with self-interest or again with much effort,
that is said to be emotional.
Action which is undertaken out of confusion
disregarding the consequence, loss, harm, and capability,
that is called dark.

"'Liberated from attachment, not egotistical,
accompanied by courage and resolution,
unperturbed in success or failure,
the actor is called good.
Passionate, wishing to obtain the fruit of action, greedy,
violent-natured, impure, accompanied by joy and sorrow,
the actor is proclaimed to be emotional.

Undisciplined, vulgar, stubborn, deceitful, dishonest,
lazy, depressed, and procrastinating,
the actor is called dark.

"'Hear the distinction of the intuition and the will
according to the threefold qualities
explained completely and distinctly, wealth winner.

"'Intuition which knows action and withdrawal,
what is to be done and what is not to be done,
what is to be feared and what is not to be feared,
bondage and liberation,
this, Partha, is good.
Intuition which distinguishes incorrectly right and wrong,
what is to be done and what is not to be done,
this, Partha, is emotional.
Intuition which thinks wrong is right,
covered by darkness, and perverted in every aim,
this, Partha, is dark.

"'The will by which one holds steady
the mind, breath, and sense functions with unbroken union,
this, Partha, is good.
But the will by which one holds to duty, desire, and wealth
with firmness, Arjuna, with attachment to desired fruits,
this, Partha, is emotional.
The will by which the stupid does not abandon
sleep, fear, sorrow, depression, and pride,
this, Partha, is dark.

"'But now hear from me, Bharata bull,
the threefold happiness one enjoys through practice
and in which one comes to the end of suffering.
That which in the beginning is like poison
but in maturity resembles nectar,
that happiness is declared good,
born from the clarity of soul intuition.
That which in the beginning
from contact between sense objects and sense resembles nectar
but in maturity is like poison,
this happiness is considered emotional.
And happiness which in the beginning and in consequence
is confusing for the soul,

arising from sleep, laziness, and negligence,
that is said to be dark.
  "'There is nothing,
either on earth or even in heaven among the gods,
no being, which can be freed
by these three qualities born of nature.
  "'The actions of the priests,
rulers, merchants, and servants,
foe scorcher, are distributed by the qualities
arising from their nature.
Calmness, control, austerity, purity, patience and sincerity,
knowledge, discernment, and piety
are priestly action born of their essence.
Valor, vigor, courage, skill in battle and also not fleeing,
charity, and leadership
are the action born of the ruler essence.
Cultivation, cow-herding, and trade
are the action born of the merchant essence.
Service-type action is born of the servant essence.
  "'Satisfied in one's own repeated action
a person attains success.
How one content in one's own action
finds perfection, hear that.
By worshipping with one's own action
that from whom is the origin of all creatures,
by whom all this is pervaded,
a human finds perfection.
  "'Better one's own duty of less quality
than another's duty well done;
performing action ordained by one's own essence
one does not incur guilt.
One should not relinquish inborn action,
Kaunteya, even though deficient,
for all undertakings are veiled with deficiency
like fire with smoke.
Unattached intuition everywhere, soul conquered,
longing disappeared, actionless perfection,
one goes by renunciation to the supreme.
  "'Learn from me briefly, Kaunteya,

how having attained perfection
one also attains God,
which is the highest state of knowledge.
United with cleansed intuition,
controlling the self with will,
and relinquishing, starting with sound, sense objects,
and rejecting passion and hatred,
living isolated, eating lightly,
controlling speech, body, and mind,
constantly intent on union meditation,
relying on detachment,
releasing ego, force, pride, desire, anger, possessiveness;
unselfish, peaceful, one is fit for oneness with God.

   "'Becoming God, soul serene,
one does not grieve nor desire,
the same among all creatures,
one attains supreme devotion to me.
By devotion to me one realizes who and what I am in truth;
then knowing me in truth one enters immediately.
Performing all actions always trusting in me,
one attains by my grace the imperishable eternal home.
Surrendering consciously all actions in me, intent on me,
constantly be conscious of me relying on intuitive union.

   "'Conscious of me,
you will transcend all difficulties through my grace;
but if through egotism you will not listen, you will perish.
If, relying on egotism, you think, "I will not fight,"
vain is this resolve; your nature will compel you.
Bound by your own essential karma, Kaunteya,
what you do not wish to do out of confusion
you will perform that even against your will.

   "'The Lord stands in the heart region
of all creatures, Arjuna,
causing to move all creatures mounted mechanically by magic.
Go to that shelter with your whole essence, Bharata.
From that grace you will attain supreme peace
and the eternal state.
Thus knowledge more secret than the secret
has been explained to you by me.

Reflecting on this completely, do whatever you wish.

"'Hear from me again the most secret supreme word.
You are surely loved by me;
therefore I shall speak for your benefit.
Become mentally me, devoted to me, sacrificing to me;
revere me, and you will come to me truly;
I promise you; you are my beloved.
Giving up all duties, take shelter in me alone.
I shall liberate you from all evils; do not grieve.

"'This is not to be told by you
to one who neglects austerity
nor to one who neglects devotion
nor to one who does not want to listen
nor to one who speaks ill of me.

"'Whoever shall explain
this supreme secret to my devotees,
performing the highest devotion to me,
will come to me without doubt.
And no one among humanity
is pleasing me more than this one,
and no other is more beloved by me on earth.
And whoever shall study this sacred dialogue of us two,
by this one with this knowledge sacrifice I may be loved;
such is my thought.

"'Also whoever may hear with faith and not scoffing,
this person, also liberated,
should attain the happy worlds of pure actions.
Has this been heard by you, Partha,
with one-pointed thought?
Has it destroyed your ignorant delusion, wealth winner?'

"Arjuna said,
'Delusion is lost, recognition gained,
through your grace by me, unchanging one.
I stand with doubt dispelled.
I shall do your word.'"

Sanjaya said,
"Thus from Vasudeva and Partha, the great soul,
I heard this marvelous dialog,
causing my hair to stand on end.

Through the grace of Vyasa
I heard this secret supreme yoga
from the Lord of yoga, Krishna,
speaking himself before my eyes.
  "O King, remembering again and again
this marvelous and holy dialog of Keshava and Arjuna,
I rejoice over and over.
And remembering again and again
that most marvelous form of Hari,
my amazement is great, King,
and I rejoice again and again.
My thought is that wherever is the Lord of yoga, Krishna,
and wherever is Partha, the archer,
there is splendor, victory, well-being, and eternal wisdom."

Union Threads (Yoga Sutras) by Patanjali

The greatest classical text from the yoga school of Indian philosophy is the *Yoga Sutras* by Patanjali, thought to have been written in the second century BC. These "threads" on yoga or union are extremely terse, stating concisely and often precisely essential points. The text may be explained and interpreted by commentaries or a teacher. Yoga practice is considered complementary to the Sankhya philosophy, the goal being the realization of freedom in Spirit from the world of Nature.

This psychological method of liberation is called *raja* or royal yoga or the yoga of the eight steps, which may be listed as follows:

1. Restraint: nonviolence, not lying, not stealing, not lusting, and not possessing;

2. Observances: cleanliness, contentment, discipline, self-study, and surrender to the Lord;

3. Posture or physical exercises;

4. Breath control;

5. Sublimation or withdrawal from the senses,

6. Attention;

7. Concentration;

8. Meditation.

1. Meditation

Now union is explained.
Union is the control of the modifications of consciousness.
Then the seer stands in its own form,
at other times identified with the modifications.

Modifications are of five kinds, painful and not painful:
knowledge, error, imagination, sleep, memory.
Perception, inference, and testimony are knowledge.
Error is false knowledge that is not formed from reality.
Sound knowledge following no object is imagination.
The absence of wakefulness is the modifying object of sleep.
The experienced object presented is memory.

By practice and detachment they are controlled.
Standing there with effort is practice.
For that, a long time of constant attention
firmly establishes it.

Getting free of the desire
for experiences heard and material objects
is by the mastery of detachment.
That is highest
when the power of the Spirit overcomes the qualities.

Reasoning, discriminating, joyful awareness
of the unity of the universe and self
is supreme meditation.
Cessation by renunciation
and constant practice in dissolving impressions
is the other,
which is undifferentiated existence,
bodilessness, absorption in supreme nature,
in others faith, enthusiasm, memory, meditation, wisdom.

To those of intense energy it comes soon.
From mild to moderate to intense practice
brings the best results;
or it is achieved by surrendering oneself to the Lord.

Untouched by afflictions, actions, and their results,
is the perfect Spirit of the Lord.
There is infinite the seed of omniscience.
That one is even the ancients' teacher,
beyond the limits of time.

Its manifest symbol is the sound current.
Constant practice of that with feeling brings success.
From that comes cosmic consciousness
and also the absence of obstacles.

Disease, laziness, indecision, apathy, lethargy,
craving sense-pleasure, erroneous perception,
lack of concentration, unstable attention,
these are the obstacles that distract consciousness.
Sorrow, worry, restlessness, and irregular breathing
accompany the distractions.
To overcome them practice that oneness.

Cultivating the feelings of
friendship, compassion, joy, and equanimity
toward those who are happy, suffering,
worthy, and unworthy,
purifies consciousness,
as does the expelling and retaining of the breath.

Also subtle vision produces
the best modification of the higher consciousness
bringing the mind into stability,
as does the transcendent inner Light,
and the consciousness that controls all passions,
and the analytical knowledge of dreams and sleep,
and concentration according to choice;
from the atom to the infinite is this mastery.

Lessened modifications become transparent
like a crystal receiver receiving knowable objects
transforming itself to the appearance of the objects.
There sound knowledge arranged meaningfully
simultaneously is thought transformation.

Memory purified so that it is empty of its own form,
the object shining alone is transformation without thought.
By this process also
with discrimination and without discrimination
subtle elements are explained.
The realm of the subtle elements
ends with undefinable nature.
These are only meditation with seed.

  Without discrimination
the undisturbed flow of the oversoul is blessed.
There wisdom is identical with direct truth.
Verbal inferences are different in essence
from these specific objects of truth.
The impression arising from this
prevents all other impressions.
Control of even that
controls everything in seedless meditation.

2. Practice

  Discipline, self-study, and surrender to the Lord
work toward union,
for the purpose of bringing about meditation
and in order to remove obstacles.
  Ignorance, egoism, attachment, aversion,
and clinging to life are the obstacles.
Ignorance is the field of the others
whether dormant, disappearing, overcome, or expanded.
Regarding the non-eternal, impure, painful non-soul
as the eternal, pure, pleasant soul awareness is ignorance.
The subject appears to be identified
with the power of seeing in egoism.
Dwelling upon pleasure is attachment.
Dwelling upon pain is aversion.
Flowing by itself even in the wise
is the established clinging to life.
  These are overcome by
reversing propagation to the subtle.
Concentration overcomes their effects.
Obstacles result in action patterns
which cause suffering in this life and the next.
Existing roots ripen into species, life, and experience.
They bear fruit as pleasure or pain
caused by virtue or vice.
By reason of the pains of change
and the opposing effects of the qualities,
all are suffering to the discriminating.

Avoidable is the suffering which has not yet come.
The cause of the avoidable
is identifying the perceiver with the perceived.
The nature of light, movement, and preservation
consisting of the elements, senses, and experience
are for the sake of liberation from the perceived universe.
Specific, not specific, definite, indefinite
are the quality states.
The perceiver is only the perception,
pure even though seeing through mental images.
That is only for the sake of
the soul of the perceived universe.
Though destroyed for the enlightened,
it is not destroyed for the community of others.

The forces of both one's own owner
attaining one's own form cause identity.
The cause of this is ignorance.
In the absence of that, in the absence of identity removed,
that is freedom of the perceiver.
Discriminating undisturbed intelligence removes suffering.

This develops through seven stages of wisdom.
By practice of the steps of union
impurities are destroyed by the light of knowledge
up to discriminating intelligence.
Restraint, observances, posture, breath control,
sublimation, attention, concentration, and meditation
are the eight steps.
There are nonviolence, not lying,
not stealing, not lusting, not possessing.
These, not limited by class, country, time, circumstance,
are the universal great vows.

Cleanliness, contentment, discipline, self-study,
and surrender to the Lord are the observances.

Overcome destructive instincts
by cultivating the opposites.
Destructive instincts are harmful thoughts
whether done, caused, or approved,
whether motivated by greed, anger, or delusion,
whether mild, moderate, or intense;

they result in endless suffering and ignorance.
Therefore cultivate the opposites.

Nonviolence confirmed,
in that presence hostility is relinquished.
Not lying confirmed, work and its fruits submit.
Not stealing confirmed, all riches approach.
Not lusting confirmed, vigor is gained.
Not possessing established,
there occurs knowledge of the birth process.

Cleanliness brings protection of one's own body
and non-infection from contact with others.
Goodness purified becomes serenity, single-mindedness,
conquest of the senses, and readiness to perceive the soul.
From contentment the best happiness is gained.
Perfection of the body's senses comes from
the destruction of impurities by discipline.
From self-study comes communion with the divine ideal.
Meditation is successfully identifying with the Lord.

Stable and pleasant is the posture.
Tension released, thought transformation is infinite.
From that, dualities do not disturb.

After that is accomplished,
regulation of inhalation and exhalation is breath control.
External, internal, and motionless are the modifications
as regulated by space, time, and number,
becoming long and subtle.
External, internal spheres cast aside is the fourth.
From this is removed the covering of the Light,
and prepared is the mind for attention.

Withdrawn from its own objects
consciousness identifies with its own form
so that the senses are sublimated.
From that comes supreme mastery over the senses.

3. Powers

Original focus of consciousness is attention.
Continuing awareness there is concentration.
When that shines light alone in its own form empty,
it is meditation.

These three working as one are inner control.
By that conquering comes the light of wisdom.
Its application is to the levels.
These three are more internal than the preceding.
Even these are external to the seedless.

 Control of destructive instincts and impressions
disappears and appears
in the highest control of joined consciousness,
as control evolves.
Its flow becomes calm by habit.
Multiplicity dissolving as oneness arises,
the consciousness of meditation evolves.
From there again past and present are similar
in the awareness of the consciousness,
as oneness evolves.
By this the elements of the senses in their evolution
of principles, characteristics, and states are explained.
Past, present, or future,
the principle closely follows the substance.
Another order causes the other to evolve.

 By inner control of the triple evolution
comes knowledge of the past and future.
Sound, meaning, and response
coinciding with one another are confused;
their analysis by inner control
brings knowledge of the sounds of all beings.
By witnessing the causes of impressions
previous lives are known.

 By awareness others' consciousness is known;
but that does not support the contents,
because that is not identified with living.
By inner control of the form of the body
the power of receiving that is blocked,
the eyes not being in contact with the light;
this is the internal value.
By this the sound of internal value is explained.

 Action has quick effects and slow effects;
by that inner control comes knowledge of death,
also by portents.

From friendship comes strength.
From strength comes the strength of an elephant.
  By directing radiant light
the subtle, hidden, and remote become known.
Cosmic knowledge comes by inner control on the sun,
on the moon, stellar knowledge;
on the pole-star, knowledge of their motions;
on the navel center, knowledge of the body's system;
on the hollow of the throat,
renunciation of hunger and thirst;
on the center of gravity, steadiness;
on the light in the head, the power of direct perception;
on intuition, comes all;
on the heart, knowledge of consciousness.

  The spirit of goodness is absolutely uncommingled;
experience is qualified by false identification,
existing for another;
by inner control of its own purpose
comes knowledge of Spirit.
From that, intuitive hearing, touching, seeing,
tasting, and smelling are produced.
They are obstacles to meditation, the worldly powers.

  By releasing the causes of bondage
and by knowledge of penetration,
consciousness can enter into others' bodies.
By conquering psychic energy,
water, mud, thorns, and the rest do not contact,
and death is overcome.

  By conquering vitality comes light.
By inner control on the ear and space comes divine hearing.
By inner control on the relationship of the body and space
comes the lightness of cotton
and the ability to levitate in space.
The external modifications become real
in the great bodiless state;
by that the light's covering is destroyed.

  Inner control on matter,
its form, subtlety, compounds, and purpose
overcomes the elements.

From that manifests minuteness and the rest,
perfection of the body
and the principle of their non-resistance.
Form, grace, strength, and thunderbolt hardness
are the body's perfection.

Inner control on sensation,
its form, analysis, decision, and purpose
overcomes the senses.
From that mental quickness and feeling without senses
nature is overcome.

Only the knowledge of discriminating
between goodness and Spirit
brings omnipotence and omniscience.
By detachment from even that,
the seed of bondage is destroyed in freedom.

On the attainment of high position
attachment to the pride of performance
again may cause the loss of position.

By inner control on moments and their succession
comes discriminating knowledge.
From this comes discernment of two similar events,
which cannot be distinguished by
class, characteristic, or position.
Understanding all objects
and every aspect of objects simultaneously
is discriminating knowledge.
When goodness and Spirit are of equal purity it is freedom.

4. Freedom

Birth, drugs, chanting, discipline, or meditation
bring about supernatural powers.
Evolution from the lower to the higher
comes by filling up nature.
The instrument does not cause manifestation, but from that
comes the destruction of the obstacles to natural energy,
as with a farmer.

Consciousness is produced by the power of the self.
Many activities are directed
by the one consciousness of innumerable minds.

There what is born of concentration leaves no effects.
Action is neither white nor black for the united,
of the three kinds in the case of others.
From those their fruition allows only
the manifestation of those tendencies.

Although separated by class, place, and time,
continuous is the correspondence of memory and impressions;
and habits have no beginning, because drives are eternal.
Cause, motive, structure, and object hold them together;
in the absence of these they are absent.
Past and future in their own form
exist exchanging cosmic principles.
Manifest or subtle, they are qualities of the soul.
The evolution of unity is the reality of things.

The object being the same, consciousness being different,
the ways of the two are different.
And it is not that the object depends on one consciousness,
because if that were not present,
then what would happen to it?
By that coloring affecting consciousness
an object is known or unknown.
Eternally known are the modifications of consciousness
to that master Spirit that is unchangeable.

They are not self-luminous, because they are perceived;
and at the same time both cannot be perceived.
Consciousness perceived by another,
intuited by another intuition is an infinite regress
and a confusion of memory.
Awareness is unchanging omniscience,
but those reflections identify with their own intuition.
The perceiver colored by the perceived
is conscious of everything.
That although equipped with innumerable tendencies,
is for the purpose of the supreme
because of its combined structure.

For the discriminating perceiver
the soul is completely detached from emotion and mind.
For then with serene discrimination
consciousness moves toward freedom.

That has intervals
of other thoughts from previous tendencies.
The removal of these is as explained with the obstacles.
  Even in the highest illumination
having no selfish attachment
from constant discriminating knowledge
comes virtue cloud meditation.
From that comes detachment from obstacle effects.
Then all the covering impurities removed,
because of infinite knowledge the universe is small.
  Then having fulfilled their purpose
the evolution of transforming qualities stops.
The continuity of moments at the end of evolution
are cognized as a distinct transformation.
Empty for the sake of Spirit
the qualities return to nature.
Freedom is established in its own form,
or it is aware energy.

Introduction to Gautama the Buddha

Siddartha Gautama (563-480 BC) was born as a prince in a small state in northern India in what is now Nepal. According to legend, several soothsayers predicted that if he stayed home, he would become a universal king; but if he left, he would become a Buddha. His mother died after one week, and Siddartha was brought up by her sister. His father surrounded him with every luxury. At the age of 16 Siddartha married Yasodhara, his cousin of the same age, and spent his time in the pleasure gardens of the palace.

When Gautama was 29, he saw the four signs which led to his renunciation of the world—first an old person, then a sick person, then a corpse being carried to a funeral, and finally a begging monk in a yellow robe. Gautama began to contemplate the meaning of life with its inevitable decay, suffering, and death; like the monk he too must find a solution to these problems. Therefore he decided to renounce everything, and he left the palace immediately after the birth of his first son.

For a while he sought enlightenment by mortifying the flesh; fasting and eating only one seed a day, he became so thin that his bones stuck out. Weak from hunger, he fainted and almost died. Then he decided that this was not the way to enlightenment. He began to beg for food and concentrated on meditation. When he gave up the austerities, his five companions in spiritual aspiration left him in disgust.

One day when he was 35, he sat under a banyan tree with the resolve not to get up until he was enlightened. Perceiving that Siddartha wanted to pass beyond his control, the tempter Mara and his armies attacked him in various ways; but each time Gautama concentrated on the ten perfections (charity, morality, renunciation, wisdom, effort, patience, truth, determination, universal love, and equanimity) and received divine protection. Mara tried to persuade him to give up his struggle and live. However, Gautama identified the ten armies of Mara as follows: lust, dislike for the spiritual, hunger and thirst, craving, laziness, cowardice, doubt, inflexibility, glamour, and finally exalting oneself while despising others. Gautama said that by conquering these one could attain bliss and that he would rather die than be defeated. Mara retired, and Gautama went into deeper meditation, realizing his former lifetimes, becoming clairvoyant, and intuiting the psychological insights that became his principal teachings.

At first people did not know what to call him and asked him if he was a god, a devil, an angel, a person or what. Gautama replied simply, "I am awake." Thus he became known as the Buddha, which means the awakened one or the enlightened one.

The first sermon included here are the words of the Buddha when he spoke in the deer park at Benares as recorded in the *Samyutta-Nikaya* V:420, one of the collections of the *Sutta Pitaka*, the largest of the "three baskets" of early Buddhist texts. Hearing this brief discourse, the five previous companions, who were at first skeptical of Buddha's new claims, were convinced and became the first five "perfected ones" in his order.

The order of monks or disciples grew, and soon the Buddha was sending out 60 of them in different directions to spread the teachings. The Buddha fulfilled his promise to return to talk with King Bimbisara after his enlightenment, and he was converted also. Although his father, King Suddhodana, did not like the idea of the Buddha begging for food, he accepted it; many of his relatives became followers also. Some of the wealthy built monasteries for the order.

Ananda, the Buddha's cousin and closest disciple, pleaded that women be allowed to join the order, and finally the order of nuns was established. Another cousin, Devadatta, wanted to become the Buddha's successor; but when he was rejected, he tried three times to kill Gautama but failed. Then Devadatta tried to split the order. However, two of the greatest disciples, Sariputta and Moggallana, were able to persuade those who had followed him to return to the Buddha. Devadatta became ill; but as he was dying, the Buddha forgave him.

When he was about 80 years old, the Buddha became seriously ill himself but felt that he should not die until he had prepared the order for his departure. Thus he fought off the illness. Ananda asked for instructions, but the Buddha said that he had not presented "the closed fist of the teacher." In other words, he had not held back any of the teachings. Not even Sariputta nor Moggallana were to be his successor; rather everything was to be decided by majority vote. He suggested that they take refuge in the teachings, but they might abolish minor rules if they wished.

Finally the Buddha instructed a friend named Cunda to prepare him a meal, which was either pork or mushrooms trodden by pigs; the leftovers were to be buried, and the other monks were to be given something else. Soon after eating this meal, the Buddha became very sick with violent pains. The Buddha declared that Cunda was to be honored as equal to the one who had given him the last meal before his enlightenment. Finally he asked the monks three times if they had any questions, but none of them spoke. Then the Buddha said his last words, "Transient are all conditioned things. Work out your salvation with diligence." The body of Gautama was cremated a week later, and an argument over the relics of the Buddha was settled peacefully by dividing them into eight portions.

Buddha's First Sermon

These two extremes, monks, are not to be practiced
by one who has gone forth from the world.
What are the two?

That joined with the passions and luxury—
low, vulgar, common, ignoble, and useless,
and that joined with self-torture—
painful, ignoble, and useless.

Avoiding these two extremes the one who has thus come
has gained the enlightenment of the middle path,
which produces insight and knowledge,
and leads to peace, wisdom, enlightenment, and nirvana.

And what, monks, is the middle path, by which
the one who has thus come has gained enlightenment,
which produces knowledge and insight,
and leads to peace, wisdom, enlightenment, and nirvana?

This is the noble eightfold way, namely,
correct understanding, correct intention,
correct speech, correct action, correct livelihood,
correct attention, correct concentration,
and correct meditation.

This, monks, is the middle path, by which
the one who has thus come has gained enlightenment,
which produces insight and knowledge,
and leads to peace, wisdom, enlightenment, and nirvana.

Now this, monks, is the noble truth of pain:
birth is painful; old age is painful;
sickness is painful; death is painful;
sorrow, lamentation, dejection, and despair are painful.
Contact with unpleasant things is painful;
not getting what one wishes is painful.
In short the five groups of grasping are painful.

Now this, monks, is the noble truth of the cause of pain:
the craving, which leads to rebirth,
combined with pleasure and lust,
finding pleasure here and there,
namely the craving for passion,

the craving for existence,
and the craving for non-existence.
  Now this, monks, is the noble truth
of the cessation of pain:
the cessation without a remainder of craving,
the abandonment, forsaking, release, and non-attachment.
  Now this, monks, is the noble truth
of the way that leads to the cessation of pain:
this is the noble eightfold way, namely,
correct understanding, correct intention,
correct speech, correct action, correct livelihood,
correct attention, correct concentration,
and correct meditation.
  "This is the noble truth of pain":
Thus, monks, among doctrines unheard before,
in me insight, wisdom, knowledge, and light arose.
  "This noble truth of pain must be comprehended."
Thus, monks, among doctrines unheard before,
in me insight, wisdom, knowledge, and light arose.
  "It has been comprehended."
Thus, monks, among doctrines unheard before,
in me insight, wisdom, knowledge, and light arose.
  "This is the noble truth of the cause of pain":
Thus, monks, among doctrines unheard before,
in me insight, wisdom, knowledge, and light arose.
  "The cause of pain must be abandoned."
Thus, monks, among doctrines unheard before,
in me insight, wisdom, knowledge, and light arose.
  "It has been abandoned."
Thus, monks, among doctrines unheard before,
in me insight, wisdom, knowledge, and light arose.
  "This is the noble truth of the cessation of pain":
Thus, monks, among doctrines unheard before,
in me insight, wisdom, knowledge, and light arose.
  "The cessation of pain must be realized."
Thus, monks, among doctrines unheard before,
in me insight, wisdom, knowledge, and light arose.
  "It has been realized."

Thus, monks, among doctrines unheard before,
in me insight, wisdom, knowledge, and light arose.
  "This is the noble truth
of the way that leads to the cessation of pain":
Thus, monks, among doctrines unheard before,
in me insight, wisdom, knowledge, and light arose.
  "The way must be practiced."
Thus, monks, among doctrines unheard before,
in me insight, wisdom, knowledge, and light arose.
  "It has been practiced."
Thus, monks, among doctrines unheard before,
in me insight, wisdom, knowledge, and light arose.
  As long as in these four noble truths
my due knowledge and insight
with the three sections and twelve divisions
was not well purified, even so long, monks,
in the world with its gods, Mara, Brahma,
its beings with ascetics, priests, gods, and men,
I had not attained the highest complete enlightenment.
This I recognized.
  And when, monks, in these four noble truths
my due knowledge and insight
with its three sections and twelve divisions
was well purified, then monks,
in the world with its gods, Mara, Brahma,
its beings with ascetics, priests, gods, and men,
I had attained the highest complete enlightenment.
This I recognized.
  Knowledge arose in me;
insight arose that the release of my mind is unshakable:
this is my last existence;
now there is no rebirth.

Path of Truth
(Dhammapada)

The *Path of Truth (Dhammapada)* is also from the *Sutta Pitaka* but in the *Khuddaka-Nikaya*. The author of these verses is unknown, although they are believed to be the teachings of the Buddha himself. The text of the *Dhammapada* was established by the time of the great Buddhist Emperor Ashoka in the third century BC. Frequent references are made to Mara, the one who tempted the Buddha.

1. The Twin-Verses

What we are is the result of what we have thought,
is built by our thoughts, is made up of our thoughts.
If one speaks or acts with an impure thought,
suffering follows one,
like the wheel of the cart follows the foot of the ox.

What we are is the result of what we have thought,
is built by our thoughts, is made up of our thoughts.
If one speaks or acts with a pure thought,
happiness follows one,
like a shadow that never leaves.

"They insulted me; they hurt me;
they defeated me; they cheated me."
In those who harbor such thoughts,
hate will never cease.

"They insulted me; they hurt me;
they defeated me; they cheated me."
In those who do not harbor such thoughts,
hate will cease.

For hate is never conquered by hate.
Hate is conquered by love.
This is an eternal law.
Many do not realize that we must all come to an end here;
but those who do realize this, end their quarrels at once.

Whoever lives only for pleasures,
with senses uncontrolled,

immoderate in eating, lazy, and weak,
will be overthrown by Mara,
like the wind throws down a weak tree.

 Whoever lives not for pleasures,
with senses well controlled,
moderate in eating, has faith and the power of virtue,
will not be overthrown by Mara,
any more than the wind throws down a rocky mountain.

 Whoever would put on the yellow robe
without having cleansed oneself from impurity,
disregarding self-control and truth,
is not deserving of the yellow robe.

 But whoever has cleansed oneself from impurity,
is well grounded in all the virtues,
and is possessed of self-control and truth,
is deserving of the yellow robe.

 Those who imagine truth in untruth
and see untruth in truth
never arrive at truth but follow vain desires.
Those who know truth as truth and untruth as untruth
arrive at truth and follow true desires.

 As rain makes its way into a badly roofed house,
so passion makes its way into an unreflecting mind.
As rain does not make its way into a well roofed house,
so passion does not make its way into a reflecting mind.

 Wrong-doers grieve in this world,
and they grieve in the next; they grieve in both.
They grieve and are afflicted
when they see the wrong they have done.

 The virtuous find joy in this world,
and they find joy in the next; they find joy in both.
They find joy and are glad
when they see the good they have done.

 Wrong-doers suffer in this world,
and they suffer in the next; they suffer in both.
They suffer when they think of the wrong they have done.
They suffer even more when going on the wrong path.

 The virtuous are happy in this world,
and they are happy in the next; they are happy in both.

They are happy when they think of the good they have done.
They are even happier when going on the good path.

Even if the thoughtless can recite many of the scriptures,
if they do not act accordingly,
they are not living the holy life,
but are like a cowherd counting the cows of others.

Even if the faithful can recite
only a few of the scriptures,
if they act accordingly,
having given up passion, hate, and folly,
being possessed of true knowledge and serenity of mind,
craving nothing in this world or the next,
they are living the holy life.

2. Awareness

Awareness is the path of immortality;
thoughtlessness is the path of death.
Those who are aware do not die.
The thoughtless are as if dead already.

The wise having clearly understood this,
delight in awareness
and find joy in the knowledge of the noble ones.
These wise ones, meditative, persevering,
always using strong effort,
attain nirvana, the supreme peace and happiness.

If a person is awake, aware, mindful, pure, considerate,
self-restrained, and lives according to duty,
that person's glory will increase.
By awakening, by awareness, by restraint and control,
the wise may make for oneself
an island which no flood can overwhelm.

Fools follow after vanity, are ignorant and careless.
The wise keep awareness as their best treasure.
Do not follow after vanity
nor after sensual pleasure nor lust.

Whoever meditates with awareness obtains great joy.
When the wise conquer thoughtlessness by awareness,
climbing the terraced heights of wisdom,
free from sadness viewing the sad crowd below,

they gaze upon the fools, like one on the mountain peak
gazes upon those standing on the plain.

Aware among the thoughtless, awake among the sleepy,
the wise advances, like a racehorse leaves behind the slow.
By awareness Indra rose to become chief of the gods.
People praise awareness; thoughtlessness is always blamed.

A mendicant who finds joy in awareness,
who looks with fear on thoughtlessness,
moves about like fire,
burning all restrictions, small or large.
A mendicant who finds joy in awareness,
who looks with fear on thoughtlessness,
cannot fall away, but is close to nirvana.

3. Thought

As fletchers make their arrows straight,
the wise make straight their wavering and unsteady thought,
which is difficult to guard and difficult to restrain.
Like a fish taken from its watery home
and thrown on the dry ground,
our thought quivers all over
in order to escape the dominion of Mara.

It is good to control the mind,
which is difficult to restrain, fickle, and wandering.
A tamed mind brings happiness.
Let the wise guard their thoughts,
which are difficult to perceive, tricky, and wandering.
Thoughts well guarded bring happiness.
Those who restrain their mind,
which travels far alone without a body, hiding in a cave,
will be free from the restrictions of death.

If a person's mind is unsteady,
if it does not know the true path,
if one's peace of mind is troubled,
wisdom is not perfected.

There is no fear for the one whose thought is untroubled,
whose mind is not confused,
who has ceased to think of good and bad,
who is aware.

Knowing that this body is like a jar,
and making one's thought strong as a fortress,
attack Mara with the weapon of wisdom,
protect what is conquered and stay always aware.
Before long, unfortunately, this body will lie on the earth,
rejected, without consciousness, like a useless log.

Whatever an enemy may do to an enemy,
or a hater to a hater,
a wrongly directed mind will do greater harm.
Neither a mother nor a father
nor any other relative will do so much;
a well-directed mind will do us greater service.

4. Flowers

Who shall conquer this world
and the world of death and the gods?
Who shall find the clear path of truth,
as a skillful person finds the flower?

The wise student will conquer this world
and the world of death and the gods.
The wise student will find the clear path of truth,
as a skillful person finds the flower.

Whoever knows that this body is like foam
and has learned that its nature is a mirage,
will break the flourishing arrows of Mara
and never see the king of death.

Death carries off a person who is gathering flowers,
whose mind is distracted,
like a flood carries off a sleeping village.
Death terminates a person who is gathering flowers,
whose mind is distracted,
before one is even satiated in pleasures.

As the bee collects nectar and departs
without harming the flower or its color or scent,
so let the sage live in a village.
Not the faults of others
nor their errors of commission or omission,
but one's own errors and omissions should the sage consider.

Like a beautiful flower, full of color, but without scent,
are the fine but fruitless words
of those who do not act accordingly.
But like a beautiful flower, full of color and full of scent,
are the fine and fruitful words
of those who do act accordingly.

As many kinds of garlands
can be made from a heap of flowers,
so many good works may be achieved by a mortal after birth.
The scent of flowers does not travel against the wind,
not even that of sandalwood, rose-bay or jasmine,
but the fragrance of good people
travels even against the wind.
A good person pervades everywhere.

Sandalwood or rose-bay or lotus or jasmine—
among these perfumes, the perfume of virtue is unsurpassed.
Limited is the scent of rose-bay or sandalwood;
but the perfume of the virtuous
rises up to the gods as the highest.

Mara never crosses the path of those who are virtuous,
who live without thoughtlessness,
and who are liberated by true knowledge.

Just as on a heap of rubbish thrown upon the highway
the lotus will grow sweetly fragrant, delighting the soul,
so also among those who are like rubbish
the wise student of the truly enlightened Buddha
shines brightly with wisdom above the blinded crowd.

5. The Fool

Long is the night to one who is awake.
Long is ten miles to one who is tired.
Long is the cycle of birth and death
to the fool who does not know the true path.

If a traveler does not meet with one who is better or equal,
let one firmly travel alone;
there is no companionship with a fool.

"These sons belong to me, and this wealth belongs to me;"
with such thoughts a fool is tormented.
One does not belong to oneself;

how much less sons and wealth?

The fool who knows one's own folly,
is wise at least to that extent;
but the fool who thinks oneself wise is really a fool.

If a fool is associated with a wise person all one's life,
the fool will not perceive the truth,
any more than a spoon will taste the soup.

If an intelligent person is associated with a wise person
for only one minute, one will soon perceive the truth,
just as the tongue does the taste of soup.

Fools of little understanding are their own worst enemies,
for they do wrong deeds which bear bitter fruits.
That action is not well done, which having been done,
brings remorse, whose result one receives crying with tears.
But that action is well done, which having been done,
does not bring remorse,
whose result one receives gladly and cheerfully.

As long as the wrong action does not bear fruit,
the fool thinks it is like honey;
but when it bears fruit, then the fool suffers grief.

Let a fool month after month
eat food with the tip of kusha grass;
nevertheless one is not worth one-sixteenth
of those who have understood the truth.

A wrong action, like newly drawn milk, does not turn soon;
smoldering, like fire covered by ashes, it follows the fool.
When the wrong action, after it has become known,
turns to sorrow for the fool,
then it destroys one's brightness and splits the head.

Let the fool wish for reputation,
for precedence among the mendicants,
for authority in the convents,
for veneration among the people.

"Let both the householders and the mendicants
think that this is done by me.
Let them always ask me
what should be done and what should not be done."

Such is the wish of the fool
of increasing desire and pride.
One road leads to wealth; another road leads to nirvana.
Let the mendicant, the disciple of Buddha, learn this,
and not strive for honor but seek wisdom.

6. The Wise

If you see a wise person who shows you your faults,
who shows what is to be avoided,
follow that wise person
as you would one who reveals hidden treasures;
you will be better not worse for following that one.
Let one admonish; let one teach; let one forbid the wrong;
and one will be loved by the good and hated by the bad.

Do not have wrong-doers for friends;
do not have despicable people for friends;
have virtuous people for friends;
have for friends the best people.

Whoever drinks in the truth
lives happily with a serene mind.
The wise are joyful in the truth
revealed by the noble ones.

Engineers of canals guide the water;
fletchers make the arrow straight;
carpenters shape the wood;
the wise mold themselves.

As a solid rock is not shaken by the wind,
so the wise are not shaken by blame and praise.
As a deep lake is clear and calm,
so the wise become tranquil after they listened to the truth.

Good people walk on regardless of what happens to them.
Good people do not babble on about their desires.
Whether touched by happiness or by sorrow,
the wise never appear elated or depressed.

Whoever for one's sake or for another's,
does not wish for a son or wealth or power,
and if one does not wish for success by unfair means,
that one certainly is virtuous, wise, and holy.

Few are those people who reach the farther shore;
the other people here run along this shore.
But those who, when the truth has been taught to them,
follow the truth, will pass over the dominion of death,
however difficult to cross.

Leaving behind the path of darkness
and following the path of light,
let the wise person go from home to a homeless state,
in retirement looking for enjoyment
where enjoyment seemed difficult.
Letting go of all pleasures, calling nothing one's own,
let the wise cleanse oneself
from all the troubles of the mind.

Those whose minds are well grounded
in the elements of enlightenment,
who without clinging to anything
find joy in freedom from attachment,
whose appetites have been conquered,
and who are full of light,
they are free in this world.

7. The Saint

There is no suffering for the one
who has completed the journey,
who is freed from sorrow,
who has freed oneself on all sides,
who has thrown off all chains.

The thoughtful exert themselves;
they do not delight in a home;
like swans who have left their lake,
they leave their house and home.

Those who have no accumulations, who eat properly,
who have perceived release and unconditioned freedom,
their path is difficult to understand,
like that of birds in the sky.

Those whose passions are stilled,
who are indifferent to pleasure,
who have perceived release and unconditioned freedom,
their path is difficult to understand,

like that of birds in the sky.
  Even the gods admire one whose senses are controlled,
like horses well tamed by the driver,
who is free from pride and free from appetites.
Such a dutiful one who is tolerant like the earth,
who is firm like a pillar,
who is like a lake without mud:
no new births are in store for this one.
  One's thought is calm;
calm is one's word and one's action
when one has obtained freedom by true knowledge
and become peaceful.
The one who is free from gullibility,
who knows the uncreated, who has severed all ties,
removed all temptations, renounced all desires,
is the greatest of people.
  In a village or in a forest, in a valley or on the hills,
wherever saints live, that is a place of joy.
Forests are delightful; where others find no joy,
there the desireless will find joy,
for they do not seek the pleasures of the senses.

8. The Thousands

  Better than a thousand meaningless words
is one sensible word if hearing it one becomes peaceful.
Better than a thousand meaningless verses
is one word of verse if hearing it one becomes peaceful.
Better than reciting one hundred verses of meaningless words
is one poem if hearing it one becomes peaceful.
  If a person were to conquer in battle
a thousand times a thousand people,
if another conquers oneself,
that one is the greatest conqueror.
  Conquering oneself is better than conquering other people;
not even a god, a spirit, nor Mara with Brahma,
could turn into a defeat the victory
of one who always practices the discipline of self-control.
  If a person month after month for a hundred years
should sacrifice with a thousand offerings,

and if but for one moment that person paid reverence
to one whose soul is grounded in knowledge,
better is that reverence than a hundred years of sacrifices.

   If a person for a hundred years
should worship Agni in the forest,
and if but for one moment that person paid reverence
to one whose soul is grounded in knowledge,
better is that reverence than a hundred years of worship.

   Whatever a person sacrifices in this world
as an offering or as an oblation
for a whole year in order to gain merit,
the whole of it is not worth a quarter.
Reverence shown to the virtuous is better.
To the one who always reveres and respects the aged,
four things increase: life, health, happiness, and power.

   Better than a hundred years
lived in vice and unrestrained
is living one day if a person is virtuous and contemplative.

   Better than a hundred years
lived in ignorance and unrestrained
is living one day if a person is wise and contemplative.

   Better than a hundred years
lived in idleness and weakness
is living one day if a person courageously makes effort.

   Better than a hundred years
of not perceiving how things arise and pass away
is living one day if a person
does perceive how things arise and pass away.

   Better than a hundred years
of not perceiving immortality
is living one day if a person does perceive immortality.

   Better than a hundred years
of not seeing the supreme path
is living one day if a person does see the supreme path.

9. Good and Bad

   A person should hurry toward the good
and restrain one's thoughts from the bad.

If a person is slow in doing good,
one's mind will find pleasure in wrong.

If a person does what is wrong, let one not do it again.
Let one not find pleasure in wrong.
Painful is the accumulation of bad conduct.

If a person does what is good, let one do it again.
Let one find joy in it.
Happiness is the result of good conduct.

Even a wrong-doer sees happiness
as long as one's wrong action does not ripen;
but when the wrong action has ripened,
then does the wrong-doer see bad.

Even a good person sees bad
as long as one's good action does not ripen;
but when one's good action has ripened,
then the good person sees the good.

Let no one underestimate evil,
thinking, "It will not come near me."
Even a water-pot is filled by the falling of drops of water.
A fool becomes full of evil
even if one gathers it little by little.

Let no one underestimate good,
thinking, "It will not come near me."
Even a water-pot is filled by the falling of drops of water.
A wise person becomes full of goodness
even if one gathers it little by little.

Let a person avoid wrong actions, as a merchant,
who has few companions and carries much wealth,
avoids a dangerous road;
as a person who loves life avoids poison.

Whoever has no wound on one's hand
may touch poison with that hand;
poison does not affect one who has no wound;
nor does evil one who does no wrong.

Whoever does wrong to an innocent person
or to one who is pure and harmless,
the wrong returns to that fool
just like fine dust thrown against the wind.

Some people are born again in the womb;
wrong-doers go to hell;
the good go to heaven;
those free from worldly desires attain nirvana.

Neither in the sky nor in the middle of the ocean
nor by entering the caves of mountains
is there known a place on earth
where a person can escape from a wrong action.

Neither in the sky nor in the middle of the ocean
nor by entering the caves of mountains
is there known a place on earth
where a person can escape from death.

10. Punishment

Everyone trembles at punishment; everyone fears death.
Likening others to oneself,
one should neither kill nor cause killing.

Everyone trembles at punishment; everyone loves life.
Likening others to oneself,
one should neither kill nor cause killing.

Whoever seeking one's own happiness
inflicts pain on others who also want happiness
will not find happiness after death.

Whoever seeking one's own happiness
does not inflict pain on others who also want happiness
will find happiness after death.

Do not speak anything harsh.
Those who are spoken to will answer you.
Angry talk is painful, and retaliation will touch you.
If you make yourself as still as a broken gong,
you have attained nirvana, for anger is not known to you.

Just as a cowherd with a staff
drives the cows into the pasture,
so old age and death drive the life of living beings.

A fool committing wrong actions does not know
that the stupid person burns through one's own deeds,
like one burned by fire.

Whoever inflicts punishment
on those who do not deserve it
and offends against those who are without offense
soon comes to one of these ten states:
cruel suffering, infirmity, injury of the body, fearful pain,
or mental loss, or persecution from the ruler,
or a fearful accusation, loss of relations,
or destruction of possessions,
or lightning fire burning one's houses,
and when one's body is destroyed the fool goes to hell.

Neither nakedness nor matted hair nor mud
nor fasting nor lying on the ground
nor rubbing with dust nor sitting motionless
purify a mortal who is not free from doubt and desire.

Whoever though dressed in fine clothes, lives peacefully,
is calm, controlled, restrained, pure,
and does not hurt any other beings,
that one is holy, an ascetic, a mendicant.

Is there in the world anyone
who is so restrained by modesty
that they avoid blame like a trained horse avoids the whip?
Like a trained horse when touched by a whip,
be strenuous and eager, and by faith, by virtue, by energy,
by meditation, by discernment of the truth
you will overcome this great sorrow,
perfected in knowledge, behavior, and mindfulness.

Engineers of canals guide the water;
fletchers make the arrow straight;
carpenters shape the wood;
good people mold themselves.

11. Old Age

Why is there laughter, why is there joy
while this world is always burning?
Why do you not seek a light,
you who are shrouded in darkness?

Consider this dressed-up lump covered with wounds,
joined with limbs, diseased, and full of many schemes
which are neither permanent nor stable.

This body is wearing out, a nest of diseases and frail;
this heap of corruption falls apart; life ends in death.

What pleasure is there
for one who sees these white bones
like gourds thrown away in the autumn?
A fortress is made out of the bones,
plastered over with flesh and blood,
and in it lives old age and death, pride and deceit.

The glorious chariots of the kings wear out;
the body also comes to old age;
but the virtue of good people never ages;
thus the good teach each other.

People who have learned little grow old like an ox;
their flesh grows, but their knowledge does not grow.

I have run through a course of many births
looking for the maker of this dwelling and did not find it;
painful is birth again and again.
Now you are seen, the builder of the house;
you will not build the house again.
All your rafters are broken; your ridgepole is destroyed;
your mind, set on the attainment of nirvana,
has attained the extinction of desires.

People who have not practiced proper discipline
who have not acquired wealth in their youth,
pine away like old cranes in a lake without fish.
People who have not practiced proper discipline,
who have not acquired wealth in their youth,
lie like broken bows, sighing after the past.

12. Self

If a person holds oneself dear,
let one watch oneself carefully.
The wise should be watchful
during at least one of the three watches.

Let each person first direct oneself to what is right;
then let one teach others; thus the wise will not suffer.
If a person makes oneself as one teaches others to be,
then being well-controlled, that one might guide others,
since self-control is difficult.

Self is the master of self;
who else could be the master?
With self well-controlled
a person finds a master such as few can find.

The wrong done by oneself, born of oneself,
produced by oneself, crushes the fool,
just as a diamond breaks even a precious stone.
The one whose vice is great brings oneself down
to that condition where one's enemy wishes one to be,
just as a creeper overpowers the entangled sala tree.
Bad actions and actions harmful to ourselves are easy to do;
what is beneficial and good, that is very difficult to do.

The fool who scorns the teaching of the saintly,
the noble, and the virtuous, and follows wrong ideas,
bears fruit to one's own destruction,
like the fruits of the katthaka reed.

By oneself is wrong done; by oneself one suffers;
by oneself is wrong left undone; by oneself is one purified.
Purity and impurity come from oneself;
no one can purify another.

Let no one neglect one's own duty
for the sake of another's, however great;
let a person after one has discerned one's own duty,
be always attentive to this duty.

13. The World

Do not follow a bad law.
Do not live in thoughtlessness.
Do not follow wrong ideas.
Do not be attached to the world.

Arise; do not be thoughtless.
Follow the path of virtue.
The virtuous rest in bliss in this world and in the next.
Follow the path of virtue; do not follow the wrong path.
The virtuous rest in bliss in this world and in the next.

Look upon the world as a bubble;
look on it as a mirage.
Whoever looks thus upon the world
is not seen by the sovereign of death.

Come, look at this world resembling a painted royal chariot.
The foolish are immersed in it,
but the wise are not attached to it.

  The one who formerly was thoughtless
and afterwards became conscientious
lights up this world like the moon when freed from a cloud.
The one whose wrong actions are eradicated by good conduct
lights up this world like the moon when freed from a cloud.

  This world is blinded; only a few can see here.
Like birds escaped from the net, a few go to heaven.
The swans go on the path of the sun;
miraculously they fly through the sky.
The wise are led out of this world,
when they have conquered Mara and the tempter's armies.

  Whoever violates the one law, who speaks lies,
and scoffs at another world,
there is no wrong that one will not do.

  Misers do not go to the world of the gods;
only fools do not praise liberality;
the wise find joy in generosity,
and because of it become blessed in the other world.

  Better than sovereignty over the earth,
better than going to heaven,
better than dominion over all the worlds
is the reward of reaching the stream.

14. The Awakened

  The one whose conquest cannot be conquered again,
into whose conquest no one in this world enters,
by what track can you lead that one,
the awakened, the omniscient, the trackless?

  The one whom no desire
with its snares and poisons can lead astray,
by what track can you lead that one,
the awakened, the omniscient, the trackless?

  Even the gods emulate those who are awakened and aware,
who are given to meditation, who are wise,
and who find joy in the peace of renunciation.

It is difficult to be born as a human being;
difficult is the life of mortals;
difficult is the hearing of the true path;
difficult is the awakening of enlightenment.

Not to do wrong, to do good, and to purify one's mind,
that is the teaching of the awakened ones.
The awakened call patience the highest sacrifice;
the awakened declare nirvana the highest good.

The one who strikes others is not a hermit;
one is not an ascetic who insults others.
Not to blame, not to strike,
to live restrained under the law,
to be moderate in eating, to live alone,
and to practice the highest consciousness—
this is the teaching of the awakened ones.

There is no satisfying lusts,
even by a shower of gold pieces.
Whoever knows that lusts have a short taste
and cause pain is wise.
Even in heavenly pleasures one finds no satisfaction;
the disciple who is fully awakened
finds joy only in the destruction of all desires.

People driven by fear go for refuge
to mountains and forests, to sacred groves and shrines.
That is not a safe refuge; that is not the best refuge.
After having got to that refuge,
a person is not delivered from all pains.

Whoever takes refuge with the awakened one,
the truth, and the community,
who with clear understanding perceives the four noble truths:
namely suffering, the origin of suffering,
the cessation of suffering, and the eightfold holy way
that leads to the cessation of suffering,
that is the safe refuge; that is the best refuge;
having gone to that refuge,
a person is delivered from all pains.

A person of true vision is not easy to find;
they are not born everywhere.
Wherever such a sage is born, the people there prosper.

Blessed is the arising of the awakened;
blessed is the teaching of the truth;
blessed is the harmony of the community;
blessed is the devotion of those who live in peace.

  Whoever gives reverence to those worthy of reverence,
whether the awakened or their disciples,
those who have overcome the army
and crossed the river of sorrow,
whoever gives reverence to such as have found deliverance
and are free of fear,
their merit cannot be measured by anyone.

15. Joy

  Let us live in joy, not hating those who hate us.
Among those who hate us, we live free of hate.
Let us live in joy,
free from disease among those who are diseased.
Among those who are diseased, let us live free of disease.
Let us live in joy, free from greed among the greedy.
Among those who are greedy, we live free of greed.
Let us live in joy, though we possess nothing.
Let us live feeding on joy, like the bright gods.

  Victory breeds hate, for the conquered is unhappy.
Whoever has given up victory and defeat
is content and lives joyfully.

  There is no fire like lust, no misfortune like hate;
there is no pain like this body;
there is no joy higher than peace.

  Craving is the worst disease;
disharmony is the greatest sorrow.
The one who knows this truly
knows that nirvana is the highest bliss.

  Health is the greatest gift;
contentment is the greatest wealth;
trusting is the best relationship;
nirvana is the highest joy.

  Whoever has tasted the sweetness
of solitude and tranquillity
becomes free from fear and sin

while drinking the sweetness of the truth.
The sight of the noble is good;
to live with them is always joyful.

Whoever does not see fools will always be happy.
Whoever associates with fools suffers a long time.
Being with fools, as with an enemy, is always painful.

Being with the wise, like meeting with family, is joyful.
Therefore, one should follow the wise, the intelligent,
the learned, the patient, the dutiful, the noble;
one should follow the good and wise,
as the moon follows the path of the stars.

16. Pleasure

Whoever gives oneself to distractions
and does not give oneself to meditation,
forgetting true purpose and grasping at pleasure,
will eventually envy the one who practices meditation.

Let no one cling to what is pleasant or unpleasant.
Not to see what is pleasant is painful,
as it is to see what is unpleasant.
Therefore do not become attached to anything;
loss of what is loved is painful.
Those who have neither likes nor dislikes have no chains.

From pleasure comes grief; from pleasure comes fear.
Whoever is free from pleasure knows neither grief nor fear.

From attachment comes grief; from attachment comes fear.
Whoever is free from attachment knows neither grief nor fear.

From greed comes grief; from greed comes fear.
Whoever is free from greed knows neither grief nor fear.

From lust comes grief; from lust comes fear.
Whoever is free from lust knows neither grief nor fear.

From craving comes grief; from craving comes fear.
Whoever is free from craving knows neither grief nor fear.

Whoever has virtue and insight,
who is just, truthful, and does one's own work,
the world will love.

The one in whom a desire for the ineffable has arisen,
whose mind is satisfied

and whose thoughts are free from desires
is called one who ascends the stream.

Family, friends, and well-wishers welcome a person
who has been away long and returns safely from afar.
Similarly, one's good actions receive the good person
who has gone from this world to the other,
as family receive a friend who is returning.

17. Anger

Give up anger; renounce pride;
transcend all worldly attachments.
No sufferings touch the person
who is not attached to name and form,
who calls nothing one's own.
Whoever restrains rising anger like a chariot gone astray,
that one I call a real driver;
others merely hold the reins.

Overcome anger by love; overcome wrong by good;
overcome the miserly by generosity, and the liar by truth.
Speak the truth; do not yield to anger;
give even if asked for a little.
These three steps lead you to the gods.

The wise who hurt no one, who always control their body,
go to the unchangeable place,
where, once they have gone, they suffer no more.
Those who are always aware, who study day and night,
who aspire for nirvana, their passions will come to an end.

This is an old saying, Atula, not just from today:
"They blame the person who is silent;
they blame the person who talks much;
they also blame the person who talks in moderation;
there is no one on earth who is not blamed."
There never was, nor ever will be, nor is there now
anyone who is always blamed
or anyone who is always praised.

But the one whom those who discriminate praise
continually day after day as without fault,
wise, rich in knowledge and virtue,
who would dare to blame that person,

who is like a gold coin from the Jambu river?
That one is praised even by the gods, even by Brahma.
  Be aware of bodily anger and control your body.
Let go of the body's wrongs
and practice virtue with your body.
  Be aware of the tongue's anger and control your tongue.
Let go of the tongue's wrongs
and practice virtue with your tongue.
  Be aware of the mind's anger and control your mind.
Let go of the mind's wrongs
and practice virtue with your mind.
  The wise who control their body,
who control their tongue,
the wise who control their mind are truly well controlled.

18. Impurity

  You are now like a withered leaf;
the messengers of death have come near you.
You stand at the threshold of your departure.
Have you made provision for your journey?
  Make yourself an island; work hard; be wise.
When your impurities are purged and you are free from guilt,
you will enter into the heavenly world of the noble ones.
  Your life is coming to an end;
you are in the presence of death.
There is no rest stop on the way,
and you have made no provision for your journey.
  Make yourself an island; work hard; be wise;
when your impurities are purged and you are free from guilt,
you will not again enter into birth and old age.
  As a smith removes the impurities from silver,
so let the wise remove the impurities from oneself
one by one, little by little, again and again.
  Just as rust from iron eats into it
though born from itself,
so the wrong actions of the transgressor
lead one to the wrong path.
  Dull repetition is the impurity of prayers;

lack of repair is the impurity of houses;
laziness is the impurity of personal appearance;
thoughtlessness is the impurity of the watcher.
Bad conduct is the impurity of a woman;
stinginess is the impurity of the giver;
wrong actions are the impurity of this world and the next.
The worst impurity of all is the impurity of ignorance.
Mendicants, throw off that impurity
and become free of all impurities.

   Life seems easy for one who is shameless,
who is a crowing hero, a mischief-maker,
an insulting, impudent, and corrupt person.
But life seems difficult for one who is modest,
who always looks for what is pure,
who is detached, quiet, clear, and intelligent.

   Whoever destroys life, whoever speaks falsely,
whoever in this world takes what is not given to them,
whoever goes to another person's spouse,
and whoever gives oneself to drinking intoxicating liquors,
even in this world they dig up their own roots.
Know this, human, that the unrestrained are in a bad way.
Do not let greed and wrong-doing bring you long suffering.

   People give according to their faith
or according to their pleasure.
Thus whoever worries about food and drink given to others
will find no peace of mind day or night.
Whoever destroys that feeling, tearing it out by the root,
will truly find peace of mind day and night.

   There is no fire like lust, no chain like hate;
there is no snare like folly, no torrent like craving.
The faults of others are easy to see;
our own are difficult to see.
A person winnows others' faults like chaff,
but hides one's own faults
like a cheater hides bad dice.
If a person is concerned about the faults of others
and is always inclined to be offended,
one's own faults grow, and one is far from removing faults.

There is no path in the sky;
one does not become an ascetic outwardly.
People delight in worldly pleasures;
the perfected ones are free from worldliness.
There is no path in the sky;
one does not become an ascetic outwardly.
No creatures are eternal,
but the awakened ones are never shaken.

19. The Just

Whoever settles a matter by violence is not just.
The wise calmly considers what is right and what is wrong.
Whoever guides others by a procedure
that is nonviolent and fair
is said to be a guardian of truth, wise and just.

A person is not wise simply because one talks much.
Whoever is patient, free from hate and fear,
is said to be wise.

A person is not a supporter of justice
simply because one talks much.
Even if a person has learned little,
whoever discerns justice with the body
and does not neglect justice is a supporter of justice.

A person is not an elder
simply because one's head is gray.
Age can be ripe, but one may be called "old in vain."
The one in whom there is truth,
virtue, nonviolence, restraint, moderation,
whoever is free from impurity and is wise,
may be called an elder.

Mere talk or beauty of complexion does not make
an envious, greedy, dishonest person become respectable.
The one in whom all these are destroyed,
torn out by the very root,
who is free from hate and is wise, is called respectable.

Not by a shaven head does one who is undisciplined
and speaks falsely become an ascetic.
Can a person be an ascetic
who is still enslaved by desire and greed?

Whoever always quiets wrong tendencies, small or large,
is called an ascetic, because of having quieted all wrong.

A person is not a mendicant
simply because one begs from others.
Whoever adopts the whole truth is a mendicant,
not the one who adopts only a part.
Whoever is above good and bad and is chaste,
who carefully passes through the world in meditation,
is truly called a mendicant.

A person does not become a sage by silence,
if one is foolish and ignorant;
but the wise one, who, holding a scale,
takes what is good and avoids what is bad,
is a sage for that reason.
Whoever in this world weighs both sides
is called a sage because of that.

A person is not a noble,
because one injures living beings.
One is called noble,
because one does not injure living beings.

Not only by discipline and vows,
not only by much learning,
nor by deep concentration nor by sleeping alone
do I reach the joy of release which the worldly cannot know.
Mendicant, do not be confident
until you have reached the extinction of impurities.

20. The Path

Best of the paths is the eightfold,
best of the truths the four;
best of the virtues is freedom from attachment;
best of the people is the one who sees.
This is the path;
there is no other that leads to the purifying of insight.

Follow this path, and Mara will be confused.
If you follow this path, you will end your suffering.
This path was preached by me
when I became aware of the removal of the thorns.
You yourself must make the effort.

The perfected ones are only preachers.
Those who enter the path and practice meditation
are released from the bondage of Mara.

"All created things perish."
Whoever realizes this transcends pain;
this is the clear path.

"All created things are sorrow."
Whoever realizes this transcends pain;
this is the clear path.

"All forms are unreal."
whoever realizes this transcends pain;
this is the clear path.

Whoever does not rise when it is time to rise,
who, though young and strong, is lazy,
who is weak in will and thought,
that lazy and idle person will not find the path of wisdom.

Watching one's speech, restraining well the mind,
let one not commit any wrong with one's body.
Whoever keeps these three roads of action clear,
will make progress on the path taught by the wise.

Through meditation wisdom is gained;
through lack of meditation wisdom is lost.
Whoever knows this double path of progress and decline,
should place oneself so that wisdom will grow.

Cut down the forest of desires, not just a tree;
danger is in the forest.
When you have cut down the forest and its undergrowth,
then, mendicants, you will be free.

As long as the desire, however small,
of a man for women is not destroyed,
so long is his mind attached,
like a sucking calf is to its mother.

Cut out the love of self,
like an autumn lotus, with your hand.
Cherish the path of peace.
Nirvana has been shown by the Buddha.

"Here I shall live in the rain,
here in winter and summer."

Thus thinks the fool, not thinking of death.
Death comes and carries off that person
who is satisfied with one's children and flocks,
whose mind is distracted,
like a flood carries off a sleeping village.

Sons are no help, nor a father, nor relations;
for one who is seized by death, there is no safety in family.
Understanding the meaning of this, the wise and just person
should quickly clear the path that leads to nirvana.

21. Miscellaneous

If by giving up a small pleasure,
one sees a great pleasure,
the wise will let go of the small pleasure
and look to the great one.

Whoever by causing pain to others
wishes to obtain pleasure for oneself,
being entangled in the bonds of hate,
is not free from hate.

By neglecting what should be done
and doing what should not be done,
the desires of the unrestrained and careless increase.
But those whose awareness is always alert to the body,
who do not follow what should not be done,
who firmly do what should be done,
the desires of such aware and wise people come to an end.

A holy person goes unscathed,
though having killed father and mother and two noble kings
and destroyed a kingdom with all its subjects.

A holy person goes unscathed,
though having killed father and mother
and two holy kings and an eminent person also.

The disciples of Gautama are always well awake;
their thought is always, day and night, set on the Buddha.

The disciples of Gautama are always well awake;
their thought is always, day and night, set on the truth.

The disciples of Gautama are always well awake;
their thought is always, day and night, set on the community.

The disciples of Gautama are always well awake;
their thought is always, day and night, set on the body.

The disciples of Gautama are always well awake;
their mind, day and night, finds joy in abstaining from harm.

The disciples of Gautama are always well awake;
their mind, day and night, finds joy in meditation.

It is hard to leave the world as a recluse
and hard to enjoy the world.
It is also hard to live at home as a householder.

Living with the unsympathetic is painful.
The life of a wanderer is painful.
Therefore do not be a wanderer and be free of suffering.

A person of faith,
who is virtuous, well-known, and successful,
is respected wherever one may be.
Good people shine from far away,
like the Himalaya mountains,
but the bad are not seen, like arrows shot at night.

Whoever can sit alone, rest alone,
act alone without being lazy, and control oneself alone
will find joy near the edge of the forest.

22. The Downward Course

Whoever says what is not goes to hell,
also whoever having done something says, "I did not do it."
After death both are equal,
being people with wrong actions in the next existence.

Many who wear the yellow robe
are ill-behaved and unrestrained.
Such wrong-doers by their wrong actions go to hell.
It would be better for a bad, unrestrained person
to swallow a ball of red-hot iron
than to live off the charity of the land.

A reckless person who wants another's wife
gains four things:
fault, bad sleep, thirdly blame, and finally hell.
There is fault and the wrong path;
there is brief pleasure

of the frightened in the arms of the frightened,
and heavy penalty from the ruler.
Therefore do not run after another's wife.

As a blade of grass wrongly handled cuts the hand,
so also asceticism wrongly practiced leads to hell.
An act carelessly performed, a broken vow,
unwilling obedience to discipline—
all these bring no great reward.
If anything is to be done, let one do it vigorously.
A careless recluse only bespatters oneself
with the dust of desires.

A wrong action is better left undone,
for a wrong action causes suffering later.
A good action is better done,
for it does not cause suffering.

Like a frontier fort
that is well guarded inside and outside,
so guard yourself.
Not a moment should escape,
for those who allow the right moment to pass
suffer pain when they are in hell.

Those who are ashamed of
what they should not be ashamed of
and are not ashamed of
what they should be ashamed of,
such people, following false doctrines, enter the wrong path.

Those who fear what they should not fear
and do not fear what they should fear,
such people, following false doctrines, enter the wrong path.

Those who discern wrong where there is no wrong
and see nothing wrong in what is wrong,
such people, following false doctrines, enter the wrong path.

Those who discern wrong as wrong
and what is not wrong as not wrong,
such people, following true doctrines, enter the good path.

23. The Elephant

I shall endure painful words
as the elephant in battle endures arrows shot from the bow;
for most people are ill-natured.
They lead a tamed elephant into battle;
the king mounts a tamed elephant.

The tamed are the best of people,
who endure patiently painful words.
Mules are good, if tamed,
and noble Sindhu horses and elephants with large tusks;
but whoever tames oneself is better still.
For with these animals no one reaches the untrodden country
where a tamed person goes on one's own tamed nature.

The elephant called Dhanapalaka is hard to control
when his temples are running with pungent sap.
He does not eat a morsel when bound;
the elephant longs for the elephant grove.

If one becomes lazy and a glutton,
rolling oneself about in gross sleep,
like a hog fed on grains,
that fool is born again and again.

This mind of mine used to wander
as it liked, as it desired, as it pleased.
I shall now control it thoroughly,
as the rider holding the hook controls the elephant in rut.

Do not be thoughtless; watch your thoughts.
Extricate yourself from the wrong path,
like an elephant sunk in the mud.

If you find an intelligent companion
who will walk with you,
who lives wisely, soberly, overcoming all dangers,
walk with that person in joy and thoughtfulness.

If you find no intelligent companion
who will walk with you,
who lives wisely and soberly,
walk alone like a king
who has renounced a conquered kingdom
or like an elephant in the forest.

It is better to live alone;
there is no companionship with a fool.
Let a person walk alone with few wishes,
committing no wrong,
like an elephant in the forest.

Companions are pleasant when an occasion arises;
sharing enjoyment is pleasant.
At the hour of death it is pleasant to have done good.
The giving up of all sorrow is pleasant.

Motherhood is pleasant in this world;
fatherhood is pleasant.
Being an ascetic is pleasant;
being a holy person is pleasant.

Virtue lasting to old age is pleasant;
faith firmly rooted is pleasant;
attainment of wisdom is pleasant;
avoiding wrong is pleasant.

24. Craving

The craving of a thoughtless person grows like a creeper.
That one runs from life to life,
like a monkey seeking fruit in the forest.

Whoever is overcome by this fierce poisonous craving
in this world has one's sufferings increase
like the spreading birana grass.

Whoever overcomes this fierce craving,
difficult to control in this world,
sufferings fall off, like water drops from a lotus leaf.

This beneficial word I tell you, "Do you,
as many as are gathered here, dig up the root of craving,
as one digs up the birana grass to find the usira root,
so that Mara may not destroy you again and again,
just as the river crushes the reeds."

As a tree, even though it has been cut down,
grows again if its root is strong and undamaged,
similarly if the roots of craving are not destroyed,
this suffering returns again and again.

The one whose thirty-six streams
are flowing strongly towards pleasures of sense,
whose thoughts are set on desires,
the waves carry away that misguided person.

The streams flow everywhere;
the creeper of craving keeps springing up.
If you see that creeper springing up,
cut its root by means of wisdom.

The pleasures of creatures
are wide-ranging and extravagant.
Embracing those pleasures and holding on to them,
they undergo birth and decay again and again.

Driven by lust, people run around like a hunted hare;
bound in chains they suffer for a long time again and again.

Driven by lust, people run around like a hunted hare;
therefore let the mendicant wishing to conquer lust
shake off one's own craving.

Whoever having got rid of the forest of desires,
gives oneself over to that forest-life,
and who, when free from the forest runs back into the forest,
look at that person, though free, running back into bondage.

Wise people do not call that a strong chain
which is made of iron, wood, or rope,
stronger is the attachment to jewelry, sons, and a wife.

Wise people call strong this chain
which drags down, yields, and is difficult to undo;
after having cut this, people renounce the world,
free from cares, leaving pleasures of sense behind.

Those who are slaves to desires follow the stream,
as a spider the web it has made for itself.
Wise people when they have cut this,
go on free from care leaving all sorrow behind.

Give up what is in front; give up what is behind;
give up what is in the middle,
passing to the farther shore of existence.
When your mind is completely free,
you will not again return to birth and old age.

If a person is disturbed by doubts,
full of strong desires,
and yearning for what is pleasurable,
craving will grow more and more,
and one makes one's chains stronger.

Whoever finds joy in quieting one's thoughts,
always reflecting, dwelling on what is not pleasurable,
will certainly remove and cut the chains of death.
Whoever has reached the goal, who is fearless,
who is without craving and without wrong,
has broken the thorns of existence;
this body will be their last.

Whoever is without craving, without greed,
who understands the words and their meanings,
who knows the order of letters
is called a great sage, a great person.
This is their last body.

"I have conquered all; I know all;
in all conditions of life I am free from impurity.
I have renounced all,
and with the destruction of craving I am free.
Having learned myself, whom shall I indicate as teacher?"

The gift of truth surpasses all gifts;
the sweetness of the truth surpasses all sweetness;
joy in the truth surpasses all pleasures;
the destruction of craving overcomes all sorrows.
Riches destroy the foolish, not those who seek beyond.
By craving for riches the fool destroys oneself,
as one destroys others.

Weeds harm the fields; lusts harm humanity;
offerings given to those free from lusts bring great reward.

Weeds harm the fields; hate harms humanity;
offerings given to those free from hate bring great reward.

Weeds harm the fields; vanity harms humanity;
offerings given to those free from vanity bring great reward.

Weeds harm the fields; desire harms humanity;
offerings given to those free from desire bring great reward.

25. The Mendicant

Control of the eye is good; good is control of the ear;
control of the nose is good; good is control of the tongue.
Control of the body is good; good is control of speech;
control of thought is good; good is control of all things.
A mendicant controlled in all things is freed from sorrow.

Whoever controls one's hand, whoever controls one's feet,
whoever controls one's speech, whoever is well-controlled,
whoever finds inner joy, who is collected,
who is alone and content they call a mendicant.

The mendicant who controls one's tongue,
who speaks wisely and calmly, who is not proud,
who illuminates the meaning of the truth,
that one's words are sweet.

Whoever lives in the truth, who finds joy in the truth,
meditates on the truth, follows the truth,
that mendicant does not fall away from the truth.

Let one not despise what one has received
nor envy others.
A mendicant who envies others does not find peace.
A mendicant, who, though receiving little,
does not despise what one has received,
even the gods praise, if one's life is pure and not lazy.

Whoever never identifies with name and form
and whoever does not grieve from not having anything
is called a mendicant.

The mendicant who lives in friendliness
with confidence in the doctrine of the Buddha
will find peace, the blessed place where existence ends.

Empty the boat, mendicant;
when emptied it will go quickly.
Having cut off desire and hate, you will go to freedom.

Cut off the five; get rid of the five; master the five.
A mendicant who has freed oneself from the five chains
is called "one who has crossed the flood."

Meditate, mendicant; do not be careless.
Do not think of pleasures
so that you may not for your carelessness

have to swallow the iron ball,
so that you may not cry out when burning, "This is painful!"
There is no meditation for one without wisdom,
no wisdom for one without meditation;
whoever has wisdom and meditation is close to nirvana.

   A mendicant who with a peaceful heart
has entered an empty house,
has more than human joy when seeing the truth clearly.
When one has comprehended
the origin and destruction of the elements of the body,
one finds happiness and joy
which belong to those who know the eternal.

   This is the beginning here for a wise mendicant:
control of the senses, contentment,
living according to the moral law,
associating with friends
who are noble, pure, and not lazy.

   Let one live in love;
let one be adept in one's duties;
then joyfully one will see the end of sorrow.
As the jasmine sheds its withered flowers,
people should shed desire and hate, mendicants.

   A mendicant is said to be calm
who has a calm body, calm speech, and a calm mind,
who has mastered oneself
and rejected the baits of the world.

   Lift up your self by yourself;
examine your self by yourself.
Thus self-protected and attentive
you will live joyfully, mendicant.
For self is the master of self;
self is the refuge of self.
therefore tame yourself,
like a merchant tames a noble horse.

   Joyful and faithful in the doctrine of the Buddha,
the mendicant finds peace,
the joy of ending natural existence.
Whoever, even as a young mendicant,
applies oneself to the path of the Buddha

illuminates this world,
like the moon when free from clouds.

26. The Holy One

Cut off the stream energetically, holy one;
leave desires behind.
Knowing the destruction of all that is created,
you know the uncreated, holy one.
When the holy one has reached the other shore
in meditation and contemplation,
all bonds vanish for the one who knows.

For the one I call holy
there is neither this shore nor that shore nor both,
who is free from fear and free from shackles.
The one I call holy is thoughtful, detached, settled,
accomplished, desireless, and has attained the highest goal.

The sun shines by day; the moon lights up the night;
the warriors shine in their armor;
the holy one shines in meditation;
but the awakened shines radiantly all day and night.

Because a person has put aside wrong, one is called holy.
Because one lives serenely, one is called an ascetic.
Because one gets rid of impurities, one is called a pilgrim.

No one should hurt a holy one,
but no holy one should strike back.
Woe to the one who hurts a holy one;
more woe to the one who strikes back.

It is no small gain to a holy one
if one holds one's mind back from the pleasures of life.
The sooner the wish to injure disappears,
the sooner all suffering will stop.
The one I call holy does not hurt by body, speech, or mind,
and is controlled in these three things.

Whoever has understood the law of justice
as taught by the well awakened one,
should revere the teacher,
as the priest worships the sacrificial fire.

Not by matted hair, not by lineage,
not by caste does one become holy.
One is holy in whom there is truth and virtue;
that one is blessed.

What is the use of matted hair, fool?
What is the use of clothes of goat-skins?
Inside you are full of craving; the outside you make clean.
The one I call holy wears thrown-away clothes,
is lean with veins showing,
and meditates alone in the forest.

I do not call one holy because of one's family or mother.
If one has property, one is called superior.
The one I call holy is free of property and all attachment.
The one I call holy has cut all chains, never trembles,
has passed beyond attachments and is independent.
The one I call holy has cut the strap, the thong,
and the chain with all their encumbrances,
has removed the bar and is awakened.

The one I call holy, though having committed no offense,
patiently bears reproach, ill-treatment, and imprisonment,
has endurance for one's force and strength for one's army.

The one I call holy is free from anger, faithful to vows,
virtuous, free from lust, controlled,
and has received one's last body.

The one I call holy does not cling to pleasures,
like water on a lotus leaf
or a mustard seed on the point of a needle.

The one I call holy
even here knows the end of suffering,
has laid down one's burden, and is detached.

The one I call holy has deep wisdom and knowledge,
discerns the right way and the wrong,
and has attained the highest end.

The one I call holy
keeps away from both householders and the homeless,
rarely visits houses, and has few desires.

The one I call holy
does not hurt any creatures, weak or strong,
and neither kills nor causes death.

The one I call holy is tolerant with the intolerant,
peaceful with the violent,
and free from greed among the greedy.
　The one I call holy
has let go of anger, hate, pride, and hypocrisy,
like a mustard seed falls from the point of a needle.
　The one I call holy speaks true words
that are useful and not harsh so that no one is offended.
　The one I call holy
does not take anything in the world
that is not given one,
be it long or short, small or large, good or bad.
　The one I call holy
has no desires for this world or the next,
is free from desires and is independent.
　The one I call holy has no longings,
in knowledge is free from doubt,
and has reached the depth of the eternal.
　The one I call holy here
has passed beyond the attachments of good and bad,
is free from sorrow, free from desire, free from impurity.
　The one I call holy is bright like the moon,
pure, serene, undisturbed,
in whom pleasure is extinguished.
　The one I call holy
has gone beyond this muddy road of rebirth and delusion,
so difficult to pass,
has crossed over and reached the other shore,
is thoughtful, not agitated,
not doubting, not attached, and calm.
　The one I call holy in this world,
giving up all desires, travels around without a home,
in whom all desire for existence is extinguished.
　The one I call holy in this world,
giving up all craving, travels around without a home,
in whom all craving for existence is extinguished.
　The one I call holy,
letting go of attachment to humans,

rises above attachment to gods,
and is independent from all attachments.

   The one I call holy
gives up what is pleasurable and what is not pleasurable,
is cool and free from any seeds of renewal,
the hero who has conquered all the worlds.

   The one I call holy
knows the destruction and the return of beings everywhere,
is free from attachment, living well, and is awakened.

   The one I call holy,
whose path is not known by gods nor spirits nor humans,
whose desires are extinct, is a saint.

   The one I call holy calls nothing one's own,
whether it be in front, behind, or between,
is poor and free from attachment.

   The one I call holy is fearless, noble, heroic,
all-wise, ever-pure, all-conquering,
has accomplished the goal and is awakened.

   The one I call holy knows one's former lives,
perceives heaven and hell,
has reached the end of births,
is a sage whose knowledge is perfect,
having accomplished complete perfection.

Introduction to Socrates and Plato

Socrates (469-399 BC) was born in Athens and spent almost all his days there. His father was a sculptor, and Socrates may have been employed on the stone-work of the Acropolis. He claimed that his mother was a midwife. Socrates' wife Xanthippe, well-known as a shrew, bore him a son, Lamprocles. When the Athenians encouraged citizens to have more children, Socrates took a second wife, Myrto, who gave birth to Sophroniscus and Menexenus.

The education of Socrates was primarily informal, but it was said that he heard Zeno, Parmenides, Prodicus, Aspasia, Anaxagoras, Damon, and Archelaus. Diogenes Laertius gives Socrates credit for having improved the study of ethics so much that he was considered its inventor. Socrates himself was always eager to discuss philosophical questions with others, but he said that he never accepted money for teaching. Some thought he might have helped Euripides with his plays. Socrates spent most of his time in public talking with anyone willing to discuss philosophy.

Socrates never traveled far from Athens except on military expeditions during the Peloponnesian Wars against Sparta. The general Laches said that he bravely fought off foes during the retreat at Delium, and Alcibiades credited Socrates with saving his life when he was wounded at Potidaea but then encouraged the generals to give the prize of valor to the officer Alcibiades rather than himself.

Socrates tried to avoid politics, because he thought it was too dangerous for a lover of truth and justice. When his tribe was serving as Prytanes he was laughed at, because he did not know how to perform his duty as president in taking the votes. While serving in the Athenian Senate at this time he refused to try together the naval commanders, who had not buried the dead after their victory at Arginusae, because he believed it was illegal to group them together, not give them time to prepare their defense, and because the assembly was not a court and had no right to condemn to death. During the oligarchy he was summoned to bring in Leon from Salamis for execution, but he refused to do so at the risk of his own life.

At the age of 70 Socrates was brought to trial for not believing in the state religion and for corrupting the youth. The story of his trial, imprisonment, and execution are told in the *Defense of Socrates, Crito,* and *Phaedo* by Plato. Xenophon also wrote about Socrates and tells us that when Hermogenes urged Socrates to prepare his defense, Socrates replied that whenever he started to do that his divine sign prevented him. This divine sign is also mentioned by Plato as a spirit that would warn Socrates not to do various things.

Plato (428-348 BC) was from an aristocratic family, and some of his mother's relatives were good friends of Socrates. Plato was one of the young men who liked to listen to the conversation of Socrates. After the execution of Socrates, Plato and some others went to Megara with Euclides, the founder of the Megarian school of philosophy. Plato then traveled extensively in Greece, Egypt, and Italy. When he was about forty, Plato founded the Academy, where he taught for nearly forty years. In his sixties Plato made two visits to Syracuse in Sicily to try to advise King Dionysius II, but these proved rather unsuccessful. Aristotle studied and taught at Plato's Academy for twenty years but left shortly after Plato died.

Many dialogs and a few letters of Plato's writings remain. Socrates is featured as a main speaker in many of the dialogs. Scholars may argue whether the ideas presented are those of Socrates or Plato, but in the final analysis what may be important is what truth the reader might find in them and what enlightenment can be gained from studying the intellectual process.

Alcibiades
by Plato

Alcibiades was about twenty years younger than Socrates. His father died in battle when Alcibiades was about 4, and he was brought up by Pericles, the eminent political leader of Athens. The *Alcibiades I* dialog is set in 432 BC when Alcibiades was 18, the same year that Socrates saved his life during the battle at Potidaea. Later in 424 BC at Delium Alcibiades stayed to protect Socrates during the retreat.

In spite of Socrates' attempts to guide him, the ambitious Alcibiades had a tumultuous career in politics, diplomacy, and war. His courage in battle and his speeches in the assembly enabled him to become a general when he was thirty. An alliance he recommended was defeated by Sparta at Mantineia in 418 BC, but he managed to escape being ostracized by political maneuvering.

His victories in the chariot races at the Olympics in 416 BC restored him to prominence, and he instigated a military expedition against Sicily. Just before sailing, the statues of Hermes were vandalized. Alcibiades was blamed and also condemned to death for profaning the Eleusinian mysteries. However, when he was recalled from Sicily, he escaped and joined the Spartans (Lacedaimonians), seduced the wife of Spartan king Agis II, stirred up revolt among Ionian allies of Athens, and tried to get financial support for Athens from Persia.

In 411 BC the Athenian fleet loyal to the democracy put him in command, and he won big victories against Sparta; in 407 BC he returned to Athens and was given supreme authority over the war. His influence declined though; when the war went badly, he took refuge in Phrygia with the Persian governor, who murdered him in 404 BC for the Spartans.

Notes to:

15: A hundred *minae* is about a hundred pounds of silver.

17: Lacedaimonian (Spartan) kings claimed to be descendants of the legendary hero Heracles. The Persian kings, such as Artaxerxes (reigned 465-425 BC), traced their ancestry to Achaemenes, who led armies against the Assyrian empire in 681 BC. Alcibiades claimed to be descended from Eurysaces, the son of Ajax, while Socrates as a sculptor claimed the legendary sculptor and architect Daedalus as his ancestor.

17: Zoroaster, also known as Zarathustra, was the great founder of the Persian religion. Horomazus probably refers to the Persian name of God, Ahura Mazda.

18: Fifty *minae* is about fifty pounds of silver.

1

SOCRATES. Child of Cleinias,
I think you may be surprised,
that being the first of your lovers,
the others having stopped, I alone have not left you,
and when the others in a crowd were conversing with you,
I have not spoken to you in years.
And the cause of this is not anything human,
but a certain divine opposition,
whose power you shall also hear of later;
but now since it no longer opposes, thus I have come;
and I am hopeful also it will not oppose anymore.

So nearby I have been observing during this time
considering how you attend to the lovers;
for though they were many and high-minded,
none not overcome by your spirit, they fled from you,
and the reason, for which they were overwhelmed,
I intend to explain.

You say you do not need any person for anything;
for your advantages are great,
so as not to need anything,
starting from the body and ending in the soul.
For you think first you are most beautiful and greatest;
and this is clear for everyone to see that it is not false;
since you are of the most dashing family in your own city,
being the greatest of the Greeks,
and there by your father for you
are many friends and relatives and the best,
who if you should need something would assist you,
and the ones by your mother are neither worse nor fewer;
and you think altogether greater than what I said
to advance you is the power of Pericles, son of Xanthippus,
whom your father left behind as guardian
for you and your brother;
who not only is able to do whatever he wishes in the city,
but in all of Greece and among many and great foreigners.
And I shall add also that of the wealth;
but you seem to me to presume least on the greatness of this.

So boasting of all these things
you have prevailed over the lovers
and they cowering under were conquered,
and these things have not been unnoticed by you;
so I know well that you are wondering why
for whatever purpose I do not leave off the love,
and having what hope do I remain when the others have fled.
    ALCIBIADES. And perhaps, Socrates,
you are not aware that you just anticipated me.
For I had in mind before going to you to ask the same thing,
what do you want
and looking for what hope are you annoying me,
always taking the utmost care to be present wherever I am;
for I really wonder what is your business,
and would be glad if I could hear of it.
    SO. Then you will listen to me, presumably, eagerly,
if, as you say, you desire to know what I mean,
and as to one listening and staying around I may speak.
    ALC. Certainly; but speak.
    SO. Look then; for it would not be surprising if,
as I had trouble starting,
so also I may have trouble stopping.
    ALC. Joyful one, speak; for I shall listen.

2
    SO. Speak I should.
Though it is hard to come near as a lover
to a man who does not yield to lovers,
but nevertheless I must venture to say what I mean.
For Alcibiades, if I saw you were content
with what I just explained
and thought it necessary to end life among these,
long ago I would have left off the love,
so at least I persuade myself;
but now I shall allege other thoughts to you,
by which you shall also know that
I have been continuously attentive to you.
    For you seem to me, if some god should say to you,
"Alcibiades, do you wish to live having what you now have,

or to die immediately,
if you are not to be permitted to gain greater?"
It seems to me you would choose to die;
but now upon what hope you really live, I shall say.
　You believe that
if you should soon come before the Athenian democracy—
and this will be in a very few days—
thus going you will point out to the Athenians
that you are more worthy of honor than either Pericles
or anyone else who has ever existed,
and having pointed this out
you will have the greatest power in the state,
and if you are the greatest here,
you are also among the other Greeks,
and not only among Greeks but also among the foreigners,
who inhabit the same continent with us.
　And if this same god should say to you
that you must have power in Europe,
but you will not be permitted to cross over into Asia
nor to interfere with the affairs there,
it seems to me you would not live on only those terms either,
if you are not to fill with your name and your power
all, as one might say, of humanity;
and I think that except for Cyrus and Xerxes
you believe no one has existed worthy of a word.
So that you have this hope, I know well and am not guessing.
　Thus perhaps you would say,
since you know what I say is true;
so what, Socrates, does this have to do with your argument?
And I shall tell you, dear child of Cleinias and Deinomache.
For the goal of all your purposes
is impossible for you to set without me;
such is the power I think I have
in regard to your business and you;
and because of this long ago I thought
the god would not allow me to converse with you,
while I was staying around for the time
when it would be allowed.

For as you have hopes of proving yourself
in the state to her that of all you are worthy,
and having proven no one else is
that immediately you will be powerful,
so I along with you hope to be more powerful
proving that of all I am worthy for you,
and neither guardian nor relative nor anyone else is adequate
to give over the power which you set for yourself
except me, with the god however.
So being in your youth and before being full of such hopes,
as it seems to me, the god did not allow conversing
so that I would not be conversing in vain;
but now he commands it; for now you will listen to me.

3
  ALC. Now, Socrates, you appear to me
even more extraordinary, since you began to speak,
than when you followed in silence;
although even then you were seen as quite excessive.
So if I intend these things or not,
as likely, you have decided,
and if I should say no,
it will not be more likely for me to persuade you.
Well; but if really I especially do intend these things,
how will it occur for me because of you
and without you it would not happen?
What do you have to say?
  SO. Then are you asking if I have to make a long speech,
which you are used to hearing?
For such is not my way;
but it is possible, as I think,
to prove to you that these things are so,
if you are willing to do me one small service.
  ALC. But if the service you mean is not hard, I am willing.
  SO. Does it seem hard to answer questions?
  ALC. Not hard.
  SO. Then answer.
  ALC. Ask.

SO. Then as to your having these intentions,
which I say you intend, I am asking.

ALC. Let it be so, if you wish,
so that I may also know what you will ask.

SO. Come now; for you intend, as I say,
to come forward in advising the Athenians in not too long;
so if when about to go up on the platform
taking hold of you I should ask, "Alcibiades,
since about something of the Athenians
you are intending to advise them,
about what are you standing up to advise them?
Then is it about what you know better than they?"
What would you answer?

ALC. I would say of course,
about what I know better than they.

SO. About what you happen to know,
you are a good adviser.

ALC. Why not?

4

SO. Then you know only the things
which you have learned from another or discovered yourself?

ALC. For what else could I know?

SO. So is it possible
that you could ever learn or discover something
not being willing to learn or inquire yourself?

ALC. It is not.

SO. But what? Would you have been willing
to inquire or learn what you thought you knew?

ALC. Of course not.

SO. Then what you happen to know now,
was there a time when you did not believe you knew it?

ALC. Necessarily.

SO. But what you have learned, I also know pretty well;
but if something has escaped me, say it.
For you really learned according to my memory
writing and the harp and wrestling;
for the flute you were not willing to learn;

this is what you know,
unless somehow you learned something escaping my notice;
but I think, neither at night nor mid-day
did you go out from inside without my noticing.

ALC. But I have not attended school
in any others than these.

SO. So which is it,
is it when the Greeks are being advised about writing,
how one should write correctly,
then will you stand up to advise them?

ALC. By God, not I.

SO. But when it is about notes on the lyre?

ALC. Not at all.

SO. Nor are they used to being advised
about wrestling in the assembly.

ALC. Of course not.

SO. So when they are being advised about what?
for surely it is not when it is about building.

ALC. Of course not.

SO. For a builder will advise on this better than you.

ALC. Yes.

SO. Nor is it when they are being advised about divination?

ALC. No.

SO. For a diviner on this is better than you.

ALC. Yes.

SO. Whether one is small or large,
whether beautiful or ugly, even noble or ignoble.

ALC. For how could it not be so?

SO. For I think concerning each the advice
is from the knowledgeable, and not from the wealthy.

ALC. For how could it not be so?

SO. But whether the one counseling is a worker or wealthy,
would make no difference to Athenians,
when they are being advised in the state
about how they should be healthy,
but they seek a physician to be the adviser.

ALC. Naturally.

SO. So what will they be considering
when you are standing up
so that you will correctly be standing up to advise them?

ALC. When it is about their own affairs, Socrates.

SO. Do you mean about shipbuilding,
what kind of ships it is useful for them to have built?

ALC. Not I, Socrates.

SO. For I think you do not know how to build ships.
Is this the cause or something else?

ALC. No, but this is it.

5

SO. But about what affairs of theirs do you mean
when they are being advised?

ALC. When it is about war, Socrates, or about peace
or other affairs of the state.

SO. Then do you mean, when they are being advised,
with whom it is useful to make peace
and on whom to make war and in what way?

ALC. Yes.

SO. And on whom it is better, should they not?

ALC. Yes.

SO. And at the time when it is better?

ALC. Certainly.

SO. And for as long a time as is better?

ALC. Yes.

SO. So if the Athenians should be advised,
with whom it is useful to wrestle close
and with whom at arm's length and in what way,
would you be the better adviser or the gymnastic trainer?

ALC. The gymnastic trainer, of course.

SO. So you have to say,
looking at what will the gymnastic trainer advise
with whom they must wrestle close and with whom not,
and when and in what way?
What I mean is: then must they not wrestle close
with these with whom it is better, or not?

ALC. Yes.

SO. Then so much as is better also?

ALC. So much.

SO. Then also at the time that is better?

ALC. Certainly.

6

SO. But also in singing is it necessary to play the harp at the time of the song and stepping?

ALC. It is.

SO. Then at the time when it is better?

ALC. Yes.

SO. And so much as is better?

ALC. I say so.

SO. So what then? Since you name "better" for both playing the harp with the song and for wrestling close, what do you call better in playing the harp, as I call gymnastic in wrestling? But what do you call that?

ALC. I do not understand.

SO. But try to imitate me. For I had the correct answer in every case, and it is correct doubtless according to the current art; or is it not?

ALC. Yes.

SO. And was not the art gymnastic?

ALC. But how could it not be?

SO. And I said in wrestling the better is gymnastic.

ALC. You did say it.

SO. Then beautifully?

ALC. It seems to me.

SO. Come then you too—for it would be fitting also for you to converse beautifully— say first, what is the art which includes playing the harp and singing and stepping correctly? What is it called all together? Is it not yet possible to say?

ALC. Not now.

SO. Try another way: who are the goddesses of the art?

ALC. Do you mean the Muses, Socrates?

SO. I do. Really look: what is the art named after them?

ALC. You seem to me to mean music.

SO. I do mean it.
So what according to this is correctly done?
As there I told you
according to the art gymnastic was correct,
and so now what do you say is so here?
How is it done?

ALC. It seems to me by music.

7

SO. You speak well.
Come now, also the better in war and in maintaining peace,
what do you name this that is better?
just as there you said the better was the more musical,
and in the other the more gymnastical;
try now also here to tell the better.

ALC. But I have no idea at all.

SO. But yet it is disgraceful,
if you were speaking and counseling someone about food
that this kind is better and now and so much,
since he would ask,
"What do you mean by 'the better,' Alcibiades?"
about these things one would have to say
that it is the more healthy,
although you do not pretend to be a physician;
and about what you pretend to be knowledgeable
and counsel standing up as one knowing,
but of this, as is fitting,
about which you were asked if you could say,
are you not ashamed? Or does it not appear disgraceful?

ALC. Very.

SO. Consider then and be ready to say,
to what does "better" refer in maintaining peace
and in warring with whom it is necessary?

ALC. But in considering I am not able to understand.

SO. Don't you know, when we make war,
with what suffering we charge each other
when we go into warring, and what we name it when we go?

ALC. I do, that someone deceived or violated or cheated.

SO. You have it; how are each of these suffered?
Try to say, what is the difference between one or another.

ALC. Do you mean by this, Socrates, justly or unjustly?

SO. The same.

ALC. But this is the whole difference and all of it.

SO. So what then?
On which are you counseling the Athenians to war,
those doing the unjust or the just?

ALC. This you are asking is tricky;
for even if someone decides that it is necessary
to war on those doing the just, he would not admit it.

SO. For this is not lawful, as is fitting.

ALC. Of course not; nor does it seem to be beautiful.

SO. Then will you make your speeches
along these lines also?

ALC. Necessarily.

SO. So what else, the better
which I was just now asking in reference to warring or not,
and with whom it is necessary and with whom it is not,
and when it is and when not,
happens to be the more just? or not?

ALC. It appears so.

8

SO. How so, dear Alcibiades?
Has it escaped your notice that you do not know this,
or did it escape me
your learning and attending school with a teacher,
who taught you to discern the more just and the more unjust?
And who is he?
And tell me so that you may introduce me too as his pupil.

ALC. You are mocking, Socrates.

SO. No, by the god of Friendship, mine and yours,
by whom I would not swear falsely in the least;
but if you have it, tell who it is.

ALC. But what if I don't have it?
Don't you think I could know about justice and injustice
in any other way?

SO. Yes, if you could discover it.

ALC. But don't you believe I could discover it.

SO. And very much, if you inquired.

ALC. Then don't you think I might inquire?

SO. I do, if you thought you didn't know.

ALC. Then was there not a time when I was that way?

SO. You speak beautifully.
Therefore you have to say this time,
when you did not think you knew the just and the unjust?
Come, was it a year ago you inquired
and didn't think you knew;
Or did you think you knew?
And answer the truth
so that the discussion may not become vain.

ALC. But I thought I knew.

SO. And the third and fourth and fifth years were you thus?

ALC. I was.

SO. But before this you were a child, were you not?

ALC. Yes.

SO. Even then I know well that you thought you knew.

ALC. How do you know it well?

SO. Many times I heard you at your teachers'
when a child and elsewhere,
and when playing dice or another children's game,
how not having any doubt about the just and unjust,
but speaking very loud and confidently
about what occurred with the children,
how one was bad and unjust and was thus doing wrong;
or do I not speak the truth?

ALC. But what was I to do, Socrates,
when someone was wronging me?

SO. But if it happened you were ignorant
whether you were wronged or not at that time,
do you mean, "What are you supposed to do?"

ALC. By God, but I was not ignorant,
but I clearly understood that I was being wronged.

SO. Then you thought you knew even as a child,
as is likely, the just and the unjust.

ALC. I did; and I did know.

SO. In what time period did you discover it?
For it was certainly not when you thought you knew.

ALC. Of course not.

SO. So when did you believe you were ignorant?
Consider; for you will not discover this period.

ALC. By God, Socrates, then I have nothing to say.

SO. Then by discovering them you do not know these things.

ALC. I appear not to at all.

9

SO. But you just said you do not know them by learning;
and if you neither discovered nor learned,
how do you know and from where?

ALC. But perhaps on this I was not answering you correctly,
appearing to know this by discovering it.

SO. But how do you have it?

ALC. I learned it, I think, and I also like the others.

SO. Again we come to the same argument.
From whom? Tell me.

ALC. From the many.

SO. Not in serious teachers are you taking refuge
in appealing to the many.

ALC. But what? Are they not capable of teaching?

SO. Not even how to play checkers and how not to;
although I think this is more trivial than justice.
But what? Don't you think so?

ALC. Yes.

SO. Then unable to teach the more trivial,
are they able to teach the more serious?

ALC. I think so; but at any rate
many are able to teach more serious things than checkers.

SO. What kind of things?

ALC. For example, I learned to speak Greek from these,
and I could not say who my teacher was,
but I attribute it to the same ones,
who you say are not serious teachers.

SO. But, noble one, the many are good teachers of this,
and may be justly praised for teaching these things.

ALC. Why?

SO. Because they have what is useful
to be good teachers of these things.

ALC. What do you mean by this?

SO. Don't you know
that it is useful for those about to teach anything
that they should first know it themselves? Or don't you?

ALC. For how could I not?

SO. Then those knowing agree with each other
and do not differ?

ALC. Yes.

SO. But if they differ on these,
will you say they know these things?

ALC. Of course not.

SO. Thus how could they be teachers of these things?

ALC. They could not at all.

SO. So what then?
Do the many seem to you to differ on what is stone or wood?
And if you asked them,
would they not agree on the same things,
and do they go after the same things
when they want to get stone or wood?
Just as also with every such thing;
for what I pretty much understand that you mean
by knowing how to speak Greek is this; or is it not?

ALC. Yes.

SO. Then on these things, as we said,
they agree with each other

and with their own selves in private,
and in democracy the states
do not disagree with each other on these,
and they do not affirm others?

ALC. They do not.

SO. Then it is likely of these things also
they will be good teachers.

ALC. Yes.

SO. Then if we should want to
make anyone know about these things,
correctly we should send him to be taught by these many?

ALC. Certainly.

10

SO. But what if we wanted to know,
not only what people are or what horses are,
but also which of them are runners and which not,
then would the many still be capable of teaching this?

ALC. Of course not.

SO. And do you have adequate proof that they neither know
nor are proficient teachers of these things,
since they do not agree themselves about them?

ALC. I do.

SO. But what if we wanted to know,
not only what people are, but which are healthy or diseased,
then would the many be adequate teachers for us?

ALC. Of course not.

SO. And would you have proof
that they are bad teachers of these things,
if you saw them differing?

ALC. I would.

SO. But what then?
Now about just and unjust people and business
do the many seem to you to agree on these themselves
or with each other?

ALC. Not in the least by God, Socrates.

SO. But what? Do they differ very much about these?

ALC. Much.

SO. Then I think you never yet saw nor heard
people differing so seriously about health and lack of it,
so as to fight because of these things and kill each other.

ALC. Of course not.

SO. But about justice and injustice I know that,
even if you have not seen it,
you have heard at any rate from many others and Homer.
For you have heard both the *Odyssey* and the *Iliad*.

ALC. Most certainly, Socrates.

SO. Then are these poems about
a difference of just and unjust?

ALC. Yes.

SO. And the battles and the deaths occurred
because of this difference
between the Achaeans and the other Trojans,
and between the suitors of Penelope and Odysseus.

ALC. You speak the truth.

SO. And I think also at Tanagra
when Athenians and Lacedaemonians and Boeotians died,
and later at Coronea, in which also your father met his end,
and concerning the former
no other difference than about the just and unjust
produced the deaths and the battles. Did it not?

ALC. You speak the truth.

SO. So are we to say these are knowledgeable,
about what they differ on so seriously,
so as to go opposing each other to their very last extremity?

ALC. It does not appear so.

SO. Then are you referring to such teachers,
whom you admit yourself do not know?

ALC. It is likely.

SO. So how is it likely
that you know the just and the unjust,
about which you go astray so
and appear not to have learned from anyone
nor discovered yourself?

ALC. From what you are saying it is not likely.

11
SO. Here again do you see
how you are not speaking beautifully, Alcibiades?

ALC. In what?

SO. In that you are saying it is me speaking these things.

ALC. But what? Are you not speaking,
how I do not know about the just and unjust?

SO. Definitely not.

ALC. But am I?

SO. Yes.

ALC. How so?

SO. Here is a way.
If I ask you between the one and the two, which is more,
will you not say that it is the two?

ALC. I shall.

SO. By how much?

ALC. By one.

SO. So which of us is saying
that the two is one more than the one?

ALC. I am.

SO. Then I was asking, and you were answering?

ALC. Yes.

SO. So do I the one questioning
appear to be the one speaking about these things,
or you the one answering?

ALC. I.

SO. But what if I ask what are the letters of "Socrates,"
and you should say; which is the one speaking?

ALC. I.

SO. Come now, in a word say:
when asking and answering is occurring,
which is the one speaking,
the one asking or the one answering?

ALC. The one answering, it seems to me, Socrates.

SO. Then so far through all the argument
was I the one asking?

ALC. Yes.

SO. And you the one answering?

ALC. Certainly.

SO. So what then?
Which of us has spoken what has been said?

ALC. I appear to have, Socrates, out of what I admitted.

SO. Then was it said about justice and injustice
that Alcibiades, the fair son of Cleinias, did not know,
but thought he did,
and was about to go into the assembly
to advise Athenians about what he does not know?
Was this not so?

ALC. It appears so.

SO. Then it follows, Alcibiades, something of Euripides:
that you are in danger of your having heard it not from me,
I am not the one speaking these things, but you,
and you blame me in vain.
And yet you also speak well.
For mad is the scheme you have in mind to attempt, best one,
to teach what you do not know, having neglected to learn it.

12

ALC. I think, Socrates, rarely are Athenians advised
and the other Greeks, which is more just or more unjust;
for such things they believe are obvious;
so passing over these
they consider which will be advantageous in practice.
For these, I think, are not the same,
the just and the advantageous,
but many really profited by committing great wrongs,
and others, I think, doing just actions gained no advantage.

SO. But what?
If the just happens to be quite another thing,
and the advantageous different,
you don't think you know these things
which are advantageous for the people, and why?

ALC. For what is to prevent it, Socrates?
Unless again you will ask me from whom I learned it
or how I discovered it myself.

SO. What a way you do this!
If you speak something not correct,
and it happens that because of the previous argument
it can be so demonstrated,
then you think it is necessary
to hear some new different demonstrations,
as though the previous ones are like a worn-out coat,
and you should no longer wear it,
if someone does not bring you a clean and undefiled proof.
But I saying goodby
passing by your advance runners of the argument
nonetheless shall ask,
again from where did you learn
how to know the advantageous,
and who is the teacher,
and all those things I asked before I shall ask as one;
for it is clear that in this you will find also
you will have no way to demonstrate
either that by discovering it you know the advantageous
or by having learned it.
But since you are fastidious
and no longer like the taste of this argument,
let me say goodby to this,
whether or not you know the advantageous for the Athenians;
but whether justice and advantage are the same or different,
why don't you demonstrate?
If you want, ask me as I did you,
or even explain it by your own argument.

ALC. But I don't know if I can explain it to you, Socrates.

SO. But joyful one, use me as assembly and democracy;
for there it will be necessary for you to persuade each one.
Will it not?

ALC. Yes.

SO. Then is the same person able to persuade
one alone and many together about what he knows,
just as a grammar school teacher can persuade

one and many about writing?

ALC. Yes.

SO. So again will not the same person persuade
one and many about arithmetic?

ALC. Yes.

SO. And he will be the one who knows, the arithmetician?

ALC. Certainly.

SO. Then too as you are able to persuade many,
is the same also so with one?

ALC. It is likely.

SO. And it is clear that these things are what you know.

ALC. Yes.

SO. So the only difference between
an orator in the democracy
and one in this kind of conversation
is that one persuades a crowd of the same things
which another does one at a time?

ALC. It may be.

SO. Come now,
since the same person appears to persuade many and one,
practice on me and try to demonstrate
how the just sometimes is not advantageous.

ALC. You are insolent, Socrates.

SO. Now at any rate with this insolence
I intend to persuade you of the opposite
of what you are not willing to persuade me.

ALC. Speak then.

SO. Only answer the questions.

ALC. No, but you speak yourself.

SO. But what? Don't you especially want to be convinced?

ALC. By all means.

SO. Then if you should say that these things are so,
would you be especially convinced?

ALC. It seems I would.

SO. Then answer; and if you don't hear from yourself,
that the just is advantageous,

you should not trust another speaking.

ALC. I won't, but let me answer;
for I don't think I shall be harmed by it.

13
SO. For you are prophetic.
And tell me: do you say
some of the just things are advantageous, but others are not?

ALC. Yes.

SO. But what? Are some of the beautiful, and some not?

ALC. How are you asking this?

SO. Did someone ever seem to you dishonorable,
but practice justice?

ALC. Not to me.

SO. But are all just things beautiful?

ALC. Yes.

SO. And what of the beautiful things?
Are they all good, or some, and not others?

ALC. I think, Socrates,
some of the beautiful things are bad.

SO. And some of the dishonorable good?

ALC. Yes.

SO. Then do you mean in such cases,
when many in war rescuing a companion or relative
received injuries or died,
but the ones not rescuing, as needed, went away healthy?

ALC. Definitely.

SO. Then such a rescue you say is beautiful
in respect to the attempt to save which was needed;
and this is courage, is it not?

ALC. Yes.

SO. But it is bad in respect to the deaths and wounding?

ALC. Yes.

SO. So then is not the courage one thing,
and the death another?

ALC. Certainly.

SO. Then it is not in respect to the same thing
the rescuing the friends is beautiful and bad?

ALC. It appears not.

SO. Then see if, what is beautiful is also good,
just as also here: for you admitted
in respect to the courage the rescue was beautiful;
So consider this same thing, the courage, is it good or bad?
But consider this way:
which would you choose for yourself, good or bad?

ALC. Good.

SO. Then the very greatest things,
and would you least accept losing such things?

ALC. For how could I not?

SO. So what do you say about courage?
at what price would you choose to lose it?

ALC. I would not even choose life as a coward.

SO. Then cowardice seems to you to be the worst of evils.

ALC. To me.

SO. Equal to dying, as is likely.

ALC. I say so.

SO. Then most opposite to death and cowardice
are life and courage?

ALC. Yes.

SO. And would you especially choose the latter for you,
and the former least?

ALC. Yes.

SO. Then is it that you believe these are best,
and the others worst?

ALC. Certainly.

SO. Then you believe courage is among the best things
and death among the worst.

ALC. I do.

SO. Then to rescue the friends in war, which is beautiful,
in respect to the doing of good by the courage,
do you name it beautiful?

ALC. I appear to.

SO. But in respect to the doing of evil by the death bad?

ALC. Yes.

SO. Then in this it is just to name each of the actions:
if really you call what produces evil bad,
and what does good must be called good.

ALC. It seems to me.

SO. So then also what does good, beautiful;
and what does bad, dishonorable?

ALC. Yes.

SO. Then saying the rescue in the war of the friends
is beautiful, but bad,
you mean nothing different than naming it good, but bad.

ALC. You seem to me to speak the truth, Socrates.

SO. Then nothing of the beautiful,
in so far as it is beautiful, is bad,
and nothing of the dishonorable,
in so far as it is dishonorable, is good.

ALC. It appears not.

SO. Then still also consider this.
Whoever acts beautifully, does he not also do well?

ALC. Yes.

SO. And are not the ones doing well happy?

ALC. For how could they not be?

SO. Then are they happy because of gaining good things?

ALC. Especially.

SO. And do they gain these things
by doing well and acting beautifully?

ALC. Yes.

SO. Then is doing well good?

ALC. But how could it not be?

SO. Then is the success beautiful?

ALC. Yes.

SO. Then it has appeared to us again
that the beautiful and the good are the same.

ALC. It appears so.

SO. Then what we find is beautiful,
we shall also find is good from this argument.

ALC. By necessity.

SO. But what? Are good things advantageous or not?

ALC. Advantageous.

SO. So do you remember what we agreed about the just?

ALC. I think the ones doing the just
must be doing the beautiful.

SO. So too the ones doing the beautiful the good?

ALC. Yes.

SO. And the good things are advantageous?

ALC. Yes.

SO. Then the just, Alcibiades, is advantageous.

ALC. It is likely.

14

SO. So what then? Are you not the one speaking,
and I the one asking?

ALC. I appear to be, as is likely.

SO. So if anyone stands up advising
either Athenians or Peparethians,
thinking he knows the just and the unjust,
and says that the just is sometimes bad,
would you do anything other than laugh at him,
since you also happen to be saying
that the same things are just and advantageous?

ALC. But by the gods, Socrates,
I do not know at all what I am saying,
but it is really like feeling strange.
For at one time during your questioning
it seems to me different,
and at another time something else.

SO. Next this, friend, are you unaware what the feeling is?

ALC. Certainly.

SO. So do you think, if someone should ask you,
do you have two eyes or three,
and two hands or four, or any other such thing,

at one time would you answer different,
and at another time something else,
or always the same?

ALC. I am already having anxiety about myself,
yet I think the same.

SO. Then is it because you know? Is this the cause?

ALC. I think so.

SO. Then about what you answer
with unwilling contradictions,
it is clear that you do not know about them.

ALC. It is likely.

SO. Then too about the just and unjust and beautiful
and dishonorable and bad and good and advantageous also
are you not saying you are going astray in your answers?
Next is it not clear that because of not knowing about them,
you are going astray over these?

ALC. To me it is.

SO. So then is it also so:
when someone does not know something,
is it necessary for the soul to go astray about this?

ALC. For how could it not?

SO. So what then?
Do you know some way by which
you could go up into heaven?

ALC. By God, not I.

SO. And does your opinion about this go astray?

ALC. Of course not.

SO. And do you know the cause, or shall I state it?

ALC. State it.

SO. Because, friend, you do not think you know it
while not knowing it.

ALC. Again what do you mean by this?

SO. You look also in common.
What is not known, and you know that it is not known,
do you go astray about these things?
For example about preparing a sauce
do you know for sure that you do not know how?

ALC. Certainly.

SO. So then do you think about these things yourself,
how it is useful to prepare it, and go astray,
or do you turn it over to one who knows?

ALC. Just so.

SO. And what if you should be sailing on a ship,
then would you think whether it is useful
to hold the tiller inward or outward,
and in not knowing you would go astray,
or turning it over to the pilot would you keep silent?

ALC. Turn it over to the pilot.

SO. Then you do not go astray about what you don't know,
as long as you know that you don't know?

ALC. It is not likely.

SO. So are you aware that
mistakes in practice are because of this ignorance,
thinking one knows when one does not know?

ALC. Again what do you mean by this?

SO. Is the time when we attempt to act,
when we think we know what we are doing?

ALC. Yes

SO. And when people do not think they know,
do they give it over to others?

ALC. Why not?

SO. Then are they of the ones who do not know
unerring in life because of turning them over to others?

ALC. Yes.

SO. So who are the ones making mistakes?
For they are not the ones who know.

ALC. Of course not.

SO. And since it is neither the ones who know
nor the ones who do not know
knowing that they have not known it,
are the others left the ones who do not know,
but think they know?

ALC. None, but these.

SO. Then this ignorance is a cause of evils
and the shameful kind of stupidity?

ALC. Yes.

SO. Thus when it is about the greatest things,
then it is most harmful and shameful?

ALC. By far.

SO. So what then?
Can you mention anything greater than the just
and the beautiful and the good and the advantageous?

ALC. Of course not.

SO. Then it is about these you say you go astray?

ALC. Yes.

SO. But if you go astray,
then is it not clear from the previous
that not only are you ignorant of the greatest things,
but also while not knowing them you think you know?

ALC. I run the risk.

SO. Then alas, Alcibiades,
what a misfortune you are suffering!
I shrink from naming it,
but nevertheless, since we are alone, let me speak.
For you are living with stupidity, best one, to the extreme,
as your argument also accuses you yourself;
and because of this you dart into politics
before being educated.
And you are not the only one to have suffered this,
but also many of the ones managing the affairs of state here,
except a few and perhaps your guardian Pericles.

15

ALC. It is said, Socrates,
he did not become wise by accident,
but associated with many also wise,
both Pythocleides and Anaxagoras;
even now at his age
he still is with Damon for this very purpose.

SO. So what then? Did you ever know anyone wise
who was unable to make someone else wise as himself?

Just as the one who taught you writing, was wise himself
and made you and the others whom he wanted to; did he not?

ALC. Yes.

SO. Then also you who learned from that one
will be able to make another wise?

ALC. Yes.

SO. And both the harpist
and the gymnastic trainer in the same way?

ALC. Certainly.

SO. For doubtless a beautiful proof
of knowing whatever one knows is this,
when one can also point out another who is knowing.

ALC. It seems to me.

SO. So what then?
Can you say whom Pericles made wise,
starting from one of his sons?

ALC. But what if the two sons of Pericles
were foolish, Socrates?

SO. But Cleinias, your brother.

ALC. But why would you say Cleinias, a mad person?

SO. Then since Cleinias is mad,
and the two sons of Pericles were foolish,
what cause are we to attribute to you,
why did he allow you to be thus?

ALC. I think I am the cause for not paying attention.

SO. But of the other Athenians
or the foreigners, slave or free,
say who has cause to have become wiser
because of being with Pericles,
just as I can say because of Zeno,
Pythodorus son of Isolochus and Callias son of Calliades,
of whom each has paid Zeno a hundred *minae*,
became wise and notable.

ALC. But by God, I cannot.

16

SO. Well; so what do you understand about yourself?
Which will it be, either as you now have it,

or taking care to do something?

ALC. Counsel in common, Socrates.
Yet I am reflecting during your talking and consent.
For the ones managing the state's affairs
seem to me to be, except for a few, uneducated.

SO. So really what is this?

ALC. If they ever were educated,
it would be necessary for one
attempting to compete with them
to be learning and practicing like an athlete;
but now since they have gone into politics as amateurs,
what need is there to practice
and take the trouble of learning?
For I know well that by nature
I shall quite completely surpass them.

SO. Alas, best one, what this is you have said!
How unworthy of your looks and of your other advantages!

ALC. What do you really mean
and why do you say this, Socrates?

SO. I am irritated on your behalf and for my love.

ALC. At what?

SO. At your expecting the competition
to be against the people here.

ALC. But against whom will it be?

SO. Is this worthy also to be asked
by a man thinking himself to be great?

ALC. What do you mean?
Is not my contest against these?

SO. But if you were intending
to pilot a trireme in fighting at sea,
would it be sufficient for you
to be best of the shipmates at piloting,
or thinking these things to be necessary qualifications,
would you regard the ones you fight against,
but not as now the ones you fight with?
Doubtless you must excel such,
so that they would not be worthy to fight against you,
but being looked down upon

to be fighting with you against the enemies,
if you really mean to show off some beautiful action
also worthy of yourself and the state.

ALC. But I do mean to.

SO. Then is it quite worthy of you to be pleased,
if you are better than the soldiers,
but do not look at the ones leading the rivals,
if ever you should become better than those,
considering and practicing against those?

ALC. But of whom are you speaking, Socrates?

SO. Don't you know each time
our state makes war on Lacedaimonians and the great king?

ALC. You speak the truth.

SO. Then if you have in mind to be leader of the state,
would you believe correctly the contest for you to be leading
is against the kings of Lacedaimonia and Persia?

ALC. You may be speaking the truth.

SO. No, joyful one,
but you must look to the quail-striker Meidias
and such others who try to manage the state's affairs,
still slavish, as the women would say,
having three parts in the soul beneath rudeness
and not having looked after it at all,
but still foreign-speaking they have come
flattering the state, but not ruling—
to these you must look, as I say,
to really neglect looking at yourself,
and not learn what has to be learned,
for one intending to compete in such a contest,
nor practice what needs practicing,
and all preparation prepared
thus to enter upon affairs of the state.

ALC. But Socrates, you seem to me to speak the truth,
yet I think the Lacedaimonian generals and the Persian king
are no different than the others.

SO. But best one, consider this thought which you have.

ALC. About what?

SO. First do you think
you would take more care of yourself,
being afraid and thinking they are terrible,
or if you are not?

ALC. Clearly if I should think they are terrible.

SO. So do you think
you will be harmed taking care of yourself?

ALC. Not at all, rather I shall derive great benefit.

SO. Then in this sense your thought is bad.

ALC. You speak the truth.

SO. Then second, that it is also false,
from the likely consideration.

ALC. How so?

SO. Which are likely to be better by nature,
those in noble races or not noble?

ALC. Clearly in the noble.

SO. Then the well born, if they are also well brought up,
thus become perfected in virtue?

ALC. By necessity.

17

SO. Let us really consider, by comparing ours with theirs,
first whether the Lacedaimonian and Persian kings
seem to be of inferior birth.
Do we not know that the former are descendants of Heracles,
and the latter of Achaemenes,
and the race of Heracles and Achaemenes
goes back to Perseus, son of Zeus?

ALC. For mine does too, Socrates, to Eurysaces,
and that of Eurysaces to Zeus.

SO. For mine does too, noble Alcibiades, to Daedalus,
and Daedalus to Hephaestus, son of Zeus.
But the ones ruling these from themselves are kings
from kings reaching back to Zeus,
either of Argos and Lacedaimonia,
or of Persia always, and often of Asia too, as also now;
but we ourselves are private persons and our fathers.
And if also one should need to show the progenitors

and Salamis, the country of Eurysaces,
or Aegina of the still earlier Aeacus
to Artaxerxes, son of Xerxes,
how much laughter do you think it would deserve?
  But look how inferior we are to the men
in pride of birth and in other upbringing.
Or have you not perceived
how great are the advantages of the Lacedaimonian kings,
whose wives are guarded at public expense by the magistrates,
so that it is not possible for the king
to be born from anyone else than from Heracleids?
  And the Persian is so far beyond,
that no one has any suspicion
that a king could have been born
from anyone other than from his own;
because of this the king's wife is not guarded
by anything other than by fear.
  And when the oldest child is born, as the ruler,
first all the subjects celebrate
in the palace of the king who should rule,
then for the rest of time on that day all of Asia
makes offerings and celebrates the king's birthday;
but at our birth, as the comic poet says,
even the neighbors hardly notice anything, Alcibiades.
  After this the child is brought up,
not by a woman nurse of little worth,
but by the eunuchs who seem to be best around the palace;
others are assigned by them to take care of the new-born,
and so that he will be made most beautiful,
reshaping and setting upright the stance of the child;
and doing these things they are held in great honor.
  And when the children become seven years old,
they are schooled on the horses and on the lessons of these,
and begin to go on the hunt;
and becoming twice seven years
those whom they name royal tutors take over the children;
and four Persians who seem best in maturity are selected,
the wisest and the most just
and the most discreet and the most courageous.

One teaches magian lore of Zoroaster, son of Horomazus;
and this is service of the gods;
and he also teaches the royal things;
and the most just to speak truth through all his life;
and the most discreet
not to be ruled by even one of the pleasures,
so as to be accustomed to be free and really a king,
ruling first what is in himself, but not being enslaved;
and the most courageous
preparing him to be fearless and secure,
how when one is afraid he is really a slave.

But for you, Alcibiades, the tutor appointed by Pericles
was the one of the household most useless by age,
Zopyrus the Thracian.
And I could describe for you
the other upbringing and education of your competitors,
if it were not much work;
and besides these things are enough to make it clear
and the others follow as much as these.
But of your birth, Alcibiades, and upbringing and education,
or of those of any other Athenians, so to speak,
nobody cares, unless it chances to be some lover of yours.

But again if you should intend to look into wealth
and luxury and robes with flowing trains
and anointments of myrrh and crowds of servants following
and the other delicacies of the Persians,
you would be ashamed at yourself,
perceiving how much you have been left behind by them.

18
And if again you intended to look into the discretion
and orderliness and dexterity and agility and magnanimity
and discipline and courage and patience and industry
and love of winning and ambition of the Lacedaimonians,
you would believe yourself a child in all these things.

And if again you are devoted to wealth
and think to be something in that,
and let this not be unsaid by us,
if you are to perceive where you are.

For in this if you intend to see
the wealth of the Lacedaimonians,
you should know that much here is left behind there.
For they have so much land of their own and Messenian,
none of ours here could compete in extent nor goodness,
nor again in acquiring captive slaves of the others
and the serfs, nor of horses,
nor how many other cattle graze in Messene;
but let us say goodby to all these things,
and there is not as much gold and silver
in all Greece as in private in Lacedaimonia;
for during many generations it has been going to them
from all of Greece, and often also from the foreigners,
and it goes out to no one,
but just as in the story of Aesop,
where the fox said to the lion,
also of the usage in Lacedaimonia it is clear
the tracks are directed going in there,
but never has anyone seen them coming out;
so that one ought to know well that
both in gold and in silver
the ones there are the wealthiest of the Greeks,
and their wealthiest is the king;
for the greatest and largest of such receipts are the king's,
and besides there is no small royal tribute,
which the Lacedaimonians pay to the king.
    And this of the Lacedaimonians
as compared to Greeks is great wealth,
but as compared to the Persians and their king it is nothing;
since once I heard from a trustworthy man
who had gone up to the palace,
who said he went along a very large and good estate,
for nearly a day's journey,
which the inhabitants call the girdle of the king's wife;
and there is also another which again is called a veil,
and many other beautiful and good regions
reserved for the adornment of the wife,
and each region is named after each of the adornments;
so that I think, if someone should say
to the king's mother, and wife of Xerxes, Amestris,

that the son of Deinomache,
whose adornment is perhaps worth fifty *minae,* if that much,
has it in mind to challenge your son,
and the son whose land at Erchiae
is not even three hundred acres,
she would wonder what this Alcibiades has in mind
to be trusting to contend with Artaxerxes,
and I think she would say that it is not possible
the man attempting this could be trusting to anything else
except to taking care and wisdom;
for these are the only things worthy of a word among Greeks.
   Since if she should learn
that this Alcibiades who now attempts this
is first not yet even twenty years old,
next completely uneducated,
and further, when his lover is telling him
that it is useful first learning and taking care of himself
and practicing thus to be contending with a king,
he is not willing, but says he is satisfied also as he is,
I think she would be surprised
and ask, "So on what is the boy to rely?"
   So if we should say that on beauty and greatness
and birth and wealth and qualities of soul,
she would believe us, Alcibiades, to be mad
in looking at all such things in comparison to them.
And I think even Lampido, the daughter of Leotychides,
and wife of Archidamus, and mother of Agis,
who all have been kings,
would wonder also the same way
in looking at their advantages in comparison,
if you have in mind to contend with her son,
being so badly led.
Yet does it not seem to be shameful,
if the wives of the enemies
should understand better about ourselves,
what is really useful in taking them on,
than we ourselves understand about ourselves?
   But blessed one, be convinced by me
and the inscription at Delphi, "Know yourself,"

that these are the competitors, but not the ones you think;
nor by any other single thing should we overcome them,
unless it be by taking care and by art.
If you are left behind in these,
you will also be left behind
in becoming notable among Greeks and foreigners,
whom you seem to me to love
more than anyone else ever loved anything.

19

ALC. So then what taking care is useful to do, Socrates?
Can you prescribe?
For more than all what you have said is likely true.

SO. Yes; but counsel in common,
as to the way by which we should become better;
for I do not speak only about your need so to be educated,
and not about mine;
for it is not that I differ from you except in one thing.

ALC. In what?

SO. The trustee who is mine is better and wiser
than Pericles, who is yours.

ALC. Who is he, Socrates?

SO. God, Alcibiades,
who before today has not allowed me to converse with you;
and trusting in it I say that your distinction
will be through no one other than through me.

ALC. You are playing, Socrates.

SO. Perhaps;
yet I speak the truth that we must take care,
as much as all people, we two also very much.

ALC. That I should, you are not lying.

SO. Nor in that I should.

ALC. So what then should we do?

SO. There must be no falling off nor weakening, companion.

ALC. These are really fitting, Socrates.

SO. None, but it must be considered in common.
And tell me: for we say that we really want to be best.
Or do we not?

ALC. Yes.

SO. Best at what?

ALC. Clearly that in which the men are good.

SO. Who are good in what?

ALC. Clearly that is the management of business.

SO. What kind? Then is it equestrian business?

ALC. Of course not.

SO. For we would be beside the horseman?

ALC. Yes.

SO. But do you mean nautical business?

ALC. No.

SO. For we would be beside the sailors?

ALC. Yes.

SO. But what kind? Who manages what?

ALC. What is the beautiful and good of Athenians.

SO. But do you mean the beautiful and good
are the sensible or the foolish?

ALC. The sensible.

SO. Then each is good in this in which he is sensible?

ALC. Yes.

SO. And bad in what he is foolish?

ALC. For how could he not be?

SO. So then is the leather-cutter
sensible in making sandals?

ALC. Certainly.

SO. Then is he good in that?

ALC. Good.

SO. But what?
In the making of clothes is not the leather-cutter foolish?

ALC. Yes.

SO. Then is he bad in this?

ALC. Yes.

SO. Then in this argument the same one is bad and good.

ALC. It appears so.

SO. Or then do you mean the good men are also bad?

ALC. Of course not.

20

SO. But whatever do you mean by the good?

ALC. I mean the ones able to rule in the state.

SO. Certainly not over horses?

ALC. Of course not.

SO. But over people?

ALC. Yes.

SO. Then when sick?

ALC. No.

SO. But when sailing?

ALC. I say no.

SO. But when harvesting?

ALC. No.

SO. But when doing nothing or when doing something?

ALC. I mean doing.

SO. What? Try and make it clear to me.

ALC. Then when they are meeting together with themselves
and using each other,
just as we live in the state.

SO. Then do you mean ruling over people
who are using people?

ALC. Yes.

SO. Then over commanders who use rowers?

ALC. Of course not.

SO. For this the pilot is best?

ALC. Yes.

SO. But do you mean ruling over flute-playing people,
who lead the people singing and use dancers?

ALC. Of course not.

SO. For again is this chorus-teaching?

ALC. Certainly.

SO. But whatever do you mean by
being able to rule over people who are using people?

ALC. I mean those sharing in the state
and meeting together with each other,
to rule over these in the state.

SO. So what then is this art?
Just as if I should ask you again the things I did just now,
what art makes one know how to rule over fellow sailors?

ALC. Piloting.

SO. And over fellow singers, as I just now said,
what knowledge makes one rule over them?

ALC. That which you just said, chorus-teaching.

SO. But what?
What do you call the knowledge of fellow citizens?

ALC. Good counsel, I call it, Socrates.

SO. But what?
Does the pilot's seem to be lack of counsel?

ALC. Of course not.

SO. But is it good counsel?

ALC. It seems so to me, in the saving of sailors.

SO. You speak well. But what?
In what is the good counsel of which you are speaking?

ALC. In the better managing and maintaining of the state.

SO. And to better manage and maintain it
what is present or absent?
For example, if you should ask me,
"To better manage a body and maintain it
what is present or absent?"
I would say that health is present, and disease absent.
Don't you think so too?

ALC. Yes.

SO. And if again you should ask me,
"And what is present when eyes are better?"
Similarly I would say that sight is present,
and blindness absent.
And also with ears deafness is absent,
and inborn hearing is best and being treated becomes better.

ALC. Correct.

21

SO. But what then?
What is present and absent when a state is best
and better treated and managed?

ALC. It seems to me, Socrates, when there is friendship
among themselves and toward each other,
and hating and rebelling are absent.

SO. So then by friendship do you mean oneness or discord?

ALC. Oneness.

SO. So through what art
are the states in oneness about numbers?

ALC. Through arithmetic.

SO. And what of the individuals? Is it through the same?

ALC. Yes.

SO. Then also is each the same with himself?

ALC. Yes.

SO. And through what art
is each one himself with himself
about a span and a cubit, which is longer?
Is it through measurement?

ALC. What then?

SO. Then also the individuals with each other
and the states?

ALC. Yes.

SO. But what about weight? Is it not similar?

ALC. I say so.

SO. And what oneness do you mean,
what is it and about what, and what art provides it?
And then is it the same in a state and individually,
with and toward oneself and toward another?

ALC. Most likely.

SO. So what is it?
You should not tire in answering, but be eager to say.

ALC. I think I mean friendship and oneness,
as when a father and mother are one in loving a son,
and brother with brother and wife with husband.

SO. So do you think, Alcibiades, a husband is able
to be one with a wife concerning wool-spinning,
not being knowledgeable next to her being knowledgeable?

ALC. Of course not.

SO. Nor has he any need;
for this is a woman's accomplishment.

ALC. Yes.

SO. But what?
Is a woman able to be one with a man
concerning politics not having learned it?

ALC. Of course not.

SO. For perhaps again you would say this is a man's.

ALC. I would.

SO. Then there are women's and men's accomplishments
according to your argument.

ALC. And how could there not be?

SO. Then in these there is no oneness
between women and men.

ALC. No.

SO. Then no friendship, if friendship is oneness.

ALC. It appears not.

SO. Then the women who are doing their own business
are not loved by the men.

ALC. It seems not.

SO. Nor then the men by the women, in doing theirs.

ALC. No.

SO. Nor then in the same way are the states well managed
when they each are doing their own business?

ALC. I think so, Socrates.

SO. How do you mean it, with friendship not present,
which we say is there to manage well the states,
and otherwise they are not?

ALC. But it seems to me also according to this
friendship arises among them,
because they each do their own business.

SO. It just was not; but now again how do you mean it?
With oneness not arising does friendship arise?
Or can oneness arise which some have known about,
and others have not?

ALC. Impossible.

SO. And are they doing justice or injustice,
when they each are doing their own business?

ALC. Justice; for how could they not be?

SO. So when the citizens are doing the just in the state
does not friendship arise toward each other?

ALC. Again it seems to me to be necessary, Socrates.

SO. So whatever do you mean by the friendship or oneness
about which we need to be wise and well-advised,
in order that we may be good men?
For I am not able to learn either what or in whom it is;
for sometimes it appears to be in them, but other times not,
from your argument.

22

ALC. But by the gods, Socrates,
I don't know myself what I mean,
but risk also having been long unaware myself
in a most shameful condition.

SO. But one should be confident.
For if you had perceived this condition at age fifty,
it would be hard for you to take care of yourself;
but now you are at the age
at which it is necessary to perceive this.

ALC. So having perceived it what should one do, Socrates?

SO. Answer the questions asked, Alcibiades;
and if you do this, God willing,
if it is necessary for someone to trust also in my prophecy,
you and I both shall become better.

ALC. These things shall be on account of my answering.

SO. Come then, what is "taking care of yourself"—
often we may not be aware
we are not taking care of ourselves,
but thinking we are—

and so when does a person do it?
Is it when one is taking care of one's things,
at that time is one also taking care of oneself?

ALC. It seems so to me at least.

SO. But what? When does a person take care of feet?
Is it when one is taking care of
those things which belong to the feet?

ALC. I don't understand.

SO. What do you call what belongs to a hand?
Does a ring belong to
any other part of a person than a finger?

ALC. Of course not.

SO. Then also a sandal to a foot in the same manner?

ALC. Yes.

SO. So then when we take care of sandals,
at that time do we take care of feet?

ALC. I don't quite understand, Socrates.

SO. But what, Alcibiades? Do you call
something taking care of whatever business correct?

ALC. I do.

SO. So what art makes sandals better?

ALC. Shoemaking.

SO. Then by shoemaking do we take care of sandals?

ALC. Yes.

SO. Also the foot by shoemaking?
Or by that by which we make feet better?

ALC. By that.

SO. And are not feet made better
by that which also the rest of the body is?

ALC. It seems to me.

SO. And is this not gymnastic?

ALC. Especially.

SO. Then by gymnastic do we take care of feet,
and by shoemaking of what belongs to the feet?

ALC. Certainly.

SO. And by gymnastic of the hands,
and by ring-engraving of what belongs to the hand?

ALC. Yes.

SO. And by gymnastic of the body,
and by weaving and the others the things of the body?

ALC. Absolutely so.

SO. Then by one art we take care of each thing itself,
but by another of what belongs to the thing itself.

ALC. It appears so.

SO. Then when you take care of what belongs to yourself,
you are not taking care of yourself.

ALC. Not at all.

SO. For the art is not the same, as likely,
by which someone may take care of oneself
and of one's things.

ALC. It appears not.

SO. Come then,
by what kind can we be taken care of ourselves?

ALC. I have nothing to say.

SO. But has so much at least been admitted,
that it is not the one
by which we would make any of our belongings better,
but by which we would make ourselves better?

ALC. You speak the truth.

23

SO. So should we ever have known
what art makes a sandal better, not knowing a sandal?

ALC. Impossible.

SO. Nor what art makes rings better,
being ignorant of a ring.

ALC. True.

SO. But what?
Then would we ever know what art makes oneself better
being ignorant of what we are ourselves?

ALC. Impossible.

SO. So then does it really happen to be easy
to know oneself,
and was it some careless person
who inscribed this in the temple at Delphi,
or is it something hard and not for everyone?

ALC. It often seemed to me, Socrates, to be for everyone,
and often quite hard.

SO. But Alcibiades, whether it is easy or not,
nevertheless for us it has to be this way;
knowing this quickly we would know
the taking care of ourselves,
but being ignorant we never would.

ALC. This is so.

SO. But come, in what way is a self itself discovered?
For thus we may quickly discover whatever we are ourselves,
but still being in ignorance of this it would be impossible.

ALC. You speak correctly.

24

SO. So it holds toward God.
With whom are you conversing now?
What other than with me?

ALC. Yes.

SO. Then also I with you?

ALC. Yes.

SO. Then Socrates is the one conversing?

ALC. Certainly.

SO. And Alcibiades the one listening?

ALC. Yes.

SO. Then Socrates converses with speech?

ALC. Well?

SO. And the conversing and the using speech
you call the same thing.

ALC. Certainly.

SO. And the one using and what is used,
are they not different?

ALC. How do you mean?

SO. For example, a leather-cutter cuts when cutting
with both a knife and with other tools.

ALC. Yes.

SO. Then is the one cutting and using it one thing,
and what is used in cutting another?

ALC. For how could it not be?

SO. So then thus also what the harpist plays
and the harpist himself would be different?

ALC. Yes.

SO. Now this is just what I was asking,
whether the one using and what is being used
always seem to be different.

ALC. It seems so.

SO. So what do we say of the leather-cutter?
Does he cut with tools alone or also with hands?

ALC. Also with hands.

SO. Then does he use these also?

ALC. Yes.

SO. Is the leather-cutter also using his eyes?

ALC. Yes.

SO. And we agree the using and what is used are different?

ALC. Yes.

SO. Then a leather-cutter and harpist are different
from hands and eyes with which they work?

ALC. It is apparent.

SO. Then also is a person using the whole body?

ALC. Certainly.

SO. And the one using and what is being used are different?

ALC. Yes.

SO. Then a person is different from one's own body?

ALC. It is likely.

SO. So whatever is a person?

ALC. I have nothing to say.

SO. So then you do have,
that at least it is the one using the body.

ALC. Yes.

SO. So what else uses it than a soul?

ALC. Nothing else.

SO. Therefore ruling?

ALC. Yes.

25

SO. And here at least I think
no one would be thinking otherwise.

ALC. What?

SO. One of three things is what the person is.

ALC. What things?

SO. Soul or body or both together, the whole of this.

ALC. What then?

SO. But did we not agree at least
this ruler of the body is the person?

ALC. We agreed.

SO. So then does a body itself rule itself?

ALC. Not at all.

SO. For we said it is ruled itself.

ALC. Yes.

SO. Really this could not be what we are seeking.

ALC. It is not likely.

SO. But then do both together rule the body,
and is this really a person?

ALC. Perhaps it is.

SO. Least of all; for they are not ruling together
when one or the other has no part in both together ruling.

ALC. Correct.

SO. But since neither body nor both together is the person,
it is left to, I think, either this is nothing,
or if it is something,
it turns out the person is nothing else than soul.

ALC. Exactly so.

SO. So what is still needed
for it to be more clearly demonstrated to you,
that the soul is the person?

ALC. By God, but it seems to me it is sufficiently so.

SO. And if not at least exactly but it is moderately,
it satisfies us;
for we shall know exactly at that time,
when we have discovered what now we really passed over
because it involves much consideration.

ALC. What is this?

SO. What was just somehow said,
that first must be considered this self itself;
but now instead of the self itself
we have been considering what each thing is.
And perhaps it will be satisfying;
for we could not say anything is more lord over ourselves
than the soul.

ALC. Of course not.

SO. Then does it hold beautifully to name it thus,
me and you using the arguments to converse with each other
by the soul to the soul?

ALC. Quite so.

SO. Then this was what we also said a little while earlier,
that Socrates is conversing with Alcibiades using argument,
not to your face, as likely,
but making the arguments to Alcibiades;
and this is the soul.

ALC. It seems to me.

SO. Then the one assigning knowing self
orders us to gain knowledge of the soul.

ALC. It is likely.

SO. Then whoever knows what belongs to the body,
has known one's things but not oneself.

ALC. This is so.

SO. Then not one of the physicians knows oneself,
as a physician,
nor any of the trainers, as a trainer.

ALC. It is not likely.

SO. Then the farmers and the other workers
are very far from knowing themselves.
For these don't even know their own things, as likely,

but even more remote than their things
according to the arts which they have;
for they know the things of the body,
with which it is served.

ALC. You speak the truth.

SO. Then if it is sensible to know oneself,
none of these are sensible in respect to the art.

ALC. None, it seems to me.

SO. Because of this also
these arts really seem to be mechanical
and not achievements of a good man.

ALC. Quite so.

SO. Then again whoever serves a body,
serves one's own things but does not serve oneself?

ALC. Could be.

SO. And whoever serves money,
serves neither oneself nor one's own things,
but what is even more remote from one's things?

ALC. It seems to me.

SO. Then the money-maker
does not even do one's own business.

ALC. Correct.

26

SO. Then if someone has been a lover of Alcibiades' body,
he is not in love with Alcibiades,
but with something belonging to Alcibiades.

ALC. You speak the truth.

SO. But your lover loves the soul?

ALC. It appears necessary from the argument.

SO. Then the one loving your body,
when the bloom ceases, going away is he gone?

ALC. It appears so.

SO. But the one loving the soul does not go away,
as long as it is getting better?

ALC. It is likely.

SO. Then I am the one who is not going away
but is remaining when the bloom of the body is ceasing,
the others having departed.

ALC. You at least are doing well, Socrates;
and you should not go away.

SO. Then be eager to be most beautiful.

ALC. But I shall be eager.

SO. So this is how it is for you;
neither was there, as likely, nor is there
a lover of Alcibiades, the son of Cleinias,
except one alone, and this beloved,
Socrates, the son of Sophroniscus and Phaenarete.

ALC. True.

SO. Then was it said my coming to you
anticipated by a little, before your coming to me,
wanting to inquire why I alone was not going away?

ALC. For that was so.

SO. Then the reason for this was that
I was the only lover of you,
but the others were of what belongs to you;
and the time of your things is ceasing,
but you are beginning to bloom.
And now if you are not corrupted by the Athenian democracy
and become shameful, I shall not forsake you.
For I am especially afraid of this,
that you might be corrupted
by becoming a lover of popularity;
for many good Athenians already have suffered this.
For a good face is the democracy of heroic Erechtheus;
but it is useful to see it stripped;
so beware of the precaution which I mean.

ALC. What?

SO. Exercise first, blessed one,
and learn what achievements are necessary
to enter the business of the state,
and which are not,
so that you might have a remedy
and not suffer anything terrible.

27

ALC. You seem to me to speak well, Socrates;
but try to explain in what manner
we may be taking care of ourselves.

SO. Then so much has been accomplished by us in advance;
for what we are, is pretty much agreed upon;
and we were afraid tripping on this
we might not notice
we are taking care of something different,
but not ourselves.

ALC. This is so.

SO. And after this really it must be
to take care of the soul and look into this.

ALC. Clearly.

SO. And give over to others
the taking care of bodies and money.

ALC. What then?

SO. So in what way could we know this most distinctly?
Since knowing this, as likely, we shall also know ourselves.
Then speaking well before God are we not comprehending
what we just now remembered of the Delphic inscription?

ALC. What kind of understanding do you mean, Socrates?

SO. I will indicate to you
what I suspect this inscription means and advises us.
For chances are not in many places is there a model of this,
but only in respect to sight.

ALC. How do you mean this?

SO. You consider also.
If to our eye just as to a person in advising
it said, "See yourself,"
how should we take up what it recommends?
Then would it not looking into this,
into what the eye is looking intend to see itself?

ALC. Clearly.

SO. What can we think of, looking into which
we may see at the same time that and ourselves?

ALC. Clearly, Socrates, into mirrors and such things.

SO. You speak correctly.
Then also in the eye by which we see
is there in it some such thing?

ALC. Certainly.

SO. So have you observed that
the face of the one looking into the eye
appears in the opposite eye as in a mirror,
and we call it the pupil,
which is a kind of image of the one looking?

ALC. You speak the truth.

SO. Then an eye seeing an eye,
and looking into this best part of it and by which it sees,
thus may see itself.

ALC. It appears so.

SO. But if it should look into any other part of the person
or at any other thing,
except into that by which this happens to be similar,
it will not see itself.

ALC. You speak the truth.

SO. Then if an eye intends to see itself,
it must look into an eye by itself,
and into that region of the eye,
in which the goodness of an eye is innate;
and is this sight?

ALC. That is so.

SO. So then, dear Alcibiades,
if soul also intends to know herself,
must she look into soul by herself,
and especially into this region of her,
in which the goodness of soul is innate, wisdom,
and into anything else which happens to be similar to this?

ALC. It seems to me, Socrates.

SO. So can we say,
is there anything of the soul more divine than this,
which is concerned with knowing and thinking?

ALC. We cannot.

SO. Then this part of her is like the divine,
and anyone looking into this

also comes to know all the divine,
and thus would especially know oneself.

ALC. It appears so.

28

SO. And to know oneself we agree is to be sensible?

ALC. Certainly.

SO. So then not knowing ourselves nor being sensible
are we able to know our own belongings bad and good?

ALC. How could this be, Socrates?

SO. For perhaps it appears to you impossible
that not knowing Alcibiades it is possible to know
that Alcibiades' belongings are Alcibiades'.

ALC. Yet it is impossible, by God.

SO. Nor even that our belongings are ours,
if we don't know ourselves?

ALC. For how could that be?

SO. And then if not our belongings,
not the business of our belongings either?

ALC. It appears not.

SO. So then we were not quite correct in just agreeing
there are some, who do not know themselves,
but know their belongings,
while others know the business of their belongings.
For it is likely
all these are to be regarded as one and a single art,
oneself, one's belongings, the business of one's belongings.

ALC. Could be.

SO. And whoever is ignorant of one's own belongings,
would also be ignorant possibly of the business of others
according to this.

ALC. What then?

SO. Then if of the business of others,
one will also be ignorant of the business of the state.

ALC. By necessity.

SO. Then such a man could never become a politician.

ALC. Of course not.

SO. Nor an economist either.

ALC. Of course not.

SO. Nor will one know what one is doing.

ALC. No.

SO. And will not the one not knowing make mistakes?

ALC. Certainly.

SO. And making mistakes will one do badly
in private and in public?

ALC. How could one not?

SO. And doing badly will one not be wretched?

ALC. Very.

SO. And what of those for whom this one is doing so?

ALC. These also.

SO. Then it is impossible,
unless one is sensible and good, to be happy.

ALC. Impossible.

SO. Then the bad people are wretched.

ALC. Very.

SO. Then it is not the one who has become wealthy
who is delivered from being most wretched,
but the one who has become sensible.

ALC. It appears so.

SO. Then it is not walls nor triremes nor shipyards
the states need, Alcibiades,
if they intend to be happy,
nor numbers nor size without goodness.

ALC. Certainly not.

29

SO. If you really intend to
manage the business of the state correctly and beautifully,
you must impart goodness to the citizens.

ALC. For how could that not be?

SO. And could anyone impart something one does not have?

ALC. And how could one?

SO. Then first you must gain goodness for yourself,
and for anyone else who intends to rule and take care of
oneself and one's belongings not in private only
but also a state and the business of the state.

ALC. You speak the truth.

SO. Then it is not power nor rule
that you must provide for yourself
to do what you want for you and the state,
but justice and discretion.

ALC. It appears so.

SO. For acting justly and sensibly
you and the state will be acting friendly to God.

ALC. It is likely.

SO. And as we said in the previous argument,
you will act looking into the divine and bright.

ALC. It appears so.

SO. But looking at this you will regard and know
both yourselves and your own good.

ALC. Yes.

SO. Then will you act correctly and well?

ALC. Yes.

SO. But acting thus
I am willing to pledge that you will be happy.

ALC. For you are an unfailing pledge.

SO. But acting unjustly,
looking into the godless and the dark,
then it is likely you will do acts similar to these
ignoring yourselves.

ALC. It is likely.

SO. For if, dear Alcibiades,
someone has the power to do what one wants,
but does not have intelligence,
what is likely to result,
for an individual or also for a state?
For example, being sick
and having the power to run where one wants,
not having medical intelligence,

but dictating so that no one would chastise one,
what would be the result?
Would not, as likely, the body be ruined?

ALC. You speak the truth.

SO. And what about in a ship,
if one had the power to do what one thought,
deprived of the intelligence and goodness of navigation,
do you see what would result for him and his shipmates?

ALC. I do, that they all would perish.

SO. Then in the same way in a state
and among all rulers and authorities lacking in goodness
does acting badly follow?

ALC. By necessity.

SO. Then dictatorship is not useful, best Alcibiades,
to be provided neither for oneself nor for the state,
if one intends to be happy, but goodness is.

ALC. You speak the truth.

SO. And until you have goodness,
it is better to be ruled by a better than for a man to rule,
not only for a child.

ALC. It appears so.

SO. Then the better is more beautiful?

ALC. Yes.

SO. And the more beautiful more fitting?

ALC. How could it not be?

SO. Then it is fitting for a bad person to serve;
for it is better.

ALC. Yes.

SO. Then vice fits the servile.

ALC. It appears so.

SO. And goodness fits the free.

ALC. Yes.

SO. Then is it useful to avoid, comrade, the servile?

ALC. Especially, Socrates.

30
SO. And now do you perceive how you are?
Fit to be free or not?

ALC. I seem to me also to be perceiving it very much.

SO. So do you know how you might escape
this state you are now in?
Let us not put this name on a beautiful man.

ALC. I do.

SO. How?

ALC. If you wish, Socrates.

SO. You don't speak beautifully, Alcibiades.

ALC. But what is useful to say?

SO. That if God wills.

ALC. I really mean it.
And yet beyond this I say that we shall be risking
exchanging characteristics, Socrates, I yours, and you mine;
for there is no way it cannot be
that I shall attend to you from this day on,
and you shall be attended by me.

SO. Noble one, then my love is not unlike a stork's,
if along with you having hatched a winged love
one is again served by this.

ALC. But it holds thus,
and I shall begin from here to take care of justice.

SO. I would like you also to continue;
but I am shuddering, not from any mistrust of your nature,
but from viewing the strength of the state,
lest it prevail over both me and you.

Defense of Socrates
by Plato

The trial of Socrates occurred in spring of the year 399 BC. He was judged by a jury of 501 Athenian men. In voting on the penalty they had to choose between the two punishments offered by the prosecution and the defendant. Little is known of his three accusers except that Anytus had been a general and recently active in overthrowing the oligarchy of the Thirty. Plato was a witness at the trial, though his account may have been written some time later by memory.

Notes to:

3: Aristophanes in 423 BC had satirized Socrates and his philosophizing in the comedy *The Clouds*, which is extant.

4: Gorgias, Prodicus, Hippias, and Evenus were professional teachers or "sophists" who accepted money from students and claimed that they could make them wiser. Callias was a wealthy man who liked to spend money entertaining sophists from abroad; however, he eventually exhausted his resources and died in poverty.

5: Chaerephon was well known to Athenians, having been satirized by Aristophanes as a bat and one of Socrates' barefoot brotherhood.

7: Socrates sometimes swore "by the dog" of Egypt, perhaps referring to Egyptian worship of the dog-star, Sirius, the brightest star in the night sky.

14: A *drachma* was a silver coin worth about a quarter.

16: In Homer's *Iliad* XVIII Achilles, the son of Thetis, prepared to kill Hector in order to avenge his friend Patroclus.

17: Socrates fought for Athens in the Pelopennesian War at Potidaea, Amphipolis and Delium.

17 and 32: Hades is the god over departed souls after death.

25: The number of votes condemning Socrates must have been 280 or less. If this is divided by three, the number of votes would have been less than one-fifth, causing the accuser to have to pay a fine of 1000 *drachmas*.

28: One *mina* was about one pound of silver and equal to one hundred *drachmas*.

1

How you, Athenian men, have been affected by my accusers,
I do not know;
but even I myself have almost forgotten myself,
so persuasively did they speak;
and yet they have spoken hardly anything of the truth.

But of the many lies they told
I was especially surprised by this one
in which they said you need to be on guard
so that you will not be deceived by me,
because I am a clever speaker.
For they ought to be ashamed
because this will be immediately refuted by me in fact,
when I do not show myself to be a clever speaker at all;
this seemed to me to be their most shameless statement,
unless they call those speakers clever who speak the truth;
for if they mean this, then I would agree,
not in their way, that I am an orator.

Thus they, as I say, have spoken little or no truth;
but you shall hear from me the whole truth.
Yet not by Zeus, Athenian men,
embellished meanings like theirs,
nor carefully arranged phrases and words,
but you will hear random meanings as the words occur;
for I believe that my plea is just,
and none of you should expect anything else.
For surely it is not fitting, men, for me at my age
to come before you like a youth making up words.

Yes, and sincerely, Athenian men,
I ask and request of you this:
if you hear me defending myself with the same words
that I am accustomed to saying
both in the marketplace and at the tables,
where many of you have heard me, and elsewhere,
do not be surprised nor interrupt on this account.

For the fact is, being seventy years old,
now is the first time I have come up before the court;
thus I am completely a stranger to the speech here.
Therefore as if I happened actually to be a stranger,

you would surely excuse me
if I spoke in that dialect and manner
in which I had been brought up,
and so now I ask you this,
a fair request as it seems to me,
that you disregard the manner of my speech—
for perhaps it might be worse, perhaps better—
but observe only this and consider this:
whether I say what is just or not;
for that is the virtue of the judge,
and the orator's is to say the truth.

2

First then it is right that I defend myself, Athenian men,
against the first false accusations against me
and the first accusers,
and then against those of the later ones.

For many accusers have come against me before you,
and long ago, for many years now, and saying nothing true;
I fear them more than those around Anytus,
although these also are dangerous;
but those are more dangerous, men,
who, educating many of you from childhood,
were persuading you and accusing me with no truth,
"There is a certain Socrates, a wise man,
who thinks about heavenly things
and examines everything under the earth
and makes the worse argument better."
These, Athenian men, who spread about this report
are my dangerous accusers.
For those hearing them believe
that such seekers do not acknowledge the gods.
Next these accusers are many
and have been making accusations for a long time already,
and furthermore saying them to you
at an age in which you would especially believe
(being children and some of you youths),
completely defaulted accusations, with no one defending.
Most unreasonable of all,
no one can know and speak their names,

unless he happens to be a comic poet.
 So many persuaded you using envy and slander—
also the same persuaded persuaded others—
all these are difficult;
for it is not possible to call them up here
nor to cross-examine any of them,
but of complete necessity
it is like fighting shadows in defense
and cross-examining with no one answering.
 You will consider then also, as I say,
that my accusers are of two kinds—
some who are just now accusing,
and others I say that are long ago,
and consider that I must first defend myself against those;
for you heard them accusing first,
and much more than these later ones.
 Well, now the defense, Athenian men,
and the attempt to remove from you the prejudice,
which you acquired over a long time,
I must do this in a short time.
Thus I wish that this would happen so,
if it is better for both you and me,
and that I might accomplish something more in my defense;
I know this is difficult,
and I am not at all deluded about its nature.
Yet may this go as it is pleasing to God,
and obeying the law I make my defense.

3
 Therefore let us take up from the beginning,
what the accusation is from which the prejudice has come,
in which Meletus also believed
in writing this indictment against me.
Well, what prejudice are the slanderers saying?
Therefore just as the charge of the accusers was,
theirs must be read:
"Socrates wrongs and meddles
by seeking the things under the earth and in the heavens
and making the worse argument better

and teaching others these things."
Such is what it is.

For you saw these also yourselves
in the comedy of Aristophanes,
a certain Socrates being carried about there,
claiming to walk on air and babbling much other nonsense,
about which I understand nothing, neither much nor little.
And not as one dishonoring such knowledge do I say this,
if anyone is wise about these things;
may I never have to flee from Meletus on these charges!

But the fact is, Athenian men,
I have nothing to do with these things.
I offer as witnesses most of yourselves,
and I ask you to teach and point out to each other,
those who have ever heard me discussing,
and there are many of you,
then point out to each other,
if ever, whether little or much,
some of you heard me discussing these things;
and from this you will understand
that such are also the other things that many say about me.

1
However, there is nothing in any of this,
nor if someone has heard that I attempt to teach people
and make money, neither is this true.
Even though this seems to me to be fine,
if someone could teach people
as do Gorgias of Leontini and Prodicus of Ceos
and Hippias of Elis.
For each of these, men, is able to go into each of the cities
to the young, who may for free
associate with whomever they wish among their citizens,—
these they persuade to abandon those associations
to associate with themselves, paying money and giving thanks.

Also another wise man is the Parian here,
whom I perceived to be in town;
for I happened to meet a man, Callias, the son of Hipponicus,
who has spent more money on sophists than all others,

So I asked him—for he has two sons—
"Callias," I said, "if your two sons were colts or calves,
we should be able to find and hire an overseer for them,
who would make them fine and good
in the appropriate virtue;
and this would be a horse-trainer or farmer.
But now since they are human,
who do you have in mind to find for them as overseer?
Who is skilled in this human and political virtue?
For I think you have looked, because you have two sons.
Is there someone?" I asked, "or not?"
    "Certainly," he said.
    "Who?" I asked, "and from where?
and for how much does he teach?"
    "Evenus," he said, "Socrates,
the Parian, for five minae."
    And I blessed Evenus,
if truly he has this art and teaches so reasonably.
Thus I myself too would be proud and conceited
if I had this skill;
however, I am not skilled, Athenian men.

5
    Therefore some of you perhaps might wonder,
"But Socrates, what is the matter with you?
From where have these slanders against you arisen?
For clearly not from your not doing anything unusual
does this fame and rumor arise,
if you do not do something other than the many?
Therefore tell us what it is,
so that we may not judge you hastily."
Those saying this seem right to me,
and I shall try to prove to you
what this is that has given me this name and slander.
    So listen.
And probably I will seem to some of you to be playing,
yet know well, I will tell you the whole truth.
For I, Athenian men, have acquired this name
on account of nothing other than a kind of wisdom.

What then is this wisdom?
Just that which is perhaps human wisdom.
For in reality I may be wise in this;
and these about whom I spoke just now
possibly may be wise
in something greater than human wisdom,
or I don't know what to say;
for I do not understand it,
and whoever says so lies and tells a slander against me.

And, Athenian men, do not interrupt me,
even if I seem to you to be boasting;
for the word I will speak is not mine,
but I refer you to the words of someone trustworthy.
For my wisdom and its nature, if it is wisdom,
I offer to you as a witness the god at Delphi.

For you surely know Chaerephon.
He was my friend from youth and a friend of your people,
and he fled with the exile and returned with you.
Also you know how Chaerephon was,
how impetuous in whatever he undertook.
And once he went to Delphi and dared to ask the oracle this:
(and, I say again, don't interrupt, men;)
for he asked if anyone was wiser than I.
Then the Pythian priestess answered that no one was wiser.
And since he has died,
his brother will testify about this to you.

6
Consider why I say these things;
for I intend to teach you how the slander against me arose.
For when I heard these things, I thought to myself:
"Whatever is the god saying, and what is the riddle?
For I myself am not aware of having any wisdom,
neither great nor little;
so whatever does it mean declaring me to be the wisest?
for clearly it does not lie, not this divine oracle."
And for a long time I was uncertain as to what it meant;
then very reluctantly I began to search somewhat as follows.

I went to one of those seeming to be wise,
because there, if anywhere, I should refute the divination
and show to the oracle, "This one is wiser than I,
but you said it was me."
So examining this one,—for I should not tell his name,
but he was one of the politicians in whose presence
I had this kind of experience, Athenian men,—
and discussing with him this man seemed to be wise
to many other people and especially to himself,
but it seemed to me not to be so;
and then I tried to show him
that he thought he was wise, but he was not.

  So as a result I was hated by him
and by many of those present;
and so going away I said to myself,
"I am wiser than this person;
for it is likely that neither of us
knows anything good and beautiful,
but he thinks he knows something not knowing,
while I, as one who does not know, do not think that I do.
Therefore I went away from him
being a little wiser in just this respect,
that what I do not know I do not think that I know."

  From there I went to another of those
who seemed to be wiser than he,
and to me these things seemed the same;
and there I was hated by that one and by many others.

7
  After this then I went to one after another
perceiving that I was hated and grieving and fearful,
yet it seemed to be necessary
to make the divine most important.
Thus I had to go, considering what the oracle means,
to all who seem to know.
And by the dog, Athenian men—
for it is necessary to tell you the truth—
amen, I experienced something like this:
the ones the most esteemed
seemed to me to be almost the most deficient,

in searching according to the god,
but others less esteemed
were more reasonable men in being sensible.
    I must describe to you
my wandering as some laboring labors
so that to me also the oracle might be proven irrefutable.
For after the politicians
I went to the poets of tragedies and songs and other things,
since I would find myself detected
as being less learned than they are.
So taking up their poems
which seemed to me especially perfected by them,
I asked them what they mean,
so that at the same time I might learn something from them.
    Thus I am ashamed to tell you, men, the truth;
but nevertheless it must be said.
For there was hardly anyone of all those present
who did not speak better on their very own compositions.
So again concerning the poets I soon became aware of this,
that what they wrote they wrote not by wisdom,
but by nature and being inspired
as are the seers and diviners;
for these also say many beautiful things,
but understand nothing of what they are saying;
such experience it appeared to me
the poets had also experienced.
At the same time I observed
that on account of their poetry they too
thought themselves in other things to be the wisest people,
which they were not.
Thus I went away also from there in the same way
thinking I surpassed them as well as the politicians.

8
    So finally I went to the artisans.
For I was aware of knowing nothing myself, so to speak,
but I knew that I might find them knowing many fine things.
And in this I was not deceived,
because they did know what I did not,
and in this they were wiser than I.

However, Athenian men, it seemed to me
that the workers also have the same fault as the poets;
on account of performing the skill well
each claimed also to be wise in other important matters,
and this false note of theirs obscured that wisdom,
so that I asked myself on behalf of the oracle,
whether I should choose to be just as I am,
neither wise in their wisdom nor ignorant in their ignorance,
or to have both of what they have.
Thus I replied to myself and the oracle
that it is better for me to be as I am.

9
Out of this examination, Athenian men,
arose against me many enmities which are harsh and severe,
so that many slanders came from them,
and this reputation of being wise is spoken.
For each time those present think I am wise
in these things in which I refute others;
but the fact is, men, in reality God is wise,
and in this oracle it is saying,
"Human wisdom is worth little or nothing."
Also this appears to say Socrates,
to use my name, making an example of me,
as if it were saying,
"This one of you, humans, is the wisest, who like Socrates
is aware that in truth his wisdom is worth nothing."
Therefore I am still even now going around
searching and inquiring according to the god,
of both citizens and strangers, who I think are wise;
and when one seems to me not so,
aiding the god I point out that they are not wise.
And because of this occupation
there is no leisure worth mentioning for me
to attend to the business of the city nor of the household,
but I am in extensive poverty on account of serving the god.

10
In addition to these things, the youth accompanying me,
who have much leisure, sons of the wealthiest,

delight in hearing people examined,
and they often imitate me, and proceed to examine others;
and then, I think, they find a great many people
who think they know something, but know little or nothing.
  So then those examined by them become angry at me,
instead of themselves, and they say,
"This is that damned Socrates who corrupts the youth."
And when someone asks them what he is doing and teaching,
they have nothing to say, but don't know,
but so that they may not seem to be confused,
they say things that are handy against all the philosophers,
"the things heavenly and below the earth"
and "not believing in gods"
and "making the worse argument better."
For the truth, I think, which they don't want to say,
is that it is being made clear
that they are claiming to know, but they know nothing.
  So, I think, being ambitious and stubborn and many
and speaking vehemently and persuasively about me,
they have filled your ears both formerly and now
with violent slanders.
Out of these Meletus attacked me, also Anytus and Lycon,
Meletus annoyed on behalf of the poets,
Anytus on behalf of the artisans and politicians,
and Lycon on behalf of the orators;
so that, as I said at first, I should be surprised
if I were able to remove this prejudice from you
in so short a time that has become so great.
  There you have the truth, Athenian men,
and concealing nothing large nor small,
I tell you without holding anything back.
And yet I know pretty well
that I am making myself hated by these same things;
and this is a sign that I say the truth
and this is the prejudice against me
and these are its causes.
And if you investigate this now or later,
you will find it so.

11

So concerning the accusations of my first accusers
against me, this is enough defense for you;
but against Meletus the good and patriotic, as he says,
and the later ones, I shall try to defend myself next.
Once more, as these are other accusers,
let us take up their affidavit.
It goes something like this:
It says that Socrates does wrong by corrupting the youth
and by not believing in the gods the state believes in,
but in other new gods.
  Such is the charge,
but let us examine each one of the charges.
He says that I do wrong by corrupting the youth.
But I, Athenian men, say that Meletus does wrong,
because in a serious matter he jokes
by frivolously bringing lawsuits against people,
claiming to be serious and concerned about these things
which he has never cared about.
That this is so I will also try to make clear to you.

12

  And tell me here, Meletus, is it not so
that you consider it important
how the youth are to be most improved?
  "I do."
  Come now, tell them who makes them better,
for clearly you know, since you care.
For you have found out who corrupts them, as you said,
you bring me before this court and accuse me;
now come tell who makes them better,
and inform these who it is.
Do you see, Meletus, that you are silent
and have nothing to say?
Yet does it not seem to you to be shameful
and a sufficient indication of what I say,
that you don't care at all?
But speak, good one, who makes them better?
  "The laws."

But this is not what I asked, excellent one,
but what person, who first knows even this thing, the laws.
"These, Socrates, the judges."
What are you saying, Meletus?
Are they able to educate the youth and make them better?
"Certainly."
Which, all? Or some of them and not others?
"All."
Well said, by Hera,
and you speak of a great abundance of helpers.
What about these?
Do the listeners make them better or not?
"These also."
And what about the senators?
"Also the senators."
But Meletus,
do the members of the assembly corrupt the youth?
Or do they also all make them better?
"They also."
So all Athenians, as it seems, make them fine and good,
except me, but I alone corrupt them.
Is this what you mean?
"I mean it very seriously."
You condemn me to great misfortune.
And answer me:
does it also seem to you to be thus concerning horses?
Are all people making them better,
but a certain one is corrupting them?
Or is it the opposite of this all,
a certain one who makes them better,
or very few, the horse-trainers;
but most if they deal with and use horses,
do they not injure them?
Is this not so, Meletus,
both concerning horses and all other animals?
Surely it is, whether you and Anytus say yes or no.
For what a great blessing it would be for the youth
if one alone corrupts them, while the others help them.

But Meletus, you demonstrate well enough
that you never consider the youth,
and you show clearly your carelessness,
that you have not cared at all about the things
on which you bring me into court.

13

Furthermore tell us, in the name of Zeus, Meletus,
which is better, to live among good citizens or bad ones?
My friend, answer; for I am not asking anything difficult.
Do not the bad work some evil always to those nearest them,
but the good some good?
"Certainly."
Then is there anyone who wishes to be harmed by associates
rather than be helped?
Answer, good one; for the law requires you to answer.
Is there anyone who wishes to be harmed?
"Of course not."
Then do you bring me here into court
for corrupting the youth and making them worse
intentionally or unintentionally?
"Intentionally, I say."
What then, Meletus?
Are you so much wiser at your age than I at my age,
that you have recognized that the evil work some evil
always to those nearest them, and the good some good;
while I have become so unlearned that I am ignorant of this,
that, if I make any of my associates wicked,
I am in danger of receiving something evil from one,
so that I do evil such as this intentionally, as you say?
I am not persuaded of these things by you, Meletus,
and I don't think any other person is either;
but either I do not corrupt,
or if I do corrupt, then unintentionally,
so that either way you are lying.
But if I corrupt unintentionally,
for such involuntary errors
the law is not to bring one into court here,
but to take one privately to teach and admonish him;

for clearly if I learn I will stop what I do unintentionally.
but you avoided associating with me and would not teach me,
and brought me here,
where the law is to bring those needing punishment,
not learning.

14
But now, Athenian men, this is clear what I said,
that Meletus never cared much nor little about these things.
Nevertheless tell us now how it is
you say I corrupt the youth, Meletus?
Or is it evident that,
according to the indictment which was written,
it is by teaching them not to believe in the gods
which the state believes in, but in other new divinities?
Do you not say that by teaching these things I corrupt them?
"Yes, I definitely say these things."
Well then, before these very gods, Meletus,
of whom we are now speaking,
explain even more clearly both to me and these men.
For I am unable to learn whether you mean
that I teach them to believe there are some gods,
and I myself then believe that there are some gods,
and I am not a complete atheist nor wronging in that way—
not those however of the state, but different,
and this is what you accuse me of, that they are different;
or whether you say I myself do not believe in the gods at all
and teach these things to others.
"I mean the latter,
that you do not believe in the gods at all."
You surprise me, Meletus; why do you say this?
Then do I not believe that the sun and moon are gods,
like other people do?
"No, by Zeus, he does not, judges,
since he says that the sun is a stone, and the moon earth."
Do you think you are accusing Anaxagoras, dear Meletus,
and do you so despise them and think they are unlettered,
that they do not know
that the books of Anaxagoras of Clazomenae

are full of these ideas?
And what is more, the youth learn these things from me,
which it is possible at times, if too much,
to buy for a *drachma* from the theatre, laughing at Socrates,
even if he claims they are his own,
especially since they are so absurd.
But before Zeus, does this seem to you
that I am not believing in any god?
  "No, by Zeus, none, not in the least."
  You are unbelievable, Meletus,
and even, as you seem to me, to yourself.
For he seems to me, Athenian men,
to be very insolent and reckless,
and actually to have written this indictment
out of some youthful insolence and recklessness.
For it is like composing a riddle for a test:
Will the wise Socrates understand my game
and my contradictory meaning,
or will I deceive him and the other listeners?
For this he says appears to me to be the opposite
of what is in his indictment,
as if he were saying,
Socrates is wrong not believing in gods,
but believing in gods.
And yet this is jesting.

15
  Consider then, men, what it appears to me he is saying,
and you answer us, Meletus;
and you people, as I asked you at the beginning,
remember not to interrupt me
if I make the argument in my accustomed manner.
Is there a person, Meletus,
who believes there are human things,
but does not believe there are people?
Let him answer, men,
and do not let him interrupt in one way or another.
Is there anyone who does not believe in horses,
but believes in the business of horsemen?
Or who does not believe there are flute-players,

but believes in the business of flute-players?
There is not, excellent man;
if you do not wish to answer,
I say it for you and these others.
But answer at least this:
Is there anyone who believes there are divine things,
but does not believe in divinities?

   "There is not."

   Thanks for answering reluctantly by compulsion of these.
Then you say I both believe in and teach divinities,
whether new or old;
but then I believe in divinities according to your meaning,
and you also swore this in your indictment.
But if I believe in divinities,
surely I must also believe in the divine.
Is this not so?
It is; for I assume you agree, since you do not answer.
But do we not think that
divinities are either gods or children of gods?
Do you say yes or no?

   "Certainly."

   Then if I believe in divinities, as you say,
if divinities are gods,
this would be the riddle and game I mention,
you are saying that not believing in gods
I believe in gods again, since I believe in divinities.
If on the other hand, divinities are bastard children
from nymphs or from any others, whoever they are said to be,
what person would think there are children of gods,
but not gods?

   For it would be just as absurd
as if one thought there are children of horses and asses,
namely mules, but did not think there are horses and asses.
But Meletus, surely you are testing us writing this charge
or else you doubt you could blame me with a real crime.
You cannot persuade any person
having even small intelligence
that it is possible for the same person
to believe in both divinities and deities

and at the same time not the divine nor gods nor heroes;
there is no way.

16

  But really, Athenian men,
as I am not wrong according to Meletus' charge,
it does not seem to me to be much defense,
but even these things are enough.
And what I said before,
how much hatred there is against me and from many people,
you well know what is the truth.
And this is what will convict me, if I am convicted,
not Meletus nor Anytus, but the prejudice and envy of many.
What has also convicted many other good men,
I know will convict again;
and there is no danger of it stopping with me.
  Then perhaps someone might say,
"Then are you not ashamed, Socrates,
of following such a pursuit
from which you are now in danger of being executed?"
  But to this I should make a just argument,
"You do not speak well, sir, if you think a man,
in whom there is even small merit,
must consider danger of life or death,
rather than looking at this alone,
whenever he acts, whether he does right or wrong
and the works of a good or evil man.
  "For in your argument
the demigods who died at Troy would be mean,
and especially the son of Thetis,
who so despised danger compared to undergoing disgrace,
that when his mother, being a goddess,
spoke to his eagerness to kill Hector,
something like this, I think,
'Child, if you avenge the death of your friend Patroclus
and kill Hector, you yourself shall die;
for at once,' she said, 'after Hector your fate is ready.'
  "But having heard this, he made little of death and danger,
but feared much more a cowardly life

which would not avenge his friends,

'At once,' he said, 'may I die,
after putting justice on the wrongdoer,
so that I may not remain here laughed at
by the curved ships, a burden on the land.'

Do you think he thought of death and danger?"

For there you have the truth, Athenian men;
wherever someone stations himself, believing it is best,
or stationed by his leader, he must be there,
as it seems to me, remaining without considering
either danger or death or anything else before disgrace.

17

Therefore I should have done a terrible thing,
Athenian men, if—
when the commanders stationed me,
whom you chose to command me,
both at Potidaea and at Amphipolis and also Delium,
I remained where they stationed me like anyone else,
even in danger of death,
and being stationed by the god, as I thought and understood,
I must live loving wisdom
and examining myself and others,—
I were to leave the station at this point
out of fear of either death or any other business whatsoever.

It would be terrible,
and truly then someone might justly bring me into court,
because I do not believe there are gods,
disobeying the oracle and afraid of death
and thinking myself wise when I am not.

For to be afraid of death, men,
is nothing other than seeming to be wise when one is not;
for it is seeming to know what one does not know.
For no one knows whether death
happens to be the greatest good of all for a person,
but it is feared as if one knows well
that it is the greatest of all evils.

And is this ignorance not the most reprehensible
which thinks one knows what one does not?
But I, men, on this point also perhaps

differ from most people in that,
even if I were to say that I am wiser, it would be in this,
that not knowing enough about Hades,
so also I do not think I know.

  But to wrong and disobey the best, both divine and human,
that I know is evil and shameful.
Thus before the evils which I know are evil
I shall never fear nor flee what I don't know
since it may happen to be good.

  So if you acquit me now, unconvinced by Anytus,
who said either I should not have been brought here at all
or, since I was brought, it was necessary to execute me,
saying before you that, if I were acquitted
your sons will all be completely corrupted
by pursuing what Socrates teaches—
if you were to say to me in addition,
"Socrates, now we are not convinced by Anytus,
but acquit you, on this condition however that you no longer
in this way seek to discuss nor philosophize;
and if you are caught doing this again, you shall die."

  Then if, as I said,
you were to acquit me on this condition,
I should say to you, "Athenian men, I respect and love you,
but I shall obey the god rather than you,
and while I breathe and am able, I shall not stop
philosophizing and urging you and demonstrating
whenever I happen to meet you, saying as I am accustomed,
'Best of men, being an Athenian of the greatest city
and famous for wisdom and power,
are you not ashamed caring for money,
how it is for you the most important,
and reputation and honor,
but you do not care and think about intelligence and truth
and the soul, how it is the best?'

  "And if any of you objects and says he does care,
I shall not let him go at once, nor shall I go away,
but I shall question and examine and test him,
and if it seems to me that he does not possess virtue,
but only appears to, I shall reproach him

for making the things most worthy of importance least,
and the worst things most important.

"I shall do these things to both the young and old,
whenever I happen to meet them,
and to stranger and citizen, but especially the citizens,
as you are more nearly related to me.
For know well God commands these things,
and I think that no greater good has ever come to the city
than my service to the god.
For I go around doing nothing else than persuading you
both young and old not to care about the body nor money
more seriously than for the soul, how it is most virtuous,
saying, 'Virtue does not come from money,
but from virtue money and every other good thing
for people both individually and collectively.'

"Thus if saying these things I corrupt the youth,
these things would be harmful;
but if someone says that I mean anything other than this,
it has no meaning.
In reference to this, I would say, Athenians,
either be convinced by Anytus or not,
and acquit or not acquit,
but I will not do anything else,
not even if I have to die many times."

18
  Do not interrupt, Athenian men,
but hold to what I requested of you,
not to interrupt what I say, but listen;
for surely I think you will benefit by listening.
For I intend now to say some other things to you,
at which you will perhaps cry out;
but by no means do this.

  For know well, if you kill me, I being what I say,
you will not do greater harm to me than to yourselves;
for neither Meletus nor Anytus will harm me; they cannot;
for I do not think that it is divine will
for a better man to be harmed by a worse.
He might kill however or perhaps banish or disenfranchise;

but by these things perhaps he and some others
might think somehow this is a great evil,
but I don't think so,
rather a much greater one is what he is doing now,
attempting to put a man to death unjustly.

So now, Athenian men, more than on my own behalf
must I defend myself, as some may think, but on your behalf,
so that you may not make a mistake
concerning the gift of god by condemning me.
For if you kill me,
you will not easily find another such person at all,
even if to say in a ludicrous way,
attached on the city by the god,
like on a large and well-bred horse, by its size and laziness
both needing arousing by some gadfly;
in this way the god seems to have fastened me on the city,
some such one who arousing and persuading
and reproaching each one of you
I do not stop the whole day settling down all over.

Thus such another will not easily come to you, men,
but if you believe me, you will spare me;
but perhaps you might possibly be offended,
like the sleeping who are awakened,
striking me, believing Anytus, you might easily kill,
then the rest of your lives you might continue sleeping,
unless the god caring for you should send you another.

That I happen to be such
who is given by the god to the city,
you may understand from this:
for it does not seem human
that I have neglected all my own affairs
and enduring this neglect of family for years,
but always attending to yours,
coming privately to each one like a father or older brother,
persuading you to care about virtue.

And if I enjoyed something from these things
and received pay for urging them,
it might make some sense;
but now you surely see that even these, the accusers,

though accusing everything so shamelessly,
have not become so shameless as to produce a witness
that I ever either required or requested pay of anyone.
For I think I present an adequate witness,
as to the truth I say, my poverty.

19

Perhaps then it may seem absurd that
I privately go around advising these things and meddling,
but publicly do not dare
to stand up in your assembly to advise the state.
But the reason for this
which you have heard me say many times and in many places
is that some godly and spiritual thing comes to me, a voice,
which also Meletus ridiculed in the indictment he wrote;
and this is some voice that began coming to me in childhood,
which when it comes always turns me away
from what I am intending to do, but never leads me on;
this is what opposes my practicing politics.
And it seems to me to oppose quite beautifully;
for know well, Athenian men,
if I had undertaken to practice political business,
I should have perished long ago
and would not have benefited you nor myself.
And don't be offended at the truth I am saying;
for the fact is that any person whatsoever to be safe
can neither honestly oppose you nor another assembly
nor prevent many injustices and illegalities in the state,
but it is necessary in really fighting for justice,
if one intends to be safe for even a short time,
to be private, rather than public.

20

I will present for you important evidence of this,
not words, but what you honor, actions.
Listen to what has happened to me,
so that you may know that I would not yield to anyone
contrary to justice from fear of death,
but not yielding I would rather perish.

I will tell you things commonplace and legalistic, but true.
  For I, Athenians,
never held any other office in the state, but senator;
and it occurred that my Antiochis tribe presided
when you wished to try together the ten generals
who had not taken up the slain from the naval battle,
illegally as it seemed to you all afterwards.
At that time I alone of those presiding opposed
doing anything contrary to the laws and voted against it,
and the speakers being ready to indict and arrest me,
and you demanding it and shouting,
with the law and justice I thought I must run the risk
rather than follow after you in not considering justice,
fearing imprisonment or death.

  And that was when the state was still democratic;
but when it became an oligarchy, the Thirty in turn
sending for me among five in the rotunda
directed us to bring from Salamis Leon the Salaminian
so that he could be executed.
And they directed many others often so
wishing to implicate as many as possible in their guilt;
however at that time I again not by word but by action
demonstrated that I do not care about death,
if it is not too crude to say, none whatsoever,
but all my care was to do neither the unjust nor the unholy.
For that government did not intimidate me,
as powerful as it was, into doing something unjust,
but when I went out of the rotunda,
the four went to Salamis and brought Leon,
but I went quietly home.
And perhaps I should have died for this,
if the government had not been quickly overthrown;
and many will be witnesses of these things for you.

21
  Then do you think that I would still be alive,
if I had done public business
and acting worthy of a good man aided what was just
and, as one should, made this most important?
Far from it, Athenian men; neither could any other person.

But during all my life even in public, if I did something,
such will appear also the same in private,
never did I yield anything contrary to justice
neither to another nor to any of those
whom the ones slandering me say are my students.

I never became anyone's teacher;
but if someone wants to hear me talking
and practicing my own things,
whether young or old, I have never objected to anyone,
nor do I converse for receiving money, but not receiving it,
and to rich and poor alike I offer my inquiry,
and if someone wishes to answer he may hear what I say.
and whether some of these become good or not,
I should not rightly bear the blame,
since I neither promised anything
nor ever gave anyone any instruction;
but if someone says that he ever learned or heard something
from me in private which all the others also did not,
know well that he is not telling the truth.

22
But why then do some like spending much time with me?
You have heard it, Athenian men;
I told you the whole truth,
that they like hearing the examination
of those who think they are wise, but are not;
for this is not unamusing.
But as I say, I have been directed to do this
by the god and from oracles and from dreams
and every way in which divine will ever directed
any person to do anything whatsoever.
This, Athenians, is both true and easily tested.

For if I do corrupt the young and have corrupted them,
certainly some of those grown older
if they are aware that I ever advised them badly,
now they ought to stand up to accuse me and be avenged;
or if they are not willing, then let some of their families,
fathers and brothers and other relatives,
now let the families of those remember and avenge
if they suffered any evil from me.

Surely many of them are present here whom I see,
first Crito here who is of my age and district
and father of Critobulus there;
then there is Lysanias the Sphettian,
father of Aeschines there;
still here is Antiphon of Cephisus, father of Epigenes;
now here are others whose brothers were involved in this,
Nicostratus, son of Theozotides, brother of Theodotus,—
though Theodotus has died,
so that he at least could not dissuade him,—
and Paralus, son of Demodocus, whose brother was Theages;
and Adeimantus, son of Aristo, whose brother Plato is here,
and Aeantodorus whose brother Apollodorus is present.
And I have many others to mention to you,
some of whom it would have been especially fitting
for Meletus to produce as witnesses in his argument;
and if he forgot then, let him call them now;
I yield, and let him speak, if he has anything to offer.
  But you will find the complete opposite of this, men,—
all are ready to help me the corrupter,
who works evil against their families,
as Meletus and Anytus say.
Yet these corrupted may possibly have reason for helping;
but the uncorrupted, already older men, their relatives,
what other reason do they have for helping me
other than right and justice,
unless they are aware that Meletus is lying,
while I am telling the truth?

23
  Well then, men, this and perhaps other such things
is nearly all that I would have to say in my defense.
Possibly some of you may be irritated
when he recalls his own,
if he even in a lesser case contesting a trial
asked and entreated the judges with many tears,
bringing up his children especially to arouse pity,
and other relatives and many friends,
but I will do none of this,
even though I seem to be in the ultimate danger of dangers.

So possibly some of the more self-willed
considering these things might hold them against me,
and upset about this might cast his vote in anger.
Now if this applies to any of you,—
though I don't claim it does; but if so,—
I think it would be reasonable for me to say to him,
"I too, excellent sir, have relatives,
for it is even the same as in Homer,
I am not 'born of oak nor of stone,' but from humans,
so that I also have relatives and, Athenian men,
three sons, one already a youth and two children;
but nevertheless I shall not bring any of them up here
to beg you to acquit me."
  Why should I not do so?
Not out of self-will, Athenian men,
nor out of disrespect for you,
but whether I have confidence in facing death or not
is another matter,
but I think both in regard to me and you and the whole state
it does not seem to me to be beautiful
for me to do any of these things at my age
and having this reputation, whether it is true or false;
nevertheless it is believed
Socrates is somehow different from most people.
  So if those of you who are supposed to be different,
whether in wisdom or courage or any other virtue,
did this it would be disgraceful;
I have often seen some of these when on trial,
who are thought to be someone,
acting strangely, as though they were thinking
they would suffer something terrible if they died,
as if they would be immortal if you did not kill them;
it seems to me they wrap the state in shame,
so that even any stranger might suppose
that those of the Athenians excelling in virtue,
whom they themselves prefer in government and other honors,
are no different than women.

For these things, Athenian men, should not be done
by those thought to be anything,
and if we do them, you should not permit it,
but make it clear that you will much more likely condemn
the one who brings in these pitiful dramas
and makes the city ridiculous
than the one who keeps quiet.

24
  But apart from appearance, men,
it does not seem right to me
to implore the judge nor to be acquitted by begging,
but to teach and persuade.
For the judge is not appointed for this purpose,
to grant favors of justice,
but to decide these things;
and he takes an oath not to favor those who appeal to this,
but to judge according to the laws.
Therefore we should not become accustomed
nor should you get into the habit of perjuring yourselves;
for neither of us would be acting piously.
  So do not require me, Athenian men,
to do such things before you,
which I consider are neither beautiful nor just nor holy,
especially by Zeus
since impiety is the charge brought by Meletus.
For clearly, if I could persuade you
and by pleading get you to break your oaths,
I would be teaching you not to consider the gods,
and in my very defense I would be accusing myself
of not believing in the gods.
  But this is far from so;
for I believe in them, Athenian men,
more than any of my accusers,
and I commit to you and to God
to decide my case however it will be best for me and for you.

25
  I am not upset, Athenian men,
at this vote that you have cast against me,

but many things contributed to it,
and it is not unexpected that this happened to me,
but I am much more surprised
by the number of votes on each side.
I did not think it would be by so little, but by much more;
but now it seems if thirty of the votes were changed,
I would have been acquitted.
So as I suppose my case, I have even now escaped Meletus,
and not only been acquitted, but it is clear to everyone,
that if Anytus and Lycon had not come forward to accuse me,
he would have been fined a thousand *drachmas*
for not receiving a fifth part of the votes.

26
  So the man proposes my death.
Well, what alternative shall I propose to you, Athenian men?
Clearly should it not be what is deserved?
What then? What do I deserve to suffer or pay,
because having learned in life I did not keep quiet,
but did not care about what most do,
money-making and property and the military
and public speaking and various offices and associations
and factions that occur in the state,
believing myself to be too reasonable
to be involved in these and be safe,
I did not go into those which would not have been a help,
neither to you nor to me,
but to each individual where the greatest good could be done,
as I say, I went into that,
trying to persuade each of you
not to care for anything of your own
before you care about yourself so as to be best and wisest,
nor of the state's interests before the state itself,
and so of others to care about them in the same way.
What then is such a one as I deserving of suffering?
  Some good, Athenian men,
if it must be proposed in truth according to deserving;
and this good thing should be what is appropriate for me.
What then is fitting for a poor man who is your benefactor,
in need of having leisure so that he can advise you?

There is nothing, Athenian men, so fitting
as providing food for such a man in the presidents' hall,
much more than if any of you
with a horse or pair of horses or a chariot won the Olympics.
For he makes you seem happy, but I to be so;
and he has no need of support, but I need it.
Thus if it must be proposed according to my just deserving,
I propose this, food in the presidents' hall.

27

  Perhaps then to you saying this also in the same way
I seem to be, as with the pity and the pleading, self-willed.
But it is not so, Athenians, but rather the following:
I am convinced I never willingly wronged any person,
but I did not convince you of this;
for we have conversed with each other for a short time;
yet, as I believe, if you had a law, even as other people do,
not to judge about death in only one day, but in many,
you would be convinced;
but now in a short time
it is not easy to be released from great prejudices.
  Really convinced that I never wronged anyone
I certainly will not wrong myself and say of my very self,
that I am deserving of bad,
and propose any such thing for myself.
What should I fear?
Is it this experience which Meletus proposes for me,
which I admit not knowing whether it is good or bad?
  Instead of this should I choose what I know well is bad,
proposing that? imprisonment?
And why should I live in prison,
always a slave to the appointed officers of the eleven?
Or a fine, and to be imprisoned until I can pay?
but to me that means the same as what I just said;
for I do not have money from which I will be able to pay.
  But then shall I propose exile?
Perhaps you will propose this for me.
However I would have much attachment to life,
if I am so irrational as not to be able to reason

that while you my fellow citizens
who could not bear my pursuits and arguments,
but they were too heavy and envy-arousing for you,
so that now you are seeking to be relieved from them;
but then would others bear the same easily?
Far from it, Athenians.
  So a fine life that would be for me
going out at my age of life
exchanging cities and being driven out from one to another!
For know well that wherever I go,
the young will listen to my talking, as they do here;
even if I drive them away,
they themselves persuading the older ones will drive me out;
but if I do not drive them away,
their fathers and relatives will for their sakes.

28
  Perhaps then someone might say,
"Socrates, are you not able to go out from us
being silent and keeping quiet?"
This is really the hardest thing for some of you to believe.
For if I say that this is disobeying the god
and because of this I am unable to keep quiet,
you will not believe me as one jesting;
and if I say that this also happens to be
the greatest good for humanity
to make arguments every day about virtue
and examine myself and others,
the unexamined life not being livable for a person,—
saying these things you would believe me even less.
Thus it is as I say, men, but to persuade you is not easy.
  Besides I am not used to myself deserving anything bad.
If I had money,
I would propose to pay as much money as I could;
for that would be no harm;
but now—for I have none,
unless you wish to propose such as I am able to pay.
Perhaps I might be able to pay you a *mina* of silver;
so I propose that.
But Plato here, Athenian men, and Crito and Critobulus

and Apollodorus bid me propose thirty *minae*,
and they will be security;
so I propose that,
and security for your silver will be those trustworthy men.

29
  On account of not much time, Athenian men,
have you gained a name and blame
by those wishing to revile the city
saying, "You killed Socrates, a wise man;"
for those wishing to reproach you will say I am really wise,
even if I am not.
So if you had waited a short time,
this would have occurred for you by itself;
for you see my age
that is already far along in life and near death.
  But I say this not to all of you,
but to those who voted for my death.
And to those I say something else also.
Perhaps you think, men,
that I am convicted for lack of such arguments,
which would have convinced you,
if I had thought it was necessary
to do and say anything in order to be acquitted.
Far from it.
  Yet I was convicted through a lack, but not of arguments,
but of impudence and shamelessness
and unwillingness to say such things to you,
which you would have liked to hear,
my wailing and moaning
and doing and saying many other things
that are also unworthy of me, as I say;
and such things you are in the habit of hearing from others.
But I did not think at the time that it was necessary
on account of the danger to do anything illiberal,
nor do I now regret the defense that was made,
but I much more prefer to die after making this defense
than to live after the other kind;
for neither in justice nor in war should I nor anyone else
contrive how to escape death by every means.

For truly in battles often it is clear
that one could escape from dying
by both abandoning weapons
and turning in supplication of the pursuers;
and there are many other contrivances
in each of these dangers in order to escape death,
if one has audacity to do and say anything.

However, this is not what is hard, men, escaping death,
but it is much harder to escape cowardice;
for it runs faster than death.
And now since I am slow and old I am caught by the slower,
but my accusers since they are clever and quick
by the faster, the bad.
And now I go away sentenced by you to death,
and they convicted by truth of wickedness and injustice.
And I abide by the penalty, even as they do.
Perhaps things had to be this way,
and I think it is fair.

30
So now after this I want to prophesy to you,
the ones who voted against me.
For I am now at the place in which people often prophesy,
when about to die.
For I say to you, men who are killing me,
punishment will come to you immediately after my death
harder by Zeus than your killing of me;
for now you did this thinking
to be relieved of giving an account of your life,
but the result will be quite contrary for you, as I say.

There will be more examining you, whom now I restrained,
though you did not realize it;
and they will be harder since they are younger,
and you will be more irritated.
For if you think killing people
will prevent someone from reproaching you
because you do not search correctly,
you do not reason correctly.
For this relief is not very effective nor beautiful,
but that both most beautiful and easiest,

is not to suppress others,
but to prepare yourself so as to be the best possible.
Thus prophesying these things to you who voted against,
I take my leave.

31
  But to those voting for
I would like to talk about this event which has occurred,
while the officials are busy
and before I go where it is necessary for me to die.
But remain with me, men, for so long;
for nothing prevents us from discussing with each other
as long as it is possible;
for to you who are friends I wish to make clear
what is the meaning of what has now happened to me.
  For to me, judges,—
for calling you judges is calling you correctly,—
a wonderful thing has occurred.
For the accustomed prophecy, the divinity,
which formerly came to me very frequently,
even about small things,
was always opposing, if I intended to do something incorrect;
but now has come upon me, as you yourselves see,
what some might think and believe to be the extreme evil,
but when I left home the sign of the god did not oppose,
nor when I came up here to court,
nor ever in my speech when I was about to say something;
and yet in other speeches
it often checked me in the middle of talking;
but now concerning this event
it has never opposed me neither in any action nor in speech.
  What then do I suppose to be the reason?
I will tell you;
for this occurrence may very likely be good for me,
and it is that we who think death is evil
do not understand it correctly.
A great proof of this has come to me;
for surely the usual sign would have opposed me,
unless what I intended to do was good.

32

Let us also consider the following:
how much hope there is that it is good.
For death is one of two things;
either the dead have no being nor perception nor anything,
or according to what is said some change of being happens
and a transmigration of the soul from here to another place.

And if it is no perception,
but a sleep when one sleeps without seeing any dreams,
then death would be a wonderful gain.
For I think if one had to pick out that night
in which one slept without seeing any dream,
and comparing this night
to the other nights and days of one's life
and considering it had to say
how many days and nights one had lived in one's life
better and more pleasantly than that night,
I think that not only a private person,
but even the great king would find these nights few
in comparison to the other days and nights.
So if death is such, I say it is a gain;
for then all of time thus appears to be
really no more than one night.

But if death is to leave here for another place,
and what is said is true that all the dead are there,
what greater good could there be, judges?
For if one arriving in Hades,
having left those claiming to be judges,
will find the true judges, who are said to judge there,
Minos and Rhadamanthus and Aeacus and Triptolemus
and others of the demigods who were just in their lives,
would the departure then be lousy?

What would any of you give to associate with Orpheus
and Musaeus and Hesiod and Homer?
For I am willing to die many times if these things are true;
since to me this life there would be wonderful,
when I might meet Palamedes and Ajax the son of Telamon,
or any other of the ancients who died
on account of an unjust judgment.

Comparing my experiences with theirs,
I think, would not be unpleasant.
And really the greatest would be in examining those there,
as I spend my time here,
and discovering who is wise and who thinks he is, but is not.
How much would one give, judges, to examine those
who led the great army against Troy or Odysseus or Sisyphus,
or countless others both men and women
whom I might mention?
To discuss and associate with and examine those there
would be infinite happiness!
At any event certainly they do not kill there for this;
For besides they are happier there than here,
and they are already immortal for the rest of time,
if what is said is true.

33
But you too, judges, must be hopeful facing death,
and consider this one truth,
that there is no evil for a good man
neither in living nor dying,
and his affairs are not neglected by the gods;
nor are mine now occurring automatically,
but this is clear to me, that it is better
for me to die now and be released from troubles.
Because of this also the sign never turned me away,
and I am not at all angry at my condemners and accusers.
Yet this was not the reason they accused and condemned me,
but thinking to harm; in this they deserve to be blamed.
However, I ask this of them:
when my sons grow up punish them, men,
by bothering them on these things as I bothered you,
if it seems to you they care about money or anything else
more than about virtue,
or if they seem to be something they are not,
reproach them as I have you,
because they do not care about what they should,
and think they are something when they are worth nothing.
And if you do these things,
I will have experienced justice from you,

both myself and my sons.

But now it is already time to go away,
I to die, and you to live;
but which of us goes to a better situation,
is unclear to all except to God.

Crito
by Plato

This dialog is set in the Athenian prison between the trial and execution of Socrates. Crito was a close friend of Socrates. According to Diogenes Laertius, he made sure that none of the needs of Socrates were left unsupplied. His sons, Critobulus, Hermogenes, Epigenes, and Ctesippus, were frequent listeners of Socrates.

Notes to:

1: The ship from Delos is explained in *Phaedo* 1.
2: The quote is from Homer's *Iliad* IX, 363.
17: Corybantes were attendants of the great Mother Goddess in a mystic cult with wild dances, which claimed to heal mental disorders.

1
SOCRATES. Why did you come at this time, Crito?
Or isn't it still early?
CRITO. It certainly is.
SOCRATES. About what time?
CRITO. Dawn is breaking.
SOCRATES. I am surprised that the prison guard
was willing to let you in.
CRITO. He is used to me already, Socrates,
on account of coming so often,
and in addition I have done something good for him.
SOCRATES. And have you just come or long ago?
CRITO. Fairly long ago.
SOCRATES. Then why did you not wake me immediately,
instead of sitting by in silence?
CRITO. No, no, by Zeus, Socrates,
I only wish I myself were not so sleepless and depressed.
But I have been marveling at you for a long time
perceiving how pleasantly you sleep;

and I did not wake you on purpose,
so that you could continue so pleasantly.
Both often and before in all your life
you have had a happy disposition,
and especially now in your present misfortune,
you bear it so easily and mildly.

SOCRATES. Surely, Crito, it would be a mistake at my age
to resent it if I must die now.

CRITO. Others, Socrates, at your age
are caught in such misfortunes,
but age does not prevent them from resenting their fate.

SOCRATES. That is true.
But why did you come so early?

CRITO. To bring a message, Socrates—
not hard for you, as it appears to me,
but to me and all your companions both hard and heavy,
which I suppose I might bear the heaviest.

SOCRATES. What is it?
Has the ship arrived from Delos,
upon whose arrival I must die?

CRITO. It hasn't arrived yet,
but it seems to me it will come today
from reports of some who came from Sunium and left it there.
So it is clear from these reports that it will come today,
and by force tomorrow, Socrates,
will be the end of your life.

2
SOCRATES. But good luck, Crito.
If this is the will of the gods, so be it.
Yet I don't think it will come today.

CRITO. What makes you think so?

SOCRATES. I will tell you.
For I must die on the day after the ship comes in.

CRITO. That is what the authorities say.

SOCRATES. Then I don't think it will come today,
but tomorrow.
I infer this from a dream

I had a little while ago during the night;
and it chanced opportunely that you did not wake me.
CRITO. What was the dream?
SOCRATES. It seemed a beautiful and good-looking woman
clothed in white, came to me,
called me and said, "Socrates,
   'On the third day you will come to fertile Phthia.'"
CRITO. A strange dream, Socrates.
SOCRATES. No, rather a plain one,
as it seems to me, Crito.

3
CRITO. Very plain, apparently.
But, dear Socrates, even now
you can still be persuaded by me and be saved;
since for me, if you die, it is not one misfortune,
but apart from losing such a companion
that I could never find anywhere,
besides it will seem to many,
who do not know me and you closely,
that I could have saved you,
if I had been willing to spend the money, but neglected to.
Yet what reputation could be more shameful than this—
to seem to make money more important than friends?
For many will not believe that while we were eager,
you yourself were not willing to escape from here.
SOCRATES. But why should you, blessed Crito,
care about what the many think?
For the most reasonable, who are more worth considering,
will think these things were done as they actually were.
CRITO. But you see that it is necessary, Socrates,
to care about the opinion of the many.
These present circumstances make it clear
that those who are many are able to accomplish
not only the smallest evil but also nearly the greatest,
if they are prejudiced against someone.
SOCRATES. If only, Crito, the many were able
to accomplish the greatest evil,
so that they would also be able to do the greatest good,

and that would be beautiful;
but now they do neither one;
for they are able to make one neither wise nor unwise,
but they do whatever happens by chance.

4
CRITO. That may be so.
But Socrates, tell me this:
are you not thinking about me and the other companions,
if you escaped from here,
the informers would cause trouble for us
for having stolen you away from here,
and we would be forced either
to lose all our property or much money
or to suffer something else in addition?
For if this is what you fear, be glad;
for it is right for us to risk this danger in saving you
and if necessary even greater than this.
But obey me and don't do otherwise.
SOCRATES. I am considering this, Crito,
and many other things.
CRITO. Then don't be afraid of this;
for surely it is not much silver,
which some would take to save you and get out of here.
Then don't you see how the informers are easily bought
and not much silver is needed for them?
My money is at your command,—which I think is enough;
and if out of some concern for me
you think mine should not be spent,
strangers here are ready to spend theirs;
and one of them has provided for this purpose enough silver,
Simmias the Theban;
and ready also is Cebes and many others.
   So, as I say, not fearing these things
do not hesitate to save yourself,
and don't you be disagreeable about what you said in court,
that if you went away
you would not know what to do with yourself.
For in many other places wherever you go they will love you;

and if you wish to go to Thessaly,
for my sake there are strangers there
who will make much of you and offer you safety
so that no one in Thessaly will bother you.

5

  Besides, Socrates, you do not seem right to me
to attempt this, giving yourself up, when you might be saved;
and you are striving to bring such things upon yourself
as also your enemies strive for
and have hastened wishing to destroy you.
  Furthermore you seem to me
to be abandoning your children,
whom you might both bring up and educate
you will depart leaving them behind,
and as far as you are concerned,
whatever chances, this they will do;
and chances are they will probably be such things
as usually occur to orphans in their destitution.
  For one either should not have children,
or should continue on in the raising and educating;
but you seem to me to choose the laziest way;
but, as a good and courageous man would choose,
you should choose these things,
having said all through your life
that you really care about virtue;
so I am ashamed both for you and for us, your companions,
lest it seem the whole affair concerning you
has been conducted in cowardice on our part,
both the bringing in of the case into court,
as it might not have been brought in as it was brought in,
and the trial of this case as it occurred,
and then this end as though a mockery of the affair
will seem to have escaped us by our baseness and cowardice,
who did not save you nor did you yourself,
which was possible, even if our help was small.
  Therefore, Socrates, see that these things
be not both bad and shameful for you and for us.
But decide, rather there is no time still to decide,

but only to have decided.
And there is one decision;
for everything must be done this coming night.
And if we delay, it can no longer be done.
But by all means, Socrates, obey me
and don't do anything else at all.

6
SOCRATES. Dear Crito, your eagerness is worth much,
if it should prove to be correct;
but if not, the greater it is, the harder.
Therefore we must look at whether I should do this or not;
since I not only now but always have been such a one
who obeys the logic which upon reasoning appears to me best.
   And the arguments which I argued before
cannot now be rejected,
since this has chanced to happen to me,
but they appear nearly the same to me,
and I rank first and honor the same ones as before;
and unless we have better arguments in the present,
know well that I shall not yield to you,
not even if the current power of the present multitude
could frighten us like children,
threatening imprisonment and death
and confiscation of money.
   So how could we look at this most reasonably?
Whether we should first take up this argument,
which you argue about opinions,
whether it was argued correctly each time or not,
that intelligence must hold to some opinions, and not others;
or was it correct before I was condemned to die,
but now it has become clear
that it was argued merely for the sake of argument,
but it was in truth play and nonsense?
   But, Crito, I am eager to examine together with you,
whether it appears something else to me, since I am here,
or the same,
and whether we should say goodby to it or obey it.
And it was argued, as I think each time,

by those thinking to argue something,
as I was just now saying,
that of the opinions which people believe
some ought to be made much of, and others not.
  Before the gods, Crito,
does this not seem to you to be argued correctly?
For you who are outside the human probability
of being about to die tomorrow,
and you not being swayed by the present misfortune:
consider then,
does it not seem to be sufficiently argued to you,
that not all the opinions of people should be honored,
but some and not others?
What do you say?
Is this not argued correctly?
CRITO. Correctly.
SOCRATES. Then should not the good ones be honored,
and not the bad ones?
CRITO. Yes.
SOCRATES. And are not the good those of the wise,
and the bad those of the unwise?
CRITO. Of course.

7
SOCRATES. Well then, how were such things argued?
Does the athletic man practicing this pay attention
to the praise and blame and opinion of every man,
or to that of only one
who happens to be a physician or trainer?
CRITO. Only the one.
SOCRATES. Then one should not be afraid of the blame,
and should esteem the praise of that one,
but not that of the many.
CRITO. Clearly.
SOCRATES. So practicing and training
and eating and drinking in this way which is
in accord with the one with knowledge and understanding
is better than that of everyone else.

CRITO. That is so.

SOCRATES. Well. But disobeying the one
and dishonoring his opinion and praises,
while honoring the arguments of the many
who have no understanding, will one not suffer harm?

CRITO. Of course.

SOCRATES. And what is this harm
and where does it extend
and into what part of the disobedient?

CRITO. Clearly into the body. For it ruins it.

SOCRATES. You argue correctly.
Then is this other also not so, Crito,
so that we do not go through them all,
furthermore concerning justice and injustice
and shame and honor and good and evil,
about which we are now deliberating,
should we obey the opinion of the many and be afraid of it,
or that of the one, if it is someone of understanding,
who should be respected and feared more than all the others?
If we do not follow that one,
we shall injure and ruin
that which is made better by justice,
and which is destroyed by injustice.
Or is this nothing?

CRITO. I believe it, Socrates.

8

SOCRATES. Come now, if what
by health becomes improved and by disease is ruined
is destroyed by obeying the opinion of those not aware,
is it still livable for us when it is ruined?
And this is the body, is it not?

CRITO. Yes.

SOCRATES. So then is the body livable for us
after it is bad and ruined?

CRITO. Certainly not.

SOCRATES. But is it livable for us after that is ruined
which is maltreated by wrong and benefited by justice?

Or do we think that that, whatever it is of ours,
which is concerned with wrong or justice,
is less important than the body?
CRITO. Certainly not.
SOCRATES. But more important?
CRITO. Much more.
SOCRATES. So, best one, we must not consider at all
what the many will say to us,
but what the aware, the one,
will say about justice and wrong, and truth itself.
So at first you brought this in incorrectly,
introducing the opinion of the many
as necessary for us to consider
concerning justice and beauty
and goodness and the opposites.
But really, some might say, the many can kill us.
CRITO. That is also clear, for it would be said, Socrates.
SOCRATES. You say the truth.
But, admirable one, this argument which we discussed
seems to me still the same as it was before;
and now see if it still holds for us or not,
that it is not living that is best, but living well.
CRITO. Yet it holds.
SOCRATES. And that this well
and beautifully and justly are the same thing
holds or does it not hold?
CRITO. It holds.

9
SOCRATES. Then out of this agreement we must look at
whether it is right for me to try to escape from here
without permission of the Athenians,
or whether it is not right;
and if it appears to be right, let us try,
but if not, let us dismiss it.
But what you say are considerations
about spending money and opinion and supporting children,
these in truth, Crito, are speculations of those many
who easily kill and would bring to life again,

if they could, with no intelligence.

But since the argument so compels,
we must consider no other than what we just now discussed,
whether we shall act justly in paying money and thanking
these here who will let me escape,
both the ones escaping and the ones escaped from,
or in truth shall we be wrong in doing all these things;
and if we appear wrong in these actions,
it may be necessary not to debate
whether it is necessary staying here and keeping quiet to die
but whether to suffer anything whatsoever before wronging.
CRITO. To me you seem to speak beautifully, Socrates;
but let's see what we should do.
SOCRATES. Let us look, good friend, together,
and if you can contradict anything I am saying,
contradict it, and I will obey you;
but if not, stop already, blessed one,
saying often to me the same argument,
that I should escape from here
without permission of the Athenians;
since I value doing these things with your approval,
but not unwillingly.
Now see if the beginning of the investigation
is sufficiently reasonable for you,
and try to answer the questioning to the best of your belief.
CRITO. I will try.

10
SOCRATES. Are we saying that
in no way are we to wrong intentionally,
or are we to wrong in some way, but not in others?
Or is it never good nor beautiful to wrong,
as we have agreed often at an earlier time?

As I also just said;
or are all those earlier agreements of ours
in these few days to be thrown out and past, Crito,
so as old men discussing seriously with each other
has it eluded us that we are not different than children?

Or above all is it as we said at that time,
whether the many say so or not,
and whether we must still suffer harder things than these
or even gentler ones,
nevertheless is not injustice both bad and shameful
to the wrong-doer in whatever way it happens?
Did we say this or not?

CRITO. We said it.

SOCRATES. Then we must never wrong.

CRITO. Of course not.

SOCRATES. Nor retaliate against wrong,
as the many think, since we must never wrong.

CRITO. Apparently not.

SOCRATES. But what? Must one do evil or not?

CRITO. Doubtless one must not, Socrates.

SOCRATES. But what? Doing evil actions against the evil,
as the many say, is just or not just?

CRITO. Never.

SOCRATES. For doing evil to people is
no different than wronging.

CRITO. You say the truth.

SOCRATES. Then one must not retaliate
nor do evil to any person,
no matter what one may suffer from them.
And see, Crito, that in conceding these things
you do not agree in a way contrary to your opinion.
For I know that these things are held
and will be held by few.
Thus those who believe this and those who don't,
on this there is no common decision,
but by force of this condemn each other,
seeing each others' decisions.

Therefore look very carefully
at whether you agree with this opinion
and let us begin with the decision here,
that it is never correct to wrong or retaliate
or suffering evil to avenge by returning evil;
or do you stand aside and not agree from the beginning?

For it seems to me thus both before and still now;
but if to you it seems anything else,
say it and teach.
But if you are holding to it as before,
listen to the next point.
CRITO. But I am holding to it and agree with you;
but say it.
SOCRATES. Then the next thing I am saying,
but rather asking is:
should someone do what he has agreed is just or deceive?
CRITO. He should do it.

11
SOCRATES. So consider what comes out of this.
By our escaping from here, not obeying the state,
are we doing evil to anyone,
and to those whom we must least of all or not?
and are we holding to what we agreed was just or not?
CRITO. I have no reply, Socrates, to the question,
for I don't understand.
SOCRATES. But look at it this way.
If we were about to run away from here,
or whatever one should name this,
the laws and the community might come and ask:
"Tell me, Socrates, what have you in mind to do?
Is this another action you are attempting to plan
to destroy our laws and the entire state
as far as you are concerned?
Or does it seem to you
that the state may exist and not be overturned,
in which court rulings have no strength,
but by private people they are made ineffective and ruined?"
  What shall we say, Crito, to this and other such things?
For one might have much to say, especially an orator,
on behalf of this destroyed law,
which directs that court judgments be effective.
Or shall we say to them,
"The state wronged us and did not judge the case correctly"?
Shall we say these things or what?

CRITO. These things by Zeus, Socrates.

12
SOCRATES. What then, if the laws should say,
"Socrates, and was this agreed to by you and us,
or was it to abide by the verdicts which the state judges?"
So if I were surprised by what they were saying,
perhaps they might say, "Socrates,
don't be surprised by what is said, but answer,
since also you are in the habit
of using questioning and answering.
Come on, what fault do you find with us and the state
that you are attempting to destroy us?
First did we not give you birth
and was it not through our security
your mother and father conceived you?
So tell those of us, the laws concerning marriage,
what do you complain is not well?"
  "I do not complain," I would say.
  "But what about those concerning nurturing and education,
in which you also were educated?
Or was it not well directed by us, the appointed laws,
instructing your father
to educate you in music and gymnastics?"
  "Well," I would say.
  "Fine. And when born and raised and educated,
would you have to say first
that you were not both our offspring and slave,
yourself and your ancestors?
And if this is so,
then do you think justice is equal for you and for us,
and whatever we may attempt to do to you,
do you think it is just for you to do this back?
Justice was not equal for you toward your father
and toward your master, if you happened to have one,
so that whatever was suffered, this also might be done back,
nor hearing bad things to talk back
nor being struck to strike back
nor many other such things;

and toward your country and the laws will it be so for you,
so that if we attempt to destroy you thinking it is just,
you also will attempt to destroy us laws and the country
as much as possible,
and will you say doing this is acting justly,
the one who in truth cares about virtue?

"Or is your wisdom such that you do not see
that more than mother and father and all other ancestors
the country is honorable and revered and holy
and in greater esteem both among the gods
and among humans who have intelligence,
also she must be revered and more yielded to and humored
when the country is angry than when the father is,
and either persuade or do what she may order,
and suffer whatever she directs be suffered,
keeping quiet, and if beaten or imprisoned
or brought to war to be wounded or killed,
these are to be done,
and justice is like this,
and not yielding nor retreating nor leaving the post,
not only in war and in court but everywhere
one must do what the state and the country may order,
or persuade her what is natural justice,
but to be violent is neither holy to mother nor father,
and even much less to one's country?"

What shall we say to this, Crito?
Are the laws telling the truth or not?
CRITO. It seems so to me.

13
SOCRATES. "Look now, Socrates,"
perhaps the laws would say, "if what we say is true,
what you are now attempting to do to us is not just.
For we gave you birth, nurtured, educated you,
giving a share of everything which is beautiful
to you and all the other citizens,
yet proclaiming permission to any Athenian wishing to do it,
when one has become a citizen
and seen the business in the state and our laws,
if we do not please,

one is allowed to take one's things
and go away wherever one wishes.
And none of our laws stand in the way nor forbid it,
if any of you wishes to go into a colony,
if we and the state do not please you,
or move your home elsewhere,
whoever wishes may go to those places keeping his things.

   "But those of you who remain,
having seen the way we judge cases
and administer other things of the state,
then we say have agreed with us in action
to what we order them to do,
and the one not obeying we say wrongs in three ways,
because of not obeying us who gave birth,
and because of those who nurtured,
and because of having agreed with us to obey
one neither obeyed nor persuaded us,
if we were not doing what is beautiful,—
also we are not proposing harsh commands
to do what we order,
but while we are offering two alternatives,
either persuade us or do it,
one does neither of these.

14

   "We say that you, Socrates,
will be liable for these responsibilities,
if you do what you have in mind,
and you not least of the Athenians, but especially."

   Then if I should say, "Why so?"
Perhaps they might justly reproach me saying,
because among the Athenians I especially
happened to have acknowledged this agreement.

   For they would say, "Socrates, we have great evidence
that we and the state pleased you;
for more than all other Athenians
you would not have particularly stayed at home in her,
if you were not particularly pleased,
and you did not go out of the state for a festival,

except once to the isthmus,
nor anywhere else, if not on military service,
nor did you make another journey anywhere like other people,
nor did you want to know other states nor other laws,
but we and our state were adequate for you;
so strongly did you prefer us and agree with our politics
that you even produced children in her,
so pleased were you with the state.

"Furthermore in this trial
you might have proposed the sentence of exile, if you wished,
and what now you are attempting against the state's will,
at that time you might have done with its permission.
But then you were proud not being upset if you must die,
but preferred, as you said, death before exile;
and now you are not ashamed of those words,
nor do you respect us laws, attempting to ruin us,
you are acting as the meanest slave would act,
attempting to run away contrary to contracts and agreements,
which you contracted with us as a citizen.

"So first reply to this,
whether we are telling the truth saying
you agreed to be a citizen according to us by action,
but not by word, or is it not true?"

What shall we say to this, Crito?
But should we not agree?

CRITO. By necessity, Socrates.

SOCRATES. "Are you not then," they would say,
"breaking these contracts and agreements with us,
not agreed to by necessity nor deception
nor forced to decide in a short time, but in seventy years,
in which you could have gone away,
if we did not please you
and the agreements did not appear to you to be just?
But you preferred neither Lacedaemon nor Crete,
which each time you say have good laws,
nor any other of the Greek states nor of the foreigners,
but you went abroad from her
less than the lame and blind and other handicapped;
so much more than other Athenians

were you pleased with the state and us the laws—is clear;
for who would be pleased with a state without its laws?
And now are you not holding to the agreements?
If you are persuaded by us, Socrates;
and you will not be ridiculous out of the state in exile.

15
   "For look, by transgressing in this
and making these mistakes,
what good are you doing for yourself or for your companions?
For that your companions themselves risk both exile
and being deprived of citizenship or loss of property,
is pretty clear;
and first if you yourself go to some nearby state,
either Thebes or Megara,—for both have good laws,—
you will go as an enemy, Socrates, to these states,
and those who care for their state, will look down on you
thinking you are a corrupter of the laws,
and you will confirm for the judges the opinion
so that they will correctly think the verdict was just;
for whoever is a corrupter of the laws,
might seriously be thought to be
a corrupter of the young and thoughtless people.
   "Then will you avoid the states with good laws
and the most civilized men?
And doing this then will life be worthwhile for you?
Or will you approach them and be unashamed of discussing—
what arguments, Socrates?
Or what you did here,
that virtue and justice are most valuable for people,
and institutions and laws?
And don't you think that Socrates' business
would appear unseemly?
One ought to think so.
   "However you will depart from these places,
and go into Thessaly along with Crito's visitors;
for there disorder and licentiousness are greatest,
and perhaps they would enjoy hearing with laughter
of your running away from prison, dressed in some disguise,
or wearing a skin or other things

in which runaways usually dress up,
and altering your appearance;
but that an old man, probably with a short time left in life,
dared so to want life shamelessly, broke the greatest laws,
will no one say it?
Perhaps, if you don't bother anyone;
but if not, Socrates,
you will hear many things unworthy of yourself.
You will live as inferior to all people and as a slave;
what will you be doing feasting in Thessaly,
as though you journeyed to Thessaly for a banquet?
And where are those arguments of ours
concerning justice and the other virtues?
   "However you may wish to live
for the sake of the children,
so that you may raise and educate them?
But what?
Bringing them into Thessaly will you raise and educate them,
making them strangers, so that they may enjoy even this?
Or maybe not this, but if they are raised during your life
will they be better raised and educated,
your not being with them?
for your companions will take care of them.
If you journey to Thessaly will they take care,
but if you journey to Hades will they not take care?
If really someone is a help
their claiming to be your companions,
one should think so.

16
   "But, Socrates, be persuaded by us who raised you,
do not make children more important
nor life nor anything else before justice,
so that going to Hades you may have all these things
to argue in your defense to those ruling there;
for it does not appear by doing these things
to be better for you here nor more just nor more holy,
nor for any of the others
nor will it be better when you arrive there.

"But now you go away wronged, if you do go away,
not by us the laws but by people;
and if you escape so shamefully
retaliating and returning bad actions,
breaking your agreements and contracts with us,
and acting bad to those whom you least should do so,—
yourself and friends and country and us,—
we shall be angry with you while you live,
and there our brothers, the laws in Hades,
will not receive you kindly,
knowing that you attempted to destroy us,
as far as you could.
But do not let Crito persuade you to do what he says
rather than what we say."

17
  My dear friend Crito, know well
that this is what I seem to hear,
as the Corybantes seem to hear the flutes,
and in myself the sound of these arguments rings,
and it makes it impossible to hear any others;
but know, as it seems now to me,
if you would argue against these, you will speak in vain.
Yet if you think you might accomplish anything, say it.
CRITO. But, Socrates, I have nothing to say.
SOCRATES. Let it be now, Crito,
and let us act this way,
since God leads this way.

PHAEDO
by Plato

Though Plato himself was apparently ill and not present at the prison on the day of Socrates' death, the discussion was surely recounted to him, perhaps much in the same way as this dialog is recounted by Phaedo for Echecrates.

Phaedo was from a noble family in Elis; but when that city was defeated in 401 BC, he was captured and forced into a house of prostitution. However, Phaedo managed to slip out to listen to Socrates, who eventually persuaded either Cebes or Alcibiades or Crito and their friends to ransom him so that he could be free and study philosophy. Echecrates was a Pythagorean.

Notes to:

5: Philolaus was a Pythagorean, who wrote a book on nature which probably later influenced Plato's cosmology.

34: Penelope was the wife of Odysseus. While waiting for her husband to return from the Trojan War, she promised to marry one of her suitors after she completed the shroud she was weaving for her father-in-law; each night she would undo what she had woven during the day.

43: Quote is from Homer's *Odyssey* XX: 17-18.

44: Cadmus was the founder of Thebes, thus representing here a Theban.

57: Telephus, a son of Heracles, gave the Greeks directions how to reach Troy.

58: The pillars of Heracles refer to the Strait of Gibraltar at the western end of the Mediterranean Sea, and the Phasis River was at the east end of the Black Sea, considered the boundary between Europe and Asia.

60: Quote is from Homer's *Iliad* VIII: 14.

60-62: Tartarus is the Greek name for purgatory where souls are punished after death.

66: Asclepius was a legendary physician who became a god of healing.

1

ECHECRATES. Were you, Phaedo, present with Socrates
on that day in which he drank the drug in prison,
or did you hear about it from someone else?

PHAEDO. Myself, Echecrates.

ECHECRATES. So what did he say before his death?
and how did he die?
For I would like to hear.
And none of the Phliasian citizens visit Athens at all now,
nor has any stranger come from there for a long time,
who could report anything definite to us about what occurred,
except that drinking the drug he died;
and nothing else has been told.

PHAEDO. Did you not even learn about the trial
and the way it went?

ECHECRATES. Yes, this someone reported to us,
and we were surprised because it occurring long before
it appeared he died much later.
So why was that, Phaedo?

PHAEDO. It was by a coincidence, Echecrates;
for it chanced on the day before the trial
the stern of the ship was crowned
which the Athenians send to Delos.

ECHECRATES. And what is this?

PHAEDO. This is the ship, as the Athenians say,
in which Theseus once sailed to Crete with those two sevens
and struggling he saved them and saved himself.
Thus they had vowed to Apollo, as it is said, at that time,
if they were saved, each year to send a mission to Delos;
so always even now out of that vow to the god
they still send it annually.
Thus when the mission begins,
it is a law for them during this time to purify the state
and no one may be publicly executed,
until the ship has gone to Delos and come back;
and sometimes it takes a long time,
when winds happen to delay them.
The beginning of the mission is
when the priest of Apollo crowns the stern of the ship;

but this chanced, as I say, on the day before the trial.
And because of this a long time passed
with Socrates in prison between the trial and his death.

2
ECHECRATES. What was his death like, Phaedo?
What was said and done,
and which of the man's companions were present?
Or did the authorities not allow them to be present,
and did he die without his friends?

PHAEDO. Not at all, but some were present, even many.

ECHECRATES. I am eager for you to relate all these things
to us as precisely as possible,
if you don't happen to be busy.

PHAEDO. But I am at leisure
and will attempt to narrate for you;
for truly to be reminded of Socrates
both speaking myself and hearing another
to me is always the greatest pleasure of all.

ECHECRATES. But Phaedo, you also
will have other such listeners;
but try to recount everything as accurately as possible.

PHAEDO. I really felt strange being with him.
For while being present at the death of my companion
I did not feel pity;
for the man appeared happy to me, Echecrates,
both in manner and words,
since he was dying fearlessly and nobly,
so that it came over me that he was not going to Hades
without there being divine providence,
and that arriving there he would do well,
if ever anyone would.

Because of this I felt no pity at all,
as might seem normal being present in mourning;
nor was the enjoyment
because we were involved in philosophy,
as we usually are; and there were such arguments;
but an extremely strange and unusual feeling came over me
mixed from the combining together of pleasure and grief,

in pondering that he was about to die.

And all those present were nearly so affected,
sometimes laughing and sometimes weeping,
and one of us particularly, Apollodorus;
for you know the man and his manner.

ECHECRATES. Of course.

PHAEDO. Now he was completely upset,
as I was myself and the others.

ECHECRATES. But who happened to be present, Phaedo?

PHAEDO. From the area was present this Apollodorus
and Critobulus and his father, and Hermogenes
and Epigenes and Aeschines and Antisthenes;
and there was also Ctesippus the Paeanian
and Menexenus and some others from the area;
but Plato, I think, was ill.

ECHECRATES. But were any foreigners present?

PHAEDO. Yes, Simmias the Theban and Cebes
and Phaedondes, and from Megara Eucleides and Terpsion.

ECHECRATES. But what?
Were Aristippus and Cleombrotus there?

PHAEDO. No; for they were said to be in Aegina.

ECHECRATES. And was there anyone else?

PHAEDO. I think these were about all there were.

ECHECRATES. So what now?
What would you say were the arguments?

3
PHAEDO. I'll try to narrate everything to you
from the beginning.
For always on the previous days I and the others
were quite accustomed to being with Socrates,
meeting at dawn in the courtroom,
in which the trial also took place;
for it was near the prison.
So we waited around each time until the prison was opened,
conversing with each other; for it was not opened early;
and when it did open, we went in to Socrates
and spent most of the day with him.

And further on that day we met together earlier.
For the day before,
when we went out of the prison in the evening
we learned that the ship from Delos had arrived.
So we passed the word along
to come as early as possible in the morning.
   And we came,
and the jailer who was accustomed to answering the door,
coming out told us to wait around
and not go in until he ordered it;
"For the eleven," he said, "are releasing Socrates
and passing the word how he is to die today."
And so after not much delay he came and ordered us to go in.
   Then coming in we found Socrates just released
and Xanthippe—for you know her—
holding her son and sitting alongside.
Then as Xanthippe saw us,
she cried out and said such things, which women usually do,
"Oh Socrates, now is the last time
your companions will speak to you and you to them."
   And Socrates looked at Crito, "Crito," he said,
"let someone take her home."
And some of Crito's people
took her away crying and mourning;
but Socrates sitting up on the bed
bent his leg and rubbed it with his hand,
and while rubbing he said, "How odd, men,
seems to be this thing, which people call pleasure;
how wonderfully is it related
to what seems to be the opposite, pain,
in that they will not come to a person at the same time,
but if someone pursues the one and gets it,
he usually is forced to get the other also,
as though out of one head the two are joined.
   "And it seems to me," he said,
"if Aesop had thought of it,
he would have composed a fable,
how God wishing to reconcile their warring,
when he could not, fastened their heads together,

and because of this when the one comes
later the other follows also.
Thus it seems just the same to me,
since the pain was in my leg from the chain,
pleasure appears to have come following it."

4

   Then Cebes interrupted, "By Zeus, Socrates," he said,
"it's good you reminded me.
For concerning the poems which you composed,
putting the words of Aesop into verse
and the hymn to Apollo,
and some others already asked me,
also Evenus the day before yesterday,
why ever did you think when you came here
to make poems when you never had before.
So if you care that I have an answer for Evenus,
when he asks me again, for I know well that he will ask,
tell me what I should say."

   "Now tell him, Cebes," he said, "the truth,
that I do not wish to compete with him
nor his poetry in composing them;
for I knew that would not be easy;
but I was checking out what the meaning is of some dreams,
and making sure lest their frequent commands
were for me to make music.
For they were something like this:
often the same dream came to me throughout my life,
appearing in one form or another, but saying the same things,
'Socrates,' it said, 'make music and work at it.'

   "And I on previous occasions interpreted it
as urging and encouraging me with what I was doing,
just as those cheering for runners,
and so the dream was encouraging me
with what I was doing, making music,
since philosophy is the greatest of the muses,
and I was practicing this;
but now since the trial occurred
and while the festival of the god delayed my execution,
it seemed to warn,

if often the dream commands me to make this popular music,
then I should not disobey it, but do it.
For it is safer not to depart before making sure
I was composing poetry, obeying the dream.

   "So first I composed to the god,
whose festival was being celebrated;
and after the god, I thought that a poet should,
if he intends to be a poet, compose myths, but not arguments,
and since I was not a storyteller,
because of this I took stories which were handy,
and knowing Aesop's, I composed them,
which I chanced on first.

5
   "So, Cebes, tell Evenus this, and to take care and,
if he is wise, to pursue me as quickly as possible.
But I depart, as it seems, today;
for the Athenians order it."
   And Simmias said, "What a thing to urge Evenus, Socrates!
For I have met the man many times;
so from what I have seen of him
he will not hardly at all be willing to obey you."
   "But why?" he said; "is not Evenus a philosopher?"
   "He seems so to me," said Simmias.
   "Then he will be willing, both Evenus
and all who are worthy of having a part in this business.
Yet perhaps he will not commit suicide;
for they say it is not divine will."
And as he was saying these things
he put his feet on the ground,
and sat thus during the rest of the conversation.
   Then Cebes asked him, "Why do you say this, Socrates,
that it is not divine will to commit suicide,
but the philosopher is willing to follow the dying?"
   "But what, Cebes? have you and Simmias
not heard about this associating with Philolaus?"
   "Nothing distinctly, Socrates."
   "But even I speak about this from hearsay;
so what I happen to have heard,

I have no objection to saying.
And indeed perhaps it is especially fitting
being about to depart to there
to examine and tell stories about the departure to there,
and what kind of place we think it is;
for what else could one do
in the time until the setting of the sun?"

6
   "So why ever do they say
it is not divine will to kill oneself, Socrates?
For I already heard Philolaus also say what you now said,
when he was staying with us, and also from some others,
how one must not do this;
but I have never heard anything definite about this."
   "But you must be ready," said he;
"for possibly you might also hear.
Perhaps however it will appear strange to you,
if this alone of all the others is absolute
and it never happens to mankind, as in other things,
when it is better to die than to live;
and to whom it is better to die,
perhaps it appears strange to you,
if for these people it is not holy for them
to do what is good for themselves,
but they must wait around for the good work of another."
   And Cebes smiling gently said, "Zeus knows,"
talking in his own dialect.
   "And indeed it seems," said Socrates,
"thus to be unreasonable;
nevertheless perhaps it has some meaning.
So what is said in secret about this matter,
that as humans we are in a kind of prison
and should not release ourselves out of this nor run away,
appears to me something great and not easy to understand;
nevertheless it seems to me, Cebes, to be well argued,
the gods are taking care of us
and we humans are possessions of the gods;
or does it not seem so to you?"

"Yes, to me," said Cebes.

"Then," said he, "and you
if one of your possessions should kill itself,
your not having indicating that you wished it to die,
would you be angry with it,
and if you could have it punished, would you punish it?"

"Certainly," said he.

"Then perhaps this is not unreasonable,
that one must not kill oneself,
until the god sends upon one some necessity,
just as even now it has come upon me."

7

"But this," said Cebes, "appears probable.
Yet what you just now said,
that philosophers easily are willing to die,
this seems, Socrates, absurd
if what you just now said is reasonable,
that God is taking care of us and we are its possessions.
For the wisest, not to be troubled departing from this care,
in which the gods who are the best of the overseers
watch over them, is not reasonable.
For this one does not think
one will be better taken care of having become free;
but an unaware person possibly might think this,
that it is better to flee from the master,
and one would not consider
that it is not necessary to flee from the good,
but rather to remain,
because one would flee unreasonably,
but the one with awareness would want always
to be with one better than oneself.
And yet, Socrates, this is probably contrary
to what was just now said;
for then it is fitting
for the wise to be troubled by dying, and the unwise glad."

So having heard,
Socrates seemed to me to be pleased at Cebes' efforts,
and looking at us he said,

"Always Cebes is searching for some arguments,
and he is not immediately willing to be persuaded
by whatever anyone says."

And Simmias said, "But Socrates, now it seems to me
there is something in what Cebes is saying;
for why should men wishing to be truly wise
flee better masters and easily release themselves from them?
and it seems to me Cebes is directing the argument at you,
because you are so easily ready to leave
both us and the gods, who are good rulers,
as you yourself agree."

"You have a right to say it," he said.
"For I think you mean that I should defend this,
as though in court."

"Certainly," said Simmias.

8

"Then," he said, "I shall try to defend myself
more persuasively to you than I did to the judges.
For if I, Simmias and Cebes," he said, "did not think
I will go first to other wise and good gods,
and secondly to people who have died, better than those here,
I should be wrong in not being troubled by death;
but now know well that I hope to come to good men;
and this I certainly would not insist upon;
yet the coming to the gods who are certainly good masters,
know well that, more than any other of these things,
I would affirm this.
So because of this similarly I am not troubled,
but I am in good hope
that something exists for those who have died and,
as has been said long ago,
it is much better for the good than for the evil."

"What then, Socrates?" said Simmias.
"Having yourself this understanding in mind
do you have to depart, or would you share it with us?
For it seems to me this good belongs in common to us also,
and it is a defense for you at the same time,
if you persuade us by what you say."

"But I shall try," he said.
"And first we shall consider Crito,
what it is he has been wishing to say,
it seems to me, for a long time."

"Only, Socrates," said Crito, "that for a long time
the one who is to give you the drug has been saying to me
that I should tell you to converse as little as possible,
for he says conversing especially heats one up,
and one must not interfere in this way with the drug
or else it is sometimes necessary for those who do this
to drink it a second or third time."

And Socrates said, "Forget it;
just let him be prepared to give it twice
or if it is necessary three times."

"But I knew almost what you would say," said Crito;
"but he has been giving me the business for some time."

"Forget it," he said.
"But now I wish to explain to you judges
the reason why it appears to me
a man who has in reality spent his life in philosophy
will naturally be confident when about to die
and has good hopes of obtaining great good there,
when one has died;
thus how this would be so, Simmias and Cebes,
is what I shall try to indicate.

9
"For those who happen to grasp philosophy correctly
risk being unrecognized by others,
because it is nothing else
but practicing how to die and be dead.
So if this is true,
it surely would be absurd
to want during all of life nothing but this,
and when it comes, to be troubled by it,
which for a long time they were wanting and practicing."

And Simmias laughed; "By Zeus, Socrates," he said,
"now I am certainly not in a laughing mood,
but you made me laugh.

For I think if the many heard this
it would seem well said about philosophers
and it would appear so to our people also,
that in reality philosophers are for death
and they are not unrecognized,
because they deserve to suffer this."

"And they would be saying the truth, Simmias,
except that they are unrecognized.
For they do not recognize in what way the truest philosophers
are for death and deserve death and what kind of death.
For let us talk," he said, "among ourselves,
forgetting about them.
Do we think death is something?"

"Certainly," replied Simmias.

"Then is it not the release of the soul from the body?
And this is death,
the body being released apart from the soul by itself,
and the soul apart is released from the body by itself?
Then is death anything else but this?"

"No, but it is this," he said.

"Now see, good sir, then if it seems to you as it does to me.
For out of this especially I think
we move into what we are considering.
Does it appear to you the philosophical man
is concerned about the so-called pleasures,
such as eating and drinking?"

"Least of all, Socrates," said Simmias.

"But what? the pleasures of love?"

"By no means."

"But what? Does it seem to you such a person
thinks highly of other cares of the body?
such possessions as special clothes
and sandals and other adornments of the body,
does it seem to you one overrates them or underrates them,
according to how necessary it is to partake of them?"

"One seems to me to underrate them," he said,
"the one who is truly a philosopher."

"Then altogether it seems to you," he said,
"such a person is not concerned

with the business of the body,
but as far as possible would withdraw from the body
and turn toward the soul?"

"Yes, to me."

"So then first in such things it is clear
the philosopher especially releases the soul
from the communion of the body,
differing from other people?"

"It appears so."

"And surely it seems, Simmias, to many people,
that such a one who takes no pleasure in these
does not deserve to live,
but one is tending near to dying
who is not thinking of the pleasures of the body."

"What you say is very true."

10
"And what about the acquiring of wisdom itself?
Is the body a hindrance or not,
if it would go along itself in the common search?
What I mean is this:
then do sight and hearing have any truth,
or are such things as the poets are always repeating to us,
that we neither hear nor see anything accurately?
And yet if these senses of the body
are not accurate nor precise,
the others are idle; for all of these are inferior;
does it not seem so to you?"

"Certainly," he said.

"Then when does the soul attain the truth?
For when it attempts to look at something with the body,
it is clear that at that time it is deceived by it."

"You say the truth."

"So then in reasoning, if in no other way,
something of the realities becomes evident?"

"Yes."

"But it reasons best at that time
when none of these things trouble it,

neither hearing nor sight nor pain nor any pleasure,
but especially when it of itself says goodby to the body
and as far as it can does not commune nor connect with it
to reach out to reality."

"That is so."

"Thus in this also the soul of the philosopher
especially underrates the body and flees from it,
and seeks to become it of itself?"

"It appears so."

"And now what about such things, Simmias?
Do we say there is such a thing as justice or not?"

"Yet we say so, by Zeus."

"And beauty and goodness?"

"Of course."

"Then have you ever seen
any of these things with your eyes?"

"By no means."

"But did you reach them with any of the bodily senses?
And I am talking about all of them,
such as greatness, health, strength,
and in a word all of the other realities,
what each one happens to be;
so is their truest essence contemplated by the body,
or does one have the way who especially prepares oneself
to understand most accurately
each thing which one considers,
thus coming nearest to knowing each?"

"Certainly."

"So then would he do this most purely,
who comes especially with the intuition itself to each,
not comparing sight in the intuition
nor dragging in any of the other senses with the reasoning,
but it of itself using unmixed the intuition attempting
to contemplate each unmixed it of itself of the realities,
being removed especially from the eyes and ears
and so to speak all of the body,
as confusing and not allowing the soul
to attain truth and wisdom, when joined;

then is this one not, Simmias, if anyone is,
the one ready for reality?"
   "Extraordinary," said Simmias,
"is the truth you say, Socrates."

11
   "Then," he said, "out of all this
it seems that the noble philosophers must come to such terms
so that even to talk to each other about such things,
that just as likely there is some path to carry us out,
with the argument which is being considered,
that, as long as we have a body
and our soul is caught up with such evil,
we shall never attain sufficiently what we want;
and we say this is the truth.
   "For the body constantly keeps us busy
by the need for food;
and if diseases fall upon it,
they hinder our search of reality.
And it fills us with many of the passions and desires
and fears and fantasies of all kinds and nonsense
so that it is said in truthful reality
because of it being inborn in us one can never think at all.
   "For wars and factions and battles
are caused by nothing other than the body and its desires.
For all wars occur because of the gaining of money,
and we need to gain money because of the body,
slaving in its service;
and out of this we bring no leisure to philosophy
because of all these things.
   "And worst of all is that
even if some leisure away from it comes to us
and we turn to considering something,
in this seeking it causes trouble to get in the way
and disturbance and distraction,
so that because of it one is unable to observe the truth,
but in reality it has been shown to us
that if we are ever to know anything clearly,
one must be released from it

and observe these same actualities with the soul itself;
and at that time for us there will likely be
what we want and say we are lovers of, wisdom,
when we are dead, as the argument indicates, but not in life.

"For if with the body one cannot have clear knowledge,
there are two alternatives,
either knowledge is not to be attained at all or having died;
for at that time the soul will be it of itself
apart from the body, but not before.

"And if we live in it thus
then it is likely we shall be nearest to knowledge,
especially if we are not in company nor joined with the body,
which is not necessarily all the time,
and are not filled by its nature,
but keep ourselves clear of it,
until God itself releases us;
and thus the clear ones released from the folly of the body,
in all probability, we shall be with these
and shall know by ourselves all that is unmixed;
and this perhaps is the truth.

"For the one not pure is not promised purity,
it not being divine will.
I think such things, Simmias,
are necessary to say to each other
and it seems to all who correctly love learning.
Or does it not seem so to you?"

"Most certainly, Socrates."

12
"Then," said Socrates, "if this is true, my friend,
there is much hope in arriving where I am going,
that there, if anywhere, this will be fully attained
for the sake of which much of the business
in the passing of our life has occurred,
so that the journey now is imposed on me with good hope
and for other men,
who think the intuition is prepared as purified."

"Certainly," said Simmias.

"And is this purification then not corresponding,
as was said long ago in the argument,
to the separating especially of the soul from the body
and the habit of bringing together and collecting
it of itself everywhere out of the body,
and to dwell as far as possible in the now present
and in it alone by itself,
released out of the body as though out of chains?"

"Certainly," he said.

"Then is this not named death,
the soul released and apart from the body?"

"Absolutely."

"But to release it, as we say,
the correct philosophers alone are also always most eager,
and is the exercise of the philosopher this same thing,
release and separation of the soul from the body, or not?"

"It appears so."

"Then, as I said in the beginning,
it would be ridiculous if a man prepared himself in a life
which is living as near as possible to dying,
and when it came to him to be troubled by this.
Is it not ridiculous?"

"Of course."

"In reality then, Simmias," he said,
the correct philosophers practice how to die,
and death is less feared by them of all people.

"And consider it this way.
For if they were in every way suspicious of the body,
and want to have the soul by itself,
and if they were afraid and troubled by this occurring,
would it not be quite unreasonable,
if they should not be glad to go there,
where those arriving are hopeful
of what they were wanting to happen throughout life;
and they were wanting wisdom;
and of being released
from their associating with this which they suspected?

"When human favorites and wives and sons have died
many have come willingly to Hades,
led by this hope of seeing there
those with whom they want to be associated;
so then someone who in reality wants wisdom
and taking seriously this same hope,
that nowhere else will one meet the same thing
that is worthy of the word than in Hades,
will one be troubled dying and not be glad one is there?
One should not think so,
if in reality one is, my friend, a philosopher;
for this will seem serious to this one,
that nowhere else will one meet pure wisdom than there.
And if this is so, as I just said,
would it not be quite unreasonable,
if such a one should fear death?"

"Very much so, by Zeus."

13
"Then is this not a sufficient indication," he said,
"if you see a man who is troubled when about to die,
that he was not a lover of wisdom but a lover of the body?
And the same thus is likely to be
both a lover of money and a lover of honor,
one or the other of these or both."

"Certainly," he said, "it is so, as you say."

"So then, Simmias," he said,
"and is not what is named courage
especially fitting to those so disposed?"

"Certainly," he said.

"And then the prudent, which also many name prudence,
concerned with not being excited by desires,
but caring little and being orderly,
then is it not for those alone especially fitting that
they care little about the body and live in philosophy?"

"Necessarily," he said.

"For if you intend to consider the courage
and prudence of others,
it will seem to you to be absurd."

"How come, Socrates?"

"Do you know that all others
think death is a great evil?"

"Quite so," he said.

"Then do not the courageous face death
in fear of greater evils, when they do face it?"

"This is so."

"Then by fearing and need are all courageous
except the philosophers.
Yet it is unreasonable for someone to be courageous
through need and fear."

"Certainly."

"And what about the orderly ones?
Do these not suffer the same thing?
Are they not prudent by a kind of indulgence?
Yet we say it is impossible,
but similarly their experience occurs
like this simplistic prudence;
for afraid of being deprived of other pleasures
and wanting them,
they abstain from some, being controlled by others.
And yet they call indulgence being ruled by pleasures.
But similarly they control some pleasures
while being controlled by other pleasures.
And this is like what I just said,
in this kind of way they are prudent because of indulgence."

"So it seems."

"Blessed Simmias, for this would not be correct
to purchase virtue, exchanging pleasure for pleasure
and pain for pain and fear for fear
and greater for less, as though by coinage,
but that alone is the right coin,
by which all those must be exchanged against, wisdom,
and by it and with it all may be coined and bought in reality
and courage and prudence and justice
and in short true virtue with wisdom,
both adding and taking away both pleasures and fears
and all other such things;
but separating wisdom and exchanging against each other

such a virtue would be some kind of sketch
and in reality servile
and there is nothing healthy nor true in it,
but truth in reality
would be a purification of all such things,
and prudence and justice and courage and wisdom itself
are some kind of cleansing.

"And probably those who established
the initiations for us were not trivial,
but in reality long ago hinted that
whoever arrives in Hades uninitiated and unaccomplished,
will lie in the mud,
but the cleansed and perfected arriving there
will dwell with the gods.
For there are, as they say in the mysteries,
many thyrsus-bearers but few mystics.
And these are according to my opinion
no other than those who have been correct philosophers.

"And as far as I could I left nothing undone in my life,
but in every way I sought to become one;
and if I sought correctly and achieved something,
going there I shall know clearly, if God wills it,
a little later, as it seems to me.

"So this, Simmias and Cebes," he said, "is my defense,
how naturally I do not bear it hard nor am I troubled
leaving you and the masters here,
and believing that there no less than here
I shall meet good masters and friends;
so if I am more convincing to you in the defense
than I was to the Athenian judges, it would be well."

14
Socrates having said these things,
Cebes replying said, "Socrates, it seems to me
the other things were well said,
but the things about the soul cause much unbelief in people,
since when it is released from the body,
it may no longer be anywhere,
but on that day the person dies it is destroyed and lost;

immediately running away from the body and going out
it is scattered like breath or smoke to depart vanishing
and it would no longer be anywhere.
Since, if it were gathered together anywhere by itself
and released from these evils which you now described,
there would be much hope and beauty, Socrates,
that it is true what you say;
but perhaps this requires not a little reassurance and faith,
how the soul of a dead person has any ability and wisdom."

    "You say the truth, Cebes," said Socrates;
"but what shall we do?
Do you wish to communicate with words about these things
whether this is probably so or not?"

    "I do," said Cebes; "I would like to hear
what opinions you have about these things."

    "Then I don't think," said Socrates,
"if anyone heard us now,
not even if one were a comic poet,
would one say that I am chattering
and making arguments about things not relevant.
So if you like, it should be examined thoroughly.

15
    "And let us consider it in this way,
whether the souls of people who died are in Hades or not.
Thus there is an ancient argument, which we remember,
that those arriving there are from here,
and again they come back and are born from the dead;
and if this is so,
the living being born again from the dying,
certainly our souls would be there;
for they would not be born again if they did not exist,
and this would be a sufficient indication of this,
if in reality it should become clear
that the living are born nowhere else than from the dead;
but if this is not so, another argument would be needed."

    "Certainly," said Cebes.

    "Now if you wish to learn easily
consider this not only in regard to people

but also in regard to all animals and plants,
and in short to whatever has birth,
let us see about all, just as all things are generated,
whether opposites are generated out of their opposites,
when there happens to be such,
beauty opposite to the ugly and justice to injustice,
and countless others having them.
Then let us consider whether it is necessary
for whatever has an opposite
to be generated from anything else but itself
or out of its opposite.
As when anything becomes greater,
by necessity was it out of the smaller
that it became greater?"

"Yes."

"So then if it becomes smaller,
was it out of the greater that later it became smaller?"

"It is so," he said.

"And out of the stronger the weaker
and out of the slower the faster?"

"Certainly."

"But what?
Does not something worse come out of the better,
and the just out of the unjust?"

"Of course."

"Then," he said, "have we taken this far enough
that everything is generated so,
the opposite circumstances out of the opposites?"

"Certainly."

"But what then? Is there also such in themselves
between all these pairs of opposites two kinds of generation,
from one over to the other,
and from the other back over to the first?
Between a larger thing and a smaller
is augmentation and decline,
and do we call one increase and the other decrease?"

"Yes," he said.

"Then also dividing and combining
and cooling and heating, and all similarly,
even if now and then we do not use names,
but in action any way everywhere is it necessarily so
that the same things born are generated
both out of each other and out of each into the other?"

"Certainly."

16

"What then?" he said. "Is there an opposite to life,
just as sleeping is to waking?"

"Certainly," he said.

"What?"

"Death," he said.

"Then are these generated out of each other,
if really opposites exist,
and are not their two origins between the two of them?"

"Of course."

"Now I shall tell you about one of the pairs
of which I just now told you," said Socrates,
"both it and the origins;
and you tell me about the other.
And I mean sleeping and waking,
and out of sleeping is generated waking
and out of waking is generated sleeping,
and their origins are falling asleep and waking up.
Is it far enough for you," he said, "or not?"

"Certainly."

"Now you also tell me," he said,
"this about life and death.
Do you not say that living is opposite to being dead?"

"I do."

"And are they generated out of each other?"

"Yes."

"Then what is generated out of the living?"

"The dead," he said.

"And what out of the dead?"

"It is necessary," he said,
"to agree that it is the living."

"Out of the dead then, Cebes,
living things and living beings are born?"

"It appears so," he said.

"Then our souls," he said, "exist in Hades."

"It seems likely."

"Then also concerning these origins
does one happen to be definite?
for surely dying is definite, is it not?"

"Certainly," he said.

"So what shall we do?
Shall we deny the opposite of birth,
and in this will nature be lame?
Or is it necessary to restore to dying an opposite origin?"

"Certainly," he said.

"What is it?"

"Coming back to life."

"Then if it really is coming back to life,
would birth into the living out of the dead
be coming back to life?"

"Certainly."

"Then for us to agree also in this
that the living are born out of the dead
no less than the dead out of the living;
and this being the case it seems to me to be proof
that it is necessary for the souls to be somewhere,
from where they are born again."

"It seems to me, Socrates," he said,
"this is necessarily so from the agreements."

17
"And so now, Cebes," he said,
"we were not wrong in agreeing, as it seems to me.
For if generating did not always give back some to the others
going around like in a circle,
but the origin out of one alone
would go straight into the direct opposite

and not bending back again to the other nor making a circle,
then do you think all things would end up the same form
and would have also the same experience
if the experiences also would stop generating?"

"What do you mean?" he said.

"It is not hard to understand what I mean;
for example if falling asleep existed,
and waking up did not give back
being generated out of falling asleep,
you know that all things would end up
showing Endymion silly and nowhere
it would appear because everything also
would be experiencing the same state, sleeping.
Or if all things were combined, and not divided,
quickly it would become Anaxagoras' 'all things together.'
And the same way, dear Cebes,
if everything would die, which should receive life,
when they should die,
the dead remaining in this form and not coming back to life,
then is it not very necessary to end up
with everything dying and nothing living?
For if out of the others the living should be born,
and the living should die,
is there any device by which
all would not be used up in dying?"

"None it seems to me, Socrates," said Cebes,
"but you seem to me to speak the absolute truth."

"For it is, Cebes," he said, "as it seems to me,
absolutely so, and we are not deceived in these agreements,
but it is in reality that the living
both come back to life and are born out of the dead
and that the souls of the dead exist."

18
"And besides," said Cebes replying,
"according to that argument, Socrates, if it is true,
which you often like to say,
that for us learning is nothing else than
being happening to recall,

and according to this it is necessary for us
in some previous time to have learned
what now we remember.
But this is impossible, if our soul did not exist somewhere
before being born in the human form;
so also in this the soul is likely to be immortal."

  "But Cebes," said Simmias replying,
"what were the demonstrations of this?
Remind me; for I'm not sure I recall at present."

  "In a word," said Cebes, "a most beautiful one
is that people being questioned, if one asks well,
they say everything themselves which is needed;
and yet if knowledge and correct reason
did not happen within them,
they could not do this.
Secondly if one leads them to a diagram
or any other such thing,
from there it is proved most clearly, that this is so."

  "And if you are not persuaded by this, Simmias,"
said Socrates, "see if it seems so to you
looking at it in this way.
For do you not disbelieve
that what is called learning is recalling?"

  "Disbelieve you I do not," said Simmias,
"but this same thing I need to learn
is what the argument is about, recalling.
And almost from what Cebes endeavored to say
already I am recalling and being persuaded;
nevertheless I should like to hear now,
what you were endeavoring to say."

  "I would say this.
For surely we agree, if anyone recalls anything,
he must know it at some previous time."

  "Certainly," he said.

  "Then also do we agree on this,
that when knowledge comes in such a way, is it recalling?
But I mean some way like this:
if someone having seen or heard
or in some other way perceived something received

knows not that alone, but also another awareness,
the knowledge of which is not the same, but something else,
then are we not correct in saying
that he recalls that which the awareness received?"

"What do you mean?"

"For example, different is knowledge
of a person and of a lyre."

"Of course."

"Then do you know that lovers
when they see a lyre or garment or something else
which their favorites like to use,
they experience this:
aware of the lyre
and in the intuition receiving the form of the favorite,
whose lyre it was?
And this is recalling;
just as someone seeing Simmias may often recall Cebes,
and there would be countless other such examples."

"Yes, countless by Zeus," said Simmias.

"Then is this kind of thing recalling?
especially when this is experienced about those things,
which through time are not examined and already forgotten?"

"Certainly," he said.

"But what? Does one seeing a drawing of a horse
and a drawing of a lyre recall a person,
and seeing a drawing of Simmias recall Cebes?"

"Certainly."

"Then also seeing a drawing of Simmias
does he recall Simmias himself?"

"Of course," he said.

19

"Then according to all these things
does it not result that recalling is from similar things,
and it is from dissimilar things?"

"It does result."

"But when one remembers something from similar things,
then is it not necessarily a special feeling,

to understand whether this left a perfect similarity
of what is recalled or not that?"
  "Necessarily," he said.
  "Now consider if this is so.
We say there is such a thing as equality.
I do not mean a stick to a stick
nor a stone to a stone nor any other such things,
but beyond these something completely different,
equality itself;
Shall we say it exists or not?"
  "Yet we shall say so by Zeus,"
said Simmias, "emphatically."
  "And do we know what it is?"
  "Certainly."
  "From where did we receive knowledge of it?
Was it not from what we just said?
Was it not from seeing equal sticks
or stones or other things,
from these we understood that which is different from these?
Or does it not appear different to you?
And consider this.
Then do not the same stones and sticks
sometimes appear equal in one way but not in another?"
  "Certainly."
  "But what?
Did the equals themselves ever appear to you unequal,
or equality inequality?"
  "Never, Socrates."
  "Then these equals and equality itself are not the same."
  "It does not appear so to me at all, Socrates."
  "But from these equals," he said,
"which are different from that equality,
did you nevertheless understand and receive knowledge of it?"
  "Most true," he said.
  "Then it is either similar to them or dissimilar?"
  "Certainly."

"But it makes no difference;
whenever seeing one thing
from this vision you understand another,
whether similar or dissimilar,
it would necessarily be," he said, "recalling it."

"Certainly."

"But what? Do we experience this concerning the sticks
and things which we just now said were equal?
Then does it appear to us they are equal
as that which is equality itself,
do they lack something from being like equality or not?"

"And they are lacking much," he said.

"Then do we agree,
that when anyone seeing anything thinks,
'This which I now see, wishes to be like something else,
and it is unable to be like that, but is inferior,'
must one necessarily think
that comes from previous knowledge
which one says it resembles but has a deficiency?"

"Necessarily."

"Then what? And did we experience this or not,
in regard to the equals and equality itself?"

"Absolutely."

"Then it is necessary for us to foreknow equality
before that time when first seeing equal things
we thought that all these things are reaching
to be like equality but have a deficiency."

"That is so."

"But we agree also that not from another is it understood
nor is it possible to be understood,
but either from seeing or touching or from some other sense;
and I mean they are all the same."

"For that is so, Socrates,
to whoever wishes to clarify the argument."

"But from the senses one must understand
that all sense objects reach for that which is equality
and are deficient of it.
Is this what we say?"

"Yes."

"Then before we began to see and hear
and use the other senses
we must somewhere have received knowledge
of that which is equality itself,
if we compared it with the equals
we understood from the senses,
that all things want to be like that,
but are inferior to it."

"It is necessary from what was said before, Socrates."

"Then being born immediately did we see
and hear and have the other senses?"

"Certainly."

"But do we say before having these
it was necessary to receive knowledge of equality?"

"Yes."

"Then before being born, since it seems likely,
it was necessary for us to receive this."

"It seems likely."

20

"Then if having received it before being born
we were born having it,
did we know both before being born and upon being born
not only equality and the greater and lesser
but also all such abstractions?
For our current argument is no more about equality
than about beauty itself and goodness itself
and justice and holiness, and, as I say,
about everything which we recognize as that which is,
both in the questioning inquiry and in choosing answers.
So it is necessary for us
to have received knowledge before being born."

"That is so."

"And if having received it we did not forget it each time,
one always is born knowing and knows throughout life;
for knowing is this,
having received knowledge and not losing it;

do we not say this forgetting, Simmias,
is throwing away knowledge?"

"Certainly, Socrates," he said.

"But I think, if having received it before being born
we should lose it when born,
but later by using the senses concerning those things
we regain that knowledge, which we also had before then,
then would not what we call learning
not be regaining the relative knowledge?"

"Certainly."

"For this appears possible, perceiving something
either seeing or hearing or receiving it by some other sense
to understand from this something different,
which had been forgotten,
with which this was associated whether dissimilar or similar;
so that, as I say, there are two alternatives,
either we are born knowing these things
and know them through all of life,
or later, what we say is learning,
is nothing but remembering these things,
and learning would be recalling."

"And that is quite so, Socrates."

21
"Then which do you choose, Simmias,
were we born knowing,
or do we remember later the knowledge we received before?"

"I have no choice at present, Socrates."

"But what about this?
You can choose, and in any way it seems to you about it:
could a knowing man give an account
about what he knows or not?"

"It is quite necessary, Socrates," he said.

"And does it seem to you everyone can give an account
about these things which we were just now discussing?"

"I would wish it," said Simmias;
"but I am rather afraid that tomorrow at this time
there will no longer be any person who could do so properly."

"Then does it not seem to you, Simmias,
that everyone knows these things?"

"By no means."

"Then they remember whatever they learned?"

"Necessarily."

"When did our souls receive knowledge of them?
For it was not after being born as humans."

"Definitely not."

"Then previously."

"Yes."

"Then, Simmias, souls existed previously,
before they were born in human form,
without bodies, and they had wisdom."

"Unless we receive this knowledge when born, Socrates;
for this time still remains."

"Well, my friend;
but at what other time do we lose them?
For we are not born having them, as we just agreed;
do we lose them at this time in which we also receive them?
Or do you have some other time to suggest?"

"Not at all, Socrates,
but I fooled myself saying nothing."

22

"Then is this how it is for us, Simmias?
If there exists what we are always repeating,
beauty and goodness and every such essence,
and we refer all things from the senses to this,
our being already existing before discovering them,
and we compare these with that,
necessarily, this just as these also exists,
and thus our soul also exists before we were born;
and if these do not exist,
would the argument thus be saying otherwise?
Then is it so, and is it equally necessary these things exist
and our souls also did before we were born,
and if these do not, neither do they?"

"Marvelously, Socrates," said Simmias,
"it seems to me to be the same necessity,
and beautifully the argument has recourse
to our soul existing before we were born
just as the essence does also, which you mention.
For nothing is so plain to me as this,
that all such things most definitely exist,
beauty and goodness and all the others
which you just now mentioned;
and it seems to me it is sufficiently proven."

"But what about Cebes?" said Socrates;
"for Cebes must also be persuaded."

"He is sufficiently," said Simmias, "as I think;
and yet he is the staunchest human in disbelieving arguments;
but I think this has not failed to persuade him,
that before we were born our soul existed.

23
"However whether also when we die it still exists,
it does not seem proven to him nor to me, Socrates,
but still the concern of the many remains,
which Cebes just now mentioned,
how the soul of the dying person is dispersed
and this is the end of its existence.
For what prevents it
from being born and brought together from somewhere else
and existing before coming into a human body,
but when it has come and left this,
from at that time both ending itself and being destroyed?"

"You speak well, Simmias," said Cebes.
"For it appears as though half of what is needed is proven,
that before we are born our soul existed;
but it is necessary to prove besides
that also when we die it will exist
no less than before being born,
if the proof is to be complete."

"It has been proven, Simmias and Cebes," said Socrates,
"even now, if you are willing to combine this argument
with the one which we agreed upon before,

that everything living is born out of the dead.
For if the soul exists also previously,
and necessarily when it comes into life and is born
it is born from nothing else than the dead and the dying,
then is it not necessary also for the dying to exist,
since it must be born again?
Thus is proved even now what you mention.

24
  "And yet you and Simmias seem to me glad
to examine this argument even more thoroughly,
and you are afraid like children
that truly when it steps out of the body
the wind may blow and disperse it,
especially if one chances to die
not in calm weather but in a great storm."
  And Cebes laughing said, "As though afraid, Socrates,
try to persuade us;
but rather not as though we are afraid,
but perhaps there is a child within us who fears such things;
therefore let us try to persuade him
not to be afraid of death as if it were a hobgoblin."
  "But," said Socrates, "you should chant to him every day,
until you charm it away."
  "Then where, Socrates," he said, "shall we find
such a good chanter, since you are leaving us?"
  "Greece is large, Cebes," he said,
"in which there are many good men,
and there are many also from foreign peoples,
all of whom you should search through seeking such a chanter,
sparing neither money nor labor,
since there is nothing more necessary
on which you could spend your money.
But you should also seek yourselves with each other;
for perhaps you would not easily find
any better able to do this than you."
  "But that will be done," said Cebes;
"but let us return to where we left off,
if it is pleasing to you."

"Truly pleasing, of course it is."
"You speak beautifully," he said.

25
"Then must we ask ourselves," said Socrates,
"something such as what kind of thing then is liable
to suffer this experience, the dispersing,
and for what kind of thing is this experience to be feared,
and for what kind of thing is it not;
and after this next to consider which the soul is,
and out of these to be encouraged,
or to be afraid on behalf of our soul?"
"You say the truth," he said.
"So then is not that which is combined and compounded
naturally liable to suffer this,
being divided in the same way as it is compounded;
and if something chances which is uncompounded,
in this alone is it liable not to suffer these things,
if really it is different?"
"It seems to be so to me," said Cebes.
"Then what is always constant and the same way,
these things very probably are uncompounded,
and what is changing and never constant,
are these compounded?"
"It seems so to me."
"Let us turn," he said,
"to what was said in the earlier argument.
Is the essence itself to which we give the meaning being
both in questioning and answering,
the same way always constant or changing?
Equality itself, beauty itself, each entity which is, really,
do they ever show any change whatsoever?
Or is each one of these which is,
being uniform it of itself, constant the same way
and does it never show any change at all to anything else?"
"The same way it is necessary," said Cebes,
"for it to be constant, Socrates."
"But what of the many,
such as people or horses or clothes or any other such things,

or equality or beauty or all which are named in that way?
Then are they constant, or in complete opposition to those
neither the same as they nor ever like each other,
so to speak, in no way constant?"

"The latter," said Cebes, "they are never the same way."

"Then these you can touch and see
and perceive with other senses,
but those that are constant are never reached
by anything except by the reasoning of the intuition,
but are these invisible and not seen?"

"You say the absolute truth," he said.

26
"Then do you wish us to assume two forms of reality,
the visible and the invisible?"

"Let us assume so," he said.

"And is the invisible always constant,
and the visible never constant?"

"Let us assume this also," he said.

"Well, is there anything else of ours but body and soul?"

"Nothing else," he said.

"Then to which do we say
the body is more similar and related?"

"This is clear to everyone," he said,
"that it is to the visible."

"And what of the soul? Is it visible or invisible?"

"Not by humans, Socrates," he said.

"But we say things are visible
and invisible to human nature;
or are you thinking of some other?"

"To humans."

"Then what do we say about the soul?
Is it seen or unseen?"

"Not seen."

"Then is it invisible?"

"Yes."

"Then the soul is more similar to the invisible

than the body, but it to the seen."
"Necessarily, Socrates."

27
"And then what we have been saying for a long time,
that the soul, when it makes use of the body
to look at something either through sight
or through hearing or through any other sense—
for this is through the body,
to look at something through the senses—
at that time is it dragged by the body
into what never is constant,
and it wanders and is confused and dizzy like one drunk
when touching such things?"
"Certainly."
"But when it looks by itself,
it departs there into the pure and eternal
which is also immortal and in the same way,
and as related to its essence it is always with that,
whenever it is by itself and is permitted itself,
and it has stopped its wandering
and concerning that is always constant in the same way,
since it is communing with such;
and has this experience of the soul been called wisdom?"
"Absolutely," he said,
"and you say the truth beautifully, Socrates."
"Then again to which does it seem to you,
in view of what was said both from before and now,
the soul is more similar and related?"
"It seems to me everyone would concede, Socrates,
from this method, even the dullest,
that the soul is wholly and completely more similar
to what is always the same way rather than to what is not."
"And the body?"
"To the other."

28
"Now see it also this way,
that, when soul and body are in the same thing,

nature directs one to serve and be ruled,
and the other to rule and be master;
and according to this again which seems to you
to be more similar to the divine and which to the mortal?
Or does it not seem to you it is natural
for the divine to rule and lead,
and for the mortal to be ruled and serve?"

"To me it does."

"Which then is the soul like?"

"It is clear, Socrates, that the soul is like the divine,
and the body like the mortal."

"Now consider, Cebes," he said,
"if from all that was said by us
it results that the soul is most similar to the divine
and immortal and intelligent and uniform and indissoluble
and always the same way being constant in itself,
and in turn the body is most like the human
and mortal and multiform and unintelligent and dissoluble
and never being constant in itself.
Do we have anything else to say on this, dear Cebes,
which has it not thus?"

"We have not."

29

"What then? Having it thus then
is it not fitting for the body to be quickly dissolved,
and for the soul to be entirely indissoluble or nearly so?"

"Of course."

"Then be aware," he said, "that when a person dies,
the seen part of him, the body, also lying in the seen,
which we call a corpse,
which is fit to be dissolved and fall away,
does not experience this immediately,
but remains for a considerably long time,
if someone has died both having the body in good condition
and especially also in a favorable season.
For the body shrunk and embalmed,
as the ones in Egypt are embalmed,
it remains almost whole for an incalculable time.

And some parts of the body, even if it decays,
bones and tendons and all such things still are,
so to speak, immortal; is it not so?"
"Yes."
"But the soul then, the invisible,
departing to another such place,
noble and pure and invisible,
into Hades in truth, to the good and wise god,
where, if God wills, soon also may my soul go,
but is this which for us has such a nature
being released from the body
immediately dispersed and destroyed, as many people say?
Far from it, dear Cebes and Simmias,
but it is much more like this:
if it departs pure, dragging nothing of the body with it,
since it did not join it in life willingly,
but avoided it and gathered itself into itself,
since it always practiced this—
but this is nothing else than correctly loving wisdom
and in reality practicing dying;
or would this not be practicing death?"
"Absolutely."
"Then being so does it go away
into what is similar to itself,
the invisible, divine and immortal and wise,
where arriving it is ready for itself to be happy,
released from wandering and folly and fear
and cruel passion and all other human evils,
and as it is said by the initiates,
in truth spends the rest of time with the gods?
Do we say this, Cebes, or not?"

30
"This by Zeus," said Cebes.
"But if, I think,
it departs polluted and impure from the body,
because it always associated with the body
and cared for this and loved it
and was fascinated by it and its desires and pleasures,

so that nothing else seemed to be true except bodily things,
which one can touch and see
and drink and eat and use for sexual love,
but what is dark and invisible to the sight
and intelligible and chosen by philosophy,
and being accustomed to hate this and tremble and avoid it,
do you think that a soul in this condition
will depart it of itself unmixed?"

"Not in the least," he said.

"But also is it interpenetrated,
I think, by bodily things,
which intercourse and association with its body
through always associating and much practice makes inborn?"

"Certainly."

"And, my friend, one should think this is weighty
and heavy and earthy and visible;
and having this such a soul is weighed down
and dragged again into the visible realm,
by fear of the invisible and Hades, as it is said,
roaming about monuments and graveyards,
about which also shadowy forms of souls have been seen,
phantoms which cause such souls to be visible,
which are not released purely,
but take part in the visible, and therefore are seen."

"It is probable, Socrates."

"Yet, Cebes, it is probable also that
these are not the souls of the good, but of the inferior,
which are compelled to wander about such places
to pay justice for former evil ways of being;
and they wander even as far as this
until being followed closely by the bodily form
by desire they are bound into the body.

31
"And they are bound, as is probable, into such a character
as they happened to have been interested in during life."

"What characters do you mean, Socrates?"

"Those such as gluttons and the insolent
and those interested in drinking

and not being wary, they are likely to be bound
into a breed of asses and such beasts.
Don't you think?"

"What you say certainly is probable."

"And those who have chosen
injustice and tyranny and robbery
go into a breed of wolves and hawks and kites;
or where else would we say such go?"

"Doubtless," said Cebes, "into such."

"Then is it clear also about the others,
where each should go,
according to what is most similar to their practice?"

"It is clear," he said, "of course."

"Then are the happiest," he said,
"of these and those going to the best place
those who have pursued democratic and political virtue,
which they call prudence and justice,
out of habit and practice without philosophy and mind?"

"How are these the happiest?"

"Because these will probably arrive again
into such a political and gentle breed,
either bees or wasps or ants
or again into the same human race,
and from them will be born moderate men."

"Probably."

32
"And when departing it is not right for anyone
who is not loving wisdom and wholly pure
to reach the family of the gods,
but for the one who loves learning.
But on account of this, dear Simmias and Cebes,
those loving wisdom correctly
keep away from all bodily desires
and are patient and do not give themselves over to them,
not from fear of household ruin and poverty,
like the many who love money;
nor is it because of anxiety
about dishonor and the disgrace of hardship,

like the lovers of power and honor,
that they keep away from them."
   "For that would not be fitting, Socrates," said Cebes.
   "Of course not, by Zeus," he said.
"Accordingly, Cebes,
those who care at all for their own souls,
but do not live working for the body,
saying goodby to that are not driven down
by those who do not know where they are going,
and themselves believing they must not oppose
the practice of philosophy and her release and purification
they turn following her wherever she leads."

33
   "How, Socrates?"
   "I'll tell you," he said.
"For the lovers of learning know
that until philosophy actually receives their soul
it is fastened and glued in the body,
being compelled to look at realities
as though through this prison but not through her own self,
and wallowing in complete ignorance,
and she looks down at the terribleness of the imprisonment
that it is through desire,
which bound itself is the main accomplice of the binding,—
so as I say, the lovers of learning know
that in this way philosophy receives their soul
and tries to gently encourage and release her,
indicating that filled with deceit
is viewing through the body,
and deceitful the ears and the other senses,
and persuading her to withdraw from them,
except so far as it is necessary to use them,
and advising her to collect and gather into herself,
and trusting nothing else but herself by herself,
except her very own intelligence of reality itself;
and whatever else is viewed in other ways is something else,
not to be believed as true,
it being so sensory and visible,

but she sees the intelligible and intangible.

"So not thinking it is necessary to oppose her release
the soul of the true philosopher thus keeps away
from pleasures and desires and griefs and fears,
so far as possible,
reasoning that whenever one has excessive pleasure
or fear or grief or desire,
he suffers such evil from them as one might think,
such as either sickness or some expenses through the desires,
but the evil which is the greatest of all and most extreme,
this he experiences and does not consider it."

"What is this, Socrates?" said Cebes.

"That which the soul of every person
is compelled at the time of excessive pleasure or pain
also to believe,
that what is especially felt
is what is most distinct and most true;
it simply does not hold;
these are mostly the visible ones, are they not?"

"Certainly."

"Thus in this which is most felt
is not the soul most bound by the body?"

"How so?"

"Because each pleasure and pain like a nail
nails and fastens itself to the body and makes it corporeal,
believing these things to be true
which the body also says are.
For from agreeing with the body
and delighting in the same things
she is compelled to adopt
the same habits and the same upbringing
and never arrives purely into Hades,
but always goes out infected by the body,
so that quickly again she falls into another body
and like scattered seed is sown,
and from this has no share in the divine and pure
and communion in the one form."

"What you say is most true, Socrates." said Cebes.

34
"Therefore on account of this, Cebes,
the true lovers of learning are well-ordered and courageous,
not on account of what the many say;
or do you think so?"
  "Of course not."
  "No, for the courageous soul of the philosopher
will reason another way,
and would not think it useful for philosophy to release her,
and released she would be bound herself fast again
in pleasures and pains
and would decline to do any of Penelope's work
by reversing the handling of the loom,
but she will prepare for calmness from these,
following reasoning and always being in this,
gazing at the truth and the divine and the undoubted
and supported by that,
she thinks it is necessary to live thus, while she lives,
and when she dies, to depart into what is akin and such,
rid of human evils.
And out of such nurturing
no one need be afraid, Simmias and Cebes,
that she will be torn apart in the departure from the body,
be dispersed by the winds
and scared of being gone and of no longer being anywhere."

35
  Then a silence occurred for a long time,
after these things were said by Socrates,
and himself on the meaning spoken,
Socrates appeared to contemplate, as did most of us.
But Simmias and Cebes conversed with each other a little;
and Socrates seeing took it up.
  "Why?" he asked.
"Does it seem to you
that what was said is insufficient argument?
For it still has many suspicions and loose ends,
if anyone cares to discuss it thoroughly.
So if you are considering something else, I say nothing;

but if anyone is in doubt about these things,
do not hesitate to say them and to go through them,
if it appears to you it somehow could have been better said,
and take me along also,
if you think you can find a better way with me."

  And Simmias said, "And really, Socrates,
I'll tell you the truth.
For a while each of us in doubt
has been pushing and urging the other to ask
because of the desire to hear,
but hesitate to cause unpleasant annoyance for you
because of the unfortunate circumstance."

  And having heard he laughed softly
and said, "Oh my, Simmias!
What difficulty I shall have persuading other people
that I do not regard my present circumstances unfortunate,
when I am not even able to persuade you,
but you are afraid
now I am apt to be more irritable than in my life before;
and probably I seem to you to be worse in prophecy
than the swans, who when they perceive that they must die,
also having sung in the previous time,
then they sing most and best,
rejoicing that they are about to go away
to the god whose ministers they are.
But people because of their own fear of death
misrepresent also the swans,
and say they sing out lamenting death under grief,
and do not reason that no bird sings when hungry
or cold or suffering any other grief,
not even the nightingale and swallow and the hoopoe,
which they say sings because of lamenting grief;
but these do not appear to me to sing grieving
nor do the swans,
but I think since they are Apollo's
and they are foreseeing the good things in Hades
they sing and celebrate on that day
more than at any previous time.
And I believe myself also to be a fellow slave of the swans
and sacred to the same god,

and to have prophecy no worse than theirs from the master,
and to be departing from life no more despondent than they.
However, one ought to speak on account of this
and ask whatever you wish,
as long as the eleven Athenians permit."

"Beautifully you speak," said Simmias;
"and I'll tell you what I doubt, and then he,
which of the things said are not accepted.
For it seems to me, Socrates, concerning these things,
perhaps as it also does to you,
that to know clearly now in life
is either impossible or most difficult;
yet not to discuss in every way the arguments about them
and to desist before exhausting every consideration
certainly would be remiss;
for about this it is necessary to accomplish
one of two things,
either to learn which has it or to discover it
or, if that is impossible,
at least taking the best of the human arguments
and hardest to refute,
and on this riding as on a boat
venturing to sail through life,
unless one can pass through safer and with less danger
on a more secure ship, by some divine word.
And so even now I am not ashamed to ask,
since you also say these things,
I will not blame myself at a later time,
that now I did not speak what it seems to me.
For to me, Socrates, when both by myself and with him
I consider the things said,
the inquiry certainly does not appear sufficient."

36
And Socrates said, "Perhaps, dear friend,
what appears to you is true;
but say then, how it is not sufficient."

"In this to me," he said,
"which also about a harmony and a lyre and its strings
one might say the same argument,

that the harmony is invisible and incorporeal
and most beautiful and divine in the tuned lyre,
but the lyre itself and the strings
are corporeal and physical and compounded and earthy
and it is related to the mortal.
Therefore when someone shatters the lyre
or cuts and breaks the strings,
if someone should maintain by the same argument as you,
that by necessity
that harmony still exists and does not perish;
for there would be no device by which
the lyre would still exist with broken strings
and the strings being mortal,
and the harmony perish
which is of the same nature
and related to the divine and immortal,
before the mortal perished;
but necessity says the harmony itself still exists somewhere,
and the wood and the strings must rot
before that could suffer anything,—
and therefore, Socrates,
I think this also must have occurred to you,
that we assume the soul is something quite like this,
as though our body were strung and held together
by heat and cold and moisture and dryness and so on,
and our soul is a combination and a harmony of these things,
when they are beautifully and properly
combined with each other.
   "Thus if it happens the soul is a harmony,
it is clear that when our body is excessively
slack or stretched by sickness and other evils,
the soul at once starts to perish,
even though it is divine,
just like other harmonies in sounds
and in all works of the artists,
and the remains of each body endure a long time
until either burnt or decayed.
So see what we shall say to this argument,
if someone claims the soul
being a combination in the body

is the first to perish in what is called death."

37
  Then Socrates looked straight,
as many times he used to do, and smiled.
"Yet what you say is right, Simmias," he said.
So if any of you is more ready than I, why not answer?
For it seems the argument touches not a trivial point.
Yet it seems to me to be useful before answering
first to hear Cebes, what he challenges in the argument
so that gaining time we shall be advised what we shall say,
and then having heard, either agree with them,
if they seem to ring true,
but if not, then plead the argument already presented.
But come on, Cebes," he said,
"tell us what it was that bothered you."

  "I will tell you," said Cebes.
"For it appears to me the argument is still the same,
and as we argued before, it has the same fault.
For that our soul existed before coming into this form,
I do not deny it was no doubt neatly,
and, if I may say so, quite sufficiently demonstrated;
but also when we are dead that it still exists somewhere,
does not seem to me so.
That the soul is not stronger
and longer lasting than the body,
I do not agree with Simmias' objection;
for it seems to me in every way it surpasses it very much.

  "'What then,' the argument might say,
'do you still disbelieve,
when you see a person dying that the weaker still exists?
And does it not seem necessary to you
the longer lasting still is preserved during the same time?'

  "So consider this, whether I am saying anything;
for it seems I need some simile, just as Simmias did.
For to me it seems similar to be saying these things,
as though someone would say about an old weaver who died
this argument, that the person did not perish,
but exists somewhere safe,

and would offer as evidence the coat
which the same weaver had woven,
that it exists safe and did not perish,
and if anyone disbelieves this,
one would ask which is longer lasting
the life of the person or a coat in use and being worn,
and someone answering that the person is much longer,
one would think it accepted that
above all the person is safe,
since the shorter lasting did not perish.

"But I think, Simmias, it is not so;
for consider also what I tell you.
For everyone understands that
whoever says this is talking folly;
for this weaver who wore out many such coats
and having woven those perished after many of them,
but before the last, I think,
and no person on this account
is poorer nor weaker than a coat.

"I think the same simile would apply for soul to body,
and someone saying the same things about them
would appear to be speaking properly,
that the soul is longer lasting,
and the body is weaker and shorter lasting;
but one might say each of the souls wears out many bodies,
especially if one lives for many years;
for if the body should melt away and corrupt
while the person is still living,
and the soul is always weaving anew what is wearing down,
then it would be necessary, when the soul should perish,
for it by chance to have on this last one woven
and to perish before this one alone,
and the soul having perished
then directly the body would show its natural weakness
and quickly would be gone to waste.
So by this argument
it is not yet worthy of being confidently believed,
that, when we die, our soul still exists somewhere.

"For if one were to concede even more
to one arguing what you argue,
granting him not only
our soul's existence at a time before we were born
but there would be nothing to prevent also when we die
the possibility of it still existing
and being born and dying again many times;
for it is so strong by nature
that the soul holds out being born many times;
and granting this one might not concede that
it does not suffer in its being born and dying many times
and does not perish completely in one of its deaths;
and this death and this dissolution of the body,
which brings ruin to the soul,
one would say no one knows;
for it is impossible for any of us to perceive it;
and if this is so,
anyone who faces death confidently is thoughtlessly confident
unless one can show that
the soul is completely immortal and imperishable;
and if not, it is necessary always
for the one who is about to die
to be afraid for one's soul
that in now being separated from the body
one may completely perish."

38
   So having heard what they said
all of us were unpleasantly disposed,
as we later said to each other,
because having been quite convinced by the previous argument
it seemed to disturb us again
and brought us down into disbelief,
not only for the past discussion
but also the latter for what was about to be said,
none of us being capable of judging
and being distrustful of these matters.
   ECHECRATES. By the gods, Phaedo,
I have sympathy for you.
For now having heard what you had to say it occurred to me,

"Then what argument shall we still believe?
since being quite convincing,
the argument which Socrates said,
now has fallen into distrust."
For wonderfully this argument has taken hold of me
both now and always,
that our soul is some kind of a harmony,
and you mentioning it has reminded me
that I myself held this before.
And now I need again as from the very beginning
some other argument, which will convince me
that at death the soul does not also die.

So say before God how Socrates went after the argument;
and whether he also, as you say you were,
was manifesting any annoyance or not,
or did he calmly assist the argument?
And did he assist adequately or deficiently?
Tell us everything as accurately as you can.

PHAEDO. Echecrates, often having marveled at Socrates
never have I admired him more than on that occasion.
So his having an argument was perhaps not unexpected;
but I was especially amazed
first at how pleasantly and gently and respectfully
he accepted the argument of the youths,
then how he perceived how sharply
we were convinced by the arguments,
then how well he healed us
and as though he called us up from flight and defeat
and turned us forward toward it
he persuaded us also to consider together the argument.

ECHECRATES. Really, how?

PHAEDO. I'll tell you.
For I happened to be sitting on his right
beside the bed on a low stool,
and he was much higher than I.
So stroking my head and grasping the hair on the neck—
for whenever it occurred,
he was in the habit of playing with my hair—
"So perhaps tomorrow, Phaedo," he said,

"this beautiful long hair will be cut off."
  "It's likely, Socrates," I said.
  "Not if you are convinced by me."
  "But why?" I asked.
  "Today," he said, "both you and I will do this,
if our argument dies and we are not able to revive it.
And if I were you, and the argument escaped me,
I would take an oath, like the Argives,
not to let it grow long
until I had conquered in a renewed fight
the argument of Simmias and Cebes."
  "But," I said, "against two
it is said not even Heracles is able."
  "But then," he said, "call me as Iolaus,
while it is still light."
  "I'll call rather," I said,
"not as Heracles, but as Iolaus."
  "It makes no difference," he said.

39
  "But first let us be careful
we do not suffer a certain emotion."
  "Of what kind?" I asked.
  "Let us not become," he said, "logic haters,
like those who become misanthropes;
since there is not," he said,
"any evil worse than this emotion of hating logic.
And logic hating and misanthropy
come out of the same manner.
For misanthropy is clothed
out of trusting someone excessively without skill,
and believing a person to be
completely true and sound and trustworthy,
then a little later finding him bad and untrustworthy
and again with another;
and when someone experiences this many times
and especially by those
who one believes are nearest and dearest,

so often taking offense he ends up hating everyone
and believes absolutely no one is sound at all.
Have you not observed this occurring?"

"Certainly," I said.

"Then," he said, "is it not shameful
and clear that such a person is without skill in human things
in attempting to deal with humans?
For if one dealt with skill, as though one has it,
then one would believe the good and bad are each very few,
and those in between most."

"What do you mean?" I said.

He said, "Just as concerning the very small and large;
do you think there is anything more rare
than to find a very large or a very small person
or dog or anything else?
or quick or slow or foul or beautiful or white or black?
Have you not observed that at the ultimate extent
all such things are rare and few,
and in between abundant and many?"

"Certainly," I said.

"Then do you think," he said,
"if a contest in evil were arranged,
certainly few also in this would appear first?"

"It is likely," I said.

"For it is likely," he said.
"But in this arguments are not similar to people,
but even now by your lead was I saying it,
rather in that,
when someone in believing the truth of an argument
being without skill in arguments,
and when a little later
is sometimes of the opinion it is false,
but sometimes it is not,
and again another and another;
and then the very ones spending time
arguing about disputations think
that finally they are the wisest and alone have discovered
that none of the matters argued are either sound or sure,
but all things being just like

the twisting in the Euripus up and down,
and nothing stays for any time at all."
  "Certainly," I said, "you tell the truth."
  "Then, Phaedo," he said,
"it would be a pitiful experience,
if there is some true and sure argument
and it can be understood,
when because of coming across such arguments
which at one time seem to be true and at another not,
one should not blame oneself for one's lack of skill,
but finally because of the hassling
gladly shift the blame from oneself to the arguments
and then for the rest of life go on hating and reviling them,
being deprived of the truth and knowledge of reality."
  "Yes, by Zeus," I said, "very pitiful."

40
  "First then," he said, "let us beware of this
and not admit into the soul that there is the danger
of arguments not being sound at all,
but rather that we are not yet sound,
and we must be courageous and willing to be sound,
thus for you and the others
and on account of all your future life,
and for me on account of this death;
since I am in danger in the present
of not being philosophical about this,
but just like the uncultured am contentious.
For when those disagree,
they do not consider which argument is so,
but how to present their own
so that they seem so to the listeners,
they are eager for this.
  "And it seems to me I differ in the present only in this:
for I will not be so eager
that what I say to those present should seem to be true,
except as a by-product,
but that it should especially seem so to me.
For I reason, dear friend, see how selfishly:

if what I say happens to be true,
then believing it is beautiful;
but if dying is nothing,
then in this time before death
I shall not yield at present to unpleasant mourning.
And this ignorance of mine will not last,
for that would be evil,
but a little later it would be left behind.

"Prepared then, Simmias and Cebes," he said,
"thus I come to the argument;
yet you, if you are persuaded by me,
will consider Socrates little, and truth much more,
if to you I seem to say the truth, agree,
but if not, oppose with every argument,
that I may not from eagerness
deceive at the same time both myself and you
and like a bee leaving the sting behind depart.

41
"But let us go on," he said.
"First remind me what you said,
if I appear not to remember.
For Simmias, I think,
both disbelieves and fears that the soul
though both more divine and beautiful than the body
may perish first being in the form of a harmony;
and Cebes it seemed to me agreed with me on this,
that the soul is longer lasting than the body,
but it was unclear to all,
whether after wearing out many bodies repeatedly
the soul at the end leaving behind the body
did itself now perish,
and that this was death, the destruction of the soul,
since the body does not ever stop perishing.
But then is this, Simmias and Cebes,
what it is necessary for us to consider?"

They both agreed it was this.

"Then," he said, "do you not accept
all of the previous arguments, or just some of them?"

"Some," they said, "but not others."

"What then," he asked, "do you say about that argument
in which we said learning is remembering,
and from this our soul necessarily has to exist
somewhere else, before it was entangled in the body?"

"I," said Cebes, "was at that time
most marvelously convinced by it
and now I remain so more than by any argument."

"I too," said Simmias, "hold it thus,
and would be very surprised,
if this should ever seem otherwise to me."

And Socrates said, "But it is necessary for you,
Theban guest, to think otherwise if you keep the opinion,
the harmony is a compound of things,
and the soul is a harmony
composed out of what is strung in the body.
For how will you not accept your own statement
that a composite harmony existed before those things
out of which it is necessary for it to be composed,
or will you accept it?"

"Not at all, Socrates," he said.

"Then do you observe," he said,
"that this agrees with what you argue,
when you say the soul exists
before it enters into the human form and body,
and it is composed out of what does not yet exist?
For surely a harmony is not such as what you compare it to,
but first both the lyre and the strings and the sounds
come into being still untuned,
and last of all is the harmony composed,
and it is the first to perish.
So how does this argument agree with yours?"

"Not at all," said Simmias.

"And yet," he said, "surely it is fitting
for there to be accord
between the other argument and what concerns harmony."

"Yes, it is fitting," said Simmias.

"Now this," he said, "is not in accord with yours;
but look, which of the arguments do you prefer,
that learning is remembering
or that the soul is a harmony?"

"Much more the former, Socrates," he said.
"For the latter came to me without demonstration
with some probability and plausibility,
which also is why it seems so to many people;
but I am aware that arguments
making demonstrations based on probability may be false,
and if one does not guard against them,
one may well be deceived,
both in geometry and in everything else.
But the argument about remembering and learning
was found to be demonstrated by worthy propositions.
For it was said how our soul exists
before it entered into the body,
just as this which is named as having the reality which is.
And I myself am convinced of this,
and I have accepted it sufficiently and correctly.
So it is necessary for me, as it seems,
because of these things
to accept the arguing neither from myself nor another
that the soul is a harmony."

42
"But what of this way, Simmias?" he asked.
"Does it seem to you a harmony or any other compound
can be in any other state
than that out of which the elements were composed?"

"Not at all."

"Nor can anything do, as I know, or experience
anything else but what they do or experience?"

He agreed.

"Then a harmony cannot lead these
out of which it is composed, but follows."

He assented.

"Then a harmony is quite unable to be moved or sounded
or be opposed by anything else opposite to its parts."

"Of course," he said.

"But what? Is it not thus
that each harmony brings forth harmony, as it is harmonized?"

"I do not understand," he said.

"Would it not," he said,
"if it was harmonized better and more,
if this is to be accepted,
be better harmonized and more,
but if worse and lesser, then worse and less?"

"Certainly."

"Is this so concerning the soul,
as even to the smallest degree
is one soul more and better
or lesser and worse a soul itself than another?"

"Not in the least," he said.

"Bear along now," he said, "toward God;
is a soul said to have intelligence and virtue
and to be good,
but another stupidity and vice and to be bad?
And are these things said true?"

"Yes, true."

"Then of those maintaining the soul is a harmony
what will one say these things in the soul are,
the virtue and evil?
that there is some other harmony and discord?
and to be harmonized, the good,
also has in its harmony reality another harmony,
but the discordant is itself and has no other in it?"

"I have nothing to say," said Simmias;
"but it is clear that the one assuming that
would say some such thing."

"But we agreed before," he said,
"that one is no better nor worse a soul than another;
and this is the equivalent to
one harmony is neither better nor more
nor worse nor less than another.
Is it not?"

"Certainly."

"And that which is neither better nor worse of a harmony
is neither better nor worse harmonized; is it so?"

"It is."

"And is that which is neither better nor worse fitting
any more or less a share of harmony, or is it equal?"

"It is equal."

"Then a soul, since it is neither better nor worse
than another soul is itself,
is it neither better nor worse harmonized?"

"Just so."

"And this would have no more
a share of discord or harmony?"

"It would not."

"And this again would have no more a share
of evil or virtue than another,
if evil was discord, and virtue harmony?"

"No more."

"But rather, Simmias, according to correct logic
no soul would have a share of evil,
if it is a harmony;
for perhaps a harmony being completely a harmony itself
it would have no share of discord."

"Of course not."

"And perhaps the soul, being completely a soul, no evil."

"For how could it out of what we said before?"

"Out of this argument then
all souls of all life will be similarly good,
if it is by nature they are similarly souls."

"It seems so to me, Socrates," he said.

"And does it seem beautiful," he said,
"that the argument would mean this
and result in these things,
if the hypothesis were correct that the soul is a harmony?"

"Not in the least," he said.

43

"But what," he asked, "of all that is in a person
do you say anything rules except the soul, and in the wise?"
  "I do not."
  "Which yields according to the feelings of the body
and which opposes?
But I mean, when it is hot and thirsty,
does it draw it in opposition, to not drink,
and when it is hungry to not eat,
and do we see how in a thousand other things
according to the body the soul opposes, or not?"
  "Certainly."
  "Then did we not agree previously that it could never,
if it be a harmony,
sound opposite to the tensions
and relaxations and vibrations and whatever other conditions
those might experience out of which it happens to be made,
but it would follow them and never lead?"
  "We agreed," he said; "for how can it not?"
  "Then what? Does it not now appear to us
to be working exactly the opposite,
leading all of those out of which one says it consists,
and opposing them in almost everything through all of life
and mastering in every way,
punishing them more harshly and with pain,
according to gymnastics and medicine,
and milder things, both threatening and admonishing them,
speaking to the desires and lusts and fears
as though it were something else other than those things?
And just as Homer composed in the *Odyssey*,
where he says of Odysseus:
  'Beating his breast he reproached his heart saying,
  "Endure it, heart;
  even more horrible have you endured."'
Do you think when these thoughts were composed
he thought of this reality as a harmony
also to be led by the conditions of the body,
but not something to lead and master these things,
and being itself much more a divine thing than a harmony?"

"By Zeus, Socrates, it seems so to me."

"Then, best one, it would not be beautiful at all
for us to say that the soul is a harmony;
for as it is likely,
we would not be agreeing with the divine poet Homer
nor with ourselves."

"That is so," he said.

44

"Well then," said Socrates, "the Theban Harmony
probably has been moderately gracious to us;
but what of Cadmus," he said,
"Cebes, how shall we find grace and with what argument?"

"It seems to me," said Cebes, "you will find it out;
at least this argument against harmony
spoke to me wonderfully beyond expectation.
For when Simmias was describing the difficulty,
I certainly wondered
if anyone could do anything with his argument;
so it seemed to me very unusual that
it did not accept the first direct approach of your argument.
Now I would not be surprised
if the argument of Cadmus experienced the same thing."

"O happy one," said Socrates, "do not talk big,
lest some envy overturn our argument
which is about to be made.
But surely this is in the care of God,
and let us being near like Homer
examine if there is anything in what you say.

"Surely the crown of what you seek is:
to prove in a way worthy of us
that the soul is indestructible and immortal,
if the philosophical man about to die,
is confident and believes dying he will do well there
differently than if in living another life he died,
he is confident that courage is not stupid and foolish.

"And dying, that the soul is something strong and divine
and existed even before we were born as people,
you say all this does not prevent it

from not revealing immortality,
but that the soul is long-lasting
and existed somewhere an extraordinarily long time before
and knew and did many things;
yet it was not any more immortal,
but its very coming into the body
was the beginning of its destruction, like a disease;
and then it lives the distress of this life
and finally perishes in what is called death.

"But now you say it does not matter
whether it enters into a body once or many times,
in reference to what each of us fears;
for it is fitting to be afraid, unless one is a fool,
if one does not know nor have an argument to give,
how it is immortal.

"Some such thing is, I think, Cebes, what you mean;
and I repeat it on purpose often
so that nothing may escape us,
and if you wish, you may add or subtract anything."

And Cebes said, "But in the present
I have nothing either to subtract or add;
and this is what I mean."

45
Then Socrates pausing for a long time
and considering something in himself
said, "It is not a trivial thing, Cebes, you are seeking;
for it is necessary to investigate completely
the cause of generation and decay.
So I will tell you
my own experience concerning these things, if you wish;
since if something appears to you useful in what I say,
you may use it for persuasion when you argue."

"I certainly do wish it," said Cebes.

"Then hear what I will say.
For I, Cebes," he said, "when young
was tremendously eager for this wisdom,
which they call the study of nature.
For it seemed to me to be magnificent,

to know the causes of each thing,
why each thing comes into being
and why it perishes and why it exists;
and I often changed myself topsy-turvy
considering first such things:
do heat and cold take some putrefaction, as some argued,
and then living things grow together;
and is it the blood by which we think,
or the air or fire, or none of these,
and is the brain what provides the sensations
of hearing and seeing and smelling,
and out of these does memory and opinion come,
and out of memory and opinion received
does knowledge according to these become stable?
And considering the ruin of these things,
and the state of heaven and earth,
until finally it seemed to be unnatural for me
to consider this matter at all.

   "And I will give you sufficient proof;
for what I knew distinctly before,
as it seemed to myself and to others,
then by that consideration thus quite blinded,
so that I unlearned even what before I was thinking to know,
about many other things and by what a person grows.
For this I was thinking before was clear to everyone,
that it is by eating and drinking;
for when out of food flesh accrues to flesh,
and bones to bones,
and thus according to the same argument also
parts of the same grow to each of the others,
and then the little bulk becomes more later,
and thus the small person becomes big;
then I was thinking thus.
Does it not seem reasonable to you?"

   "Yes," said Cebes.

   "Then consider this also.
For I was thinking it seemed to me adequate,
whenever some person stood alongside
the big one would appear to be larger

than the small one by a head,
and a horse with a horse;
and still more palpably than this,
ten seemed to me to be more than eight
because two was added to it,
and the two-cubit to be larger than the cubit
because of being twice as long."
   "And now," said Cebes, "what do you think about this?"
   "By Zeus," he said, "my place is far from thinking
I know the cause of any of these things,
who does not accept myself at all that,
when one is added to one,
whether the one to which was added became two,
or the one added, _____
or whether the one added and the one to which was added
because of the addition one to the other became two;
for I wonder if, when each of them was without the other,
each was then one and they were not then two,
and when they were brought near to each other,
then this was the cause of their becoming two,
the putting of them closer together with each other.
And still I am not persuaded that, if one is divided,
the division causes it to become two;
for then they arose because one was near to each other
and added to another,
and now because one is subtracted
and separated from another.
Because of this I no longer believe I know even
the meaning of how one or anything else is generated
or perishes or exists, according to this type of method,
but I made at random another way myself,
and I do not accept this anymore.

46
   "But when I heard someone reading out of a book,
as he said, of Anaxagoras, and arguing that
it is the mind which sets in order and causes everything,
I was pleased by this cause
and it seemed to me good to have some way
for the mind to be the cause of everything,

and I thought, if this is so,
the mind in ordering orders everything
and puts each thing itself how it is best to have it;
so if anyone wishes to discover the cause of each,
how it is generated or perishes or exists,
one must discover about it,
how it is best for it either to be
or to experience anything whatsoever or to do.
And then out of this argument nothing else is fitting
for a person to consider concerning both it and others,
but the virtue and the best.
And it is necessary to know this and the worst;
for the knowledge about them is the same.

"Contemplating these things I was glad to think
I had discovered a teacher of the causes of reality
according to my mind in Anaxagoras,
and to me would be shown first
whether the earth is flat or round,
and when shown, he would explain the cause and necessity,
arguing the better and why it was better for her to be such;
and if he said she was in the center,
he would explain how it was better
for her to be in the center;
and if these things would be proved,
I was prepared to yearn no longer
for any other kind of cause.

"And I was prepared also thus about the sun,
learning in like manner about both the moon
and the other stars,
the speed toward each other and courses
and the other phenomena,
how it is better for each of them
both to do and undergo what is undergone.

"For I never thought that,
having said they were ordered by mind,
any other cause would be offered for them
than that it is best to have them so as they are;
so having given a cause to each and to all in common
I was thinking it was being explained

what was best for each and good for all in common;
and I would not give up these hopes for a great deal,
but taking the books very seriously
I read them as quickly as I could in order to know
as quickly as possible the best and the worst.

47
   "So from this wonderful hope, friend, I was swept away,
when advancing in reading
I saw the man made no use of the mind
nor did he charge any causes in the ordering of things,
but air and ether and water
and many other oddities were charged.
   "And it seemed to me it was most like experiencing as if
someone said that Socrates does everything he does by mind,
and when attempting to explain the causes of each thing I do,
should say first that because of these things
I am now sitting here:
my body being composed out of bones and muscles,
and the bones are hard
and have joints separating them from each other,
and the muscles can be contracted and relaxed,
surrounding the bones with the flesh
and skin which contains them;
so raising the bones in their sockets
loosening and tightening the muscles
makes possible the bending which is now my care,
and because of this cause
I am sitting here in a bent position;
and concerning the discussion with you
he would argue other causes
such as voice and air and hearing and many other such causes,
neglecting to say the true causes that,
since it seemed to the Athenians it was best to condemn me,
and so because of these things
it seemed to me best to sit here,
and more right staying to undergo
whatever judgment they order;
since by the dog,
I fancy long ago these muscles and bones

would have been either around Megara or Boeotia,
carried by an opinion of the best,
if I did not think it was more just and beautiful
before fleeing and escaping
to undergo the judgment which the city may impose.

"But to call such things causes is very odd;
and if anyone should say that without having such things
as bones and muscles and other things I have,
I could not have done what seemed to me best,
one would be saying the truth;
yet to say because of these things I do what I do
and I do these by mind,
but not from choosing what is best,
would be a far-fetched and rash way of speaking.
For the discussion is unable to distinguish that
the cause is in reality something else,
and the other is that without which
the cause could never be a cause;
so it appears to me many are groping as in the dark,
attaching a false name to a stranger,
when they address a cause this way.

"And so someone by putting a whirlwind around the earth
makes the earth remain below heaven,
and another as a flat trough
supported on a foundation of air;
but of the power which is able now to establish these
placing them as is best,
they neither seek this
nor do they think it has any divine force,
but they believe they can discover an Atlas
stronger and more immortal and all-embracing than this,
and in truth they do not think at all of the good
which must both unite and embrace.

"Therefore of such causes
I would like to become a student
wherever, whenever, from anyone;
but since I was deprived of this and did not find it
nor was I able to learn it from another,
about the second voyage seeking for the cause

which I conducted,
do you wish me," he asked, "to add what I did, Cebes?"
  "I do wish it enormously," he said.

48
  "It seemed to me then," he said, "after this,
since I had failed in considering the realities,
it was necessary to be careful that I should not suffer
as those who watch and look at the sun during an eclipse;
for some ruin their eyes,
unless they look at it in water or something like that.
And I understood this,
and was afraid lest the soul would be completely blinded
looking at the things with the eyes
and attempting to perceive them with each of the senses.
  "So it seemed to me necessary
to take refuge in the meanings
to consider in them the truth of the realities.
Perhaps then the way I represent some is not accurate.
For I do not at all concede
that considering the realities in their meanings
is to consider them in images any more than in actions;
but then in this way I began,
and hypothesizing each argument
which I judge to be most sound,
whatever seems to me to agree with this,
I assume as being true,
both concerning causes and any other thing whatever,
and what does not, as not true.
But I wish to tell you more clearly what I mean;
for I think now you do not understand."
  "No, by God," said Cebes, "certainly not."

49
  "Well," he said, "I mean this, nothing new,
but as always and elsewhere and in the past argument
I have not stopped saying it.
For I am going to try to explain to you
the form of the cause which I have been working on,

and I am back again on those much repeated things
and begin from those,
hypothesizing there is a certain beauty in and of itself
and goodness and greatness and all the rest;
which if you grant me and agree these exist,
I hope out of this to explain to you the cause
and discover how the soul is immortal."

"Truly," said Cebes, "as it is granted to you
quickly conclude."

"Consider then next," he said, "these things,
if they seem to you as they do to me.
For it appears to me,
if anything else is beautiful except beauty itself,
for no other reason is it beautiful
than for the reason that it shares in that beauty;
and so I say this of all things.
Do you consent to such a cause?"

"I consent," he said.

"Now then," he said, "I do not yet understand
nor am I able to know these other wise causes;
but if anyone tells me the reason
why anything whatever is beautiful
is either its flowery color or shape
or anything else of that kind whatever,
I let the other things go,
for I am confused by all the others,
and this I hold simply and absolutely
and perhaps simplistically by myself,
that nothing else makes it beautiful
except either the presence or communion of that beauty
in whatever way that may also come to it;
for this is still not confirmed,
but that all beautiful things become beautiful by beauty.
For this seems to me to be the most sure thing to answer
both to myself and another,
and holding to this I believe it will never fall,
but it is safe both for me and anyone else to answer
that beautiful things are beautiful by beauty;
or does it not seem so to you too?"

"It does."

"And great things are great
and the greater greater by greatness,
and the lesser are less by smallness?"

"Yes."

"And you would not accept it,
if someone said one is greater than another by a head,
and the smaller smaller in the same way,
but you would affirm that you say nothing else
but that every greater thing is greater than another
by nothing else than greatness,
and on account of this greater, because of greatness,
and the smaller is smaller by nothing else than by smallness,
and on account of this smaller, because of smallness,
fearing I think, lest some opposite argument met you,
if you said someone is greater by a head and smaller,
first that the greater is greater by the same thing
and the smaller smaller,
since the greater is greater by a head which is small,
and this is monstrous,
that something is great by something small;
or would you not be afraid of this?"

  And laughing Cebes said, "I would."

  "Then," he said, "would you be afraid to say
ten is two more than eight,
and surpasses it on account of this cause,
but rather it counts more also on account of counting?
And the two-cubit is greater than the one-cubit by half,
but not by greatness?
For the same fear is there."

  "Certainly," he said.

  "But what? Would you not avoid saying that
in adding one to one addition is the cause of the two
or division of the dividing?
And you would shout loudly
that you know of no other way each thing is generated
than by sharing in the essential idea
of each thing in which it shares,
and in these you do not have any other cause

of the generating of the two than sharing in duality,
and it is necessary for things intending to be two
to share in this,
and whatever intends to be one in unity,
and you would let go of these divisions
and additions and other such subtleties,
passing yourself for the wiser to answer;
and you would be afraid, as in the saying,
of your own shadow and ignorance,
having that sure hypothesis, would you answer thus?

"And if anyone should challenge this hypothesis,
you would let it go and not answer
until you should consider the things that come from that,
whether to you they agree with each other or disagree;
and when you have to give the meaning of that principle,
you would give it in the same way,
by hypothesizing another hypothesis,
which should appear best of the higher ones,
until you should come to what was sufficient,
and at the same time you would not mix,
as the contentious do
in discussing about the beginning
and what comes out of that,
if you wish to find any of the realities.
For perhaps none of those think at all about this argument;
for adequate by their common wisdom
in mixing everything up
nevertheless they can be satisfied with this themselves;
but if you are a philosopher,
I think you should do as I say."

"You tell the truth," said Simmias and Cebes together.

ECHECRATES. By Zeus, Phaedo, reasonably said;
for amazingly it seems to me how distinctly
even to one having small intelligence he said these things.

PHAEDO. Certainly, Echecrates,
and it seemed so to everyone present.

ECHECRATES. Also for us not present, but hearing now.
But what was the discussion after this?

50

PHAEDO. As I believe,
when these things were consented to by him,
and they had agreed each of these forms exists
and other things sharing in these have their names,
then after this he asked, "So if you say these things thus,
do you not, when you say Simmias is greater than Socrates,
but smaller than Phaedo,
say then there is in Simmias both greatness and smallness?"

"I do."

"But," he said, "you agree
that Simmias exceeding Socrates
is not as stated in that phrase also true.
For not by having been born
does Simmias exceed Socrates in this,
but by the greatness which he happens to have;
nor does he exceed Socrates because Socrates is Socrates,
but because Socrates has smallness
next to that one's greatness."

"True."

"And he is not exceeded by Phaedo,
because Phaedo is Phaedo,
but because Phaedo has greatness
next to the smallness of Simmias."

"This is so."

"Thus Simmias has the name small and large,
being in between the two,
by exceeding in greatness he is exceeding the smallness,
and submitting to the greatness exceeding his smallness."
And at once smiling he said, "I am speaking like a book,
but then anyway it is as I say."

He agreed.

"And I am talking this way on account of
wishing for it to seem to you as it does to me.
For it appears to me not only that greatness itself
will never be at the same time great and small,
but also that the greatness in us will never accept the small
nor will it be exceeded by it,
but one of two things,

either it flees and withdraws,
when its opposite, the small, comes toward it,
or by that one coming near it perishes;
but it will not in surviving and accepting smallness
be other than as it was.
Just as I accepted and survived smallness,
and still being as I am, I am this same small person;
and the greatness has not endured being small;
as also the same way the smallness in us
will never become and be great,
nor will any other opposite, which is still as it was
become and be at the same time opposite,
but it either goes away or perishes in this experience."

"Absolutely," said Cebes, "thus it appears to me."

51
And one of those present hearing said—
who it was I don't clearly remember:
"Before the gods,
is not what we agreed to in the previous argument
the very opposite of what is being said now,
out of the lesser the greater is generated
and out of the greater the lesser,
and simply the very generation of opposites
is out of their opposites?
But now it seems to me it is being said
that this could never occur."

And Socrates turning his head and listening,
said, "Like a man you have spoken,
yet you do not understand the difference
between the meaning of now and then.
For then it was said
out of the opposite thing
the opposite thing is generated,
but now, that the opposite itself
could never become its own opposite,
neither in us nor in nature.
For then, friend, we were talking about
things having opposites, naming these by those names,
but now about those themselves,

which having have the name named;
and those themselves we say
will never accept generation from each other."
And looking at Cebes at the same time he said, "Cebes,
are you at all bothered by any of the things which he said?"

  "Not so much," said Cebes,
"though I am not saying that many things don't bother me."

  "Then we are agreed," he said, "plainly on this,
an opposite is never to be an opposite to itself."

  "Completely," he said.

52
  "So still also consider," he said,
"if you agree with me on this.
Do you call anything heat and cold?"

  "I do."

  "Then is it the same as snow and fire?"

  "By God, no."

  "But something other than fire is heat
and something other than snow is cold?"

  "Yes."

  "But here, I think, it seems to you,
if snow ever accepted heat,
as in the previous argument,
it will no longer be as it was, snow and warm,
but encountering heat
will either withdraw itself or perish."

  "Certainly."

  "And fire encountering cold
either withdraws itself or perishes,
yet it can never endure accepting the cold
and still be as it was, fire and cold."

  "You say the truth," he said.

  "Then it is," he said, "concerning some of these,
that not only the form itself
is worthy of its name into the eternity of time,
but also something else, which is not that,
but has the shape of that always whenever it exists.

But still in the following
perhaps it will be clearer what I am saying.
For the odd it is always necessary for this name to occur,
as now we are saying; or is it not?"

"Certainly."

"Then is it the only one, for I am asking this,
or is there something else also,
which is not the same as the odd,
but similarly it is necessary to call this also
with its own name always because of its nature,
so that it never is separated from the odd?
And I mean the same is also possible
in the case of three and many others.
But consider the three.
Then does it not seem to you
it may always be addressed by its own name
and as odd, which is not the same as three?
But similarly thus in the case of both the three
and the five and half of all the numbers,
so that not being the same as the odd
each of them is always odd;
and in the same way the two
and the four and all in the other series of numbers
not being the same as the even
similarly each of these is always even;
do you agree or not?"

"Of course," he said.

"Now," he said, "observe what I wish to clarify.
And here it is, that it appears
not only are those opposites not accepting each other,
but also opposites which not being opposites to each other
always have opposites,
these similarly do not accept that form
which is opposite to the reality in them,
but in its approach they perish or withdraw;
are we not saying the three will perish or anything else
before it will submit to becoming even
while it is still remaining three?"

"Certainly," said Cebes.

"But," he said, "two is not opposite to three."

"No."

"Then not only opposite forms
approaching each other do not remain,
but also certain other opposites approaching do not remain."

"You say the truth," he said.

53

"Then do you wish," he said, "if we can,
to determine what these are?"

"Certainly."

"Then Cebes," he said, "will they be those which,
when they take possession,
not only compel it to take its own form,
but also always of some opposite?"

"What do you mean?"

"The same as we just said.
For you know of course that
those forms which take possession of the three,
must be in themselves not only three but also odd."

"Certainly."

"So still such, we said, the opposite forms to that shape,
which make it this, never could be."

"No."

"And does the odd make it?"

"Yes."

"And is the even opposite to this?"

"Yes."

"Then the three will never come to the form of the even."

"Of course not."

"So the three has no part in the even."

"No part."

"Then the three is uneven."

"Yes."

"Now what I said is to be determined is
what things not being opposites to something
nevertheless do not accept the opposite itself,

as now the three in not being the opposite to the even
does not any the more accept it,
for it always brings forth the opposite to it,
and the two to the odd
and fire to the cold and all the rest—
but see if you note this,
not only the opposite does not accept the opposite,
but also that, which brings forth something opposite to that,
which it approaches,
will never accept the oppositeness of the very thing brought.
  "And again recall,
for there is no harm in hearing it often.
The five will not accept the even,
nor the ten, the double, the odd;
so this itself is also not opposite to the other,
but nevertheless it will not accept that of the odd;
nor the half nor such others that of the whole,
also in turn a third and all such things,
if you follow and agree on this."
  "Very certainly I both agree," he said, "and follow."

54
  "So again," he said, "tell me from the beginning.
And do not answer me what I ask, but imitate me.
And I mean beyond what was first said, that safe answer,
seeing now another safe one out of what was said.
For if you ask me what makes something hot,
I will not tell you that safe ignorant answer
that it is heat,
but out of the more refined now, that it is fire;
and if you ask, what makes a body ill,
I will not say that it is an illness, but a fever;
and what makes a number to be odd,
I will not say oddness, but a one, and so on.
But see if already you sufficiently understand what I mean."
  "But quite sufficiently," he said.
  "So answer," he said, "what makes the body to be alive?"
  "The soul," he said.
  "Then is this always the case?"

"Of course," he said.

"Then the soul that takes possession of it,
does it always come bringing life to that?"

"It does," he said.

"And first is there anything opposite to life or not?"

"There is," he said.

"What?"

"Death."

"Then will the soul ever accept the opposite
to what it always brings,
as out of the previous agreement?"

"Most certainly not," said Cebes.

55

"What then?
So now what do we name the form not accepting the even?"

"Uneven," he said.

"And what does not accept the just and the musical?"

"Unmusical," he said, "and the unjust."

"Well; and what does not accept death, we call what?"

"Immortal," he said.

"Then does the soul not accept death?"

"No."

"So the soul is immortal."

"Immortal."

"Well," he said; "then shall we say
this is demonstrated; how does it seem?"

"And most sufficiently, Socrates."

"What then, Cebes?" he said.
"If it was necessary for the uneven to be indestructible,
what else than indestructible would the three be?"

"For how could it not?"

"Then if also it was necessary
for the heatless to be indestructible,
whenever any heat approached snow,
would the snow withdraw to be safe and unmelted?

for it could not have perished,
nor could it remaining have accepted the heat."

"You say the truth," he said.

"In the same way, I think, also
if the coldless were indestructible,
whenever anything cold approached fire,
it would never be extinguished nor perish,
but having gone away safe it would endure."

"By necessity," he said.

"Then also," he said,
"is it not necessary to say this about the immortal?
If the immortal is also indestructible,
it is impossible for the soul,
when death comes upon it, to perish;
for out of what was said before
it will not accept death nor will it be dead,
just as we said the three will not be even, nor will the odd,
nor fire cold, nor the heat in the fire.

"But what prevents, someone might say,
the odd from becoming even when approached by the even,
as we agreed,
but perishing the even becomes it instead of that?

"To the one saying this
we would have nothing to contend that it does not perish;
for the uneven is not indestructible;
since if this were conceded to us,
we could easily contend that when the even approaches
the odd and the three withdrawing are gone;
and we could contend this about fire and heat and the others.
Or could we not?"

"Certainly."

"So too now concerning the immortal,
if it is conceded to us also to be indestructible;
but if not, another argument would be needed."

"But it is not needed," he said, "on account of this;
for scarcely anything else would not accept ruin,
if the immortal which is eternal will accept ruin."

56
  "But God, I think," said Socrates,
"and the form of life itself,
and if there is anything else immortal,
by all it would be agreed they will never perish."

  "Of course by all people, by God," he said,
"and even more, I think, by gods."

  "Since then the immortal is also incorruptible,
the soul, if it happens it is immortal,
also would be indestructible?"

  "Very definitely."

  "Then when death comes upon a person
the mortal part of one, it seems, dies,
and the immortal, safe and incorruptible,
going away is gone, withdrawing from death."

  "It appears so."

  "Then more than all, Cebes," he said,
"the soul is immortal and indestructible,
and in reality our souls will exist in Hades."

  "So I, Socrates," he said,
"have nothing else to say along these lines
nor can I disbelieve the arguments.
However, if Simmias or anyone else has anything to say,
he would do well not to keep silent;
as I do not know any other time to which it could be delayed
other than now in the present,
if anyone is wishing
either to say or hear anything about such things."

  "But," said Simmias,
"I myself have no disbelief from the discussion;
yet under the greatness which the arguments are about,
and not esteeming human weakness,
I still must have disbelief
along my lines about what was said."

  "Not only that, Simmias," said Socrates,
"but also the first hypotheses,
even if they are believed by you,
similarly should be more carefully examined;
and if you analyze them sufficiently,

I think, you will follow the argument
as closely as it is possible for a human to do;
and if this itself becomes clear,
you will not seek further."
  "You tell the truth," he said.

57
  "But, men," he said, "it is right to understand that,
if the soul is immortal,
then it is necessary to take care of her
not only for this time which we call life, but for all time,
and the danger now also seems to be terrible
if one does not take care of her.
For if death were a release from everything,
it would be a god-send for the evil
who in dying would be released from the body
and at the same time from their evils with the soul;
but now since it appears to be immortal,
no one can escape from evils nor be saved in any other way
except by becoming as good and wise as possible.
  "For the soul goes into Hades having nothing else
except her education and nurture,
which it is said greatly helps or harms the dead
in the very beginning of the journey there.
And so it is said, that then each angel
of each of the dead, as assigned in life,
attempts to lead them into a place,
where those gathered must be judged to pass into Hades
with that guide who has been appointed
to conduct them from here to there;
and there occurring that which must happen
and remaining for the necessary time
another guide brings them here again
after many long periods of time.
  "And the journey is not as Aeschylus's Telephus says;
for that one says a simple path brings one into Hades,
but it appears to me to be neither simple nor single.
For it would not need guides;
for no one could ever stray from a single road.

But now it seems to have many forks and circuits;
I speak from the signs of the holy rites and customs here.
   "Therefore the orderly and sensible soul follows
and does not ignore the present;
but the one having desires of the body,
as I said previously,
excited about that for a long time
and around the visible place,
after much resistance and much suffering,
departs led by force and with pain by the appointed angel.
   "And arriving where the others are,
the impure and any having done such a thing
as taking part in unjust murders or other such actions,
which happen to be brother acts of these and of sister souls,
it is avoided and shunned by all
who also are not willing to become its companion nor guide,
but she wanders by herself in complete confusion,
until it should be a certain time,
when going out by necessity
she is carried into her proper home;
but those who passed through life purely and moderately,
and getting divine companions and guides,
each lives in her proper place.
And there are many marvelous regions of the earth,
and she is neither in size
nor in any way what she is imagined
by those who are used to talking about the earth,
as I am persuaded by someone."

58
   And Simmias said, "What do you mean by that, Socrates?
For I have heard much about the earth myself,
yet not the things you believe;
so gladly I would listen."
   "Well then, Simmias, it does not seem to me
to be the art of Glaucus to narrate what she is;
yet as truth,
it appears to me to be harder than by the art of Glaucus,
and at the same time perhaps I would not be able to,

and besides, even if I knew how,
it seems to me my life, Simmias, would be over
before the argument is adequate.
Yet nothing prevents my telling what I believe to be
the form of the earth and her regions."

"But," said Simmias, "that will be adequate."

"I believe then," he said, "that first,
if she is in the middle of the heavens being carried round,
she needs neither air nor any other such necessity
for her not to fall,
but sufficient to maintain her
are the likeness of heaven to all of it
and the equal balance of the earth herself;
for something equally balanced
put in the middle of something similar
will not incline at all more nor less,
but similarly stays unswerving.
First," he said, "I believe this."

"And correctly," said Simmias.

"Next then," he said, "she is something very large,
and those of us living
between the pillars of Heracles and the Phasis river
live in a small portion around the sea,
like ants or frogs around a pond,
and many others elsewhere live in many such places.
For there are everywhere around the earth
many hollows of all sorts both in form and greatness,
into which the water and the mists and the air
have flowed together;
but the earth pure herself is situated in the pure heaven,
in which the stars are,
which is called ether
by many who are used to talking about such things;
of which these are the sediment
and flow together always into the hollows of the earth.

"So our living in her hollows is unnoticed,
and we think we are living up on the earth,
just as if someone who lived at the bottom of mid-ocean
should think one lived on the sea,

and through the water seeing the sun and the other stars
should believe the sea to be heaven,
and because of slowness and weakness
never reached the surface of the sea nor ever seen,
getting out and popping up out of the sea into this place,
which happens to be more pure and beautiful than theirs,
nor having heard from another who had seen.

"And this is the same thing we have experienced;
for living in some of the hollows of the earth
is to think one is living above her,
and to call the air heaven,
since because of this heaven the stars really move;
but the fact is, by weakness and slowness
we are not able to go through to the utmost air;
since, if anyone should go to the top of it
or becoming winged should reach it, popping up to look down,
just as the fish popping up out of the sea see things here,
so someone there also could look down on things,
and if by nature were capable to hold up to the looking,
would recognize that that is truly heaven
and truly the light and so truly the earth.

"For this earth and the stones and the whole region here
are corrupted and devoured,
just like things in the sea by the brine,
and nothing worth any meaning grows in the sea,
nor, as one might say, is anything perfect,
but it is caves and sand and endless mud and mire,
where there would be earth also,
and nothing is in any way worthy to be judged beautiful
compared to our things;
but those things would appear
to surpass even much more ours.
For if it is necessary also to tell a story,
worth hearing, Simmias,
it hits upon the things on the earth
which are below the heavens."

"But Socrates," said Simmias,
"we would gladly listen to this story."

59
"Then it is said, friend," he said,
"first that to see the earth is such,
if one looked from above, as twelve spheres,
varied, with distinct colors,
for which also the colors are like patterns,
with which the painters color;
but there the whole earth is made out of these,
and out of even brighter and purer ones than these;
for the purple also is of amazing beauty, and the golden,
and the white whiter than chalk or snow,
and she is composed likewise out of the other colors,
still more amazing and beautiful than the ones we see.
For these very same hollows which are full of water and air,
present a form of color
shining among the other varied colors,
so that in her continuous form she appears varied.

  "And in this same reality
growing things grow in proportion,
trees and flowers and the fruits;
and further the mountains likewise and the stones
are by the same ratio smoother and transparent
and the colors more beautiful;
and the pebbles which here are these prized ones,
sards and jaspers and emeralds and all such gems;
but there what is not such
is even more beautiful than these.
And the reason for this is that those stones are pure
and not devoured and corrupted as those here are
by rottenness and brine flowing together here,
which also produce in stones and earth
and the other animals and plants deformity and disease.
And the earth herself has been arranged with all these
and also with gold and silver and other such things.
For showing forth these have grown, being many,
abundant and large and in many places of the earth,
so that seeing her is a blessed sight to see.

  "And upon her there are many other animals and people,
some living inland, and some around the air,
as we around the sea,

and some on islands
which the air flows around being next to the mainland;
and in a word,
what the water and the sea are to us for our use,
there the air is this,
and what the air is to us, the ether is to them.

  "And its seasons have such temperature,
that they have no diseases
and a lifetime is much longer than here,
and sight and hearing and sensibility and all such things
stand apart from ours in the same way as
air stands apart more pure than water and ether than air.

  "So also even their groves and sacred places are divine,
in which gods are really living,
and speaking and prophecies and visions of the gods
and such communions occur with these to them;
and the sun and moon and stars
are seen by them as they really are,
and otherwise happiness is in accord with these.

60
  "And so the whole earth has such a nature
and the things around the earth;
but in her, down in her hollows
round about the whole are many regions,
some deeper and more spread out than those in which we live,
and some deeper having a narrower opening than our region,
and some are shorter in depth than here and are wider;
but all these are connected to each other by the earth
in many places down both narrower and wider,
and having passages through which much water flows
from one to another like in a basin,
and ever flowing rivers extraordinarily large under the earth
and of warm and cold waters,
and much fire and great rivers of fire,
and many streams of mud both thinner and thicker,
like in Sicily the rivers of mud flowing before the lava
and the lava itself;
and so which fill each of the regions,
as to each by chance the flowing around each time occurs.

And all these move up and down
like some oscillation within the earth;
and so this oscillation through nature is some such thing.
  "One of the chasms of the earth
happens to be greater than the rest
and is bored right through the whole earth,
this of which Homer himself says,
    'Far off, where deepest beneath the earth is an abyss;'
and which elsewhere
he and many other poets have called Tartarus.
For all the rivers flow together into this chasm
and flow out of it again;
and each becomes such,
as the earth through which it also flows.
  "And the cause of all the streams
flowing in and out of here
is that this liquid has no foundation nor base.
So it oscillates and waves up and down,
and the air and the wind around it do the same thing;
for they follow it
both when it moves into the other side of the earth
and when it moves into this side,
and like the breath stream of the breathing
always blows out and blows in,
so too there the wind oscillates with the liquid
and produces some terrible and extraordinary winds
both going out and going in.
  "Therefore when the water withdraws
into the region called the lower,
it flows into the streams down there through the earth
and fills them like pumps;
and when it sinks from there, and moves here,
it fills the ones here again,
and being filled they flow through the passages
and through the earth,
and into the regions they each reach,
into which each makes a path,
and they make seas and marshes and rivers and springs;
and from there again sinking beneath the earth,

some going around larger regions and more,
and others lesser and smaller,
again emptying into Tartarus,
some much below where they were emitted, and some a little;
but all flow in below the exit.

   "And some flow in opposite where they came out,
and others below the same part;
and there are some going completely around in a circle,
either once or even many times
wound around the earth like snakes,
descending as low as possible emptying in again.
And it is possible to go down both ways
as far as the center, but no further;
for it is uphill to both streams
from either side of the center.

61
   "So then these streams are many
and great and of all kinds;
and it happens then that among these many are four streams,
the greatest and outermost of which flows in a circle
and is called Oceanus,
and opposite this flowing oppositely is Acheron,
which flows through other desert regions
and flowing under the earth arrives into the Acherusian lake,
at which the souls of most of the dead arrive
and having stayed for the time due,
some longer, and some shorter,
again are sent out to be born into living creatures.
   "And the third river comes out between these,
and near its exit it falls into
a great region burning with much fire,
and it makes a lake greater than the sea by us,
boiling with water and mud;
and from there it withdraws in a circle turbid and muddy,
and winding around to another place
it arrives also at the edge of the Acherusian lake,
not mingling with its water;
but winding around many times beneath the earth
empties lower than Tartarus;

and this is what they name Pyriphlegethon,
from which also the lava streams drawn off
spout up wherever they happen to on the earth.

"And opposite this the fourth falls
first into a region terrible and wild, as it is said,
the whole of which having a dark blue color,
which they name Stygian,
and the lake, which the river emptying makes, Styx;
and having fallen in here
and received terrible powers in the water,
passing beneath the earth,
winding around it withdraws opposite to the Pyriphlegethon
and meets it in the Acherusian lake from the other side;
and also this water does not mingle with any,
but this too going around in a circle
empties into Tartarus opposite to the Pyriphlegethon;
and the name of this is, as the poets say, Cocytus.

62
"Such is the nature of these,
when the dead arrive at the place
where the angel brings each,
first they are judged,
those who lived well and piously and those who did not.

"And the ones judged not to have lived moderately,
going to the Acheron, embarking on ships which are for them,
arrive in them at the lake,
and there they live and are purified of the wrongs
making amends they are forgiven,
if someone did something wrong,
and of the good deeds they gain something
each according to merit;
but the ones judged to have incurable wrongs
because of the greatness of the faults,
or who committed many and great sacrileges
or unjust murders and many crimes,
or who happened to do any other such things,
the fitting destiny casts these into Tartarus,
from where they never get out.

"But the curable ones,
judged to have committed great crimes,
who in anger did something violent to father or mother,
and lived the rest of their life in repentance,
or who were manslaughterers in some other such way,
they fall into Tartarus by necessity,
they having fallen and also having been there a year
the wave throws them out,
the manslaughterers by the Cocytus,
the father-beaters and mother-beaters by the Pyriphlegethon;
and when they have been carried by the Acherusian lake,
from there they cry and call,
to those they killed, and to those they offended,
and calling they beg and ask to allow them
to get out into the lake and be accepted,
and if they persuade them,
they get out and they cease the evils,
but if not, they are carried again into the Tartarus
and from there again into the rivers,
and these sufferings do not stop
until they persuade those they wronged;
for this is the sentence imposed on them by the judges.

   "But the ones judged to have lived excelling in holiness,
these are free from these regions in the earth
and released as from prisons,
and arriving up into the pure home they dwell on earth.
And of these those purified sufficiently by philosophy
live without bodies altogether in the time thereafter,
and arrive into homes even more beautiful than these,
which are not easy to describe
nor is there sufficient time in the present.
However, on account of these things we discussed
we ought to do everything
so as to share in virtue and thoughtfulness in life;
for the contest is beautiful and the hope great.

63
   "So for such things to be relied upon as being thus,
as I described,
it is not fitting for a man having intelligence;

yet that it is this or some such thing
concerning our souls and the homes,
since the soul appears to be immortal,
this also seems to me fitting
and a venture worthy of imagining it is so;
for the venture is beautiful;
and such things are useful in singing to oneself,
wherefore I also have lengthened the past story.

"However on account of these things
it is useful for a man to take courage concerning his soul,
who in life renounced the other pleasures of the body
and its ornaments, as being alien,
believing even more it is another thing to be perfected,
and has been serious about learning things
and has adorned the soul not with something alien
but with her own order,
discretion and justice and courage and freedom and truth,
thus one waits for the journey into Hades,
as passing when destiny should call.

"So you, Simmias," he said, "and Cebes and the others,
hereafter in some time each will pass;
but now already it calls me,
a man of tragedy would say, destiny,
and the hour is close for me to turn to the bath;
for it is better to be bathed to drink the drug
and not cause the women the trouble of bathing the corpse."

64
When he had said these things,
Crito said, "Well, Socrates, what do you direct me to do
either concerning the children or anything else
which we could do for you as a special favor?"

"As I always say, Crito," he said, "nothing new;
that taking care of yourselves
you are doing a favor both to me and mine and yourselves,
if you do, even if now you do not promise;
but if you neglect yourselves
and are not willing to live as on the track
of these speeches now and the previous ones,

no, even if you promise much in the present and vehemently,
you will not do any better."

  "Accordingly we shall be eager," he said, "to do so;
but in what manner shall we bury you?"

  "However you wish," he said,
"if you can catch me and I do not escape from you."
And laughing gently and at once looking toward us he said,
"I have not convinced Crito, men, that I am this Socrates,
who now is conversing and arranging each part of the arguing,
but he thinks I am that corpse
which he will see a little later,
and so he asks how he should bury me.
And though I have just made much argument, that,
when I drink the drug, I shall no longer stay with you,
but I shall go away into the joys of the blessed,
these things about me to him I seem to say otherwise,
encouraging at once both you and myself.

  "So you will give me a pledge to Crito," he said,
"the opposite than the one which you pledged to the judges.
For that one was to remain;
but you will pledge I am not to remain, when I die,
but I shall go away,
so that Crito may bear it more easily,
and seeing my body either burned or buried
would not be upset on my behalf as terrible suffering,
nor say at the funeral
that Socrates is being displayed or carried out or buried.
for know well, excellent Crito," he said,
"to say what is not beautiful not only is wrong by itself,
but also it produces evil in the souls.
But you must have courage and say this body is being buried,
and bury it thus as is pleasing to you
and as you believe is most customary."

65
  Having said this he stood up
to go into a room for bathing,
and Crito followed him, and he ordered us to wait.
Thus waiting we were discussing among ourselves

about the things said and examined,
and then about the circumstances gone through,
how it would come to be for us,
really believing as though deprived of a father
we would spend life thereafter as orphans.

And when he had bathed
and the children had been brought to him—
for there were two of his small sons, and one big one—
and the women of the family had arrived,
having conversed with them facing Crito
and commanded some things he wished,
he ordered the women and the children to go away,
and came himself to us.

And it was already near sunset;
for he spent a long time inside.
And coming he sat down having bathed,
and after that not much was discussed,
and the servant of the eleven came and stood by him;
"Socrates," he said, "I shall not condemn you
as I condemn others, who are angry with me and curse,
when I give them the word
to drink the drug compelled by the rulers.
And I have known you to be otherwise in this time
the noblest and gentlest and best man who ever arrived here,
and even now I know well that you are not angry with me,
but with those, for you know the ones responsible.
Now, for you know what I came to announce,
goodby and try to bear the constraints as easy as possible."
And at once bursting into tears turning he went away.

And Socrates looking up at him said, "And goodby to you,
and we shall do these things."
And at once to us he said, "What a charming person!
and during all the time he has come to me
and conversed sometimes and was the most agreeable of men,
and now how nobly he weeps for me.
But come now, Crito, let us obey him,
and let someone bring the drug, if it has been ground;
and if not, let a person grind it."

And Crito said, "But I think, Socrates,
the sun is still on the mountains and has not yet set.
And at the same time I know also others drank it quite late,
when the word should be given to them,
they have dined and drank quite well,
and kept company with some whom they happened to desire.
But do not hurry at all;
for it is still permitted."
    And Socrates said, "Naturally, Crito,
those do these things, which you say,
for they think they gain by doing them,
and I naturally shall not do these things;
for I think I would not gain anything
by drinking it a little later
other than to bring on ridicule for myself,
clinging to life and sparing it
when there is nothing still in it.
But come," he said, "obey and do not do otherwise."

66
    And Crito having heard nodded to the boy standing nearby.
And the boy going out and spending a long time
came leading the one intending to give the drug,
bringing it in a cup ground;
and Socrates seeing the person said, "Well, best one,
for you have knowledge of these things,
what is necessary to do?"
    "Nothing," he said, "except drinking it
to walk around until your legs become heavy, then lie down;
and thus it will do it itself."
    And at the same time he held out the cup to Socrates;
and taking it and very gently, Echecrates,
not trembling nor changing color or expression,
but as he was accustomed to doing,
looking up like a bull toward the person, he said,
"What do you say about pouring out a libation to someone?
Is it allowed or not?"
    "We grind such amount, Socrates," he said,
"as we think to be the measure to drink."

"I understand," he said;
"but it is allowed and useful to pray anyway to the gods,
that the change of residence from here to there be fortunate;
which now also I pray and may it be so."
And having said these things at once holding it up
he drank it off very accommodatingly and calmly.

And most of us up to this time
were reasonably able to restrain from weeping,
but as we saw him drinking and having drunk it,
no longer could we, but in spite of myself even
my tears were coming not in drops,
so that hiding my face I was wailing;
for it was not for him, but for my own fortune,
of a man who was being deprived of such a companion.

And Crito got up even before I,
when he could not restrain his tears.
But Apollodorus even in the previous time
did not stop weeping,
and so then really roaring out the wailing was so upsetting
that there was no one who did not break down
of those present except Socrates himself.

But he said, "What sort of things
you are doing, you wonders!
Yet not least did I send away the women on account of this,
so that they would not offend in such ways;
for I have heard that it is useful to die among praising.
But keep quiet and be patient."

And we having heard were ashamed
and restrained the weeping.
And walking around, when he said his legs were heavy,
he lay down on his back;
for the person ordered this;
and at once this giver of the drug grasping him,
after a time he examined his feet and legs,
and when he had pressed hard his foot he asked if he felt it;
"No," he said;
and after this in turn the calves;
and going up thus he showed us that
he was growing cold and stiff.

And again he touched him and said that
when it reached his heart, then he would be gone.
   So already the cooling was nearly about his abdomen,
and uncovering his head, for he had covered it up,
he said, which he really uttered dying,
"Crito," he said, "we owe to Asclepius a cock;
but pay it and do not neglect it."
   "But this shall be done," said Crito;
"but see, if you have anything else to say."
Having asked him this he no longer answered,
but a short time after he moved,
and the person uncovered him,
and his eyes were set;
and Crito seeing it closed his mouth and eyes.

67
   Such was the end, Echecrates, of our companion,
a man, as we might say,
of those we had experience of at that time
who was best and besides most sensible and most just.

Ethical Writings of Epicurus

Epicurus was born in 340 BC and was raised at Samos by his schoolmaster father. As an Athenian citizen he reported for two years of military service when he was eighteen. He taught philosophy in Asia Minor before buying a home and the Garden at Athens, where he taught from 306 BC until his death in 270 BC. According to the biography by Diogenes Laertius, Epicurus wrote extensively, but only a few letters and short sayings remain. His atomistic philosophy was later described in the poem *On the Nature of Things* by Lucretius. Epicurus summarized his ethical teachings in a *Letter to Monoeceus* and his forty *Authoritative Doctrines*. A 14th-century manuscript discovered in 1888 from the Vatican library included many more sayings by Epicurus and is entitled *Pronouncements of Epicurus*. Other "fragments" are *Quotations of Epicurus* from other classical writers. The quote in the *Letter to Monoeceus* about dying soon after being born is from the poet Theognis.

Epicurus' Letter to Menoeceus

Epicurus to Menoeceus, greeting:
Let no one who is young delay loving wisdom
nor let the aging tire of philosophy;
for no age is too early or too late for a healthy soul.
Saying that the season for loving wisdom
has not arrived or that it is past
is like saying that the time for happiness
has not yet come or is gone.
Therefore both young and old must love wisdom
so that while aging one may be young in good things
by the grace of what has been
while the young may at the same time also be old
because of not fearing the future.
So we should care for the things that make happiness,
since if this is present, we have everything;
but if it is absent, everything we do is to gain this.
I have been constantly recommending
that you practice and care for these things,
holding them to be the elements of a beautiful life.

First think of the living God, immortal and blessed,
as the common idea of God is engraved on minds
and do not attribute to this anything alien
to its incorruptibility or its blessedness,
but believe about this
all that upholds its incorruptiblity and blessedness.
For gods do exist.
The knowledge of them is clear,
but they are not what many think,
for most do not uphold the same ideas about them.
And impious is not the one who denies the gods of many
but the one who imposes on the gods the opinions of many.
For the statements of many about the gods
are not true conceptions but false assumptions,
thus it is that great harms come to the bad
from the gods and help to the good.
For being accustomed to their own virtues
they welcome those like themselves
while rejecting all others as alien.

   Accustom yourself to thinking that death is nothing to us;
for all good and bad is in perception,
and death is the deprivation of perception.
Thus the right understanding that death is nothing to us
makes the mortality of life enjoyable,
not by adding to life infinite time
but by removing the yearning for immortality.
For life has no terror for the one who truly understands
that there is nothing terrible in not living.
So one is foolish saying one is afraid of death,
not because it will be painful in the future but in the present.
For whatever does not annoy in the present
is a meaningless pain in expectation.
So the most terrifying of evils, death, is nothing to us,
since when we are, it is not present;
and when death is present, then we do not exist.
So it is nothing either to the living or to those who have ended,
since for the former it does not exist,
and the latter no longer exist.

   But many avoid death now as the greatest of evils
but then welcome it as rest from things in life.

The wise neither declines life nor fears not living;
for life does not offend him
nor does he believe that not being alive is bad.
Just as food is not chosen
only for the larger portion but for the more pleasant,
so the wise enjoy the time that is not longer but happier.
   The one who advises the young to live well
and the aging to make a fine end is foolish,
not only because of life being welcome
but also because a fine life and dying well are the same care.
Much worse is the one who says it is well not to be born.
   "But once born pass quickly through the gates of Hades."
For if one says this from conviction
why does he not depart from life?
For it is easy to do this if one is firmly resolved on this;
but if mocking, it is vain to those allowing it.
   We must remember that the future is neither ours
nor wholly not ours
so that we cannot completely expect it as existing
nor despair of it completely as not existing.
   It should also be recognized that of desires
some are natural, but others are vain.
Of the natural some are also necessary,
and others are only natural.
Of the necessary desires some are necessary for happiness,
some for the repose of the body, and others for life itself.
For whoever has a clear and certain understanding
of these things will direct every preference and aversion
toward the health of the body and an untroubled soul,
since this is the goal of a blessed life.
For we do all things for the sake of this,
how to have neither grief nor fear.
Once this has occurred for us,
the storm of the soul is dissolved,
and the living creature does not have to proceed
searching for what is lacking nor for anything else
by which the good of the soul and the body will be fulfilled.
For then we have the need of pleasure
when we are pained from pleasure not being present;

but when we are not pained, we no longer need pleasure.
And because of this we say that
pleasure is the beginning and end of a blessed life.
For we recognize pleasure as the first and innate good,
and from this we originate every choice and aversion,
and we return to this as the measure of feeling
for judging every good.

Also since this is our first and native good,
for this reason we do not choose every pleasure;
but we may pass over many pleasures
when a greater annoyance accompanies them,
and often we consider pains better than pleasures
when submission to the pains for a long time
results in greater pleasure for us.
So every pleasure because of its natural relationship is good,
though not all are chosen,
just as every pain is bad,
and not all are always to be avoided.
Yet by measuring one against another
and by looking at the advantages and disadvantages
all these things must be judged.
For sometimes we experience the good as bad
and other times the bad as good.

Also we consider self-sufficiency a great good,
not so that we use little in all cases
but in order to be content with little if we do not have much,
being truly persuaded that
they have the sweetest enjoyment who least need it,
and as the natural is easily obtained; but the vain is hard.
For simple foods bring as much pleasure as expensive ones
once the pain of need has been removed;
and bread and water produce the highest pleasure
when they are brought to those in need.
Becoming accustomed therefore
to a simple and inexpensive diet
supplies both the fullest health
and makes a person alert for the necessities of life,
and it puts us in better condition
when we come at intervals to the expensive,
and it prepares us to be fearless toward chance.

So when we say that pleasure is the goal,
we do not mean
the pleasures of the prodigal and idle enjoyment
as some think in ignorance and in not agreeing
or taking it badly,
but not to feel pain in the body nor to be troubled in the soul.
For it is neither drinking nor carousing together
nor enjoying children and women
nor fish and other things brought to an expensive table
which produce a pleasant life,
but sober reasoning and examining the motives
for every choice and avoidance
and eliminating those beliefs through which
the greatest confusion takes hold of the soul.
    Of all these the first and greatest good is prudence,
thus making prudence even more valued than philosophy.
From it all remaining virtues are derived
as it teaches it is not possible to live pleasantly
without living prudently, nobly, and justly,
nor can one live prudently, nobly, and justly
without living pleasantly.
For the virtues have grown into the life of pleasure,
and the life of pleasure is inseparable from these.
    Then who do you think is better
than the one who has holy beliefs about the gods
and about death no fear at all
and has considered the end of nature,
and realizes that the limit of the goods
is easily fulfilled and obtained,
while the time or pain of evils is slight?
Laughing at fate brought in by some as master of all,
rather he says that some things occur by necessity,
some by chance, and others by ourselves
because of seeing that necessity is irresponsible
and chance unstable,
but what is by us is not despotic,
and to it naturally follows blame and the opposite,
since it is better to accept the myths of the gods
than to be enslaved by the fate of scientists.

For by honoring the gods
one underwrites hope of intercession,
while necessity has no intercession.
Holding that chance is not a god, as many think,
for there is no disorder in the acts of God,
nor is it an uncertain cause,
he does not believe that good or evil
are given by this to people for a blessed life,
though it may supply the beginning of great good or evil,
thinking that the misfortune of the logical is better
than the good fortune of the illogical.
For it is better in this for actions well judged
not to be made right by chance.

Therefore take care of these things and related ones
by yourself and with someone like yourself day and night,
and never while awake or dreaming be disturbed,
and you will live as a god among humans.
For a human living among the immortal goods
is not like a mortal animal.

Authoritative Doctrines of Epicurus

1. What is blessed and incorruptible has no troubles itself
nor does it produce them for any other,
and so it embraces neither anger nor partiality;
for all such things are in the weak.

2. Death is nothing to us;
for the dissolved has no perception,
and what has no perception is nothing to us.

3. The greatest pleasure is the removal of all pain.
When pleasure is present, as long as it is there,
there is neither pain nor mental stress nor both together.

4. Continuous pain does not last long in the flesh;
rather, extreme pain is present for the shortest time,
and even what exceeds the pleasure in the flesh
does not continue for many days.
Chronic illnesses allow more pleasure than pain in the flesh.

5. Living pleasantly is not possible
without living prudently and well and justly,
nor can one live prudently and well and justly

without living pleasantly.
Whenever one of these is not there, such as living prudently,
even though both living well and justly are there,
it is not possible to live pleasantly.

6. In order to be courageous in regard to people
any way of procuring this is a natural good.

7. Some people intended to become notable and admired,
thinking this would make them secure from people.
So if the life of such people really was secure,
they attained the natural good;
but if it was not secure, they have not attained
what they sought at the beginning by natural instinct.

8. No pleasure is by itself bad;
but the things which produce some pleasures
bring on disturbances many times greater than the pleasures.

9. If every pleasure could be intensified,
both in time and about the whole organism
or in the most important parts of nature,
the pleasures would never be different from each other.

10. If the things producing the pleasures of profligates
could loosen the fears of the mind
about the heavens and death and pain,
and if also they taught the limit of desires,
we would never have a reason to blame them;
they would be filling themselves
with pleasures from everywhere
and would have neither pain nor stress, which is the real evil.

11. If we had never been bothered by suspicions of the heavens
and about death, whether it ever affects us,
and if we did not observe the limits of pains and desires,
we would not need natural science.

12. It is impossible to dispel anxieties
about the most important things
if one does not understand the nature of the universe,
but suspects there is something in the myths.
Thus without natural science
it is impossible to attain the pleasures uncontaminated.

13. There is no profit in procuring security against people
if we suspect what is ordained from above

and from under the earth and absolutely in the infinite.

14. When security from people
based somewhat on the power of expelling occurs,
security also occurs by the simplest prosperity
from a quiet life and withdrawal from the many.

15. Nature's wealth is both limited and easy to obtain,
but that of vain fancies is driven to infinity.

16. Chance seldom interferes with the wise;
the greatest and most important things
have been, are, and will be directed by reason
throughout the time of one's life.

17. The just is most free of trouble,
but the unjust has the largest load of trouble.

18. Pleasure in the flesh is not increased
once the pain of need is removed; but it only varies.
The limit of pleasure in the mind is reached
by the calculation of these themselves and by these relations
which prepare the greatest fears for the mind.

19. Infinite and limited time have equal pleasure,
if we measure the limits by reason.

20. The flesh takes the limits of pleasure as infinite,
and infinite time is prepared for it;
but the mind taking account of the end and limit of the flesh
and banishing the fears of eternity
prepares for a complete life
and no longer requires infinite time.
Yet it does not avoid pleasure
even when circumstances prepare one
for being led out of life
so that leaving, it does not turn down the best life.

21. Whoever understands the limits of life
knows how easy it is to obtain enough
to remove the pain of need
and to establish the whole life complete;
thus one no longer needs business earned by struggle.

22. It is necessary to consider the established end
and all manifestation to which we refer our opinions;
or else everything will be full of uncertainty and confusion.

23. If you fight all the sensations
you will have no standard by which
you may judge even those which you say are false.

24. If you reject absolutely any sensation
and do not discriminate between
opinion waiting for confirmation
and what is already present in sensation and feeling
and every imagined attempt of the mind
you confuse even the remaining sensations by a rash opinion
so that you will reject the criterion altogether.
But if you consider both
what in your opinion is waiting confirmation
and what is not witnessed,
you will not escape error,
as you will be maintaining all the ambiguity
whenever judging right and not right.

25. If you do not in every case refer each of the actions
toward its natural end,
but when avoiding or choosing
turn aside to something else,
your actions will not follow your words.

26. Of desires all that do not lead to pain
when they are not gratified are not necessary,
but the craving is easily diverted
when it is difficult or expected to produce harm.

27. Of what wisdom prepares for the most blessed whole life,
by far the greatest is obtaining friends.

28. The same conviction that creates confidence
that nothing terrible is eternal or even long-lasting
also enables us to see that in these defined things
friendship especially is seen as accomplishing security.

29. Of desires some are natural and necessary;
others are natural and not necessary;
others are neither natural nor necessary
but come from vain opinion.

30. Among those natural desires
which do not all lead to pain when not gratified,
though undertaken with intense effort,
these also occur because of vain opinion,

and it is not because of their own nature
but because of human vanity.

31. Natural justice is a contract of expediency
to prevent people from harming or being harmed by another.

32. Those animals which are incapable of making compacts
for the sake of not harming or being harmed,
for these nothing is either just or unjust.
Just so also are tribes which either could not or would not
make compacts for the sake of not harming or being harmed.

33. There was never any justice by itself,
but at gatherings in various times and places
a compact with each other
for the sake of not harming or being harmed.

34. Injustice by itself is not bad,
but in the feared consequence that you may be caught
by the appointed punisher of such things.

35. It is not possible for anyone secretly violating
what was agreed with others in not harming or being harmed
to believe that one will not be caught,
even if one has violated up to the present ten thousand times.
For until the catastrophe it is unclear if one will be caught.

36. In general justice is the same for all,
for it is something brought together
in community with each other;
but applied specifically in various countries and times
the same does not turn out to be just for all.

37. The testimony that is brought together
in useful ways in community with each other
being thought to be just has the character of justice,
whether or not it is the same for all.
If some law is made
but does not prove expedient with each other in community,
this no longer has the nature of the just.
Yet if the expedient according to justice changes,
and only for a time corresponds with the previous,
nevertheless for that time it was just
as long as they are not bothered by empty speeches
but look simply at the facts.

38. In cases where the circumstances are not new
and the conventional laws are shown
not to be fitting to the previous in practice,
these are not just.
But in cases where the circumstances are new,
the same actions that were held as just
no longer are expedient;
in that case they were just then when they were expedient
for each other in the community of citizens;
but later they were no longer just,
when they were not expedient.

39. Whoever is best at organizing against external danger
builds the ablest clan,
and those not able are not aliens;
but those not able who are not this are unsocial,
and it is better to exclude these.

40. Those who have the power of courage
to be prepared especially from neighbors
so live pleasantly with each other, having the surest trust,
and enjoying the fullest intimacy
they do not pity the dying as a catastrophe.

Pronouncements of Epicurus

4. All pain is easily disregarded, for severe stress is brief,
and what lasts in the flesh has mild stress.

7. It is difficult for those doing wrong to escape detection,
and assurance that one will escape being caught is impossible.

9. Necessity is bad, but one need not live with necessity.

11. Most people rest in torpor and march in rage.

14. We are born once, and it is not possible to be born twice,
but for eternity must be no more.
But you, though not lord of tomorrow, put off happiness.
We waste our lives in procrastination,
and each of us dies without having had leisure.

15. We value our character as individuals for ourselves,
whether we have esteem and are admired by people or not;
therefore esteem neighbors if it is fitting.

16. No one seeing the bad chooses it,
but lured as to a good better than an evil, one is caught.

17. The young is not blessed, but the old having lived well;
for the young at the height of power
is bewildered by raving chance.
But the old has anchored in old age as in a harbor
and holds in secure and happy memories unexpected goods.

18. Remove sight and company and contact,
and erotic passion is loosened.

19. One becomes old on the day
one forgets the good that has been.

21. One must not violate nature but obey;
we shall obey if we fulfill the necessary desires
and also the physical if they do not harm
while sharply rejecting the harmful.

23. Every friendship is chosen for itself,
but at the beginning it is taken for its help.

24. Dreams are drawn
neither by divine nature nor by prophetic power,
but they come from spitting images.

25. Poverty measured by the purpose of nature is great wealth;
but wealth not bounded is great poverty.

26. One must assume that the long argument and the short
are directed to the same purpose.

27. In other pursuits the fruit comes hardly after completion,
but in philosophy delight concurs with knowledge;
for enjoyment does not occur after learning,
but enjoyment and learning occur at the same time.

28. In friendship neither those at hand nor those hesitating
are to be approved;
but one must even run risks for the sake of friendship.

29. For frankly in studying nature
I would rather speak in oracles the advantages for all people,
even if no one understood,
than conform to opinions
to win the solid approval offered by many.

31. One can provide security against anything else,
but in regard to death all people live in an unfortified city.

32. Venerating the wise is a great good for those venerating.

33. The flesh cries out not to be hungry, thirsty, or cold.
For anyone having these and expecting to have them
may compete with Zeus for happiness.

34. We have need not so much of the need from friends
as of the confidence concerning the need.

35. One must not ruin the things present
with desire for things absent,
but consider that even these things were prayed for.

37. Nature is weak toward the bad, not toward the good;
for it is saved by pleasures but destroyed by pains.

38. Small in every way is the one
who has many reasons for departing from life.

39. Neither the one who is always seeking help
nor the one who never has contact is a friend;
for one trades gratitude for payment,
and the other cuts off hope for the future.

40. The one saying that all things occur by necessity
has no charge against the one saying that
not all things occur by necessity;
for he says this occurs by necessity.

41. At the same time it is necessary to laugh and philosophize
and manage the household and use the remaining faculties
and never cease proclaiming
the sayings of the right philosophy.

42. The same moment is both the origin
and the enjoyment of the greatest good.

43. The love of money, if unjust, is impious,
but if just, shameful;
for to be sparing sordidly is unseemly even with justice.

44. The wise in being accustomed to necessities
is more in charge of giving a share than of receiving a share,
having found such a treasure of self-sufficiency.

45. The study of nature does not prepare one for boasting
nor for the sound of working
nor for displaying education that is fought for by many,
but for being haughty and self-sufficient
and proud of the greatness of themselves,

not of their business.

46. May we completely drive out our bad habits
like cowardly men who were doing great harm for a long time.

48. We must attempt to make the later
better than the previous as long as we are on the way;
but when we arrive at the limit, we must be equally glad.

51. I learn from you that the stimulus of the flesh
makes you too disposed to sexual intercourse.
Provided that you do not break the laws
nor the established noble customs nor annoy any neighbors
nor waste away your flesh nor squander the necessities,
you may indulge yourself as you wish.
Yet it is impractical that you will not be restrained
by one or another of these;
for sexuality has never benefited,
and one is beloved if one is not harmed.

52. Friendship dances around the world
summoning us all to awaken to the blessing.

53. Envy no one; for the good do not deserve envy,
and the wicked, the luckier they are,
the more they ruin themselves.

54. We must not pretend to study philosophy,
but really study it;
for it is not seeming healthy that we need, but true health.

55. Let us heal circumstances by gratitude for what has been
and in being aware that it is not possible
to make undone the past.

58. Let us release ourselves
from the prison of cycles and politics.

59. Insatiable is not the stomach, as many say,
but the false opinion on behalf of the stomach
that it can be indefinitely filled.

60. All go out of life as if just born.

62. For if the anger of parents for their children is needed,
it is certainly foolish to fight against it
and not to intercede for pardon;
but if it is not needed but irrational,
it is very ridiculous to ignite the irrational temper,

and not to seek amendment in other considerate ways.

63. There is also a boundary to frugality,
and whoever disregarding it sails past
may experience by no boundary a shipwreck.

64. One must follow the natural praise from others,
but our concern is our own treatment.

65. It is vain to beg from the gods
what one is competent to supply for oneself.

66. Let us sympathize with our friends,
not by mourning but by meditating.

67. A free life cannot obtain many possessions,
because business is not easy
without serving masses or dynasties;
but it has acquired all things in unfailing abundance,
and if perhaps by chance much property,
these things too are easily distributed to kind neighbors.

68. Nothing is enough for the one to whom enough is little.

69. The ungrateful greed of the soul makes the animal
into unlimited greed for a diet of variety.

70. Let nothing be done by you in life
which will cause you fear
if your neighbor becomes aware of it.

71. For all desires one must introduce this question:
what will happen to me
if the desire sought after is accomplished,
and what if it is not accomplished?

73. Also the occurrence of some pains concerning the body
is advantageous for guarding against similar ones.

74. In philosophical debate
the one defeated gains more by learning more.

75. Ungrateful to the goods one has lived
is the saying "Observe the end of a long life."

76. You are aging just as I recommend,
and you have discerned how to love wisdom
for yourself and for Greece;
I rejoice with you.

77. The greatest fruit of self-sufficiency is freedom.

78. The well-born is especially concerned
with wisdom and friendship;
of these one is a mortal good, the other immortal.

79. The untroubled for oneself and the other is undisturbed.

80. The first part of safety is watching youth
and guarding against the pestering desires
that defile all things.

81. The soul's trouble is not released
nor is worthwhile happiness created
either by possessing the greatest wealth
or by honor and respect by many
or by anything else which is from unlimited causes.

Quotations of Epicurus

29. We admire self-sufficiency
not so that we may always use the frugal and plain
but so that we may have courage for these.

43. I never reached out to conciliate the many.
For what conciliated them I did not learn;
and what I knew was far from their perception.

44. Do not believe it unnatural
that the soul cries out when the flesh cries out.
The flesh cries not to be hungry nor thirsty nor cold.
Also it is hard for the soul to hinder these,
and it is precarious to disregard the summoning of nature
because of clinging to her own daily self-sufficiency.

45. So the one who follows nature
and not vain opinion in all things is self-sufficient;
for with what is sufficient in nature
every possession is wealth,
but with unlimited appetites
even the greatest wealth is poverty.

46. If you are in difficulty,
you are in difficulty in so far as you forget nature;
for you throw yourself into unlimited fears and desires.

48. It is better for you to have courage laying down on straw
than to be troubled having a golden couch and a rich table.

50. Sweet is the memory of a dead friend.

51. Do not avoid doing small favors,
for you will seem like one who does great ones.

52. Do not turn away from your enemy's worthy demand;
except keep yourself safe; for not one differs from a dog.

54. Vain is the argument of that philosopher,
which does not heal human suffering;
for as there is no benefit in medical treatment
if it does not expel the diseases of the body,
so there is none in philosophy
if it does not expel the suffering of the soul.

58. If God followed the prayers of humans,
all humans would quickly be destroyed,
many praying also continually against each other.

59. The beginning and root of all good
is the pleasure of the stomach;
even wisdom and extravagance have this reference.

61. What makes unsurpassed joy
is having avoided a great evil;
and this is the nature of good,
if someone applies it correctly, then establishes it,
and does not walk chattering idly about the good.

62. It is better to endure some labors
so that we may enjoy greater pleasures;
it is expedient to abstain from some pleasures
so that we may not suffer harder pain.

63. Let us not blame the flesh as the cause of great evils
nor turn to business for our troubles.

64. Great labors lead us out shortly,
but lasting ones are not great.

65. Excessive labor will bring you death.

66. By loving true philosophy
every troublesome and laborious desire is released.

67. Thanks to the blessing of nature
that made necessities easy to procure
and the things difficult to procure unnecessary.

68. It is not rare to find a person
poor toward the purpose of nature
and wealthy toward vain opinions.

For none of the fools is satisfied with what one has,
but rather is distressed about what one does not have.
Just as the feverish through the illness
always are thirsty and desire the deleterious,
so too the ones having a badly disposed soul
are always poor in everything
and by gluttony fall into ever changing desires.

69. The one not satisfied with little is satisfied with nothing.

70. The self-sufficient is most wealthy of all.

71. Most fearing frugality through this fear proceed to actions
that especially bring this about.

72. Many fortunate with wealth
have not found an escape from evils
but a change to greater ones.

73. From the work of a beast
one may heap up an abundance of substance,
but a miserable life results.

74. For through fear or unlimited and vain desire
someone may be unhappy;
which if one can restrain,
one may preserve for oneself blessed reason.

75. Labor is not being deprived of these,
but rather bearing the useless labor from vain opinion.

76. The low soul is puffed up by good times
and purged by the expedient things.

77. Nature teaches one to consider things from chance smaller,
and to know that being fortunate is unlucky,
and being unfortunate
not to assume that good fortune is great,
and to receive undisturbed the good things from chance,
and to stand prepared for the evil things
that seem to come from this;
as ephemeral is all the good and bad of the many,
and wisdom has nothing in common with chance.

78. The one least in need of tomorrow
is most glad to meet tomorrow.

79. I spit upon the beautiful and those who vainly admire it
when it never creates pleasure.

80. The greatest fruit of justice is being untroubled.

81. Laws are established for the sake of the wise,
not so that they may not do wrong
but so that they may not be wronged.

82. Even if one can escape,
it is not possible to be confident one will escape being caught;
thus fear of the future always pressing
does not let them be happy or have courage in the present.

83. When no one is present,
the one attaining the goal of the race is coming near the good.

84. The one who is causing fear is not fearless.

85. Happiness and blessing are not an abundance of property
nor a sizeable business nor having some office nor power,
but painless and gentle feelings
and a disposition of soul
according to the boundaries of nature.

86. Live unnoticed.

87. It is necessary to say
how the best may maintain the purpose of nature,
and how one will not willingly
from the first aim at public offices.

Wisdom of Solomon

Solomon was the son of David and Bathsheba, and he succeeded David as king of Israel, ruling for about forty years in the middle of the tenth century BC. Solomon headed a large commercial empire, accumulating 700 wives (according to *I Kings*), many of whom represented diplomatic alliances. He was famous for his wealth and wisdom and for building the Temple in Jerusalem. When two women asked him to settle their dispute over a baby they both claimed, he ordered the child cut in two, then gave the child to the woman who preferred to lose the child to seeing it killed.

The poetic *Song of Solomon* is credited to him, as are the aphorisms in the book of *Proverbs*. However, the *Wisdom of Solomon* appears only to use him as a literary figure, while wisdom is personified as feminine. Scholars agree that the *Wisdom of Solomon* was almost certainly written by a Jew in Alexandria in the first century BC. It is one of the apocryphal works written between the *Old* and *New Testaments*, but it was included in the ancient Greek edition of the *Old Testament* called the *Septuagint*. The original text was probably written in Greek, and Greek fragments were found in the Essene library at Qumran in Palestine.

The speaker, identified as Solomon only by the title, describes his love of wisdom, as though he were Solomon. In the tenth chapter references to early Biblical stories include Adam, Cain, Noah, Abraham, Lot, Jacob, Joseph, and Moses. Chapters 11, 12, and 16-19 contrast God's treatment of the Israelites led by Moses with that of the Egyptians.

1

Love justice, judges of the earth;
think about the Lord in goodness
and in singleness of heart seek it,
because it is found by those who do not test it,
and appears to those who do not distrust it.

For crooked calculations are separate from God,
and having been tested the power convicts the foolish;
because into a wily soul wisdom will not enter
nor will it dwell in a body abused by sin.

For a holy and educated spirit will flee trickery
and will stand apart from stupid calculations
and will disprove the approach of injustice.

For wisdom is a humane spirit
and will not let a blasphemer off for one's lip service,
because God is a witness of one's inmost feelings
and a true observer of one's heart
and a listener of the tongue.

Because the spirit of the Lord has filled the world,
also that which holds all things together knows its voice.
On account of this no one speaking injustice is unnoticed,
nor will justice pass them by when convicting.

For the deliberations of the profane will be reviewed,
and a report of their words will come to the Lord
to convict them of lawlessness;
since zealous ears hear all things,
and muttered murmurings are not kept hidden.

Watch out then for useless murmuring
and spare the tongue from slander;
since secret vanity will not pass unnoticed,
and a lying mouth contradicts the soul.

Do not vie with death in the wandering of your life
nor bring on ruin by the work of your hands;
since God did not make death
and does not enjoy the destruction of the living.

For it brought all things into being,
and the generations of the world are preserved,
and there is no destructive drug in them

nor is the sovereignty of Hades on earth.
For justice is immortal.
  But the profane by their words and deeds summon him,
believing him friendly they languished
and made a contract with him,
because they are deserving of being a part of that.

2
  For they said to themselves reasoning incorrectly,
"Our life is short and painful,
and there is no remedy in the termination of a person,
and release from Hades is not known.
Because we were born offhand
and after this we shall be as though we had never existed;
because the breath in our nostrils is smoke,
and reason is a spark in the movement of our hearts,
which being extinguished the body will turn to ashes
and the spirit will dissolve like empty air.
  "Also our name will be forgotten in time,
and no one will remember our work;
and our life will be undone like the trace of a cloud
and will be dispersed like mist
pursued by the rays of the sun
and oppressed by its heat.
For our time is a passing shadow,
and there is no calling back our end,
because it is sealed up and no one returns.
  "Therefore come and let us enjoy the good things
and we shall use the creation like youths seriously;
Let us be filled with expensive wine and perfumes,
and may no flower of spring pass us by;
let us be crowned with rosebuds before they wither;
let no one be without the meadows' share of our glory;
everywhere let us leave signs of the festivity,
since this is our share and this our lot.
  "Let us put down the just poor,
nor should we spare the widow
nor respect the gray hairs of old age;
and let our might be the law of right,

for the weak is proven useless.

"Let us ambush the just, who is hard for us to use
and opposed to our work
and reproaches us for legal wrongs
and accuses us for our wrongs of education;
he professes to have knowledge of God
and calls himself a child of the Lord;
he became for us a confutation of our ideas,
even seeing is burdensome to us,
because his life is unlike others,
and his habits are completely changed;
we are considered by him among the base,
and he avoids our ways as coming from impurities;
he blesses the final end of the just
and pretends God is father.

"Let us see if his words are true,
and let us test what will happen to him;
for if the just is son of God, it will assist him
and rescue him out of the hand of the adversaries.
Let us impose on him insult and torture,
so that we may know his tolerance
and let us test his endurance of evil;
let us condemn him to a shameful death,
for from his words it will watch over him."

These things they argued, and were going astray;
for their vice blinded them,
and they did not know the mysteries of God
nor hope for the reward of holiness
nor choose the prerogative of a blameless soul.

"Since God created the human for incorruption
and made them in its own image of eternity;
but by envy of the devil death entered into the world,
and they tempt those who are of that part.

3
But the souls of the just are in the hand of God,
and no torment will ever touch them.
In the eyes of the foolish they seem to be dead,
and their departure was considered distressing

and their passing from us crushing,
but they are at peace.

For though in the sight of humans they were punished,
their hope of immortality is fulfilled;
and being educated a little they will receive great good,
because God tested them
and found them worthy of itself;
like gold in a crucible it tested them
and like a whole-fruit offering accepted them.

Also in the time of their visitation they will revive
and run like sparks through straw;
they will judge nations and rule the common people,
and the Lord will reign over them into eternity.
Those trusting on this will understand truth,
and the faithful will wait for this in love;
because grace and mercy are in its holy ones
and watchfulness in its chosen ones.

But the profane as they reason will have pay,
who neglected justice and rejected the Lord;
for whoever disregards wisdom and education is miserable,
and their hope is vain, and their labors unprofitable,
and their work useless.
Their wives are foolish,
and their children bad,
their family cursed.

Since blessed is the barren woman who is undefiled,
who has not known a bed in transgression,
for she will have fruit in the visitation of souls,
also the eunuch who works nothing lawless in hand
nor thinks anything bad toward the Lord,
for special grace will be given him for trusting
and a place in the temple of the Lord more pleasing.
For the fruit of good work is a good report,
and unfailing is the root of understanding.

But children of adulterers will be immature,
and seed coming out of an unlawful bed will disappear.
For even if they are long-lived, they amount to nothing,
and at last their old age is without honor;
if they die young, they will have no hope

nor consolation on the day of decision;
for the end of an unjust generation is hard.

4
 Better is childlessness with virtue;
for immortality is in its memory,
because it is known both by God and by humans.
When present they imitate it
and yearn for it when gone away;
and in eternity it proceeds crowned
winning prizes in contests of the undefiled.
 But prolific progeny of the profane will not be useful
and none of their bastard offshoots will strike a deep root
nor take a firm hold;
for even if in slips they shoot up for a while,
having started insecurely they will be shaken by the wind
and by force of wind they will be rooted out.
Immature branches will be broken,
and their useless fruit, unripe for eating
and good for nothing;
for children born of unlawful sleep
are bad witnesses against their parents in examination.
 But the just even if dying sooner, will rest;
for old age is not honored for long life
nor measured by the number of years,
but understanding is gray hair for humans
and a blameless life is ripe old age.
 There was one well-pleasing and loved by God
who living in the middle of sinners was translated;
snatched away, lest evil change his conscience
or cunning deceive his soul;
for the slander of vice obscures the beautiful,
and roaming desire perverts an innocent mind.
 Being perfected in a short time he fulfilled a long time;
for his soul was pleasing to the Lord,
because of this he was quickly out of the middle of pain;
but the people seeing also were not perceiving
nor putting this to understanding,
that grace and mercy are in its chosen ones

and watchfulness in its holy ones.

And the late just condemn the living profane
and perfected youth quickly the many old years of the unjust;
for they will see the end of the wise
and will not understand what was intended for him
and for what the Lord kept him safe.

They will see and make nothing of it;
and the Lord will laugh at them,
and after this they will become dishonored corpses
and an outrage among the dead forever,
since it will make them speechless head down
and shake them from the foundations,
and until at last they are dried out
and will be in pain,
and the memory of them perishes.
They will come in the summing up of their sins cringing,
and their lawless things will convict against them.

5
Then the just will stand in great openness
facing those who pressed him
and those making light of his sufferings.

Seeing they will be troubled with terrible fear
and will be amazed at the unexpected salvation;
they will talk among themselves repenting
and because of narrowness of spirit they will wail,
"This was the one whom we were once laughing at
and the fools made into a byword of reproach;
and we considered his life madness
and his end without honor.
How is he counted among the sons of God
and why is his lot among the holy?

"Then we were straying from the way of truth,
and the light of justice did not shine on us,
and the sun did not rise upon us;
we were filled up with thorns of lawlessness and destruction
and traveled through trackless deserts,
and did not know the way of the Lord.
What has arrogance gained us?

and what has wealth with pretense brought us?
"All those things passed by like a shadow
and like news ran by;
like a ship going through swelled water,
of whose passage there is no trace to find
nor of its inflexible keel in the waves;
or like a bird flying through the air
no evidence of a passage is found,
and by the stroke of wings lashing the light breeze
and divided by force of the rushing
of moving wings comes through,
and after this no sign of its approach is found in it;
or like an arrow shot at a target,
the air cut immediately is returned into itself
so that its path through is unknown;
thus we too being born failed
and we had no sign of virtue to show,
and in our evil we were squandered."

Since hope of the profane is like fuzz carried by wind
and like thin frost driven away by a hurricane
and like smoke it is dispersed by wind
and like the memory of a one-day guest passed on.

But the just live forever,
and in the Lord is their reward,
and the care of them by the highest.
On account of this they will receive the palace of dignity
and the crown of the beautiful out of the hand of the Lord,
because by the right hand it will protect them
and by the arm will shield them.

It will receive its zeal as full armor
and will make creation tools for warding off the hostile,
will put on justice as a breastplate
and wear unhypocritical judgment as a helmet,
will receive holiness as an invincible shield,
and will sharpen cut-off anger into a sword,
and the world will join in war against the deranged.

Well aimed bolts of lightning will be conveyed
and as from a well-rounded bow of clouds will roam on target,
and from rock-throwing full of courage hail will be hurled;

the water of the sea will rage against them,
and rivers will wash together relentlessly;
a powerful wind will oppose them
and like a hurricane it will winnow them out;
and lawlessness will make a desert of the whole earth,
and bad enterprises will overthrow thrones of the powerful.

6

 Hear therefore, kings, and understand;
learn, judges of earth's opposites;
listen, you who are ruling people
and being proud over a crowd of nations;
for the rule was given you by God
and the power by the highest,
who will examine your work and question your plans;
since as servants of its sovereignty
you did not decide correctly
nor did you observe the law
nor proceed according to the plan of God.
 Horribly and quickly it will come to know you,
because abrupt judgment comes to those on top.
For the lowest is pardonable by mercy,
but the powerful will be powerfully tested;
for the master of all will not prevaricate before any
nor respect greatness,
because it made the small and great itself
and provides similarly concerning all,
but severe questioning is imposed on the rulers.
 For you, then, tyrants, are my words,
so that you may learn wisdom and not fall along the way;
for those observing divine laws in holiness will be purified,
and those being taught them will find a defense.
Therefore set your heart on my words,
yearn and you will be educated.
 Wisdom is brilliant and unfading
and easily contemplated by those who love her
and is found by those who search for her,
is sooner to be understood by the eager.

Whoever rises early will not get tired of her;
for one will find her sitting beside one's entrance.
For the one thinking deeply about her accomplishing purpose,
and the wakeful will be quickly free of worry through her;
because she goes around searching for those worthy of her
and graciously appears to them in their routines
and in every thought replies to them.

For the beginning of her is the truest educational desire,
and concern for education is love,
and love is keeping her laws,
and attention to laws is confirmation of incorruption,
and incorruption makes one be near God;
thus desire for wisdom leads to sovereignty.
So if you like thrones and scepters, tyrants of people,
honor wisdom, so that you may reign forever.

What wisdom is and how she was born, I shall relate
and I will not conceal mysteries from you,
but from the beginning of birth I shall complete
and put the knowledge of her into the light
and will not pass by the truth.

Neither will I travel with sickly envy,
because this does not share with wisdom.
A majority of the wise is salvation of the world,
and a sensible sovereign stability of the commons.
Therefore learn from my words, and you will be helped.

7

I too am mortal equal to every human
and descendant of the first-formed earthborn;
and in a mother's womb shaped into flesh
in ten months' time built in blood
out of the man's seed and pleasurable coming together in bed.
And being born I sucked in the common air
and fell down on the sympathetic earth,
the first sound just like the crying of everyone;
I was wrapped up in diapers and cared for.
For no king was different at the beginning of birth,
and everyone comes into life and goes out the same way.

Because of this I prayed, and understanding was given me;
I called upon it, and the spirit of wisdom came to me.
I preferred her to scepters and thrones
and wealth I believed nothing in comparison to her;
nor did I liken a priceless stone to her,
since all gold in her sight is a little sand,
and silver is considered as clay before her;
above health and beauty I loved her
and I chose to have her instead of light,
because her light is unsleeping.

And all good things came to me along with her
and uncounted wealth in her hands;
and I enjoyed all, because wisdom leads them,
not knowing their origin to be her.

What I learned without deceit I share ungrudgingly,
nor do I hide her wealth;
for it is an unfailing treasure to humans,
who acquiring it are fit for friendship with God
because of the gifts of education being allied.

God grant me to speak according to knowledge
and to infer conclusions worthy of what has been given,
since it is the guide even of wisdom
and the corrector of the wise.
For both we and our words are in its hand,
all understanding and knowledge of working.

For it gave me unerring knowledge
to know the structure of the world and operation of elements,
the beginning and end and middle of times,
change of directions and transition of seasons,
cycles of the year and the constellations of stars,
the nature of animals and the hearts of beasts,
the force of spirits and considerations of humans,
the varieties of plants and the virtues of roots,
both what is secret and what is visible I learned;
for the builder of all things, wisdom, taught me.

For in her is a spirit, intelligent, holy,
singly born, of many parts, subtle,
mobile, clear, unpolluted,
manifest, harmless, good-loving, sharp,

unhindered, doing well, humane,
secure, certain, unworried,
omnipotent, watching over all
and moving through all spirits
intelligent, pure, and most subtle.

For wisdom is more mobile than every motion,
and extends and moves through all by purity;
for she is a breath of God's power
and an emanation of the unmixed glory of the all-ruling;
because of this nothing tainted steals into her.
For she is the brilliance of eternal light
and an unstained mirror of God's energy
and an image of its goodness.

One being can do all things
and remaining in herself she makes all things new
and each generation she passes into holy souls
and makes them friends of God and prophets;
for God loves nothing as much as those living with wisdom.

For she is more beautiful than the sun
and beyond every constellation of stars.
Compared with light she is found brighter;
for this is succeeded by night,
but evil does not prevail over wisdom.

8
She extends from end to end strongly
and manages all things beneficially.

I loved her and sought her from my youth
and sought to take her as a bride for myself
and I fell in love with her beauty.
Living with God magnifies nobility,
and the master of all loves her;
for she is an initiate of God's knowledge
and a chosen one of its work.

If wealth is a desirable possession in life,
what is richer than wisdom working all things?

And if understanding works,
who more than she is the builder of what exists?

And if someone loves justice,
her labors are excellent;
for she teaches discretion and understanding,
justice and courage,
than which nothing is more beneficial in human life.

And if someone longs for much experience,
she knows the ancient and infers the things to come,
understands turns of logic and solutions of riddles,
foreknows signs and wonders
and the outcome of seasons and times.

So I decided to take her to live together
aware that she will be a counselor of good to me
and an advisor of concerns and grief.

Because of her I shall have fame among the crowd
and honor from elders as the young one;
I shall be found sharp in judgment
and in the sight of the powerful will be admired;
being silent they wait for me
and in talking they will pay attention
and speaking at length
they will put their hands on their mouths.

Because of her I shall have immortality
and leave an eternal memory to the ones after me.
I shall govern peoples, and nations will be subject to me;
horrible tyrants hearing of me will be afraid;
among people I appear good and in war courageous.

Entering my house I shall rest with her;
for her companionship has no bitterness
nor does living with her have any pain,
but gladness and joy.

Considering these things in myself
and contemplating in my heart,
that in relationship with wisdom is immortality
and in her friendship pure delight
and in the labor of her hands unfailing wealth
and in her company while exercising together understanding
and in partnership with her words good reputation,
I went around searching how I could get her for myself.

As a child I was good natured
and was granted a good soul,
or rather being good I came into an undefiled body.
Aware that I would not be master any way unless God gave it,
and this was understanding to know someone's grace,
I pleaded with the Lord and begged him
and said from my whole heart:

9

"God of fathers and Lord of mercy,
who made all things in your logic
and by your wisdom prepared humanity,
so as to be master of the created beings under you
and manage the world in holiness and justice
and decide judgments in openness of soul,
give me the wisdom sitting beside your throne
and do not reject me from your servants;
since I am your slave and son of your servant-girl,
a person weak and short-lived
and lesser in understanding of judgment and laws;
for even if someone is perfect among sons of humans,
absent from your wisdom one is considered nothing.

"You selected me sovereign of your common people
and judge of your sons and daughters;
you said to construct a temple on your holy mountain
and an altar in your city of encampment,
a copy of the holy tent, which was prepared from the start.

"Also with you is the wisdom which knows your work
and was present when you made the world,
and knows what is acceptable in your sight
and what is in line with your commands.

"Send her out from the holy heavens
and from the throne of your glory send her,
so that being present with me she may work hard,
and I may know what is acceptable before you.

"For she knows and understands all things
and will guide me wisely in my actions
and watch over me in her glory;
and my work will be acceptable,

and I shall judge your common people justly
and shall be worthy of my father's throne.

"For what human knows the plan of God?
Or who can be conscious of what the Lord wills?
For the calculations of mortals are poor,
and our designs precarious;
for a perishable body burdens the soul,
and the earthy tent weighs down a thoughtful mind.

"Also we hardly guess at things on earth
and things in hand we find with labor;
but who traced out the things in heaven?
Who knew your plan, unless you have given wisdom
and sent your holy spirit from the highest?

"And thus the paths of those on earth were set right,
and the things acceptable to you were taught to humans,
and they were saved by wisdom."

10
She watched over the first-formed father of the world
being created alone
and delivered him from a peculiar transgression,
and gave him strength to rule everything.

But standing apart from her an unjust one in his anger
perished in the spirit of brother-murdering.
By this the earth being flooded again wisdom saved
by paltry wood steering the just.

Also when the nations were confused in vicious agreement
she knew the just and kept him blameless for God
and guarded the strength in the feelings for the child.

She rescued the just when the profane were perishing
escaping the fire falling down on the Five Cities,
of which there is still evidence of the viciousness
in a continually smoking barren land
and the incomplete seasons of fruit-bearing plants,
a standing monument of an unbelieving soul, a pillar of salt.

For passing by wisdom
not only were they blocked from knowing beautiful things,
but also left a reminder of the folly for the living,
so that among these the mishap could not go unnoticed.

Wisdom rescued out of troubles those serving her.
When a just person fled a brother's anger
she led in straight paths,
showed him the sovereignty of God
and gave him knowledge of the holy ones,
supplied him in hardship
and made full his labors,
in the greed of the overpowering stood by him
and enriched him,
protected him from enemies
and assured against ambushings,
and in stiff competitions arbitrated for him,
so he would know that piety is more powerful than everything.

A just person being sold she did not leave him behind,
but out of failure rescued him,
went down with him into a pit
and in prison did not leave him,
until she brought him a scepter of sovereignty
and authority over his tyrants,
and showed him the lies of the accusers
and gave him eternal glory.

A holy people and blameless seeds
she rescued out of a nation of oppressors;
she entered into the soul of a servant of the Lord
and stood up to terrible kings with signs and wonders.

She gave to the holy the reward of their labors,
led them on a marvelous way
and for them turned into a shelter by day
and into flames of stars at night.

She brought them over the Red Sea
and led them through deep water,
but drowned their enemies
and tossed them up from the depth of the abyss.

On account of this the just plundered the profane
and sang hymns, Lord, to your holy name
and praised with one accord your defending hand;
because wisdom opened the mouth of the dumb
and made the tongues of babes clear.

11

She prospered their work in the hand of a holy prophet.
They journeyed through an uninhabited desert
and pitched tents in inaccessible places;
they stood up to wars and warded off enemies.
They were thirsty and called upon you,
and water was given them out of sharply cut rock
and healing of thirst out of hard stone.

For through that by which their enemies were punished,
through these they being at a loss were served well.
Instead of a fountain of an ever-flowing river
troubled with the defiled gore of blood
in confutation of the baby-killing order
you gave them abundant water unexpectedly
showing through the thirst then
how the adversaries were punished.

For when they were tested, though being educated in mercy,
they knew how being judged in anger the profane were tried;
for you tested them like a father in admonition,
but those you examined like an abrupt king in sentencing.
Both the absent and the present were similarly distressed;
for a double grief took hold of them
and a moaning at the memory of what had passed;
for when they heard that through their own punishments
they were being served well, they became aware of the Lord.

For in the exposing long before
they scoffing denied the cast-off,
at the end of the escape they marveled
thirsting not like the just.
In return for their misunderstanding unjust calculations,
in which straying they worshipped
irrational reptiles and mean beasts,
you sent upon them many irrational animals in avenging,
so that they would know that
one is punished through the things by which one sins.

For your omnipotent hand was not at a loss
also having created the world out of formless matter
to send upon them many bears or bold lions
or newly created unknown beasts full of rage

or such as breathe fire-breathing gasps
or a roar scattering smoke
or terrible lightning sparks from the eyes,
of which not only could the damage exterminate them,
but even the sight could destroy them out of fear.
  Even without these they could fall in one breath
being pursued by justice
and scattered by your powerful spirit,
but you arranged everything
by measure and number and weight.
For it is always possible for you to greatly prevail,
and who can stand against the rule of your arm?
Since like a turn of the scale is the whole world before you
and like a drop of morning dew falling on the earth.
  But you are merciful to all,
because you can do everything,
and you overlook human sins into repentance.
For you love all beings
and you are nauseated by none of the things you made;
for you would not hate anything you built.
How would anything remain, if you had not willed it,
or what was not called forth by you be maintained?
You spare all, because they are yours, life-loving master.

12
  For your incorruptible spirit is in all.
Therefore you refute a little at a time the fallen ones
and reminding admonish for the things in which they sin,
so that releasing the vice they will trust in you, Lord.
  For even those inhabiting your holy land long ago
you hated for practicing hostility,
works of drugs and unholy rites
and merciless murdering of children
and sacrificial feasting on human flesh and blood,
out of the middle of a secret cult
and autocratic parents of helpless lives,
you planned to destroy by the hands of our fathers,
so that the most valuable land of all for you
might receive a settlement worthy of God's servants.

But even these you spared as humans
sending wasps in advance of your army,
so that they would be destroyed gradually.
Not unable in battle to give the profane to the just hands
or to terrible reptiles
or to wipe them out at once by an abrupt word,
but judging gradually giving an opportunity of repentance
not being ignorant that their origin was bad
and their vice implanted
and that their calculating would never change.
For the seed was cursed from the beginning,
and not from deference to anyone
did you grant amnesty to them for sin.
    For who will say, "What did you do?"
Or who will stand against your judgment?
Who will accuse you for destroying nations which you made?
Or who will come into an institution to you
without law concerning unjust persons?
    For neither is there a god except you,
who cares about all,
so that you should show that you did not judge unjustly,
nor can a king or tyrant confront you about those punished.
Being just you manage all things justly
believing it alien to your power
to condemn one not deserving to be punished.
    For your strength is the first cause of justice,
and your mastering all makes you spare all.
For to show strength the disbelieving of complete power
also you refute among those knowing courage;
you of masters' strength judge in fairness
and with much restraint you manage us;
for the power is present for you whenever you will it.
    You taught the common people through such work
that the just must be humane,
and you made your sons have good hope
that you would grant repentance for sins.
For if the enemies of your servants also deserving death
with such attentive vengeance and indulgence
given time and opportunity by which they may give up vice,

with what precision did you judge your sons,
to whose fathers you gave
oaths and covenants of good promise?

So educating us our enemies got ten thousand scourges,
so that when judging we may meditate on your goodness,
and being judged we may expect mercy.
From this also those in folly of life living unjustly
through their own abominations you tormented;
for they also wandered farther on paths of error
taking gods even in animals dishonored of the shameful
being deceived after the manner of foolish children.

On account of this like thoughtless children
you sent judgment for mocking.
But those not being admonished by censure for mockery
will experience the merited judgment of God.
For upon this suffering they are irritated,
upon those they believed were gods being punished with them
seeing, whom before they refused to know,
recognizing the true God;
wherefore the end of judgment came upon them.

13

For all persons vain by nature who were ignorant of God
and from good sights were not able to know the existing
nor observing the work did they recognize the artisan,
but either fire or wind or swift air
or the circle of stars or forceful water
or the lights of heaven presiding over the world
they assumed were gods.

If enjoying the beauty they took these as gods
let them know how much better than these is the master,
for the architect of beauty created these;
and if by power and good work they were astonished,
let them be aware from these
how much more powerful is the one who arranged these;
for out of the greatness and beauty of creation
analogously their maker is contemplated.

Nevertheless on these there is little blame,
for perhaps they go astray

seeking and wishing to find God;
for in returning to its works they search
and trust the sight, because beautiful things are seen.
   But again not even these are pardoned;
for if they were able to know so much
that they could guess the age,
why did they not find the master of these sooner?
   But the miserable and their hopes in dead things,
who call gods the works of human hands,
gold and silver of skilled practice
and models of animals
or a useless stone work of an ancient hand.
   If some skilled woodcutter
sawing down an easily moved tree
stripped off deftly all its bark
and crafting it well
prepared a useful implement for the service of life,
and the thrown away things of the work
spent for preparing food he ate his fill,
but thrown away from these good for nothing,
a stick crooked and full of knots,
taking he carves with care in his idleness
and by practice of recreation shapes it,
forming it in the image of a person
or likens it to some cheap animal
applying red and coloring its surface red
and applying it to every blemish on it
and making a dwelling for it worthy of it
he puts it in a wall securing it with iron.
Thus so it may not fall, he provides for it
knowing that it cannot help itself;
for it is an image and has need of help.
   And praying about possessions and marriage and children
he is not ashamed of talking to a lifeless thing
and concerning health he calls upon a weak thing,
and concerning life thinks fit a dead thing,
and concerning aid asks the most inexperienced,
and concerning a journey what cannot take a step,
and concerning procuring and working and success with hands

he asks the most inactive for active hands.

14
 Again someone sailing and intending to venture wild waves
cries out to wood more fragile than the ship carrying him.
For desire of gain contrived that,
and the technician wisdom built it;
but your providence, father, steers it through,
because you gave it both a way in the sea
and on waves a safe path
showing that you could save it from everything,
so that even someone without skill may go on.
 You will your works of wisdom not be undone;
because of this also humans trust lives to the smallest wood
and coming through waves on a boat are preserved.
For even at the start when arrogant giants were perishing
the hope of the world escaping on a boat
left to the ages seeds of generation by your guiding hand.
 For praised be the wood by which justice comes;
but the hand-made is cursed itself and the one who made it,
because he did the work,
and the corruptible was named a god.
For equally hated by God are the profane and his profanity;
for the action will also be punished with the doer.
 Because of this too on idols of nations will be oversight,
since in the creation of God they fell into abomination
and into traps for human souls
and into snares for the feet of fools.
 For the concept of idols
was the beginning of prostitution,
and their discovery corruption of life.
For neither was it from the beginning nor will it be forever;
for by the delusion of humans it came into the world,
and on account of this their shortened end was conceived.
 For a father consumed by untimely mourning
made an image of a child suddenly taken away
then honored a human now dead as a god
and gave over to those under him mysteries and rites;
then in time the profane custom held to was kept as a law.

And by orders of tyrants the carvings were worshipped,
whom humans could not honor in person
due to living far away
impressing again the sight from a distance
they made a visible image of the honored king,
so that the absent as present they might flatter by zeal.

The ambition of the technician urged also
the ignorant into the duty of worship;
for perhaps wishing to please the ruling
he forced out by skill resemblance to the beautiful;
and many attracted by the popularity of the work
considered the one honored a little before as a person
now a religious object.
And this became for the living an ambush,
since persons enslaved by either circumstance or tyranny
conferred the unshareable name on stones and wood.

Next it was not enough to err about knowledge of God,
but also living in a great war of ignorance
they label such evils peace.
For whether child-murdering rites or clandestine mysteries
or celebrating frantic revels of peculiar institutions
they no longer keep lives nor marriages pure,
but either take off another by ambush
or pain another by adultery.

All is promiscuous blood and murder, theft and deceit,
corruption, mistrust, disorder, perjury,
confusion of the good, forgetfulness of favors,
pollution of souls, perverting of generation,
marriage disorders, adultery and licentiousness.

For the worship of nameless idols
is the beginning and cause and end of every vice;
for either cheering they go mad or prophesy lies
or live unjustly or quickly commit perjury;
for trusting in lifeless idols
swearing viciously they do not expect to be wronged.

But the just avenge them both ways
since they thought viciously about God praying to idols
and swore unjustly in deceit disdaining holiness;
for not the power of the things sworn,

but the justice due from the sinning
always prosecutes the deviation of the unjust ones.

15
  But you, our God, are kind and true,
patient and merciful managing all things.
For even if we sin, we are yours, knowing your rule;
but we shall not sin, knowing that we are considered yours.
For to know you is complete justice,
and to know your rule is the root of immortality.
  For neither did the design of humans' evil arts mislead us
nor the fruitless labor of painters,
a figure stained with varied colors,
whose sight returns fools into desire,
and they yearn for the lifeless form of a dead image.
Lovers of vices and those deserving of such hopes
are the ones doing and desiring and worshipping.
  For potters pressing hard on the soft earth
mold each one for our service;
but remodel out of the same clay
furnishings serving both the clean work
and the opposite, all similarly;
but what the use of each of these is
the clay-workers decide.
Also by bad labor an idle god out of the same clay they mold
who a little before were made out of earth
after a while they go to that out of which they were taken,
the debt of the soul being demanded.
  But it is no concern to them
that they are about to retire
or that they have a short life,
but they compete with goldsmiths and silversmiths
and imitate copper-molders
and believe it glory that they mold counterfeits.
  Their heart is ash, and cheaper than earth their hope,
and less honored than clay their life,
because they were ignorant of the one who molded them
and inspired them with an energized soul
and breathed into them living spirit,

but they considered our life a game
and living a festival for profit,
for it is necessary, they say,
to procure it from whatever source, even from vice.
For they above all know that they sin
making fragile furnishings of earth and carvings of wood.

But most foolish and wretched beyond an infant soul
are all the enemies who oppressed your common people,
since they thought all the idols of the nations were gods,
which neither have use of eyes for sight
nor nostrils for drawing together air
nor ears to hear
nor fingers of hands for touching
and their feet inactive for walking.

For a person made them,
and the spirit that has been borrowed molded them;
for no person can mold a god like oneself;
being mortal one works the dead with lawless hands;
for one is better than one's religious objects,
being oneself alive, but those never.

They even worship the most hated animals;
for judging by ignorance they are worse than the others;
and even as animals the beauty of sight is not to be desired,
but they have fled from both God's approval and its praise.

16
Because of this they were
deservedly punished by similar ones
and were tormented by many beasts.
Instead of punishment you worked well your common people
into a desire of appetite for a strange taste
having prepared quails for food,
so that those desiring food
due to the loathsomeness of what was sent to them
might turn away the necessary appetite,
and these being needful for a short while
also might partake of a strange taste.

For inevitable poverty must come upon those tyrants,
while to these it was only shown

how their enemies were tormented.

For when the terrible beasts' rage came upon them
and they were destroyed by the biting of twisting snakes,
your anger did not continue until the end;
as a warning they were disturbed for a short while
having an omen of safety
as a reminder of your law's command;
for the one who turned was saved not by the seeing,
but by you, the savior of all.

Also in this way you convinced our enemies
that you are the rescuer from every evil;
for the bites of locusts and flies killed them,
and no healing was found for their soul,
because they deserved to be punished by such things;
but the teeth of poisonous snakes did not conquer your sons,
for your mercy came by opposite and healed them.
for they were bitten as a reminder of your oracles
and swiftly were delivered,
lest falling into deep forgetfulness
they might become unresponsive to your good work.
For neither herb nor poultice cured them,
but Lord, your all-healing word did.

For you have authority over life and death,
and you lead down into the gates of Hades and up again;
a person kills by one's vice,
but the spirit that went out does not return
nor is the soul taken over released.

To escape from your hand is impossible;
for refusing to know you the profane
were whipped by the strength of your arm
pursued by strange rains and hails and sweeping storms
and consumed by fire;
for, most incredible, in the water which quenches all
the fire was fully active,
for the universe is the defender of the just;
for at one time the flame was subdued,
lest it burn up the animals sent upon the profane,
so that they seeing this might know that
they were driven by the judgment of God;

and at another time even in the middle of water
it burned more dynamically than fire,
so that it might ruin the crops of an unjust land.

   Instead of this you fed your common people angels' food
and provided for them effortlessly handy bread from heaven
satisfying every pleasure and suited to every taste;
for your sustenance manifested sweetness to your children,
and serving the desire of those using it
it was transformed to whatever one wished.

   Snow and ice submitted to fire and did not melt,
so that they would know that the fruits of the enemies
were destroyed by the fire blazing in the hail
and flashing in the rain;
but this again was so that the just might eat,
and it forgot about its own power.

   For the creation serving you who made it
stretches for the punishment of the unjust
and relaxes for good work on behalf of those who trusted you.

   On account of this also then changing into all things
it served your all-nourishing gift
according to the will of the needing,
so that your sons whom you loved, Lord, might learn
that the production of fruits does not feed a person,
but your saying maintains those trusting in you.

   For what was not ruined by fire
simply melted when warmed by a brief ray of sun,
so it may be known that it is necessary
to first come giving thanks to you before the sun
and before the rising of the light meet with you;
for the hope of the ungrateful will melt like winter frost
and run off like useless water.

17
   For great are your judgments and hard to describe;
on account of this uneducated souls have gone astray.
For assuming power over the holy nation the lawless
captives of the dark and prisoners of the long night
lay enclosed under roofs fugitives from eternal providence.

For thinking to be unnoticed in their secret sins
by the obscure curtain of forgetfulness
they were dispersed astounded terribly
and agitated by apparitions.
For not even the closet holding them kept them fearless,
but shattering sounds roared around them,
and downcast phantoms with unsmiling faces appeared.

Also no force of fire was able to light,
nor did the bright flames of stars
manage to shine on that gloomy night.
Shining through to them alone was
a self-moving fearful fire,
and frightened by what was not seen of that sight
they believed the things looked at were worse.

Tricks of magic art were laid down,
and the pretense of boasted wisdom was refuted;
for those promising to drive off
the frights and agitation of a sick soul,
these deriding caution became sick.

For even if nothing agitating frightened them,
scared by the passage of monsters and hissing reptiles
they perished trembling
refusing to look even at the air from nowhere avoided.

For miserable cowardice testifies condemned by itself,
it always takes hold of difficulties oppressed by conscience;
for fear is nothing but giving up the helps from reason,
and the inner expectation being weak
counts on full ignorance of the cause promising torture.

On the really powerless night
and out of the powerless recesses of Hades coming upon
the ones sleeping the same sleep
monstrous things of phantoms drove them,
and things of the soul paralyzed by betrayal;
for unforeseen and unexpected fear poured over them.

So whoever was there fell down,
thusly they were kept shut up in an ironless prison;
for whether someone was a farmer or a shepherd
or a worker laboring in the desert,
being seized one endured the inescapable fate,

for with one chain of darkness all were bound;
whether a hissing wind
or melodious sounds of birds in widespreading branches
or rhythm of water moving by force
or the harsh crash of rocks thrown down
or leaping animals running unseen
or the sound of howling rough beasts
or an echo bounced back out of most hollow mountains,
terrorizing paralyzed them.
   For the whole world was illuminated with bright light
and was held together with unhindered work;
but over those alone heavy night was spread,
an image of the darkness about to take its turn.
But they were heavier to themselves than darkness.

18
   But for your holy ones there was great light;
who hearing the sound but not seeing the form,
since also those not having suffered, were blessed,
because the ones wronged before were not harming,
being thankful they even asked pardon for being different.
Against which you provided a pillar of flaming fire
as a guide for their unknown journey,
and a harmless sun of foreign ambition.
   For those deserved to be deprived of light
and kept in the dark,
the ones guarding your sons as prisoners,
through whom the incorruptible light of law
was about to be given to the ages.
   When they were planning
to kill the babies of the holy ones,
and one child had been exposed and saved,
in confutation many of their children were taken away
and in like spirit destroyed in violent water.
   That night was known before by our fathers,
so that securely knowing the promises in which they trusted
they might be heartened.
The salvation of the just and the destruction of the enemies
were expected by your common people;

for in the same way you avenged the opposition,
you calling us forward glorified us.

For in secret the holy children of the good sacrificed
and in unity agreed to the most divine law
similarly both their goods
and dangers the saints were sharing
already singing the fathers' praises.

But the discordant cry of the enemies resounded,
and the pitiable wailing sound for the children was borne;
by a like sentence a slave was punished along with a master
and the people suffered the same things as a king,
and in like spirit all in one name of death
had uncounted dead;
for the living ones were not even enough for the burial,
since in one moment their honored generation was destroyed.

For mistrusting all because of drugs
upon the death of the first-born
they acknowledged common people to be God's son.
For with still silence surrounding all things
and night in its swiftness half spent
by your omnipotent word from heaven out of a royal throne
a ruthless warrior wandered in the middle of the ruined land
carrying the sharp sword of your unanswered injunction
and stood filling all things with death
and reached heaven while walking on earth.

Then on the spot phantoms in terrible dreams agitated them,
and unexpected fears set upon them,
and here and there hurled half-dead
through which they showed the reason for death;
for disturbing dreams forewarned them of this,
lest they perish ignorant of why they badly suffer.

The experience of death reached also the just,
and a plague came to many in the desert.
However the anger did not remain for long;
for a blameless man hurried to defend
bringing his personal shield of ministry,
prayer and propitiating incense;
standing up to the anger he also put an end to the event
showing that he is your servant;

he conquered the anger not by strength of body,
nor by activity of weapons,
but by logic he subordinated the ones punishing
reminding them of the fathers' promises and covenants.

  For the dead having fallen on each other in heaps
standing between he drove back the anger
and severed through its way to the living.
For on a robe to the feet was the whole world,
and fathers' glories were carved on four rows of stones,
and your majesty on the crown on his head.
To these the destroyer yielded, and these he feared;
for the trial of the anger alone was enough.

19
  The profane were set upon until the end by pitiless anger,
for it knew ahead even their intentions,
that they being committed to the departing
and with speed sending them forth
regretting it they would pursue.

  For while they were still mourning
and lamenting at the graves of the dead
they fixed on another foolish reason
and those whom begging they threw out,
these as fugitives they pursued.

  For the fate they deserved drew them on to this end
and made them forget what had happened,
so that they might fill up the punishment
with what remained of the torments,
and your common people experience an incredible journey,
and those might find a strange death.

  For the whole creation in particular
came to be reformed again from above
complying with your orders,
so that your children might be kept unharmed.

  The cloud overshadowed the encampment,
and out of what was water before
dry land was seen coming up,
an unhindered way out of the Red Sea
and a plain of green grass out of the violent surf;

where the whole nation came through sheltered by your hand
seeing marvelous wonders.
  For like horses they were grazing
and like lambs were leaping
praising you, Lord, who rescued them.
For they still remembered their sojourning,
how instead of producing animals
the earth brought forth gnats,
and instead of emptying itself of water
the river was full of frogs.
Later they also saw a new generation of birds,
when desire led them to ask for luxurious meats;
for their relief quails came up from the sea.
  Also the vengeance did not come upon the sinners
without previous signs by the force of thunderbolts;
for justly they suffered for their bad peculiarities,
for also they practiced the harsher hating of strangers.
  For some did not receive the ignorant who passed by;
but these enslaved beneficial strangers.
Not only that, but some oversight will be theirs,
since hatefully they received the aliens;
but the ones with celebrations
whom they already received having shared the same rights
they treated badly with terrible toil.
  Also they were struck with loss of sight
as those were at the door of the just,
when surrounded by yawning darkness
each of them tried to find the way through their door.
  For the elements being corrected by themselves,
as on a harp notes vary the kind of rhythm
all the time continuing by ringing,
this is inferred out of clearly seeing what happened;
for land things were transformed into water things,
and the swimming changed to walk on earth;
fire maintained in water its own power,
and water forgot its quenching nature;
flames contrary to destroying animals
did not wither the flesh of those walking around,
nor did they melt the crystals

of the easily melted type of ambrosial food.
  For in all things, Lord,
you exalted and glorified your common people
and not overlooking stood by in every time and place.

Introduction to Jesus the Christ

Though the numbered years of our common era were supposed to have been based on the birth of Jesus, the one called Christ, it is likely that he was born about 6 BC. According to evidence in the *Gospel of John* the public ministry of Jesus lasted about three years. Jesus was executed by the Roman punishment of crucifixion in Jerusalem about 30 CE.

Jesus was the oldest child in his family but had four brothers: James, Joseph, Judas, and Simon, and also sisters. Apparently after witnessing the resurrection James became the acknowledged leader of the early Christians in Jerusalem. The letter in the *New Testament* by James is attributed to him. According to the Jewish historian Josephus, James was accused by Ananus, the high priest in Jerusalem, of breaking the Jewish law. James was stoned to death in the year 62; this caused Ananus to lose his position, because he had not gained Roman approval for the capital punishment.

No evidence of any writing by Jesus exists, and what we know of his life is contained in the *Gospels*. The word "Gospel" is a Middle English translation of the Greek *Euangelion*, which means literally a good message or good news; the word "angel" comes from the Greek word for a messenger.

Scholars generally agree that *Mark* was the first gospel to be written but probably not until about thirty years after the crucifixion. According to Papias, the bishop of Hierapolis in the early second century, John the elder said that Mark had been Peter's interpreter and wrote down as accurately as he could everything he heard from Peter of the Lord's sayings and actions. Though shorter because of fewer parables and teachings, Mark gives more details on specific incidents than the other Gospels.

Papias also wrote that Matthew compiled the sayings of Jesus in the original Aramaic language, and everyone had to translate them as best they could. The *Gospel according to Matthew* in the *New Testament*, like all the books in that collection, is in Greek. It was attributed to Matthew or Levi the tax collector who became one of the twelve disciples.

The *Gospel according to Luke* and the *Acts of the Apostles* are attributed to a physician and companion of the apostle Paul.

Both *Matthew* and *Luke* were probably written a few years after *Mark*. The *Gospel according to John* is attributed to the beloved disciple, but scholars do not think it was written until about 100 CE.

A collection of sayings by Jesus known as the *Gospel of Thomas*, thought to have been written in the early second century, was found in Naj Hammadi, Egypt, in 1945, written in Coptic. This text was probably used by Gnostics who claimed mystical knowledge; some of its ideas were considered too esoteric or heretical to be included in orthodox theology. Thomas was the disciple called the Twin and may have traveled to Persia and India.

The Good Message of Jesus the Christ is a synthesis of the *Gospels of Mark, Matthew, Luke,* and *John,* with a few additions from the sayings of *Thomas.* For the most part these four versions of the life and teachings of Jesus harmonize with each other rather well, but each includes many things not found in the others. By putting all of the elements together in one compilation, the reader can most easily understand the actions and teachings of Jesus as a whole. The only major elements left out from the four gospels are the two contradictory genealogies of Joseph and the opening dedication to Theophilus in *Luke.*

The word "amen" has not been translated but left as it is, because it means much the same today as it did then, a term of confirmation usually used at the end of a liturgy. Jesus departed from tradition by using it at the beginning of statements.

The silver coin *denarius* was considered the average daily wage for a worker and has been translated as such even though it was worth a little less than a *drachma*, which was another silver coin worth about a quarter of a dollar. A talent was worth well over a thousand dollars. The word "stadium" has been left as such, because it was about the length of a stadium, actually 607 feet.

The twelve hours of the day were counted from sunrise to sunset; the night had watches of two hours each such that the fourth watch was the first two hours after midnight.

The Pharisees were a major religious party of Jews who emphasized the oral tradition as well as the written law and were more liberal in regard to spiritual ideas such as immortality, resurrection, divine retribution, free will, and angelic spirits than were the Sadducees who denied these things, controlled the temple, and tended to be wealthy conservatives favoring strict punishments for violations of written law.

Notes to:

2: Herod reigned over Judea from 37 BC to 4 BC; late in his life he suffered from arteriosclerosis and manifested irrational behavior.

6: The Roman emperor Caesar Augustus (ruled 31 BC-14 CE) did order a census, which began in 8 BC and could have taken a couple years to reach provinces like Judea.

8: The term "magi" refers to priests of the Zoroastrian religion who were usually knowledgeable in astrology. According to the astronomer and astrologer Johannes Kepler, a conjunction of major planets in the sign of Pisces occurred in 6 BC. The precession of the equinoxes, which is a 25,868-year cycle, at that time was moving from Aries to Pisces. Now it is moving from Pisces to Aquarius.

8: Jeremiah was a prophet and reformer of Judah who lived about 650-570 BC. Ramah was a transit point for those being deported into exile to Babylon. Rachel, Jacob's wife, had trouble bearing children and finally died in childbirth.

8: Archelaus reigned in Judea from 4 BC-6 CE, when he was replaced by a Roman procurator.

10: Since Tiberius Caesar was invested with equal authority in the provinces two years before the death of Augustus, the fifteenth year of his government there refers to 26 or 27 CE. Pontius Pilate was appointed procurator of Judea in 26, was unpopular for flaunting pagan religious symbols, and was finally removed in 36 for executing people without proper trials. Herod Antipas and Philip were the sons of Herod who divided the remainder of their father's kingdom.

10: Annas had been high priest but still retained influence during the high-priesthood of his son-in-law Caiaphas.

10, 11, 19, 21, 26, and 79: *Second Isaiah* (Chapters 40-66) was written by an anonymous prophet during the Babylonian exile in the sixth century BC.

17: The Samaritans were not allowed to help build the second temple of Jerusalem after the Babylonian exile, and therefore built their own at Mt. Gerizim.

19, 36, 44, and 79: *Isaiah* (Chapters 1-40) was called to be a prophet to Israel in the year 742 BC. In 701 he opposed going to war against the Assyrians.

19: Elijah was a Hebrew prophet in the 9th century BC who emphasized the reality of one God. After prophesying a drought he was directed by God to go stay with the widow Zarephath.

19: Elisha, also in the ninth century, succeeded Elijah as the prophet of Israel; he told Naaman to wash seven times in the Jordan river, which cured him of his leprosy.

25: Herodians supported Herod and his sons.

76: The author of the prophetic book of *Daniel* was a Jew who lived under the persecution of Antiochus IV Epiphanes between 175 and 164 BC.

The Good Message of Jesus the Christ

1

  In the beginning was the Word,
and the Word was with God,
and God was the Word.
This was in the beginning with God.
All things came to be through him,
and without him not one thing has come to be.
  In him was life,
and the life was the light of human beings;
the light shines in the darkness,
and the darkness has not comprehended it.
It was the true light coming into the world
which enlightens every person.
  He was in the world,
and the world through him came to be,
and the world did not know him.
He came to his own,
and his own did not accept him.
  But as many as did accept him,
he gave them authority to become children of God,
to those believing in his name,
who were born not from blood nor from the will of flesh
nor from the will of man, but from God.
  The Word became flesh and resided among us,
and we saw his glory,
glory as the one who came from the Father,
full of grace and truth.
  For from his fullness we all received,
and grace upon grace;
for the law was given through Moses;
grace and truth came through Jesus Christ.
No one has ever seen God;
the only born God who is in the breast of the Father,
that one has made him known.

2

In the days of Herod, king of Judea,
there was a priest named Zacharias of the Abijah division,
and his wife Elizabeth was from the daughters of Aaron.
They were both correct before God,
proceeding blamelessly in all the commandments
and requirements of the Lord.
They had no child, because Elizabeth was barren;
and they were both advanced in their days.

It happened that in the order of his division
while he served as priest before God,
according to the custom of the priesthood
it was his lot to burn incense
entering the temple of the Lord,
and all the assembly of the people
were praying outside at the hour of the incense.

An angel of the Lord appeared to him
standing on the right of the altar of incense.
Zacharias seeing it, was troubled, and fear fell upon him.

But the angel said to him, "Fear not, Zacharias,
for your prayer has been heard,
and your wife Elizabeth will bear you a son,
and you shall call his name John;
there will be joy and gladness for you,
and many will be great in the presence of the Lord,
and he may not drink wine nor alcohol;
he will be filled with the Holy Spirit
even from his mother's womb,
and he will turn many of the sons of Israel
to the Lord their God;
he will go before him in the spirit and power of Elijah
to turn the hearts of the fathers to the children,
and the disobedient into the wisdom of the just
to make ready for the Lord a people prepared."

Zacharias said to the angel, "How will I know this?
For I am old and my wife is advanced in her days."

The angel answered him, "I am Gabriel,
standing in the presence of God,
and I was sent to speak to you

and to tell you these good messages;
look, you shall be silent and unable to speak
until the day these things happen,
because you did not believe my words,
which will be fulfilled in their time."

The people were expecting Zacharias,
and they wondered about his delay in the temple.
Coming out he was unable to speak to them,
and they realized that he had seen a vision in the temple;
he was nodding to them, and he remained dumb.
When the days of his service were completed,
he went away to his home.

After these days Elizabeth his wife conceived,
and she hid herself for five months,
saying, "The Lord has done this for me in these days in which
he looked favorably in taking away my shame among people."

3
In the sixth month the angel Gabriel was sent from God
to a town of Galilee named Nazareth,
to a virgin betrothed to a man named Joseph,
from the house of David,
and the name of the virgin was Mary.

Coming to her he said,
"Hello, favored one, the Lord is with you."

She was confused by the words,
and she pondered what sort of greeting this might be.

The angel said to her, "Fear not, Mary;
for you have found grace with God.
Look, you will conceive in the womb and bear a son,
and you shall call his name Jesus.
He will be great and will be called the son of the highest,
and the Lord God will give him
the throne of his father David;
he will reign over the house of Jacob forever,
and his kingdom will have no end."

Mary asked the angel,
"How will this be, since I know no husband?"

The angel answered her,
"The Holy Spirit will come upon you,
and the power of the highest will overshadow you;
and so the holy one born will be called the son of God.
Look, Elizabeth, your relative,
also conceived a son in her old age,
and this is the sixth month with her who was called barren;
for every saying will not be impossible with God."
   Mary said, "Look, the servant of the Lord;
let it be to me according to your saying."
And the angel departed from her.
   The birth of Jesus the Christ was like this.
His mother Mary being betrothed to Joseph,
before they came together
she was found to be pregnant from the Holy Spirit.
Joseph her husband, being just and not wishing to expose her,
decided to divorce her secretly.
   But as he considered these things,
look, an angel of the Lord appeared to him in a dream,
saying, "Joseph, son of David,
do not be afraid to take Mary as your wife;
for what is conceived in her is from the Holy Spirit.
She will bear a son, and you shall call his name Jesus;
for he will save his people from their sins."
   All this occurred so that what was spoken by the Lord
through his prophet might be fulfilled:
     **"Look, the virgin will be pregnant and bear a son,
     and they will call his name Immanuel,"**
which is translated "God with us."
   Joseph rising from the sleep did
as the angel of the Lord ordered him and accepted his wife;
he did not know her until she bore a son,
and he called his name Jesus.

4

   Standing up in those days
Mary traveled to the hill country
with haste to a town of Judah,
and she entered the home of Zacharias and greeted Elizabeth.

As Elizabeth heard Mary's greeting
the baby leaped in the womb,
and Elizabeth was filled with the Holy Spirit;
she cried out with a great shout and said,
"Blessed are you among women,
and blessed is the fruit of your womb.
Why is this for me, that the mother of my Lord comes to me?
For look, as the sound of your greeting came into my ears,
the baby leaped in gladness in my womb.
Blessed is she who believed that
what has been spoken to her from the Lord will be completed."

Mary said, "My soul magnifies the Lord,
and my spirit is glad in God my savior;
for he looked upon the humble state of his servant.
For look, from now on
all generations will consider me blessed,
because the powerful one did great things for me.
Holy is his name,
and his mercy is on generations and generations revering him.
He did a mighty deed with his arm,
scattered the proud in the understanding of their hearts,
brought down the powerful from thrones
and lifted up the humble;
he filled the hungry with good things
and sent the rich away empty.
He took the part of Israel his servant, remembering mercy,
as he spoke to our fathers, to Abraham and his seed forever."

Mary stayed with her about three months,
and returned to her home.

5
The time was fulfilled for Elizabeth to bear,
and she gave birth to a son.
The neighbors and her relatives heard
that the Lord had magnified his mercy with her,
and they rejoiced with her.

On the eighth day they came to circumcise the child,
and they were calling him
by the name of his father Zacharias.

His mother answered, "No, he shall be called John."

They said to her, "There is no one among your relatives
who is called by this name."
They nodded to his father what he might wish to call him.

Requesting a tablet, he wrote, "John is his name."
They were all surprised.
His mouth and his tongue were opened at once,
and he spoke praising God.

Fear came upon all their neighbors,
and throughout the hill country of Judea
all these sayings were discussed,
and all who heard put it into their hearts,
saying, "What then will this child be?"
For the Lord's hand was with him.

Zacharias, his father, was filled with the Holy Spirit
and prophesied, "Praised be the Lord God of Israel,
for he has visited and redeemed his people,
and raised a horn of salvation for us
in the house of his servant David,
as he has spoken
through the mouth of his holy prophets from the ages,
salvation from our enemies
and from the hand of all who hate us,
to perform mercy with our fathers
and remember his holy covenant,
the oath he swore to our father Abraham,
to give us fearlessly from the hand of enemies deliverance
to serve him in holiness and justice
in his presence all our days.

"You also, child, will be called a prophet of the highest;
for you will go before in the presence of the Lord
to prepare his ways,
to give knowledge of salvation to his people
in forgiveness of their sins,
through the tender mercy of our God,
in which sunrise from on high will visit us to shine
upon those sitting in darkness and the shadow of death,
to guide our feet into the way of peace."

The child grew and became strong in spirit,
and he was in the deserts
until the days of his manifestation to Israel.

6

In those days a decree went out from Caesar Augustus
to have registered all the inhabited world.
This was the first registration
when Quirinius governed Syria.
Everyone went to be registered, each to his own town.

Joseph also went up from the town Nazareth of Galilee
into Judea to the town of David which is called Bethlehem,
because he was from the house and family of David,
to be registered with Mary, his bride, who was pregnant.

While they were there
the days were fulfilled for her to give birth,
and she bore her first-born son;
she wrapped him in swaddling clothes
and laid him in a manger,
because there was no place for them in the inn.

Shepherds were in that country living in the fields
and keeping watch at night over their flock.
An angel of the Lord came to them,
and the glory of the Lord shone around them;
and they were in great awe and fear.

The angel said to them, "Do not be afraid;
for look, I bring you a good message of great joy
which will be for all the people,
for today in the town of David was born to you a savior,
who is Christ the Lord.
This is a sign for you: you will find a baby
wrapped in swaddling clothes and lying in a manger."

Suddenly there was with the angel
a multitude of the heavenly host praising God
and saying, "Glory in the highest to God
and on earth peace among people of goodwill."

As the angels went away from them into heaven
the shepherds spoke to each other,
"Let us go then to Bethlehem

and see this thing that has happened
which the Lord made known to us."

   They went hurrying,
and found Mary and Joseph and the baby lying in the manger;
and having seen they made known the saying
spoken to them about this child.

   All who heard marveled
at the things spoken to them by the shepherds;
but Mary kept all these sayings,
pondering them in her heart.

   The shepherds returned glorifying and praising God
for everything they had heard and seen
as it was spoken to them.

7

   At the completion of eight days when he was circumcised,
he was called the name Jesus,
which he was called by the angel
before he was conceived in the womb.

   When the days of their purification were completed
according to the law of Moses,
they took him into Jerusalem to present him to the Lord,
as it is written in the law of the Lord,

   "Every male opening the womb
   shall be called holy to the Lord,"

and to offer a sacrifice
according to what is said in the law of the Lord,

   "a pair of doves or two young pigeons."

   There was a person in Jerusalem named Simeon,
and this person was just and devout,
waiting for the consolation of Israel,
and the Holy Spirit was upon him;
it had been revealed to him by the Holy Spirit
that he was not to see death
before he had seen the Lord's Christ.

   He came in the spirit into the temple;
and as the parents brought in the child Jesus
to perform for him according to the custom of the law,
he took him in his arms and praised God

and said, "Now you may release your servant, master,
according to your saying in peace;
for my eyes have seen your salvation,
which you prepared in the presence of all peoples,
a light for revelation to the nations
and a glory of your people Israel."

His father and mother were marveling
at the things spoken about him.

Simeon blessed them and said to Mary, his mother,
"Look, this one is appointed
for the fall and rising of many in Israel
and for a sign spoken against,
and also a sword will pierce your soul,
so that the thoughts of many hearts may be revealed."

Also there was Anna, a prophetess,
daughter of Phanuel from the tribe of Asher;
she was advanced many days
having lived with her husband seven years from her virginity,
and as a widow until she was eighty-four years old;
she did not leave the temple,
serving with fasting and prayer night and day.

Coming in at that hour she gave thanks to God
and spoke about him to all
who were waiting for the redemption of Jerusalem.

8
Jesus having been born in Bethlehem of Judea
in the days of King Herod,
look, magi from the east arrived in Jerusalem,
saying, "Where is the one born king of the Jews?
For we saw his star in the east and came to worship him."

King Herod having heard was disturbed,
and all Jerusalem with him,
and assembling all the high priests
and scholars of the people
he inquired of them where the Christ was to be born.

They told him, "In Bethlehem of Judea;
for thus has it been written through the prophet:

'And you, Bethlehem, in the land of Judah,
are by no means least among the governors of Judah.
For from you will come a governor,
who will shepherd my people Israel.'"
  Then Herod secretly calling the magi
ascertained from them the time of the star's appearance,
and sending them to Bethlehem he said,
"Go examine carefully about the child;
and when you find him, report back to me,
so that I too may come worship him."
  Having heard the king they set out;
and look, the star, which they had seen in the east,
went ahead of them
until it came to stand above where the child was.
Seeing the star they rejoiced with extremely great joy.
  Coming into the house
they saw the child with Mary, his mother,
and falling down they worshipped him;
opening their treasures they offered him gifts,
gold and frankincense and myrrh.
Having been warned in a dream not to return to Herod,
they withdrew by another way into their country.
  When they had withdrawn,
look, an angel of the Lord appeared in a dream to Joseph,
saying, "Get up, take the child and his mother,
and flee to Egypt, and be there until I tell you;
for Herod intends to search for the child to destroy it."
  Getting up he took the child and his mother by night
and withdrew into Egypt,
and he was there until the death of Herod
so that what was spoken by the Lord
through the prophet might be fulfilled:
  "Out of Egypt have I called my son."
  Then Herod, seeing that he was tricked by the magi,
became very angry,
and sending out he annihilated all the little boys
in Bethlehem and all its regions
from two years and under, according to the time
which he had ascertained from the magi.

Then was fulfilled what was spoken
through the prophet Jeremiah:

> "A voice was heard in Ramah,
> weeping and lamenting much;
> Rachel wept for her children
> and would not be comforted,
> for they are not."

But Herod having died,
look, an angel of the Lord
appeared in a dream to Joseph in Egypt
saying, "Get up, take the child and his mother,
and travel into the land of Israel,
for those who sought the child's life have died."

Getting up he took the child and his mother
and entered the land of Israel.
But hearing that Archelaus was king of Judea
instead of his father Herod,
he was afraid to go there;
and having been warned in a dream
he withdrew into parts of Galilee,
and he lived in a town called Nazareth;
so it was fulfilled what was spoken through the prophets:

> "He shall be called a Nazarene."

9

The child grew and became strong, being filled with wisdom,
and the grace of God was upon him.
His parents went every year to Jerusalem
for the feast of the Passover.

When he was twelve years old,
they were going up according to the custom of the feast,
and the days being finished,
on their return the boy Jesus stayed back in Jerusalem,
and his parents were not aware of it.
Thinking he was in their company they went a day's journey,
and they looked for him
among their relatives and acquaintances;
not finding him they returned to Jerusalem looking for him.

After three days they found him in the temple
sitting in the middle of the teachers
both listening to them and questioning them;
all who heard him
were astonished at his intelligence and his answers.
    Seeing him they were upset,
and his mother said to him,
"Child, why did you do this to us?
Look, your father and I
have been anxiously searching for you."
    He said to them, "Why were you searching for me?
Did you not know that I must be about my Father's business?"
    They did not understand the saying he spoke to them.
He was obedient to them
and went down with them and came to Nazareth.
But his mother kept all these sayings in her heart.
    Jesus progressed in wisdom and age
and in favor with God and people.

10
    In the fifteenth year of the government of Tiberius Caesar,
when Pontius Pilate was governing Judea,
and Herod was tetrarch of Galilee,
his brother Philip tetrarch
of the Iturea and Trachonitis country,
and Lysanias tetrarch of Abilene,
during the high-priesthood of Annas and Caiaphas,
the word of God came
to John, Zacharias's son, in the desert.
    He went into all the country around the Jordan
preaching a baptism of repentance
for the forgiveness of sins,
saying, "Change your mind,
for near is the sovereignty of heaven,"
as it has been written in the book of Isaiah the prophet;
    "Look, I send my messenger ahead of you,
    who will prepare your way;
    a voice crying in the desert:
    Get ready the way of the Lord;

make straight his paths.
Every valley shall be filled
and every mountain and hill shall be made low,
and the crooked shall be made straight,
and the rough roads smooth;
and all flesh shall see the salvation of God."

John was dressed in camel's hair
with a leather belt around his waist,
and he was eating grasshoppers and wild honey.
Then Jerusalem and all Judea
and all the country around the Jordan went out to him,
and they were baptized in the Jordan River by him,
confessing their sins.

Seeing many of the Pharisees and Sadducees
coming to the baptism he said to them, "Products of vipers!
Who warned you to flee from the coming wrath?
Produce then fruit worthy of repentance;
and do not presume to say among yourselves,
'A father we have in Abraham;'
for I tell you that God can
from these stones raise up children for Abraham.
Already the ax is laid to the root of the trees;
therefore every tree not producing beautiful fruit
is cut down and thrown into the fire."

The crowds questioned him, "What then should we do?"

He answered them,
"Let whoever has two coats share with the one having none,
and let whoever has food do likewise."

Tax collectors also came to be baptized
and said to him, "Teacher, what should we do?"

He told them, "Collect no more than is required of you."

The soldiers also questioned him, "And what should we do?"

He told them, "Do not shake down anyone nor harass them,
and be satisfied with your pay."

11

A person was sent from God by the name of John;
this one came as a witness
so that he might testify about the light,

so that all might believe through him.
He was not that light but testified about the light.
John testified about him and cried out,
"This is the one of whom I said, 'The one coming after me
has become ahead of me, because he was before me.'"
    The people were in expectation
and all were considering in their hearts concerning John,
whether he might be the Christ.
When the Jews sent to him from Jerusalem priests and Levites
so that they might ask him, "Who are you?"
he acknowledged, "I am not the Christ."
    They asked him, "Who then? Are you Elijah?"
    He said, "I am not."
    "Are you the prophet?"
    He answered, "No."
    So they said to him, "Who are you?
that we may give an answer to those who sent us;
what do you say about yourself?"
    He said, "I am a voice crying in the desert:
    'Make straight the way of the Lord,'
as said Isaiah the prophet."
    The ones sent were from the Pharisees,
and they asked him, "Why then do you baptize
if you are not the Christ nor Elijah nor the prophet?"
    John answered them,
"I baptize you with water for repentance;
but the one coming after me is stronger than I,
whose sandals I am not worthy to carry;
he will baptize you with the Holy Spirit and fire;
his winnowing fork is in his hand
to clean out his threshing floor
and to gather the wheat into his storehouse,
but the chaff he will burn with inextinguishable fire."
    So with many different appeals
he brought the good message to the people
in Bethany beyond the Jordan, where John was baptizing.

12

Then Jesus came from Nazareth of Galilee
to be baptized in the Jordan by John.
He saw Jesus coming toward him and said,
"Look, the lamb of God who lifts away the sin of the world!
This is he of whom I said,
'After me comes a man who has become ahead of me,
because he was before me.'
I did not know him,
but that he might be revealed to Israel,
for this reason I came baptizing with water."
   John said to Jesus, "I need to be baptized by you,
and do you come to me?"
   Jesus answered him, "Let it be so now;
for thus it is fitting for us to fulfill all correctness."
   When Jesus had been baptized,
immediately coming up out of the water he was praying,
and the heavens were opened,
and the spirit of God came down upon him like a dove;
and there was a voice out of the heavens:
"You are my beloved son; with you I am well pleased."
   And John witnessed saying, "I have seen the Spirit
coming down like a dove from heaven,
and it remained on him.
I have not known him,
but the one who sent me to baptize with water,
that one said to me,
'On whomever you see the Spirit
coming down and remaining upon him,
this is the one baptizing with the Holy Spirit.'
I have seen, and I have testified
that this is the son of God."
Jesus beginning his ministry was about thirty years old.

13

   Then Jesus was led into the desert by the Spirit
to be tested by the devil,
and he was with wild beasts.

Having fasted forty days and forty nights,
afterward he was hungry.
The tempter approaching said to him,
"If you are the son of God, tell this stone to become bread."
Jesus answered him, "It has been written:

'Not on bread alone shall the human live,
but on every saying coming out of the mouth of God.'"

Then the devil took him along to the holy city of Jerusalem
and set him on the pinnacle of the temple,
and said to him, "If you are the son of God,
throw yourself down from here;
for it has been written,

'He will command his angels for you to protect you,
and on hands they will lift you up
lest you strike your foot against a stone.'"

Jesus answered him, "Again it has been written:

'You shall not tempt the Lord your God.'"

Again the devil took him along to a very high mountain
and showed him in a moment of time
all the sovereignties of the world,
and he said to him,
"I will give you all this authority and their glory,
for it has been given over to me
and to whomever I wish to give it;
therefore if falling down you will worship me,
it will all be yours."
Jesus answered him, "Go, Satan;
for it has been written:

'You shall worship the Lord your God,
and this only shall you serve.'"

Having completed every test,
the devil went away from him until an opportune time;
and look, angels approached and ministered to him.

14

On another day again
John was standing with two of his disciples,
and seeing Jesus walking he said, "Look, the lamb of God."
The two disciples heard him speaking and followed Jesus.

Jesus turning and seeing them following
said to them, "What are you looking for?"
  They said to him, "Rabbi"
(which translated means "Teacher"),
"where are you staying?"
  He said to them, "Come, and you will see."
So they went and saw where he was staying,
and they stayed with him that day;
it was about the tenth hour.
  Andrew, the brother of Simon Peter,
was one of the two who had heard John and followed him;
first he found his own brother Simon
and told him, "We have found the Messiah"
(which is translated "Christ").
  He led him to Jesus.
Looking at him Jesus said, "You are Simon, the son of John;
you shall be called Cephas" (which is translated "Peter").
  The next day he wished to go out to Galilee,
and he found Philip.
Jesus told him, "Follow me."
Philip was from Bethsaida,
from the town of Andrew and Peter.
  Philip found Nathanael and told him,
"We have found him
about whom Moses and the prophets wrote,
Jesus, son of Joseph, from Nazareth."
  Nathanael said to him,
"Can anything good be from Nazareth?"
  Philip said to him, "Come and see."
  Jesus saw Nathanael coming toward him and said about him,
"Look, a true Israelite, in whom there is no deceit."
  Nathanael said to him, "From where do you know me?"
  Jesus answered him, "Before Philip called you,
while you were under the fig tree I saw you."
  Nathanael answered him, "Rabbi, you are the son of God;
you are king of Israel."
  Jesus answered him, "Because I told you
that I saw you underneath the fig tree, do you believe?

You shall see greater things than these.
Amen, amen, I tell you, you shall see heaven opened
and the angels of God going up
and coming down upon the human son."
    On the third day there was a wedding in Cana of Galilee,
and the mother of Jesus was there;
and both Jesus and his disciples were invited to the wedding.
    Running out of wine,
the mother of Jesus said to him, "They have no wine."
    Jesus said to her, "What is that to me and you, woman?
My hour has not yet come."
    His mother said to the servants,
"Do whatever he tells you."
Lying there were six stone water jars
according to the purifications of the Jews,
each holding twenty or thirty gallons.
    Jesus told them, "Fill the jars with water."
They filled them up to the top.
    He told them, "Draw now and carry to the headwaiter."
They carried it.
    When the headwaiter tasted it, the water had become wine;
and he did not know where it was from,
but the servants who drew the water knew.
    The headwaiter called the bridegroom and said to him,
"Everyone first puts out the fine wine,
and when they are drunk the lesser;
you have kept the fine wine until now."
    This beginning of the miracles
Jesus did in Cana of Galilee;
he manifested his glory,
and his disciples believed in him.
    After this he went down to Capernaum,
he and his mother and brothers and his disciples,
and there they stayed not many days.

15
    It was near the Passover of the Jews,
and Jesus went up to Jerusalem.

When he was in Jerusalem at the Passover feast,
many believed in his name,
seeing his miracles which he was doing;
but Jesus himself did not trust himself to them,
because he knew all,
and had no need for anyone to testify about a person;
for he knew what was in a person.

There was a person from the Pharisees named Nicodemus,
a ruler of the Jews.
This one came to him at night and said to him,
"Rabbi, we know that you have come from God as a teacher;
for no one can do these miracles which you do,
unless God is with one."

Jesus answered him, "Amen, amen, I tell you,
unless one is born from above,
one cannot see the sovereignty of God."

Nicodemus said to him,
"How can a person be born who is old?
Can one enter into the womb of one's mother
a second time and be born?

Jesus answered, "Amen, amen, I tell you,
unless one is born of water and spirit,
one cannot enter into the sovereignty of God.
What has been born of flesh is flesh,
and what has been born of the spirit is spirit.
You should not wonder because I told you:
'You must be born from above.'
The spirit breathes where it wills,
and you hear its sound,
but you do not know where it comes from and where it goes;
So it is with everyone who has been born of the spirit."

Nicodemus asked him, "How can these things happen?"

Jesus answered him, "You are a teacher of Israel,
and you do not know these things?
Amen, amen, I tell you that what we know we speak
and what we have seen we testify to,
and you do not accept our testimony.
If I told you earthly things, and you do not believe,
how will you believe if I tell you heavenly things?

"No one has gone up into heaven
except the one who has come down from heaven,
the human son.
As Moses lifted up the snake in the desert,
so the human son must be lifted up,
so that everyone believing in him may have eternal life.

"For God so loved the world that he gave the only son,
that everyone believing in him should not perish
but have eternal life.

"For God did not send the son into the world
in order to judge the world,
but so that the world might be saved through him.
Whoever believes in him is not judged;
whoever does not believe has already been judged,
because he has not believed
in the name of the only son of God.

"This is the judgment:
that the light has come into the world,
and people loved the darkness rather than the light;
for their actions were bad.
For everyone who does evil hates the light
and does not come to the light,
lest one's actions be exposed;
but whoever does what is true comes to the light,
so that one's actions may be manifested
that they are accomplished in God."

16

After this, Jesus and his disciples
went into the Judean country,
and he spent time there with them and baptized.

John was also baptizing at Aenon near Salim,
because there was much water there,
and they came and were baptized;
for John had not yet been thrown into prison.

So there was a discussion between the disciples of John
and a Jew about purification.
They came to John and said to him,
"Rabbi, the one who was with you beyond the Jordan,

about whom you have testified,
look, this one baptizes, and everyone is going to him."
   John answered, "A person cannot receive anything
unless it has been given to one from heaven.
You yourselves witnessed me when I said,
'I am not the Christ, but I am sent ahead of that one.'
The one having the bride is the bridegroom;
but the friend of the bridegroom,
standing by and hearing him,
rejoices with joy because of the voice of the bridegroom.
Therefore this joy of mine has been fulfilled.
   "That one must grow, but I must diminish.
The one coming from above is over all;
the one from the earth is of the earth
and speaks of the earth.
The one coming from heaven is over all;
what he has seen and heard, this he testifies,
and no one accepts his testimony.
The one accepting his testimony certified that God is true.
For the one whom God sent speaks the sayings of God;
for not out of a measure does one give the spirit.
   "The Father loves the son,
and has given everything into his hand.
Whoever believes in the son has eternal life;
and whoever disobeys the son will not see life,
but the wrath of God remains upon one."
   So when the Lord knew that the Pharisees had heard
that Jesus was making and baptizing more disciples than John
(although Jesus himself did not baptize, but his disciples),
he left Judea and went away again into Galilee.

17
   He had to pass through Samaria.
So he came to a town in Samaria called Sychar,
near the place which Jacob gave to his son Joseph;
and there was Jacob's well.
So Jesus, tired from the journey, sat thus at the well;
it was about the sixth hour.

A woman from Samaria came to draw water.
Jesus said to her, "Give me a drink."
For his disciples had gone away into the town to buy food.

So the Samaritan woman said to him,
"How is it that you, a Jew,
ask for a drink from me, a Samaritan woman?"
(For Jews do not associate with Samaritans.)

Jesus answered her, "If you knew the gift of God,
and who it is saying to you, 'Give me a drink,'
you would have asked him,
and he would have given you living water."

She said to him, "Lord, you have no bucket,
and the well is deep;
where then do you have living water?
Are you greater than our father Jacob, who gave us the well,
and drank from it himself with his sons and his cattle?"

Jesus answered her,
"Everyone who drinks from this water will thirst again,
but whoever drinks from the water which I will give one,
will never thirst,
but the water which I will give one will become in one
a fountain of water springing up to eternal life."

The woman said to him, "Lord, give me this water,
so that I may not thirst nor come through here to draw water."

He said to her, "Go call your husband and come here."

The woman answered, "I have no husband."

Jesus said to her, "You say correctly, 'I have no husband;'
for you have had five husbands,
and now the one you have is not your husband;
this you have said truly."

The woman said to him, "Lord,
I see that you are a prophet.
Our fathers worshipped on this mountain,
and you say that in Jerusalem
is the place where one must worship."

Jesus said to her, "Believe me, woman,
that the hour is coming
when neither on this mountain nor in Jerusalem

will you worship the Father.
You worship what you do not know;
we worship what we know,
because salvation is from the Jews;
however, the hour is coming and now is,
when the true worshipers
will worship the Father in spirit and truth;
for the Father seeks such worshipers of him;
God is spirit,
and those worshipping must worship in spirit and truth."

The woman said to him,
"I know that Messiah is coming (the one called Christ);
when that one comes, he will announce everything to us."

Jesus said to her, "I am the one, who is speaking to you."

Upon this his disciples came,
and they were surprised that he was speaking with a woman;
though no one said, "What do you want?"
or "Why do you speak with her?"

So the woman left her water jar
and went away into the town,
and she said to people,
"Come see a person who told me all I ever did;
is this not the Christ?"
They went out of the town and came to him.

In the meantime the disciples said to him, "Rabbi, eat."

But he said to them, "I have food to eat
which you do not know about."

Therefore the disciples asked each other,
"Has anyone brought him something to eat?"

Jesus said to them, "My food is that I may do the will
of the one who sent me and complete this work.
Do you not say that
there is still four months, and the harvest comes?
Look, I tell you, lift up your eyes and see the fields,
because they are white for the harvest.
Already the reaper receives pay
and gathers fruit for eternal life,
so that the sower and the reaper may rejoice together.
For in this the word is true

that one is the sower and another the reaper.
I send you to reap what you have not labored over;
others have labored, and you have entered into their labor."

Out of that town many of the Samaritans believed in him
because of the word of the woman's testimony,
"He told me everything I did."
Therefore when the Samaritans came to him,
they asked him to stay with them;
and he stayed there two days.

And many more believed because of his word;
to the woman they said,
"We no longer believe because of your talk;
for we ourselves have heard,
and we know that this is truly the savior of the world."

After two days he went out from there into Galilee.

18
Herod the tetrarch, having been criticized by John
concerning Herodias, his brother's wife,
and all the evil things which Herod did,
added also this above all: he locked up John in prison.

After the arrest of John
Jesus came in the power of the Spirit into Galilee,
saying, "The time has been fulfilled,
and near is the sovereignty of God;
change your minds and believe in the good message of God."

News went out
through the whole country around concerning him,
and he taught in their synagogues, being praised by all.
The Galileans welcomed him,
for they too had gone to the feast
and had seen everything he had done
in Jerusalem at the feast.

So he came again to Cana of Galilee,
where he had made the water wine.
There was a certain royal official
whose son was ill at Capernaum;
this one having heard
that Jesus had come from Judea to Galilee,

went to him and asked that he come down and cure his son;
for he was about to die.

So Jesus said to him, "Unless you see miracles and omens,
you will not believe at all."

The royal official said to him,
"Lord, come down before my child dies."

Jesus said to him, "Go, your son lives."

The person believed the word which Jesus said to him,
and he went; and as he was going down,
the servants met him, saying that his boy lives.

So he inquired of them
the hour in which he had gotten better;
they said to him,
"Yesterday at the seventh hour the fever left him."

Therefore the father knew that that was the hour
in which Jesus said to him, "Your son lives."
And he and his whole household believed.
This second miracle Jesus did coming from Judea to Galilee.

19

He came to Nazareth, where he had been brought up;
and according to his custom on the day of the Sabbath
he entered the synagogue, and he stood up to read.
A scroll of the prophet Isaiah was handed to him,
and having opened the scroll
he found the place where it was written,

"The Spirit of the Lord is upon me,
for which he anointed me
to bring the good message to the poor;
he has sent me to proclaim to the captives release,
and to the blind, sight;
to send the oppressed release;
to proclaim the year of the Lord's favor."

Having rolled up the scroll
and having given it back to the attendant, he sat down,
and the eyes of everyone in the synagogue
were fixed upon him.

He began to speak to them,
"Today this scripture has been fulfilled in your hearing."

Everyone witnessed him
and marveled at the words of grace coming out of his mouth,
and they said, "Isn't this the son of Joseph?"
He said to them, "Surely you will quote me this proverb:
'Physician, heal yourself;
what we have heard of happening in Capernaum,
do here in your homeland.'
Amen, I tell you that no prophet is accepted in his homeland.
"But in truth I tell you,
many widows were in Israel in the days of Elijah,
when the heavens were shut for three years and six months,
when great famine came upon all the earth,
and to none of them was Elijah sent
except to the widow Zarephath of Sidon.
"Also many lepers were in Israel
in the time of Elisha the prophet,
and none of them were cleansed except Naaman the Syrian."
Everyone in the synagogue hearing these things
was filled with anger,
and getting up they threw him out outside the town,
and led him to the cliff of the mountain
upon which their town was built,
in order to throw him down;
but passing through between them he traveled on.
Leaving behind Nazareth
he settled in Capernaum by the sea
in the regions of Zebulun and Naphtali;
that what was spoken through the prophet Isaiah
might be fulfilled:
   "Land of Zebulun and land of Naphtali,
   way by the sea, beyond the Jordan,
   Galilee of the nations,
   the people sitting in darkness saw a great light,
   and to those sitting in the country
   and the shadow of death,
   a light has dawned for them."

20
As the crowd was pressing him
and listening to the word of God,

he was standing beside the lake Gennesaret.
He saw two boats standing beside the lake;
the fishermen having gone away from them
were washing the nets.
Embarking in one of the boats, which was Simon's,
he asked him to put out a little from the land;
and sitting he taught the crowds from the boat.

When he stopped speaking, he said to Simon,
"Put out into the deep,
and let down your nets for a catch."

Simon answered, "Master,
laboring through the whole night we took nothing,
but upon your saying I will let down the nets."

Having done this they enclosed a large quantity of fish,
and their nets were being torn.
They signaled to the partners in a different boat
to come help them,
and they came and filled both boats
so that they were sinking.

Simon Peter seeing fell down at the knees of Jesus
saying, "Go away from me, for I am a sinful man, Lord."
For wonder seized him and all those with him
at the catch of fish which they took.

Jesus said to Simon and his brother Andrew, "Fear not;
come after me, and from now on you will take living people."

Bringing in the boats to land
and leaving everything they followed him.

He saw James and John, sons of Zebedee,
who were Simon's partners,
and immediately he called them.
Leaving their father Zebedee in the boat with the hired men
they went away after him.

21

They went down into Capernaum, a town of Galilee.
Entering the synagogue on the Sabbath he was teaching them,
and they were amazed at his teaching;
for his word was with authority, not like the scholars.

In their synagogue was a person
with an unclean demon spirit,
and he cried out in a loud voice, "Eah!
Why are you among us, Jesus Nazarene?
Did you come to destroy us?
I know who you are, the holy one of God."
   Jesus reprimanded him, "Be quiet and come out of him."
Throwing him down and convulsing him
and crying in a loud voice
the unclean spirit came out of him without harming him.
   Everyone was astounded,
so that they debated with each other,
"What is this word?
A new teaching with authority,
that with power he even commands the unclean spirits,
and they obey him."
And his fame went out everywhere
in the whole region of Galilee.
   Going out of the synagogue they came into the home
of Simon and Andrew with James and John.
The mother-in-law of Simon was laying down fever-stricken,
and they asked him about her.
As he touched her hand, the fever left her,
and she rose at once and served them.
   While the sun was setting and evening was coming,
they brought to him
all those who were ill and demon-possessed
so that the whole town was gathered at the door,
and putting his hands on each one of them he healed them.
   Thus was fulfilled
what was spoken through Isaiah the prophet:
   "He took our ailments and bore our diseases."
   With a word he expelled demons out of many,
some shouting, "You are the son of God."
Reprimanding them he would not allow them to speak,
for they knew he was the Christ.
   Getting up very early in the night he went out
and went away into a deserted place, and there he prayed.
Simon and these with him searched for him,

and finding him they said to him,
"Everyone is looking for you."

He said to them,
"Let us go elsewhere into the neighboring towns,
so that there also I may preach
the good message of the sovereignty of God,
because for this I was sent."

He went around throughout Galilee,
teaching in their synagogues
and preaching the good message of the sovereignty
and healing every disease
and every malady among the people.

His fame went into all of Syria;
they brought to him all who were ill with various diseases
and those suffering pain,
the demon-possessed and lunatics and paralytics,
and he healed them.
Large crowds followed him from Galilee and Decapolis
and Jerusalem and Judea and beyond the Jordan.

While he was in one of the towns,
a leper came and kneeled before him appealing to him,
"Lord, if you are willing, you can cleanse me."

In compassion reaching out his hand he touched him
saying, "I am willing; be cleansed."
Immediately the leprosy went away from him,
and he was cleansed.

Warning him sternly Jesus sent him away,
ordering him, "See that you tell no one anything,
but go show yourself to the priest
and offer for your cleansing what Moses commanded,
as testimony to them."

But going out he began to proclaim many things
and spread the word,
so that he was no longer able to enter the towns openly,
but he was withdrawing into the deserts and praying;
yet the crowds came to him from everywhere.

22

After some days embarking in a boat he crossed over
and entered again into his own town Capernaum.
It was heard that he was at home,
and many were gathered,
so there was no longer any room at the door.
Pharisees and law-teachers were sitting
who had come from every village
of Galilee and Judea and Jerusalem;
he spoke to them the word,
and the power of the Lord was in him to cure.

They came bringing to him on a bed
a person who was paralyzed being carried by four,
and they tried to bring him in and lay him before him.
Not being able to bring him in to him because of the crowd,
they took the roof off where he was,
and tearing out the tiles they lowered the mattress
on which the paralytic was laying
letting him down in the middle in front of Jesus.

Seeing their faith he said to the paralytic,
"Have courage, child; your sins are forgiven."

The scholars and Pharisees were pondering in their hearts,
"Why does this one speak thus? He blasphemes.
Who can forgive sins except God alone?"

Jesus recognizing in his spirit
that they were reasoning so among themselves, said to them,
"Why do you think these bad things in your hearts?
Which is easier:
to say to the paralytic, 'Your sins are forgiven,'
or to say, 'Rise and pick up your mattress and walk'?
But so that you may know that
the human son has authority on earth to forgive sins,"
he said to the paralytic, "I tell you, rise,
pick up your mattress and go into your home."

Standing up at once before them,
picking up what he was laying on,
he went away into his home praising God.

They were all bewildered and filled with awe,
and they praised God for giving such authority to humans,

saying, "We never saw anything like this;
we saw wonderful things today."

23
He went out again by the sea;
all the crowd came to him, and he taught them.
Passing by he saw a tax collector named Levi
sitting at the tax office,
and he said to him, "Follow me."
Standing up he followed him.
Levi made a great banquet for Jesus in his home,
and many tax collectors and sinners were dining
with him and his disciples;
for there were many disciples who followed him.
The scholars and Pharisees seeing that
he was eating with sinners and tax collectors
complained to his disciples,
"Why does he eat and drink with tax collectors and sinners?"
Jesus hearing said to them,
"The healthy have no need of a physician, but the ill do.
Go learn what it is: 'I wish mercy and not sacrifice;'
I did not come to call the just, but sinners to repentance."
John's disciples and the Pharisees were fasting,
and they came and said to him,
"Why do John's disciples and the Pharisees' disciples fast,
but your disciples do not fast?"
Jesus said to them, "What sin, then, have I committed,
or in what have I been overcome?
Can the wedding attendants fast
while the bridegroom is with them?
But the days will come
when the bridegroom may be taken away from them,
and then they will fast on that day.
"No one sews a patch of unshrunk cloth on an old garment;
if one does, the new takes fullness from the old,
and a worse tear occurs.
And no one puts new wine into old wineskins;
if one does, the new wine will burst the skins;
the wine would be spilled, and the skins would be ruined;

and old wine is not put into a fresh skin, lest it spoil it.
But new wine must be put into fresh skins,
and both are preserved.
No one having drunk the old wants the new,
for one says, 'The old is good.'"

24
  After this there was a Jewish feast,
and Jesus went up to Jerusalem.
In Jerusalem at the sheep gate is a pool,
which in Hebrew is called Bethzatha, having five porticoes.
  In these lay a multitude
of the ailing, blind, lame, withered,
waiting for the moving of the water;
for at certain times
an angel of the Lord coming down stirred the water;
whoever went in first after the stirring
was cured of whatever disease one had.
  A certain person was there
who had his ailment for thirty-eight years;
seeing this one lying down,
and knowing that it already had been a long time,
he said to him, "Are you willing to become healthy?"
  The ailing one answered him, "Lord, I have no person,
so that when the water is stirred
one may put me into the pool;
but while I am going, another goes down before me."
  Jesus said to him, "Rise,
pick up your mattress and walk."
Immediately the person became healthy,
and he picked up his mattress and walked.
  It was a Sabbath on that day.
Therefore the Jews said to the one who had been healed,
"It is a Sabbath,
and it is not permitted for you to carry the mattress."
  But he answered them, "The one who made me healthy,
that one told me, 'Pick up your mattress and walk.'"
  They asked him, "Who is the person who told you,
'Pick it up and walk'?"

But the one cured did not know who it was;
for Jesus had withdrawn, as there was a crowd in the place.
After this, Jesus found him in the temple and said to him,
"Look, you have become healthy;
sin no more, lest something worse happen to you."
The person went away and told the Jews
that it was Jesus who made him healthy.
For this reason the Jews pursued Jesus,
because he did this on a Sabbath.
But he answered them, "My Father is working until now,
and I am working."
So for this reason the Jews tried even more to kill him,
because he not only broke the Sabbath,
but also he called God his own Father,
making himself equal to God.
So Jesus answered them, "Amen, amen, I tell you,
the son cannot do anything by himself;
except what he sees the Father doing;
for whatever that one does,
this also the son does likewise.
For the Father loves the son
and shows him everything he does,
and greater works than these will he show him,
so that you may marvel.
For as the Father raises the dead and gives life,
so also the son gives life to whom he will.
"For the Father does not judge anyone,
but has given all judgment to the son,
so that everyone may honor the son as they honor the Father.
Whoever does not honor the son
does not honor the Father who sent him.
"Amen, amen, I tell you that whoever hears my word
and believes in the one who sent me has eternal life
and does not come into judgment,
but has passed over from death into life.
Amen, amen, I tell you that the hour is coming and now is
when the dead will hear the voice of the son of God
and the ones hearing will live.

"For as the Father has life in himself,
so also he granted the son to have life in himself.
He gave him authority to make judgment,
because he is the human son.

"Do not be surprised by this,
because the hour is coming in which all those in the tombs
will hear his voice and will come out—
those who have done good into a resurrection of life,
those who have done bad into a resurrection of judgment.

"I can do nothing by myself;
as I hear I judge, and my judgment is just,
because I do not seek my will,
but the will of the one who sent me.

"If I testify about myself, my testimony is not true;
there is another who testifies about me,
and I know that his testimony about me is true.
You have sent to John, and he has testified to the truth;
though I do not take testimony from a person,
but I say this so that you may be saved.
That one was a burning and shining lamp,
and you were willing to rejoice for an hour in his light.

"But I have testimony greater than John's;
for the works which the Father has given me to complete,
these works which I do, testify about me
that the Father has sent me.
The Father who sent me, that one has testified about me.
You have neither heard his voice nor seen his form,
and you do not have his word abiding in you,
because you do not believe this one whom that one sent.

"You study the scriptures,
because you think in them you have eternal life;
and those are the ones testifying about me;
and you are not willing to come to me
so that you may have life.

"I do not accept praise from humans,
but I have known you,
that you do not have the love of God in you.
I have come in the name of my Father,
and you do not accept me;

if another comes in his own name,
that one you will accept.
How can you believe, accepting praise from each other,
and not seek the praise from the only God?

"Do not think that I will accuse you before the Father;
there is accusing you Moses,
in whom you have put your hope.
For if you believed Moses, you would believe me;
for he wrote about me.
But if you do not believe his writings,
how will you believe my sayings?"

25

In that season on a Sabbath
Jesus was passing through the grain fields;
his disciples were hungry
and began to make a path picking the wheat,
and rubbing it in their hands they ate the wheat.

Some of the Pharisees seeing said to him,
"Look, your disciples are doing
what is not permitted on a Sabbath."

Jesus answered them, "Have you never read what David did,
when he was in need and hungry, he and those with him?
how he entered into the house of God
in Abiathar's high-priesthood
and taking the consecrated bread ate it
and gave it to those with him,
which only the priests are permitted to eat?

"Or have you not read in the law that on the Sabbath
the priests in the temple desecrate the Sabbath
and are blameless?

"I tell you that one greater than the temple is here.
If you had known what is 'I wish mercy and not sacrifice,'
you would not have condemned the blameless.
The Sabbath was made because of the human,
and not the human because of the Sabbath;
so the human son is also Lord of the Sabbath."

On another Sabbath he entered the synagogue and taught.
A person was there who had a withered hand,

and the scholars and the Pharisees watched him
to see if he would heal on the Sabbath,
so that they might find something to accuse him of.

But he knew their reasoning
and said to the person with the withered hand,
"Rise and stand in the middle;" and he stood up.

Jesus said to them,
"I ask you if it is permitted on the Sabbath
to do good or to do harm, to save life or to destroy?"

But they were silent.

He said to them, "What person is there among you
who has one sheep, if it falls into a ditch on the Sabbath,
will not seize it and lift it out?
By how much, then, does a person differ from a sheep!
So it is permitted to do good on the Sabbath."

Then looking around at them with anger,
grieved at the hardness of their hearts,
he said to the person, "Hold out your hand."

He held it out,
and his hand was restored as healthy as the other.
The Pharisees were filled with fury,
and going out they plotted with the Herodians against him,
how they might destroy him.

26

Jesus with his disciples withdrew to the sea,
and a great many from Galilee followed;
from Judea and from Jerusalem and from Idumea
and beyond the Jordan and around Tyre and Sidon,
a great many, hearing what he was doing, came to him.

He told his disciples
that a small boat should be ready for him
because of the crowd, lest they press upon him.
For he had healed many,
so those who were suffering fell upon him
so that they might touch him.

The unclean spirits, when they saw him,
fell before him and cried out, "You are the son of God."
He strongly warned them

that they should not make him known.

Thus what was spoken through the prophet Isaiah
was being fulfilled:

> "Look, my servant whom I chose,
> my beloved in whom my soul is delighted;
> I will put my Spirit upon him,
> and he will proclaim justice to the nations.
> He will not quarrel nor shout,
> nor will anyone hear his voice in the streets.
> A bruised reed he will not break
> and a smoldering wick he will not quench,
> until he leads justice to victory.
> And in his name nations will hope."

In these days he went up on the mountain to pray,
and he spent the night in prayer to God.

When day came, he called his disciples,
and he appointed twelve so that they might be with him,
and so that he might send them out to preach
and to have authority to expel the demons.

Appointing the twelve he laid the name Peter on Simon,
and on James, the son of Zebedee, and John, his brother,
he laid the name Boanerges, which means sons of thunder;
there was also Peter's brother Andrew
and Philip and Bartholomew and Matthew the tax collector
and Thomas and James, son of Alphaeus,
and Thaddaeus and Simon the Zealot
and Judas Iscariot, who even gave him over.

27

Seeing the crowds he went up on the mountain;
as he sat, his disciples came to him.

Lifting up his eyes to his disciples he said,
"Blessed are the poor in spirit,
for yours is the sovereignty of heaven.

"Blessed are those who mourn,
for you shall be comforted.

"Blessed are the gentle,
for you shall inherit the earth.

"Blessed are those who hunger and thirst for justice,
for you shall be satisfied.

"Blessed are the merciful,
for you shall be shown mercy.

"Blessed are the pure in heart,
for you shall see God.

"Blessed are the peacemakers,
for you shall be called sons of God.

"Blessed are those persecuted on account of justice,
for yours is the sovereignty of heaven.

"Blessed are you when people hate you
and insult you and persecute you,
and when they exclude you and reject your name
and say every bad thing against you falsely
on account of the human son.
Rejoice and be glad, for your reward is large in heaven;
for thus their fathers persecuted the prophets before you.

"But woe to the rich,
for you have received your comfort.

"Woe to those who are full now,
for you shall hunger.

"Woe to those who laugh now,
for you shall mourn and weep.

"Woe when all the people speak well of you,
for their fathers did the same to the false prophets.

"You are the salt of the earth; salt is fine;
but if even the salt becomes tasteless,
with what will it be seasoned?
Neither for soil nor manure is it fit;
it is no longer good for anything
except to be thrown out and trampled under by people.

"You are the light of the world.
A city cannot be hidden set on a mountain;
no one lighting a lamp hides it or puts it under a basket,
but one puts it on the lampstand
so that it shines for everyone in the house.
Let your light so shine before people,
that they may see your good works

and praise your Father in heaven.

28
"Do not think that I came
to abolish the law or the prophets;
I did not come to abolish but to fulfill.
For amen, I tell you, until heaven and earth pass away,
not one 'i' nor one dot shall pass away from the law
until everything is accomplished.

"Therefore whoever breaks one of the smallest
of these commandments and teaches people thus,
will be called smallest in the sovereignty of heaven.
But whoever performs and teaches,
this one will be called great in the sovereignty of heaven.
For I tell you that unless your justice
surpasses that of the scholars and Pharisees,
you will not enter into the sovereignty of heaven.

"You heard that it was said to the ancients,
'You shall not murder;
and whoever murders will be liable to the judgment.'
But I tell you that everyone who is angry with his brother
will be liable to the judgment;
and whoever says to his brother, 'Numskull,'
will be liable to the council;
and whoever says, 'Fool,'
will be liable to the hell of fire.

"Therefore if you are offering your gift at the altar
and there remember
that your brother has something against you,
leave your gift there before the altar,
and go first be reconciled to your brother;
then come offer your gift.

"Why do you not judge even by yourselves what is right?
As you go with your opponent to a ruler be agreeable quickly
and work hard to be released from him on the way,
lest the opponent drag you to the judge,
and the judge give you over to the officer,
and the officer throw you into prison;
amen, I tell you, you will not come out from there

until you pay back the last penny.

"You heard that it was said,
'You shall not commit adultery.'
But I tell you that everyone looking at a woman with desire
already has committed adultery with her in his heart.

"If your right eye offends you,
take it out and throw it away from you;
for it is better for you to lose one of your parts
and not let your whole body be thrown into hell.

"If your right hand offends you,
cut it off and throw it away from you;
for it is better for you to lose one of your parts
and not let your whole body go away into hell.

"It was said, 'Whoever separates from his wife
must give her a divorce.'
But I tell you that everyone separating from his wife,
except for reason of fornication,
makes her commit adultery;
everyone leaving his wife and marrying another
commits adultery;
and whoever marries the one left by the husband
commits adultery.

"Again you heard that it was said to the ancients,
'You shall not break your oath,
but keep your oaths to the Lord.'
But I tell you not to swear at all:
neither by heaven, for it is the throne of God;
nor by the earth, for it is the footstool of his feet;
nor by Jerusalem, for it is the city of the great king;
nor swear by your head,
for you cannot make one hair white or black.
Let your word be 'Yes,' or 'No;'
but more than these is from evil.

"You heard that it was said,
'An eye for an eye and a tooth for a tooth.'
But I tell you not to resist the evil;
but whoever strikes you on your right cheek,
turn to him the other also;
to the one wishing to judge you and take your coat,

let him have your shirt also;
whoever forces you to go one mile, go with him two.

"Give to the one asking you;
do not turn away from the one wishing to borrow from you;
and do not demand your things back
from the one taking them.
What you would like people to do to you, do likewise to them.

"You heard that it was said,
'You shall love your neighbor and hate your enemy.'
But I tell you: love your enemies,
do good to those who hate you,
bless those cursing you,
pray for those abusing you,
so that you may become sons of your Father in heaven;
for his sun rises on the bad and good,
and it rains on the just and unjust.

"If you love those who love you,
what credit is that to you?
Even tax collectors and sinners love those who love them.

"For even if you do good to those who do good to you,
what credit is that to you?
Even the sinners do the same.

"If you greet only your brothers,
are you doing anything extra?
Do not even other nations do the same?

"If you lend to those from whom you hope to receive,
what credit is that to you?
Even sinners lend to sinners
so that they may receive back an equal amount.

"But love your enemies and do good
and lend expecting nothing;
and your reward will be large,
and you will be sons of the highest,
for he is kind to the ungrateful and bad.
Therefore become compassionate and perfect,
as your heavenly Father is compassionate and perfect.

29
"When you pray, do not be like the hypocrites;
for they love to pray in the synagogues
and standing on the street corners,
so that they may be visible to people;
amen, I tell you, they received their reward.

"But when you pray,
go into your room and having closed your door
pray to your Father in secret;
and your Father who sees in secret will give back to you.

"And in praying do not babble like the nationalities;
for they think that in their many words they will be heard.
Therefore do not be like them;
for your Father knows what needs you have
before you ask him.

"Therefore pray you thus:
Our Father in heaven;
holy be your name;
may your sovereignty come;
may your will be done,
as in heaven also on earth.
Give us today our daily bread;
and forgive us our debts,
as we forgave also our debtors;
and do not bring us into temptation,
but rescue us from the evil.

"For if you forgive people their transgressions,
your heavenly Father will also forgive you;
but if you do not forgive people,
neither will your Father forgive your transgressions.

"When you fast, do not look gloomy like the hypocrites;
for they disfigure their faces
so they may show to people they are fasting;
amen, I tell you, they received their reward.

"But when you are fasting,
anoint your head and wash your face,
so you may not show to people you are fasting
but to your Father in secret;
and your Father who sees in secret will give back to you.

"Be careful not to do your rightness before people
to be seen by them;
otherwise you have no reward from your Father in heaven.

"Therefore when you perform charity,
do not trumpet it before you,
as the hypocrites do in the synagogues and in the streets,
so that they may be praised by people;
amen, I tell you, they received their reward.

"But performing your charity
let not your left know what your right does,
so that your charity may be in secret;
and your Father who sees in secret will give back to you.

"Do not store up for yourselves treasures on the earth,
where moth and eating destroy,
and where thieves break in and steal;
but store up for yourselves treasures in heaven,
where neither moth nor eating destroy,
and where thieves do not break in nor steal;
for where your treasure is, there also will be your heart.

"The eye is the lamp of the body.
Therefore if your eye is clear,
your whole body is also illuminated;
but if your eye is bad,
your whole body is also dark.
Therefore if the light in you is dark,
how great the darkness!
But if your whole body is illuminated,
not having any part dark,
it will be completely illuminated
as when the lamp by gleaming lights you.

"No one can serve two lords;
for either one will hate the one and love the other,
or one will hold to one and disregard the other.
You cannot serve God and money.

"For this reason I tell you:
do not worry about your life—
what you should eat or what you should drink,
nor about your body—what you should wear.
Is not life more than food and the body more than clothes?

Look at the birds of heaven,
for they do not sow nor reap nor gather into barns,
and your heavenly Father feeds them;
are you not worth more than they?
Who among you by worrying can add one hour to his life?
If then you cannot do the smallest thing,
why worry about the rest?
  "And why worry about clothing?
Observe the lilies of the field, how they grow:
they do not labor nor spin;
yet I tell you, not even Solomon in all his splendor
was dressed like one of these.
But if God so clothes the grass of the field
which exists today and tomorrow is thrown into an oven,
will he not much more clothe you, you of little faith?
  "Therefore do not be anxious saying,
'What should we eat?'
or 'What should we drink?'
or 'What should we wear?'
For the nations of the world strive for all these things;
and your heavenly Father knows that you need all of them.
  "But seek first the sovereignty and his justice,
and all these things will be provided for you.
Therefore do not be anxious about tomorrow,
for tomorrow will be anxious for itself;
each day has enough trouble of its own.

30
  "Do not judge, and you may not be judged;
for by what condemnation you judge, you will be judged.
Forgive, and you will be forgiven;
give, and it will be given to you;
a good measure, pressed down, shaken, and running over,
they will put in your lap;
for by what measure you measure
it will be measured back to you.
  "Can the blind guide the blind?
Will not both fall into a ditch?
Why do you look at the speck in your brother's eye,

but the plank in your own eye you do not consider?
How can you say to your brother:
'Let me take the speck out of your eye,'
while not seeing yourself the plank in your eye?
Hypocrite, first take the plank out of your eye,
and then you will see clearly
to take the speck out of your brother's eye.

"Do not give what is holy to the dogs,
lest they throw it on the dung-heap.
Do not throw your pearls to the pigs,
lest they trample them under their feet
and turning tear you apart.

"Let one who searches,
not cease searching until one finds;
and when one finds, one will be troubled;
and when one has been troubled, one will marvel,
and one will reign over all.

"Ask, and it will be given to you;
search, and you will find;
knock, and it will be opened to you.
For everyone asking receives,
and whoever searches finds,
and to the one knocking it will be opened.

"What father is there among you,
if his son asks him for bread, would give him a stone?
or if he asks for a fish, would give him a snake?
If, then, you who are bad
know to give good gifts to your children,
how much more will your Father in heaven
give the Holy Spirit to those who ask him.

"Thus everything which you wish
that people should do to you,
you should do so to them also;
for this is the law and the prophets.

"Enter through the narrow gate;
for wide is the gate and broad the road
that leads away into destruction,
and there are many entering through it;
but narrow is the gate and hard the road

that leads into life,
and there are few finding it.

  "Watch out for false prophets,
who come to you in sheep's clothing,
but inside are ravenous wolves.
By their fruit you will recognize them.
Does anyone pick grapes from thorns or figs from thistles?

  "Thus every good tree produces beautiful fruit,
but the rotten tree produces bad fruit.
A good tree cannot bear bad fruit,
nor can a rotten tree bear beautiful fruit;
for each tree is known by its own fruit.
Every tree not producing beautiful fruit
is cut down and thrown into fire.
So by their fruit you will recognize them.

  "Not everyone saying to me, 'Lord, Lord,'
will enter into the sovereignty of heaven,
but the one doing the will of my Father in heaven.
Why do you call me, 'Lord, Lord,' and not do what I say?

  "Many will say to me on that day: 'Lord, Lord,
did we not prophesy in your name,
and in your name expel demons,
and in your name perform many powerful things?'

  "Then I will declare to them, 'I never knew you;
depart from me workers of lawlessness.'

  "Therefore everyone who hears these words of mine
and practices them,
will be like a sensible man building a house,
who dug deep and laid a foundation on the rock.
The rain came down, and the winds blew,
and a flood occurring the river crashed against that house;
and it was not able to shake it, because it was well built;
it did not fall, for it had been established on the rock.

  "But everyone hearing these words of mine
and not practicing them
will be like a foolish man, who built his house on the sand.
When the rain came down and the winds blew
and the river pounded against that house,
it collapsed and fell;

and the ruin of that house was great."

When Jesus finished these words,
the crowds were amazed at his teaching;
for he was teaching them as one having authority,
and not as their scholars.

As he was coming down from the mountain,
large crowds followed him.

31

He entered Capernaum.
A certain centurion's servant, who was valued by him,
being ill was about to die.
Having heard about Jesus he sent to him Jewish elders,
asking him to come so that he might save his servant.

Coming to Jesus they pleaded with him urgently,
saying, "He is worthy for whom you should grant this;
for he loves our nation,
and he built the synagogue for us."
Jesus went with them.

While he was not far from the house,
the centurion approached and pleaded with him,
"Lord, my boy has been laid up in the house paralyzed,
suffering terribly."

He said to him, "I will go heal him."

But the centurion answered, "Lord,
I am not worthy that you should enter under my roof;
but only say the word, and my boy will be cured.
For I am a person appointed under authority,
having soldiers under me,
and I say to this one, 'Go,' and he goes,
and to another, 'Come,' and he comes,
and to my servant, 'Do this,' and he does."

Having heard this, Jesus marveled
and turning to those following he said,
"I tell you, from no one in Israel have I found such faith.
Amen, I tell you that many will come from east and west,
and will recline with Abraham and Isaac and Jacob
in the sovereignty of heaven;
but the sons of the sovereignty

will be thrown out into the outer darkness;
there will be the weeping and the gnashing of teeth."
   And Jesus said to the centurion,
"Go, as you believed, let it be for you."
Returning to the house he found the servant cured.
   On the next day he went into a town called Nain,
and his disciples and a large crowd went along with him.
As he came near the gate of the town,
a mother's only son having died was being carried out;
she was a widow,
and a considerable crowd from the town was with her.
   Seeing her the Lord felt compassion for her
and said to her, "Do not cry."
Approaching he touched the coffin,
and the bearers stood still;
he said, "Young man, I tell you, arise."
And the one dead sat up and began to speak,
and he gave him to his mother.
   Fear took hold of them all, and they praised God
saying, "A great prophet has arisen among us,"
and "God has visited his people."
This word about him went out
throughout Judea and all the region around.

32
   John's disciples reported to him in prison
about all these things.
Calling to him two of his disciples John sent to the Lord.
   Coming to him the men said,
"John the Baptist sent us to you asking,
'Are you the coming one, or should we expect another?'"
   Jesus answered them,
"Go report to John what you hear and see:
the blind regain sight, and the crippled walk;
lepers are cleansed, and the deaf hear;
the dead are raised, and the poor receive the good message;
and blessed is the one who is not offended by me."
   As John's messengers were going away,
he began to speak to the crowds about John:

"What did you come out into the desert to see?
A reed shaken by the wind?
But what did you come out to look at?
A person clothed in soft garments?
Look, the ones used to soft garments and luxury
are in the palaces.
But why did you come out?
To look at a prophet?
Yes, I tell you, and more than a prophet.
This is the one about whom it has been written:
    'Look, I send my messenger ahead of you,
    who will prepare your way before you.'
    "Amen, I tell you,
there has not risen among those born of women
anyone greater than John the Baptist;
but the smallest in the sovereignty of heaven
is greater than he.
From the days of John the Baptist until now
the sovereignty of heaven is forced,
and the forceful seize it.
For all the prophets and the law prophesied until John;
and if you are willing to accept it,
he is Elijah who intended to come.
Let whoever has ears hear."

All the people who heard, even the tax collectors,
acknowledged the justice of God,
having been baptized by John's baptism;
but the Pharisees and the lawyers
rejected the purpose of God for themselves,
not having been baptized by him.

"To what, then, should I compare
the people of this generation?
They are like children sitting in the marketplaces
who call to others,
'We played the flute for you, and you did not dance;
we sang dirges, and you did not mourn.'

"For John the Baptist came
neither eating bread nor drinking wine,
and you say, 'He has a demon.'

"The human son came eating and drinking,
and you say, 'Look, a gluttonous and wine-drinking person,
a friend of tax collectors and sinners.'
Yet wisdom is justified by her deeds."

33
   Then he began to reproach the cities
in which most of his powerful deeds occurred,
because they did not change their minds.
"Woe to you, Chorazin! Woe to you, Bethsaida!
For if the powerful deeds which occurred among you
had occurred in Tyre and Sidon,
long ago they would have repented
sitting in sackcloth and ashes.
But I tell you, it will be more bearable
for Tyre and Sidon on the day of judgment than for you.
   "And you, Capernaum,
will you be lifted up as high as heaven?
You shall go down as low as Hades;
for if the powerful deeds which occurred among you
had occurred in Sodom, it would have remained until today.
But I tell you that it will be more bearable
for the land of Sodom on the day of judgment than for you."
   In that moment Jesus said, "I acknowledge you, Father,
Lord of heaven and earth,
that you hid these things from the wise and intelligent,
and revealed them to infants;
yes, Father, that this was pleasing before you.
   "Everything was given over to me by my Father;
no one recognizes the son except the Father,
nor does anyone recognize the Father except the son
and to whomever the son chooses to reveal him.
   "Come to me all who labor and are burdened,
and I will refresh you.
Take my yoke upon you and learn from me,
for I am gentle and humble of heart;
and you will find rest for your souls,
for my yoke is kind and my burden is light."

34

One of the Pharisees asked him to eat with him,
and entering the Pharisee's home he sat down.
A woman who was a sinner in the city,
also having discovered
that he was dining in the Pharisee's home,
brought an alabaster jar of perfume
and standing behind at his feet weeping,
she began to wet his feet with her tears,
and she wiped them off with the hair of her head,
and kissed his feet and anointed them with the perfume.

But the Pharisee who invited him seeing
said within himself, "If this one were a prophet,
he would have recognized
who and what kind of woman was touching him,
for she is a sinner."

Jesus answered him, "Simon,
I have something to tell you."

He said, "Teacher, say it."

"There were two debtors to a certain creditor;
the one owed five hundred days' wages, the other fifty.
Neither of them having it to pay back he pardoned both.
Therefore which of them will love him more?"

Simon answered,
"I suppose the one for whom he pardoned more."

He said to him, "You judge correctly."
Turning toward the woman he said to Simon,
"Do you see this woman?
I entered into your home;
and you did not give me water for my feet;
but she wet my feet with her tears
and wiped them off with her hair.
You did not give me a kiss;
but from the time I entered
she has not left off kissing my feet.
You did not anoint my head with olive oil;
but she anointed my feet with perfume.
Because of this I tell you,
her many sins have been forgiven,

for she loved much;
but whoever is forgiven little, loves little."
  Then he said to her, "Your sins have been forgiven."
  The guests began to say among themselves,
"Who is this, who even forgives sins?"
  He said to the woman,
"Your faith has saved you; go in peace."
  After this he traveled to each town and village
preaching the good message of the sovereignty of God.
The twelve were with him, and certain women
who were healed from bad spirits and illnesses:
Mary the one called Magdalene,
from whom seven demons had gone out,
and Joanna, wife of Chuza, Herod's manager, and Susanna
and many others who supported them from their possessions.

35
  He went into a house, and again a crowd gathered,
so that they were not able to eat bread.
His relatives hearing went out to get him;
for they said, "He is out of it."
  Then was brought to him a demoniac blind and dumb;
and he healed him, so that the one dumb spoke and saw.
  All the crowds were astonished and said,
"Is this the son of David?"
  The scholars and Pharisees who came down from Jerusalem
said, "He expels the demons by Beelzebub,
the ruler of the demons."
  But aware of their thoughts he said to them,
"How can Satan expel Satan?
If a sovereignty is divided against itself,
that sovereignty cannot stand;
and if a house is divided against itself,
that house cannot stand.
Also if Satan stood up against himself and was divided,
how then would his kingdom stand?
If I expel demons by Beelzebub,
by whom do your sons expel them?
Because of this they will be your judges.

But if I expel demons by the Spirit of God,
then the sovereignty of God has come upon you.

"How can someone enter the house of the strong
and rob his property, unless one first binds the strong?
Then one will rob his house.

"When the armed strong man guards his courtyard,
his belongings are in order;
but when a stronger one than he attacking overcomes him,
one takes his armor, upon which he had relied,
and distributes his spoils.

"Whoever is not with me is against me,
and whoever is not gathering with me scatters.

"Because of this I tell you,
every sin and slander will be forgiven people,
but the slander of the Spirit will not be forgiven.
Whoever says a word against the human son,
it will be forgiven one;
but whoever speaks against the Holy Spirit,
it will not be forgiven one
neither in this age nor in the coming one.

"Either make the tree beautiful and its fruit beautiful,
or make the tree rotten and its fruit rotten;
for by the fruit the tree is known.

"Products of vipers,
how can you speak good things being bad?
For from the overflow of the heart the mouth speaks.
The good person from the good treasure puts out good things,
and the bad person from the bad treasure puts out bad things.

"But I tell you that every idle saying which people speak,
they will pay for concerning its meaning
on the day of judgment;
for by your words you will be justified,
and by your words you will be condemned."

Then some of the scholars and Pharisees answered him,
"Teacher, we wish to see a sign from you."

He answered them,
"A bad and adulterous generation demands a sign,
and a sign will not be given to it
except the sign of Jonah the prophet.

For as Jonah was in the belly of a sea monster
three days and three nights,
so will the human son be in the heart of the earth
three days and three nights.

"The men of Nineveh will stand up at the judgment
with this generation and condemn it;
for they changed their minds at the preaching of Jonah,
and look, one greater than Jonah is here.

"The queen of the south will arise at the judgment
with this generation and condemn it;
for she came from the ends of the earth
to hear the wisdom of Solomon,
and look, one greater than Solomon is here.

"When an unclean spirit comes out of a person,
it goes through waterless places searching for rest,
and does not find it.
Then it says,
'I will return to my house where I came from;'
and going it finds it empty, swept, and put in order.
Then it goes and brings along with it
seven spirits worse than itself,
and entering it lives there;
and the last state of that person
becomes worse than the first.
Thus will it be also for this bad generation."

While he was speaking to the crowds,
his mother and brothers stood outside
trying to speak with him,
and they were not able to join him because of the crowd.

Someone reported to him,
"Look, your mother and your brothers
are standing outside wishing to see you."

He answered the one talking to him,
"Who is my mother, and who are my brothers?"

Looking around at those sitting in a circle around him
he said, "Look, my mother and my brothers.
Whoever does the will of my Father
is my brother and sister and mother."

A woman raising her voice from the crowd said to him,
"Blessed is the womb that bore you
and the breasts that nourished you."
   But he said,
"Blessed are those hearing the word of God and keeping it."

36
   On that day Jesus going out of the house
sat beside the sea;
the crowd gathering by him was so large
that embarking he sat in a boat on the sea,
and all the people stood on the beach.
   He taught them many things in parables,
and he said to them in his teaching, "Listen.
The sower went out to sow his seed.
In his sowing some fell along the way
and were trampled under,
and the birds of heaven came and ate them up.
   "Others fell on rocky ground
where they did not have much earth,
and immediately they sprang up
because of not having depth of earth;
when the sun rose, they were scorched;
and because of not having roots they dried up.
   "Others fell in the middle of the thorns,
and the thorns came up and choked them;
and they gave no fruit.
   "Others fell into the good earth and gave fruit;
coming up and growing
they produced thirty, sixty, and a hundred.
Let the one who has ears to hear hear."
   When he was alone,
the ones around him with the twelve
asked him about the parable.
   He said, "To you it has been given
to know the mysteries of the sovereignty of God,
but to those outside all things are in parables,
because looking they do not see
and listening they do not hear nor understand.

Fulfilled in them is the prophetic saying of Isaiah:
   'In listening you will hear and not understand,
   and watching you will look and not see.
   For fattened is the heart of this people,
   and they hardly heard with their ears,
   and they closed their eyes;
   lest they should see with their eyes
   and hear with their ears
   and understand with the heart and turn around,
   and I would cure them.'
   "But blessed are your eyes because they see,
and your ears because they hear.
For amen, I tell you that many prophets and just people
wished to see what you see and did not see it,
and to hear what you hear and did not hear it.
Therefore you shall hear the parable of the sower.
   "The sower sows the word of God.
The ones along the way,
when they hear the word and do not understand,
the devil comes and snatches away
what was sown in their hearts,
lest believing they may be saved.
   "What was sown on the rocky ground,
when they hear the word,
they immediately accept it with joy;
yet they have no root in themselves but are temporary;
when oppression or persecution occurs because of the word
they immediately are offended.
   "What was sown into the thorns,
these are the ones hearing the word,
and worries of the age and the deception of wealth
and desires for the pleasures of life
come in and choke the word,
and it becomes unfruitful and does not mature.
   "What was sown on the beautiful earth,
these are the ones hearing the word
in a beautiful and good heart,
and understanding they hold on to it
and bear fruit with patience,
some thirty, others sixty, and others a hundred.

"No one having lit a lamp hides it with furniture
or puts it under a couch,
but one puts it on a lampstand,
so that those coming in may see the light.

"Know what is in front of you,
and what is hidden from you will be revealed to you.
For there is nothing hidden that will not become manifest,
nor concealed that will not be known
and come out into the open.

"Therefore watch how you listen and look at what you hear,
for whoever has,
it will be given to one, and one will have abundance;
but whoever has not,
even what one seems to have will be taken from one."

37
He said, "Thus is the sovereignty of God:
as a person might throw seed on the earth,
and might sleep and rise night and day,
and the seed sprouts and lengthens,
though one does not know how.
By itself the earth bears fruit,
first grass, then an ear, then full grain in the ear.
When the fruit is ripe, immediately one sends the sickle,
for the harvest has arrived."

He put another parable to them:
"The sovereignty of heaven is like
a person sowing beautiful seed in his field.
At night while the people were sleeping his enemy came
and sowed weeds in between the wheat and went away.
When the grass sprouted and produced fruit,
then the weeds appeared also.

The servants approaching the master of the house
said to him, 'Lord,
did you not sow beautiful seed in your field?
Where then have the weeds come from?'

"He said to them, 'An enemy did this.'

"The servants asked him,
'Then do you want us to go gather them?'

"But he said, 'No, lest pulling up the weeds
you should uproot with them the wheat.
Let both grow together until the harvest;
and in the season of the harvest I will say to the reapers:
"First gather the weeds
and tie them into bundles to burn them,
but gather the wheat into my barn."'"

He said, "How shall we describe the sovereignty of God,
or by what parable may we compare it?
It is like a mustard seed,
which when it is sown on the earth,
is smaller than all the seeds of the earth,
but when it comes up and grows,
it is greater than the vegetables and becomes a tree,
so that the birds of heaven come and dwell in its branches."

He spoke another parable to them:
"The sovereignty of God is like yeast,
which a woman took and hid in three measures of flour,
until the whole of it was lightened."

Jesus spoke all these things in parables to the crowds,
so that what was said through the prophet might be fulfilled:
  "I will open my mouth in parables;
  I will utter what has been hidden from creation."

Then leaving the crowds he went into the house.
His disciples approached him saying,
"Explain to us the parable of the weeds of the field."

He answered,
"The sower of the beautiful seed is the human son;
the field is the world;
the beautiful seed, these are the sons of the sovereignty;
the weeds are the sons of the evil one,
and the enemy sowing them is the devil;
the harvest is the completion of the age,
and the reapers are angels.

"Therefore as the weeds are gathered and burned with fire,
so will it be at the completion of the age:
the human son will send his angels,
and they will gather out of his sovereignty
all the offenses and ones doing wrong,

and will throw them into the oven of fire;
there will be the weeping and the gnashing of teeth.
Then the just will shine out as the sun
in the sovereignty of their Father.
Let the one having ears hear.

"The sovereignty of heaven is like
a treasure hidden in a field, which finding a person hid,
and from his joy he goes and sells whatever he has
and buys that field.

"Again the sovereignty of heaven is like
a merchant seeking beautiful pearls;
and finding one very precious pearl,
going away he sold everything he had and bought it.
You too search for imperishable and enduring treasure,
where no moth comes near to devour, and no worm destroys.

"Again the sovereignty of heaven is like
a net cast into the sea gathering from every kind,
which when filled was brought up on the shore,
and sitting they gathered the beautiful into baskets,
and threw out the bad.

"So will it be at the completion of the age;
the angels will go out
and separate the bad from among the just,
and will throw them into the oven of fire;
there will be the weeping and gnashing of teeth.
Have you understood all these things?"

They said to him, "Yes."

He said to them, "For this reason every scholar
who has become a disciple of the sovereignty of heaven
is like a master of a house
who brings out of his treasure the new and old."

When Jesus finished these parables, he moved from there.

38

Jesus seeing the crowd around him
gave orders to go away to the other side.
A scholar said to him, "Teacher,
I will follow you wherever you go."

Jesus said to him,
"The foxes have holes and the birds of heaven nests,
but the human son has no place
where he may lay his head and rest."

He said to another, "Follow me."

But he said, "Lord, permit me first
to go away and bury my father."

But Jesus said to him,
"Let the dead bury the dead themselves,
but you go announce the sovereignty of God."

Another also said, "I will follow you, Lord;
but first permit me to say goodby to the ones in my home."

But Jesus said to him,
"No one putting his hand on the plow
and looking at the things behind
is fit for the sovereignty of God."

He said to them on that day as evening came,
"Let us go over to the other side."
Leaving the crowd they took him along,
as he was in the boat.
They put out; and as they sailed he fell asleep.
A whirlwind came down onto the lake,
and the waves broke into the boat,
so that now the boat was being filled up
and they were in danger.
He was in the stern sleeping on a pillow.

Approaching they woke him up saying, "Lord, save us!
Don't you care that we are perishing?"

Waking up he reprimanded the wind
and said to the sea, "Be quiet! Shut up!"
The wind ceased, and it became very calm.

He said to them, "Why are you such cowards?
How come you have no faith?"

They were afraid with great awe and marveled,
saying to each other, "Who then is this,
that he commands even the wind and the sea,
and they obey him?"

They came to the other side of the sea
to the country of the Gerasenes, which is opposite Galilee.
As he was coming out of the boat,
a man from the tombs having demons met him,
and for a considerable time he had not worn clothes;
he did not stay in a house but among the tombs.
No one could bind him with a chain anymore,
for he had often been bound with shackles and chains,
and the chains and shackles had been broken
and torn apart by him,
and no one was strong enough to control him;
through all the night and day
among the tombs and in the mountains
he was crying out and cutting himself with stones;
he was extremely violent,
so that no one could pass through that way.

Seeing Jesus from a distance he ran and fell before him,
and crying out with a loud voice he said,
"What are you to me, Jesus son of God the highest?
I implore you by God, do not torture me!"

For he had said to him,
"Come out unclean spirit from this person."

Then Jesus questioned him, "What is your name?"

He said to him, "My name is Legion, for we are many."

They begged him much
that he should not send them outside the country.
There near the mountain was a large herd of pigs feeding;
the demons begged him, "If you expel us,
send us into the pigs, that we may enter into them."

He permitted them to do so, saying, "Go."
Coming out from the person the demons entered into the pigs,
and the herd rushed down the steep slope into the sea,
about two thousand of them; and they were drowned.
The ones feeding them fled
and reported in the city and in the country,
and they came out to see what happened.

They came to Jesus
and saw the demoniac sitting clothed and sensible,
the one who had had the legion, and they were afraid.

Those who saw related to them how the demoniac was healed.
All the population of the Gerasene neighborhood
began to beg him to go away from their region,
because they were distressed with great fear.

As he embarked in the boat,
the man from whom the demons had gone out
asked to be with him, but he sent him away
saying, "Return to your home to your people,
and report to them
what the Lord has done for you and the mercy shown you."
So he went away and began to proclaim in the Decapolis
what Jesus had done for him, and everyone marveled.

39
When Jesus had crossed over in the boat again
to the other side, a large crowd welcomed him;
for they were all waiting for him.

One of the synagogue rulers named Jairus came,
and seeing Jesus he fell at his feet and begged him much
saying, "My little daughter is dying;
come lay your hands on her,
so that she may be saved and live."

Rising Jesus and his disciples followed him.
As he was going,
a large crowd followed and pressed upon him.
A woman who had a flow of blood for twelve years
and had suffered many things under many physicians,
having spent all she had,
and not being helped but rather getting worse,
heard about Jesus,
and approaching behind touched the fringe of his robe;
for she said to herself,
"If I may touch even his robe, I shall be saved."

At once the flow of her blood stopped.
Immediately Jesus recognizing in himself
the power going out from him,
turning around in the crowd said, "Who touched my clothes?"

Peter said, "Master, the crowds press upon you and push,
and you say, 'Who touched me?'"

He looked around to see who had done this.

The woman afraid and trembling,
knowing what had happened to her
and seeing that she was not unnoticed,
came and falling before him declared before all the people
the reason why she touched him,
and how she was cured at once.

He said to her, "Have courage, daughter;
your faith has saved you;
go in peace, and be healed from your suffering."

While he was speaking,
someone came from the synagogue ruler's saying,
"Your daughter has died; why still bother the teacher?"

But Jesus overhearing the word spoken
said to the synagogue ruler, "Fear not;
only believe, and she will be saved."

He did not let anyone accompany him
except Peter and James and John, the brother of James.
They came into the home of the synagogue ruler,
and seeing the flute players
and the distress of weeping and wailing,
he said to them, "Why be distressed and weep?
The child did not die, but is sleeping."

They laughed at him, knowing that she had died.
Putting everyone out he went in where the child was,
taking the father of the child and the mother
and the ones with him.

Holding the hand of the child
he said to her, "Talitha koum,"
which is translated, "Little girl, I tell you, arise."

Her spirit returned, and she stood up at once and walked;
for she was twelve years old.
Her parents were greatly amazed.
He gave strict orders that no one should know this,
and he directed that she be given something to eat.

Passing along from there two blind people followed Jesus
shouting and saying, "Have mercy on us, son of David!"

Coming into the house the blind ones approached him,
and Jesus said to them, "Do you believe that I can do this?"

They said to him, "Yes, Lord."

Then he touched their eyes
saying, "According to your faith may it be for you."

And their eyes were opened.
Jesus warned them sternly, "See that no one should know."

But going out they spread the news about him
throughout the land.

As they were going out,
they brought to him a dumb demoniac.
The demon being expelled the one dumb spoke.
The crowds marveled saying,
"Never has such appeared in Israel."

But the Pharisees said,
"By the ruler of the demons he expels the demons."

He went out from there and came into his homeland,
and his disciples followed him.
The Sabbath occurring he began to teach in the synagogue,
and many hearing were astonished
saying, "Where did he get these things,
and what is this wisdom given to him?
Such powerful deeds are occurring through his hands!
Isn't this the son of the carpenter, the son of Mary
and brother of James and Joses and Judas and Simon?
Aren't his sisters here with us?"
They were offended by him.

But Jesus said to them, "A prophet is not unhonored
except in his homeland
and among his relatives and in his home."
He did not do so many powerful deeds there
because of their lack of faith,
except laying on his hands he healed a few sick people.

Jesus went around to all the towns and villages,
teaching in their synagogues
and preaching the good message of the sovereignty
and healing every disease and every illness.

Seeing the crowds he was compassionate about them,
because they were troubled
and laying like sheep without a shepherd.
Then he said to his disciples, "The harvest is large,
but the workers are few;
therefore ask the Lord of the harvest
so he may send out workers for his harvest."

40
He called to him the twelve
and began to send them out two by two,
and he gave them authority over unclean spirits
so as to expel them,
and power to heal every disease and illness.
Sending out the twelve disciples Jesus instructed them:
"Do not go off into the way of the nations,
and do not enter into a town of the Samaritans;
but go rather to the lost sheep of the house of Israel,
and going preach, 'The sovereignty of heaven is near.'
Heal the ailing; raise the dead;
cleanse lepers; expel demons.
"Freely you received; freely give.
Do not take gold nor silver nor copper in your belts,
nor a bag for the road
nor two shirts nor extra sandals nor a staff.
"In whatever town or village you enter,
inquire who in it is worthy.
Entering a house greet it, 'Peace to this house.'
If there is a son of peace there,
let your peace rest upon it;
if not, let your peace return to you.
Stay in the same house, eating and drinking with them;
for the worker is worthy of one's pay.
Do not move from house to house.
In whatever town you enter where they welcome you,
eat what they put before you, and heal the sick in it.
"Whoever does not welcome you or listen to your words,
going out of the house into their streets
or outside that town

say, 'Even the dust clinging to our feet from your town
we shake off to you;
yet know this: that the sovereignty of God has come near.'
Amen, I tell you, it will be more bearable
for the land of Sodom and Gomorrah on judgment day
than for that town.

"Look, I send you out as lambs in the middle of wolves;
therefore be wise as serpents and innocent as doves.
Watch out for people;
for they will give you over to councils,
and in their synagogues they will punish you;
on account of me
you will be led before governors and also kings,
for testimony to them and to the nations.

"When they bring you in
before synagogues and rulers and authorities,
do not worry about how you should defend yourself
or what you should say;
for the Holy Spirit will teach you in that hour
what you should say;
for you are not the ones speaking,
but the Spirit of your Father is the one speaking in you.

"Brother will give over brother into death
and the father the child,
and children will rebel against parents
and will put them to death.
You will be hated by everyone because of my name;
but whoever endures to the end will be saved.
When they persecute you in one town, flee to another;
for amen, I tell you,
you will not complete the towns of Israel
before the human son comes.

"A disciple is not above the teacher
nor a servant above his lord.
But every disciple who has been prepared
will become like his teacher,
and the servant like his lord.
If they called the master of the house Beelzebub,
how much more the members of his house.

"So do not be afraid of them;
for nothing has been veiled which will not be unveiled,
and hidden which will not be known.
What I tell you in the dark, say in the light;
and what you hear in your ear, proclaim on the housetops.

"Do not be afraid of those who kill the body
and after that do not have anything more they can do,
not being able to kill the soul;
but rather be afraid of the one able to ruin
both soul and body in hell.

"Are not two sparrows sold for a penny?
Yet not one of them will fall upon the earth
without your Father.
Even the hairs of your head are all numbered.
So do not be afraid;
you are worth more than many sparrows.

"Therefore everyone who acknowledges me before people,
I will also acknowledge him before my Father in heaven;
but whoever denies me before people,
will also be denied before my Father in heaven.

"Do not think that I came to bring peace upon the earth;
I did not come to bring peace, but a sword.
For I came to turn a person against his father
and a daughter against her mother
and a bride against her mother-in-law,
and a person's enemies will be the members of his house.

"The one loving father or mother above me
is not worthy of me;
and the one loving son or daughter above me
is not worthy of me;
and whoever does not take one's cross and follow after me,
is not worthy of me.
The one finding one's life will lose it,
and the one losing one's life for my sake will find it.

"The one welcoming you welcomes me,
and the one welcoming me welcomes the one who sent me.
The one welcoming a prophet in the name of a prophet
will receive a prophet's reward,
and the one welcoming a just person in the name of justice

will receive a just person's reward.
Also whoever gives one of these little ones
a cup of cool water to drink
only in the name of a disciple,
amen, I tell you, will not lose one's reward."
  When he finished instructing his twelve disciples,
going out they preached that they should change their minds,
and they expelled many demons
and anointed with oil and healed many sick people;
Jesus moved on from there to teach and preach in their towns.

41
  At that time King Herod heard the rumors about Jesus,
and he said, "John the Baptist has been raised from the dead,
and because of this the powers are at work in him."
  But others said, "He is Elijah;"
and others said, "He is a prophet like one of the prophets."
  But Herod having heard said,
"John whom I beheaded, this is him raised."
  For Herod himself having sent out
seized John and bound him in prison,
because he had married Herodias,
the wife of his brother Philip,
and John had said to Herod, "It is not permitted
for you to have your brother's wife."
  So Herodias resented him and wished to kill him,
and she could not; for the crowd held him as a prophet,
and Herod feared John,
knowing him to be a just and holy man.
He protected him,
and having heard him much he was in doubt;
yet he listened to him gladly.
  An opportune day occurring
when Herod produced his birthday banquet for his courtiers
and local rulers and the foremost of Galilee,
the daughter of Herodias entered and danced in the middle,
pleasing Herod and the guests.
  So the king said to the girl,
"Ask me for whatever you wish,

and I will give it to you;"
and he swore to her, "Whatever you request I will give you,
up to half my kingdom."

Having gone out she asked her mother,
"What should I ask for?"

She said, "The head of John the baptizer."

Going in immediately with haste to the king
she requested, "I wish that at once you may give me
on a platter the head of John the Baptist."

The king, grieved
because of the oaths and the dinner guests,
did not wish to refuse her.
Sending out immediately,
the king ordered an executioner to bring his head.
Going away he beheaded him in the prison
and brought his head on a platter and gave it to the girl,
and the girl gave it to her mother.

His disciples having heard
came and took his corpse and buried it,
and going they reported to Jesus.

42
Having returned, the apostles gathered together with Jesus
and reported to him everything they did and taught.

He said to them, "Come privately yourselves
into a deserted place and rest a little."
For many were coming and going,
and they had no opportunity to eat.

They withdrew in a boat to a deserted place privately.
Many saw them going and recognized them,
and they ran there on foot from all the towns
and came before them.

Jesus went up to a mountain
and sat there with his disciples;
it was near the Passover, the Jewish feast.
Lifting up his eyes
and seeing a large crowd coming toward him,
he welcomed them
and taught them about the sovereignty of God,

and he had compassion on them and healed their sick.

Already the hour becoming late,
his disciples approached him saying,
"The place is a desert, and the hour has already passed;
release the crowd, so that going into the villages
and farms around they may buy themselves food to eat."

Jesus said to them, "They do not need to go away;
you give them something to eat."

Philip answered him,
"Going away we may buy bread for two hundred days' wages,
and shall we give them it to eat?
It is not enough so that
each of them may take a little bit."

He said to him, "How many loaves do you have? Go see."

One of his disciples, Andrew, the brother of Simon Peter,
said to him, "A boy is here
who has five barley loaves and two cooked fish;
but what are these among so many?"

But he said, "Have them sit down
in groups of about fifty each."

There was much grass in the place, and they all sat down.
Taking the five loaves and the two fish,
looking up into heaven he blessed them,
and breaking the loaves
he gave them to the disciples to set before them,
and he distributed the two fish to everyone.
They all ate and were satisfied.

When they were full, he told his disciples,
"Gather the leftover pieces,
so that nothing may be wasted."

They picked up twelve baskets
full of pieces and from the fish,
and about five thousand men were eating,
besides women and children.

So the people seeing the miracle he performed said,
"This is truly the prophet who is coming into the world."

So Jesus knowing that they intended to come and seize him
so that they might make him king,

immediately made his disciples embark in the boat
and go ahead of him to the other side to Bethsaida,
while he released the crowd.
Saying goodby to them
he went up on the mountain privately to pray.
As evening came, he was there alone.

Already it had become dark,
and the boat was in the middle of the sea.
The sea was roused by a great wind blowing against them,
and they were straining in the rowing,
harassed by the waves.

In the fourth watch of the night
he came toward them walking on the sea;
he wished to pass by them.
But the disciples seeing him walking on the sea
were disturbed saying, "It is a phantom,"
and they cried out from fear.

Immediately Jesus spoke to them,
"Have courage, it is I; do not be afraid."

Peter answered him, "Lord, if it is you,
command me to come to you on the water."

He said, "Come."

Going down from the boat
Peter walked on the water and came toward Jesus.
But looking at the wind he was afraid,
and beginning to sink he shouted, "Lord, save me."

Immediately Jesus holding out his hand caught him
and said to him, "Little faith, why did you doubt?"
As they went up into the boat, the wind ceased.
In themselves they were extremely astounded;
for some did not understand about the loaves,
but their hearts were hardened.
Others in the boat worshipped him
saying, "Truly you are God's son."

Having crossed over to the land
they came to Gennesaret and anchored.
As they came out of the boat,
the men of that place recognizing him
sent throughout that country

and began to carry around on stretchers those who were ill,
wherever they heard that he was.
Wherever he went into villages or into towns or into farms,
in the marketplaces they put the ailing,
and they begged him
that they might only touch the fringe of his robe;
and as many as touched him recovered.

43

The next day the crowd standing across the sea
saw that no other boat had been there except one,
and that Jesus had not entered the boat with his disciples,
but his disciples had gone away alone;
other boats from Tiberias came near the place
where they ate the bread, the Lord having given thanks.
Therefore when the crowd saw
that Jesus was not there with his disciples,
they embarked in the boats
and came to Capernaum seeking Jesus.
Finding him across the sea
they said to him, "Rabbi, when did you come here?"
Jesus answered them, "Amen, amen, I tell you,
you seek me not because you saw miracles,
but because you ate from the loaves and were satisfied.
Do not work for the food which spoils,
but for the food which continues into eternal life,
which the human son will give you;
for God the Father certified this one."
So they said to him, "What should we do
that we may do the works of God?"
Jesus answered them, "This is the work of God,
that you believe in that one whom he sent."
So they said to him, "Then what sign do you perform,
that we may see and believe you?
What work do you do?
Our fathers ate manna in the desert,
as it is written:
'He gave them bread from heaven to eat.'"

Therefore Jesus said to them, "Amen, amen, I tell you,
Moses has not given you the bread from heaven,
but my Father gives you the true bread from heaven;
for the bread of God is the one coming down from heaven
and giving life to the world."

So they said to him, "Lord, always give us this bread."

Jesus said to them, "I am the bread of life;
whoever comes to me does not hunger,
and whoever believes in me will never thirst.
However, I told you that you have even seen me
and do not believe.

"Everyone whom the Father gives me will come to me,
and whoever comes to me I will not throw out outside,
because I have come down from heaven
not that I may do my will,
but the will of the one who sent me.

"This is the will of the one who sent me,
that everyone whom he has given me
I shall not lose any of them,
but I shall raise them up on the last day.
For this is the will of my Father,
that everyone seeing the son and believing in him
may have eternal life,
and I shall raise the same up on the last day."

Therefore the Jews grumbled about him
because he said, "I am the bread coming down from heaven,"
and they said, "Is this not Jesus the son of Joseph,
whose father and mother we know?
How does he now say, 'I have come down from heaven'?"

Jesus answered them, "Do not grumble with each other.
No one can come to me
unless the Father who sent me draws one,
and I shall raise the same up on the last day.
It is written in the prophets:
    'They shall all be taught by God;'
everyone having heard from the Father and learning
comes to me.

"Not that anyone has seen the Father,
except the one from the Father;

this one has seen the Father.
Amen, amen, I tell you, whoever believes has eternal life.
  "I am the bread of life.
Your fathers ate the manna in the desert and died;
this is the bread coming down from heaven,
so that anyone may eat of it and not die.
I am the living bread which came down from heaven;
if anyone eats of this bread, one will live into eternity;
and also the bread which I will give
is my flesh for the life of the world."

  Therefore the Jews quarreled with each other
saying, "How can this one give us his flesh to eat?"

  Therefore Jesus said to them, "Amen, amen, I tell you,
unless you eat the flesh of the human son
and drink his blood,
you do not have life in yourselves.
Whoever eats my flesh and drinks my blood has eternal life,
and I shall raise the same up on the last day.
For my flesh is true food, and my blood is true drink.
Whoever eats my flesh and drinks my blood
remains in me and I in the same.

  "As the living Father sent me
and I live because of the Father,
also whoever eats me,
that one will also live because of me.
This is the bread which came down from heaven,
not like the fathers ate and died;
whoever eats this bread will live into eternity."
These things he said teaching in a synagogue in Capernaum.

  Therefore many of his disciples having heard
said, "Hard is this word; who can listen to it?"

  But Jesus aware in himself
that his disciples were grumbling about this,
said to them, "Does this offend you?
So what if you see
the human son going up where he was before?
The Spirit is life-giving;
the flesh benefits nothing;
the sayings which I have spoken to you

are Spirit and are life.
However, there are some of you who do not believe."

For Jesus knew from the beginning
who were the ones not believing
and who was the one giving him over.

He said, "Because of this I have told you
that no one can come to me
unless it is given to one from the Father."

From this, many of his disciples went away
into the things behind and no longer walked with him.

Therefore Jesus said to the twelve,
"Do you also wish to leave?"

Simon Peter answered him, "Lord, to whom shall we go?
You have the sayings of eternal life,
and we have believed and known
that you are the holy one of God."

Jesus answered them, "Did I not select you twelve?
and one of you is a devil."
He told of Judas, son of Simon Iscariot;
for this one of the twelve was intending to give him over.

44
Pharisees and scholars coming from Jerusalem
were gathering by him,
and they saw some of his disciples
eating bread with unwashed hands,—
for the Pharisees and all the Jews do not eat
unless they wash their hands first,
holding to the tradition of the elders;
they do not eat from markets unless they rinse;
and they hold to many other things which they received,
washing of cups and pitchers and copper pots,—
and the Pharisees and the scholars questioned him,
"Why do your disciples break the tradition of the elders?
For they do not wash their hands whenever they eat bread."

He answered them, "And why do you
break the commandment of God because of your tradition?
For Moses said, 'Honor your father and mother,'
and 'Let whoever speaks evil of his father or mother

be put to death.'

"But you say, 'A person may say to his father or mother:
"Whatever you might have been benefited from me is a gift,"'
and you no longer let one
do anything for one's father or mother,
nullifying the word of God
by your tradition which you have received;
and you do many such similar things.

"Hypocrites! Isaiah prophesied well about you,
as it has been written:
  'This people honors me with the lips,
  but their heart is far away from me;
  and in vain they worship me,
  teaching as teachings the commands of people.'
Letting go of the commandment of God
you hold to the tradition of people."

  Calling to the crowd he said,
"Everyone listen to me and understand.
There is nothing outside of a person
which entering into one's mouth can defile one;
but what comes out from the mouth, this defiles a person."

  When he went into the house away from the crowd,
his disciples said to him, "Do you know that
the Pharisees who heard the word were offended?"

  He answered, "Every plant that
my heavenly Father did not plant will be uprooted.
Let them go; they are blind guides of the blind;
and if the blind guide the blind,
they will both fall into a ditch."

  Peter said to him, "Explain to us the parable."

  He said, "Are you also so unintelligent?
Do you not understand that everything outside
entering into a person's mouth cannot defile one,
because it does not enter into one's heart,
but it goes into the stomach
and is thrown out into a latrine, thus purifying all foods?

  The thing coming out of the mouth
is what defiles the person.
For from within come out

the bad thoughts from the heart of people:
murders, adulteries, fornications, thefts,
false testimonies, greeds, malice, deceit,
lewdness, an evil eye, slander, arrogance, foolishness;
all these evils come out from within and defile a person,
but to eat with unwashed hands does not defile a person."

  After these things Jesus walked in Galilee;
for he did not wish to walk in Judea,
because the Jews were trying to kill him.

45

  Going out from there
Jesus withdrew into the region of Tyre.
Entering into a house he did not wish anyone to know;
but it could not be kept secret,
and a Canaanite woman having heard about him came out;
the woman was Greek, born a Syrophoenician.

  She shouted, "Have mercy on me, Lord, son of David;
my daughter is badly demonized."

  But he did not answer her a word.
His disciples came to him requesting, "Release her,
for she is screaming after us."

  But he answered, "I was not sent to anyone
except the lost sheep of the house of Israel."

  But she came and knelt before him
saying, "Lord, help me."

  He said to her, "Allow the children
to be satisfied first;
for it is not nice to take the children's bread
and throw it to the dogs."

  She answered him, "Yes, Lord;
yet even the dogs underneath the table
eat from the children's crumbs."

  Then Jesus said to her, "O woman, your faith is great!
Because of this word, go;
let it be for you as you wish."

  Her daughter was cured from that hour;
having gone away into her home
she found the child lying on the bed,

and the demon had gone out.

Again going out of the regions of Tyre
he came through Sidon to the sea of Galilee
in the middle of the districts of Decapolis.
They brought to him a deaf person with a speech impediment,
and begged him to put his hand on him.

Taking him away from the crowd privately
he put his fingers into his ears
and spitting touched his tongue,
and looking up into heaven he sighed
and said to him, "Ephphatha," which is "Be opened."

And his ears were opened;
and immediately the bond of his tongue was loosened,
and he spoke correctly.

He ordered them not to tell anyone;
but as much as he ordered them,
so much more did they proclaim it.
They were overwhelmingly amazed
saying, "He has done everything well;
he makes both the deaf hear and the speechless speak."

Moving from there Jesus went along the sea of Galilee,
and going up on the mountain he sat there.
Large crowds approached him having with them
the lame, crippled, blind, dumb, and many others,
and they laid them at his feet; and he healed them,
so that the crowd marveled
seeing the dumb speaking, the crippled healthy,
the lame walking, and the blind seeing;
and they praised the God of Israel.

There being a large crowd and not having anything to eat,
calling his disciples he said to them,
"I empathize with the crowd,
because already they are staying three days with me
and they do not have anything they may eat;
and I am not willing to let them go away hungry,
lest they faint on the way;
and some of them are from far away."

His disciples answered him,
"From where will anyone be able to get bread

to satisfy such a crowd here in the desert?"
    Jesus asked them, "How many loaves do you have?"
    They said, "Seven, and a few small fish."
He instructed the crowd to sit down on the ground;
taking the seven loaves and giving thanks
he broke and gave them to his disciples
so that they might serve it, and they served the crowd.
Blessing the fish also he told them to serve these.
    They all ate and were satisfied,
and they picked up seven baskets full of leftover pieces.
The ones eating were four thousand men,
besides women and children.
    Having let the crowds go away
he embarked in the boat with his disciples,
and he went into the regions of Dalmanutha and Magadan.
    The Pharisees and Sadducees came out
and began to debate with him
asking him to show them a sign from heaven, testing him.
    Sighing a deep breath he said,
"Why does this generation seek a sign?
As evening comes you say, 'Fair weather,'
for heaven is fiery;
and in early morning: 'Stormy today,'
for heaven is fiery and gloomy.
You know how to discern the face of heaven,
and can you not discern the signs of the times?
A bad and adulterous generation searches for a sign,
and no sign will be given to it except the sign of Jonah."
    Leaving them behind again
embarking he went away to the other side,
and the disciples forgot to take bread;
except for one loaf they had none with them in the boat.
    Jesus warned them, "See that you watch out for
the yeast of the Pharisees and Sadducees
and the yeast of Herod."
They discussed it with each other because they had no bread.
    But knowing he said to them,
"Why do you discuss that you have no bread?
Still do you not see nor understand?

Have you hardened your hearts?
Having eyes do you not see, and having ears do you not hear?
Do you not remember,
when I broke the five loaves for the five thousand,
how many baskets full of pieces you picked up?"
  They said to him, "Twelve."
  "When the seven for the four thousand,
how many baskets full of pieces did you pick up?"
  They said, "Seven."
  "How come you do not realize
that I was not telling you about bread?
But be careful of the yeast
of the Pharisees and Sadducees."
  Then they understood that he was not saying
to be careful of the bread's yeast,
but of the teaching of the Pharisees and Sadducees.
  They came to Bethsaida.
They brought to him a blind person
and begged him to touch him.
Taking the hand of the blind one
he led him outside the village,
and spitting in his eyes, putting his hands on him,
he asked him, "Do you see anything?"
  Looking up he said,
"I see people that look like trees walking."
  Then again he put his hands on his eyes,
and he looked straight and was restored
and saw everything clearly.
  He sent him to his home saying,
"You should not go into the village."

46
  Jesus went out into the villages of Caesarea Philippi,
and on the way he questioned his disciples,
"Who do people say I am?"
  They answered, "Some John the Baptist,
and others Elijah, and others Jeremiah
or that one of the ancient prophets rose up."

He said to them, "But who do you say I am?"

Simon Peter answered, "You are the Christ,
the son of the living God."

Jesus answered him, "Blessed are you, Simon Barjonah,
because flesh and blood did not reveal this to you
but my Father in heaven.
I also tell you that you are Peter,
and on this rock I shall build my church,
and the gates of Hades will not overpower it.

"I shall give you the keys of the sovereignty of heaven,
and whatever you bind on the earth
will be bound in heaven,
and whatever you release on the earth
will be released in heaven."

Then he warned them
that they should tell no one that he is the Christ.

From then on Jesus began to teach his disciples
that the human son must go away into Jerusalem
and suffer many things,
and be rejected by the elders and high priests and scholars
and be killed and on the third day be raised.
He spoke the word frankly.

Taking him aside Peter began to reprimand him
saying, "God help you, Lord! This shall not be."

But turning and looking at his disciples
he reprimanded Peter and said, "Get behind me, Satan;
you are a temptation to me,
for you do not think of God's things but of humans'."

Then Jesus said to his disciples,
"If anyone wishes to come after me,
let one deny oneself and take up one's cross, and follow me.
For whoever wishes to save one's life, will lose it;
and whoever loses one's life on account of me, will save it.
For what does it benefit a person
to gain the whole world and damage one's soul?
For what could a person give in exchange for one's soul?

"For whoever is ashamed of me and my words
in this adulterous and sinful generation,
the human son will also be ashamed of the same

when he comes in the glory of his Father
with the holy angels;
then he will give back to each according to one's action.
Amen, I tell you
that some who are standing here may not taste death
until they see the sovereignty of God has come with power."

47
  After six days Jesus took along Peter and James and John,
and brought them up onto a high mountain privately to pray.
In his praying the appearance of his face became different,
and he was transformed before them;
his face shone like the sun,
and his clothes became as white as the light.
  There appeared to them Moses and Elijah,
and they spoke with Jesus about his exodus,
which he was about to fulfill in Jerusalem.
Peter and the ones with him were heavy with sleep;
but awakening they saw his glory
and the two men standing with him.
  As they were parting from him Peter said to Jesus,
"Rabbi, it is good we are here; let us make three tents,
one for you and one for Moses and one for Elijah."
But he did not know what he was saying,
for he was terrified.
  While he was still speaking,
a bright cloud overshadowed them;
a voice came from the cloud saying, "This is my beloved son,
in whom I am well pleased; listen to him."
The disciples hearing fell on their faces
and were much afraid.
  Jesus approached and touching them said,
"Rise and do not be afraid."
Lifting up their eyes
they saw no one except Jesus himself alone.
  As they were coming down from the mountain,
Jesus commanded them, "Tell no one the vision
until the human son is raised from the dead."

They kept the word to themselves,
discussing what it is to be raised from the dead.
They questioned him,
"Why do the scholars say that Elijah must come first?"
He answered, "Elijah coming first
does restore all things;
and how has it been written that the human son
should suffer many things and be treated with contempt?
But I tell you that in fact Elijah has already come,
and they did not recognize him,
but did to him what they wished;
so too the human son is going to suffer by them."
Then the disciples understood
that he told them about John the Baptist.

As they were coming down
from the mountain to the disciples,
they saw a large crowd around them
and scholars debating with them.
All the people seeing him were amazed,
and running up to him they greeted him.
He questioned them, "What are you debating with them?"
One of the crowd answered him, "Teacher,
I brought my only son, because he is a lunatic and ill,
having a speechless spirit;
wherever it seizes him, it throws him down,
and he foams at the mouth
and grinds his teeth and becomes rigid;
I asked your disciples to expel it, and they could not."
Jesus answered, "O faithless and perverted generation,
how long shall I be with you?
How long shall I endure you?
Bring him to me here."
So they brought him to him.
Seeing him the spirit immediately
threw him down and convulsed,
and he rolled on the ground foaming at the mouth.
He questioned his father,
"How long has this been happening to him?"

He said, "From childhood;
and often it threw him both into fire and into water
so that it might destroy him;
but if you can do anything, help us;
have compassion on us."

Jesus said to him, "The 'If you can!'
All things are possible to the one believing."

Immediately crying out the father of the child said,
"I believe; help my disbelief!"

Jesus seeing that a crowd was running together
reprimanded the unclean spirit
saying to it, "Speechless and deaf spirit, I command you,
come out of him, and you may no longer enter into him."

Having cried out and convulsed much it came out;
and he became as though dead,
so that many were saying that he died.

But Jesus taking his hand raised him, and he stood up.
He gave him back to his father,
and they were all amazed at the grandeur of God.

When he entered a house,
his disciples privately questioned him,
"Why were we not able to expel it?"

He said to them, "Because of your little faith;
for amen, I tell you, if you have faith like a mustard seed,
you will say to this mountain, 'Move from here to there,'
and it will be moved;
and nothing will be impossible for you."

48

Going out from there they passed through Galilee,
and he did not wish anyone to know;
for he was teaching his disciples,
and he said to them, "Put these words into your ears:
the human son is going to be given over
into the hands of people,
and they will kill him,
and being killed after three days he will rise up."

But they were ignorant of this saying;
it was hidden from them lest they should perceive it,

and they were afraid to ask him about this saying.

As they were coming into Capernaum,
the ones receiving the two-*drachma* tax approached Peter
and said, "Doesn't your teacher pay the two-*drachma*?"

He said, "Yes."

When he came into the house,
Jesus anticipated him saying, "What do you think, Simon?
From whom do the kings of the earth receive duty or tax?
From their sons or from others?"

He having said, "From others,"
Jesus said to him, "Then the sons are free.
But so that we should not offend them,
go to the sea, cast a hook
and take the first fish coming up,
and opening its mouth you will find a four-*drachma* coin;
taking that give it to them for yours and mine."

49

When they were in the house at Capernaum,
he questioned them, "What were you discussing on the way?"

They were silent;
for they had discussed with each other on the way
who was greater.

Sitting he called the twelve and said to them,
"If anyone wants to be first,
he will be last of all and servant of all."

Calling a child he set it in the middle,
and taking it in his arms
he said to them, "Amen, I tell you,
unless you change and become like children,
you may not enter into the sovereignty of heaven.
Therefore whoever humbles oneself like this child,
this one is the greater in the sovereignty of heaven.
Whoever welcomes one such child in my name, welcomes me;
and whoever welcomes me, welcomes the one who sent me."

John said to him, "Teacher,
we saw someone expelling demons in your name,
and we forbade him, because he does not follow with us."

But Jesus said, "Do not forbid him;
for there is no one who will do a powerful deed in my name
and quickly be able to speak evil of me;
for whoever is not against us, is for us.

"For whoever gives you a cup of water in the name,
because you are Christ's,
amen, I tell you that one will not lose one's reward.
But whoever offends one of these small ones believing in me,
it would be better for one
if a millstone were laid around one's neck
and one was thrown into the sea and drowned.
Woe to the world from the offenses, for offenses must come;
but woe to the person through whom the offense comes.

"If your hand or your foot offends you,
cut if off and throw it away from you;
it is better for you to enter into life deformed or lame,
than having two hands or two feet to be thrown into hell.

"If your eye offends you,
take it out and throw it away from you;
for it is better for you to enter one-eyed into life,
than having two eyes to be thrown into the fire's hell,
where their worm does not die
and the fire is not extinguished.

"For everyone will be salted with fire.
Salt is fine;
but if the salt becomes saltless,
with what will you season it?
Have salt in yourselves and be at peace with each other.

"See that you do not look down on one of these small ones;
for I tell you that their angels in heaven
see through everything the face of my Father in heaven.

"Watch yourselves;
and if your brother sins,
go correct him between you and him alone.
If he repents, forgive him.
If he sins against you seven times a day
and seven times turns to you
saying, 'I repent,' forgive him.
If he listens to you, you gained your brother;

but if he does not listen,
take along with you one or two more,
so that by the mouth of two or three witnesses
every saying may be established;
but if he ignores them, tell the congregation;
and if he ignores also the congregation,
let him be as a national and tax collector.

"Amen, I tell you that if two of you agree on the earth
about any action which you may request,
it will come to be for you from my Father in heaven.
For where two or three are gathered in my name,
I am there with them."

Then Peter approaching said to him, "Lord, how many times
will my brother sin against me and shall I forgive him?
Up to seven times?"

Jesus said to him, "I do not tell you up to seven times,
but up to seventy times seven.

"For this reason the sovereignty of heaven is like a king,
who wished to settle accounts with his servants.
As he began the accounting,
one debtor of ten thousand talents was brought to him.
As he did not have it to pay back,
the lord commanded him and his wife and children
and everything he had to be sold, and it be paid back.

"So the servant fell on his knees to him saying,
'Be patient with me,
and I will pay back everything to you.'
Empathizing with that servant
the lord released him and forgave the loan.

"But going out that servant
found one of his fellow servants,
who owed him a hundred days' wages
and grabbing him he choked him
saying, 'Pay back if you owe anything.'

"So falling down his fellow servant begged him
saying, 'Be patient with me, and I will pay you back.'
He did not want to,
but going away he threw him into prison
until he should pay back the debt.

"So seeing what happened
his fellow servants were deeply grieved,
and coming explained to the lord themselves
everything that happened.

"Then his lord calling him said to him, 'Bad servant,
I forgave you all that debt, since you begged me to;
must not you also have mercy on your fellow servant,
as I had mercy on you?'

"Being angry his lord gave him over to the jailers
until he should pay back all the debt to him.
Thus also my heavenly Father will do to you,
unless you each forgive your brother from your hearts."

50

The Jewish feast of tabernacles was near.
Therefore his brothers said to him,
"Leave here and go into Judea,
so that your disciples also
will see your works which you do;
for no one does anything in secret
and seeks to be in the open himself.
If you do these things, show yourself to the world."
For his brothers did not believe in him.

So Jesus said to them, "My time has not yet arrived,
but your time is always ready.
The world cannot hate you, but it hates me,
because I testify about it that its works are bad.
You go up to the feast; I am not going up to this feast,
because my time has not yet been fulfilled."
Saying these things to them he stayed in Galilee.

But after his brothers went up to the feast,
then he also went up, not openly but in secret.
As the days of his going up were being fulfilled
he set his face to go up into Jerusalem
and sent messengers ahead of him.
Proceeding they entered a Samaritan village,
to prepare for him;
but they did not welcome him,
because he was heading for Jerusalem.

The disciples James and John seeing
said, "Lord, do you want us
to tell fire to come down from heaven and destroy them?"

But turning he reprimanded them,
and they proceeded into a different village.

Therefore the Jews were looking for him at the feast
and said, "Where is that one?"

There was much murmuring about him among the crowds;
some said, "He is good;"
but others said, "No, he misleads the crowd."
However, no one spoke openly about him
because of fear of the Jews.

The feast being already half over,
Jesus went up to the temple and taught.

So the Jews were surprised saying,
"How does this one know literature not having studied?"

So Jesus answered them, "My teaching is not mine,
but from the one who sent me;
if anyone is willing to do his will,
one will know about the teaching,
whether it is from God or whether I speak from myself.
The one speaking from himself seeks his own glory;
but the one seeking the glory of the one who sent him,
this one is true, and injustice is not in him.
Did not Moses give you the law?
Yet none of you practices the law.
Why are you trying to kill me?"

The crowd answered, "You have a demon;
who is trying to kill you?"

Jesus answered them, "I did one work,
and you are all surprised.
For this reason Moses has given you circumcision,
not that it is from Moses but from the fathers,
and on a Sabbath you circumcise a person.
If a person receives circumcision on a Sabbath
so that the law of Moses may not be broken,
are you angry with me,
because I made a whole person healthy on a Sabbath?
Do not judge according to appearance,

but judge a just judgment."

Therefore some of the Jerusalemites said,
"Isn't this the one they are trying to kill?
And look, he speaks openly, and they say nothing to him.
Have the authorities really concluded
that this is the Christ?
But we know where this one is from;
and when the Christ comes,
no one will know where he is from."

So Jesus cried out in the temple teaching
and saying, "You know me, and you know where I am from;
yet I have not come from myself,
but he is true who sent me, whom you do not know;
I know him, because I am from him and that one sent me."

So they tried to arrest him;
yet no one laid a hand on him,
because his hour had not yet come.

But many of the crowd believed in him and said,
"When the Christ comes,
will he do more miracles than this one did?"

The Pharisees heard the crowd
murmuring these things about him,
and the high priests and the Pharisees
sent attendants to arrest him.

So Jesus said, "I am with you only a short time,
and I go to the one who sent me.
You will look for me and not find me,
and where I am you cannot come."

Then the Jews said to themselves,
"Where is he about to go, that we will not find him?
Is he about to go to the dispersion among the Greeks
and teach the Greeks?
What is this word which he said,
'You will look for me and not find me,
and where I am you cannot come'?"

51

On the last day of the feast, the great day,
Jesus stood and cried out saying,

"If anyone thirsts, let him come to me and drink.
Whoever drinks from my mouth will become like me;
and I myself will become he,
and the secrets will be revealed to him.
Whoever believes in me, as the scripture said,
rivers of living water will flow from him."

But this he said about the Spirit
which the ones believing in him were going to receive;
for it was not the Spirit yet,
because Jesus was not yet glorified.

So some of the crowd hearing these words
said, "This is truly the prophet;"
others said, "This is the Christ;"
but others said, "No,
for does the Christ come from Galilee?
Doesn't the scripture say
that the Christ comes from the seed of David,
and from Bethlehem the village where David was?"

Thus a division occurred among the crowd because of him;
and some of them wished to arrest him,
but no one laid a hand on him.

So the attendants went to the high priests and Pharisees,
and those said to them, "Why did you not bring him in?"

The attendants answered,
"A person never spoke thus, as this person speaks."

So the Pharisees answered them, "Have you been misled too?
Did any of the rulers or Pharisees believe in him?
But this crowd not knowing the law is cursed."

Nicodemus, the first one of them to come to him,
said to them, "Does your law judge a person
unless it first hears from him and knows what he does?"

They answered him, "Aren't you from Galilee too?
Investigate and you will see
that a prophet is not raised from Galilee."

They each went into his house,
but Jesus went to the Mount of Olives.

At dawn he appeared again in the temple;
all the people came to him, and sitting he taught them.

The scholars and the Pharisees
brought a woman caught in adultery,
and standing her in the middle they said to him, "Teacher,
this woman has been caught in the act of adultery;
and in the law Moses ordered us to stone such a woman;
therefore what do you say?"
They said this tempting him,
so that they might have something to accuse him of.
  But Jesus bending down
wrote down with his finger on the ground.
As they kept asking him, he straightened up and said to them,
"Let whoever among you who is without sin
throw the first stone at her."
  Again bending down he wrote on the ground.
Having heard they went out one by one
beginning with the elders;
he was left alone, and the woman was in the middle.
  Straightening up Jesus said to her,
"Woman, where are they?
Did no one condemn you?"
  She said, "No one, lord."
  Jesus said, "Neither do I condemn you;
go, from now on sin no more."

52
  So again Jesus spoke to them:
"I am the light of the world;
the one following me will not walk in darkness,
but will have the light of life.
I am the light that is over all.
I am the all;
the all came out of me, and the all returned to me.
Split wood: I am there;
lift the stone, and you will find me there."
  Therefore the Pharisees said to him,
"You testify about yourself;
your testimony is not true."
  Jesus answered them, "Even if I testify about myself,
my testimony is true,

because I know where I came from and where I go;
but you do not know where I come from or where I go.
You judge according to the flesh; I do not judge anyone.
But even if I judge, my judgment is true,
because I am not alone,
but it is I and the one who sent me.
It has even been written in your law
that the testimony of two people is true.
I am testifying about myself,
and my Father who sent me testifies about me."

So they asked him, "Where is your father?"

Jesus answered, "You know neither me nor my Father;
if you knew me, you would also know my Father."
These sayings he spoke in the treasury
while teaching in the temple;
and no one arrested him, because his hour had not yet come.

So again he said to them, "I am going,
and you will look for me, and you will die in your sin;
where I am going you cannot come."

Therefore the Jews said, "Will he kill himself,
for he says, 'Where I am going you cannot come'?"

He said to them, "You are from below; I am from above.
You are of this world; I am not of this world.
So I told you that you will die in your sins;
for if you do not believe what I am,
you will die in your sins."

So they asked him, "Who are you?"

Jesus said to them, "The beginning.
Why do I even speak to you?
I have many things to speak and judge about you;
but the one who sent me is true,
and what I heard from him,
these things I speak to the world."
They did not know that he told them of the Father.

Therefore Jesus said, "When you lift up the human son,
then you will know what I am; from myself I am nothing,
but as the Father taught me, these things I speak.
The one who sent me is with me;
he did not leave me alone,

because I always do what pleases him."

As he was speaking these things, many believed in him.
So Jesus said to the Jews who had believed him,
"If you continue in my word, you are truly my disciples,
and you will know the truth, and the truth will free you."

They answered him, "We are Abraham's seed,
and we have never been enslaved to anyone;
how can you say that we will become free?"

Jesus answered them, "Amen, amen, I tell you
that everyone performing sin is a slave of sin.
But the slave does not stay in the house forever;
the son stays forever.
If then the son frees you, you will be really free.
I know that you are Abraham's seed;
but you are trying to kill me,
because my word finds no room in you.
What I have seen with the Father I speak;
and you, therefore, do what you heard from the Father."

They answered him, "Our father is Abraham."

Jesus told them, "If you are children of Abraham,
do the works of Abraham;
but now you are trying to kill me,
a person who has spoken the truth to you,
which I heard from God;
Abraham did not do this.
You are doing the works of your father."

They told him, "We were not born of fornication;
we have one Father, God."

Jesus said to them, "If God were your Father,
you would have loved me;
for I came out of God and am present;
for I have not come from myself, but that one sent me.
Why do you not know my speech?
Because you cannot hear my word.
You are of the devil father,
and you want to perform your father's desires.
That one was a murderer from the beginning,
and he did not stand in the truth,
because truth is not in him.

When he speaks a lie, he speaks of his own,
because he is a liar and the father of lying.

"But because I say the truth, you do not believe me.
Which of you convicts me of a sin?
If I am telling the truth, why do you not believe me?
The one who is of God listens to the sayings of God;
for this reason you do not listen,
because you are not of God."

The Jews answered him, "Do we not say well
that you are a Samaritan and have a demon?"

Jesus answered, "I do not have a demon,
but I honor my Father, and you dishonor me.
I do not seek my glory; there is one seeking and judging.
Amen, amen, I tell you, if anyone keeps my words,
he will not see death at all ever."

The Jews said to him, "Now we know that you have a demon.
Abraham died and the prophets,
and you say, 'If anyone keeps my word,
he will not taste death at all ever.'
Are you greater than our father Abraham, who died?
and the prophets died;
whom are you making yourself?"

Jesus answered, "If I glorify myself, my glory is nothing;
my Father is the one glorifying me,
of whom you say, 'He is our God,'
and you have not known him, but I know him.
If I say that I do not know him,
I shall be a liar like you;
however I do know him, and I keep his word.
Your Father Abraham was glad to see my day,
and he saw and rejoiced."

Therefore the Jews said to him,
"You are not yet fifty years old
and have you seen Abraham?"

Jesus said to them, "Amen, amen, I tell you,
before Abraham was born, I am."

So they picked up stones
so that they might throw them at him;
but Jesus was hidden and went out of the temple.

53
  Passing along he saw a person blind from birth.
His disciples asked him, "Rabbi, who sinned,
this one or his parents, that he was born blind?"

  Jesus answered, "Neither this one nor his parents sinned,
but it happened so that
the works of God may be manifested in him.
We must do the works of the one who sent me while it is day;
night is coming when no one can work.
While in the world, I am the light of the world."

  Having said this,
he spat on the ground and made mud out of the saliva,
and he put mud on his eyes and said to him,
"Go wash in the pool of Siloam"
(which is translated "Sent").

  So he went away and washed, and came seeing.
Therefore the neighbors and the ones seeing him before
when he was a beggar,
said, "Isn't this the one who sits and begs?"

  Others said, "This is the one;"
others said, "No, but he is like him."

  That one said, "I am the one."

  So they said to him, "How then were your eyes opened?"

  That one answered, "A person called Jesus made mud
and anointed my eyes and told me, 'Go to Siloam and wash;'
so going away and washing I gained sight."

  They said to him, "Where is that one?"

  He said, "I don't know."
They led him to the Pharisees, the one blind at one time.
It was a Sabbath on the day
Jesus made mud and opened his eyes.
Therefore the Pharisees also asked him again how he saw.

  He said to them, "He put mud on my eyes,
and I washed, and I see."

  Therefore some of the Pharisees said,
"This person is not from God,
for he does not keep the Sabbath."

But others said,
"How can a sinful person do such miracles?"
Thus there was division among them.

So they said to the blind one again,
"What do you say about him, since he opened your eyes?"

He said, "He is a prophet."

Yet the Jews did not believe about him
that he was blind and gained sight,
until they called the parents of him who gained sight,
and asked them, "Is this your son,
whom you say was born blind?
How then does he see now?"

So his parents answered, "We know that this is our son
and that he was born blind;
but how he now sees we do not know,
or who opened his eyes we do not know.
Ask him; he is of age; he will speak about himself."

This his parents said because they feared the Jews;
for already the Jews had agreed
that if anyone should acknowledge him as Christ,
he would be expelled from the synagogue.
Because of this his parents said,
"He is of age; question him."

So they called the person who was blind a second time,
and said to him, "Give praise to God;
we know that this person is sinful."

So that one answered, "I don't know if he is sinful;
one thing I know, that having been blind now I see."

So they said to him, "What did he do to you?
How did he open your eyes?"

He answered them, "I told you already,
and you didn't listen;
why do you want to hear it again?
Do you want to become his disciples too?"

And they berated him and said,
"You are a disciple of that one,
but we are disciples of Moses;
we know that God has spoken to Moses,

but we don't know where this one is from."

The person answered them,
"Then in this is the marvelous thing,
that you don't know where he is from,
and he opened my eyes.
We know that God does not listen to the sinful;
however if someone is godly and does his will,
he listens to him.
From eternity it has not been heard of
that anyone opened the eyes of one born blind;
if this one were not from God, he could not do anything."

They answered him, "You were born completely in sin,
and do you teach us?"
And they threw him outside.

Jesus heard that they threw him outside,
and finding him he said, "Do you believe in the human son?"

That one answered, "Who is he, lord,
that I may believe in him?"

Jesus said to him, "You have both seen him,
and the one speaking with you is that one."

He said, "I believe, Lord;" and he worshipped him.

Jesus said, "For judgment I came into this world,
so that the ones not seeing may see
and the ones seeing may become blind."

The Pharisees who were with him heard these things
and said to him, "Are we blind too?"

Jesus said to them, "If you were blind,
you would not have sin;
but now that you say, 'We see;' your sin remains.

54
"Amen, amen, I tell you,
the one not entering through the door into the sheepfold
but going up another way, is a thief and a robber;
but the one entering through the door
is the shepherd of the sheep.
The doorkeeper opens to him,
and the sheep listen to his voice;
and he calls his own sheep by name and leads them out.

When he has put out all of his own,
he goes in front of them,
and the sheep follow him, because they know his voice;
and they will not follow a stranger, but will flee from him,
because they do not know the voice of strangers."

Jesus told them this allegory,
but those did not know what it was that he spoke to them.

Therefore Jesus said again, "Amen, amen, I tell you
that I am the door for the sheep.
All who came before me are thieves and robbers;
but the sheep did not listen to them.
I am the door;
if anyone enters through me, one will be saved,
and one will come in and come out and find pasture.
The thief does not come
except to steal and kill and destroy;
I came so that they may have life and have abundance.

"I am the noble shepherd.
The noble shepherd lays down his life for the sheep;
the hired hand not being a shepherd,
the sheep are not his own;
he sees the wolf coming and leaves the sheep and flees,
and the wolf seizes them and scatters them;
for he is a hired hand and does not care about the sheep.

"I am the noble shepherd;
and I know mine, and mine know me,
as the Father knows me, and I know the Father;
and I lay down my life for the sheep.
I also have other sheep which are not from this fold;
and I must bring those, and they will listen to my voice
and will become one flock, one shepherd.

"For this reason the Father loves me,
because I lay down my life, that I may receive it again.
No one took it from me, but I lay it down by myself.
I have authority to lay it down,
and I have authority to receive it again;
this commandment I received from my Father."

Again there occurred division among the Jews
because of these words.

Many of them said, "He has a demon and is crazy;
why listen to him?"

Others said, "These sayings are not a demoniac's;
can a demon open the eyes of the blind?"

55

After these things the Lord appointed seventy-two others
and sent them two by two ahead of him
into every city and place where he intended to go.

He said to them, "Whoever listens to you listens to me,
and whoever rejects you rejects me;
and whoever rejects me rejects the one who sent me."

And the seventy-two returned with joy
saying, "Lord, even the demons submit to us in your name."

He said to them,
"I saw Satan fall like lightning from heaven.
Look, I have given you the authority
to tread on serpents and scorpions,
and on all the power of the enemy,
and nothing will harm you at all.
Yet do not rejoice in this that the spirits submit to you,
but rejoice that your names have been recorded in heaven."
In the same hour he was overjoyed by the Holy Spirit.

A certain lawyer stood up to test him
saying, "Teacher, by doing what may I obtain eternal life?"

He said to him, "What has been written in the law?
How do you read it?"

He answered, "Love the Lord your God
from your whole heart
and with your whole soul
and with your whole strength
and with your whole mind,
and your neighbor as yourself."

He said to him, "You answer correctly;
do this and you will live."

But wishing to justify himself
he said to Jesus, "And who is my neighbor?"

Taking him up Jesus said,
"A certain person was going down from Jerusalem to Jericho,

and he fell in among robbers,
who both beating him and stripping him
went away leaving him half dead.
By coincidence a certain priest was going down on that road,
and seeing him he passed by on the opposite side.
Likewise also a Levite coming upon the place
and seeing passed by on the opposite side.

"A certain Samaritan traveling came upon him
and seeing was compassionate;
approaching he bound up his wounds
pouring on oil and wine,
and putting him on his own pack-animal
he brought him to an inn and took care of him.
On the next day taking out two days' wages
he gave it to the innkeeper and said, 'Take care of him,
and whatever you spend in addition
I on my return will pay back to you.'

"Which of these three seems to you to have been a neighbor
to the one falling in among the robbers?"

He said, "The one who demonstrated mercy with him."

Jesus said to him, "Go, and you do likewise."

56
As they were proceeding, he entered a certain village;
and a woman named Martha welcomed him into her home.
Her sister was called Mary,
who sitting at the Lord's feet listened to his word.

But Martha was busy with much serving;
and standing she said, "Lord, doesn't it matter to you
that my sister left me alone to serve?
So tell her that she should help me."

The Lord answered her, "Martha, Martha,
you are worried and bothered about many things,
but there is need of few things or one;
for Mary selected the good part,
which will not be taken from her."

When he was praying in a certain place,
as he stopped, one of his disciples said to him, "Lord,
teach us to pray, just as John also taught his disciples."

He said to them, "When you pray, say:
'Father, let your name be holy;
let your sovereignty come;
give us our daily bread each day;
and forgive us our sins,
for we ourselves also forgive everyone owing us;
and do not bring us into temptation.'"
  Also he said to them, "Suppose one of you has a friend,
and he goes to him in the middle of the night
and says to him, 'Friend, lend me three loaves of bread,
since my friend has come to me from a journey
and I have nothing that I may set before him;'
and that one inside answers, 'Don't bother me;
the door has already been locked,
and my children are with me in bed;
I can't get up to give to you.'
I tell you, even if he will not give to him,
getting up because he is his friend,
yet because of his persistence,
rising he will give him whatever he needs."

57
  A Pharisee asked him to dine with him,
and entering he sat down.
But the Pharisee seeing was surprised
that he did not first wash before the dinner.
  The Lord said to him,
"Now you Pharisees clean the outside of the cup and dish,
but inside you are full of greed and corruption.
Fools!
Did not the one who made the outside also make the inside?
Yet give the inner things as charity,
and look, everything is clean for you.
  "But woe to you Pharisees,
because you tithe the mint and the rue and every herb,
and pass by justice and the love of God;
and these are necessary to do, not passing by those either.
  "Woe to you, Pharisees,
because you love the best seat in the synagogues

and the greetings in the marketplaces.

"Woe to you, because you are like unmarked graves,
and the people walking over do not know it."

One of the lawyers answered him, "Teacher,
by saying these things you insult us also."

He said, "Woe to you lawyers also,
because you took the key of knowledge;
you yourselves did not enter,
and you hindered the ones entering.
For you are like a dog sleeping in the manger of the oxen;
neither does he eat nor does he let the oxen eat."

As he went out from there,
the scholars and the Pharisees began to be terribly hostile
and to interrogate him about numerous things,
lying in wait for him to catch something from his mouth.

While a crowd of thousands was gathering,
stepping on each other,
he began to say to his disciples first,
"Beware yourselves of the yeast of the Pharisees,
which is hypocrisy."

Someone from the crowd said to him, "Teacher,
tell my brother to divide the inheritance with me."

But he said to him, "Human,
who appointed me a judge or divider over you?"
He turned to his disciples and said to them,
"I am not a divider, am I?"

He said to them, "See that you guard against every greed,
for a person's life does not consist of
the abundance of his possessions."

He told to them a parable:
"The land of a certain wealthy person yielded well,
and he reasoned within himself saying, 'What should I do?
for I have nowhere I may store my fruit.'
Then he said, 'I will do this:
I will tear down my barns and build larger ones;
there I will store all my grain and goods,
and I will say to my soul, "Soul,
you have many goods laid up for many years;
rest, eat, drink, be merry."'

But God said to him, 'Fool,
this night they demand back your soul from you;
and the things you prepared, whose will they be?'
   "Thus is the one treasuring for himself,
and not being wealthy in God.
Fear not, little flock;
for your Father is pleased to give you the sovereignty.
Sell your possessions and give charity;
make yourselves purses that do not get old,
inexhaustible treasure in heaven,
where a thief does not come near nor does a moth destroy;
for where your treasure is, there also will be your heart.
   "I came to throw fire on the earth,
and I wish it were already kindled.
But I have to be baptized with a baptism,
and how I am absorbed until it be completed.
Do you think that I have come to give peace on earth?
No, I tell you, but rather division.
For there will be from now on five in one house divided;
three will be divided against two and two against three,
father against son and son against father,
mother against daughter and daughter against the mother,
mother-in-law against her daughter-in-law
and daughter-in-law against the mother-in-law."
   He also said to the crowds,
"When you see a cloud rising in the west,
immediately you say that a rainstorm is coming,
and so it occurs;
and when a south wind is blowing,
you say that it will be hot, and it occurs.
Hypocrites, you know how to examine
the face of the earth and of heaven,
but do you not know how to examine this time?"

58
   Some were present at that time
reporting to him about the Galileans
whose blood Pilate had mixed with their sacrifices.

He answered them, "Do you think that these Galileans
were sinners beyond all the Galileans,
because they have suffered this?
No, I tell you, but unless you change your minds,
you will all die similarly.
Or those eighteen
on whom fell the tower in Siloam killing them,
do you think they are debtors
beyond all the people living in Jerusalem?
No, I tell you, but unless you change your minds,
you will die all the same."

He told this parable:
"Someone had a fig tree planted in his vineyard,
and he went looking for fruit on it and did not find any.
He said to the gardener, 'Look, for three years
I have come looking for fruit on this fig tree,
and I do not find any;
cut it down; why should it even waste the land?'

"But he answered him, 'Lord, leave it again this year,
until I dig around it and throw on dung;
it might produce fruit in the future;
but if not, cut it down.'"

He was teaching in one of the synagogues on the Sabbath.
There was a woman who had an ailing spirit eighteen years,
and she was bent over and unable to straighten up at all.

Seeing her Jesus called her forward and said to her,
"Woman, you have been released from your ailment,"
and he put his hands on her;
at once she straightened up, and she praised God.

But answering, the synagogue ruler,
angry that Jesus healed on the Sabbath, said to the crowd,
"There are six days on which work is to be done;
therefore come be healed on them
and not on the day of the Sabbath."

But the Lord answered him, "Hypocrites!
Does not each of you on the Sabbath
untie his ox or donkey from the manger
and leading it away give it something to drink?
And this woman being a daughter of Abraham,

whom Satan bound for ten and eight years,
should she not be released from this bond
on the day of the Sabbath?"

   When he said this,
all the ones opposing him were humiliated,
and all the crowd was glad
at all the glorious things done by him.

59

   Then the dedication festival occurred in Jerusalem;
it was winter;
and Jesus walked in the temple in Solomon's colonnade.
   So the Jews surrounded him and said to him,
"Until when will you keep us in suspense?
If you are the Christ, tell us openly."
   Jesus answered them, "I told you, and you do not believe;
the works which I do in the name of my Father,
these testify about me;
however, you do not believe,
because you are not sheep from my flock.
My sheep listen to my voice;
I know them, and they follow me;
and I give them eternal life, and they never die;
and no one will snatch them out of my hand.
My Father who has given them to me is greater than all,
and no one can snatch them out of the Father's hand.
The Father and I are one."
Again the Jews picked up stones so that they might stone him.
   Jesus answered them,
"I showed you many noble works from the Father;
because of which work do you stone me?"
   The Jews answered him,
"We do not stone you for a noble work but for blasphemy,
and because you being human make yourself God."
   Jesus answered them, "Is it not written in your law,
   'I have said, "You are gods"'?
If he called those gods to whom the word of God came,
(and scripture cannot be broken),
are you telling the one the Father sanctified

and sent into the world,
'You blaspheme,' because I said, 'I am God's son'?
If I do not do the works of my Father, do not believe me;
but if I do,
even if you do not believe me, believe the works,
so that you may know and be aware
that the Father is in me and I am in the Father."

So they tried to arrest him again,
and he went out out of their hands.
He went away again across the Jordan
to the place where John was first baptizing,
and he stayed there.

Many came to him and said, "John performed no sign,
but everything John said about this one was true."
And many believed in him there.

60
He traveled through towns and villages teaching
and making a journey to Jerusalem.
Someone said to him, "Lord, are only a few being saved?"

He said to them, "Strive to enter through the narrow door,
because many, I tell you, will try to enter
and will not be able to.
As soon as the master of the house rises and shuts the door,
you will begin to stand outside and knock on the door,
saying, 'Lord, open for us,'
and he will answer you, 'I don't know where you are from.'
Then you will begin to say, 'We ate before you and drank,
and in our streets you taught;'
and he will say to you, 'I don't know where you are from;
keep away from me, all you workers of injustice.'

"There will be the weeping and the gnashing of teeth,
when you see Abraham and Isaac
and Jacob and all the prophets
in the sovereignty of God, but you are outside thrown out.
They will come from east and west and from north and south,
and they will recline in the sovereignty of God.
There are last ones who will be first,
and there are first ones who will be last."

In the same hour some Pharisees approached saying to him,
"Go out and leave here, because Herod wishes to kill you."
    He said to them, "Go tell that fox:
look, I expel demons and perform cures today and tomorrow,
and on the third day I am perfected.
Nevertheless today and tomorrow and on the following day
I must travel,
for it is not permitted
for a prophet to die outside of Jerusalem."
    As he went into the home of one of the Pharisees' leaders
on a Sabbath to eat bread, they were watching him closely.
A certain person in front of him had edema.
    Jesus answered the lawyers and Pharisees saying,
"Is it permitted to heal on the Sabbath or not?"
    But they were silent.
Taking hold of him he cured him and let him go.
    To them he said, "Which of you
if your son or ox falls into a pit,
would not also immediately pull him up on a Sabbath day?"
    They could not reply to this.
    He told a parable to the ones invited,
noticing how they selected the best seats:
"When you are invited by someone to a wedding,
do not sit in the best seat,
lest someone more honored than you be invited by him;
and when he comes, the one who invited you
will say to you, 'Give this one a place,'
and then you will begin with shame to take the last place.
But when you are invited, go sit in the last place,
so that when the one who invited you comes,
he will say to you, 'Friend, go up higher;'
then you will be praised
before all the ones sitting with you.
For whoever exalts oneself will be humbled,
and whoever humbles oneself will be exalted."
    He also said to the one who invited him,
"When you give a luncheon or dinner,
do not call your friends nor your brothers
nor your relatives nor wealthy neighbors,

lest they also invite you in return
and it becomes repayment to you.
But when you give a banquet,
invite the poor, crippled, lame, and blind;
and you will be blessed,
because they have nothing to repay you;
for it will be repaid to you
in the resurrection of the just."

Having heard this, one of those sitting with them
said to him, "Blessed is the one
who will eat bread in the sovereignty of God."

He said to him,
"A certain person gave a great dinner and invited many,
and he sent his servant at the hour of the dinner
to say to those invited, 'Come, for it is already prepared.'
Yet they all began to decline, one after another.

"The first said to him, 'I bought a farm,
and I must go out to see it; I will have no time.
I ask you, let me be excused.'

"Another said, 'I bought five yoke of oxen,
and I am going to try them out;
I ask you, let me be excused.'

"Another said, 'I married a woman,
and for this reason I can't come.'
Coming back the servant reported these things to his lord.

"Then getting angry the master of the house
said to his servant,
'Go out quickly into the streets and alleys of the city,
and bring in here the poor and crippled and blind and lame.'

"The servant said, 'Lord, what you ordered has occurred,
and there is still room.'

"So the Lord said to the servant,
'Go out to the roads and hedges and have them come in,
so that they may dine and my house may be filled;
for I tell you
that none of those invited will taste my dinner.'"

61
  Large crowds were traveling with him,
and turning he said to them, "If anyone comes to me
and does not hate one's father and mother
and wife and children and brothers and sisters,
and even his own life also,
one cannot be my disciple.
Whoever does not bear one's cross and come after me,
cannot be my disciple.

  "For which of you intending to build a tower
does not first sit so one may calculate the cost,
whether one has enough for completion?
lest when one has laid a foundation
and is not able to finish
all those seeing will begin to make fun of one, saying,
'This person began to build and was not able to finish.'

  "Or what king going to attack another king in war
will not sit so he may decide
whether he is able with ten thousand
to oppose the one with twenty thousand coming upon him?
If not, while he is still far away,
sending an embassy he asks for peace.

  "So also everyone of you
who does not give up all one's possessions
cannot be my disciple.

  "Which of you having a servant plowing or herding,
when he is coming in from the field
will tell him, 'Come sit down at once,'
but will not tell him, 'Prepare something so I may dine,
and girding yourself serve me until I eat and drink,
and after that you may eat and drink'?
Does he thank the servant
because he did what he was ordered?

  "So you also, when you do all that you are ordered to do,
say, 'We are useless servants;
we have done what we ought to do.'
Let the one having ears to hear hear."

62
All the tax collectors and sinners
were drawing near him to listen to him.
Both the Pharisees and the scholars grumbled
saying, "This one welcomes sinners and eats with them."
  He told them this parable:
"What person among you having a hundred sheep
and losing one of them wandering astray
does not leave the ninety-nine on the hills
and go search for the wandering one until one finds it?
and finding it one puts it on one's shoulders rejoicing,
and going home one calls together friends and neighbors,
saying to them, 'Rejoice with me,
for I found my lost sheep.'
  "I tell you that there will be more joy in heaven
over one sinner repenting than over ninety-nine just persons
who have no need of repentance.
Thus it is not your Father's will in heaven
that one of these small ones should be lost.
  "Or what woman having ten silver coins,
if she should lose one coin,
does not light a lamp and sweep the house
and search carefully until she finds it?
and finding it she calls together friends and neighbors
saying, 'Rejoice with me, for I found the coin which I lost.'
  "Thus I tell you, there is joy before the angels of God
over one sinner repenting."
  He said, "A certain person had two sons.
The younger one said to the father,
'Father, give me my share of the estate.'
So he divided his living between them.
  "After not too many days the younger son
getting everything together moved away to a far country,
and there he squandered his property in profligate living.
When he had spent everything,
a severe famine occurred throughout that country,
and he began to be in need.
So going he was hired
by one of the citizens of that country,

and he sent him into his fields to feed pigs;
he longed to fill his stomach
from the carob pods which the pigs ate,
and no one gave him anything.

  "But coming to himself he said,
'My father has so many hired laborers
and abundance of bread,
but I am dying of hunger here.
Getting up I will travel to my father and say to him,
"Father, I sinned against heaven and before you;
no longer am I worthy to be called your son;
make me like one of your hired laborers."'

  "So getting up he went to his own father.
But while he was still far away,
his father saw him and was compassionate,
and running he embraced his neck and kissed him.
The son said to him, 'Father,
I sinned against heaven and before you;
no longer am I worthy to be called your son.'

  "But the father said to his servants,
'Quickly bring out my best robe and put it on him,
and put a ring on his hand and sandals on his feet,
and bring the fattened calf, sacrifice it,
and eating let us celebrate,
for this son of mine was dead and lives again,
was lost and is found.'

  "So they began to celebrate.
But his older son was in the field;
and as he was coming near the house,
he heard music and dancing,
and calling to one of the servants
he inquired what this might be.
He told him, 'Your brother has come,
and your father sacrificed the fattened calf,
for he has gotten him back safe and sound.'

  "He was angry and did not wish to go in,
but his father coming out pleaded with him.
But he answered the father,
'Look, so many years I serve you,

and never did I go against your command,
and you never gave a goat to me
so that I might celebrate with my friends;
but when this son of yours
who ate up your living with prostitutes came,
you sacrificed for him the fattened calf.'

"He said to him, 'Child, you are always with me,
and all my things are yours;
but we must celebrate and rejoice,
because this brother of yours was dead and lives,
and was lost and is found.'"

63

He also said to his disciples,
"There was a rich person who had a manager,
and charges were brought to him
that this one was squandering his possessions.
Calling him he said to him, 'What is this I hear about you?
Give back the account of your management;
for you can no longer be manager.'

"The manager said to himself, 'What should I do,
since my lord is taking away the management from me?
I am not strong enough to dig; I am ashamed to beg.
I know what I should do,
so that when I am removed from the management
they may welcome me into their houses.'

"So calling each one of his lord's debtors
he said to the first, 'How much do you owe my lord?'

"He said, 'A hundred baths of oil.'

"He said to him, 'Take your bill
and sitting quickly write fifty.'
Then he said to another, 'And how much do you owe?'

"He said, 'A hundred barrels of wheat.'

"He told him, 'Take your bill and write eighty.'

"The lord commended the manager of injustice
because he acted shrewdly;
for the sons of this age are more shrewd
with their own generation than the sons of light.

"I tell you, make friends for yourselves
from the money of injustice,
so that when it fails
they may welcome you into eternal dwellings.

"The one faithful with the smallest
is also faithful with much,
and the one unjust with the smallest
is also unjust with much.
Therefore if you were not faithful with the unjust money,
who will trust you with the true?
If you were not faithful with another's,
who will give you ours?

"No domestic can serve two lords;
for either one will hate the one and love the other,
or one will hold to one and disregard the other.
You cannot serve God and money."

The Pharisees being money-lovers
heard all this and sneered at him.

He said to them,
"You are the ones justifying yourselves before people,
but God knows your hearts;
for what is highly valued by people
is an abomination before God.
The law and the prophets were until John;
since then the sovereignty of God is the good message
and everyone is pushing into it.

"There was a rich person,
and he wore purple and fine linen
celebrating splendidly every day.
Someone poor named Lazarus had been laid at his gate,
covered with sores and longing to satisfy his hunger
from the things falling from the table of the rich one;
moreover dogs coming licked his sores.

"It happened that the poor one died,
and was taken away by the angels to the bosom of Abraham;
and the rich one also died and was buried.
In Hades lifting his eyes, while in torment,
he saw Abraham from a distance and Lazarus in his bosom.
Calling he said, 'Father Abraham,

have mercy on me and send Lazarus
so that he may dip the tip of his finger in water
and cool down my tongue,
for I am in pain in this flame.'

"But Abraham said, 'Child, remember
that you received your good things during your life,
and Lazarus similarly the bad things;
now he is comforted here, but you are in pain.
Besides all this,
between us and you a great chasm has been fixed,
so that those wishing to pass from here to you cannot,
and no one may cross from there to us.'

"He said, 'Then I ask you, father,
to send him into my father's house;
for I have five brothers; so that he may warn them,
lest they also come to this place of torment.'

"But Abraham said, 'They have Moses and the prophets;
let them listen to them.'

"But he said, 'They don't, father Abraham,
but if someone from the dead goes to them,
they will change their minds.'

"He said to him,
'If they don't listen to Moses and the prophets,
neither will they be convinced
if someone rises from the dead.'"

64
There was someone ailing, Lazarus from Bethany,
from the village of Mary and her sister Martha.
It was Mary who anointed the Lord with perfume
and wiped off his feet with her hair,
whose brother Lazarus was ailing.

So the sisters sent to him saying, "Lord,
look, the one you love is ailing."

Jesus having heard said, "This ailment is not for death
but for the glory of God,
so that the son of God may be glorified by it."

Jesus loved Martha and her sister and Lazarus.
So when he heard that he was ailing,

first he stayed in the place he was for two days;
then after this he said to the disciples,
"Let us go into Judea again."
   The disciples said to him, "Rabbi,
the Jews were just trying to stone you,
and are you going back there again?"
   Jesus answered, "Are there not twelve hours of day?
If one walks by day, one does not stumble,
because one sees by the light of this world;
but if one walks at night, one stumbles,
because there is no light in one."
   He said these things, and after this he said to them,
"Lazarus our friend has fallen asleep;
but I am going so I may awaken him."
   Therefore the disciples said to him, "Lord,
if he has fallen asleep, he will be saved."
But Jesus had spoken about his death;
and those thought that he was talking about ordinary sleep.
   So then Jesus told them plainly, "Lazarus died,
and I am glad for your sake, so that you may believe,
that I was not there;
but let us go to him."
   Therefore Thomas,
who was called Twin by his fellow disciples,
said, "Let us go also so that we may die with him."
   So going Jesus found him
having already been in the tomb for four days.
Bethany was near Jerusalem about fifteen stadiums away.
Many of the Jews had come to Martha and Mary,
so that they might console them about the brother.
   So when Martha heard that Jesus was coming,
she went to meet him; but Mary sat in the house.
So Martha said to Jesus, "Lord,
if you had been here, my brother would not have died.
Even now I know that whatever you ask of God,
God will give you."
   Jesus said to her. "Your brother will rise up."
   Martha said to him, "I know that he will rise up
in the resurrection on the last day."

Jesus said to her, "I am the resurrection and life;
whoever believes in me even though one dies one will live,
and all who live and believe in me never die;
do you believe this?"

She said to him, "Yes, Lord;
I have believed that you are the Christ,
the son of God, the one coming into the world."

Having said this she went away
and called her sister Mary secretly
saying, "The teacher is here and is calling you."

When she heard, she rose quickly and went to him;
Jesus had not yet come into the village,
but he was still in the place where Martha met him.
Therefore the Jews who were with her in the house
and consoling her,
seeing that Mary quickly got up and went out,
followed her, thinking that she was going to the tomb
so that she might weep there.

So when Mary came to where Jesus was,
seeing him she fell at his feet, saying to him, "Lord,
if you had been here, my brother would not have died."

So when Jesus saw her weeping
and the Jews coming with her weeping,
he was deeply moved in his spirit and troubled,
and he said, "Where have you put him?"

They said to him, "Lord, come and see."

Jesus wept.
Therefore the Jews said, "See how he loved him!"

But some of them said, "Could not this one
who opened the eyes of the blind
make it so that this one also would not die?"

So Jesus again deeply moved within himself
came to the tomb;
it was a cave, and a stone lay upon it.

Jesus said, "Take away the stone."

Martha, the sister of the one who died, said to him,
"Lord, by now he will smell; for it is the fourth day."

Jesus said to her, "Did I not tell you
that if you believe, you will see the glory of God?"
  So they took away the stone.
Jesus lifted up his eyes and said, "Father,
I thank you that you did hear me.
I knew that you always do hear me;
however, because of the crowd standing around I said it,
so that they may believe that you sent me."
  Having said this
he cried out with a loud voice, "Lazarus, come out!"
  The one who had died came out,
his feet and hands bound with bandages,
and his face had been wrapped around with a handkerchief.
  Jesus said to them, "Untie him and let him go."
  Therefore many of the Jews, who had come to Mary
and had seen what he did, believed in him;
but some of them went away to the Pharisees
and told them what Jesus did.
  So the high priests and the Pharisees assembled a council
and said, "What do we do,
for this person performs many miracles?
If we let him go on like this, everyone will believe in him,
and the Romans will come
and will take both our place and the nation."
  But one of them, Caiaphas, who was high priest that year,
said to them, "You don't know anything,
nor do you reason that it is better for us
that one person should die on behalf of the people
than that the whole nation should perish."
  But he did not say this from himself,
but being high priest of that year he prophesied
that Jesus was about to die on behalf of the nation,
and not on behalf of the nation alone,
but also so that he might gather into one
the scattered children of God.
  So from that day they plotted so that they might kill him.
Therefore Jesus no longer walked openly among the Jews,
but he went away from there to the country near the desert,
to a town called Ephraim;

and there he stayed with his disciples.

65
In traveling to Jerusalem
he passed through the middle of Samaria and Galilee.
As he entered a certain village, ten lepers met him;
they stood at a distance and lifted their voices
saying, "Jesus, master, have mercy on us."
Seeing he said to them,
"Go show yourselves to the priests."
As they were going, they were cleansed.
But one of them, seeing that he was cured,
turned back with a loud voice praising God,
and he fell on his face at his feet thanking him;
he was a Samaritan.
Jesus answered, "Were not ten cleansed?
Where are the nine?
Was no one found turning back to give praise to God
except this foreigner?"
He said to him, "Stand up and go;
your faith has saved you."
Questioned by the Pharisees
when the sovereignty of God is coming,
he answered them,
"The sovereignty of God is not coming with observation,
nor will they say, 'Look, here,' or 'There;'
for look, the sovereignty of God is within you.
"If those who lead you say to you,
'Look, the sovereignty is in heaven,'
then the birds of heaven will precede you.
If they say to you, 'It is in the sea,'
then the fish will precede you.
But the sovereignty is within and outside you.
When you know yourselves, then you will be known
and you will know that you are the sons of the living Father.
But if you do not know yourselves,
then you are in poverty, and you are poverty."
He told them a parable toward the necessity
of their always praying and not despairing:

"There was a judge in a certain town
neither fearing God nor regarding a person.
A widow was in that town, and she came to him
saying, 'Vindicate me against my opponent.'
He would not for some time;
but after awhile he said to himself,
'Even though I do not fear God or regard a person,
because this widow keeps causing me trouble
I will vindicate her,
lest in the end she wear me out with her coming.'
  "Listen to what the judge of injustice said.
Will not God also make vindicated his chosen ones
who cry to him day and night,
and be patient with them?
I tell you that he will make them vindicated quickly.
Nevertheless when the human son comes,
will he find faith on the earth?"
  He also said this parable
to some of those confident by themselves
that they are just and despising the rest:
"Two people went up to the temple to pray,
one a Pharisee and the other a tax collector.
The Pharisee standing prayed to himself these things:
'God, I thank you that I am not like the rest of humanity,
greedy, unjust, adulterers, or even like this tax collector;
I fast twice a week,
and I tithe a tenth of everything I acquire.'
  "But the tax collector standing at a distance
would not even lift his eyes to heaven, but beat his breast,
saying, 'God, be gracious to me, a sinner.'
I tell you, this one went down to his home
justified rather than the other;
for everyone exalting oneself will be humbled,
and the one humbling oneself will be exalted."

66
  When Jesus finished these words, getting up from there
he went into the region of Judea across the Jordan.
Again crowds traveled with him,

and he taught and healed them there.

Pharisees approaching to test him asked, "Is it permitted
for a man to divorce his wife for any cause?"

He answered them, "What did Moses command you?"

They said, "Moses allowed one
to write a divorce certificate to divorce."

But Jesus said, "For your hardness of heart
he wrote you this commandment.
But from the beginning of creation
he made them male and female;
on account of this a person will leave his father and mother
and be united with his wife,
and two will be one flesh;
so they are no longer two, but one flesh.
Therefore what God joined together,
let a person not separate.

"I tell you that whoever divorces his wife,
except for fornication,
and marries another, commits adultery;
and if she having divorced her husband marries another,
she commits adultery."

In the house again the disciples said to him,
"If such is the case of a person with a wife,
it is better not to marry."

He said to them, "Not all can accept this word,
but those to whom it has been given.
For there are eunuchs who were born so
from a mother's womb,
and there are eunuchs who were made eunuchs by people,
and there are eunuchs who made themselves eunuchs
because of the sovereignty of heaven.
Let the one who can accept this accept it."

They brought to him children
so that he might touch them and pray;
but the disciples reprimanded them.

But Jesus called them to him saying,
"Allow the children to come to me and do not prevent them;
for of such is the sovereignty of God.
Amen, I tell you,

whoever does not welcome the sovereignty of God like a child,
may not enter it.
The person old in days will not hesitate
to ask a child of seven days about the place of life,
and he will live."

   And taking them in his arms he blessed them
putting his hands on them.

67

   As he went out on his way,
one running and kneeling before him questioned him,
"Good teacher, what should I do
so that I may obtain eternal life?"

   Jesus said to him, "Why do you call me good?
No one is good except God alone.
There is one good;
if you intend to enter into life, keep the commandments."

   He asked him, "Which ones?"

   Jesus said, "Do not murder, do not commit adultery,
do not steal, do not testify falsely, do not defraud,
honor your father and mother,
and you shall love your neighbor as yourself."

   He said, "All these things
I have guarded against from my youth."

   Jesus looking at him loved him and said to him,
"You are missing one thing;
if you intend to be perfect,
go sell all your possessions and give to the poor,
and you will have treasure in heaven;
and come follow me."

   Shocked at the word
he went away distressed and became very sad,
for he had many possessions and was quite rich.

   Looking around Jesus said to his disciples,
"How hard it is for those having property
to enter the sovereignty of God."

   The disciples were amazed at his words,
and Jesus again answered them, "Children,
how hard it is to enter the sovereignty of God;

it is easier for a camel to go through the eye of a needle
than for a rich person to enter the sovereignty of God."

The disciples hearing were even more astonished,
saying to themselves, "Who then can be saved?"

Looking at them Jesus said,
"With humans this is impossible, but not with God;
for all things are possible with God."

Peter began to say to him, "Look,
we left everything and followed you."

He said to them, "Amen, I tell you
there is no one who has left home or brothers or sisters
or mother or father or wife or children or fields
on account of me
and the good message of the sovereignty of God,
who will not receive manifold now in this time
homes and brothers and sisters
and mothers and children and fields
with persecutions, and in the coming age eternal life.

"Amen, I tell you that you who have followed me,
in the rebirth
when the human son sits on his throne of glory,
you also will sit on twelve thrones
judging the twelve tribes of Israel.
But many first will be last, and the last first;
and they will become a single one.

"For the sovereignty of heaven is like
a master of an estate,
who went out early in the morning
to hire workers for his vineyard.
Agreeing with the workers on a day's wages
he sent them into his vineyard.

"Going out about the third hour he saw others
standing in the marketplaces idle, and to those he said,
'You go also into the vineyard,
and whatever is fair I will give you.'
So they went.

"Again going out about the sixth and the ninth hour
he did the same thing.

"Going out about the eleventh hour
he found others standing, and he said to them,
'Why are you standing here the whole day idle?'
   "They told him, 'Because no one hired us.'
   "He said to them, 'You go also into the vineyard.'
   "When evening had come,
the lord of the vineyard said to his foreman,
'Call the workers and pay the wage,
beginning from the last up to the first.'
   "Those coming about the eleventh hour
each received a day's wages.
Those coming first thought that they would receive more;
and they also each received a day's wages.
Receiving it they complained to the master of the estate
saying, 'These last ones did one hour,
and you made them equal to us
who bore the burden of the day and the heat.'
   "But he answered one of them,
'Friend, I am not unfair to you;
did you not agree with me on a day's wages?
Take yours and go;
but I wish to give this last one
as I have given also to you;
is it not permitted for me
to do what I wish with my own things?
Or is your eye bad because I am good?'
Thus the last will be first, and the first last."

68
   They were going up on the way to Jerusalem;
Jesus was leading them.
They were surprised, while those following were afraid.
   Taking aside again the twelve he began to tell them
what was about to happen to him:
"Look, we are going up to Jerusalem,
and everything written through the prophets
about the human son will be completed;
for the human son will be given over
to the high priests and the scholars;

they will condemn him to death
and give him over to the nations,
and they will mock him and spit on him
and whip him and kill him;
and on the third day he will rise."

None of them understood these things;
this saying was hidden from them,
and they did not know what he meant.

Then the mother of James and John,
the two sons of Zebedee,
approached him with her sons bowing and asking him,
"Teacher, we wish that whatever we ask you, you do for us."

He said to them, "What do you wish me to do for you?"

She said to him, "Grant that
these two sons of mine may sit one on your right
and one on your left in your sovereignty."

Jesus said to them, "You do not know what you are asking.
Can you drink the cup which I am about to drink,
or be baptized with the baptism with which I am baptized?"

They said to him, "We can."

Jesus said to them, "The cup which I drink you will drink,
and with the baptism with which I am baptized
you will be baptized;
but to sit on my right or on my left is not mine to grant,
but it is for those
for whom it has been prepared by my Father."

The ten hearing began to be
indignant about James and John.
Calling them forward Jesus said to them,
"You know that those thinking to rule the nations
lord it over them,
and their great ones exercise authority over them.
But it is not so among you;
instead whoever wishes to become great among you,
shall be your servant,
and whoever wishes to be first among you,
shall be slave of all;
just as the human son did not come to be served,
but to serve and to give his life as a ransom for many."

They came to Jericho.
As he and his disciples and a considerable crowd
were going out of Jericho,
the son of Timaeus, Bartimaeus, a blind beggar,
was sitting beside the road.
Hearing a crowd passing through
he inquired what this might be.
They reported to him that Jesus the Nazarene was going by.

So he cried out, "Jesus, son of David, have mercy on me!"
The ones leading reprimanded him so that he would be quiet;
but he shouted even more, "Son of David, have mercy on me!"

Stopping, Jesus said, "Call him."
They called the blind one saying to him,
"Courage; rise; he calls you."
Throwing away his garment and jumping up he came to Jesus.

Jesus questioned him,
"What do you want that I may do for you?"
The blind one said to him, "Rabbi, that I may see again."

Feeling compassion Jesus touched his eyes
and said, "Go, your faith has saved you."

Immediately he saw again,
and he followed him on the road praising God.
Also all the people seeing gave praise to God.

69
Having entered Jericho he passed through.
There was a man named Zacchaeus;
he was a chief tax collector, and he was rich.
He tried to see who Jesus was;
and he was not able to from the crowd,
because he was short in height.
Running ahead in front he climbed up on a sycamore tree,
so that he might see him;
for he was about to pass through that way.

As he came upon the place, looking up Jesus said to him,
"Zacchaeus, hurry, come down;
for I must stay in your house today."

So hurrying he came down and welcomed him gladly.
Everyone seeing grumbled
saying that he went to lodge with a sinful man.

Standing Zacchaeus said to the Lord, "Look, Lord,
half of my possessions I give to the poor,
and if I have extorted something from someone,
I pay back fourfold."

Jesus said to him,
"Today salvation has come to this house,
because even he is a son of Abraham;
for the human son came to seek and save the lost."

As they were listening to this,
he went on to tell a parable,
because he was near Jerusalem and it seemed to them
that the sovereignty of God was about to appear at once;
therefore he said, "A certain person of noble birth,
traveling to a far country
to receive a kingdom for himself and return,
called his own servants
and gave over to them his possessions;
to one he gave five talents, and to another two,
and to another one, each according to his own ability.
He said to them, 'Do business until I come.'
Then he left home.

"But his citizens hated him,
and sent a delegation after him saying,
'We do not want this person to be king over us.'
Immediately proceeding the one receiving five talents
traded with them and gained five more;
similarly the one with two gained two more.
But the one receiving one went away
and dug into the ground and hid the silver of his lord.

"After a long time the lord returned
having received the kingdom.
He asked those servants to be called to him
to whom he had given the money,
so that he might know what business they had transacted.

"The one who received five talents
approaching brought five more talents

saying, 'Lord, you gave over five talents to me;
look, I have gained five more talents.'

"His lord said to him,
'Well done, good and faithful servant,
since with the smallest you have been faithful,
I will put you in charge of much;
you are to have authority over five cities.
Come in to the joy of your lord.'

"Approaching also the one with two talents
said, 'Lord, you gave over two talents to me;
look, I have gained two more talents.'

"His lord said to him,
'Well done, good and faithful servant,
since with the smallest you have been faithful,
I will put you in charge of much;
you are to be over two cities.
Come in to the joy of your lord.'

"Approaching also the one who received one talent
said, 'Lord, knowing you that you are a strict person,
taking what you did not put in,
and reaping what you did not sow,
and being afraid
I went away and hid your talent in the ground;
look, you have yours.'

"But his lord answered him, 'Bad and lazy servant,
out of your own mouth I will judge you.
Did you know that I am a strict person,
taking what I did not put in,
and reaping what I did not sow?
Why did you not deposit my silver at the banker's table?
And coming I would have collected it with interest.'
To those standing by he said, 'Take from him the talent
and give it to the one who has ten talents.'

"They said to him, 'Lord, he has ten talents.'

"'I tell you that to everyone having it will be given,
and he will have abundance;
but from the one not having
even what one has will be taken away from one.
Throw out the useless servant into the outer darkness;

there will be the weeping and the gnashing of teeth.
Nevertheless bring here those enemies of mine,
the ones not wanting me to be king over them,
and slaughter them in front of me.'"
  Having said these things
he traveled in front going up to Jerusalem.

70
  It was near the Jewish Passover,
and many went up to Jerusalem from the country
before the Passover, so that they might purify themselves.
  So they were looking for Jesus
and said to each other standing in the temple,
"What do you think?
that he may not come to the feast at all?"
  The high priests and the Pharisees had given commands
that if anyone knew where he was one should make it known,
so that they might arrest him.
  So six days before the Passover Jesus came to Bethany,
where Lazarus was, whom Jesus had raised from the dead.
When they drew near to Jerusalem
and came to Bethphage and Bethany at the Mount of Olives,
then Jesus sent two disciples saying to them,
"Go into the village opposite you,
and immediately upon entering it you will find a colt tied
upon which no person has ever sat; untie it and bring it.
If anyone asks you, 'Why are you untying it?'
say, 'The Lord has need of it,
and immediately he will send it back here.'"
  This happened so that it might be fulfilled
what was spoken through the prophet:
    "Tell the daughter of Zion:
    Look, your king comes to you
    gentle and riding on a donkey's colt."
His disciples did not understand this at first;
however, when Jesus was glorified, then they remembered
that this was written about him and they did this for him.
  They went away
and found a colt tied at a door outside in the street.

As they were untying the colt,
the owners of it standing there said to them,
"What are you doing untying the colt?"
They told them just what Jesus said, and they let them go.

They brought the colt to Jesus,
and throwing their clothes on the colt Jesus sat upon it.
A large crowd hearing that Jesus was coming into Jerusalem
took the branches of palms and went out to meet him,
and as he was drawing near already
to the descent from the Mount of Olives,
all the many disciples
began joyfully to praise God with loud voices
about all the powerful deeds they had seen.

Those leading and following shouted, "Hosanna!
Praised is the one coming in the name of the Lord!
Praised is the coming sovereignty of our father David!
In heaven peace and glory in the highest!"

Some of the Pharisees from the crowd said to him,
"Teacher, reprimand your disciples."

He answered, "I tell you,
if these will be quiet, the stones will shout."

So the crowd who was with him
when he called Lazarus out of the tomb
and raised him from the dead was testifying.
For this reason also a crowd met him,
because they heard that he had performed this miracle.

Therefore the Pharisees said among themselves,
"You see that you do not help at all;
look, the world has gone away after him."

As he drew near, seeing the city he wept over it,
saying, "If you only knew on this day,
even you, the things for peace;
but now they have been hidden from your eyes.
For days will come upon you
when your enemies will put up a palisade to you
and surround you and attack you on all sides;
they will raze you to the ground and your children in you,
and they will not leave a stone upon a stone in you,
in return for your not knowing the time of your visitation."

As he was entering Jerusalem
all the city was stirred saying, "Who is this?"
The crowds said,
"This is the prophet Jesus from Nazareth of Galilee."
The blind and lame approached him in the temple,
and he healed them.
But when the high priests and the scholars
saw the marvels which he did
and the children shouting in the temple
and saying, "Hosanna to the son of David,"
they were indignant
and said to him, "Do you hear what these are saying?"
Jesus said to them, "Yes; have you never read,
   'Out of the mouth of infants and suckling ones
   you prepared praise'?"
So leaving them behind
he went out outside the city to Bethany,
and he spent the night there with the twelve.

71
Early the next day as they were coming from Bethany
he was hungry.
On the way seeing from a distance a fig tree having leaves
he came to see if he would find something on it,
and coming upon it he found nothing except leaves;
for it was not the season of figs.
He said to it, "May no fruit come from you ever again."
His disciples heard it.
They came into Jerusalem, and entering the temple
he found those selling cattle and sheep and doves,
and the money-changers seated.
Having made a whip out of rope
he threw them all out of the temple,
the sheep and the cattle,
and he poured out the coins
and overturned the tables of the money-changers
and the seats of those selling doves,
to whom he said, "Take these away from here;
do not make my Father's house a market."

He did not allow anyone
to carry property through the temple,
and he said to them, "It has been written,
  'My house shall be called
  a house of prayer for all the nations,'
but you have made it a den of robbers."
  His disciples remembered that it is written:
  "Zeal for your house will consume me."
  Therefore the Jews answered him,
"What sign do you show us, since you do these things?"
  Jesus answered them, "Destroy this temple,
and in three days I will raise it."
  So the Jews said,
"This temple was built in forty-six years,
and will you raise it in three days?"
  But he was talking about the temple of his body.
So when he was raised from the dead,
his disciples remembered that he said this,
and they believed the scripture
and the word which Jesus said.
  He was teaching daily in the temple;
but the high priests and the scholars
and the foremost of the people sought to destroy him,
and they did not discover what they should do;
for they feared him,
because all the people were hanging out listening to him.
  When it got late, he went out outside the city.
Passing along early in the morning
they saw the fig tree dried up from the roots.
  Peter remembering said to him, "Rabbi, look,
the fig tree which you cursed has dried up."
  The disciples marveled
asking, "How was the fig tree dried up?"
  Jesus answered them, "Amen, I tell you,
if you have faith in God and do not doubt in your heart
but believe that what you speak happens,
not only will you do what was done with the fig tree,
but also if you say to this mountain,

'Be picked up and thrown into the sea,' it will happen.
   "For this reason I tell you,
everything for which you pray and ask,
believe that you received it, and it will be for you.
When you stand praying,
forgive if you have anything against anyone,
so that your Father in heaven
may also forgive you your transgressions."

72
   During the days he was in the temple teaching,
and going out he spent the nights
on the mountain called Olives'.
All the people came to him early in the morning
to listen to him in the temple.
Again they came into Jerusalem.
   As he was walking in the temple and teaching,
the high priests and the scholars and the elders
approached him asking,
"By what authority are you doing these things?
Or who gave you this authority
so that you could do these things?"
   Jesus answered them, "I also will ask you one question;
if you answer me, I will tell you
by what authority I do these things.
Was the baptism of John from heaven or from humans?
Answer me."
   They discussed it among themselves saying,
"If we say, 'From heaven,'
he will say, 'Then why did you not believe him?'
But if we say, 'From humans,'
we are afraid the crowd will stone us down;
for everyone holds that John was really a prophet."
   So answering Jesus they said, "We don't know."
   Jesus said to them, "Neither will I tell you
by what authority I do these things.
   "What do you think? A person had two children.
Approaching the first he said, 'Child,
go work today in the vineyard.'

"He answered, 'I am going, lord,' and he did not go.

"Approaching the second he said the same thing.
He answered, 'I will not;' later regretting it he went.

"Which of the two did the will of the Father?"

They said, "The latter."

Jesus said to them, "Amen, I tell you
that the tax collectors and the prostitutes
are going ahead of you into the sovereignty of God.
For John came to you with a way of justice,
and you did not believe him;
but the tax collectors and the prostitutes believed him;
but you seeing did not regret later
changing to believe him.

73

"Listen to another parable.
A master of an estate planted a vineyard,
And he put a fence around it
and dug in a wine-press and built a tower;
then he rented it to farmers and went away on a journey.
When the season of the fruit drew near,
he sent a servant to the farmers
so that from the farmers
he might receive from the fruit of the vineyard;
taking him they beat him and sent him away empty-handed.
Again he sent to them another servant,
and that one they hit in the head and insulted.
He sent another in addition, and that one they killed.
There were many others also, some beaten, others killed.

"The lord of the vineyard said, 'What should I do?
I will send my beloved son;
perhaps this one they will respect.'

"But the farmers seeing the son
said among themselves, 'This is the heir;
come let's kill him,
so that the inheritance may become ours.'
Taking him they threw him out of the vineyard
and killed him.

"When the lord of the vineyard comes,
what will he do to those farmers?"
They said to him, "The bad ones he will destroy,
and the vineyard he will rent to other farmers,
who will give him back the fruit in their seasons."
Jesus said to them,
"Have you never read in the scriptures:
'A stone which the builders rejected,
this became the corner-stone;
it was from the lord,
and it is marvelous in our eyes'?
The one falling on this stone will be shattered;
but whomever it falls upon, it will crush him.
For this reason I tell you
that the sovereignty of God will be taken from you
and will be given to a nation producing its fruit."

The high priests and the Pharisees hearing his parables
knew that he was talking about them;
they tried to arrest him,
yet they were afraid of the crowd,
since they held him as a prophet.

Jesus again spoke to them in parables.
"The sovereignty of heaven is like a king,
who gave a wedding for his son.
He sent his servants to call those invited to the banquet,
and they would not come.
Again he sent other servants saying, 'Tell those invited:
look, I have prepared my luncheon;
my oxen and fattened calves have been butchered,
and everything is ready; come to the banquet.'
But not caring they went off,
one to his field, another to his business;
and the rest seizing his servants insulted and killed them.
The king became angry, and sending his armies
he destroyed those murderers and burned their city.

"Then he said to his servants, 'The banquet is ready,
but those invited were not worthy;
therefore go to the street corners,
and call as many as you find to the banquet.'

Those servants going out into the streets
gathered everyone they found, both bad and good;
and the wedding hall was filled with guests.

  "But coming in to see the guests
the king saw there a person not wearing wedding clothes;
and he said to him, 'Friend,
how did you get in here without having wedding clothes?'
He was silent.

  "Then the king said to the attendants,
'Tying his feet and hands
throw him out into the outer darkness;
there will be the weeping and the gnashing of teeth.'
For many are called, but few are selected."

74
  Then the Pharisees took advice how they might trap him,
and watching carefully they sent to him their disciples
with the Herodians as spies who were pretending to be just
so that they might catch him by a word
in order to give him over
to the rule and authority of the governor.

  Coming they questioned him, "Teacher, we know that
you are honest and do not care about anyone's opinion;
for you do not look at the appearance of people,
but teach truthfully the way of God;
therefore tell us, what do you think?
Is it permitted for us to pay tax to Caesar or not?
Should we pay or shouldn't we?"

  But aware of their cunning malice he said to them,
"Why are you testing me, hypocrites?
Bring me the coin of the tax so that I may see it."

  They brought him a coin.
He said to them, "Whose image and inscription is this?"

  They said, "Caesar's."

  Jesus said to them, "Then pay back
Caesar's things to Caesar and God's things to God."

  They could not catch him by his saying
in the presence of the people,
and marveling at his answer they were silent;

leaving him they went away.

  On that day some of the Sadducees,
who say there is no resurrection,
approaching questioned him, "Teacher, Moses wrote for us
that if someone's brother dies
and leaves behind a wife and no child,
the brother should take his wife
and raise up seed for his brother.
Now there were seven brothers;
the first having taken a wife died childless,
and not having seed he left his wife to his brother;
the second took her, and he died leaving behind no seed;
the third similarly up to the seventh,
and the seven left no seed.
Last of all the woman died too.
In the resurrection then, when they rise again,
whose wife will she be?
For the seven had her as a wife?"

  Jesus answered them,
"Do you not go astray because of this,
not knowing the scriptures or the power of God?
The sons of this age marry and are given in marriage,
but those considered worthy
of attaining that age and the resurrection
neither marry nor are they given in marriage;
for they can no longer die,
but they are like angels in heaven;
they are sons of God being sons of the resurrection.

  "Concerning the dead that they are raised,
even Moses made known at the part about the bush
when God said to him, 'I am the God of Abraham
and the God of Isaac and the God of Jacob.'
He is not God of the dead but of the living;
for to him everyone lives.
You are going far astray."

  Some of the scholars answered, "Teacher, well said."
The Pharisees, hearing that he silenced the Sadducees,
gathered together.

One of the scholars who heard them debating,
aware that he answered them well,
asked him, "What is the foremost of the commandments?"

Jesus answered, "The foremost is: 'Hear, Israel,
the Lord your God is one Lord,
and you shall love the Lord your God
with your whole heart
and with your whole soul
and with your whole intelligence
and with your whole strength.'
The second is like it:
'You shall love your neighbor as yourself.'
On these two commandments
hang the whole law and the prophets."

The scholar said to him, "Beautifully said, teacher,
in truth you say that there is one
and there is no other except him;
and the love for him from the whole heart
and from the whole intelligence
and from the whole strength
and the love for the neighbor as oneself
is more than all the burnt offerings and sacrifices."

Jesus, seeing that he answered intelligently,
said to him, "You are not far from the sovereignty of God."

The Pharisees being gathered together
Jesus questioned them, "What do you think about the Christ?
Whose son is he?"

They said to him, "David's."

He said to them, "How is it then that David himself
said in the Holy Spirit, 'The Lord said to my Lord:
Sit on my right until I put your enemies under your feet.'
If David calls him Lord, then how is he his son?"

No one was able to answer him a word,
nor did anyone dare from that day to question him any more;
but the large crowd listened to him gladly.

75
Then Jesus spoke to the crowd and to his disciples,
"On the seat of Moses sit the scholars and the Pharisees.

Therefore do and keep whatever they tell you,
but do not do according to their actions;
for they talk and do not do.
They burden people with heavy loads hard to bear,
but they themselves are not willing
to move them with their finger.
Watch out for the scholars who devour the houses of widows
and in pretense make long prayers.

"All their actions they do to be seen by people;
for they broaden their phylacteries and lengthen the tassels,
and they love the places of honor at the dinners
and the best seats in the synagogues and walking in robes
and the greetings in the marketplaces
and to be called by people 'Rabbi.'

"But you are not to be called 'Rabbi;'
for one is your teacher, and you are all brothers.
Call no one your father on earth;
for one is your heavenly Father.
Nor be called leaders,
because your leader is one, the Christ.
The greatest of you will be your servant.
Whoever will exalt oneself will be humbled,
and whoever will humble oneself will be exalted.

"But woe to you, scholars and Pharisees, hypocrites,
because you shut the sovereignty of heaven
in front of people;
for you do not enter,
nor do you allow those coming in to enter.

"Woe to you, scholars and Pharisees, hypocrites,
because you go around the sea and the dry land
to make one convert; and when he becomes one,
you make him twice the son of hell you are.

"Woe to you, blind guides who say,
'Whoever swears by the temple, it is nothing;
but whoever swears by the gold of the temple,
he is obligated.'
Fools and blind ones, for which is greater,
the gold or the temple sanctifying the gold?
Also you say, 'Whoever swears by the altar, it is nothing;

but whoever swears by the gift upon it,
he is obligated.'
Blind ones, for which is greater,
the gift or the altar sanctifying the gift?

"Therefore whoever swears by the altar
swears by it and everything on it;
whoever swears by the temple
swears by it and the one dwelling in it;
and whoever swears by heaven
swears by the throne of God and the one sitting on it.

"Woe to you, scholars and Pharisees, hypocrites,
because you tithe mint and dill and cumin,
and have left the weightier part of the law,
justice and mercy and faith;
but these are necessary to do,
and those are not to be left either.
Blind guides, who strain out the gnat,
but swallow the camel.

"Woe to you, scholars and Pharisees, hypocrites,
because you clean the outside of the cup and the dish,
but inside they are full of greed and self-indulgence.
Blind Pharisee, clean first the inside of the cup
so that the outside of it may also be clean.

"Woe to you, scholars and Pharisees, hypocrites,
because you resemble whitewashed tombs,
which outwardly appear pleasant,
but inside they are full of the dead's bones
and everything unclean.
So also you outwardly appear to be just people,
but inside you are full of hypocrisy and lawlessness.

"Woe to you, scholars and Pharisees, hypocrites,
because you build the tombs of the prophets
and adorn the monuments of the just,
and your fathers killed them.
You say, 'If we had been in the days of our fathers,
we would not have participated with them
in the blood of the prophets.'
So you testify against yourselves
that you approve of your fathers' deeds;

for they killed them, and you build their tombs.
Snakes, products of vipers!
How are you to escape from the judgment of hell?

　"For this reason also the wisdom of God said,
'I will send you prophets and the wise and scholars;
some of them you will kill and crucify,
and some of them you will whip in your synagogues
and persecute from town to town;'
so comes upon you all the just blood shed on earth
from the blood of the just Abel
up to the blood of Zacharias, son of Barachiah,
whom you murdered between the sanctuary and the altar.
Amen, I tell you, all these will come upon this generation.

　"Jerusalem, Jerusalem, who kills the prophets
and stones those sent to you,
how often have I wished to gather your children,
the way a bird gathers her young under her wings,
and you were not willing.
Look, your house is forsaken.
For I tell you, you may not see me
until the time comes when you say,
'Praised be the one coming in the name of the Lord.'"

　Sitting opposite the contribution box
he saw how the crowd was putting money into the box;
many rich people put in large amounts;
and one poor widow coming put in two copper coins,
which is a penny.

　Calling to his disciples he said to them,
"Amen, I tell you that this poor widow
has put in more than all those contributing;
for they all put in gifts out of their abundance,
but she out of her need put in everything she had,
her whole living."

76
　As he was going out of the temple,
one of his disciples said to him, "Teacher,
look, what beautiful stones and buildings!"

Jesus said to them, "Do you see these great buildings?
Amen, I tell you, days will come in which
no stone will be left here on a stone
which will not be thrown down."

As he was sitting on the Mount of Olives
opposite the temple,
Peter and James and John and Andrew
questioned him privately, "Tell us,
when will these things be,
and what is the sign
when all these things are about to be accomplished
and of your presence and of the ending of the age?"

Jesus answered them, "See that no one leads you astray.
For many will come in my name saying, 'I am he,'
and 'The time has drawn near;'
and they will lead many astray.
Do not go after them.

"When you hear of wars, rumors of wars, and revolutions,
do not be disturbed;
for it must happen, but it is not yet the end.
For nation will be raised against nation
and sovereignty against sovereignty;
there will be earthquakes
and plagues and famines in various places,
and there will be terrors and great signs from heaven;
but all these things are the beginning of birth pangs.

"But watch yourselves;
before all these things
they will lay their hands on you and persecute you;
they will give you over to councils,
and you will be beaten in synagogues,
and you will stand before governors and kings for my sake,
for testimony to them.

"When they lead you delivering you,
do not worry about what you should say,
but put it into your hearts
not to practice beforehand your defense;
for I will give you a mouth and wisdom,
and whatever is given to you in that hour, speak that;

for it is not you speaking but the Holy Spirit,
which all those opposing you
will not be able to resist or contradict.

"Brother will give over brother to death and father child,
and children will rebel against parents
and put them to death;
and you will be hated by all the nations because of my name.
Many false prophets will be raised
and will lead many astray,
and because of the increase of lawlessness
the love of many will grow cold.

"Yet not a hair of your head will perish;
by your patience you will win your souls.
The one enduring to the end, this one will be saved.
This good message of the sovereignty will be preached
in the whole world as a testimony to all the nations,
and the end will come.

"So when you see the devastating abomination
spoken of through the prophet Daniel
standing in the holy place,
(let the one reading understand,)
and when you see Jerusalem surrounded by armies,
then know that its devastation has drawn near.

"Then let those in Judea flee to the mountains,
and let those in the middle of it depart,
and let those in the country not go into it;
let the one on the roof
not come down to take things out of his house,
and let the one in the field
not turn back to get one's coat;
for these are days of punishment
to fulfill all that has been written.

"Woe to those in pregnancy and nursing in those days,
and pray that your flight not be in winter or on a Sabbath;
for there will be great distress on the earth
and wrath upon this people,
and they will fall by the edge of the sword
and will be led captive to all the nations;
and Jerusalem will be trampled on by nations,

until the seasons of the nations are fulfilled.
  "Those will be days of great affliction,
such as has not occurred
from the beginning of God's creation of the world until now
and which may never happen.
Unless the Lord had not cut short those days,
no flesh would be saved;
but because of the chosen ones he selected,
he will cut short the days.

  "Then if anyone tells you,
'Look, here is the Christ, look there,' do not believe;
for false Christs and false prophets will be raised,
and they will perform miracles and wonders,
in order to lead astray, if possible, even the chosen ones.

  "But you watch; I have foretold you everything.
Days will come when you will long to see
one of the days of the human son,
and you will not see it.
So if they say to you,
'Look, he is in the desert,' do not go out;
'Look, in the inner rooms,' do not pursue it.
For as the lightning flashes out of the east
and shines to the west,
so will be the presence of the human son.

  "After the affliction of those days
the sun will be darkened;
the moon will not give its light;
and the stars will fall from heaven.
There will be signs in sun and moon and stars,
and on the earth anguish of nations in confusion
at the noise of the sea and waves,
people fainting from fear and expectation
of what is coming to the world;
for the powers of heaven will be shaken.

  "Then will appear the sign of the human son in heaven,
and then all the tribes of earth will mourn
and will see the human son coming
in a cloud of heaven with power and much glory.
Then he will send his angels with a great trumpet,

and they will gather his chosen ones out of the four winds
from the end of earth to the end of heaven.
  "As these things begin to happen,
stand up and lift your heads,
because your redemption is drawing near.
From the fig tree learn the parable:
when its branch is already tender and the leaves sprout,
you know that summer is near;
so also when you see all these things happening,
know that it is near at the doors.
Amen, I tell you that this generation may not pass away
until all these things happen.
Heaven and earth will pass away,
but my words will not pass away.

77
  "But about that day and hour no one knows,
neither the angels of heaven nor the son,
but only the Father.
As it was in the days of Noah,
so will be the presence of the human son.
For as they were in those days before the flood
eating and drinking, marrying and giving in marriage,
until the day Noah entered the ark,
and they knew nothing until the flood came and took all;
so also will be the presence of the human son.
  "Similarly as it was in the days of Lot,
they were eating, drinking,
buying, selling, planting, building;
but on the day Lot went away from Sodom,
it rained fire and sulfur from heaven and destroyed all.
It will be the same way
on the day the human son is revealed.
Remember the wife of Lot.
  "Whoever seeks to preserve one's life, will lose it;
and whoever will lose it, will give it life.
I tell you, on that night there will be two in one bed;
one will be taken, and the other will be left.
There will be two in the field;

one is taken, and one is left.
Two will be grinding in the mill;
one is taken, and one is left."

  They asked him, "Where, Lord?"

  He said to them, "Wherever the corpse may be,
there also the eagles will be gathered together.

  "Watch, keep awake;
for you do not know when your Lord is coming.
It is like a person away from home leaving his house
and giving his servants authority, to each his work,
and he commands the doorkeeper to be alert.
Therefore be alert;
for you do not know when the lord of the house is coming,
whether late or at midnight
or at cockcrow or in the morning;
lest coming suddenly he should find you sleeping.

  "What I tell you, I tell everyone: be alert.
Pay attention to yourselves
lest your hearts become burdened
with dissipation and drunkenness and the anxieties of life,
and that day appear to you suddenly like a trap;
for it will come upon everyone
sitting on the face of all the earth.
But be awake in every season
asking that you may be able to escape
all these things that are about to happen,
and be able to stand in front of the human son.

  "Let your loins be girded and your lamps be burning;
and be like people waiting for their lord
to return from the wedding,
so that when he comes and knocks
they may immediately open to him.

  "Blessed are those servants,
whom the lord will find awake when he comes;
amen, I tell you that he will gird himself
and invite them to dine and coming by he will serve them.
If he comes in the second or third watch and finds such,
blessed are those.

"But be aware that if the master of the house
knew at what hour the thief was coming,
he would be alert
and would not have allowed him to break into his house.
For this reason you also be ready,
because in the hour you do not think,
the human son is coming."

Peter said, "Lord,
are you telling this parable to us, or to everyone?"

The Lord said,
"Who then is the faithful, sensible manager,
whom the lord will put in charge of his household
to give out food allowance at the proper time?
Blessed is that servant,
whom his lord will find doing so when he comes;
amen, I tell you that he will
put him in charge of all his possessions.

"But if that servant says in his heart,
'My lord is taking a long time to come,'
and starts to beat his fellow servants,
and to eat and drink with those getting drunk,
the lord of that servant will come
on a day he does not expect and in an hour he is not aware,
and he will cut him in two
and put his part with the unfaithful hypocrites.

"That servant who is aware of his lord's will
and not ready or not doing according to his will
will be beaten much;
but the one who is not aware,
but doing things deserving of blows,
will be beaten a little.
Everyone to whom much was given,
much will be demanded from one;
and whomever was entrusted with much
they will ask one for much more.

"Then the sovereignty of heaven will be like ten virgins,
who taking their lamps
went out to a meeting with the bridegroom.
Five of them were foolish, and five were wise.

For the fools taking their lamps did not take oil with them,
but the wise took oil in flasks with their lamps.
The bridegroom being delayed they all dozed off and slept.

"In the middle of the night there was a shout:
'Look, the bridegroom is going out to a meeting.'
Then all those virgins got up and trimmed their lamps.

"The fools said to the wise, 'Give us some of your oil,
for our lamps are going out.'

"But the wise answered,
'There may not be enough for us and for you;
go instead to those selling and buy for yourselves.'

"While they were going away to buy, the bridegroom came;
and the ones who were ready
went in with him to the wedding,
and the door was shut.
Later the rest of the virgins also came
saying, 'Lord, lord, open for us.'

"But he answered, 'Amen, I tell you, I do not know you.'
Therefore be alert,
for you do not know the day nor the hour.

78

"When the human son comes in his glory
and all the angels with him,
then he will sit on his glorious throne;
all the nations will be gathered before him,
and he will separate them from each other,
as a shepherd separates the sheep from the goats;
he will put the sheep on his right,
and the goats on his left.

"Then the king will say to those on his right,
'Come blessed ones of my Father,
inherit the kingdom prepared for you
from the foundation of the world.
For I was hungry, and you gave me something to eat;
I was thirsty, and you gave me a drink;
I was a stranger, and you welcomed me;
I was naked, and you clothed me;
I was ailing, and you visited me;

I was in prison, and you came to me.'

"Then the just will answer him, 'Lord,
when did we see you hungering and feed you,
or thirsty and give you a drink?
When did we see you a stranger and welcome you,
or naked and clothe you?
When did we see you ailing or in prison and come to you?'

"The king will answer them,
'Amen, I tell you, as you did it
for one of the smallest of these brothers of mine,
you did it for me.'

"Then also he will say to those on the left,
'Go from me cursed ones into the eternal fire
prepared for the devil and his angels.
For I was hungry, and you did not give me anything to eat;
I was thirsty, and you did not give me a drink;
I was a stranger, and you did not welcome me;
I was naked, and you did not clothe me;
I was ailing and in prison, and you did not visit me.'

"Then they also will answer, 'Lord,
when did we see you hungry or thirsty or a stranger
or naked or ailing or in prison and not minister to you?'

"Then he will answer them, 'Amen, I tell you,
as you did not do it for one of the smallest of these,
you did not do it for me.'

"These will go away into eternal punishment,
but the just into eternal life."

79

When Jesus finished all these words,
he said to his disciples,
"You know that after two days the Passover occurs,
and the human son is given over to be crucified."

Then the high priests and the elders of the people
gathered in the court of the high priest called Caiaphas,
and they plotted so that by deceit
they might arrest and kill Jesus;
but they said, "Not at the feast,
lest there be a disturbance among the people."

Some of those going up
to worship at the feast were Greeks;
therefore these approached Philip,
the one from Bethsaida of Galilee,
and they asked him, "Lord, we wish to see Jesus."
Philip went and told Andrew;
Andrew and Philip went and told Jesus.

Jesus answered them, "The hour has come
so that the human son may be glorified.
Amen, amen, I tell you,
unless a grain of wheat falling into the earth dies,
it remains alone;
but if it dies, it bears much fruit.

"Whoever loves one's life loses it,
and whoever hates one's life in this world
will preserve it for eternal life.
If anyone serves me, let him follow me;
and where I am, there also my servant will be;
if anyone serves me, the Father will honor him.

"Now my life has been troubled, and what should I say?
Father, save me from this hour.
But for this reason I came to this hour.
Father, glorify your name."

So a voice came out of heaven:
"I glorified it, and I will glorify it again."

Therefore the crowd standing and hearing
said thunder had occurred;
others said, "An angel has spoken to him."

Jesus answered, "Not for me has this voice occurred,
but for you.
Now is the judgment of this world;
now the ruler of this world will be thrown out;
and if I am lifted from the earth,
I will draw everyone to myself."
He said this signifying what death he was about to die.

Therefore the crowd answered him,
"We heard from the law that the Christ remains forever,
and how is it you say that the human son must be lifted up?
Who is this human son?"

So Jesus said to them,
"For a short time longer the light is among you.
Walk while you have the light, lest darkness overtake you;
and whoever walks in the dark
does not know where one is going.
While you have the light, believe in the light,
so that you may become sons of light.

"If they say to you, 'Where have you come from?'
say to them, 'We have come from the light,
where the light has originated through itself.
It revealed itself in their image.'

"If they say to you, 'Who are you?'
say, 'We are his sons,
and we are the elect of the living Father.'

"If they ask you,
'What is the sign of your Father within you?'
say to them, 'It is a movement and a rest.'

"The images appear to people,
and the light which is within them
is hidden in the image of the light of the Father.
He will manifest himself;
his image is concealed by his light."
Jesus spoke these things,
and going away he was hidden from them.

As many miracles as he had performed before them,
they still did not believe in him,
so that the word of Isaiah the prophet might be fulfilled:

"Lord, who has believed our report?
and to whom has the arm of the Lord been revealed?"

For this reason they could not believe,
for again Isaiah said,

"He has blinded their eyes and hardened their heart,
lest they should see with their eyes
and understand with their heart
and turn, and I would cure them."

These things Isaiah said because he saw his glory,
and he spoke about him.

Nevertheless even many of the rulers believed in him,
but because of the Pharisees they did not admit it,

lest they be put out of the synagogue;
for they loved human glory more than the glory of God.
  Jesus shouted, "Whoever believes in me
does not believe in me but in the one who sent me,
and whoever sees me sees the one who sent me.
I have come as light into the world,
so that everyone who believes in me
may not remain in the dark.
  "If anyone hears my sayings and does not keep them,
I do not judge him;
for I did not come so that I might judge the world,
but so that I might save the world.
Whoever rejects me and does not accept my sayings
has judging him the word which I have spoken;
that will judge him on the last day.
  "For I have not spoken from myself,
but the Father who sent me he has given me commands
what I should say and what I should speak.
I know that his command is eternal life.
Therefore what I speak is just as the Father has said to me;
that I speak."

80
  While he was in Bethany in the home of Simon the leper,
they made a dinner for him there;
Martha served, and Lazarus was one of those dining with him.
  As he was sitting,
Mary took a pound of expensive genuine nard perfume
and breaking the alabaster flask
she poured it on his head and anointed the feet of Jesus
and wiped off his feet with her hair;
and the house was filled with the odor of the perfume.
  Some of the disciples seeing
were angry saying to themselves,
"Why has this waste of the perfume happened?"
  Judas Iscariot, one of his disciples,
who was about to give him over, said,
"Why was this perfume not sold
for three hundred days' wages

and given to the poor?"
He said this not because he cared about the poor,
but because he was a thief
and having the money box
he used to lift what was put into it.

But Jesus said, "Let her go; why are you bothering her?
She did a beautiful thing for me;
for you have the poor with you all the time,
and whenever you wish, you can do good for them;
but me you do not have all the time.
What she had she did;
beforehand she has anointed my body for burial.
Amen, I tell you,
wherever this good message is preached in the whole world,
what she did will also be spoken in memory of her."

So a large crowd of Jews became aware that he was there,
and they came not because of Jesus alone,
but so that they might also see Lazarus
whom he raised from the dead.
The high priests decided that they should kill Lazarus too,
because many of the Jews went because of him
and believed in Jesus.

Then Judas Iscariot, one of the twelve,
going to the high priests
said, "What are you willing to give me,
if I give him over to you?"

Hearing they were glad
and promised to give him thirty silver coins.
He consented,
and from then on he looked for an opportunity
to give him over to them apart from the crowd.

81

On the first day of unleavened bread,
when they sacrifice the Passover lamb,
he sent Peter and John, saying,
"Go prepare for us the Passover, so that we may eat."

They asked him, "Where do you wish us to prepare it?"

He said to them, "As you are entering the city,
you will meet a person carrying a jar of water;
you will follow him to the house that he enters,
and you will tell the master of the house
that the teacher says, 'Where is the guest room
where I may eat the Passover with my disciples?'
That one will show you a large upper room already furnished;
there prepare for us."
   The disciples went out and came into the city
and found it as he had told them,
and they prepared the Passover.
   Evening coming he arrived with the twelve disciples.
He said to them, "With longing I have desired
to eat this Passover with you before my suffering;
for I tell you that I will not eat it any more
until it is fulfilled in the sovereignty of God."
   Also a competition occurred among them,
which of them was considered to be greater.
He said to them,
"The kings of the nations lord it over them,
and those having authority over them are called benefactors.
But let it not be so with you,
rather let the greater among you become like the younger,
and the governing like the serving.
For who is greater, the one dining or the one serving?
Is it not the one dining?
But I in the middle of you am like one serving.
   "You are the ones remaining with me during my tests;
and I confer upon you
as my Father conferred upon me a sovereignty,
so that you may eat and drink at my table in my sovereignty,
and you will sit on thrones
judging the twelve tribes of Israel."
   At the Passover feast, Jesus aware that his hour had come
to pass over from this world to the Father,
having loved his own in the world,
he loved them to the end.
   During dinner, as the devil had already
put into the heart of Judas Iscariot, son of Simon,

that he should give him over,
aware that the Father had given all things into his hands,
and that he came out from the Father and goes to the Father,
he rose from the dinner and put aside his clothes,
and taking a towel he wrapped it around his waist;
next he poured water into a basin,
and he began to wash the feet of the disciples
and wipe them off with the towel
which was wrapped around him.

So he came to Simon Peter;
he said to him, "Lord, do you wash my feet?"

Jesus answered him, "What I am doing
you do not understand now, but you will afterward."

Peter said to him, "You shall never wash my feet."

Jesus answered him, "Unless I wash you,
you have no part with me."

Simon Peter said to him, "Lord, not only my feet,
but also my hands and head."

Jesus said to him, "One who has bathed
has no need to wash except for the feet,
but he is completely clean;
and you are clean, but not everyone."
For he knew who was giving him over;
for this reason he said, "You are not all clean."

So when he had washed their feet
and taken his clothes and sat down again,
he said to them, "Do you know what I have done for you?
You call me 'Teacher' and 'Lord,'
and you are right; for I am.
Therefore if I, Lord and teacher, washed your feet,
you also ought to wash each other's feet;
for I gave you an example
so that as I have done for you, you also should do.
Amen, amen, I tell you, no servant is greater than his lord,
nor is the messenger greater than the one sending him.
If you know these things, you are blessed if you do them.

"I am not talking about everyone;
I know those I have selected;
but so that scripture may be fulfilled:

'The one eating my bread
has lifted his heel against me.'
I am telling you now before the occurrence,
so that you may believe when it occurs that I am he.
  "Amen, amen, I tell you,
whoever accepts anyone I may send accepts me,
and whoever accepts me accepts the one who sent me."

82
  Saying these things as they were sitting and eating,
Jesus was troubled in the spirit and said,
"Amen, I tell you that one of you will give me over,
one who is eating with me."
  The disciples looked at each other
uncertain about whom he meant.
One of his disciples, whom Jesus loved,
was sitting by the chest of Jesus;
so Simon Peter nodded to this disciple
and said to him, "Ask who it is he means."
  That disciple leaning thus on Jesus's chest
said to him, "Lord, who is it?"
  Becoming very sad
each one began to say to him, "Is it I, Lord?"
  Jesus answered,
"The one who is dipping his hand with me in the dish,
he will give me over.
The human son is going as it has been written about him,
but woe to that person through whom
the human son is given over;
it would have been better for him
if that person had not been born."
  Dipping the piece of bread
was Judas Iscariot, son of Simon,
and after the piece of bread
then Satan entered into that one.
Judas, the one giving him over, answered, "Is it I, Rabbi?"
  Jesus said to him, "You said it;
what you are doing do quickly."

But none of those dining knew why he told him this;
for some thought, since Judas had the money box,
that Jesus was telling him, "Buy what we need for the feast,"
or that he should give something to the poor.
Taking the piece of bread that one went out immediately;
it was night.

When he went out, Jesus said,
"Now the human son is glorified,
and God is glorified in him;
God will both glorify him in himself,
and will immediately glorify him.
Children, for a little while I am still with you;
you will search for me,
and just as I told the Jews
that where I am going you cannot come,
I say it also to you now.

"I give you a new commandment, that you love each other;
as I have loved you, so also you love each other.
By this everyone will know that you are my disciples,
if you have love for each other."

As they were eating, taking bread and blessing it
he broke it and gave it to the disciples,
saying, "Take it, eat; this is my body."
Taking a cup and giving thanks he gave it to them,
saying, "Take this and share it among yourselves;"
and they all drank from it.
He said to them, "This is my blood of the covenant
which is shed on behalf of many for the release of sins.
Do this in remembrance of me.
Amen, I tell you that
I will not drink any more from the fruit of the vine
until that day when I drink it anew
with you in the sovereignty of God.

83
"Do not let your heart be troubled;
trust in God, and trust in me.
In my Father's house are many rooms;
if not, I would have told you;

for I am going to prepare a place for you;
and if I go and prepare a place for you,
I will come again and welcome you to myself,
so that where I am you may be also.
Where I am going you know the way."

   Thomas said to him, "Lord,
we don't know where you are going;
how can we know the way?"

   Jesus said to him, "I am the way and the truth and life;
no one comes to the Father except through me.
If you had known me, you also would have known my Father.
From now on you know him and have seen him."

   Philip said to him, "Lord, show us the Father,
and it is enough for us."

   Jesus said to him, "So long have I been with you
and have you not known me, Philip?
Whoever has seen me has seen the Father;
how can you say, 'Show us the Father'?
Do you not believe that I am in the Father
and the Father is in me?
The sayings which I tell you I do not speak from myself;
but the Father living in me does his works.
Believe me that I am in the Father and the Father in me;
or else believe because of the works themselves.

   "Amen, amen, I tell you, whoever believes in me
the works which I do that one also will do,
and one will do greater than these,
because I am going to the Father;
whatever you ask for in my name, this I will do,
so that the Father may be glorified by the son.
If you ask me for anything in my name, I will do it.

   "If you love me, keep my commandments.
I will ask the Father,
and he will give you another intermediary,
so that he may be with you forever, the spirit of truth,
which the world cannot accept,
because it neither sees it nor knows it;
you know it, because it stays with you and will be in you.

"I will not leave you orphans; I am coming to you.
A little while and the world no longer sees me,
but you see me, because I live and you will live.
On that day you will know that I am in the Father
and you are in me and I in you.

"Whoever has my commandments and keeps them,
that one is the one loving me;
and whoever loves me will be loved by my Father,
and I will love him and will reveal myself to him."

Judas (not Iscariot) said to him, "Lord,
but what has happened
that you are about to reveal yourself to us
and not to the world?"

Jesus answered him, "If someone loves me,
he will keep my word;
and my Father will love him,
and we will come to him and make our home with him.
Whoever does not love me does not keep my words;
and the word which you hear is not mine
but the Father's who sent me.

"These things I have spoken to you remaining with you;
the intermediary, the Holy Spirit
which the Father will send in my name,
that one will teach you everything
and remind you of everything I told you.

"Peace I leave with you; my peace I give you;
not as the world gives do I give to you.
Do not let your heart be troubled nor timid.
You heard that I told you,
'I am going and am coming to you.'
If you loved me,
you would be glad that I am going to the Father,
for the Father is greater than I.

"Now I have told you before it happens,
so that when it happens you may believe.
I will not speak much longer with you,
for the ruler of the world is coming;
he has nothing on me,
but so that the world may know that I love the Father,

and as the Father commands me, thus I do.

84
 "I am the true vine, and my Father is the farmer.
Every branch in me not bearing fruit, he removes it;
and every branch bearing fruit,
he cleans so that it may bear more fruit.
You are already clean
because of the word which I have spoken to you;
remain in me, and I in you.
As the branch cannot bear fruit from itself
unless it remains on the vine,
so neither can you unless you remain in me.
 "I am the vine, you the branches.
The one remaining in me and I in him,
this one bears much fruit,
for without me you cannot do anything.
If someone does not remain in me,
he is thrown out like the branch and dried out;
and they gather them and throw them into the fire,
and they are burned.
If you remain in me and my sayings remain in you,
ask for whatever you wish, and it will happen to you.
By this my Father is glorified, that you bear much fruit
and you will be my disciples.
 "As the Father loved me, I also loved you;
remain in my love.
If you will keep my commandments,
you will remain in my love,
as I have kept my Father's commandments
and I remain in his love.
These things I have spoken to you
so that my joy may be in you,
and your joy may be fulfilled.
This is my commandment,
that you love each other as I loved you.
 "No one has greater love than the one,
who lays down one's life on behalf of one's friends.
You are my friends, if you do what I command you.

I no longer call you servants,
for the servant does not know what his lord does;
but I have called you friends,
because everything I heard from my Father
I made known to you.
You did not select me, but I selected you;
and I have appointed you so that you may go and bear fruit,
and your fruit may remain,
that whatever you ask the Father for in my name
he may give you.

"This I command you, that you love each other.
If the world hates you,
know that it has hated me before you.
If you were from the world,
the world would have loved its own;
but you are not from the world,
because I selected you out of the world;
for this reason the world hates you.

"Remember the word which I told you:
a servant is not greater than his lord.
If they persecuted me, they will also persecute you;
if they kept my word, they will also keep yours.
But they will do all these things to you because of my name,
for they do not know who sent me.
If I had not come and spoken to them,
they would not have sin;
but now they have no excuse for their sin.
Whoever hates me also hates my Father.
If I had not done works among them
which no other person did,
they would not have sin,
but now they have both seen and hated
both me and my Father.
But it is so that the word written in their law
may be fulfilled:
    'They hated me without reason.'
"When the intermediary comes
whom I will send to you from the Father,
the spirit of truth which proceeds out from the Father,

that one will testify about me;
and you also will testify,
because you have been with me from the beginning.

85
"I have spoken these things to you
so that you may not fall away.
They will make you excommunicated;
but the hour is coming when everyone who kills you
may think he is offering a service to God.
They will do these things
because they do not know the Father or me.
But I have spoken these things to you
so that when their hour comes you may remember them,
what I told you.

"I did not tell you these things from the beginning,
because I was with you.
But now I am going to the one who sent me,
and none of you asks me, 'Where are you going?'
But because I have spoken these things to you,
grief has filled your heart.

"But I tell you the truth;
it is to your advantage that I should go away.
For unless I go away, the intermediary may not come to you;
but if I go, I will send it to you.
That one coming will correct the world
concerning sin and justice and judgment:
concerning sin, because they did not believe in me;
concerning justice, because I am going to the Father
and you will see me no more;
and concerning judgment,
because the ruler of this world has been judged.

"I still have many things to tell you,
but you cannot bear them now;
but when that one comes, the spirit of truth,
it will guide you into all truth;
for it will not speak from itself,
but whatever it hears it will speak;
and it will report to you what is coming.

That one will glorify me,
because it will receive from me and report to you.
Everything which the Father has is mine;
for this reason I said
that it receives from me and will report to you.
A little while and you will no longer see me,
and a little while again and you will see me."

So some of his disciples said to each other,
"What is this he tells us:
'A little while and you will not see me,
and a little while again and you will see me'?
and 'Because I am going to the Father'?"

So they said, "What is this he says, 'A little while'?
We don't understand what he is saying."

Jesus knew that they wished to ask him,
and he said to them,
"Concerning this are you searching with each other
because I said, 'A little while and you will not see me,
and a little while and you will see me'?
Amen, amen, I tell you that you will weep and mourn,
and the world will rejoice;
you will be grieved, but your grief will turn into joy.

"The woman when she gives birth has grief,
because her hour has come;
but when the child is born,
she no longer remembers the pain
because of the joy that a person was born into the world.

"You therefore now have grief;
but I will see you again, and your heart will rejoice,
and no one can take your joy away from you.

"On that day you will not ask me anything.
Amen, amen, I tell you, whatever you ask the Father
he will give you in my name.
Until now you have not asked for anything in my name;
ask, and you will receive, so that your joy may be filled.
I have spoken these things to you in allegories;
an hour is coming
when I will no longer speak to you in allegories,
but I will announce to you openly about the Father.

"On that day you will ask in my name,
and I am not saying that I will ask the Father about you;
for the Father himself loves you,
because you have loved me
and have believed that I came from God.
I came out of the Father and have come into the world;
again I am leaving the world and going to the Father."

His disciples said, "Look, now you are speaking openly,
and you are telling no allegory.
Now we understand that you know everything
and have no need for anyone to question you;
by this we believe that you came from God."

Jesus answered them, "Do you now believe?
Look, an hour is coming and has come
when you will be scattered each to his own things,
and you will leave me alone;
yet I am not alone, for the Father is with me.
I have spoken these things to you
so that in me you may have peace.
In the world you have affliction;
but courage! I have overcome the world."

86
Jesus spoke these things, and lifting his eyes to heaven
he said, "Father, the hour has come;
glorify your son, so that the son may glorify you,
as you gave him authority over all flesh,
so that everyone you have given to him
he may give to them eternal life.
This is eternal life,
that they may know you, the only true God,
and whom you sent, Jesus Christ.

"I glorified you on earth,
completing the work which you have given me to do;
and now you glorify me, Father, with yourself
with the glory I had with you before the world existed.

"I revealed your name
to the people you gave me out of the world.
Yours they were and to me you gave them,

and they have kept your word.
Now they know that everything you gave me was from you,
because the sayings you gave me I have given to them;
they accepted them, and truly know that I came from you;
and they have believed that you sent me.

"I ask about them; I do not ask about the world,
but about those you have given me, because they are yours;
all mine are yours, and yours are mine,
and I have been glorified in them.
I am no longer in the world;
yet they are in the world,
and I am coming to you.
Holy Father, keep them in your name
which you have given me,
so that they may be one as we are.

"When I was with them,
I kept them in your name which you have given me;
I guarded them, and none of them was lost
except the son of destruction,
so that the scripture might be fulfilled.

"But now I am coming to you,
and I speak these things in the world
so that they may have my joy fulfilled within themselves
I have given them your word,
and the world hated them, because they are not of the world
just as I am not of the world.

"I do not ask that you take them out of the world,
but that you keep them out of evil.
They are not of the world just as I am not of the world.
Sanctify them in the truth; your word is truth.
Just as you sent me into the world,
I also sent them into the world;
and on their behalf I sanctify myself,
so that they also may be sanctified in truth.

"But I do not ask only about these,
but also about those believing in me because of their word,
so that everyone may be one,
just as you, Father, are in me and I in you,
that they also may be in us,

so that the world may believe that you sent me.
I have given to them the glory which you have given to me,
so that they may be one just as we are one:
I in them and you in me,
so that they may be perfected into one,
that the world may know that you sent me
and loved them just as you loved me.
   "Father, what you have given to me,
I wish that where I am those also may be with me,
so that they may see my glory, which you have given me
because you loved me before the foundation of the world.
Just Father, even the world did not know you,
but I know you, and these know that you sent me;
I made known your name to them and will make it known,
so that the love with which you loved me
may be in them and I in them.
Rise, let us go from here."

87

   Having sung a hymn they went out to the Mount of Olives.
Then Jesus said to them,
"You will all fall away from me on this night;
for it has been written:
   'I will strike the shepherd,
   and the sheep of the flock will be scattered.'
But after I am raised, I will lead you to Galilee."
   Simon Peter asked him, "Lord, where are you going?"
   Jesus answered, "Where I am going
you cannot follow me now, but you will follow later."
   Peter said to him, "Lord, why can't I follow you now?
Even if everyone falls away from you, yet I will not."
   Jesus said to him, "Amen, I tell you
that today on this night before the cock crows
you will deny knowing me three times."
   Peter spoke with greater emphasis,
"Even if I must die with you, I will not deny you."
All the disciples said the same thing.
   Jesus said, "Simon, Simon, look,
Satan demanded to sift you like wheat;

but I begged for you so that your faith might not fail;
and when you have returned, support your brothers."
  He said to them,
"When I sent you without purse and wallet and sandals,
were you lacking anything?"
  They said, "Nothing."
  He said to them, "But now
whoever has a purse let him take it, likewise also a wallet,
and whoever does not have one
let him sell his clothes and buy a sword.
For I tell you
that what has been written must be completed in me:
    'And he was counted with transgressors;'
for the thing about me has an end."
  They said, "Lord, look, here are two swords."
  He said to them, "It is sufficient."

  Across the ravine of Kidron
they came to a garden called Gethsemane,
and he said to his disciples,
"Sit here while I go over there to pray."
  Taking along Peter and James and John with him
he began to be sad and anxious.
Then he said to them, "My soul is sorrowful till death;
stay here and keep awake with me.
Pray not to enter into temptation."
  Going forward about a stone's throw away from them
he fell upon the ground and prayed
that if it was possible the hour might pass away from him,
saying, "Abba, Father, all things are possible with you;
if you choose, remove this cup from me;
nevertheless, not what I will, but let your will be done."
  He came to his disciples
and found them sleeping from the sorrow,
and he said to Peter, "Simon, are you asleep?
Were you not able to keep awake with me for one hour?
Keep awake; stand up and pray,
lest you enter into temptation;
the spirit is eager, but the flesh is weak."

Going away again a second time he prayed saying,
"My Father, if this cannot pass away unless I drink it,
let your will be done."

Coming again he found them sleeping,
for their eyes were weighed down,
and they did not know what they should answer him.

Leaving them again he went away and prayed a third time,
saying the same word again.
An angel from heaven appeared to him strengthening him.
Being in agony he prayed more fervently,
and his sweat was like drops of blood
falling down upon the ground.

Standing up from the prayer he came to his disciples
and said to them, "Sleep the remainder and rest up;
it is enough; the hour has come;
look, the human son is given over into the hands of sinners.
Rise, let us go;
look, the one giving me over has drawn near."

88
As he was still speaking,
Judas, one of the twelve, arrived;
he also knew the place,
for often Jesus met there with his disciples.
Judas taking the cohort
and officials from the high priests and Pharisees
had with him a large crowd
with torches and lanterns and swords and clubs.

The one giving him over had given them a signal
saying, "Whomever I kiss is he;
seize him and lead him away securely."

So Jesus aware of everything that was coming upon him
went out and said to them, "Who are you looking for?"

They answered him, "Jesus the Nazarene."

He said to them, "I am he."

Judas, the one giving him over also stood with them.
So when he told him, "I am he,"
they went back and fell on the ground.
Judas drew near to Jesus to kiss him,

but Jesus said to him, "Judas,
do you give over the human son with a kiss?"
    Immediately approaching Jesus
he said, "Hello, Rabbi," and kissed him.
    Jesus said to him, "Comrade, what have you come for?"
    Then approaching
they laid their hands on Jesus and seized him.
So again he questioned them, "Who are you looking for?"
    They said, "Jesus the Nazarene."
    Jesus answered, "I told you that I am he;
therefore if you are looking for me, allow these to go;"
so that the word which he said might be fulfilled:
"Those you gave me, I have not lost any of them."
    Those around him seeing what was going to happen
said, "Lord, shall we strike with a sword?"
    Simon Peter having a sword drew it
and struck the high priest's servant
and cut off his right ear;
the name of the servant was Malchus.
    Jesus said to Peter, "No more of this!
Put the sword into the sheath;
for all who take a sword will die by a sword.
Or do you think that I cannot appeal to my Father,
and he will provide me now
with more than twelve legions of angels?
Then how may the scriptures be fulfilled
that it must happen like this?
The cup which the Father has given to me,
shall I not drink it?"
    Touching the ear of the servant he cured him.
Jesus said to the high priests and officers of the temple
and elders who had come against him,
"As against a robber
have you come out with swords and clubs to arrest me?
I was with you every day teaching in the temple,
and you did not reach out your hands
against me and seize me;
but this is your hour and the authority of darkness.
This whole thing has happened

so that the scriptures of the prophets may be fulfilled."
  Then leaving him, all the disciples fled.
A certain youth accompanied him
wearing a tunic over his nakedness,
and they seized him;
and leaving behind the tunic he fled naked.

89
  So the cohort and the commander
and the officials of the Jews
arrested Jesus and bound him,
and they led him to Annas first;
for he was the father-in-law of Caiaphas,
who was high priest that year;
Caiaphas was the one who had advised the Jews
that it was advantageous for one person to die
on behalf of the people.
  The high priest asked Jesus about his disciples
and about his teaching.
  Jesus answered him, "I have spoken clearly to the world;
all the time I taught in synagogues and in the temple,
where all the Jews come together,
and in secret I spoke nothing.
Why are you asking me?
Ask those who have heard what I have spoken to them;
look, these people know what I said."
  As he was saying these things,
one of the officials standing by gave Jesus a slap
saying, "Do you answer the high priest so?"
  Jesus answered him, "If I have spoken wrongly,
testify about the wrong;
but if I have spoken correctly, why do you hit me?"
So Annas sent him bound to Caiaphas, the high priest.
  The ones who had seized Jesus led him away
and brought him into the house of the high priest,
where all the high priests and the elders and the scholars
were assembled.
  Simon Peter and another disciple
followed Jesus from a distance.

That disciple was known to the high priest,
and he entered with Jesus
into the courtyard of the high priest,
and Peter stood at the door outside.
So the other disciple who was known to the high priest
went out and told the doorkeeper, and brought in Peter.
Entering inside he was sitting with the attendants
and warming himself by the fire to see the end.

The high priests and the whole council
were looking for testimony against Jesus
to put him to death,
and they did not find any;
though many falsely testified against him,
the testimonies did not agree.

But later two coming forward said, "This one said,
'I will tear down this handmade temple of God,
and in three days I will build another not handmade.'"
Even this testimony of theirs did not agree.

Standing up in the middle the high priest
questioned Jesus, "Are you not going to answer anything
of what these are testifying against you?"

But he was silent and did not answer anything.

Again the high priest questioned him,
"I adjure you by the living God that you should tell us
if you are the Christ, the son of God."

Jesus said, "If I tell you, you will not believe;
and if I were to question you, you would not answer.
But from now on you will see the human son
sitting at the right hand of power
and coming on the clouds of heaven."

They all said, "Then are you the son of God?"

He said to them, "You are saying that I am."
Then the high priest ripped his clothes
and said, "He blasphemed!
What need have we of any more witnesses?
Now you have heard the blasphemy from his mouth.
What does it look like to you?"

They all condemned him to be deserving of death.
Then the men holding him

began to spit in his face and beat him,
and they mocked him covering his face and slapping him
saying, "Prophesy to us, Christ;
who is the one who struck you?"

90
  The servants and attendants had kindled a fire
in the middle of the courtyard, because it was cold,
and standing they were warming themselves;
Peter was also standing with them and warming himself.
The doorkeeper seeing him sitting by the light
and staring at him said, "Are you not also
one of the disciples of the Nazarene Jesus?"
  But he denied it saying,
"I don't know nor understand what you mean, woman."
  He went outside into the forecourt,
and after a short while another saw him
and said to those standing by, "This one is one of them."
  But Peter denied it again saying, "Man, I am not."
  After about one hour intervened
another servant of the high priest,
who was a relative of the one whose ear Peter cut off,
said, "Didn't I see you in the garden with him?"
And he insisted saying,
"Upon the truth you are also one of them,
for you are also a Galilean;
even your speech makes it clear."
  Then Peter began to curse and swear,
"I don't know this person you mean."
Immediately while he was speaking, the cock crowed.
  The Lord turning looked at Peter,
and Peter remembered the saying as Jesus had told him,
"Before the cock crows today you will deny me three times."
Going outside he broke down and wept bitterly.
  Early in the morning
all the high priests with the scholars
and the elders of the people and the whole council
formed a plan against Jesus in order to put him to death;
and having bound him they led him away

and gave him over to Pilate, the governor.

Then Judas, who had given him over,
seeing that he was condemned,
regretted it and returned the thirty silver coins
to the high priests and elders
saying, "I sinned giving over innocent blood."

They said, "What is that to us? You see to it."

Throwing the silver into the temple he withdrew,
and going away he hanged himself.

But the high priests taking the silver
said, "It is not permitted to put this into the treasury,
since it is the price of blood."

Forming a plan they bought with it
the potter's field for the burial of foreigners.
This is why that field
has been called the field of blood to this day.
Then was fulfilled
what was spoken through Jeremiah the prophet:

> "And they took the thirty silver coins,
> the price of him on whom a price had been set
> by some of the sons of Israel,
> and they gave them for a potter's field,
> as the Lord directed me."

91

So they led Jesus from Caiaphas to the praetorium;
it was early morning,
and they did not enter the praetorium,
so that they might not be defiled
but might eat the Passover.

Therefore Pilate went outside to them and said,
"What accusation are you bringing against this person?"

They answered him, "If he were not doing evil,
we would not have given him over to you;"
and they began to accuse him,
"We found this one perverting our nation
and forbidding us to pay taxes to Caesar,
and saying that he himself is Christ a king."

Pilate said to them, "You take him,
and judge him according to your law."

The Jews said to him,
"It is not permitted for us to kill anyone;"
so that the word of Jesus might be fulfilled
which he said signifying by what death he was about to die.

So Pilate went back into the praetorium and called Jesus
and asked him, "Are you the king of the Jews?"

Jesus answered, "You say it.
Do you say this from yourself,
or did others tell you about me?"

Pilate answered, "Am I a Jew?
Your nation and the high priests gave you over to me;
what did you do?"

Jesus answered, "My sovereignty is not of this world;
if my sovereignty were of this world,
my attendants would have fought,
so that I might not be given over to the Jews;
but now my sovereignty is not from here."

Therefore Pilate asked him, "So are you a king?"

Jesus answered, "You say that I am a king.
I have been born for this
and for this I have come into the world,
so that I might testify to the truth;
everyone who is of the truth hears my voice."

Pilate said to him, "What is truth?"
Having said this he went out again to the Jews,
and he said to them, "I find no guilt in this person."

But they insisted saying, "He stirs up the people,
teaching throughout all Judea,
beginning from Galilee even up to here."

When he was accused by the high priests and elders,
he did not answer at all.

Then Pilate questioned him again,
"Are you not answering anything?
Don't you hear how many things
they are testifying against you?"

Jesus did not answer him with even one word,
so that the governor really wondered.

Pilate having heard the Jews,
questioned if the person was Galilean,
and discovering that he was under the authority of Herod,
he sent him up to Herod,
as he was also in Jerusalem during these days.

Seeing Jesus, Herod was very glad;
for he had been wanting to see him for a long time
because he had heard about him,
and he hoped to see some miracle performed by him.
He questioned him with considerable words;
but he did not answer anything.

The high priests and the scholars stood
accusing him vehemently.
Herod with his soldiers having despised him and mocked him,
dressing him in bright garments
they sent him back to Pilate.
Herod and Pilate became friends with each other on that day;
for previously they had been at enmity with each other.

92
Pilate calling together
the high priests and the rulers of the people said to them,
"You brought me this person as one alienating the people,
and look, I having examined him before you
found nothing in this person guilty
of what you accuse against him.
Neither has Herod, for he sent him back to us.
Look, nothing has been done by him that is worthy of death;
therefore disciplining him I will release him."

At the feast he released to them
one prisoner whom they requested.
They had then a notorious prisoner called Barabbas,
who had committed murder in a rebellion in the city
and was thrown into prison with the rebels.
The crowd going up began to request
that he do it for them as usual.

Pilate answered them, "It is your custom
that I should release one to you at the Passover;
therefore will you choose
that I may release to you Barabbas
or Jesus the one called Christ, the king of the Jews?"
For he knew that the high priests
had given him over because of envy.

As he was sitting on the judicial bench,
his wife sent to him saying,
"Have nothing to do with that just person,
for I suffered many things today in a dream because of him."

But the high priests and the elders persuaded the crowds
that they should request Barabbas and destroy Jesus.

The governor answered them,
"Which of the two do you want me to release to you?"

But they altogether shouted, "Take this one,
and release to us Barabbas."

Pilate again answered them,
"Then what should I do with Jesus called Christ
whom you call king of the Jews?"

They shouted, "Crucify him!"

So then Pilate took Jesus and whipped him.
The soldiers having woven a crown out of thorns
put it on his head, and dressed him in a purple robe,
and came to him and said, "Hail, king of the Jews;"
and they gave him slaps.

Pilate went outside again and said to them,
"Look, I am bringing him out to you,
so that you may know that I find no guilt in him."
So Jesus came outside,
wearing the thorn crown and the purple robe.
He said to them, "Look, the person."

So when the high priests and the assistants saw him,
they shouted, "Crucify, crucify!"

A third time Pilate said to them,
"Then what evil has this one done?
I found nothing deserving of death in him;
therefore having disciplined him I will release him."

Even more they shouted, "Crucify him!"

Pilate said to them, "You take him and crucify him,
for I find no guilt in him."

The Jews answered him, "We have a law,
and according to the law he ought to die;
for he made himself son of God."

So when Pilate heard this word, he was even more afraid;
he went back into the praetorium
and said to Jesus, "Where are you from?"

But Jesus did not give him an answer.

So Pilate said to him, "Aren't you speaking to me?
Don't you know that I have authority to release you
and I have authority to crucify you?"

Jesus answered, "You do not have any authority against me
unless it has been given to you from above;
for this reason the one who gave me over to you
has a greater sin."

From this, Pilate tried to release him;
but the Jews shouted, "If you release this one,
you are not a friend of Caesar;
everyone who makes oneself king speaks against Caesar."

So Pilate having heard these words brought Jesus outside,
and he sat on the judicial bench
in a place called Stone Pavement, and in Hebrew Gabbatha.
It was the preparation day of the Passover,
about the sixth hour;
he said to the Jews, "Look, your king."

So those shouted, "Take him; take him; crucify him!"

Pilate said to them, "Shall I crucify your king?"

The high priests answered,
"We have no king except Caesar."
They insisted with loud voices, and their voices prevailed.

Pilate seeing that nothing was helping
but instead an uproar was occurring,
taking water washed his hands in front of the crowd
saying, "I am innocent of this blood; you see to it."

All the people answered,
"His blood be on us and on our children."

Pilate choosing to satisfy the crowd
released to them Barabbas,
who had been thrown into prison
because of rebellion and murder,
and having whipped Jesus
he gave him over to be crucified.

93
Then soldiers of the governor
took Jesus into the praetorium,
and calling together the whole cohort
they gathered around him.
Having dressed him in purple with the thorn crown on him,
they put a reed in his right hand,
and kneeling they worshipped him
and began to salute him, "Hail, king of the Jews!"
Spitting on him they took the reed and beat his head.
When they had mocked him,
they took the purple off him and dressed him in his clothes,
and they led him away to crucify him.
They enlisted passing by Simon, a Cyrenian,
coming from the country, the father of Alexander and Rufus.
Grabbing him they put the cross on him
to carry it behind Jesus.
A large number of the people followed him
and women who mourned and lamented him.
Turning to them Jesus said, "Daughters of Jerusalem,
do not weep for me;
but weep for yourselves and for your children,
for days come on which they will say,
'Blessed are the barren,
and the wombs that have not borne,
and breasts that have not nursed!'
Then they will begin to say to the mountains, 'Fall on us,'
and to the hills, 'Cover us;'
for if they do these things when the wood is green,
what will happen when it is dry?"
Also two different criminals were led with him
to be executed.

They brought him to a place called Golgotha,
which translated means the place of the skull.
They gave him myrrh-flavored wine mixed with gall to drink,
but tasting it he would not drink it.

There they crucified him and with him the two robbers,
one on his right and one on his left,
and in the middle Jesus.

Jesus said, "Father, forgive them;
for they do not know what they are doing."

It was the third hour when they crucified him.
Pilate also wrote a title and put it on the cross,
and the inscription of the charge
written above his head was:
THE KING OF THE JEWS.
Therefore many of the Jews read this title,
for the place where Jesus was crucified was near the city;
and it was written in Hebrew, Latin, and Greek.

Therefore the high priests of the Jews said to Pilate,
"Do not write, 'The king of the Jews,'
but that that one said, 'I am king of the Jews.'"

Pilate answered, "What I have written, I have written."

The soldiers, when they crucified Jesus,
took his clothes and made four parts,
to each soldier a part, and the tunic.
But the tunic was seamless, woven from the top throughout.

So they said to each other, "Let us not split it,
but decide about it by lot whose it shall be;"
that the scripture might be fulfilled:

> "They divided my clothes themselves
> and over my robe they threw lots."

The soldiers did these things,
and sitting they kept watch over him there.
The people stood watching,
and those passing by reviled him shaking their heads
and saying, "Ah, the one tearing down the temple
and building it in three days!
Save yourself, if you are the son of God,
and come down from the cross."

Likewise also the high priests
mocking with the scholars and elders
said, "He saved others; he cannot save himself;
let the Christ, the king of Israel,
come down now from the cross,
so that we may see and believe in him.
He has trusted in God;
let him rescue him now if he wants him;
for he said, 'I am God's son.'"

The soldiers approaching also mocked him saying,
"If you are the king of the Jews, save yourself."

One of the criminals crucified with him also insulted him
and reviled him, "Are you not the Christ?
Save yourself and us."

But the other answering
reproached him, "Do you not fear God,
for you are under the same verdict?
And we justly, for we did things deserving
of what we are receiving back;
but this one did nothing out of place.
Jesus, remember me when you come into your kingdom."

He said to him, "Amen, I tell you,
today you will be with me in paradise."

There stood by the cross of Jesus his mother
and his mother's sister, Mary, wife of Clopas,
and Mary Magdalene.

So Jesus seeing his mother
and the disciple standing by whom he loved,
he said to his mother, "Woman, look, your son."

Then he said to the disciple, "Look, your mother."
From that hour the disciple took her into his home.

94

At the sixth hour darkness came over the whole earth
until the ninth hour as the sun was eclipsed.

About the ninth hour Jesus cried out in a loud voice,
"*Eli, Eli, lama sabachthani?*" which is translated,
"My God, my God, why have you forsaken me?"

Some of those standing by there hearing
said, "He is calling Elijah."

After this Jesus aware
that everything was already completed,
so that the scripture might be completed,
he said, "I thirst."

A jar full of vinegar was there,
and someone running having filled a sponge with vinegar
putting it around a hyssop reed gave it to him to drink.

But the rest said, "Let go;
let us see if Elijah comes to save him."

When Jesus had taken the vinegar
he said, "It is completed,"
and shouting in a loud voice he said,
"Father, into your hands I entrust my spirit."

Saying this and bowing his head he expired.
The curtain of the temple
was split in two from top to bottom;
the earth was shaken, and rocks were split;
tombs were opened,
and many bodies of sleeping saints were raised;
and coming out of the tombs after his resurrection
they went into the holy city and appeared to many.

The centurion and those with him keeping watch on Jesus,
seeing the earthquake and the things happening,
were greatly afraid and said,
"Truly this person was the son of God."

All the crowds who were gathered at this sight
watching what was happening
turned back beating their chests.
There were also women there watching from a distance,
who followed Jesus from Galilee ministering to him,
among whom were Mary Magdalene,
Mary, the mother of James the younger and Joses,
Salome and the mother of the sons of Zebedee,
and many others who had come up with him to Jerusalem.

So the Jews, since it was preparation day,
that the bodies might not stay on the cross on the Sabbath,
for that Sabbath was a high day,

asked Pilate that their legs be broken
and they be taken down.
 Therefore the soldiers came
and broke the legs of the first
and of the other crucified with him;
but coming upon Jesus, as they saw he had already died,
they did not break his legs;
but one of the soldiers pierced his side with a spear,
and immediately blood and water came out.
The one who saw it has testified,
and his testimony is true;
that one knows that he says the truth,
so that you may also believe.
For these things happened
so that the scripture might be fulfilled:
    "No bone of his will be shattered."
Again different scripture says,
    "They will look on him whom they pierced."

95
 Evening already coming on preparation day,
which is before the Sabbath,
Joseph, a prominent member of the council,
a wealthy person from Arimathea, a Jewish town,
a man good and just
who was himself also expecting the sovereignty of God
and was not agreeing with the council and their action,
who himself also had become a disciple of Jesus
but secretly because of the fear of the Jews,
coming and having summoned his courage
he went in to Pilate and requested the body of Jesus.
 Pilate wondered if he had already died,
and calling forward the centurion
he asked him if he had already died;
and discovering it from the centurion
he granted the corpse to Joseph.
 Having bought linen he came and took his body down.
Nicodemus also, who had come to him by night at the first,
came bringing a mixture of myrrh and aloes

of about a hundred pounds.
So they took the body of Jesus and wrapped it in clean linen
and bound it in bandages with the spices,
as it is the custom to bury the Jews.

At the place where he was crucified there was a garden,
and in the garden his new tomb
which he had hewn in the rock,
in which no one had ever been laid.
Therefore due to the Jewish preparation day,
because the tomb was near, they laid Jesus there,
and having rolled a big stone to the door of the tomb
they went away.

Mary Magdalene and Mary, the mother of Joses,
following behind and sitting opposite the grave
saw the tomb and how his body was laid,
and returning prepared spices and ointment.
They rested on the Sabbath according to the commandment.

The next day, which is after preparation day,
the high priests and the Pharisees assembled before Pilate
saying, "Lord, we were reminded that
that deceiver said while living, 'After three days I rise.'
Therefore command the grave to be secured
until the third day,
lest the disciples coming should steal him
and say to the people, 'He was raised from the dead,'
and the last deception will be worse than the first."

Pilate said to them, "Take a guard;
go secure it as you know how."
So proceeding they secured the grave
sealing the stone with the guard.

96
After the Sabbath, at dawn on the first day of the week,
Mary Magdalene, Mary, the mother of James, and Salome
came upon the tomb
bringing the spices which they had prepared.
As the sun was rising, they said to each other,
"Who will roll the stone away
from the door of the tomb for us?"

Looking up they saw that the stone had been rolled back,
for it was extremely big.

  Entering they did not find the body of the Lord Jesus.
While they were confused about this, they saw a youth;
for an angel of the Lord had come down from heaven
and approaching had rolled away the stone.
His appearance was like lightning,
and he was sitting on the right
dressed in a gleaming white robe.
From fear of him those keeping watch were shaken
and had become like the dead.

  As the women became frightened
and bowed their faces to the ground,
the angel answered them, "Do not be alarmed;
for I know that you are looking for Jesus
the crucified Nazarene.
But why are you looking for the living with the dead?
He is not here, for he was raised just as he said;
look at the place where they laid him.
But go tell his disciples and Peter
that he was raised from the dead,
and that he is leading you into Galilee;
there you will see him.
Remember how he spoke to you while he was still in Galilee,
saying, 'The human son must be given over
into the hands of sinful people
and be crucified and on the third day rise up.'
Look, I have told you."

  They remembered his sayings.
Going out they fled from the tomb,
for they were trembling and bewildered;
and they did not tell anyone anything,
for they were afraid;
but going away quickly with fear and great joy
they ran to report to his disciples.

  Returning from the tomb
they reported all these things to the eleven
and to all the rest.
It was Mary Magdalene and Joanna

and Mary, the mother of James,
and the rest of the women with them
who told these things to the apostles.

These sayings seemed to them like nonsense,
and they disbelieved them.

So Mary Magdalene hurried and came to Peter
and to the other disciple whom Jesus loved,
and said to them, "They took the Lord out of the tomb,
and we don't know where they put him."

So Peter and the other disciple went out,
and they came to the tomb.
The two hurried together;
the other disciple ran ahead quicker than Peter
and came to the tomb first;
bending over he saw the bandages lying there,
though he did not go in.

Then Simon Peter also came following him,
and he went into the tomb and saw the bandages lying there;
the handkerchief, which had been on his head,
was not with the bandages lying there
but had been folded up separately in one place.

So then the other disciple who had come to the tomb first
also entered the tomb, and he saw and believed;
for they did not yet know the scripture,
that he must rise up from the dead.
So the disciples went away again to their homes.

But Mary stood outside the tomb weeping.
So as she was weeping, she bent over into the tomb;
and she saw two angels in white sitting,
one at the head and one at the feet,
where the body of Jesus had lain.

Those said to her, "Woman, why are you weeping?"

She said to them, "They took my Lord,
and I don't know where they put him."

Saying these things she turned around,
and she saw Jesus standing,
but she did not know that it was Jesus.

Jesus said to her, "Woman, why are you weeping?
Who are you looking for?"
  She, thinking that it was the gardener,
said to him, "Lord, if you carried him away,
tell me where you put him, and I will take him."
  Jesus said to her, "Hello, Mary."
  She turning said to him
in Hebrew, "Rabboni" (which means Teacher),
and approaching she grabbed his feet and worshipped him.
  Then Jesus said to her, "Do not be afraid;
do not hold on to me,
for I have not yet ascended to the Father.
But go report to my brothers
so that they may go away to Galilee,
and there they will see me;
tell them: I am ascending to my Father and your Father
and my God and your God."
  So he appeared first to Mary Magdalene,
from whom he had expelled seven demons.
She went announcing to the disciples
who were mourning and weeping,
"I have seen the Lord,"
and that he had told her these things;
those hearing that he was alive
and was seen by her disbelieved.
  Some of the guard coming into the city
reported to high priests everything that had happened.
Assembling with elders and forming a plan
they gave considerable silver to the soldiers,
saying to them, "Say: 'His disciples coming at night
stole him while we were sleeping.'
If this is heard by the governor,
we will persuade him and keep you out of trouble."
Taking the silver they did as they were taught.
This account has been spread by the Jews even to this day.

97

  On the same day two of them were traveling to a village
sixty stadiums away from Jerusalem, by the name of Emmaus,

and they were conversing to each other
about all these things that had come about.
During their conversation and discussion
Jesus himself coming near traveled with them;
but their eyes were kept from recognizing him.

He asked them, "What are these accounts
you are exchanging with each other while walking?"

They stood still, depressed.
One named Cleopas answered him,
"Are you only a stranger in Jerusalem
and are you not aware of the things
happening in it on these days?"

He asked them, "What things?"

They said to him, "About Jesus the Nazarene,
who was a powerful prophet in deed and word
before God and all the people,
how both the high priests and our rulers
gave him over to the verdict of death and crucified him.
But we were hoping
that he was the one who was going to redeem Israel;
moreover with all these things
this is the third day since this happened.

"But also some of our women astounded us,
having been at the tomb early in the morning,
and not finding his body
they came saying also they had seen a vision of angels,
who said that he was alive.
Some of those with us went away to the tomb,
and found it just as the women had said,
but him they did not see."

He said to them, "O unintelligent and slow of heart
to believe in all that the prophets have spoken!
Did not the Christ have to suffer these things
and enter his glory?"

So beginning from Moses and from all the prophets
he explained to them
the things about himself in all the scriptures.
They came near to the village to which they were traveling,
and he made as though he were traveling farther.

But they prevailed upon him saying, "Stay with us;
for it is nearly evening, and the day has already faded."
So he went in to stay with them.
As he was sitting down with them
taking the bread he blessed it,
and breaking it he gave it to them;
then their eyes were opened, and they recognized him;
and he disappeared from their sight.
They said to each other,
"Were not our hearts burning within us,
as he spoke to us on the way,
as he opened the scriptures to us?"
Getting up at the same hour they returned to Jerusalem,
and they found gathered the eleven and those with them,
saying, "The Lord was really raised and appeared to Simon."
So they related what happened on the way
and how he was known to them in the breaking of the bread.

98
While it was evening on that first day of the week,
the doors having been locked where the disciples were
because of fear of the Jews,
as they were dining and speaking these things
Jesus came and stood in the middle,
and said to them, "Peace to you."
But becoming terrified and frightened
they thought they saw a spirit.
He said to them, "Why are you troubled,
and why are doubts coming up in your hearts?
See my hands and my feet, for I am myself;
touch me and see,
for a spirit does not have flesh and bones
as you see me having."
Saying this he showed them both his hands and his side.
While they were still disbelieving from joy and wondering,
he said to them, "Do you have any food here?"
They handed him part of a broiled fish;
and taking it he ate it in front of them.
Therefore the disciples were glad seeing the Lord.

He reproached their disbelief and hardness of heart
because they had not believed
the ones who had seen him raised.

Then Jesus said to them again, "Peace to you;
as the Father has sent me, I also send you."

Saying this he breathed on them
and said to them, "Receive the Holy Spirit.
Whosoever sins you forgive, they are forgiven them;
whosoever sins you retain, they have been retained."

But Thomas, one of the twelve called the Twin,
was not with them when Jesus came.
So the other disciples told him, "We have seen the Lord."
But he said to them,
"Unless I see the mark of the nails on his hands
and put my finger into the place of the nails
and put my hand into his side,
I will not believe it."

After eight days his disciples again were inside,
and Thomas with them.
Jesus came, the doors having been locked,
and he stood in the middle and said, "Peace to you."

Then he said to Thomas,
"Bring your finger here and see my hands,
and bring your hand and put it into my side,
and do not be faithless but faithful."

Thomas answered him, "My Lord and my God."

Jesus said to him,
"Because you have seen me, have you believed?
Blessed are those not seeing yet believing."

So Jesus also did many other signs
in front of the disciples,
which are not written in this book;
but these have been written so that you may believe
that Jesus is the Christ, the son of God,
and so that believing you may have life in his name.

99

After this Jesus manifested himself again
to the disciples on the sea of Tiberias;

and he appeared in this way.
Simon Peter and Thomas, called the Twin,
and Nathanael from Cana of Galilee and the sons of Zebedee
and two other disciples of his were together.

   Simon Peter said to them, "I am going fishing."

   They said to him, "We are also going with you."

   They went out and embarked in the boat,
and on that night they caught nothing.

   But when it was already early morning,
Jesus stood on the shore;
though the disciples did not know that it was Jesus.

   So Jesus said to them, "Children, do you have any fish?"

   They answered him, "No."

   He said to them,
"Cast the net on the right side of the boat,
and you will find some."

   So they cast it,
and they were no longer able to haul it
from the quantity of fish.

   So that disciple whom Jesus loved
said to Peter, "It is the Lord."

   So Simon Peter, hearing that it was the Lord,
tied a coat around him, for he was naked,
and threw himself into the sea;
but the other disciples came in the boat,
dragging the net full of fish,
for they were not far from land
but about two hundred cubits away.

   So when they got out on the land,
they saw a charcoal fire laid
and a cooked fish lying on it and bread.

   Jesus said to them,
"Bring some of the fish that you have just caught."

   Simon Peter went up and dragged the net on to the land
full of big fish, a hundred fifty-three;
and though there were so many, the net was not torn.

   Jesus said to them, "Come have breakfast."

None of the disciples dared
to inquire of him, "Who are you?"
knowing that he was the Lord.

Jesus came and took the bread and gave it to them,
and the fish likewise.

This was now the third time
Jesus was manifested to the disciples raised from the dead.

So when they had had breakfast,
to Simon Peter Jesus said, "Simon, son of John,
do you love me more than these?"

He said to him, "Yes, Lord, you know that I love you."

He said to him, "Feed my lambs."
He said to him again a second time,
"Simon, son of John, do you love me?"

He said to him, "Yes, Lord, you know that I love you."

He said to him, "Be shepherd of my sheep."
He said to him for the third time,
"Simon, son of John, do you love me?"

Simon was sad
that he said to him for the third time, "Do you love me?"
and he said to him, "Lord, you know everything;
you know that I love you."

Jesus said to him, "Feed my sheep.
Amen, amen, I tell you, when you were younger,
you dressed yourself and walked where you wished;
but when you grow old, you will reach out your hands,
and another will dress you
and carry you where you do not wish."
This he said signifying by what death he would glorify God.

Saying this he said to him, "Follow me."
Peter turning saw the disciple whom Jesus loved following,
who also at the dinner had leaned on his chest
and had said, "Lord, who is the one giving you over?"

So Peter seeing this one
said to Jesus, "Lord, what about him?"

Jesus said to him, "If I wish him to stay until I come,
what is that to you?
You follow me."

So this word went out to the brothers
that that disciple would not die;
but Jesus did not say to him that he would not die,
but: "If I wish him to stay until I come,
what is that to you?"
   This is the disciple
who testified about these things and wrote them,
and we know that his testimony is true.

100
   The eleven disciples traveled to Galilee,
to the mountain where Jesus had directed them;
and seeing him they worshipped him, but some doubted.
   Jesus approaching said to them, "These are my words
which I spoke to you while I was still with you,
that everything written in the law of Moses
and the prophets and psalms about me must be fulfilled."
   Then he opened their mind to understand the scriptures;
and he said to them, "Thus it was written
for the Christ to suffer
and rise up from the dead on the third day,
and to be preached in his name
repentance for the forgiveness of sins
to all the nations, beginning from Jerusalem.
   "You are witnesses of these things.
Look, I am sending out the promise of my Father upon you;
but sit in the city
until you are dressed with power from on high.
All authority in heaven and on earth has been given to me.
   "Therefore traveling into all the world
preach the good message to all creation
and make disciples of all the nations,
baptizing them in the name of the Father
and the son and the Holy Spirit,
teaching them to observe all that I have commanded you.
Whoever believes and is baptized will be saved,
but whoever disbelieves will be condemned.
   These signs will accompany those believing:
in my name they will expel demons,

speak in new languages, pick up snakes,
and if they drink anything deadly it will not harm them;
they will put their hands upon the sick,
and they will get well.
Look, I am with you all the days
until the completion of eternity."

  After speaking to them
the Lord Jesus led them out as far as Bethany,
and lifting his hands he blessed them.
While he was blessing them, he parted from them
and was taken up into heaven
and sat at the right hand of God.

  They returned to Jerusalem with great joy,
and were continually in the temple praising God.
Those going out preached everywhere,
as the Lord was working with them
and confirming the word through the accompanying signs.

  There are also many other things which Jesus did,
which if every one were written
I do not think the world would have room
for the books written.

Manual of Epictetus
by Arrian

Epictetus, who was a native of Phrygia, is known by a name which means "newly acquired," because he was a slave of Epaphroditus in the court of Rome during the reign of Emperor Nero (54-68 CE).

The early Christian, Origen, quoted an account by Celsus about Epictetus and the greatness of his words under suffering similar to that of Jesus. Celsus wrote, "Take Epictetus, who, when his master was twisting his leg, said, smiling and unmoved, 'You will break my leg;' and when it was broken, he added, 'Did I not tell you that you would break it?'" Epictetus spent the rest of his life with a crippled leg.

While a slave Epictetus managed to attend lectures of the Stoic philosopher, Musonius Rufus, who made his listeners feel that they were personally being accused. Epictetus gained his freedom and was expelled from Rome by Emperor Domitian about 90 CE with other philosophers suspected of republicanism.

Epictetus settled in Nicopolis in Greece, where he lived in poverty with only "earth, sky, and a cloak." Epictetus lived and taught a long time and probably died late in the reign of Hadrian (117-138).

Among his students coming from various parts of the empire was Flavius Arrian, who became a consul under Emperor Hadrian and wrote a history of Alexander the Great. Arrian collected the teachings of Epictetus into eight books of *Discourses*, the first four of which survive, and in a brief compendium of these teachings called the *Encheiridion* or *Manual of Epictetus*.

Notes to:

15: Diogenes in the fourth century BC founded the Greek philosophical sect called Cynics. He challenged social conventions with his ascetic and homeless life-style, his outspoken criticisms, and his shamelessness.

15: Heracleitus of Ephesus lived about 540-480 BC and for a while he lived in the mountains on grass and herbs. His pithy book, mostly lost, influenced Socrates and others.

25: An *obol* was one-sixth part of a day's wage or about four cents.

29: Euphrates lectured on Stoic philosophy and was highly praised by Pliny.

31: Polyneices and Eteocles were the sons cursed by Oedipus who fought over the kingship of Thebes and killed each other in single combat.

33: Zeno about 300 BC founded the Stoic school of philosophy by teaching from a porch *(stoa)* in Athens.

49: Chrysippus lived in Athens during the third century BC. He was a student of Cleanthes and Zeno and wrote several hundred books expounding on logic and Stoic philosophy.

53: The last two quotes refer to Socrates facing death after having been prosecuted by Anytus and Meletus. The prayer to Zeus is from a poem by Cleanthes, and the second quote is from Euripides.

1

Of existing things some are in our power,
others not in our power.
In our power are conception, effort, desire, aversion
and in a word whatever are our actions;
but not in our power are the body, property, reputation,
rulers and in a word whatever are not our actions.

Also things in our power are by nature
free, unhindered, unimpeded,
but things not in our power are
weak, slavish, hindered, belonging to others.

So remember, that if
what is by nature slavish you think free
and what is others' your own,
you will be hindered, you will mourn, you will be disturbed,
and you will blame both gods and humans,
but if you think only yours is yours,
and another's, just as it is, another's,
no one will ever compel you, no one will hinder you,
you will not blame anyone, nor accuse someone,
not one thing will you do unwilling,
no one will harm you, you will have no enemy,
for you will suffer no harm from anyone.

So aiming at such great things, remember that
it is not necessary moderately moving to take hold of them,
but to give up some things completely,
and carry over others for the present.

Even if you intend these things
and to rule and be wealthy,
perhaps you may not bring about these latter
because of also aiming at the former,
and you may fail to get these,
by which alone freedom and happiness are gained.

So at once practice saying to every disturbing impression,
"You are an impression and not the complete manifestation."
Then examine it and test it by these rules which you have,
first and foremost of which is this:
whether it concerns things in our power or not in our power;
and if it does not concern something in our power,

let the reason for that be handy, "It is nothing to me."

2

Remember that the promise of desire
is the attainment of what you desire,
the attainment of aversion
not to fall into that which is avoided,
and whoever fails in desire is unfortunate,
and whoever falls into what is avoided has misfortune.

If then you avoid things against nature in your power,
you will fall into none which you may avoid;
but if you are averse to sickness or death or poverty,
you will have misfortune.

So remove aversion from all things not in your power
and transfer it to things against nature in your power.
But for the present remove completely the desire;
for if you desire some of the things not in our power,
you must be unfortunate,
and of those in our power,
however beautiful it would be to desire them,
none would ever come forward for you.
But use only impulse and departing,
and yet even lightly with exceptions and unconstrained.

3

To each of the allurements
or things providing use or contentment
remember to say, "What quality is it?"
beginning from the smallest things.

If you like a jug, say, "I like a jug;"
for when it breaks you will not be disturbed.
If you should kiss your child or wife,
say that you are kissing a person;
for when one dies, you will not be disturbed.

4

When you are about to take on some work,
remind yourself, what kind of work it is.
If you are going out to bathe,

put before yourself things occurring in a bathhouse,
the splashing, the pushing, the insulting, the stealing.
And thus you will take on your work more safely,
if at once you say to yourself, "I intend to bathe
and to watch keeping my preferring according to nature."

Also do the same in each action.
For thus if something got in the way of bathing,
a handy reason for that will be:
"But this was not the only thing I intended,
but also to watch keeping my preferring according to nature;
but I shall not be observing it,
if I am annoyed at the things occurring."

5

Actions do not disturb people,
but opinions about actions;
for example, death is nothing terrible,
or else it would have appeared so to Socrates also,
but the opinion about death, that it is terrible,
that is what is terrible.

So when we are hindered or disturbed or grieved,
let us never accuse another, but ourselves,
that is, our own opinions.

To charge others is the work of the uneducated,
in whose power the self is doing badly;
beginning to be educated is to charge oneself;
having been educated neither another nor oneself.

6

Do not be excited by any advantages of others.
If the horse being excited should say,
"I am beautiful," it could be endured;
but when you being excited say, "I have a beautiful horse,"
be aware that you are excited about a good of the horse.

What then is yours?
The use of impressions.
Therefore, when you have the use of impressions
according to nature, then get excited;
for then you will be getting excited

about something good in your power.

7

Just as on a voyage the ship being anchored
if you should go out to draw water,
along the way you might pick up both shell-fish and bulbs,
it is necessary to pay attention to the ship
and continually turn towards it,
lest the captain ever call,
and if he calls, to give up all those things,
unless you want to be thrown on like the sheep.

Thus also in life, if instead of a bulb and shell-fish
a wife and child is given, no one will hinder;
but if the captain should call,
run to the ship giving up all those and not turning back.

If you are old, do not ever get far away from the ship,
lest when called you may be left behind.

8

Do not strive for things occurring to occur as you wish,
but wish the things occurring as they occur,
and you will flow well.

9

Sickness is a hindrance of the body,
but not of preferring, unless this wills it.
Lameness is a hindrance of the leg, but not of preferring.
Also say this upon each thing happening;
for you will find this a hindrance of something else,
but not of yourself.

10

Upon each thing happening remember turning upon yourself
to seek what ability you have for the use of it.
If you see someone handsome or beautiful,
you will discover self-control the ability for these;
if labor is imposed, you will discover endurance;
if insults, you will discover patience.
And so becoming accustomed
the impressions will not grab you.

11

Never say about anything, "I lost it,"
but "I gave it back."
Did the child die? It was given back.
Did the woman die? She was given back.
"The farm was taken away." So this also was given back.
"But the one taking it away was bad."
What do you care by whom the giver took it back?

So long as one gives it, as a stranger's take care of it,
just as the ones passing by do of an inn.

12

If you intend to advance, give up such inferences.
"If I neglect my things, I shall have no support."
"Unless I punish the servant, he will be bad."
For it is better to die of hunger
becoming sorrowless and fearless
than live in abundance being disturbed.
And it is better for your servant to be bad
than for you to be unhappy.

Begin therefore from the small things.
The oil is poured out; the wine is stolen;
say, "Such is the price of calmness, of being undisturbed."
Nothing is gained gratis.

When you call the servant,
realize that he may not be able to comply
and having complied may not do what you intend;
however it is not so well for him
that it should be in that one's power
for you to be disturbed at all.

13

If you intend to advance,
daring on account of external things
to be thought unintelligent and silly,
do not wish to be known for knowing anything;
and if some should believe you to be something,
distrust yourself.

For be aware that it is not easy
to watch keeping your preferring according to nature
and the externals too,
but taking care of one of these,
one must neglect the other altogether.

14
If you wish that your children and wife and your friends
live forever, you are silly;
for you are wishing that
things not in your power be in your power
and others' things be yours;
thus if you wish that the servant not fail, you are a fool;
for you are wishing that vice not be vice,
but something else.
But if you wish not to fail in desiring, this can be done.
Therefore exercise this, what can be done.
The lord of each is the one having authority
over what that one is wishing or not wishing
in the obtaining or taking away.
So whoever would be free,
let them neither wish anything nor avoid anything
in the power of others;
or else be by necessity enslaved.

15
Remember that you ought to conduct yourself
as at a banquet.
When something is passed around to you,
stretching out your hand partake of it politely.
It passes on; do not hold it back.
It has not arrived yet; do not project the desire forward,
but wait around until it comes to you.
Do so toward children, do so toward a wife,
do so toward officers, do so toward wealth;
and then you will be worthy of the gods' banquets.
But if you do not take what is put before you,
but look down on it,
then not only will you share in the banquet of the gods

but also in ruling with them.
For by doing thus Diogenes and Heracleitus and similar ones
were deservedly divine and called so.

16
  When you see someone crying in sorrow,
either a child having gone abroad
or one's things having been ruined,
be careful that the impression does not grab you
as being in one's external ills,
but at once let be handy,
"What happened does not distress this person
(for it does not distress another),
but their opinion about it."
  Yet as far as words go
do not hesitate to sympathize with them,
and if it so chances, even to lament with them;
yet be careful not to lament also inside.

17
  Remember that you are an actor in a play,
which the playwright wills;
if short, short; if long, long;
he may intend you to play a beggar
so that also you might act this naturally;
or a cripple, an official, or a private person.
For this is yours, to play the given role beautifully;
but the selection of it is another's.

18
  When a raven does not crow auspiciously,
do not let the impression carry you away;
but at once distinguish for yourself and say,
"None of these are significant for me,
but either for my body or my property
or my reputation or the children or wife.
  "For me every portent is significant, if I wish;
for whatever turns out,
it is in my power to benefit from it."

19

You can be invincible,
if you never go into a contest,
which is not in your power to win.

Look out lest seeing some more honored
or with great power or otherwise blessed with fame,
you are ever carried away by the impression.

For if the essence of the good is in your power,
neither envy nor jealousy have a place;
and you yourself will not wish to be a magistrate,
nor a president or consul, but free.

There is one way to this,
looking down upon things not in your power.

20

Remember that not the one abusing or beating is insulting,
but the opinion about these is insulting.
So when someone irritates you,
be aware that your assumption has irritated you.
Thus at first try not to be carried away by the impression;
for once you get time and delay,
you will more easily control yourself.

21

Let death and exile and all things appearing terrible
be before your eyes each day, but most of all death;
and then you will neither take to heart the mean
nor will you desire anything very much.

22

If you desire philosophy,
prepare now as one being ridiculed,
as you are being mocked by many,
who are saying, "Suddenly a philosopher has returned to us"
and "From where has this high brow come to us?"

But you should not have a high brow;
but hold thus to what is appearing best to you,
as to that place assigned by God;
and remember that if you remain in the same,

these ridiculing you before will later be amazed,
but if you are overcome by them,
you will receive ridicule twice.

23

  If it should ever happen that you turn outside
because you wish to please someone,
be aware that you lost the management.

  Therefore be sure in everything to be a philosopher,
if you also plan to seem one,
and you will be capable also of showing it.

24

  Do not let these considerations oppress you:
"I shall live unhonored and no one anywhere."
For if the lack of honor is bad,
you cannot be in evil through another,
any more than in shame.

  So is it your work to get office
or be invited to a feast?
Not at all.
How then can this still be lack of honor?
and how will you be no one anywhere,
when it is necessary to be someone
only in those things which are in your power,
in which it is possible for you to be worthy of the greatest?

  But will your friends be helpless?
What do you mean "helpless"?
They will not have small change from you;
nor will you make them citizens of Rome.

  So who told you that these things are in your power,
and not others' work?
Who can give another what one does not have oneself?

  "So acquire," one says, "so that you shall have."
If I can acquire keeping myself modest
and faithful and high-minded,
show the way and I shall acquire.
But if you expect me to lose the good things that are mine,
so that you may obtain things that are not good,

you see yourselves how unfair and unkind you are.
And what do you want more?
silver or a faithful and modest friend?
Therefore rather assist me into this
and do not expect me to do those things,
by which I may lose these things.
"But the country, as far as it is in my power,"
one says, "will be helpless."
Again, what kind of help is this also?
It will not have porticoes nor baths through you.
And what is this?
For neither does it have shoes through the blacksmith
nor arms through the cobbler;
but it is sufficient if each fulfills one's own work.
If you furnished for it
another faithful and modest citizen,
would you not be benefiting it?
"Yes."
Then you yourself would not be unbeneficial to it.
"So what place," one says, "shall I have in the state?"
Whichever you can
guarding at the same time fidelity and modesty.
But if wanting to benefit it you lose these things,
what benefit would you be for it,
if you ended up shameless and unfaithful?

25
Is someone honored before you at a feast
or in greeting or in being invited in to counsel?
If these things are good,
you must be glad that that one got them;
but if bad, do not be distressed that you did not get them.
Remember that not doing the same things
toward getting things not in your power,
you cannot be expected to get an equal share.
For how can one have an equal share
not frequenting someone's door with the one frequenting it?
not escorting with the one escorting?
not praising with the one praising?

  Thus you would be unjust and insatiable,
if not paying things for which those are sold,
you wish to receive them free.
But for how much is lettuce sold?
For an obol, perhaps.
So if someone paying an obol receives lettuce,
and you not paying do not receive it,
in no way have you less than the one receiving.
For as that one has lettuce,
so you an obol, which you have not given.
  Now it is the same way also here.
You have not been invited to someone's feast?
For you have not given to the one calling
as much as the dinner is sold for.
It is sold for praise, it is sold for service.
So give the price, if it profits you, for which it is sold.
But if you intend both not to pay and receive these,
you are insatiable and silly.
So do you have nothing instead of the dinner?
Thus you have the not praising one whom you did not wish to,
the not having to endure those at his entrance.

26
  The will of nature is to be learned out of things
in which we do not differ from each other.
For example, when another's servant breaks the cup,
it is handy at once to say, "It is of the things happening."
So be aware that when your cup is broken,
you should be such, as when that of another is broken.
  Thus alter also the greater things.
Another's child or wife has died;
There is no one who would not say that it is human.
However when someone of one's own dies,
at once "Ah me! I am wretched."
But one must remember,
what we suffer hearing about the same of others.

27
  Just as a mark is not set up in order to be missed,
so neither does the nature of evil occur in the universe.

28

If someone turned over your body to anyone,
you would be upset;
but that you turn over your mind to any chance,
so that, if they insult you, it is disturbed and troubled,
are you not ashamed on account of this?

29

In each action consider the leading things
and its following things and so upon the action itself.
If not, you will come to it at first enthusiastically
without having thought of the next things,
but later when some difficulties show up
you will withdraw disgracefully.
   Do you wish to win the Olympics?
I do too, by the gods; for it is exquisite.
However consider the leading things and the things following
and so take hold of the action.
It is necessary for you to be disciplined,
to eat strictly, to keep off sweets,
to exercise under compulsion, at an appointed hour,
in heat, in cold, not to drink cold water,
nor wine, as it chances,
absolutely as to a physician
to give yourself over to the trainer,
when in the contest to dig in alongside,
it is possible then to throw out a hand,
to sprain an ankle, swallow much sand, perhaps be beaten,
and with all these things be defeated.
   Having considered these things,
if you still intend to, enter upon athletics.
If not, you will be turning back like children,
who now play at wrestling, and now at single combat,
and now at athletics, then at tragedy;
so also you are now an athlete, and now a gladiator,
then an orator, then a philosopher,
but with the whole soul nothing;
but like an ape imitate everything which you see
and one after another whatever strikes you.

For you did not go into anything
with consideration nor circumspection,
but rashly and according to cold desire.

Thus some having seen a philosopher
and having heard thus someone talking,
like Euphrates talks (Yet who can speak like him?),
they wish also to philosophize themselves.

Person, first consider, what is the matter;
and then learn your nature, if you can bear it.
Do you wish to be in the pentathlon or a wrestler?
Look at your arms, thighs, study the loins.
For another has a nature for another thing.

Do you think that doing these things
you can eat the same way, drink the same way,
get angry similarly, be displeased similarly?
It is necessary to stay awake, to work,
to go away from the household, to be condemned by a servant,
to be ridiculed by everyone, to have the worst in everything,
in honor, in office, in justice, in every affair.

Consider these things, if you are willing to exchange
for these calm, freedom, tranquillity;
but if not, do not approach, not like children,
now a philosopher, but later a tax collector,
then an orator, then an administrator of Caesar.
These things do not harmonize.

But you must be one person either good or bad;
you must work out of yourself
either the leading or the externals;
either to love the art concerning inside things
or concerning outside things;
that is, either take the position of a philosopher
or of an average person.

30
Proper things in general are measured by the conditions.
It is a father; one is required to take care,
to yield in all things, to hold up when insulted, struck.
"But the father is bad."
What then, you were not related to a good father by nature?

But to a father.
"The brother is unjust."
So then maintain your position to him;
do not consider what he does,
but what you are doing
to keep your preferring according to nature.

For another will not harm you if you are not willing;
but then you will be harmed,
when you assume you are harmed.
So then from the neighbor, from the citizen, from the general
you will discover the proper thing,
if you are in the habit of seeing the conditions.

31
Concerning piety toward the gods
be aware that the most lordly is that,
to have correct conceptions about them as existing
and administering the things whole beautifully and justly,
and to have appointed yourself into this,
to obey them and to submit to everything happening
and to follow voluntarily
as being accomplished by the best intelligence.
For thus you will never blame the gods
nor accuse them for neglecting.

But no other way can this happen,
than by withdrawing from things not in your power
and putting good and bad only on things in your power.
Since if you conceive of any of the former as good or bad,
by absolute necessity, when you fail in things you wish
and fall into things you do not wish,
you will blame and hate those responsible.

For this is the nature of all living things
to flee and turn aside from things appearing harmful
and things responsible for them,
and to go after and admire things beneficial
and things responsible for them.

Thus it is impractical for someone
thinking they are being harmed
to be glad at what seems to be harming,

just as it is impossible to be glad at the harm itself.

Therefore even a father is insulted by a son,
when he does not share with the child what seems to be good;
and this made Polyneices and Eteocles enemies to each other
thinking tyranny was good.

Because of this also the farmer insults the gods,
because of this the sailor, because of this the merchant,
because of this the ones who have lost wives and children.
For where the profit is, there also is piety.

Therefore, whoever is careful of desire and aversion
as one should, at the same time also is taking care of piety.
But it is fitting to pour libations and offer and sacrifice
according to ancestral ways each time purely and not slovenly
nor carelessly nor sparingly nor beyond ability.

32
When you undertake divination,
remember that what the outcome will be, you do not know,
but you have come inquiring it from the diviner,
and you have come knowing what sort it is,
if you are a philosopher.
For if it is anything not in your power,
it is absolutely necessary
for it to be neither good nor bad.

So do not bring to the diviner desire or aversion
nor approach them trembling,
but resolving that every outcome
is indifferent and nothing to you,
and whatever it may be, it will be beautifully useful to one,
and no one will prevent this.

So be confident in going to the gods as to counselors;
and leaving, when some counsel is given to you,
remember whom you have taken as counselors
and whom you disregard disobeying.

But go to divination, just as Socrates went,
in things where all speculation has reference to the outcome
and neither from logic nor from any other skill
is it given to begin to view the thing exposed.

Therefore, when one should incur danger
with a friend or country,
do not divine if the danger should be incurred.
For if the diviner foretells to you the omens are poor,
it is clear that death is indicated
or maiming of some part of the body or exile;
but reason requires even with this to stand by the friend
and incur danger with the country.

Therefore pay attention to the greater diviner,
the Pythian, who threw out of the temple
one who had not helped a friend being murdered.

33
Appoint for yourself already some character and model,
which you may keep by yourself and meeting with people.

And be silent most of the time
or talk the necessities and in few words.
But rarely, when opportunity invites speaking, speak,
but about none of the ordinary things;
not about gladiators, not about horse-races,
not about athletes, not about food or drink,
things said everywhere,
and especially not about people
faulting or praising or comparing.

So you may be able to change it by your words
and those of the companions to what is proper.
But if you are caught by chance among strangers, be silent.

Do not laugh much nor at many things nor unrestrained.
Decline an oath, if possible at all,
but if not, it is out of one's power.

Avoid feasts of those outside and average persons;
but if at some time an opportunity occurs,
let your attention be alert,
never then slip into mediocrity.
For be aware that if the companion be defiled,
also the one rubbing up against them must be defiled,
even though one happens to be clean.

In things concerning the body
take only the bare necessities,

such as food, drink, clothing, shelter, servants;
but draw the line at all glamour and luxury.
Concerning sexuality be as pure as possible before marriage;
but in engaging participate in what is lawful.
However do not be annoying
nor examining to those indulging;
nor bring forward often the fact that one does not indulge.

   If someone reports to you
that a certain person speaks badly of you,
do not defend against the things said, but answer,
"For they did not know the other bad approaches to me,
otherwise these would not be the only things said."

   It is not necessary to go to shows often.
But if at some time there is an opportunity,
do not show seriousness for anyone other than yourself,
that is, wish only for the things happening to happen
and only for those winning to win;
for thus you will not be thwarted.
But refrain completely from shouting and laughing at anyone
or from being much stirred up.

   Also after leaving
do not discuss much about what occurred,
except as it bears on your improvement;
for it appears from such that the sight was amazing.

   Do not go rashly nor readily to people's readings;
but going be solemn and steady
and at the same time keep inoffensive.

   When you are about to meet someone,
especially those held in eminence,
propose to yourself,
what would Socrates or Zeno have done in this situation,
and you will not be at a loss
to make proper use of the event.

   When you resort to some of great power,
propose that you will not find them in,
that you will be shut out,
that the doors will be slammed on you,
that they will pay no attention to you.
And if it is proper to go into this,

go bearing what happens
and never say to yourself, "It was not so great;"
for the average person also is offended by externals.

  In your conversation stay away from
remembering much and excessively
your own actions or dangers.
For it is not as pleasant for others
thus also to hear of your adventures
as it is pleasant for you to remember your dangers.

  Stay away also from arousing laughter;
for the slippery manner relaxes into vulgarity
and at the same time the respect of neighbors for you.
It is also precarious to go on into foul language.
So when some such thing occurs, if it be well-timed,
even reprove the one going into it;
and if not, keep silent and blush and frown
to make clear you are displeased by the word.

34

  When you receive an impression of some pleasure,
as with others, watch yourself, not to be carried off by it;
however let it wait upon your business,
and get some delay for yourself.

  Next remember both the times,
when you will enjoy the pleasure,
and when having enjoyed it
later you will repent and reproach yourself;
and against these refraining
how much you will be glad and commend yourself.

  But if an opportunity appears to you
to engage in the action,
be sure you are not overcome
by its softness and pleasure and attraction;
but set against it, how much better is the awareness
for yourself to have won a victory over it.

35

  When you have decided to do something,
that it is to be done,

never avoid being seen doing it,
even though many people will likely suppose
something different about it.
   For if you are not acting correctly,
avoid the action itself;
but if you are acting correctly,
why should you fear those chastising not correctly?

36
   Just as "It is day" and "It is night"
in separation have great value,
but in combination are without value,
so also to select a larger portion
for the body may have value,
but in community at a feast,
one should be able to observe,
it is without value.
So when you are eating with another,
remember, look at not only the value
of what is presented for the body,
but also keep respect for the host.

37
   If you take up some role beyond your power,
both are you in this dishonored, and,
you are unable to fulfill what you left behind.

38
   Just as you pay attention in walking around,
not to step on a nail or sprain your foot,
so be sure also not to hurt your leadership.
And if we observe this in each action,
we shall reach more security of action.

39
   The body of each is the measure of property
as the foot of the shoe.
So if you establish this, you will keep the measure;
but if you go beyond it,
as down from a cliff you must be carried;

so also with the shoe, if you go beyond the foot,
the shoe becomes gilded, then purple, embroidered.
For once beyond the measure there is no limit.

40
  Women right after fourteen years
are called ladies by the men.
Therefore seeing that there is nothing else for them,
but only to sleep with men,
they begin to beautify themselves
and in this put all hopes.
  So it is valuable to make sure they understand
that they are honored for nothing else
than to appear orderly and modest.

41
  It is a sign of the unnatural
to waste time on what concerns the body,
as on much exercise, on much eating, on much drinking,
on much defecating, copulating.
However these may be done in passing;
but let all the attention be concerning the mind.

42
  When someone treats you badly or speaks badly,
remember that thinking it is proper they do or say so.
So they are not able to follow what appears so to you,
but to themselves,
so that, if it appears wrong to them,
they are hurt, who are also deceived.
  For if someone supposes that a compound truth is false,
the compound truth is not hurt, but the one deceived.
So starting from this you will be gentle to the insulting.
For declare each time, "It seemed so to them."

43
  Every matter has two handles,
one for carrying, the other not for carrying.
If your brother wrongs, do not take hold of it from here,
that he wrongs (for this is the handle not to carry it by),

but rather from there, that he is a brother,
that you were nurtured together,
and you will take it as it is carried.

44

  These reasonings are not coherent:
"I am wealthier than you; thus I am better than you."
"I am more eloquent than you; thus I am better than you."
  But these are more coherent:
"I am wealthier than you;
thus my property is better than yours."
"I am more eloquent than you;
thus my speech is better than yours."
  But you are neither property nor speech.

45

  Someone bathes quickly;
do not say that it is bad, but that it is quick.
  Someone drinks much wine;
do not say that it is bad, but that it is much.
  For until you understand the belief,
how do you know whether it is bad?
  Thus it will not result for you
to receive some repressed impressions,
but agree to others.

46

  Never say you are a philosopher
nor speak much among average people about principles,
but do what follows from principles;
for example at a banquet do not say how one should eat,
but eat as one should.
  For remember how thus Socrates completely avoided display,
such that they came to him
wishing to be introduced to philosophers by him,
and he took them along.
Thus he bore being overlooked.
  And if some argument about principle
arises among average people,

be silent most of the time;
for great is the danger you will immediately vomit out
what you have not digested.

And when someone says to you that you know nothing,
and you are not stung,
then be aware that you may be beginning the action.

Since even sheep do not bring fodder to the shepherds
to show how much they have eaten,
but digesting pasture inside produce outside wool and milk;
and you then do not show off principles to average people,
but the actions from their having been digested.

47
When you are adapted frugally according to the body,
do not embellish on this at all,
do not, if you drink water,
on every occasion say that you drink water.
and if you ever intend to train for endurance,
do it for yourself and not for the ones outside;
do not embrace statues;
but when very thirsty draw in cold water
and spit it out and say nothing.

48
Position and character of the average:
never from themselves do they expect benefit or harm,
but from ones outside.

Position and character of a philosopher:
every benefit and harm is expected from oneself.

Signs of the progressing:
they blame no one, praise no one,
fault no one, accuse no one,
say nothing about themselves
as though being someone or knowing something.

If someone praises them,
they laugh to themselves at the one praising;
if blamed, they make no defense.

They go around like the feeble,
taking care about moving any of what is set,

until it has been fixed.
   They keep out of themselves every desire;
and they transfer aversion
only to things against nature in our power.
   They use unrestrained effort toward everything.
If they seem foolish or unlearned, they do not care.
In a word, as a treacherous enemy they guard themselves.

49
   When someone thinks they can expound and interpret
the books of Chrysippus,
say to yourself, "If Chrysippus had not written obscurely,
this one would have nothing upon which to interpret."
   But what do I want?
To understand nature and follow her.
So I seek someone who is expounding;
and having heard that Chrysippus does, I go to him.
But I do not understand what has been written;
so I seek the one expounding.
And so far of these there is nothing holy yet.
But when I find the one expounding,
it remains to use the instructions;
this itself is alone the holy.
   But if I admire this expounding itself,
what other accomplishment is it other than grammatical
instead of philosophical?
Except that instead of Homer it is expounding Chrysippus.
So rather, when someone says to me,
"Read to me Chrysippus,"
I blush, when I cannot show similar actions
harmonizing with the words.

50
   Whatever is proposed, stay with these like laws,
as though it would be profane for you to overstep them.
But whatever anyone may say about you, pay no attention;
for this is still not yours.

51

For how much longer will you put off
valuing yourself worthy of the best
and in nothing step over logical distinctions?
You received the principles with which you should agree,
and you have agreed.

So what kind of teacher are you still expecting,
that you postpone for that
making corrections of yourself?

You are no longer a boy, but already a grown man.
If now you are careless and take it easy
and always make advances out of advancement
and schedule for other days upon other days,
after which you will pay attention to yourself,
escaping yourself you will not progress,
but you will continue in mediocrity both living and dying.

So already value your life as perfect and progress;
and let everything appearing best to you be unchangeable law.
And if you meet anything laborious or sweet
or notable or unnotable,
remember that now is the contest
and already present are the Olympics
and it is not possible to put it off any longer
and that on a single day and in one matter
progress is both lost and saved.

Thus Socrates became accomplished,
by paying attention in every encounter of his
to nothing else but reason.
And even if you are not yet a Socrates,
as one wishing to be a Socrates you ought to live.

52

The first and most necessary topic in philosophy
is the using of principles, such as not lying;
The second is demonstrating, such as why should one not lie?
The third is confirming and discriminating from these,
such as how does this demonstrate it?

For what is a demonstration, what a consequence,
what a conflict, what true, what false?

Therefore the third topic is necessary because of the second,
and the second because of the first;
and most necessary and where one should halt is the first.

But we do the contrary;
for we spend time on the third topic
and all our effort is concerning that;
while we completely neglect the first.

Therefore we lie,
but we have handy how to demonstrate
that one should not lie.

53

Upon every occasion one must have handy these things:
"Lead me, Zeus, and you also Destiny,
to where I am assigned by you;
as I follow untiring; and if I am not willing,
becoming bad, nonetheless I shall follow."
"Whoever with necessity complies well,
is wise by us, and in things divine skilled."
"But, Crito, if this is friendly to the gods,
let it be this."
"Anytus and Meletus can kill me, but not hurt me."

Introduction to Boethius

Anicius Manlius Severinus Boethius was born about 480 CE into an aristocratic Roman family which had been Christian for a century. It was said that he studied for eighteen years in Athens under the influence of the Neo-Platonist Proclus and his disciples, but Proclus died in 485. The father of Boethius had been consul of Rome in 487 but died shortly after that. Boethius was raised by Symmachus, who later became his father-in-law when he married his daughter Rusticiana.

The lifetime goal of Boethius was to translate the complete works of Aristotle and all the dialogs of Plato, showing by his commentaries that the two could be harmonized, because they agree at philosophically decisive points. He did translate into Latin Porphyry's introduction to Aristotle's *Categories* and all of Aristotle's works on logic, which later had a great influence on the history of medieval philosophy, these being the most available works of Aristotle or Plato in Latin. He also translated from Greek into Latin the geometry of Euclid, the music of Pythagoras, the arithmetic of Nicomachus, the mechanics of Archimedes, and the astronomy of Ptolemy. He could explain a sun-dial and a water-clock.

In 510 Boethius became consul under the Ostrogoth Theodoric, who had become king of Italy. Although Theodoric was an Arian Christian, Boethius wrote *Theological Tractates* on the trinity, attempting to explain with logic the unity of God as substance and the three divine persons in terms of relation and to describe the Christ as both human and divine by defining substance, relation, and nature.

About 520 Theodoric appointed Boethius the master of the offices, heading all the government and court services. In 522 Boethius reached the height of his fortune as his two sons became consuls together.

A 35-year schism between Rome and Constantinople had been resolved in 519, and apparently Theodoric was fearful of the Eastern emperor. The senator Albinus was accused of having written a letter to Emperor Justin, and Boethius openly came to his defense. Boethius was charged with treason and also with practicing magic or sacrilege.

In political life Boethius had often stood up for justice at his own risk. He and Saint Epiphanius had persuaded Theodoric to remit by two-thirds the tax his nephew Odoacer had imposed on the farmers of Campania. The eloquence of Boethius had rescued Paulinus from the intriguers in the palace. He had criticized the Goths Conigastus and Trigulla, and he had sided with the culture of the larger Roman empire against the Gothicizing circle of Cyprian. Now the "honorable" Basilius and Opilio were saying that Boethius had treasonous designs.

Boethius was locked up in Pavia three hundred miles from Rome while a sentence was passed against him and confirmed by the Senate, probably under pressure from Theodoric. While Boethius was in captivity and deprived of the use of his library, he wrote *The Consolation of Philosophy*. In 524 a strong cord was tied so tightly around his head that his eyes bulged out; then he was beaten with a club until he died. Shortly after that, his father-in-law, the senator Symmachus, was taken from Rome to Ravenna and was also executed.

The historian Procopius wrote how Theodoric was stricken with guilt soon after this when the head of a large fish was served him, reminding him of the head of Symmachus. Terrified, he caught a chill, which piles of blankets could not smother. He lamented the wrongs he had done against Symmachus and Boethius and died in 526.

The Consolation of Philosophy became one of the most popular books throughout the middle ages. It was translated into Old, Middle and Elizabethan English by Alfred the Great, Chaucer, and Queen Elizabeth respectively.

Notes to Book 1:

1: The *Pi* and *Theta* represent the first letters of Greek words describing philosophy from the practical to the theoretical.

1: The Eleatic school of philosophy was founded by Parmenides a little before Socrates and emphasized the unity of being. The Academics were those who studied at the Academy founded by Plato.

3: The Epicureans followed the philosophy of Epicurus (341-270 BC) which believed in maximizing pleasure and minimizing pain. The Stoics included Zeno of Citium, Epictetus, and Marcus Aurelius.

3: Anaxagoras was condemned for impiety and exiled from Athens about 450 BC. Socrates was executed by the Athenians in 399 BC. Zeno of Elea was tortured for challenging the tyranny of Nearchus about 440 BC.

3: Canius was executed by Caligula in 40 CE. Seneca was forced to commit suicide by Nero in 65 CE, and Soranus was condemned to death by Nero in 66.

4: A Greek proverb referred to those who would not listen any better than a donkey to a lyre.

4: Plato discussed the importance of having wise rulers in his *Republic* V and VI (473, 487).

4: Gaius Caesar, son of Germanicus, is better known as the Roman Emperor Caligula, who reigned 37-41 CE.

4: The mystical Pythagorean brotherhood began in the sixth century BC with Pythagoras and his school at Krotona in Italy.

VI: The sun is in the sign of Cancer during the first month of summer.

VI: Bacchus was also known as Dionysus, a god of fruitfulness as well as wine and ecstasy.

The Consolation of Philosophy
by Boethius

Book 1

I

Songs which once I wrote in flourishing description,
  tearful, alas, I am forced to form into gloomy measures.
Look how the torn Muses dictate to me writing,
  and elegies bathe my face with real tears.
Not even terror could overcome these
  from proceeding as our companions along the way.
Once the glory of my happy and green youth,
  they now console my fate of gloomy old age.
For hurried unexpected age comes with evils,
  and sorrow has ordered her time to come in.
From the head unseasonable gray hairs are spreading,
  and slack skin trembles on an exhausted body.
Human death is lucky which in sweet years itself
  does not intrude and comes when often called by sorrows.
Alas, how it turns aside the wretched by a deaf ear
  and cruelly refuses to close weeping eyes!
While fortune may have favored by wrong trust in easy goods
  a sad hour nearly overwhelmed my head;
now because the clouds have changed their deceitful face
  vicious life is dragged out by unwelcome delays.
Why did you so often consider me happy, friends?
  Whoever has fallen, that one was not in a steady position.

1

  While I was silently thinking over these things in myself
and noting mournful complaints by a pen's service
there stood over head visions for me,
a woman of very majestic appearance,
with eyes shining and sharp beyond common human health,
from vivid color and of inexhaustible vigor,
yet so mature in age as almost to be believed of our time,
the height of doubtful determination.

  For at one time she held herself to common human measure,
while at another time in height she actually

seemed to strike the heaven of the highest summit;
which when her head was raised higher
even penetrated heaven
and was frustrating the observation of the humans looking.

Her clothes with the finest threads were by delicate skill
from the imperishable material of perfection,
which, as I have since learned from her coming out,
she wove herself with her own hands;
just as it usually does smoky pictures,
a kind of fog of neglected antiquity covered their form.

On the lowest border of these a Greek Pi was embroidered,
while on the highest a Theta could be read,
and between both letters could be seen
in the manner of stairs a kind of marked grade,
by which the ascent should be
from the lower to the higher element.

However the hands of some violent ones had torn this dress
and had taken away whatever particulars each could.
At any rate in her right hand were books,
while in the left she was carrying a scepter.

When she saw the poetic Muses standing by our bed
and dictating words for my tears,
upset for a little while and inflamed with wild lights:
"Who," she asked, "allowed the actress harlots
to approach this sick person?
These sorrows not only have not encouraged any cures,
but they actually nourish them further with sweet drugs.
For these are the ones
who with the unproductive thorns of passion
kill the fertile crop of reason with its fruits
and accustom human minds to stress;
they do not liberate.

"Now if your allurements had drawn off someone profane,
as it is usual with you in the crowd,
I would think it bringing in less annoyance,
since then none of our work would be harmed;
while this one has been nurtured
in Eleatic and Academic studies.
But rather depart, Sirens pleasant all the way into ruin,

and leave him to caring and healing by my Muses."
   That sad chorus reprimanded by this
cast a gloomier look on the ground
and having confessed shame by a blush went out the door.
   But I, whose sight immersed by tears may have been dimmed
so that I could not distinguish
who this woman of such imperious authority might be,
was astounded, and I fixed my sight on the earth
to wait in silence for what action would begin next.
   Then personally approaching
she sat down on the farthest part of my bed
and observing my face heavy from mourning
and so cast down by gloom,
about the disturbance of our mind
the complaint is in these verses:

II
   "Alas, how immersed in the deep of the ruined
a mind is dull and by proper light abandoned
stretches to go into external darkness
as often as it is enlarged by terrestrial breezes
guilty care arises in immensity!
Once this one was free to the open heaven
accustomed to going into ethereal movements
he was perceiving the lights of the rosy sun,
seeing the constellations of the cold moon
and wherever a star winding practices
its wandering returns through various orbits
the victor was having counted with numbers;
why and again from where do the noisy winds
stir up causes from the sea's surface,
what spirit turns the stable world
or why does the western constellation on the wave
falling rise red from the east,
what in truth would moderate the calm hours
so that it may adorn the land with rosy flowers,
who gives so that in a full year the fertile
autumn may flow into the loaded grapes
it is the custom to examine and so to report

various causes of a secret nature:
now it is neglected by the exhausted light of the mind
and the neck pressed by heavy chains
and bearing under a burden the sloping face
it is compelled, alas, to perceive the dull earth.

2
   "But," she said, "it is the time
of medicine rather than of complaining."
Then with her eyes completely intent on me, she said:
"Are you not that one who once was nurtured by our milk,
educated by our nourishment
until you had come out in a manly hardness of spirit?
And yet we contributed retaliatory weapons
which if you had not previously thrown away
would have protected you with invincible firmness.
   "Don't you recognize me?
Why are you silent?
Have you been silenced by shame or by bewilderment?
I would prefer by shame,
but, as I see, bewilderment overwhelms you."
   When she saw me not only silent
but absolutely speechless and mute,
she softly put her hand on my chest and said:
"There is no danger; he is experiencing drowsiness,
a common disease of mental delusions.
For a little while he has forgotten himself.
He will be recollected easily
if in fact he recognizes us as before;
and so that he can, in a little while let us wipe
from his eyes the cloudy fogginess of mortal things."
   She said this, and gathering her dress into a fold
she dried my eyes weeping with tears.

III
Then with night dispelled the darkness left me
   and the previous energy returned to the eyes,
as with the rushed northwest wind the stars are gathered
   and in storms the rainy pole stood,

the sun hides and not yet in heaven with the coming stars
  is the night from above spilled on the earth;
but if the north wind sent out from a Thracian cave
  beats and unlocks enclosed day
the sparkled sun shines out and suddenly by light
  dazzles admiring eyes with its rays.

3
  In no other way with clouds of sadness dissolved
did I drink in heaven,
and mind I regained in recognizing the physician's face.
And so when I was brought back
and concentrated my eyes upon her watching,
I looked back at my nurse, Philosophy,
in whose liberality from youth was I turned out.
  "And why," I asked,
"have you come into these lonely places of our exile,
O mistress of all virtues,
fallen down from the pole above?
Or is it that you too with me may be a defendant
persecuted by false accusations?"
  She replied, "Surely I would not desert you, a pupil,
and not share the burden which you have taken on
from the envy of my name by work communicated to you?
Yet it was never right for Philosophy
to abandon unaccompanied the way of the innocent.
Should I no doubt be afraid of my accusers
and as if something new had struck should I tremble?
  "Now then do you think it is the first time
wisdom is among bad morals challenged by dangers?
Did we not among the old too
before the great age of our Plato
often contend in disputes with the thoughtlessness of folly
and by the same superstition his teacher Socrates
earned the victory of an unjust death by my assistance?
  "The inheritance of which since successively
the crowd of Epicureans and Stoics and others
each having plundered to the best of their ability
they tried to go on

and me crying out and resisting
they carried off for part of the plunder,
a dress they cut up which I had woven with my own hands
and with rags dragged from it went away
believing I had completely yielded to them.
Since among them were seen some traces of our dress,
the imprudent having supposed them to be familiar with me
some of them were undone by the common multitude's error.

"But if you have not learned of the flight of Anaxagoras
nor the poisoning of Socrates nor the tortures of Zeno,
since they are foreigners,
at least Canius, Seneca, and Soranus could be known,
whose memory is neither antiquated nor unhonored.
Nothing else dragged them down into ruin
except that in the studies of our education
they seemed most different from the morals of the bad.

"And so it is no wonder if in this sea of life
we are driven by whirling hurricanes,
in which this plan is precisely to displease the worst.
although in fact the troublesome group is numerous
it nevertheless is rejecting,
since it is not guided by any leader
but is agitated by so much rash error as random distraction.

"The one who if when building a point against us
has taken pains more vigorously,
our leader in fact assembles her resources inside,
while those around are busy seizing useless baggage.
Yet each one taking the most worthless of things
we are laughing at from above
safe from all the frantic disturbance
and on that fortified rampart on which
it should not be right for the raging of folly to attain.

IV
"Everyone clear in an orderly age
may set overbearing fate underfoot
and watching fortune straight in both directions
can maintain an invincible expression;
the fury and threats of the sea

turned not that tide utterly with the disturbing
nor so often as the unsettled bursting forge
hurls the smoky fires of Vesuvius
or to strike the eminent towers of custom
the way of the burning thunderbolt was moving.
  "Why are so many of the wretched amazed
at cruel tyrants raging without powers?
You should neither hope for anything nor be afraid,
and you would have disarmed the anger of the powerless;
yet every anxious one who fears or wishes,
which may not be steady and independent,
throws away a shield and having changed place
binds a chain which can drag.

4
  "Do you understand," she asked,
"and do these work into your soul
or is it 'the donkey lyre'?
Why are you crying, why do you yield to tears?
    'Speak out, do not conceal your mind.'
If you expect the service of a physician,
you should uncover the wound."
  Then I recovered the powers in the soul:
"Is there still a need for a reminder
and does not the cruel severity of fortune
by itself stand out in us enough?
Doesn't the appearance of this place itself move you?
Is this the library, which you yourself assigned
as a most certain seat for you in our home,
in which residing with me you often discussed
about knowledge of human and divine matters?
  "Was the condition such and expression such,
when I would search with you the secrets of nature,
when you would describe for me
with a rod the ways of the stars,
when you would shape our morals
and the whole system of life
according to the example of the heavenly order?
Are these the rewards we receive for complying with you?

"Yet you sanctioned this doctrine from Plato's mouth
that commonwealths would be blessed
if either those studious in wisdom were ruling
or their rulers came to study wisdom.
You from the mouth of the same man
advised this to be a necessary reason
for the wise to go into politics,
that for the government of the city
to be left to the bad and disgraceful citizens
would be ruin and destruction for the good.

"Therefore having operated on this authority
what I learned from you in quiet privacy
I wished to transfer into the act of public administration.
You and God who serves you in the minds of the wise
are aware that I never offered myself to any office
unless it was the study of all goods in common.

"Then with the bad came
serious and inexorable disagreements and,
because freedom of conscience holds, for watching justice
always the scorned displeasure of the more powerful.

"How often did I in the way catch Conigastus
making an attack on the fortunes of someone helpless,
how often did I put down Trigulla,
the overseer of the royal palace,
from attempting a wrong he was already carrying forward,
how often did I protect by authority exposed to dangers
the miserable who were vexed with unending prosecutions
by the ever unpunished greed of barbarians!

"Never has anyone pulled me away from justice to wrong.
I have felt sorry no differently than those
who suffered their provincial fortunes to be ruined
not only by private robbery but by public taxation.
When in the time of the bitter famine
an oppressive and inexplicable sale was considered
putting a ruinous price on Campania province scarcity,
I undertook a contest against the praetorian commander
on account of the common interest;
by the king learning of it I fought and defeated it
and the sale was not enforced.

"Paulinus, a brave consul, whose resources
the Palatine dogs in hope and ambition had already devoured,
I drew from their gaping jaws.
The penalty of a prejudiced accusation
might have seized another brave consul, Albinus,
had I not exposed myself
to the hatred of the informer Cyprian.

"Do I seem to have aroused great enough discord on me?
But I should have been more protected among the others,
I who by my love of justice
reserved nothing among the courtiers
by whom I might have been more protected.

"Now by which informers was I knocked down?
One of them, Basilius, once expelled from royal service
was forced into the denouncing of our name
by the necessity of debt.

"While Opilio and Gaudentius
when for countless and various frauds
royal decree decided they should go into exile
and when evidently unwilling they themselves
were looking to temple sanctuary for defense
and it was found out by the king,
he said unless they withdrew by a specified day from Ravenna
they would be expelled from the city
with distinguishing marks on their foreheads.
What does it seem could be added to this severity?
Yet on that day the denouncing of our name
by the same informers was undertaken.

"Then why? So did our virtues deserve this
or did prejudged condemnation make these accusers right?
So does nothing shame fortune
if not in the innocence of the accused
at least the cheapness of the accusers?

"But you investigate the sum of the charge
for which we are blamed.
It was said I wished the Senate to be safe.
You want the method.
I was charged with having hindered an informer,
lest he bring proof by which

he could make the Senate a defendant for treason.

"So what do you think, o teacher?
Shall we deny the crime, lest we be a shame to you?
But I did wish it, and I shall never cease to wish it.
Shall I confess?
But I stopped hindering the work of the informer.
Or should I call it wrong
having wished the welfare of that order?

"In fact by its own decrees about me
it tried to prove how this was wrong.
But imprudence ever deceiving itself
cannot change the merits of things,
nor for me by Socratic resolve do I think it is right
either to have the truth concealed
or to have a lie conceded.

"In whatever way it may be true,
I leave the valuing to you and to the judgment of the wise.
The sequence and truth of which matter
cannot escape the notice of posterity,
as I have committed the history to writing.

"Now why would it pertain to tell about the forged letters
by which I am blamed for having hoped for Roman liberty?
Their fraud would have been made clear if only for us
by the confession of the informers themselves,
since in every business it has the most strength,
granted that it had been allowed.

"Now what freedom can be left to be hoped for?
And if only there could be any!
I would have answered in the words of Canius, who
when he was accused by Gaius Caesar, the son of Germanicus,
of being aware of a plot against himself:
replied, 'If I had known, you would not have known.'

"For that reason grief has not dulled our feelings so far
that I should complain of the wicked
working impiety against the virtuous,
but I am surprised they hoped to be effective violently.
Now to wish it might be perhaps
weakness from our lower nature,
to be able to do against the innocent

what every wicked one has conceived
with God looking on is quite monstrous.

  "Thus it is not wrong that
a certain follower of yours has questioned:
'If in fact God exists,' he asks, 'where is evil from?
While where is good from, if it does not exist?'

  "But it might be possible for criminal persons,
who aim at the blood of all the good and the entire Senate,
also having wished us to go to ruin,
whom they had seen fight for the good and the Senate.
But surely we did not deserve the same from patriots too?

  "You remember, I think, since you yourself always
were present guiding me in whatever words and action,
you remember," I said, "at Verona
when the king eager for its common outcome
tried to transfer the charge of treason
by which Albinus was accused
to the whole order of the Senate, a Senate entirely innocent
which in spite of the danger to my safety I defended.

  "You know this I am mentioning is both true
and I am not at any time boasting in praise of myself;
for the mystery of conscience
is lessened in some way in approving itself,
as often as anyone accepts the reward of fame
for displaying what was done.

  "But you see the result followed after our innocence;
instead of the rewards of true virtue
we undergo the penalties of a falsified crime.
Did ever a clear confession of any action
so find the judges agreed on severity
that some were not moderated
either by the human nature of error itself
or by the uncertain condition of fortune for all mortals?

  "If it were said we had wished to burn sacred temples,
or to murder priests with an impious sword,
or to plot the slaughter of all the good,
even then I would have been present for the sentence,
at least confessed or convicted before being punished;

"Now about five hundred miles away mute and defenseless
on account of inclining affection toward the Senate
I am condemned to death and proscription.
O for such a crime no one can deserve to be convicted!

"Even those who indicted me saw the honor of the charge;
considering how much some were blackening it
with the mixture of some crime,
they were lying that I had polluted my conscience
by sacrilege out of ambition for position.

"And yet you implanted in us
expelled from the seat of our spirit
all desire of mortal things,
and under your eyes room for sacrilege was not possible.
For you were instilling in my ears and daily thoughts
that Pythagorean saying, 'Follow God.'

"Nor was it proper for me
to try for the support of the meanest characters,
in this excellence which you were composing
considering how you made me just like a god.

"Further the interior innocence of the home,
the meeting of most honored friends,
besides my father-in-law
pious and equal to you yourself in veneration
defend us from every suspicion of this crime.

"But—oh the shame!
while those take from you the trust of such a crime
and we seem by this itself to have been allied with mischief
because we are steeped in your teachings,
educated in your morals.

"So it is not enough
that your reverence has been of no benefit to me,
but besides you may be torn by the offense rather than me.
But certainly this even adds to the mass of our evils,
because the opinion of most
does not look at the merits of things
but at the results of fortune
and at the same time judges foresight to be worth
what luck has approved;
thus it is that the good opinion of all

first deserts the unlucky.

"What now are the rumors of the people,
how discordant and various the opinions,
I dislike recalling;
this I would rather say is
the ultimate burden of adverse fortune because,
as long as some crime is fastened on the wretched,
what they endure they are believed to have deserved.
And I in fact driven from all good things,
stripped of positions, disgraced in reputation
for kindness I bore punishment.

"Now I seem to see the criminal workshops of the wicked
flowing with delight and joy,
the most desperate threatening new and false denunciations,
the good lying low prostrated by terror of our crisis,
the profligate daring in fact any act with impunity,
while encouraged in accomplishing it by rewards,
and the harmless deprived not only of safety
but even of defense itself.

"Therefore it is pleasing to cry out:

V
"O builder of the starry orbit,
who is set on a universal throne
you turn heaven in a swift spiral
and compel the stars to submit to law,
so that at one time bright with a full horn
exposed to all the brother's flames
the moon conceals the lesser stars,
at another time paled by a dark horn
nearer it loses the lights from the sun
and who at the earliest time of night
rising drives the cooling western ones
again may alter the usual reins
paling the morning star with the rising of the sun:
you in the leaf-stripped cold of winter
draw tight the light to a shorter span,
you when the fervid heat comes
divide the agile hours of night.

"Your power regulates the diverse year,
so that the leaves which the north wind took away
the mild west wind brings back,
all the seeds Arcturus has seen
Sirius may parch as high crops:
nothing exempt from the ancient law
leaves the work of its proper station.

"Certainly governing all things by an end
the act of humans alone you refuse
as a guide to restrain by merit only.
For why does fleeting Fortune
keep changing conditions so much?

"The harmful penalty due the wicked presses the innocent,
but the morals of the perverted residing on a high throne
trample on the pious,
and the guilty in retaliation trample on the wrong necks.
Hidden in dark unconsciousness is concealed bright virtue,
and the just bear the crime of the unfair.

"For themselves fraud harms neither the perjured
nor the ones embellished with a colorful lie.
But since the strong ones liked to use them,
they are glad to subdue the highest rulers
whom countless people fear.

"O directly look to the wretched lands,
whoever binds the agreements of things!
Not a poor part of such great work
humans are shaken on the sea of fortune.
Check, guide, the impetuous floods
and where you rule immeasurable heaven
confirm in federation the steadfast lands."

5
When in continued sorrow I poured these out,
she with a calm expression and not moved by my complaints
said, "When I saw you mourning and crying
I knew instantly you were wretched and in exile;
but how long the exile was I would not have known
unless your speech had revealed it.

"But you have not even been pushed so far from home,
but strayed and, if you think you were pushed,
rather you expelled yourself;
for it is the case concerning you
what never would have been right for anyone else.

"For if you remember the country from which you descended,
not as Athens was formerly ruled by command of a crowd,
but 'It is one ruler, one king'
who rejoices in crowds of citizens not in rejection;
to be led by those reins and so comply
is the freedom of justice.

"Or are you ignorant of that oldest law of the community
whereby it is a sacred right for that one not to be an exile
who has preferred to establish a seat in it?
For the one who is contained by its fort and defense,
there is no fear of exile being deserved;
but whoever wishes to abandon living there
equally abandons also the deserving.

"And so not so much of this place moves me as your face,
nor do I need library walls arranged with ivory and glass
rather than the seat of your mind, in which are no books
but that which creates value in books,
sentences of my books I once arranged.

"And it is true about your services to the common good,
but as for the many carried out by you few have you told.
Of objections to you either honest or false
you have mentioned what is noted by all.

"Of the accusations by the wicked and fraudulent
you have correctly thought to touch on them slightly,
since they are repeated by the mouth of the public
better and more fully reviewing them all.

"Also you have vehemently noised about
the action of the unjust Senate.
About us also have you grieved for the slander;
for hurts damaging our reputation too have you wept.

"The last sorrow got hot against fortune
and in outcry of its not repaying the equal reward of merit;
in the extreme poetry of raging, you proposed prayers
that the peace which rules heaven should rule lands too.

"But since the most emotional disturbance broods over you,
and varied sorrow, anger and mourning are distracting you,
so that you are now of a mind,
not yet do the more powerful remedies take hold of you.

"And so let us use milder ones for a little while,
so that which in flowing disturbances hardens into swelling
may soften by a coaxing touch
until the taking of the medicine of sharper power.

VI
"When with severe rays of the sun
the constellation of Cancer scorches,
then whoever in declining plenty
entrusted seeds to the furrow
cheated by the promise of Ceres
must go to the oak trees.

"Never look in purple woods
for a couch of violets
when the hissing plain bristles
with the fierce north wind;
nor would you look with eager hand
to prune the vines in spring
if you would enjoy the taste of grapes;
rather in autumn
Bacchus confers his gifts.

"God designates the times
adapting to the proper functions,
and these cycles which it itself controlled
it does not allow to be mixed.

"Thus because a way of violence
abandons reliable order
it does not have a pleasant outcome.

6
"First then will you open to me the state of your mind
to undertake and test it with a very few questions,
so that I may understand
what should be the method of your treatment?"

"Certainly," I said, "in your judgment
whatever request you will wish I shall answer."
   Then she said, "Do you suppose this world
is led by random and chance accidents
or do you believe there is any rule of reason in it?"
   "No," I said, "I don't at all think that
such certain accidents would be changed by chance;
truly I know the founder God presides over its work
nor ever would there be a day
which will dislodge me from this true belief."
   "So it is," she said;
"for you even recited it a little before
and deplored humans being so much outside of divine care;
for concerning the others nothing would change
that they are ruled by reason.
But ooh, I wonder very much why
one placed in so healthy an attitude should be ill.
Let us search deeper for the truth;
I cannot but think some interpretation is missing.
But tell me, since you do not doubt God rules the world,
do you also pay attention by which governments it is ruled?"
   "Scarcely," I said, "do I recognize
the meaning of your question,
much less can I reply to the inquiry."
   "Surely," she said, "I am not mistaken
that something is missing,
in that as with an opening in a hard fortification
emotional disease has insinuated itself into your spirit?
But tell me, do you remember what the end of things may be,
the intent toward which all of nature is aiming?"
   "I have heard it," I said,
"but mourning has dulled the memory."
   "Yet you know from where all things have proceeded."
   "I know," I said, and I answered it is God.
   "And how could it happen that
in having understood the origin
you should be ignorant of what the end of things should be?
Yet it is true the behavior of these disturbances is strong,
so that it can in fact change a person's position,

but it cannot destroy and uproot the whole for oneself.
But I should like you to answer this too:
do you remember that you are a person?"

"Why should I not remember?" I replied.

"Can you then reveal what a person should be?"

"Are you asking this,
whether I am sure I am an animal by the rational and mortal?
I know it, and I confess myself to be it."

And she said, "Do you know yourself to be nothing else?"

"Nothing."

"Already I know," she replied,
"the other very greatest cause of your illness;
you have stopped knowing what you should be yourself.
Thus I have come upon fully the reason for your sickness
and the approach for the restoring of safety.

"For since you are confused in your forgetfulness,
you also have grieved that
you are exiled and robbed of your personal goods;
while since you are ignorant
of what should be the end of things,
you think worthless and criminal people
are powerful and happy;
while since you have forgotten
by which governments the world is ruled,
you estimate these changes of fortune
to waver without a guide:
great causes not only of illness, but truly of death too.

"But give thanks to the author of safety,
because your whole nature has not yet forsaken you.
We have the greatest spark of your health,
the true judgment about the government of the world,
because you believe it is not subject to the fall of chance
but to divine reason;
therefore be alarmed at nothing,
already for you from this smallest little spark
a vital heat will blaze.

"But since it is not yet time for stronger remedies,
and it is agreed to be the nature of minds
that as often as they will abandon truths,

they will assume false opinions,
from which the fog of emotions sprang
which confuses that true insight,
I shall attempt for a little while to reduce this
with the mild and moderate ones,
so that with the shadows of the deceitful emotion dispersed
you can recognize the clarity of true light.

VII
    "Stars concealed
by black clouds
can shed
no light.
    "If the sea is rolling
the troubled south wind
mixes the surf,
just now a glassy wave
and like the clear ones
the wave for days
soon released
filthy mud
obstructs with sights,
and what is wandering
from the high mountains
the flowing river
often stops
freed from rock
thrown against a boulder.
    "You also if you wish
clear light
to perceive the truth,
by the straight path
to travel the foot-path:
pleasures drive out,
drive out fear
and banish hope
and sorrow may not appear.
    "The mind is cloudy
and defeated by restraints
when these are ruling."

Notes to Book 2:

2: According to the history of Herodotus, after the Persian king Cyrus II the Great had defeated the Lydians in battle at Sardis in 546 BC., Croesus was to be burned on a pyre; but moved by the change of fortune of this king, Cyrus ordered the flames extinguished. However, they could not be quenched until Croesus called on Apollo and a rain doused the fire.

2: Aemilius Paulus, consul of Rome, defeated Perses, the last king of Macedonia at Pydna in 168 BC.

6: Diogenes Laertius tells the story of two different philosophers who bit off their tongues and spat them at tyrants: Zeno of Elea about 460 BC and Anaxarchus about 330 BC.

6: The Roman general Regulus was defeated by the Carthaginians in 255 BC. According to Cicero he was sent to Rome with a proposal for a prisoner exchange, which he counseled against, then returned a prisoner himself to Carthage.

VI: Nero ruled the vast Roman empire from 54 to 68 CE, ordering the murder of his step-brother Britannicus and his mother Agrippina.

VII: Fabricius was a Roman general and consul in the third century BC known for his integrity and refusal to accept a bribe from Pyrrhus.

VII: Brutus led the overthrow of the last Tarquin king and became the first consul of Rome in 509 BC. A later Brutus led the conspiracy which assassinated Julius Caesar in 44 BC.

VII: Cato the Elder (234-149 BC) was famous for upholding strict Roman standards of morality and for his orations against Carthage. Cato the Younger (95-46 BC) committed suicide after Pompey's defeat by Caesar, because he feared it was the end of the republic.

Book 2

1

After this she was quiet for a little while,
and when she had gathered my attention by her modest silence
she began as follows:
"If I have understood thoroughly
the causes and condition of your sickness,
you are wasting away
in fondness and desire of former fortune;
this change has upset so much of your spirit
just as you imagine it for yourself.

"I understand the manifold pretenses of that monster
and how far with these she depends on
the most flattering intimacy to delude them
until she confuses with irresistible sorrow
those whom she has abandoned unexpectedly.

"If you remember her nature, morals and merit,
you will know that you neither had in her
nor lost in her any beauty at all;
but, as I suppose, I shall not have to work much
to recall this to your memory.
For you used to attack with brave words
both her presence and flattery
and from our sanctuary criticize her with quoted sentences.

"Truly every sudden change of things does not happen
without a certain kind of disturbance of minds;
so the fact is that you too for a little while
have deviated from your calmness.

"But it is time for you to take and taste
something soft and pleasing,
which passing through to the interior
will make way for healthier drinks.
Thus may the persuasion of sweet argument assist,
which then proceeds so much by a straight path
when it does not desert our principles,
and when by this native music of our household god
it may chime in now lighter then heavier meters.

"What is it then, O human,
that has thrown you down in melancholy and mourning?

You have seen, I believe, something new and unusual.
You think fortune is changed toward you:
you are mistaken.

"These are always her morals; that is her nature.
She has preserved around you her peculiar constancy
rather by her very own mutability;
such it was when she was flattering,
when she played with you
by the attractions of false happiness.

"You have detected the blind goddess's ambiguous face.
Though she still veils herself to others,
to you she has become completely known.
If you approve, you may use it for behavior, don't complain.
If you are horrified at dishonesty,
reject and abandon playing at ruin;
for she who now is so great a cause of mourning
ought to have been a cause of calmness.
For she left you,
she whom no one can ever be sure will not leave.

"Or do you really find valuable happiness that goes away,
and is a fortune not reliable in staying present dear to you
and which when it has departed brings mourning?
But if one cannot keep it through control
and fleeing it causes the disastrous,
what else is it but a kind of indication of future disaster?

"For it will never be sufficient
to look at the situation that is in front of one's eyes;
prudence measures the outcome of things;
and in the same way mutability into one or the other
makes both the terrors of fortune to be less
and the longings not alluring.

"Finally you should bear with an even spirit
whatever is produced within fortune's area
since you first put your neck in her yoke.
But if you wish to write the law of staying and going
for the one whom you have freely chosen as your mistress
will you not be wrong,
and will not impatience aggravate a fate
which you cannot exchange?

"If you commit a sail to the winds,
not where your will aims will you advance
but where the breezes will drive;
if you entrust seeds to the fields,
will you not weigh out mutually fruitful and barren years.

"You have given yourself to fortune's ruling;
you should comply with the behavior of the mistress.
Do you really want to hold back
the impetus of her rolling wheel?
But, most stupid of all mortals,
if it begins to stop it ceases to be chance.

I

"As her arrogant right hand turns the alternations
and is heaving like the surge of Euripus,
just now she crushes cruelly terrible kings
and a deceptive face raises the lowly conquered.
She does not hear the wretched or care for the weeping
and on the other side the groaning,
which she made them endure, she ridicules.
So she plays, so she proves her powers
and with surprises shows a great display, to see if
anyone may be seen prostrate and happy in the same hour.

2

"Now I might be willing to deliberate briefly with you
in the words of Fortune herself;
then you censure, or the law may prosecute.

"'Why do you, human,
make me a defendant with daily complaints?
What injury have we done to you?
Have we taken away from you your goods?
With a judge from anywhere contend with me
about the possession of wealth and position,
and if you show that any part of these is properly mortals'
I will then freely allow you
to take back what was to have been yours.

"'When nature produced you from your mother's womb,
I received you naked of all things and helpless,

kept you warm with my resources and,
whereas now it makes you impatient with us,
I brought you up under the easy favor of indulgence,
surrounded you with all the abundance and splendor
which are right for me.

"'Now it pleases me to withdraw my hand:
be grateful as for the use of another's;
you have no right of complaining
as if you absolutely lost yours.
Why then do you groan?
No violence is brought against you from us.

"'Wealth, honors and the rest of such things
are right for me.
The servants recognize the mistress:
they come with me; with my going away they depart.
Boldly I declare, if these were yours
which you bemoan are missing,
you never would have lost them.

"'Or am I alone kept from exercising my right?
Heaven is permitted to reveal bright days
and to conceal the same with dark nights;
the year is permitted to redeem the face of the land
at one time with flowers and fruits
at another to confound it with clouds and frosts;
it is right for the sea
at one time to charm with a level surface
at another to tremble with storms and waves:
is incessant human greed to bind us
to a consistency alien to our morals?

"'This is our power; we play this continuous game:
we turn the wheel in a revolving cycle,
we like to change the lowest to the highest,
the highest to the lowest.
Ascend if it pleases,
but choose it, only if you will not think it an injury
when the procedure of my game requires you to descend.

"'Or are you ignorant of my morals?
Don't you know about Croesus, king of Lydia,
who a little before terrified Cyrus,

next was pitifully thrown on a pyre committed to the flames
then protected by rain from heaven?
Surely it has not escaped you that Paulus spent holy tears
for the defeats of Perses the king captured by him?

"'What else is the clamor of tragedies lamenting
but the indiscriminate blows of fortune
overturning happy sovereignties?
Did you not learn in adolescence of two vessels,
one filled with bad, and the other with good
standing in Jove's entranceway?

"'What if you have taken more fully from the good part?
What if I have not gone away from you completely?
What if this mutability of mine itself
is a fair cause for your hoping for better things?
In any case should you waste away in spirit,
and do you want to live by your own law
placed within a sovereignty in common with all?

II
"'If the roused sea turns up
   as many sands with swift breezes
or as many as high stars shine
   in the starry night sky
so much wealth may Plenty with a full horn scatter
   and not draw back her hand,
still the human race would never stop
   crying its wretched complaints.
Although prayers a willing God may receive
   wasteful of much gold
and fit out the greedy with bright honors,
   already the possessions seem nothing,
but swallowing the gains cruel rapacity
   stretches a gaping mouth elsewhere.
What bridle now would hold back
   headlong lust by a definite end,
when fluent with rather ample rewards
   the thirst of having burns?
Never does the rich one lead who anxiously sighing
   believes oneself needing.'

3

"Then if Fortune spoke in this way for herself to you,
certainly you would not have anything
you could utter in reply;
or if there is anything by which
you may be rightly protected in your complaint,
you should mention it;
we will give space for talking."

Then I said, "In fact yours are plausible,
and smeared over with the honey of rhetoric and sweet music
such that when they are heard they amuse,
but for the wretched it is a deeper feeling of evils;
and so when these stop sounding on the ears
an implanted sadness weighs down the spirit."

And she said, "So it is;
for these are not yet your illness's remedies,
but so far they are a sort of bandage
for the stubborn sorrows opposing the treatment;
for the ones which will penetrate in deep themselves
I will apply when it would be timely.

"Yet truly you may not wish to consider yourself wretched;
or have you forgotten
the number and measure of your happiness?
I say nothing about how abandoned by a parent
the care of the greatest men took you
and gathered you into the city's most eminent family,
because the most valuable kind of relationship is,
you had begun to be dear before being kin.

"Who did not proclaim you most happy
with such magnificent in-laws with a modest wife
besides suitable male offspring too?
I go past—for it pleases to go past the common—
positions assumed in youth denied to the old;
one is glad to come to
the unique culmination of your happiness.

"If the enjoyment of mortal things
has any weight of happiness,
can the memory of that brightness be destroyed
by as great a mass of heaping evils as can be

when you saw your two sons consuls together
transported from home among the numerous senators
among the cheerful common people,
when they were officially seated in the Senate
you as speaker praising the king
earned the glory of genius and eloquence,
when in the circus in the middle of the two consuls
you satisfied the expectations of the surrounding crowd
by a triumphal distribution?

  "You devoted, as I suppose, words to Fortune
as long as she stroked you,
as long as she cherished you as her darling.
A gift that she never gave to an individual you took away.
Will you not then reckon up accounts with Fortune?

  "Now is the first time
she has dazzled you with a black eye.
If you consider the number and measure
of your glad and sad times,
so far you will not be able to deny your happiness.

  "But if for this reason
you don't value your being fortunate
since what then seemed pleasing went away,
in that you should not think you are wretched,
since now what they believe is sad will pass.

  "Or have you come on this stage of life
now for the first time by surprise and as a stranger?
Do you think there is any consistency in human affairs
when often a quick hour has destroyed a person?

  "For even if faith in the chances of remaining is thin,
nevertheless the last day of life
is a kind of death of the fortune still remaining.
What then do you think to answer:
do you desert her by dying, or she you by fleeing?

III
"When by the pole the sun in a rosy chariot
  begins to disperse its light,
the dawning face fades the dulled
  stars with tightening flames.

When the grove by the breeze of the warming west wind
  has been reddened with spring roses,
the cloudy south wind may blow furiously,
  by then with thorns the beauty goes away.
Often in calm serenity shines
  the sea with motionless waves;
often the north wind stirs up raging hurricanes
  on the upset sea.
If her form in the world seldom is constant,
  if the alterations vary so much,
trust in the failing fortunes of humans,
  trust in transient goods!
It is constant and fixed by eternal law
  that nothing born may be constant."

4
  Then I said, "You are recalling truths,
nurse of all virtues,
nor can I deny my fastest progress of success.
But this is because reflecting boils it more vehemently;
for in all the adversity of fortune
the unhappiest kind of misfortune is to have been happy."
  "But because you," she said,
"may be atoning for the punishment of false opinion,
you cannot rightly blame it for things.
For if this empty name of accidental happiness moves you,
you may consider with me
how you may be abundant with more and the greatest.
  "Then if you were possessing what is rated
the most valuable in all your fortune
that is preserved for you by the divine
unhurt still and inviolable,
can you while retaining the better ones
pretend rightly it is because of misfortune?
  "And yet thrives safe
that most valuable ornament of the human race
your father-in-law Symmachus and,
because you are under an obligation
not to be lazy at the cost of life,

a complete man made out of wisdom and virtues:
in his security he sighs for your injuries.

"Your modest wife lives with character,
excelling in shy chastity and,
as I include all her gifts concisely,
she is like her father;
she lives, I say, and for you
she preserves so much spirit by the detesting of this life,
perhaps I myself too must grant
I have reduced your happiness by one;
in longing for you she languishes in tears and sorrow.

"What should I say about the sons of consular rank,
whose example of character now just as in boyhood
outshines that of either father or grandfather?

"Then since the principal care for mortals
is holding on to life,
you, if you knew your blessings, should be happy,
to whom are available even now
what no one doubts are more dear than life.

"Therefore dry the tears already;
not yet is every single fortune detested,
nor has too strong a storm fallen upon you
since your firm anchors hang on
which allow neither relief in the present
nor hope of future opportunity to go away."

"And I pray they do hang on," I said;
"for in their remaining, however things may hold themselves,
we shall stay afloat.
But you see how many of our distinctions may have ceased."

And she said, "We have moved forward somewhat
if you are no longer annoyed with all of your lot.
But I cannot bear your whims,
whereby you bewail with so much sorrow and trouble
that there is something lacking in your happiness.

"For whose happiness is so constructed
that one has no quarrel from any side
with the quality of one's status?
For the condition of human welfare is a troubled thing,
and either its wholeness never appears

or its continuation never holds out.

"Property for this one abounds,
but the degenerate blood is a shame;
the nobility of another is made known,
but the one shut in prefers
the household scarcity of things to be unknown.

"And that one overflowing with both
laments life unmarried;
that one happy in marriage who is childless
nourishes property to be inherited by strange children;
another rejoicing in offspring
weeps in mourning for the wrongs of a son or daughter.

"For that reason no one easily agrees
with the condition of one's fortune;
for in each one the thing not experienced is unknown,
which having been experienced is terrifying.

"Add that the feeling of the happiest is most delicate,
and unless all things are supplied to one's command
unaccustomed to every adversity
one is thrown by the smallest things:
so very small are the things
which pull down the highest from the happiest blessings.

"How many do you conjecture there are
who would consider themselves near heaven
if the smallest part of your remaining fortune came to them?
This place itself, which you call exile,
is the homeland of those inhabiting it.

"Thus nothing is wretched except when you think so,
and conversely every fate is blessed
by the evenmindedness of being patient.
Who is so happy, who when one yields to impatience
a hand would not wish to change it's status?

"With how much bitterness
is the sweetest of human happiness sprinkled!
For even if enjoying it seems to be delightful,
nevertheless one cannot retain it when it would go away.

"Then it is evident how wretched
may be the happiness of mortal things,
which neither endures forever among the evenminded

nor delights entirely the troubled.
Why then, o mortals, do you aim outside
for the happiness placed inside you?
You are confused by error and ignorance.

"I will show you briefly
the axis of the highest happiness.
Is there anything you value more than your very self?
'Nothing,' you will answer.
Then if you would be in control of yourself,
you will possess something you would never want to lose
nor could fortune take it away.

"And yet as you would recognize that
happiness cannot be constant in these accidental things,
check this out.
If happiness is the highest good
of a nature living by reason,
and the highest good is not
what can be torn away by any method,
since what cannot be taken away surpasses it,
it is obvious that the instability of fortune
cannot aspire to gaining happiness.

"Besides, such failing happiness carries along one
who either knows it or does not know it to be changeable.
If one does not know,
what happy fate can there be in the blindness of ignorance?
If one knows, one must be apprehensive of losing
that which one doubts not can be lost;
therefore continuous fear does not allow one to be happy.
Or perhaps if one should lose it,
does one think it indifferent?
So too it is a very small good
whose loss may be borne with an even mind.

"And since you are the same one whom I know
was persuaded and informed by very many proofs
that human minds are in no way mortal,
and since it should be clear that
chance happiness is ended by the body's death,
it cannot be doubted, if this can carry off happiness,
that the entire race of mortals

is collapsing in misery at death's boundary.

"But if we know that many have sought
the true enjoyment of happiness
not by death alone but also by sorrows and sacrifices,
in what way can the present make them happy
which finished does not make them wretched?

IV
"Whoever wishes to build
  an unfailing secure foundation
and be steady and not overthrown
  by the noise from the breezes of the east wind
and takes care to reject
  the threatening sea with its waves,
should avoid the high mountain peak,
  the thirsty deserts;
the former the insolent south wind
  presses with all its strength,
the latter loose decline
  to bear the hovering weight.
Fleeing the dangerous fate
  of an elegant foundation
remember to be certain to fix
  the home on humble rock.
However much it may thunder with destruction
  the wind mixing the level sea,
you built on the calm
  happy in fortified vigor
lead a serene life
  smiling at the sky's angers.

5
"But since already the medicines of my reason
are sinking into you,
I am thinking of using somewhat stronger ones.
Well then of course, supposing for the purpose of argument
the property and gifts of fortune were not momentary,
what is there in them which either could ever become yours
or not cheapen upon examination and inspection?

"Are riches valuable either from your nature or theirs?
Which of them is more so?
Gold or the power of accumulated money?
And yet this shines better spent more than heaped up,
if in fact avarice always causes hatred,
generosity distinction.

"But if what cannot remain with one
is transferred to another,
then money is valuable when
having been transferred by bestowing it on others for use
it ceases to be possessed.

"But the same, if it were collected by one
wherever the amount is among the people,
it would make the rest destitute of it.
And a voice in fact fills equally all the many who heard it,
but your riches unless diminished cannot pass to more;
because when it is done,
it is necessary to make poor those whom it leaves.

"Oh then scant and helpless are riches,
which to have them all with more is not right
and they do not come to anyone
without impoverishing the rest.

"Or does the brightness of jewels attract the eyes?
But if what is in this luster is anticipated,
that is the light of the jewels, not of the humans;
in fact I am surprised humans eagerly admire them.
For why is the lacking of movement and structure of spirit
that which rightly seems to be beautiful
to a reasonable and animated nature?

"Although they may be works of their maker
and attract somewhat the lowest distinction of beauty,
all the same placed below your excellence
they are not at all deserving of your admiration.

"Or does the beauty of the land amuse you? Why not?
For it is a very beautiful portion of a beautiful work.
As sometimes we delight in the appearance of a calm sea,
so we admire sky, stars, moon and sun.
Surely none of these touches you;
surely you dare not boast of any such splendor?

Perhaps you yourself are adorned by the flowers of spring
or is it your fertility that swells the fruits in summer?

"Why are you seized by empty delights?
Why do you embrace external goods for yourself?
Fortune will never make yours
what the nature of things made for others.

"In fact the fruits of the earth
far from doubt ought to be nourishment for animals;
but if you wish to fill the need that is enough for nature,
there is nothing that you should seek
from the abundance of fortune.
For nature is content with a few and little;
upon which sufficiency if you wish to impose excess,
what you pour in will be either unpleasant or harmful.

"Now you really think beauty shines in various clothes.
If looking at them is a pleasant sight,
I would admire either the nature of the material
or the ability of the maker.

"Or does a long line of servants really make you happy?
Who if they should be corrupt in morals,
are a ruinous burden to the house,
and quite unfriendly to the master himself;
while if they are honest,
how may the honesty of others be counted as your wealth?

"Out of all these goods which you consider yours
none of them may clearly be shown to be your good.
If none of this beauty is obtained by grasping,
what is that for which
either having lost you should grieve
or having retained you should be glad?

"But if by nature they are beautiful,
what does it matter to you?
For these by themselves would have been pleasing
though separated from your wealth.
For they are not valued
for the reason of coming into your riches,
but since they seem valuable
you prefer to add them to your riches.

"Now why do you desire such clatter from fortune?
To banish need, I think, you seek plenty.
And yet this turns out for you in the reverse;
of course by more supports the work is different
in the guarding of your valuable furniture,
and it is true that
those who possess very much need very much,
and conversely the least
those whose abundance is measured by the necessity of nature
not by the excess of courting.

"Now is there no personal good inside you
that you seek your goods in things outside and remote?
So is the condition of things turned
so that reason's animal deservedly divine
is not otherwise to be bright for itself
unless it is seen in possession of inanimate furniture?

"Also others at any rate are content with their own,
but you, just like a god in mind,
chase after from the lowest things
decorations of an outstanding nature,
nor do you understand how much
you may do injury to your maker.
That one willed the human race
to be superior to all earthly things,
yet you throw down your dignity below the lowest.

"For if by everyone each's good is agreed to be
more valuable than that to which it belongs,
since you judge your goods to be the poorest of things
to these same things you lower yours in reputation.
Which in fact does not happen at all unjustly.

"Since this is the condition of human nature
that one may surpass other things
only when one is aware of oneself,
nevertheless one is reduced below a beast
if one ceases to know oneself;
for to other animals it is natural
to be ignorant of oneself;
with humans it comes by vice.

"How really extensive is this error of yours is evident,
whereby you think someone
can be adorned by strange decorations!
But it cannot be done;
for if anything should shine from the additions,
the additions themselves are in fact what are praised,
while it endures from these that covering and disguise
no less in its own foulness.

"Certainly I deny anything is good
which harms the one having it.
Surely I am not lying about it, am I?
'Not at all,' you will say.
And yet riches very often are harmful in possessing them,
since every worst one all the more covetous of another
thinks it is oneself alone
who is in any way most worthy of gold and jewels.

"You then, who now agitated are alarmed by club and sword,
if you had traveled the path of this life an empty traveler
you might sing in person by the bandit.
How very bright the happiness of mortal wealth,
when you have attained it you stop being secure!

V
"Happy the very great previous age
content with faithful fields
not ruined by idle debauchery,
with ease when late it was the habit
to dissolve hunger by nuts.

"They did not know the rewards of Bacchus
to mingle in a sweet liquid
nor bright woolly silk
to mix with Tyrian dye.

"Grass gave them healthy sleep,
the sliding stream a drink too,
the tallest pine shade.

"Not yet were they operating on the sea's depths,
nor with costly picked items on every side
did a foreigner see new shores.

"Then the cruel battle trumpets were silent,
nor with bitter hatred
did spilt blood soak the rugged fields.

"For why should the previous wish to provoke
with any arms a hostile furor,
since they never saw cruel wounds
nor any rewards for bloodshed?

"If only our times would return
to the morals of the ancients!
But more cruel than the fires of Aetna
the boiling love of having burns.

"Alas, who was that first one
who wanting to hide
weights of hidden gold and gems
dug expensive dangers?

6
"But why should I discuss positions and power,
which you unaware of true position and power
equate with heaven?
Which if they had fallen into the worst somehow,
which in the belching flames of Aetna,
then would they have yielded such masses of deluge?

"Surely, as I think you remember,
command by the consul, that had been a principle of liberty,
on account of consular arrogance
your ancestors wanted to abolish it,
just as on account of the same arrogance before
the title of king had been taken away from the state.

"But if when, because it is very rare,
they are conferred on the honest,
what is pleasing in this other than honesty being employed?
Thus honor does not come to the virtuous from position
but from virtue honor comes to position.

"While what is your coveted and bright power?
Do you not, o terrestrial animal, consider
over whom you are looking to preside?
Now if you saw among mice one
claiming some right and power for itself before the rest,

with how much laughter would you be moved!
  "While what, if you look at the body,
can you find weaker than a human,
whom often too either a bite or entrance in secret
of any creeping thing into the muscles may kill?
  "How can anyone really exercise a right upon any other
except upon the body alone and—
I speak of fortune—what is below the body?
Surely you will not impose anything on a free spirit?
Surely you will not remove from its state of calmness
a mind stable in its coherent reason?
  "When a certain tyrant was thinking that a free man
compelled by punishments himself so that he might betray
the ones guilty of conspiring in a plot against himself,
that one bit and cut off his tongue
and raging threw it in the face of the tyrant;
thus the torture,
which the tyrant was thinking was the substance of cruelty,
the wise man made into courage.
  "But why is it that everyone can do to another,
what one cannot control from another oneself?
We have heard how Busiris accustomed to killing strangers
was sacrificed by the stranger Hercules.
Regulus drove many Carthaginian prisoners of war in bonds,
but soon held out his own hands to the victor's chains.
  "Then do you think anything of that person's power
who oneself can do to another
what one could not make sure one may survive
when the other does it to oneself?
  "Besides, if in positions and powers themselves
there belonged any natural and innate good,
they never would come to the worst.
For opposites are not accustomed to uniting with each other;
nature rejects that contraries should be joined together.
  "So since it may not be doubted that
generally the worst do function in these positions,
certainly it is clear that that is not natural good itself
which is allowed to cling to the worst themselves.
That in fact can be judged more worthy

from all the rewards of fortune,
which come more fully to the most dishonest.

"From which also I am thinking of considering this,
because no one doubts courage is in the one whom
one has observed to be courageous
and it is also obvious
speed is present in the one who is fast;
thus for instance music makes musicians,
medicine doctors, rhetoric orators:
for the nature of each thing acts because it is appropriate
and is not mixed up with the effects of contrary things
and even expels those which are opposite.

"Nevertheless wealth cannot quench incessant greed,
nor does power cause control of oneself for the one whom
corrupt desires hold back tightly with unbreakable chains,
and position collected by the dishonest
not only does not make them worthy
but rather it betrays and exposes the unworthy.

"Why does it come out so?
It is because you like to call things themselves
having different qualities with false names,
which easily are refuted by the effect of their realities;
and so neither those riches nor that power
nor this position can rightly be called so.

"Finally the same may be concluded about all fortune,
in which nothing is to be sought;
it is obvious nothing of native goodness is in it,
which does not always join itself with the goods,
and it does not make good
those with whom it may have been joined.

VI
"We know how many ruins it yielded
with the city burned and fathers slashed
by a brother who once wild destroyed
and dripped with the profuse blood of his mother,
the body and cold sight perusing
the area he did not wet with tears, but he could be
censor of the decorum of the one extinguished.

"Nevertheless he with a scepter was ruling people
whom the sun sees until its rays
are concealed under the waves,
with the last coming from the beginning,
whom the seven frosty constellations overrule,
whom the raging South with its dry heat
parches recooking the shining sands.

"Surely in the end lofty power could not
turn the perverse madness of Nero?
Alas the heavy fate, how often the unequal
sword is added to cruel poison!"

7

Then I said, "You know yourself
the ambition of mortal things
has had the least mastery over us;
but we have chosen the opportunity of managing things
so that virtue will not grow old unmentioned."
And she said, "Yet this is one thing
which could attract in fact outstanding natural minds
but which are not yet guided by perfection
to the finishing touch of virtues,
the desire of course for glory
and of best deserving fame in public business.

"Consider how thin it may be and so empty of all weight.
The whole circumference of the earth,
as you have interpreted by astrological demonstration,
compared with the space of heaven
corresponds to holding the calculation of a point, that is,
if it were compared in greatness to the celestial sphere,
it would be judged to have absolutely no space at all.

"Then of this so very meager region in the world
about a fourth portion is,
as you have learned from the proof of Ptolemy,
inhabited by animals which are known to us.
From this fourth if you subtracted in thought
how much is sunk in sea and marsh
and how much may be extended in desolate territory,
barely the narrowest area is left for inhabiting by humans.

"Then in this least point
which you fenced around and enclosed by a point
do you think about making public fame,
about publishing a name,
as though glory so compressed by narrow and meager limits
may have eminence and greatness?

"Add that many nations inhabit this same small living area
diverse in respect to language, customs, their whole life,
to which then the difficulty of travel
besides the difference in speaking plus the rarity of trade
not only the fame of a single human
but that of cities in fact is not able to reach.

"Finally in the time of Cicero,
as he indicates opportunely, the fame of the Roman republic
had not yet passed beyond the Caucasus mountains,
and it was even then mature
terrifying to Parthians and other nations of that region.

"Don't you see then how narrow,
how compressed the glory may be,
which you are laboring to expand and propagate?
Or may the glory of a Roman person advance
where the fame of the Roman name is unable to pass?

"Moreover, don't the morals and also the traditions
of different nations disagree between themselves,
so that what is judged praiseworthy among some
may be worthy of punishment among others?

"Thus if someone delights in this commendation of fame
in most populations it is of no use to publish a name.
Then each will be content
having spread glory among one's own,
and within the boundaries of one nation
that bright immortality of fame will be confined.

"But how many men, the most eminent in their times,
does oblivion blot out in need of writers!
And yet why should the writings themselves profit,
which with their authors longer and obscure age covers?

"While you seem to propagate immortality for yourselves
when you imagine fame in a future time.
But if you study about the infinite extent of eternity,

what do you have that you will enjoy
from the long duration of your name?
    "In fact the character of one moment
if it is compared with ten thousand years,
since both ways it is a definite period,
may nevertheless have some very small portion;
but this very number of years
and the multiplication of this as much as you like
cannot even be compared to interminable duration.
    "Though compared to themselves
there might be some mutuality with finite things,
with the infinite and the finite
there could never really be a comparison.
So it happens that fame
for however long of a time one may like,
if it is thought of with unexhausted eternity,
may be seen to be not small but plainly non-existent.
    "Now you unless for popular sounds and idle rumors
are unable to act correctly,
and having abandoned the pre-eminence
of conscience and virtue
you demand rewards from strange gossip.
    "Listen how humorously someone ridiculed
in the lightness of this method of arrogance.
For when a certain person was attacked with insults,
who not for the practice of true virtue
but for false overbearing glory
had assumed for himself the name of philosopher,
and added one might know then oneself
whether that one was a philosopher,
if in fact one could bear
inflicted wrongs gently and patiently,
he for a little while assumed patience
and accepted the assaults as he was taunting.
'Now at last,' he said,
'do you understand me to be a philosopher?'
    "Then that one said too sharply,
'I would have understood, if you had kept silent.'

"Why is it that to outstanding men—
for the discussion is about these—
who seek glory from virtue,
why, I ask, is it that one should seek for this from fame
after the body is released by the moment of death?

"For if, because our reasons forbid the belief,
humans die completely, there is no glory at all,
since the one of whom it is said to be
does not exist at all.

"While if the mind correctly conscious in itself
released free from its earthly prison seeks heaven,
does it not spurn all earthly business,
while enjoying itself in heaven
it is glad to be exempt from earthly things?

VII
"Whoever alone by headlong mind seeks
  and believes glory is the highest,
should perceive the wide open regions of the ethereal
  and the compressed situation of the world;
not being able to fill up the small circle
  one will be ashamed of an enlarged name.
Why are the proud eager to lighten
  the mortal collar from their necks in vain?
Although diffuse fame through distant peoples passing
  may develop languages,
and a great house may shine with bright titles,
  death scorns high glory,
rolls on the humble and lofty head alike
  and makes the low equal to the highest.
Where do the bones of the loyal Fabricius remain now?
  Why is Brutus or Cato stiff?
Surviving shallow fame marks a name
  with a very few letters in vain.
But because we have known the noble terms
  surely it is not given to know the destroyed?
Consequently you lay absolutely unknown,
  and fame does not make them known.
But if you suppose life is drawn out longer
  by the aura of a mortal name,

when a later day snatches this from you too
  then the second death awaits you.

8
  "But do not think I wage inexorable war against fortune:
there is a time when not deceptive about humans
she may be well served,
at the time of course when she opens herself,
when she uncovers her facade and declares her morals.
By chance you do not yet understand what I mean;
it is strange what I am eager to say,
and so far I can hardly explain the meaning in words.
  "As a matter of fact I think adversity
is more beneficial for humans than fortune;
for the latter always with the pretense of happiness,
when it seems charming, is lying;
the former always is true,
when it shows itself inconstant with change.
  "The latter deceives; the former instructs;
the latter a lie by pretense of goods
ties the minds of those enjoying them,
the former by awareness of the fragility of happiness
absolves them;
and so you may see that the latter is fickle, lax
and always ignorant of herself,
the former sober and prepared
and through its adversities wise by experience.
  "Finally happiness by devious allurements
draws one from the truly good,
and adversity generally leading one back to the truly good
draws one back with a hook.
  "Or are you thinking of valuing this among the least
because this rough, this terrifying fortune
describes for you the minds of faithful friends?
She has differentiated for you
the reliable faces of the companions and the doubtful ones;
departing she has taken away hers, left yours.
  "For how much might you have let this go intact and,
as you were seeming to yourself, fortunate?

Now you complain about lost resources:
when you have found out that
friends are the most precious kind of riches.

VIII
  "Because the universe by steady faith
varies harmonious successions,
because struggling seeds
maintain a continuous treaty,
because the sun the rosy day
advances in a golden car,
while the moon may command in the nights
which the western star has led,
while the greedy ocean wave
encloses a definite boundary,
it may not stretch with wandering lands
the wide bounds,
love ties this sequence of things
guiding lands and the open sea
and commanding in heaven.
  "If this should relax the reins,
whoever now loves each other
would wage war continuously
and what now associates by faith
inspire with beautiful movements
they would compete to dissolve the scheme.
  "This by a sacred treaty too
holds peoples united;
this also the sacredness of marriage
binds with chaste loves;
this again dictates their rights
to trusted companions.
  "O happy human race,
if love guides your souls
as heaven is guided!"

Notes to Book 3:

I: Ceres, goddess of agriculture, was Demeter to the Greeks.

4: A poem of Catullus about 60 BC referred to Nonius.

4: Decoratus was quaestor in 508 CE.

5: Dionysius the Elder, tyrant of Syracuse (405-367 BC), invited Damocles, who envied royal happiness, to a banquet and seated him beneath a sword hanging by a thread.

5: The philosopher and tragedian Seneca was the tutor and advisor of Emperor Nero, but after retiring he was ordered to commit suicide by Nero in 65 CE.

5: Papinianus (140-212) wrote influential books on Roman law and held office under Emperor Severus, but he was ordered killed by the next emperor Caracalla for refusing to justify Caracalla's fratricidal murder of his brother Geta.

V: To the Romans Thule represented the most remote island in the north or west, possibly Iceland.

6: The tragedy quoted is *Andromache* (l. 319) by Euripides.

7: The statement of Euripides on children is also found in *Andromache* (l. 420).

8: Lynceus was an Argonaut famous for his sharp vision.

8: The great philosopher Aristotle lived from 384 to 322 BC.

8: Alcibiades (450-404 BC) was considered quite handsome. (See *Alcibiades* by Plato.)

XI: How knowledge comes from remembering is discussed in Plato's *Meno* 82-86 and *Phaedo* 17-21.

12: Parmenides of Elea lived about 500 BC; his philosophy emphasized the unity of being. He was considered the first to declare that the earth is a sphere.

12: Plato discusses the relation between discourse and subject matter in *Timaeus* 29b.

XII: The legendary Thracian musician Orpheus descended to the underworld in an attempt to reclaim his dead wife Eurydice. There he charmed the three-headed dog Cerberus by the door; the avenging goddesses, the Furies, were so moved that they let up on their punishments of Ixion, Tantalus, and Tityos. Because Orpheus violated the condition laid down by the placated Pluto, the god of the underworld, by looking back at Eurydice at the last moment of their departure, she was lost to him.

Book 3

1

  She had already finished the song,
while the soothing of the poetry bewitched me
eager and amazed with the ears of listening still roused.
And so after a moment I said,
"O highest solace of tired spirits, how you have revived me
either by the weight of the sentences
or else by the delight of the singing,
so much that now after this
I should not think myself
to be unequal to the blows of fortune!
And so not only am I not trembling at the remedies
which you were saying are a little sharper,
but quite eager of hearing I urgently demand it."

  Then she said, "I sensed it,
when silent and attentive you seized upon our words,
and either I was waiting for that condition of your mind
or, what is more true, I caused it;
such are certainly the ones which remain
though in fact biting to the taste,
yet taken inside they should become sweet.
But because you mention your desire of hearing,
in how much ardor would you be blazing
if you recognized where I am undertaking to lead you!"

  "Where?" I asked.

  "To true happiness," she said,
"about which your soul dreams too,
but in being busy near the images
the sight cannot look at that itself."

  Then I said, "Do it, I implore,
and explain what that truth may be without delay."

  "I'll do so," she said, "for your sake gladly;
but what is better known to you,
before that I'll try to sketch and define in words,
so that from this perspective
when you have turned your eyes on the opposite side
you may be able to recognize the form of true happiness.

I

"Whoever wants to plant the native land
first clears the fields from bushes,
cuts back with a sickle brambles and the fern,
so that Ceres may go heavy under new fruit.

"The labor of the bees is all the more sweeter
if previously the mouth should eat a bad taste.
Stars shine with more grace where the south wind
has ceased to bring rainy sounds.
As soon as the lightbringer has pushed away the shadows
the beautiful day drives the rosy horses.

"You too having looked on false good previously
begin to draw back your neck from the yoke:
truths next will come to the soul."

2

Then under concentrated sight for a short moment
and just as she got back into the majestic seat of her mind
she began as follows:
"Every care of mortals
which the labor of various studies exercises
advances in fact by a different path,
but it is striving to reach
all the same toward the one end of happiness.

"Now the good is that in which
anyone in having attained it
should be able to desire nothing further.
Which in fact is the highest of all goods
and containing all goods within itself;
in which if anything is missing it could not be the highest,
since something is left outside that could be wished for.
Then it is clear that happiness is a state
perfected by the union of all goods.

"This, as we said, by a different trail
all mortals are trying to attain;
for there is inserted in human minds by nature
desire of the true good,
but devious error leads them away to the false.

"Some of them in fact are believing
the highest good is to need nothing,
so that they work hard for abundant riches,
while others the good they depend on is
what may be most worthy of respecting
judging by veneration for their civic honors attained.

"There are some who decide that the highest good
is in the highest power;
these either wish to rule themselves
or they try to adhere to the ones ruling.
And these for whom a certain celebrity seems best
hurry to propagate a glorious name
either by the arts of war or peace.

"While most measure the fruit of the good
by enjoyment and delight;
these think it happiest to melt away in pleasure.
There are even some who exchange
the aims and causes of these one with the other,
as those who desire riches
for the sake of power and pleasures
or who seek power whether for the purpose of money
or of publishing a name.

"In these then and others like them
human motives and the intention of prayers are engaged
such as nobility and popular favor,
which seem to provide some distinction,
wife and children, which are sought for the charm of delight;
while of friends the kind which is in fact most sacred
is not to be counted in fortune but in virtue,
while what is left is taken
either for the purpose of power or of amusement.

"Then truly it is evident that the body's goods
may be ascribed to the ones above;
for strength and size seem to be better for vigor,
beauty and speed for celebrity, health for pleasure.

"By all these happiness alone is clearly desired;
for what each aims at before the rest
one judges it to be the highest good.
But we have defined the highest good to be happiness;

therefore one judges to be a happy state
what everyone desires before the rest.

"Then you have before your eyes almost
the proposed form of human happiness:
wealth, honors, power, glory, pleasure.
Considering these in fact alone Epicurus accordingly
determined for himself the highest good to be pleasure,
because all others seemed to bring enjoyment to the soul.

"But to return to human inclinations,
their soul even though memory is fading
nevertheless goes back to the highest good,
but like a drunk doesn't know on which trail to return home.

"Surely these do not seem to err
who are striving to need nothing?
Yet there is nothing else which could complete happiness
as well as the plentiful situation of all goods
and not needing of another but providing for oneself.

"While surely these are not wavering
who may think what is best
may also be most worthy of respect by the cultivated?
Not at all; nor is it something being disparaged by the poor
because the intention of almost all mortals
labors to attain it.

"Or is power not being counted among the good?
Why then, surely it is not valued as weak and without force
what of all things is agreed to be pre-eminent?
Or is distinction being thought of as nothing?
But it cannot follow but that
what may be most excellent to all
it also seems to be most distinguished.

"For what is important to say is that
happiness is not troubled and sad
nor is it subject to sorrows and annoyances,
since in the smallest things too is it not trying to get
what is a delight to have and enjoy?

"Yet these are what humans wish to attain
and for this reason they desire
riches, positions, domains, glory and pleasures
because through these they believe

sufficiency, respect, power, celebrity, joy
may be coming to them.
   "It is the good then that humans seek
by such different pursuits;
it is easily demonstrated
how much strength of nature may be in that,
since in spite of various and disagreeing opinions
all the same they agree on the goal
in the choosing of the good.

II

   "How many reins of things
powerful nature may turn, by which laws
providence serves the immeasurable world
and may draw together tying it tight
by a single bond, it is pleasing to produce
melodious music with lingering lyres.
   "Although the Punic lions may wear
beautiful chains and may try to catch
food given by hands and may fear
the savage master to bear the lashes of custom,
if blood soaks their shaggy mouth,
once idle spirits return
and by serious roaring to remember themselves,
they undo the knots freeing the neck
and first torn by their bloody teeth
the tamer wets the raving anger.
   "The babbling bird which sings on high branches
is confined in a hollow cage;
in this it is allowed a bedaubed cup of honey
and ample meals with sweet affection
the playing care of humans supply;
yet if leaping from the restricted web
it should see the welcome shadows of forests,
having scattered it with its feet it tramples the food,
it misses the woods with so much sadness,
it murmurs for the woods in a sweet voice.
   "Once driven downward by strong forces
the tree-top twig bends;

if arching the right hand releases this,
as an upright pole it faces the sky.

"The sun falls into the western waves,
but by a secret trail back
it turns the car toward the usual risings.

"All go back to their own recourse
and are pleased by their individual return,
nor does the entrusted order stay with any
unless that has joined the rising with the end
and has made its orbit steady.

3

"You too, o terrestrial creatures, although poor
imagine nevertheless your beginning in dreams
and you perceive that true goal of happiness
though in the least sharp awareness all the same,
and by it natural intention leads you both to true good
and manifold error leads away from the same.

"Consider for example whether through these
by which humans think they may attain happiness
they will be able to arrive at the determined goal.
For if either money or honors and the rest of such
bring that to someone who seems to lack none of the goods,
let us also acknowledge that
some do become happy by the attainment of these.
But if they are not able to accomplish what they promise
and are missing many goods,
clearly is not a false pretense of happiness caught in them?

"First then you yourself,
who a little before was abundant with riches I ask:
during that most abundant wealth
did anxiety never confuse your spirit
out of any concept of injustice?"

"Yes," I said, "I cannot remember in my spirit
ever to have been free but that there was some distress."

"Was it not because either
what you were not wishing to be missing was missing
or what you did not wish to be present was present?"

"It is so," I said.

"Then were you desiring the presence of the former
and the absence of the latter?"

"I admit it," I said.

"Is everyone really," she asked,
"in want of what one desires?"

"Everyone is in want," I said.

"While the one who is in want of something at every moment
is not providing for oneself."

"Not at all," I said.

"And so you full of this insufficiency," she asked,
"were you supported by wealth?"

"Of course not," I said.

"Then wealth could do nothing for need and sufficiency,
and this was what it seemed to promise.
Yet this too I am especially thinking of considering
that money may have nothing in its own nature
so that from these by whom it is possessed
it could not be carried off against their will."

"I acknowledge it," I said.

"Why not acknowledge it, since any day
someone stronger may rob it against one's will?
From where are public complaints,
unless moneys which were stolen either by force or by fraud
are being reclaimed from the unwilling ?"

"It is so," I said.

"Then everyone will be in want," she said,
"from the outside in asking for protection
from one who will guard their money."

"Who would deny it?" I said.

"Yet one would not be in want from it
unless one were possessing money, which one could lose."

"I cannot doubt it," I said.

"Then the matter is fallen back into the opposite;
for wealth which was thought to make one self-sufficient
rather makes a need for the protection of another.
But what is the method by which
need may be expelled by riches?

For surely the rich are not unable to be hungry,
or unable to be thirsty,
or don't the limbs of the moneyed feel the cold of winter?

   "But there is support, you may say, for the wealthy
by which they may satisfy hunger,
by which they may remove thirst and cold.
Though need in fact can be consoled in this way by riches,
they cannot take it away entirely;
for though this is ever gaping
and requiring that something be filled up by wealth,
there must be remaining what could be filled up.

   "I do not mention that the least is enough for nature,
that nothing is enough for greed.
Therefore if wealth cannot remove need
and makes its own for itself,
why is it that you should believe
it is responsible for sufficiency?

III

"Although rich from an affluent flood of gold
   the greedy may not compel wealth to be filled up
and may load necks with pearls from the Red Sea's shores
   and may plow a hundred fat estates by the ox,
nor will biting care abandon the surviving
   and at death easy wealth will not be accompanying.

4

   "But positions give back honor and respect
to the one whom they might have prospered.
Surely this power is not with the offices
so that into the minds of the employed
they should insert virtues or expel vices?

   "Yet they are accustomed not to banish them,
but rather to make famous the worthless.
Thus it is that we are indignant
that these often came to the worst people;
so although Nonius was sitting as a magistrate
Catullus nevertheless calls him a tumor.

"Don't you see how much disgrace
positions may add to the bad?
Yet their unworthiness will be less exposed
if they are not made famous by any honors.

"You too surely could not finally
have been led into so many dangers
while you were thinking to manage the office with Decoratus,
since you were looking back so long
into the mind of the worst jester and informer?
For we cannot on account of honors judge worthy of respect
those whom we judge unworthy of honors themselves.
But if you see someone endowed with wisdom,
surely you cannot but consider them worthy of either respect
or at least the wisdom with which one is endowed?"

"At least."

"For then the position is appropriate to the virtue,
which it transmits directly into those
in whom the connection is made.
Because popular honors cannot create that,
it is clear
they don't have the position's proper excellence.

"On which that is paying more attention:
for if one is more degraded from it
by which everyone is more despised by more people,
since it cannot make respected those whom it shows to more,
position makes the dishonest more despicable.
True not with impunity;
for indeed the dishonest give back
an equal recompense to the positions,
which they stain by their contamination.

"And so that you may recognize that true respect
cannot be reached through these shadowy positions:
if one who functioned as consul many times
came by chance into foreign nations,
would honor make him venerated by foreigners?
Yet if this service were natural in positions,
they would in no way be remiss from their duty
anywhere in the world,
just as the fire of lands everywhere never stops being hot.

"But since it is not a proper power for them
but the false opinion of humans connects it,
they disappear instantly when they might have come
to those who do not value these as positions.

"But this is among outside nations:
while between these among whom they are born
surely they do not endure forever?
Though the great praetor was once powerful,
now it is an empty name
and a heavy burden on a senator's property;
whoever might be administering the people's grain market
was once held great;
now why is this superintendence more degraded?

"For as we said a little before,
what has no elegance of its own,
by the opinion of those employing it
sometimes receives luster, sometimes loses it.

"If then positions cannot cause respect,
if besides they become dirty
by the contamination of the dishonest,
if by the change of times they stop shining,
if they are cheap in the estimation of nations,
why is it that they should have
covetings of excellence in themselves,
much less may they be better than others?

IV
"However much the arrogant Nero might dress himself
  in the proud purple of Tyre and in snowy gems,
hated nevertheless by all he was thriving
  in the cruelties of luxury;
but once the dishonest was giving to venerable
  senators indecent offices.
Who then would consider those honors blessed
  which the wretched bestow?

5
"Perhaps sovereignties and familiarity with royalty
can really bring about power?

Why not, when their happiness endures forever?
Yet antiquity is full of examples,
full also is the present age,
with monarchs who changed happiness to calamity.
O brilliant power, which is not found
capable enough even for its own preservation!
    "But if this power of rulers is the author of happiness,
may it not, if it has failed in any part,
be reducing happiness, bringing in misery?
But however widely human empires may be spread,
there must remain more nations
over whom not any monarch may command.
While in whatever part power stops making them blessed
there comes in by this impotence what makes them wretched;
in this way then there must belong to monarchs
a greater portion of misery.
    "A tyrant having experienced the fear
of the dangers of one's royal fate represented it
by the terror of hanging a sword above the head.
What then is this power,
which cannot expel the bite of anxieties,
nor avoid the stings of horrors?
Yet they themselves might wish to have lived in security,
but they cannot;
then immediately they boast about power.
    "Perhaps you rate powerful one whom you may see
might wish for what one could not bring about,
or do you rate powerful
one who walks abroad with an attendant
who oneself is more afraid of those one terrifies,
who so that one may seem to be powerful
is lying in the hand of those serving?
    "For why should I discuss the intimates of royalty,
when monarchies themselves
are proven full of so much weakness?
These in fact the royal power ruins often while unharmed,
often on the other hand when fallen.
    "Nero forced his intimate and mentor Seneca
toward picking the decision of death;

Papinianus long a power among the courtiers
Antoninus threw to the soldiers' swords.
Yet both were willing to renounce their powers,
of whom Seneca even tried to transfer his wealth to Nero
and go into retirement;
but as long as the bulk itself draws things to be ruined,
neither accomplished what he wanted.

   "What then is your power, which alarms those having it,
which when you may wish to have it you are not safe
and when you may desire to lay it down
you may not be able to get rid of it?

   "Or are friends for protection
whom not virtue but fortune reconciles?
But a friend whom happiness made misfortune makes hostile.
While what plague is more effective in harming
than an intimate enemy?

V
   "Whoever wishes oneself to be powerful,
should tame the insolent spirits
nor collared by lust
should one submit to vile reins;
and although in far off India
the country may be afraid of your laws
and most remote Thule may serve,
nevertheless it is not power
not to be able to drive out black cares
and banish wretched complaints.

6
   "Truly how deceptive glory often is, how ugly!
Thus not wrongly the tragedian exclaims:
   'O glory, glory, thousands of mortals
   of no live substance have you puffed up great.'
For many often obtained a great name
from the false opinions of the public.
What can be contrived uglier than that?
For those who are praised falsely
must themselves blush at their praises.

"Even if they may be collected by merit,
what could they add to the conscience of the wise,
who measures one's good not by popular rumor
but by the truth of conscience?
But if this seems beautiful to have spread a name,
it is logical that not to have extended it is judged vile.

"But since, as I explained a little before,
it may be necessary for there to be many nations
to whom the fame of a single person cannot come,
it arises that the one whom you estimate to be glorious
seems inglorious in the next part of the world.
While between these I think popular favor
is not even worth mentioning,
which neither comes by judgment nor ever remains stable.

"Now really who could not see how empty it may be,
how futile a name of nobility?
Which if it is ascribed to distinction, it is another's;
for nobility seems to be a kind of praise
coming from the merits of parents.

"But if commendation causes distinction,
those must be distinguished who are commended;
therefore if you don't have your own brilliance,
the distinction of others doesn't cause it.

"But if there is anything good in nobility,
I think it is this alone,
that the necessity imposed on the noble ones seems
not to degenerate from the virtue of the ancestors.

VI
"The birth of every person on earth
arises from a similar origin.
For there is one father of things; one serves all.
That gives to the sun rays, and gives horns to the moon;
that also gives humans to lands as stars to the sky;
this imprisoned in members fallen souls from a high abode:
then it produced all mortals from a noble germ.
Why should you rattle on about birth and ancestors?
If you should look at your beginning and author, God,
no one is degenerate unless cherishing worse faults

one should desert one's proper source.

7
   "Now what should I speak about the body's pleasures,
of which the craving is in fact full of anxiety,
while the satiety is full of remorse?
How many diseases, how much unbearable sorrow
as if those are accustomed to return to bodies
some fruit of the enjoying evils!
Of these I am ignorant
what impulse of delight it might have;
the outcome of pleasures being truly sad,
whoever is willing to remember their passions understands.
   "If these can open up blessings,
there is no reason why sheep too may not be called blessed,
whose every intention hurries
toward filling up a bodily pit.
   "The enjoyment of marriage and children
may in fact be most honored;
but too much from nature is the proverb for the ignorant
who have found their sons to be tormentors.
However bitter the condition of those may be
it is not necessary to advise you
since you neither experienced it at one time
nor is it a worry now.
In that I prove the sentence of my Euripides,
who said being unfortunate in lacking children is lucky.

VII
   "Every pleasure has this:
the stimulus drives the ones enjoying
and like the bee flying
where it scattered pleasing honey
it fled and with too much grip
it hit the struck hearts with a sting.

8
   "Then there is no doubt but that
these roads to happiness may be kind of devious,
nor are they able to lead anyone through it to what

they may be promising to lead them through themselves.
I'll show very briefly with how many evils
they may really be entangled.

   "Well? Will you not try to collect money?
But you rip it off from the one having it.
Do you wish to be illustrious in positions?
You will entreat with the one granting them,
and if you desire to precede others in honor
you are cheapened by the humility of asking.

   "Are you not longing for power?
In ambushes of neighbors
you are liable to be connected to dangers.
Do you aim at glory?
But having been distracted through all the violent things
you cease to be secure.
Would you live a pleasurable life?
But who would not spurn and abandon slavery
to the most cheap and fragile thing, the body?

   "While already those who display the goods of the body,
how brief, how fragile the possession they depend on!
For surely you will not be able to surpass
elephants in bulk, bulls in strength,
nor will you outstrip tigers in speed?

   "Look again at heaven's space, stability, quickness
and for a while stop admiring the cheap.
Because in fact heaven is not more admired for these
than for its reason by which it is guided.
While the form's sleekness is as swift, as fast
and more fleeting than the changeability of spring flowers!

   "But if, as Aristotle says,
humans could use the eyes of Lynceus,
so that their sight might penetrate obstructions,
in having looked into the organs might not
that superficially most beautiful body of Alcibiades
seem most ugly?

   "Then you do not seem beautiful by your nature,
but the weakness of the eyes looking represent it.
But estimate how excessive are the goods of the body's face,
as long as you know that however much you admire this

it can be destroyed by the fire of three days' fever.

"Out of all these to reduce that into a summary
it is admitted that
these cannot perform the good which they promise
nor are they perfected by the union of all goods,
nor do they lead to happiness as if by a sort of path
nor do they make them blessed.

VIII
"Alas, what ignorance leads away on a trail
  the devious wretched!
You do not search for gold on a green tree
  nor from the vine do you pick gems,
nor do you hide nets on high mountains
  so that you may feast on a fish banquet,
nor if it would please you to follow goats
  do you catch them in the Tyrrhenian Seas;
rather they know also places hidden by the waves
  in the recess of the sea,
which waters are more productive with snowy gems
  or which of the red purple-fish
and which shores not with delicate fish or with bitter ones
  provide sea-urchins.
But where it may escape notice that they desire good
  the blind maintain they are ignorant,
and sunk in the ground they seek
  what goes beyond the starry pole.
What should I invoke fitting for stupid minds?
  They may court wealth and honors,
and when they may have procured the false in a heavy bulk
  then they may recognize true goods.

9
"Thus far it has been enough
to have exposed the form of deceptive happiness;
which if you have observed clearly,
next in order is to demonstrate what may be the true."

"Yes, I see," I said,
"it is not possible to reach sufficiency by wealth
nor power by monarchies nor respect by positions

nor celebrity by glory nor joy by pleasures."

"Perhaps also you detected the reason why it may be so?"

"I grasped it in fact just as I seem to observe a crack,
but I would rather learn it more clearly from you."

"Yet the reason is most obvious.
For what is simple and by nature indivisible,
human error separates and transforms
from the true and thus perfect
to the false and imperfect.

"Or do you think that what may need nothing lacks power?"

"Not at all," I said.

"You are correct in fact;
for whatever may be weaker in anything though strong,
in this it must be lacking in support from another."

"So it is," I said.

"Then the nature of sufficiency and power
is one and the same."

"It seems like it."

"Truly do you think that such should be rejected
or on the contrary be most worthy of all things in respect?"

"But this," I said, "cannot be doubted at any rate."

"Then let us add respect to sufficiency and power,
so that we may judge these three to be one."

"Let us add it,
if in fact we wish to acknowledge the truth."

"What," she asked, "do you really think this is
dark and unknown or most bright in every celebrity?
Consider truly, it is conceded
that it needs nothing, that it is most powerful,
that in honor it is most worthy,
whether it is lacking in brightness,
which it could not provide for itself,
and so on account of it
it should seem somehow partly more contemptible."

"I cannot," I said, "but confess this
granted that it is even so most celebrated."

"Then it is logical that we should acknowledge that
brightness does not differ from the previous three."

"It is logical," I said.

"Then what should be in need of nothing from another,
what could be whole in its own powers,
what should be bright and so venerable,
is it not also established this is most joyful?"

"But I cannot in fact imagine from where," I said,
"any sadness might creep into such a thing;
thus it is necessary to confess that it is full of joy,
if in fact the previous qualities will remain."

"Yet that is also necessary by the same reason,
the names of sufficiency, power, brightness,
respect, enjoyment in fact being different,
that the substance does not really disagree in any way."

"It is necessary," I said.

"This then which is one and single by nature
human depravity divides
and while one tries to acquire a part
of a thing which is lacking in parts,
one does not attain a portion, which does not exist,
nor itself, which it is not aspiring to at all."

"How is that?" I asked.

"The one who seeks riches," she said,
"by the avoidance of want, does nothing for power,
prefers to be cheap and unknown,
and deprives oneself of many natural pleasures too,
lest one lose the money which one has procured.
But in this way not even sufficiency
comes to one whom strength abandons, whom trouble stings,
whom cheapness degrades, whom obscurity hides.

"While the one who desires ability alone spends wealth,
despises pleasures and honor lacking power,
also values glory as nothing.
But you see this too how much they may forsake;
for it happens that sometimes one may need necessities,
that one may be bit by anxieties,
may not be able to remove these at any time,
besides what one is aiming at most,

to be powerful, may stop.

"One may argue similarly about honors, glory, pleasures;
but since each one of these should be the same as the others,
anyone aiming at one of these without the others
does not even take hold of that in fact which one wants."

"Then what," I asked, "if one should desire
to acquire all at the same time?"

"That one wants in fact the sum of happiness;
but surely one will not find it in these
which we have demonstrated
cannot confer what they promise?"

"Not at all," I said.

"Then in these which are believed to provide individually
certain of the things being coveted
in no way is happiness being discovered."

"I admit it," I said, "and nothing truer could be said."

"Then you have," she said,
"both the false form of happiness and the causes.
Now turn the mind's observation into the opposite;
for there you will see at once
the truth which we have promised."

"Yet this," I said, "is even clear to the blind,
and you showed it a little before
when you tried to explain the false causes.
For unless I am mistaken,
true and perfect happiness is that which may make one
sufficient, powerful, respected, celebrated, and joyful.
And so that you may learn
that I have paid attention inwardly,
I know which one of these, since they are all the same,
truthfully can prove this to be
full happiness without ambiguity.

"O you, pupil, by this opinion are happy," she said,
"if in fact you may have added this!"

"What?" I asked.

"Do you think there is anything
in these mortal and perishable things
that could bring about such a state as this?"

"Not at all," I said, "and I think it is proved by you,
so that nothing more is desired."

"These then seem to give to mortals
either images of the true good or a kind of incomplete good,
but they cannot confer the true and complete good."

"I agree," I said.

"Then since you have known that which may be true,
the ones which moreover imitate happiness,
now it remains that you recognize
from where you could aim at this true one."

"For that in fact," I said,
"already I have been waiting eagerly for a long time."

"But since, as in the Timaeus it pleased our Plato,"
she said, "in the smallest things too
one should invoke divine assistance,
what now do you think we should be doing
so that we may deserve to find out
the foundation of that highest good?"

"Call upon," I said, "the father of all things,
so that in having neglected nothing
the beginning is properly secured."

"Correct," said she;
and at once the following was sung:

IX
"O you who rule the universe by perpetual reason,
sower of earth and heaven,
you who from eternity order time to pass
and remaining stable permit all things to be moved,
whom no external causes pushed to form
a true work of flowing material by an innate form
of the highest good free of envy, by a celestial example
you lead all, the most beautiful itself managing by mind
a beautiful universe and shaping it in a similar image;
and ordering the perfect to finish the perfect parts,
you bind the elements with numbers, as winters with flames,
the dry lands harmonize with waters, purer fire
may not fly off nor do weights bring down sunken lands.

"You released an intermediary soul of triple nature
connecting together the moving through concordant members;
which when cut gathered movement into two circles,
in self returning it passes and goes round the vast mind
and turns heaven in a similar image.

"From like causes you carry forward souls and lesser lives
and fitting the sublime with the light vehicles
you plant in heaven and earth, which converted by benign law
you cause to be led back to you by fire returned.

"Permit, father, the mind to mount this majestic throne,
permit it to scan the source of good,
permit discoveries by light
to concentrate perceptive visions of the soul on you.

"Scatter the mists of earth and the massive burdens
and so sparkle in your splendor; for you are fair,
you are the tranquil rest of the pious,
to perceive you is the goal,
beginning, carrier, leader, way, likewise the boundary.

10
"Then since you have seen
what may be the form of the imperfect,
as well as the form of the perfect good,
now I am thinking of explaining
where the perfection of this happiness may be established.

"In this I think first it must be inquired whether
any good of this kind as defined a little before
could exist in the nature of things,
lest an empty image of thought
deceive us about the truth of the subject matter.

"But it cannot be denied but it should exist
and may be this as a kind of source of all goods;
for everything that is said to be imperfect
is held to be imperfect by the impairment of the perfect.

"Thus, if in any class whatever
something may seem to be imperfect,
it may be necessary for something perfect to be in it too;
unless raised by perfection somehow or other
that which is held imperfect cannot even come to be formed.

"For the nature of things does not take initiative
from the diminished and uncompleted,
but progressing from the whole and complete
it disintegrates into these extremes and so is exhausted.
But if, as we have shown a little before,
there is a kind of imperfect happiness of a fragile good,
it cannot be doubted that something is solid and perfect."

"Most sure," I said, "and most true is the conclusion."

"While as to where it lives," she said, "consider this.
The common conception of the human spirit proves that
God, the principle of all things, is good;
for since nothing better than God can be thought of,
who may doubt that what nothing is better than is good?

"So reason demonstrates that God is really good
so that one may be convinced that the perfect is in it too.
For if it were not such,
it could not be the principle of all things;
for there would be something more outstanding in it
possessing the perfect good,
which may seem to be before this and so more ancient;
for all the perfect ones have become clear
to be prior to the less complete ones.

"Therefore lest the argument proceed into infinity,
it is being acknowledged that the highest God
is most full of the highest and perfect good;
but we established perfect good to be true happiness:
then it is necessary for true happiness
to be situated in the highest God."

"I accept it," I said,
"nor is it what can be spoken against in any way."

"But," she said, "I ask you,
see that you approve it solemnly and so inviolably
what we said about the highest God
being most full of the highest good."

"In what way?" I asked.

"It is not asserted that this father of all things
either has received from outside
that highest good of which it is full
nor should you presume it keeps so naturally

as if you should think the substance of the God having it
and the condition of happiness to be different.

"For if you should think it received from outside,
you could judge that which gave it more outstanding
than that which received it;
but we most properly acknowledge this to be
the most excellent of all things.
Because if in fact it belongs by nature
but is different by reason,
when we speak of God as the principle of things,
one may imagine what can have joined these differences.

"Finally, what is different from any thing
is not that from which it is understood to be different;
therefore what is different from the highest good
by its own nature, that is not the highest good;
because it is wrong to think that about it,
when it is established that nothing is more outstanding.

"For surely the nature of any thing
could not be better than its principle;
therefore I would conclude by the truest reasoning
that what may be the principle of all
is actually by its essence the highest good."

"Most correct," I said.

"But the highest good is conceded to be happiness."

"So it is," I said.

"Then," she said, "it must be acknowledged
that God is happiness itself."

"I cannot," I said,
"oppose the preceding with any propositions,
and from those I perceive this to be logically inferred."

"Look again," she said, "whether from this too
the same is more strongly proven,
because there cannot be two highest goods
which may be different from each other.
For it is evident that goods which disagree with each other
are not what the other may be;
therefore neither could be perfect,
since each is lacking the other.

"But it is obvious that
what may not be perfect is not the highest;
then in no way can those
which are the highest goods be different.
Yet we inferred both happiness and God
to be the highest good;
therefore it must be the highest happiness itself
which should be the highest divinity."

"Nothing," I said, "can actually be concluded that is
truer or stronger in reasoning or more worthy of God."

"Beyond this," she said,
"then as geometricians are accustomed
to infer something from proven propositions,
which they themselves call deductions,
so I too shall give one to you as a corollary.

"Now since humans become blessed
by the attainment of happiness,
while happiness is divinity itself,
it is obvious that they become blessed
by the attainment of divinity.
But just as by the attainment of justice they become just,
by wisdom they become wise,
so it is necessary by similar reasoning
to become gods by having attained divinity.
Then everyone blessed is a god.
But God is one in fact by nature;
while nothing prevents as many as possible
from being it by participation."

"This is both beautiful and so valuable," I said,
"whether it be called either a deduction or a corollary."

"Yet too nothing is more beautiful than this
which reason persuades is to be connected to these."

"What?" I asked.

"Since happiness," she said, "may seem to contain much,
should all these join together as one
like a body of happiness from a kind of variety of parts
or should some of them
which may complete the essence of happiness,
while others may be referred to this?"

I said, "I would like you to make it clear
by recollection of the things themselves."

"Do we not," she said, "think happiness is good?"

"And in fact the highest," I said.

"You may impart this," she said, "to all of them.
For the highest sufficiency is the same,
the highest power the same, respect too,
distinction and pleasure are judged to be happiness.
What then, are all these,
the good, sufficiency, power and the others,
are they like some kind of members of happiness
or are they all referred to the good as to a head?"

"I understand," I said, "what investigating you propose,
but I long to hear what you may decide."

"Take the discernment of that thing as follows.
If these all were members of happiness,
they would in turn disagree with each other too;
for this is the nature of the parts
that different ones may compose one body.
And yet all these are shown to be the same.
Then at least they are not members;
otherwise happiness would seem to be
joined together out of one member, which cannot be."

"That in fact," I said, "is not doubtful,
but I am waiting for what remains."

"While it is well known the others refer to the good.
For that reason sufficiency is sought,
since it is judged to be good;
for that reason power, since it too is believed to be good;
one may infer the same for respect, distinction, enjoyment.
Then the sum and so the cause of all the aiming is the good;
for that which does not retain in itself any good
whether by reality or imitation can in no way be sought out.

"On the other hand those which are not by nature good
nevertheless they are desired
if they may seem to be as if they were from a true good.
Thus goodness is rightly believed to be
the sum, axis and so the cause of all aiming.

"While the cause of that which is sought out
seems to be chosen most,
just as if someone who wishes to ride for reason of health,
desires the riding not so much for the movement
as much as for the effect of health.
Then since all those are sought for the sake of the good,
not those but rather the good itself is desired by all.

"But on account of what we have conceded happiness to be
the others are chosen;
thus here too happiness alone is sought.
From which it is clearly apparent that
the substance of the good itself and of happiness
is one and so the same."

"I do not see how anyone could disagree."

"But we have shown that God and true happiness
are one and so the same."

"Yes," I said.

"Safely then one may conclude that the essence of God too
is situated in the good itself and nowhere else.

X
"Come here equally all the caught,
whom the deceptive binds with dishonest chains
lust inhabiting earthly minds:
this will be for you the labors' rest,
this harbor remaining quietly calm,
this single open sanctuary for the wretched.

"Not even the Tagus with its golden sands
bestows nor the reddening Hermus shore
nor the Indus near the torrid zone
mingling green gems with the white
may illuminate the sight and all the more close
blind souls into their darkness.

"This, whatever pleases and excites minds,
earth has nourished in the lowest caves;
the splendor by which heaven is guided and flourishes
avoids the dark ruins of the soul;
whoever will be able to note this light
will decline the bright rays of the sun."

11

"I agree," I said, "for it all is established
tied by the strongest arguments."

Then she asked, "How highly would you value it,
if you might have recognized what the good itself may be?"

"Infinitely," I said,
"if in fact it brings me at the same time
to recognize God too, who is the good."

"And yet this," she said,
"I may make clear by the truest reasoning,
should what was concluded a little before remain."

"They will remain."

"Have we not shown," she asked,
"that these which are desired by most
for this reason are not true and perfect goods
since they disagree from each other in turn,
at any time one is missing from the other
not being able to bring about full and complete good,
but then to become true good
when they are gathered as into a single form and operation,
so that what sufficiency is may be the same as
power, respect, distinction and enjoyment,
unless they all may be really one and so the same,
does it not hold that
they are to be counted among the things sought out?"

"It is proven," I said,
"nor can it in any way be doubted."

"Which then when they disagree are not at all good,
while when they may have begun to be one become good,
does this not happen so that
they may become good by the attainment of unity?"

"It seems so," I said.

"But do you concede that every good is good
by participation of the good, or not?"

"So it is."

"Then you may concede by a similar reason
that the one and so the good ought to be the same;
for the substance of those of which naturally

it is not a different effect is the same."

"I cannot deny it," I said.

"Then did you not learn," she said, "everything that is
remains and so continues for as long as it may be one,
but perishes and is dissolved at the same time
as soon as it may have ceased to be one?"

"In what way?"

"As in animals," she said,
"while the soul and body combine and persist as one
it is called an animal,
while when this unity is dissolved by separation of both
it is clear the animal perishes and no longer exists;
in the body itself too
while it persists in one form by the union of members
the human appearance is seen,
but if divided and segregated parts of the body
tear apart the unity
it ceases to be what it had been;
and in this way going through the others
beyond a doubt it will be evident that
each one continues as long as it is one,
while when it ceases to be one it perishes."

"In having considered more," I said,
"it seems to me no other."

"Then is there anything," she asked,
"which, in as much as it may act naturally,
having abandoned the craving for continuing
may long to come to destruction and corruption?"

"If I may consider animals," I said,
"which have some nature of willing and refusing,
I find nothing that with no outside forcings
would throw away the intention of remaining
and spontaneously hurry toward destruction.
For every animal labors to protect its welfare,
while it avoids death and ruin.
But what about plants and trees,
what about inanimate things in general?
In short I doubt the agreement for things."

"And yet about this too it is not what you could argue,
since you may observe plants and trees
first grow in places convenient to them,
where, as much as their nature could,
they should not be able to dry up quickly and die.
For some in fact spring up in plains, some in mountains,
marshes produce some, some cling to rocks,
barren sands are fertile for some, which would dry up
if someone tried to transfer them to another place.

"But nature gives to each what is appropriate, and,
as long as they can remain, labors so they may not perish.
Why do they all draw nourishment by the roots
as if from a mouth submerged in the soils,
and so through the pith the wood and bark spreads out?
Why is everything which is most tender,
as in fact the pith is,
always stored away in an interior site,
while by a kind of strength of the wood outside,
the most remote bark is set against intemperate weather
as if it were a patient averter of wrong?

"While now how great is the diligence of nature
that they should all be propagated by seed multiplication!
Who does not know of them all remaining not only for a time,
actually by species too as it were lasting forever
as if to be some kind of machines?

"Even these which are believed to be inanimate
does not each long for what is theirs by a similar reason?
For why does lightness convey flames in fact upwards,
while weight presses down the lands,
unless it is because
these places and motions are appropriate to each one?

"Moreover, the individual preserves
what is in keeping with itself,
just as they ruin things which are unfriendly.
While now things which are hard like stones
stick most persistently with their parts
and resist being easily dissolved;
while fluids which are like air and water
yield easily in fact to being divided,

but quickly glide back again into that
from which they are cut off;
while fire flees every section.

"Now we are not dealing with
the voluntary movements of an understanding soul,
but with natural intention,
just as it is accepted that we digest food without thought,
that unknowing we draw breath in sleep.
For not even in animals does the love of remaining
come out of the will of the soul,
but truly out of the principles of nature.

"For often the will embraces death,
which nature dreads, for compelling reasons,
and on the other hand that by which alone
the long life of mortal things endures,
the work of procreating, which nature always desires,
the will occasionally represses.

"So this love of oneself comes not out of animal motion,
but out of natural intention;
for providence has given to creatures from things themselves
this very greatest cause of remaining
so that naturally they should long
to remain as long as they can.

"Therefore there is no way that you can doubt that
all things which are
naturally desire constancy of persisting, to avoid ruin."

"I confess," I said, "to discerning now without my doubt
what a moment ago seemed uncertain."

"Moreover," she said,
"what seeks to hold out and persist longs to be one;
for if this is removed in fact, nothing will persist."

"It is true," I said.

"Then all," she said, "long for the one."

"Agreed."

"But we have shown this one itself to be what is good."

"So it is in fact."

"Then all things seek the good,
which you may in fact describe as being the good itself

which should be longed for by all."

"Nothing," I said, "can be thought out more truthfully;
for either all things are brought back to no one thing
and will flow abandoned as if without one guiding head,
or if there is something universal
toward which they accelerate
it will be the highest of all goods."

And she said, "I am very glad, o pupil;
for you have fixed mentally the note of the central truth.
But in this it has opened to you
what you were saying you didn't know a little before."

"What?" I asked.

"What might be," she said, "the end of all things.
For it is certainly what is longed for by all;
because we have inferred that to be good,
we should acknowledge the end of all things to be the good.

XI

"Whoever with a deep mind investigates the truth
and desires to be deceived by no deviations
should turn back into oneself the light of the inner sight
and bending should force the long movements into a circle
and should teach the soul that whatever is built outside
it possesses withdrawn in its treasures;
what a while ago the gloomy cloud of error covered
will shine more clearly than the sun itself.

"For the body carrying a forgetful bulk
did not expel light from every mind;
there certainly lingers inside the seed of truth
which is awakened by instruction fanning it;
for why when asked do you spontaneously answer correctly
unless sunk in a deep heart a spark might live?
But if the Muse of Plato rings true,
what everyone learns is recalled from the forgotten."

12

Then I said, "I agree very much with Plato;
for this is already the second time
you have reminded me of these,

the first time I lost the memory by bodily contact,
the next when pressed by a mass of grief."
 Then she said,
"If you should look back at previous admissions,
that in fact might no longer be absent
but rather you might recall
what you just now confessed not knowing."
 "What?" I asked.
 "By which governments," she replied,
"the universe may be guided."
 "I remember," I said, "that I had confessed my ignorance,
but what you bring up, may already be foreseen,
nevertheless I long to hear it from you more plainly."
 "That this universe," she said, "is guided by God
a little before you were not even thinking of doubting."
 "Not even now am I thinking it," I said,
"nor was I ever thinking of doubting it,
and let me briefly explain by which reasons I came to this.
This universe would not have come together into one form
out of such diverse and opposite parts
unless there were one
who might join together such differences.
 "While the very diversity of natures in turn discordant
might dissociate and so tear apart the joined
unless there were one who should hold together what it tied.
While so definite an order of nature might not go on,
nor might such arrangements of motion unfold
in places, times, efficiency, spaces, qualities
unless there were one who should arrange
these varieties of changes while remaining itself.
This, whatever it is,
by which created things remain and so are motivated
with the designation usual to all I name God."
 Then she said, "Since you may feel this is so,
I think there is little work left for me
so that safely in control of happiness
you may revisit your homeland.
But let us look into what we have proposed.
Have we not included sufficiency in happiness,

and have we not agreed that God is happiness itself?"

"Yes in fact."

"And then," she said, "for guiding the universe
it will not need any supports from outside;
if it should be in need of anything else by which to do so,
it would not have full sufficiency."

I said, "It is so of necessity."

"Through itself then alone does it arrange all things?"

"I cannot deny it," I said.

"And yet God is shown to be the good itself."

"I remember," I said.

"Through the good then it arranges all things,
if in fact it guides all through itself
which we have agreed to be the good,
and this is like a kind of rudder and so a helm by which
the universal machine is preserved stable and uncorrupted."

"I very much agree," I said,
"and a little before though I was restrained by suspicion
I foresaw it would be said by you."

"I believe it," she said; "for already, as I think,
you focus your eyes more carefully on discerning truths.
But what I may say is no less open to being observed."

"What?" I asked.

"Since God," she said, "is rightly believed
to steer all by the rudder of goodness,
and all these, just as I have taught,
by natural intention accelerate toward the good,
surely it cannot be doubted but that
they may be guided voluntarily and by themselves
toward the will of the one arranging
as if harmony and the moderate
should turn round unaided by the guide?"

"It must be so," I said;
"nor would the guidance seem to be blessed,
if in fact it was a yoke of the resisting,
not the welfare of the complying."

"Is there nothing then,
which serving nature attempts to go against God?"

"Nothing," I said.

"But if one attempts it," she went on,
"surely at last it does not profit
against that which we rightly conceded to be
the greatest power of happiness?"

"Absolutely nothing could," I said.

"Is there not then anything
which either would or could resist this highest good?"

"I don't think so," I said.

"Then it is the highest good," she said,
"which bravely guides and pleasantly arranges all things."

Then I said, "How not only these
which are the highest conclusions of arguments,
truly much more these very words which you used please me,
so that now at last one should be greatly ashamed
of one's foolish abusing!"

"You have heard," she said,
"in fables about Giants challenging heaven;
but it had arranged those too,
as it was appropriate, by a kind courage.
But do you want us to bring these very arguments
into conflict with each other?
Perhaps out of a conflict of this kind
some beautiful spark of truth may fly off."

"By your decision," I said.

She said, "No one would doubt God to be the power of all."

"At any rate," I said,
"no one who depends on a mind would argue."

"While for the one who is all-powerful," she said,
"there is nothing which that one could not do."

"Nothing," I said.

"Then surely God cannot do evil?"

"Not at all," I said.

"Then evil," she said, "is nothing,
since that one could not do it
for whom nothing is impossible."

"Are you playing with me," I asked,
"weaving an inextricable labyrinth with arguments,
which at one time where you may come out you may go in,
while at another
where you may have gone in you may come out,
or are you complicating
some wonderful circle of divine simplicity?

"For a little before beginning from happiness
you were saying it is the highest good,
speaking how it is situated in the highest God.
You were explaining that God itself too
is the highest good and full happiness,
out of which you were granting a small present
that no one is to be blessed
except one who might equally be God.

"Again you were saying that the very form of the good
is the essence of God and of happiness,
and you were teaching that the one itself is the good itself
which is sought by all from the nature of things.
You were arguing that God also guides the universe
by the helms of goodness and that all willing things obey
nor does any nature of evil exist.
And you were explaining these with no outside assumptions,
but from one to the other getting credence
with innate and internal approvals."

Then she said, "We were not playing at all,
and we have examined the greatest matter of all
by the grace of God, to whom we were just now praying.
For the form of the divine substance is such
that it is not dissolved in externals
nor would it itself take into itself anything external,
but, as Parmenides puts it,

'well-rounded on all sides like a sphere's mass'

it rotates the mobile circle of things
while it preserves itself immobile.
But if you should seek reasons too not outside
but inside of the matter which we were tossing around
we have deliberated on things established,
there is no reason to be surprised,

since you have learned from Platonic ordaining
that the relations about the matters which are spoken
ought to be the discourses.

XII
  "Happy, the one who can see
the clear source of good,
happy, the one who can release
the chains of heavy earth.
Once the prophet of Thrace
mourning his dead wife
when with tearful music
he compelled nimble forests to run,
the rivers to stand
and deer joined unafraid
beside the fierce lions
and the rabbit did not fear the sight
of the dog already calm from the song,
when hotter inside
the fervor of feeling burned
and the measures of the one who had subdued all
could not soothe the master,
lamenting the inexorable gods above
he went to the lower worlds.

  "There by sounding strings
moderating charming tunes
whichever he drew
from the special source of the mother goddess,
which powerless lamentation was giving,
which love bewailing lamentation
the lower world moving weeps
and by a sweet prayer asks
the lords of the ghosts for indulgence.

  "The threefold porter is astonished
captured by the new song;
the avenging goddesses of crimes
who drive the guilty by fear
next are drenched by tears of grief;
the head of Ixion is not
thrown down by the fast wheel,

and ruined by long thirst
Tantalus spurns the streams;
now the vulture is sated by the music
and does not pull at the liver of Tityos.
   "Finally 'We are conquered'
the pitying witness of the ghosts declares.
'We bestow on the man the accompanying
wife bought by a song;
but a law controls the gift,
until she has left the underworld
to turn the eyes would not be allowed.'
   "Who would give a law to lovers?
A greater law is love to itself.
Alas, near the boundary of night
Orpheus upon his Eurydice
looked, lost, fell.
   "This fable looks back to you
whoever of you into the day above
seeks to lead the mind;
for the one who in the chasm of the underworld
having been conquered has turned the eyes,
whatever special one carries off
one loses when one sees the lower worlds."

Notes to Book 4:

III: Ithaca's leader was Odysseus (Ulysses). His visit to the island of the magical Circe and his rescue by the Arcadian god Hermes are described in Homer's *Odyssey* book X.

V: Arcturus is the brightest star in the northern constellation Bootes and is in direct line with the tail of the Great Bear (Ursa Major); Arcturus in Greek means "bear guard."

6: The poet Lucan (39-65 CE.) in *Pharsalia* I, 128 referred to Caesar's victory at Thapsus in 46 BC which led to Cato's suicide.

VII: Agamemnon, the son of Atreus, fought the Trojans for ten years in Phrygia, because the wife of his brother Menelaus was taken by them; to gain favorable winds for sailing he sacrificed his daughter Iphigenia.

VII: Odysseus (Ulysses) of Ithaca had some of his crew eaten by the Cyclops Polyphemus; but getting him drunk, Odysseus blinded the one-eyed giant.

VII: Hercules is credited with accomplishing twelve great labors for which he won a heavenly reward. These included overcoming the half-human half-horse Centaurs, killing the Nemean lion, destroying the many-headed Hydra by fire and the Stymphalian birds with arrows, picking the golden apples of the Hesperides that were guarded by a dragon, capturing the triple-headed dog Cerberus, overcoming the river god Achelous, outwrestling Antaeus the king of Libya, helping king Evander and punishing Cacus for stealing cattle, and for a while taking the weight of heaven off the shoulders of Atlas.

Book 4

1

When with dignity of expression and a serious face
Philosophy recited this service gently and pleasantly,
then I not yet having forgotten the depth of sorrow inside
broke off something she was still intending to say
and said, "O foreseer of true light,
which right up to now your speech has shed
the unconquered have been evident
not only by their divine observation but by your arguments,
and these even if recently forgotten
because of the pain of the wrong to me
nevertheless you have not spoken of
what was completely unknown previously.

"But this itself is even the greatest cause of our grief
which, when a good guide of things should emerge,
either evils could not exist at all
or they may escape unpunished;
you should certainly consider with so much surprise
that it alone may be fitting.

"Yet to this another even greater is attached;
for by commanding and prospering worthlessness
virtue not only lacks rewards,
but is even subject to being trampled
under the feet of the wicked
and pays the punishment in place of the criminals.
For it to happen in the reign of God
the all-knowing, the all-powerful, but willing only good
no one can either wonder or complain enough."

Then she said, "And it would be of infinite bewilderment
and more terrible with all monstrous things if,
as you estimate, in such
as in the most arranged home of the master of an estate
the cheap dishes might be cherished, the expensive trashed.
But it is not so;
for if these which were concluded a little before
are preserved undestroyed,
from the very originator of whose reign we are now speaking
you understand in fact goods always are powerful,

while bads always are contemptible and so helpless,
neither is vice ever to be without penalty
nor virtues without reward;
to the good happiness always comes,
to the bad misfortune and many things of that kind,
which with your complaints calmed
it may corroborate in firm solidity.

"And since the form of true happiness
you have just now seen from my demonstrating,
you have also recognized where it may be situated,
from all the maneuvers which I think necessary to precede
the proven way that brings you back to your home.
Also I may fasten wings to your mind
by which it could lift itself into heaven,
so that with confusion removed you may return safe
into your country by my guidance, my path, and my vehicles.

I
"In fact swift wings are mine
  which climb the heights of the pole;
which when the quick mind has put on for itself
  it looks down on detested lands,
rises above the globe of vast atmosphere
  and sees the clouds left behind
and which is warmed by the agile motion of the sky,
  passes beyond the peak of fire,
until it may rise into the home of the stars
  and join the ways of the sun
or it follows the route of the old in the cold,
  the soldier of the shimmering constellation
or wherever sparkling night is pictured
  recurs the orbit of stars
and so when it might already be exhausted enough
  it may leave the farthest pole
and press the ridges of the fast sky
  in control of the respected light.
Here the master of kings holds the scepter
  and regulates the reins of the orbit
and steady it steers the flying car,
  the shimmering arbiter of things.

If the way should bring you back returned here
  which now forgetful you request,
'These I remember,' you will say, 'the country is mine,
  from this source, here I stand firm.'
But if it should please you to visit
  the night of earthly things left behind,
you will perceive grim dictators exiled
  whom the wretched peoples fear."

2
  Then I said, "Wow, what greatness you promise!
Not that I doubt you could accomplish it,
and don't delay what you have just excited."
  "Then first," she said, "you should recognize that
power always supports the good,
the bad are devoid of all strengths;
in fact each of these is explained from the other.
For since good and bad should be opposites,
if power consisted of being good
the helplessness of the bad is evident,
or if the fragility of bad should be clear
the firmness of good is noted.
But so that confidence in our opinion may be more abundant,
I may proceed by both paths now from here
then from there confirming the propositions.
  "There are two things,
in which every effect of human actions is established,
will, of course, and power,
of which if one or the other has been left off,
there is nothing which can be accomplished.
For in lacking will
no one in fact undertakes what is not picked,
but if power be absent the will may be in vain.
Thus, if you should see that
one wishes to attain what may not be attained,
you cannot doubt one has been missing the ability
for obtaining this which one has wanted."
  "It is clear," I said, "and in no way can it be doubted."

"While if you should see someone has accomplished
what one has wanted,
surely you will not actually doubt one to have been able?"

"Not at all."

"Truly everyone is rated effective
in that which one can do,
while one is helpless in this which one cannot."

"I admit it," I said.

"Then do you remember," she asked,
"that it was inferred from the preceding arguments
that every intention of human will,
which is acted on by various pursuits,
accelerates toward happiness?"

"I remember," I said, "that to be proven too."

"Surely you may recall that the good is happiness itself
and in this way, since happiness is sought,
the good is desired by everyone?"

"I recall," I said, "since I hold it fixed in memory."

"Then all humans, good and bad alike,
by indistinguishable intention
are striving to come to the good?"

"Accordingly," I said, "it is logical."

"But it is certain they become good
by attainment of the good?"

"It is certain."

"Then do the good attain what they desire?"

"So it seems."

"While if the bad should attain what they desire,
the good, they could not be bad."

"So it is."

"Then since both may seek the good,
but these in fact should attain it, while those do not,
surely it is not doubted that the good are in fact powerful,
while the ones who are bad should be helpless?"

"Whoever doubts it," I said, "can consider
neither the nature of things nor the logic of arguments."

"Again," she said, "if there be two
for whom the same purpose may be second nature,
and one of them by a natural function
should act and complete the thing itself,
while the other cannot manage that natural function,
but by another method which is not suited to nature
in fact should not fulfill one's purpose
but is imitating the fulfilling,
which of these do you determine is more capable?"

"Even if I infer," I said, "what you want,
nevertheless I long to hear it more plainly."

"Surely you will not deny," she said,
"that the motion of walking is second nature for humans?"

"Not at all," I said.

"And surely you do not doubt that
feet are the natural function of that?"

"Not in this case," I said.

"If someone then with feet is able to advance walking
and another, who lacking this natural function of the feet,
is attempting to walk leaning on the hands,
which of these can be considered rightly more capable?"

"Devise other riddles," I said, "for no one could argue
but that the one with the power of the natural functions
should be more capable than the same."

"But the highest good,
which is equally the purpose of the bad and good
the good in fact seek by the natural function of virtues,
while the bad through a different desire,
which is not the natural function for attaining the good,
are attempting to attain the very same;
or do you consider it otherwise?"

"No," I said, "for even what is following is obvious.
For out of this which I should have conceded
it is necessary that the good in fact are powerful,
while the bad are helpless."

"You anticipate it correctly," she said,
"and, as doctors are accustomed to hope,
the indication is now of a nature uplifted and resistant.

But since I am perceiving you
to be understanding most readily,
I shall accumulate crowded arguments;
for look how obvious the weakness of vicious humans may be,
who cannot even come to this to which their nature leads
and intention almost compels them.

"And what if they were deprived of going forward
with so great and nearly invincible assistance of nature?
Truly consider how much impotence
the wicked humans should have.
For neither easy nor sporting are the rewards they seek
which it follows also they could not obtain,
but concerning the very highest and top of things they fail
and from that in miseries success is not reached
for which alone the days and nights are working;
in which thing the strengths of goods excel.

"For if one who is advancing on foot
toward that place up to which one could have arrived
beyond which lay nothing accessible to attack
you would consider that one to be most capable of walking,
so the one who takes hold of the goal of aiming
beyond which is nothing
you must judge is most capable.
Thus, what is opposite to this,
seeing that it is the same for the wicked
they seem to be abandoned by all the strengths.

"For why having been left by virtue do they chase vice?
Is it ignorance of the goods?
But what is weaker than the blindness of ignorance?
Or have they known chasing, but does lust throw them across?
So too is excess fragile,
which cannot struggle against vice.

"Or do the knowing and willing desert the good
and turn aside to vice?
But in this way they abandon not only being capable,
but being entirely;
for they too equally stop being
who abandon what is the common goal of all who are.

"It may in fact seem rather strange to some
that we should say the bad, who are the majority of humans,
that these same ones do not exist;
but the reality in themselves has it so.
Now I am not denying those who are bad are the bad ones,
but I do plainly and simply deny that these exist.

"For though you might say a corpse is a dead person,
you simply could not really call it a person,
so I might concede that the vicious are in fact bad,
but I cannot confess they exist completely.
For it is what retains order and preserves nature;
while what defects from this being,
which is situated in its nature, also abandons it.

"But they are capable, you say, of bad;
I would not even deny it,
but this power of theirs comes
not from strengths but from helplessness.
They can do bad things,
which they would not have been able to do
if they could have stayed in the effectiveness of goods.
Which capability shows more clearly they can do nothing;
for if, as we inferred a little before, the bad is nothing,
since they could do only bad things,
it is evident the dishonest can do nothing."

"It is clear."

"And so that you may understand
what the strength of this power may be:
we have defined a little before
nothing to be more powerful than the highest good."

"So it is," I said.

"But the same," she said, "is unable to do bad."

"No."

"Is there then," she asked,
"anyone who thinks that humans can do everything?"

"Unless someone may be insane, no one."

"And yet the same can do bad."

I said, "I wish in fact they couldn't!"

"Then since only one capable of goods could do everything,
while those capable of evils still could not do everything,
it is obvious those who can do evils can do less.
Moreover we have indicated that
all power among aims being counted
and all aims are to be referred to the good
as to a kind of summit of their natures.
But the possibility of committing a crime
cannot be referred to the good;
then it is not aiming.
Yet all power is aiming;
then it is evident the capability of evils is not power.

"Out of all these the power of goods is fact,
while the weakness of evils appears not doubtful at all,
and that true sentence of Plato is evident
that it is the wise alone who can do what they may desire,
truly the dishonest in fact practice what may please,
while they cannot fulfill what they desire.

"For they do what pleases,
as long as they think through things in which they delight
they will attain for themselves the good which they desire;
but they are not attained,
because abuses do not come to happiness.

II

"Those eminent kings you see sitting on a lofty throne,
bright in gleaming purple, walled in with sad weapons,
threatening from a grim face, panting in the heart's fury,
if someone should take away from the arrogant
the vain's cultured covering,
then one will see inside masters bearing tight chains;
for here lust twists hearts with greedy poisons,
here troubled anger raising a flood whips the mind,
captured grief either tires or slippery hope tortures.
So when you may perceive one head bear so many tyrants,
it does not do what it chooses itself,
oppressed by unjust masters.

3
"Do you see then in how much filth abuses are maintained,
by which light honesty may shine?
In this it is clear never are rewards for the good missing,
never for the wicked their punishments.
And as a matter of fact of the things which are produced
that reward can not seem to be wrong
on account of which everyone of the same is produced,
as with running in the stadium
the garland is the reward for which one is running.

"But we have indicated happiness is the same good itself
for which all things are produced;
then it is for human actions the good itself
just as if the proposed reward is in common.
And yet this cannot be separated from the good ones—
for besides the one who may be missing the good
will not be rightly called good;
therefore honest morals do not forsake their rewards.

"Then however much the bad may rage,
nevertheless the garland of the wise
does not fall off, does not dry up;
nor does dishonesty by another
pluck off personal honor from honest souls.

"But if one is glad for credit from outside,
this could be taken away either by someone else
or even by the very one who conferred it;
but since honesty confers one's own on each,
then one will lack one's reward
only when one stops being honest.

"Finally, since every reward is desired
for the reason that it is believed to be good,
would someone judge the experienced
in control of a good reward?
But of which reward?
The most beautiful and greatest of all;
remember that corollary I emphasized a little before,
and conclude as follows.

"Since happiness should be the good itself,
it is evident that all the good who should be good

become blessed by that itself.
But it is agreed that those who may be blessed are gods.
Then it is the reward of the good to become gods,
which no time may erase, no power may lessen,
no dishonesty may darken.

"Since this should be so, the wise cannot doubt
the inevitable punishment of the bad too;
for since good and bad,
like the opposites of punishment and reward
should disagree broadly,
the reward which we see taken in by the good must match
the same penalty opposite on the side of the bad.

"Then just as honesty itself
becomes a reward for the honest
worthlessness itself is a punishment for the dishonest.
While surely whoever is afflicted by bad
does not doubt oneself to be suffering a penalty.
If then they themselves may be willing to judge themselves,
could they seem to themselves not free of punishment,
which not only afflicts them with the worst of all evils,
worthlessness, but also actually infects them violently?

"Now from the opposite side of the good ones
look at the penalty which accompanies the dishonest;
for example you learned a little before
that everything which may be is one
and that the one itself is good;
from which it is logical that
everything which may be also may be seen to be good.

"Then in this way
whatever defects from the good ceases to be.
Thus the bad should stop being what they had been.
But the form of the human body still left them
proves that they had been humans;
therefore to be turned into evil
is to lose human nature too.

"But since honesty alone
could advance someone beyond humans,
it is necessary that the ones
whom dishonesty throws down from the human condition

it may deservedly push down below humans;
then it turns out that you could not judge as human
one whom you may see is transformed by vices.

  "A violent robber burns from greed of others' wealth:
you might say is like a wolf.
One insolent and so restless
exercises the tongue with quarrels:
you will compare to a dog.

  "The hidden ambusher likes to steal with frauds:
and is equal to a little fox.
The intemperate roars with anger:
and is believed to carry about the spirit of a lion.

  "The terrified and timid fears things not to be feared:
and may be held like deer.
The lazy and stupid is dumb:
and lives as an ass.

  "The trivial and so fickle changes parties:
and is no different from birds.
One is immersed in foul and dirty lusts:
and is held back by the sordid pleasure of swine.

  "Thus the one who deserts honesty ceases to be a person,
since one could not change the condition into the divine,
one may be turned into a beast.

III
  "The sails of Ithaca's leader
and the wandering rafts on the open sea
the east wind drove to an island,
where was residing a beautiful goddess
descended from the seed of the sun;
she mixes for her new guests
potions influenced by song.

  "Whereby her herb-powerful hand
turns them into various shapes,
the face of a boar covers this one,
that one appears as an African lion
with a fang and claws;
here recently added were wolves
while intending to weep one howls,

that one like a tiger from India
gently prowls around the house.
 "But although in various misfortunes
the divinity reared in Arcadia
pitying the covered leader
released him from the plague of the hostess,
though the crew had already
drunk by the mouth the evil potions;
by then the pigs had turned
from cereals to acorn fodder,
and nothing remains intact
with voice, body in ruins.
 "The mind alone staying steady
bewails the monsters which suffer.
O too slight the hand
and not potent the herbs,
which though they could turn the limbs,
are not able to turn the hearts!
 "Inside is the energy of humans
established by a hidden fortress.
More powerful are these dreadful drugs
which going deep inside
withdraw the human from oneself
and not harmful to the body
they cruelly wound the mind."

4
 Then I said, "I acknowledge and see that
it is not wrong to say that the vicious,
although they may preserve the form of the human body,
nevertheless in the quality of their souls
may be changed into beasts;
but that their fierce and wicked mind
rages with the ruin of the good
I would have refused to allow this itself for them."
 "It is not allowed," she said,
"as will be shown with an appropriate argument,
but nevertheless, if this itself should be taken away,
which it is believed is permitted to them,

the punishment of wicked humans
would be to a great extent relieved.
In fact, what may seem to anyone as perhaps incredible,
it must be the bad are more unhappy
when they might carry through desires
than when they could not fulfill things which they desire.

  "For if it is wretched to have wanted the perverse,
it is more wretched to have been able to get it,
without which the wretched will's effect would be weak.
And so since one's own misery may be single,
they must be urged as triply unfortunate
whom you may see willing, able, and performing crime."

  "I agree," I said, "but so that they may be freed soon
from this misfortune of suffering crime
I desire strongly that it to be removed from the ability."

  "They will be free of it," she said,
"sooner than either you may wish perhaps
or those may guess themselves to be freed;
for there is nothing in such brief lives apprehended so late
that especially the immortal soul
should think it has to wait a long time.

  "Their great hope and eminent scheme of crimes
often are destroyed by a sudden and unexpected end,
which in fact imposes a limit on their misery;
for if worthlessness makes them wretched,
the longer one is worthless the more wretched one must be.

  "I would judge them to be most unhappy
if final death at least should not finish their malice;
and in fact if we have concluded truly
about the misfortune of depravity,
it is evident that infinite is the misery
which is agreed to be eternal."

  Then I said, "At any rate
it is a strange inference and hard concession,
but I know it fits too well
with these which previously were conceded."

  "You evaluate it correctly," she said,
"but one who thinks it is reasonable
that it is hard to come to a conclusion

either should point out that something false has preceded it
or show the arrangement of propositions
of the necessary conclusion not to be effective;
otherwise with the preceding concessions
there is absolutely nothing
which may excuse one from the inference.

"For this too which I am going to say
may not seem any less strange,
but from these which are assumed it is equally necessary."

"What?" I asked.

"That the dishonest are happier paying the punishments
than if no penalty of justice should stick to them.
Now I am not devising what may come into anyone's mind,
that perverted morals be corrected by revenge
and be led away toward the right by fear of punishment,
to be an example to others also fleeing blaming;
but in another way I think
the unpunished dishonest are unhappier,
even if no method of correction is being considered,
nor the respect for example."

"And what other way would it be besides these?" I asked.

And she said, "Did we not concede that
the good are happy, while the bad are wretched?"

"So it is," I said.

"If then," she said, "something good
may be added to the misery of someone, is not one happier
than the one whose pure and solitary misery
is without any admixture of good?"

"So it seems," I said.

"But if with the same misery,
the one who may be free from all goods,
besides this by which one is wretched
should have something bad connected to them,
is it not agreed that this one is much more unhappy
than the one whose misfortune
is relieved by the participation of good?"

"Why not?" I asked.

"But for the dishonest to be punished is just,
while to get off unpunished is obviously unfair."

"Who would deny it?"

"But no one at any rate," she said;
"will deny that what is just is good
and the contrary that what is unjust is bad."

I answered that it is clear.

"Then the dishonest have when they are punished
in fact some connection of the good,
the punishment itself of course,
which is good by reason of the justice,
and the same when they are free of punishment
something extra of the bad belongs to them,
the impunity itself, which in being deserving of adversity
you have confessed is bad."

"I cannot deny it."

"Then of the dishonest presented
the ones unjust by impunity are much more unhappy
than the just ones punished by revenge."

Then I said, "Your consequences from these are in fact
what was concluded a little before;
but I ask you, don't you allow for any punishments of souls
after the body is discharged by death?"

"Yes, great ones in fact," she said,
"of which some are to be carried out by severe penalty,
while others I think by purgatorial mercy;
but it is not my purpose to discuss these now.

"While so far we have managed it so that
what will seem to you the most unworthy power of evils
might be understood to be nothing,
and dishonesty's unpunished
about whom you seem to complain
never are free of their punishment,
the licentiousness which you were asking to be soon ended
you might learn is not long
and if longer will be more unhappy,
while most unhappy if it should be eternal;
after this more wretched are the dishonest
let go by unjust impunity

than the ones punished by just revenge.
With this sentence it is logical that
not till then may they be oppressed by heavy punishments
when they are believed to be unpunished."

Then I said, "When I consider your arguments,
I think nothing could be said more truly;
but if I should turn back to the judgment of humans,
is there anyone to whom these things would seem
not only believable but even understandable?"

"So it is," she said.
"For they are unable to lift up eyes
accustomed to the dark to the light of clear truth
and like birds whose sight night illuminates, day blinds;
for as long as they are looking not at the order of things
but at their feelings, they may think
either the license or the impunity of the wicked is happy.

"But see what eternal law sanctifies.
You might have shaped the soul with better things:
there is no need for a reward from a conferring judge,
you have added yourself to the more excellent;
you might have perverted study to worse things:
you should not look for an avenger outside,
you have thrust yourself into the inferior—
just as if you should look back
by turns at the sordid earth and heaven,
in discerning by reason all the loiterings outside yourself
you seem to be between now the mud then the stars.

"But the crowd does not look back at yours.
What then, should we agree with these
whom we have shown are like beasts?
What if someone who utterly lost vision itself
also has forgotten ever having had sight oneself
and thought oneself lacking nothing for human perfection,
surely we the seeing should not think the same as the blind?
For they do not even acquiesce to that
which equally rests on valid supports of arguments;
unhappier are those who do than those who suffer injury."

"I should like to hear these very reasons," I said.

"Surely you do not deny," she asked,
"that everyone dishonest is deserving of punishment?"

"Not at all."

"While it is abundantly evident that
those who may be dishonest are unhappy."

"Yes," I said.

"Then you do not doubt that
those who are deserving of punishment are wretched?"

"It is agreed," I said.

"Then if you might be the idle attorney," she said,
"upon which would you think of putting the punishment,
on the one who did it
or on the one who endured the injury?"

"I would not waver," I said, "but in making amends
to the one who suffered from the trouble."

"Then to you the bringer of the injury
seems to be more wretched than the receiver."

"It follows," I said.

"Then it appears from this and other causes
resting on this foundation
that baseness makes one wretched by its own nature,
the misery put on anyone injured
being not the recipient's but the perpetrator's."

"It appears so," I said.

"And yet now," she said, "the speakers do the opposite;
for they try to arouse the pity of the jurors
for these who suffered severely and who are bitter,
when more justly the pity should be for those committing it;
whom should be led to trial not by the angry
but rather by gracious and pitying accusers
as the sick are to the doctor
so that the fault's diseases may be cut short by treatment.

"By this contract the works of the defenders
either would completely fall flat
or if one would rather be useful to humans
it could be turned into the practice of prosecution.

"The very dishonest too, if it were possible for them
by some crack to catch sight of abandoned virtue

and they could see themselves laying down the dirt of vices
by the tortures of penalties,
from the compensation of acquiring honesty
they would not consider these to be torture
and they would refuse the work of the defenders
and entrust themselves completely to the prosecutors.

　"Thus among the wise
absolutely no place would be left for hatred.
For who but the most foolish would hate the good?
While one does not have any reason to hate the bad.

　"For just like the feebleness of bodies
so vice is like a certain disease of souls,
since we should not judge the sick in body
as deserving hatred but rather pity,
much more deserving not being persecuted but being pitied
are the minds whose dishonesty oppresses
by a more dreadful disease than any feebleness.

IV
"Why is one glad to excite so much emotion
　and to disturb fate with one's own hand?
If you seek death, it is near itself
　of its own accord nor does it delay swift horses.
Those a snake, lion, tiger, bear and boar by a fang attack
　nevertheless they themselves attack the same with a sword.
Or is it because morals are diverse and different,
　that they provoke unjust battles and cruel wars
and want to perish by one weapon after another?
　It is not a just enough reason for fury.
You want to give back merits suitable in turn:
　esteem rightly the good and feel pity for the bad."

5
　At this point I said, "I see that
either happiness or misery may be established
in the very merits of the honest and dishonest.
But in this way I find fortune itself
to be in some good people and in some bad;
for no one wise would be an exile, destitute and degraded
rather than strong in business, respected in honor,

effective in power to prosper permanently in one's city.
    "For thus the duty of wisdom
is handled more clearly and publicly,
when the happiness of the ruling
is in a way transfused into the contacting people,
especially when prison, murder,
and the other tortures of legal penalties
should be rather for the ruinous citizens
for whom they are actually established.

    "Then why these should be turned in reverse
and crimes' punishments should press on the good,
while the bad should snatch the rewards of virtues,
I am very much amazed,
and I long to know from you
what reason may be seen for such confusions of the unjust.

    "And in fact I would be less amazed if I could believe
everything to be mixed up with chance accidents.
Now the divine guide heightens my bewilderment.
Since one may concede that the one who often may assign
delights to the good, the bitter to the bad
and on the contrary the hard to the good, wishes to the bad,
unless the cause is detected,
what is it that seems to differ from chance accidents?"

    "It is no wonder," she said,
"if what is unknown of the order by reason
may be believed accidental and confused;
but although you may be ignorant
of the cause of so great an arrangement,
nevertheless, since a good guide regulates the universe,
you should not doubt that all things happen correctly.

V
    "If someone is ignorant of Arcturus
the star sinking near the highest pole,
why the slow Bootes should steer the Great Bear
and sink its late flames into the horizon,
although very quickly it unfolds its rising,
one will marvel at the law of high heaven.

"The unfinished horns of the full moon become pale
by the dark of fearful night,
and the moon uncovers the diffused stars,
which she had covered with her shining face:
public error agitates the nations
and they tire from repeatedly striking cymbals.

"No one wonders at the northwest winds
beating the coast with roaring waves
nor the mass hardened by the snow's cold
being dissolved by the burning heat of the sun.
For here it is easy to discern the causes,
there hidden things disturb the feelings.

"Age promotes all things which are rare,
and the fickle crowd is stunned by sudden things,
but should the cloudy error of ignorance depart,
with progress they cease to seem strange!"

6
"So it is," I said;
"but since it should be in your duties
to unfold the causes of things hiding
and to explain the reasons veiled by mist,
I ask that you may determine what is here;
since this marvel especially upsets me,
you should explain it in detail."

Then smiling for a moment she said,
"By a question you call me to the greatest matter of all,
on which hardly anything would be enough to exhaust it.
For the matter is such that
one head having been cut off by doubt
countless others like the hydra's grow back;
nor would there be any limit
unless someone should enclose them
with the most lasting fire of the mind.

"For in this one is accustomed to inquiring
about the singleness of providence,
about the sequence of fate,
about the chances of a sudden event,
about divine cognition and predestination,

about freedom of decision,
which you weigh yourself how much of a load they may be.

"But since it is part of your medicine
for you to know some of these too,
although fenced in by a narrow limit of time
nevertheless I'll try to determine some of them.
But if the musical amusements of song delight you,
you should delay this pleasure for a while
until I weave in their order the entwining arguments."

"As you please," I said.

Then as though starting from another beginning
she examined it as follows:
"The generation of all things
and the whole progress of mutable natures
and whatever is moved in any way
draw causes, order and forms
out of the stability of the divine mind.

"This in the regular arc of its singleness
established a manifold method for producing things.
Which method when it is observed in itself
by the purity of divine intelligence,
is named providence;
while when it refers to what moves and so arranges,
it is called by tradition fate.

"It will soon be evident how different these are
if someone might observe mentally the force of both;
for providence is that very divine reason
established in the highest principle of all
which arranges all things,
while fate is the arrangement inherent in moveable things
through which providence ties everything in its order.

"For providence embraces all things together
however different however infinite,
while fate divides the individual things distributed
in motion with places, forms and times,
so that providence may be
this impotent unfolding of the temporal order
in the perspective of the divine mind,
while the same impotence divided

and so unfolded in times may be called fate.

"Although these may be different,
nevertheless one depends on the other;
for the destined order comes forth
out of the singleness of providence.
For just as an artist perceiving mentally
the form of the thing being made
puts in motion the accomplishment of the work
and what one had foreseen simply and immediately
one constructs through the temporal order,
so God by providence in fact
arranges the things being done individually and reliably,
while fate manages variously and temporally
this itself which has been arranged.

"Then whether fate is carried out by divine spirits
in some kind of serving of providence
or by a soul or by all nature submitting
or by the motions of the stars in the heavens
or by angelic virtue or by the varied skill of spirits
whether by some of these or by all
the fatal sequence is woven,
it is certainly obvious that
providence is the unchanging and single form
of the things being produced,
while fate is the changing bond and temporal order of those
which the divine singleness producing them has arranged.

"Thus all things which are under fate
should be subject to providence too,
to which fate itself is even subject,
while some things which are placed under providence
may rise above the sequence of fate;
these truly are the things which
reliably fixed near the primary divinity
exceed the order of destined mobility.

"For as in the case of circles
turning themselves around the same pole
the one which is innermost
goes toward the singleness of the center
and it exists as a kind of pole of the others placed outside

around which they are turned,
while the outermost rotated in a greater circuit
by however much it is away from the indivisible center point
so much is it extended in a larger space;
while whatever connects and unites itself to that center
is gathered into singleness
and ceases to be diffused and flow away:
by a similar argument
whatever goes farther away from the primary mind
is entwined in greater bonds of fate,
and something is so much freer from fate
by however much closer it aims at that pole of things;
but if it should cling to the firmness of the supernal mind,
being free of the motion of fate it too surpasses necessity.

   "Then as reasoning is to understanding,
that which is produced to that which is,
time to eternity, a circle to the centerpoint,
so is the mobile sequence of fate
to the stable singleness of providence.

   "This sequence moves heaven and the stars,
regulates the elements mutually in themselves
and transforms them one after another by change,
the same renews all things being born and dying
through the similar progress of breeding and procreation.

   "This also constrains the actions and fortunes of humans
by the imperishable connection of causes;
which since it originates
from the immovable beginnings of providence,
it is necessary for these to be unchangeable too.

   "Accordingly things are guided best
if the singleness remaining in the divine mind
brings out the unavoidable order of causes;
while this order by its own unchangeableness
should control mutable things
or else they would float about at random.

   "Thus, although to us not able to contemplate this order
all things may seem confused and disordered,
nonetheless however its method may arrange
the directing of all things toward the good.

"For there is nothing which may happen because of evil
nor even from the dishonest themselves;
whom, as is most amply explained,
perverse error diverts the ones looking for the good,
much less would the order
profiting from the pole of the highest good
turn aside anywhere from its beginning.

"'What truly,' you may ask,
'can any confusion be more unfair than that
now set-backs should affect the good then successes,
while now wishes should affect the bad then hates?'

"Surely then humans do not pass these
with such integrity of mind
that those whom they rate honest or dishonest
must also be as they judge?
And yet on this human courts fight hard,
and those whom some think fit for a reward
others think fit for punishment.

"But let us concede that
someone could discern good and bad;
surely then one will not be able to
look into that innermost temperature of souls,
just as temperature is usually told in bodies?

"For it is no less a miracle to the ignorant
why sweet things for instance
may be suited to some healthy bodies
while bitter things may be suited to others,
why certain of the sick are likewise helped by mild things
while others are helped by sharp ones.
But a doctor, who distinguishes the method and temperament
of health itself and so of sickness,
is not surprised by this at all.

"While what else other than honesty
is seen to be the health of souls,
what the sickness other than vice?
Who else other than God the guide and healer of minds
is either preserver of the good or remover of the bad?
When this one who has looked back
out of the deep mirrors of providence,

recognizes what may be proper to each one
and has learned what to apply it accommodates.

   "Here already arises that destined
distinguishing marvel of order,
when from the knowing is produced
what may astound the ignorant.

   "Now considering how few words
human reason is capable of,
I'll touch lightly on divine profundity;
about this which you think is most just
and most protective of equality
to the omniscience of providence it seems different.

   "As our familiar Lucan suggested,
the conquering cause pleased the gods,
while the conquered pleased Cato.
Then whatever you may see here short of hope
with things to be produced the order is in fact correct,
while in your opinion it is perverse confusion.

   "But someone may be so well mannered that about him
divine and human judgment may agree together,
but in the strengths of soul he is weak,
and if something adverse should happen to him
he might perhaps stop cultivating the innocence
through which he could not retain fortune:
and so a wise dispensation spares
the one whom adversity could make worse,
lest it not be fitting to work for one who may suffer.

   "Another is complete in all the virtues
and holy and so near God:
providence judges it would be so wrong
for this one to be touched by any adversity whatever
that he is not allowed to be agitated
by bodily diseases for instance.
For as someone better than I put it:

   'So the ethers build the body of a sacred man.'

   "Moreover it often happens that
the highest guiding of things is conferred upon the good
so that abounding dishonesty may be checked.
To others a certain one distributes a mixture

according to the quality of the souls:
Some she torments lest they be luxuriant in long happiness;
others may be agitated by hardships
so that they may reinforce the virtues of the soul
by the use and exercise of patience.
Some are too afraid of what they can bear;
others look down too much on what they cannot bear;
these she leads into proof with their sad things.

"Some revering the ages
have earned a name of glory at the price of death;
the impregnable by other sacrifices
have held out a certain example
of virtue being unconquered by evils;
there is no doubt how correctly these may happen
and so to whom they seem to come
by arrangement and out of their good.

"For that too is induced out of the same causes,
because now sadness then wishes come to the dishonest.
As to the sad ones in fact no one is surprised,
because everyone thinks them deserving of bad;
whose punishments in fact then deter others from crimes
by which then they are driven themselves to improve.
While the glad ones speak a great argument to the good,
about how they ought to judge this kind of happiness
which they should discern often serves the dishonest.

"There is another thing also I believe to be regulated
which is someone's nature
being perhaps so headstrong and insolent
that domestic material poverty
could rather irritate one into crimes;
for an illness of this kind
providence heals with the remedy of collected money.

"Here one viewing the conscience fouled by abuses
and comparing it with one's fortune perhaps is very alarmed
lest the loss of that of which the use is pleasing be sad;
then one will change morals
and so as long as one is afraid to lose a fortune
one forsakes wrong.

"Happiness shamefully spent
has thrown others into deserved ruin;
for some the right of punishing is permitted
so that it might be a cause of exercise for the good
and of punishment for the bad.
For just as there is no treaty
between the honest and dishonest
so among themselves the dishonest are not able to agree.

"Why not, since with vices tearing apart the conscience
by the selves themselves everyone disagrees,
and they often may do things
which when they may have managed them
they may decide they should not be managing them?

"Out of which that highest providence
often brought forth a distinguishing marvel,
so that the bad might make the bad good.
For while they seem to allow
a certain inequality to themselves from the worst,
burning with hatred of the guilty ones
they return to the fruit of virtue,
until they apply themselves
to be unlike those whom they hate.

"For it is divine force alone
for which evils may be goods too;
when using them competently
it elicits the effect of something good.
For a certain order embraces all things,
so that what has departed
the place assigned by reason of order
this nevertheless falls back into order, though another one,
lest anything in the realm of providence be left to chance.

'But it is difficult for me
to proclaim all these things as a god.'

For it is not possible for a human
either with genius to comprehend
all the engines of the divine work
or to explain them by language.

"It may be sufficient to have observed this enough
that the same God, the producer of all nature,

directing all may arrange them for the good,
and while it hastens to retain this
which it has brought forth in its likeness,
it may eliminate through the sequence of destined necessity
all evil from the boundaries of its republic.
Thus what is believed to abound on earth,
if you should look at the providential arrangement,
you would judge nothing at all to be evil.

"But I have seen for a long time that you are
both overloaded by the weight of the question
and exhausted by the length of the argument
waiting for some poetry's sweetness;
take then a drink by which refreshed
you may strive farther stronger.

VI
"If you wish to discern the laws
of the high Thunderer with a clear and clever mind,
focus on the summit of the highest heaven;
there by a fair agreement of matters
the stars preserve the ancient peace.

"The sun roused by red fire
does not obstruct the cold axis of the moon
nor does the Bear which by the world's highest pole
turns its swift movements
never washed in the western deep
perceiving other stars to be sunk
desire to dip its flames in the ocean;
always by equal intervals of time
does the evening star announce the late shadows,
and Venus brings back the nourishing day.

"Thus does mutual love
restore the eternal courses;
thus discordant war
is an exile of the stellar face.

"This concord regulates
the first principles by equal measures,
so that by fighting
wet may by successions yield to dry

and cold things may join faith with flames;
a flickering fire should rise into heaven,
and heavy earthly things by their weight should sink.

  "Truly from these causes of warming
the flowery year breathes the odors,
summer heat dries the grain,
autumn comes back heavy with fruit,
falling rain irrigates the winter.

  "This temperature nourishes and brings forth
whatever breathes life in the world;
the same snatching conceals and takes them away
burying the born in a final death.

  "Meanwhile the creator sits on high
and guiding turns the reins of things,
king and master, source and origin,
law and wise judge of the just,
and what stirs by angry emotion
it may check drawing it back
and so strengthen the wavering;
for unless the movement recalling the corrected
winding again collected them in cycles,
which now a stable order contains
the separated would be split from their source.

  "Here love is common to all,
and they go back to be held by the goal of the good,
because in no other way are they able to endure
unless turned back around by love
the causes which gave them being may flow again.

7
  "By now then do you see what all these things are
which follow from what we have said?"
  "What?" I asked.
  "That all fortune," she said, "is absolutely good."
  "And how can that be?" I asked.
  "Listen," she said.
"Since all fortune whether pleasant or difficult
is brought about for the sake of
at one time rewarding or disciplining the good

at another punishing or correcting the dishonest,
everything which consists of being
either just or useful is good."

"In fact," I said, "the argument is very true, and,
if I should consider the providence or fate
which was taught a little before,
the sentence rests upon firm strength.
But if it seems good,
let us count it among those which a little before
were set down as inconceivable."

"Why?" she asked.

"Because the common talk of people says of it,
and in fact frequently,
that the fortune of some is bad."

"Do you wish then," she asked, "that for a little while
we should not go too far from the talk of the crowd
as we would seem to have departed
from the experience of humanity?"

"As it pleases," I said.

"Then don't you consider what is productive to be good?"

"So it is," I said.

"While what either disciplines or corrects,
is it productive?"

"I admit it," I said.

"Then is it good?"

"Why not?"

"But this is theirs who either
set in virtue wage war against difficulties
or turning aside from vices take the way of virtue."

"I am unable to deny it," I said.

"What about the truly pleasant,
which as a reward is bestowed upon the good,
surely the crowd does not consider it to be bad?"

"Not at all, as it is true
so too one rates it to be the best."

"What about the rest,
which since it may be difficult

curbs the bad by just punishment,
surely the people do not think it good?"

"No," I said, "of all which can be imagined
one judges it to be most wretched."

"Watch out then lest following the opinion of the people
we might formulate something quite inconceivable."

"What?" I asked.

"For out of these," she said, "which are conceded
it turns out that all the fortune of those who either are
or are in possession of or are advanced in
or are in the attainment of virtue may be entirely good,
while for those staying in dishonesty
all fortune is the worst."

"This is true," I said,
"although no one would dare confess it."

"Accordingly," she said,
"a wise hero should not become annoyed
whenever struggle is drawn into fortune,
just as it is not proper for a brave hero to be indignant
whenever the tumult of war is noisy.

"For both the difficulty itself is an opportunity
for the latter in fact in extending glory
while for the former in shaping wisdom.
From which even virtue is named,
which thriving on its strengths
is not overcome by adversities;
nor have you positioned in the advancement of virtue come to
melting away in delights and wasting away in pleasure.

"You are engaged in a battle for passions
with every sharp fortune
lest either the sad should oppress you
or the pleasant should corrupt you.
Occupy the middle with firm strengths;
whatever either stops lower or advances beyond
has the contempt of happiness,
does not have the reward of labor.

"For in your hands is situated
the kind of fortune you prefer to form for yourself;
for everything which seems difficult,

unless it either disciplines or corrects, punishes.

VII
"Wars for twice five years occupied
the avenging son of Atreus in the ruins of Phrygia
where he expiated his brother's lost marriage-beds;
when that one wished to set sail with a Greek army
and in bloodshed ransomed the winds,
he put off paternal pity and as a sad priest
marred the throat of his daughter.

"The Ithacan mourned for his lost companions,
whom the savage Polyphemus reclining in a vast cave
plunged into his monstrous stomach;
but nevertheless frenzied by a blind face
delight compensated for the sad tears.

"Hard labors glorify Hercules:
that one tamed the arrogant Centaurs,
carried away the spoils from the fierce lion,
pierced with unerring arrows the birds,
snatched fruits from the perceiving dragon
in a left hand heavier with golden quarry,
dragged Cerberus with a triple chain;
the victor is said to have set the inexorable
master as fodder for the fierce team of four;
Hydra perished in burned up poison;
the river Achelous disfigured in appearance
submerged its modest face under the banks;
he threw down Antaeus on the Libyan sands;
Cacus appeased the anger of Evander,
the shoulders which the deep world was to press
the bristly one marked with foams;
the last labor lifted heaven
with an unbent neck and earned again
the heavenly prize of the last labor.

"Go now, brave ones, where the lofty way
of the great leads by example.
Why do you lazy ones expose your backs?
The earth surpassed, the stars are bestowed."

Notes to Book 5:

1: Aristotle in his *Physics* II, 3 defined the material, formal, efficient, and final causes of things.

II: The Homer quote is said of the sun in the *Iliad* III, 277 and in the *Odyssey* XI, 109.

3: Horace (65-8 BC) made fun of the legendary soothsayer Tiresias in his *Satires* II, 5.

4: The Roman statesman and prolific writer Cicero (106-43 BC) discussed providence in his *Divination* II, 8.

IV: The Stoics, named after the porch in Athens where Zeno of Citium taught in the early third century BC, recognized the impressions of the senses and imagination and attempted to rise above them.

6: Aristotle discussed whether the heavens and the universe are eternal in book I of *On the Heavens*, concluding that only the ungenerated can be eternal.

6: Plato's ideas on the eternity of the universe can be found in the *Timaeus* 28 and 37.

Book 5

1

She had spoken and was turning the direction of the speech
toward handling and explaining other subjects.

Then I said, "Your encouragement is in fact correct
and absolutely most worthy of your responsibility,
but what you just now said about providence
being a question complicated by many other things
I am experiencing in reality.
For I am asking whether you think
chance is anything at all and what it is."

Then she said, "I am in a hurry
to pay off the debt of the promise
and open up for you the way by which you may go back home.
But these things though very useful to have acknowledged
nevertheless for a little while
are averse from the trail of our purpose,
and there is a concern lest tired out by side-trips
you may not be capable of traversing the straight journey."

"Have absolutely no concern for that," I said;
"for instead it might be a rest for me
to understand that by which I am most charmed.
At the same time, when the flank of your argument
might be established by every undoubted belief,
none of the consequences may be argued."

Then she said, "I will humor you,"
and at the same time the beginning was as follows:
"If in fact," she said, "one may define chance to be
some event produced by accidental movement
and by no connection of causes,
I would confirm chance to be nothing at all
and except for an indication of the subject matter
I would determine it to be an absolutely empty word.
For with God confining all things in order
can there be any place left for randomness?

"For it is a true sentence
that nothing arises out of nothing,
which none of the ancients ever opposed,
though they might not lay it down as a working principle

but as a subject of the material
as if this were a kind of foundation
of all reasonings about nature.

"But if something should arise from no causes at all,
it will seem to be arisen from nothing;
but if this is unable to arise,
it is not possible for chance at any rate
to be like this which we defined a little before."

"What then," I asked, "is there nothing
which can rightly be called either chance or accidental?
Or is there something, even though the crowd may miss it,
for which such words may be appropriate?"

"My Aristotle," she said, "defined it in his *Physics*
both briefly and by reason near the truth."

"In what way?" I asked.

"Whenever," she said, "something is managed
for the sake of some matter and something other
than what was intended from the purposes happens
it is called chance,
as if someone in digging the ground
for the purpose of cultivating a field
should come upon a mass of buried gold.

"Then this is believed to have happened by accident,
not from nothing it is true,
for it has its own causes,
whose unforeseen and unexpected coincidence
seems a chance occurrence.
For if the cultivator was not digging the field's ground,
if the depositor had not buried his money in that place,
the gold would not have been discovered.

"So these are the causes of the accidental saving,
which comes about from the causes
exposed to it and flowing together with it,
not from the intention of the one managing it.

"For neither the one who buried the gold
nor the one who cultivated the field
intended that this money should be discovered,
but, as I said, it coincided that
what the former buried the latter dug up,

and so it concurred.

"So it is all right to define chance to be
an unexpected event from causes flowing together in these
which are managed for the sake of something else.
While that order makes causes concur and so flow together
proceeding from the inevitable connection
which descending from the source of providence
arranges all things in their places and times.

I
"In Persian rock cliffs, where turned on one following
    a fugitive shoots aggressive darts in their breasts,
Tigris and Euphrates release themselves from one source
    and soon disunite into unjoined waters.
If they should combine course and return again into one,
    each shoal's stream which draws may flow together,
ships and trunks plucked by the river come together
    and the mixed stream may entwine accidental ways;
nevertheless the very steepness of chance's earthy abyss
    and the order of the falling flow guide these wanderings.
Thus luck which seems to float with reins surrendered
    submits to bridles and goes itself by law."

2
    "I am paying attention," I said,
"and agree that it is just as you say.
But in this sequence of causes clinging to itself
is there any freedom for our judgment
or does the fatal chain constrain
the very movements of human souls too?"
    "There is," she said;
"nor could there be any rational nature
unless freedom of judgment should support the same.
For whatever by reason can use it naturally
has the judgment by which it may discern each one;
by itself then it may distinguish avoiding or choosing.
Truly everyone seeks what one judges one to be choosing,
while one shuns what one evaluates one is avoiding.

"Therefore reason belongs in the very ones in which
the freedom of willing and of refusing also belong,
but I am not establishing that this is equal in all.
For in celestial and divine substances there is
both sharp judgment and uncorrupted will
and the effective power of the readily chosen.

"While human souls must in fact be more free
when they keep themselves in contemplation of divine mind,
while less when they fall out toward bodies,
and even less when they may be compressed in earthly limbs;
while the last is slavery when addicted to vices
they have fallen from the possession of their own reason.

"For when they have lowered their eyes
from the light of the highest truth to lower and dark things,
soon they become misty from a cloud of ignorance,
are disturbed by ruinous moods,
in which approaching and agreeing
they encourage slavery which has been brought on themselves
and are in a way captured by their own freedom.

"Nevertheless that intuition discerns from the eternal
the whole of providence which is watching
and arranges everything predestined by their merits.

II
"'It oversees all and listens to all,'
sings Homer with the honey-flow of the mouth
about the bright sun with its clear light;
nevertheless the weakness of its rays
is not able to break through with light
the innermost bowels of the earth or of the sea.

"Not so the creator of this great world:
for this one watching all from heaven
none blocks it with a pile of earth,
nor does night obstruct it with black clouds;
what may be, what might have been and may come
in one stroke of the mind it discerns;
because it alone looks back at everything
you could call it the true sun."

3

Then I said, "Look,
again I am confused by more difficult ambiguity."
   "What is that?" she asked.
"Of course I am already guessing
by which things you may be upset."
   "It seems," I said, "to oppose and so disagree too much
for God to foreknow the universe
and for freedom's judgment to exist for anyone.
For if God foresees all and cannot in any way be mistaken,
what providence has foreseen to be the future must result.
   "Therefore if from eternity it foreknows
not only the actions of humans
but also the deliberations and wishes,
there will be no freedom of judgment;
for neither any other action
nor any will whatever could exist
except what an infallible divine providence
might have preconceived.
   "For if things were able to be turned aside
differently from how they are foreseen,
the foreknowledge of the future will not already be sure,
but opinion rather is uncertain;
which to believe about God I judge is wrong.
   "For I do not approve of that argument
by which some believe themselves able
to unloose this question's knot.
For they say the reason why the future of events exists
is not because providence has foreseen it to be,
but on the contrary rather because what the future is
cannot escape the notice of divine providence
and by that method this must fall back on the opposite side.
   "For they say it is not necessary
for that which is foreseen to happen,
but it is necessary that future things are to be foreseen—
as if truly which may be the cause of which thing,
whether foreknowledge is the work of necessity's futures
or necessity the work of providence's futures,
and so should we not press on to demonstrate that,

howsoever the order of the causes may hold itself
the result of the foreknown matters is necessary
even if foreknowledge of the resulting
does not seem to impose necessity on future matters.

"And in fact if someone should sit,
the opinion which infers that one is sitting must be true;
and so again from the converse,
if concerning someone the opinion be true because one sits,
one must be sitting.

"Then it is necessary in both cases,
in this fact of the sitting,
but certainly in the other of its truth.
But not for this reason is someone sitting
because the opinion is true,
but rather this is true
because someone sitting has preceded.
So though the cause of the truth
may proceed from another side,
nevertheless a common necessity belongs to both.

"It is similarly evident to argue this
about providence and future matters.
For even if for this reason they are foreseen
because they are future things,
truly the reason they result
is not because they are foreseen,
nonetheless either the things coming must be foreseen by God
or the things foreseen must result as foreseen,
which alone is adequate for destroying freedom of judgment.

"Now really how absurd it is
that the result of temporal matters
is said to be the cause of eternal foreknowledge!
What other reason is there to think that
God foresees future things because they are about to result
than to suppose that what has happened only once
is the cause of that highest providence?

"Besides, just as when I know what is
it itself must be so
when I have learned what the future is
it itself must be the future;

so it arises then that
the result of the foreknown matter could not be avoided.

"Finally if someone should think that
something is different from the reality it has itself,
it is not only not knowledge,
but it is a false opinion
very much different from true knowledge.

"Therefore if what is such a future
that its result may not be certain and so necessary,
how could it be foreknown that it is to result?
For just as knowledge itself is impervious to falsity
so that which is conceived by it
also cannot be conceived otherwise.

"For indeed the reason why
knowledge should be free from deception is because
it must have such a reality as this by itself
so that the knowledge comprehends that it has it by itself.

"What then, in what way does God foreknow
these uncertain future things?
For if it thinks coming things inevitable
which it is actually possible may not result,
it is mistaken;
which it is not only wrong to feel
but even to mention aloud.

"But if accordingly it determines future things
to be just as they are such that it may recognize
equally whether they are to arise or possibly not arise,
what foreknowledge is this,
which comprehends nothing certain, nothing stable?
Or does this refer to that ridiculous prophecy of Tiresias

'Whatever I may say either will be or not'?

"Also how would divine providence be better than opinion
if like humans it judges things uncertain
whose result is uncertain?
But if with that most certain source of all things
nothing can be uncertain,
certain is the result of these
which that might have foreknown firmly as future things.

"Therefore there is no freedom
in human deliberations and actions,
which the divine mind
foreseeing all things without the error of falsity
binds to the one and constrains the result.

"Once this is accepted it is clear
how much the downfall of human matters follows.
For in vain are rewards or penalties
set before the good and bad,
which no free or voluntary movement of souls has earned,
and what now is judged most fair
will seem most unfair of all,
either to punish the dishonest or reward the honest,
whose own will does not emit one or the other
but necessity compels the certainties of the future.

"Then neither vices nor virtues would be anything,
but rather there would be
a mixed and so indiscriminate confusion of all merits;
also nothing more wicked can be contrived,
since every order of things should be drawn from providence
and nothing should be permitted to human deliberations,
it arises that our vices too
should be traced back to the author of all goods.

"Then there is no reason in either
hoping for or praying to avert anything;
for what would anyone either hope for or even pray to avert
when an inflexible sequence
connects all the things being chosen?

"Taken away then is that unique commerce
between humans and God,
evidently of hoping for and praying to avert,
if in fact for the price of fair humility
we deserve the inestimable recompense of divine grace;
which is the only way by which humans seem able
to converse with God and join with that inaccessible light
before they too should obtain it themselves
by means of praying.

"If in having accepted the necessity of future things
these may be believed to have none of the powers,

what will there be by which we could connect
and so adhere to that highest principle of things?
Therefore it will be necessary for the race of humans,
just as you were singing a little before, to crack
having been separated and so removed from its source.

III
  "What discordant cause released
the agreements of things? What God
established such wars between two truths
so that what at different points may exist as single
the same mixed should refuse to be coupled?

  "Or is there no discord between the truths
and do they always cohere with themselves definitely,
but is the mind covered over by the blind body parts
unable by the fire of suppressed light
to recognize the thin grip of things?

  "But why does it burn with such love
to discover the hidden signs of truth?
Does it know what troubles it is desiring to learn?
But why does it work to know the signs?

  "Or if it is ignorant, why does it seek blindly?
For who unaware would wish for anything?
Or who could pursue the unknown
or where would one come upon it?
Who ignorant could recognize the discovered form?

  "Or when it perceives the deep mind
does it know alike the highest and the single,
now built by the cloud of body parts
has it not on the whole forgotten itself
and losing the sum holds the individual?

  "Then whoever searches for truths
is in neither condition; for one does not know
nor yet is one thoroughly ignorant of everything,
but retaining the highest which it remembers
one deliberates from above reconsidering the visions,
so that one could add the forgotten parts
to the ones preserved."

4

Then she said, "Old is this complaint about providence
Cicero when he distributed 'Divination' eagerly ridiculed,
and the matter was questioned absolutely
by you yourself long and often,
but not by any means has it been explained by any of you
thus far diligently and powerfully enough.

   "The cause of such mist is that
the movement of human reasoning is not able
to apply to the singleness of divine foreknowledge,
which if in any way could be contemplated,
absolutely nothing would remain ambiguous.
So this at last I'll attempt to make clear and so explain,
if before that I deal with what you set in motion.

   "For I am wondering why you should think
that refuting argument less effective
which because it considers foreknowledge
not to be the cause of the necessity for future matters
thinks freedom of judgment not hindered by foreknowledge.

   "For surely you do not draw
the argument of the necessity of future things
from anywhere but from the fact that
things which are foreknown cannot not result?

   "If then forethought does not add
any necessity to future matters,
which you even acknowledged a little before,
why is it that the outcome of voluntary matters
should be compelled toward a certain result?

   "Now for the sake of argument,
so that you may turn to what should follow,
let us propose that no foreknowledge exists.
Then surely, as many things as pertain to this,
which come from judgment
may not be compelled toward necessity?"

   "Not at all."

   "Let us propose secondly it does exist,
but it imposes nothing of necessity on things;
the same freedom of will, as I believe,
will remain whole and so complete.

"'But,' you may say,
'although foreknowledge of events
is not a necessity for future things,
nevertheless it is a sign they are of necessity coming.'

"Then in this case, even if there were no forethought,
the outcome of future things would still be necessary;
and in fact every sign only shows what may be,
while it does not cause what it designates.

"Therefore the previous demonstration is that
nothing happens except out of necessity,
so that it may be apparent that
forethought is a sign of this necessity;
otherwise if the latter does not exist,
the former in fact could not be a sign
of that thing which does not exist.

"While already the proof is established
supported by a strong argument,
not from signs nor from evidence sought outside
but from agreeing and necessary causes being drawn.

"But how could it arise that
what are foreseen to be future things may not come about?
Truly it is as if we should believe that
future events do not exist
which providence foreknows do exist,
and so instead of that rather we should think,
although they may result,
yet they have had nothing of necessity in their nature
so that they should result.

"What here you may easily weigh will be allowed:
and in fact as long as more subjects arise
we observe them with the eyes,
just as those drivers who perform in chariots
in restraining and turning are watched,
and in this way others also.
Surely then necessity does not compel
any of those things to so occur?"

"Not at all; for the effect of skill would be in vain
if all things should be moved by compulsion."

"Then since the same things which occur
are free of arising by necessity
before they may occur
future things are without necessity.
Therefore there are some things about to happen
whose outcome may be unrestricted by any necessity.

"For in fact I think there is no one who will say
that what occurs now might not exist
before coming events should occur.
Then even these forethoughts have free results.

"For just as knowledge of present things
brings in of necessity nothing for these which occur
so foreknowledge of future things
brings in of necessity nothing for these which are coming.

"'But,' you may say, 'this is the very thing to be doubted
whether there could be any forethought of those things
which have no necessary outcomes.'
And as a matter of fact they seem to disagree,
and you think if they may be foreseen necessity follows,
if necessity ceases very little is foreknown,
and nothing can be grasped by knowledge except the certain.

"But if outcomes which are uncertain
are foreseen as if they were certain,
it is the mist of opinion, not the truth of knowledge;
for to think a thing should have
anything different from itself
you believe to be opposite from the integrity of knowledge.

"The cause of this error is because
all things which are known which anyone knows
one thinks to be understood
so much from the power and so the nature of themselves.

"But it is the complete opposite;
for everything which is understood is grasped
not according to its own power
but rather according to the ability of those understanding.

"For as may be made clear by this brief example,
in one way sight in another way touch
recognizes the same roundness of a body;
the former staying at a distance

looks at it all at once by the rays it has thrown,
while the latter clinging to the sphere
the connected movement around the circumference itself
also grasps the roundness in parts.

"Also in one way sensation, in another imagination,
in another reason, in another intelligence
observe the same person.
For sensation examines the shape
constituted in the subject matter,
while imagination examines the shape alone without matter;
while reason transcends this too
and weighs by universal consideration the appearance itself
which belongs to the individualities.

"While the eye of intelligence rises higher;
for having surpassed the circumference of the universal
it observes that single form itself
by the clear apprehension of the mind.
In which the greatest consideration is this:
for the higher power of grasping encircles the lower,
while the lower in no way rises up to the higher.

"For sensation is not able to grasp anything except matter
nor does imagination observe universal appearances
nor does reason catch the single form;
but intelligence as if looking from above
by the conceived form differentiates all
which actually are underneath,
but by this method it grasps the form itself,
which could be known to no other.

"For it understands both the universal of reason
and the shape of the imagination and sensible material
nor is it by using reason or imagination or the senses,
but by that one stroke of the mind formally,
as I may say it thus, watching all.

"Reason too when it looks back at some universal
using neither imagination nor the senses
grasps the imaginable or the sensible.
For this is what so defines
by the universal of its conception:
a human is a rational two-footed animal.

"This not only may be a universal idea,
but no one is ignorant that
the imaginable and sensible are a reality
because that considers it not in imagination or sense
but in a rational conception.

"Imagination too, even though it has taken its beginning
of seeing and forming shapes from the senses,
nevertheless in the absence of sense
it surveys every sensible thing
not by the sensible but judging by imagined reason.

"Do you see then that in understanding
all things should use their own ability
rather than those of the things which are understood?
Nor is it wrong;
for since every judgment is an act of the one judging,
it is necessary that everyone should carry out their work
not from another but from one's own capability.

IV
"Formerly the Stoics brought forth
old ones too hidden
who could believe the senses and images
from bodies outside
were impressed on minds,
just as formerly with a swift pen
the practice was to fix pressed letters
on a smooth page which should have no marks.

"But the mind if thriving with its characteristics
explains nothing with its impulses,
but lays experiencing so much
subdued by the marks of bodies
and empty like in a mirror
it represents the images of things,
from where does this idea so thrive
in souls discerning all things?

"What power sees through the individuals
or what differentiates the things learned?
What recovers the things differentiated
and selecting one course after another

now engages its head in the highest things
now departs into the lowest,
then bringing itself back to itself
refutes the false with the true?

"This is an efficient cause
very much more powerful
than that which only experiences
the impressed marks of matter.

"Nevertheless it precedes rousing
and so moving the powers of the soul
in the passive living body
when either light strikes the eyes
or the voice makes noise in the ears.

"Then the aroused energy of the mind
holds the appearances which are inside
calling similar ones into motion,
attaches them to marks from outside
and inside mingles the images
with the stored away forms.

5
"But if in feeling bodies,
however much otherwise exposed qualities
may affect the instruments of the senses
and the body's experience may precede
the energy of the active soul,
which in itself may provoke the action of the mind
and arouse meanwhile on the inside the dormant forms,
if in feeling bodies, I say,
the soul is not distinguished by the experience,
but out of its own power judges
the experience subjected to the body,
how much more do those
who are unqualified by all the moods of the body
not follow external objects in distinguishing,
but extricate the action of their own mind!

"And so by this argument various ideas
might yield to diverse and different means.
For sense alone went to all the other immobile animals

destitute of ideas, such as are the sea's shellfish
and others which are raised clinging to the rocks;
while imagination is for mobile beasts,
in whom some already seem to be endowed
with avoiding and desiring;
while the reason of the human race is so important
just as intelligence alone is of the divine:
thus this idea may be better than others
which by its own nature understands not only its own
but subjects of other ideas too.

  "What then, if sense and imagination
are opposed to reasoning saying that
that from the universal is nothing
which reason may think it contemplates by itself?

  "For that which is sensible or imaginable
cannot be universal;
then either the judgment of reason is true
and the sensible is not anything
or, since there may be known to be
more subjects in the senses and imagination,
the concept of reason is empty,
because it might consider
what should be sensible and so individual
as if they were something from the universal.

  "To this if reason itself should answer in reply in fact
that it perceives both what may be sensible
and what imaginable in the logic of the whole,
while those cannot attain the understanding of the whole
since their idea could not exceed corporeal shapes,
while concerning the understanding of things
it is rather trusting in stronger and more perfect judgment:
in a dispute like this then should not we,
in whom belongs the power of such great reasoning
as well as of imagining and also of feeling,
rather approve the position of reason?

  "It is similar to how human reason thinks that
divine intelligence does not contemplate future things
except as it understands them itself.
For so you discuss it:

If in these which don't seem to have
certain or necessary results
their coming cannot be foreknown for certain.
Then there is no foreknowledge of these things;
if we actually may believe that to be in these,
there will be nothing that does not happen out of necessity.

"If then just as we are reason's participants
so we could have the judgment of the divine mind,
just as we have judged
imagination and sense ought to yield to reason
so we shall assess it most just
for human reason to submit itself to the divine mind.

"Therefore, if we can, let us rise up
to the summit of that highest intelligence;
for there reason will see
what it cannot contemplate in itself:
and that is, where in a moment
even what doesn't have a certain outcome
certain and definite forethought nevertheless may see,
and it would not be opinion
but rather the inclusive singleness
of the highest knowledge with no boundaries.

V
"In how many varied shapes do animals move on the lands!
For some are in a stretched body and sweep the dust
and drag a continuous furrow by the breast's roused force;
some are wanderers for whom the wings' lightness beats winds
and swims in fluid flight in the vast space of the sky;
and some like to press these footprints only on steps
either to pass over green plains or to go under forests.

"Though you may see all differ in various forms,
yet sense is able to weigh downward the stupid faces;
the unique race of humans lifts the lofty summit higher
and stands in an easy upright body and looks down on lands.

"This figure advises, unless earthly you fool with evil:
You who in an upright look seek heaven and reveal the front,
to the sublime should bear the soul too,
lest weighed to the ground the mind should sink lower

than the higher lifted body.

6

"Then since, as was shown a little before,
everything which is known is understood
not from its own nature but from comprehending,
let us examine now as much as possible
what may be the condition of the divine substance,
so that we could also recognize what its knowledge may be.

"Then that God is eternal
is the judgment by the common reason of all peoples.
Then let us consider what eternity may be;
for this will make clear to us at once
divine nature and knowledge.
Then eternity is at once
the total and perfect possession of interminable life.
This is more clearly evident
from comparison of the temporal.

"For whatever lives in time
that present proceeds from the past into the future
and nothing is established in time
which could embrace at once the entire space of its life,
but in fact it does not yet apprehend tomorrow
while it has already lost yesterday;
in life today too you do not live more fully
than in that passing and transitory moment.

"Then what submits to the condition of time,
that may, just as Aristotle supposed about the universe,
never begin to be nor does it cease
and its life is extended in the infinity of time,
nevertheless it is not yet such
that it rightly may be believed to be eternal.
For not all at once is it permitted
to comprehend and so grasp the space of infinite life,
but the future not yet, it does not have the past already.

"So what comprehends and so possesses at once
the entire fullness of interminable life,
to whom nothing of the future may be absent
nor has anything of the past vanished,

it is rightly asserted to be eternal
and it must be both present in control of itself
to always stand by itself
and have present the infinity of passing time.

   "Thus not correctly do some,
who when they hear this universe viewed by Plato,
neither to have had a beginning of time
nor is there to be a failure of conditions,
in this way they think the created universe
is co-eternal with the creator.

   "For it is one thing to be led through interminable life,
which Plato attributed to the universe,
another for the presence of the interminable life
to be embraced all at once,
which it is obvious is a characteristic of the divine mind.
Nor should God be seen as older
than the created things in the amount of time
but rather in the property of a single nature.

   "For that infinite movement of temporal things
imitates this state of the present immobile life,
and since it could not represent and so equal it,
from immobility it falls into movement,
from singleness of the present it degenerates
into the infinite quantity of the future and so the past,
and since it is unable to possess
all at once the fullness of its life,
this by itself which in some way never ceases to be that
to some it seems to emulate
what it cannot fulfill and so express
binding itself to whatever presence
of this brief and fleeting moment,
which since it carries a certain image
of that remaining presence,
with whatever it has touched it stands out
so that they seem to be.

   "While since it could not remain,
the infinite march of time took hold of it
and the action from that method is that
it might continue the same life the fullness of which

it has not been able to embrace by enduring.
And so if we wish to apply worthy names to things,
following Plato let us say that God is in fact eternal,
while the universe is perpetual.

   "Since then every judgment comprehends
according to its nature things which are subject to it,
it is moreover with God
always an eternal and so an immediate state;
knowledge too having surpassed every motion of that time
remains in the singleness of its present
and embracing the infinite spaces of the past and future
it contemplates all things
as if they were already produced in its single cognition.

   "And so if you wish to consider the foreseeing
by which it distinguishes all,
you will more correctly evaluate it
not to be foreknowledge as if of the future
but knowledge of a never failing presence.
Thus it is called not foreseeing but rather providence,
because established far from things below
it may watch all as if from the eminent summit of things.

   "Why then do you claim that necessary things should arise
which are illuminated by divine light,
since humans in fact may not cause
necessary things to be which they may see?
For your having observed the present which you perceive
surely does not add any necessity to them, does it?"

   "Not at all."

   "Yet if the worthy comparison is
of the divine and the human present,
as you see certain things in this your temporary present
so that perceives all things in its eternal one.
Therefore this divine forethought
does not change the nature and property of things
and looks at the presence of such things with itself
even as future things one day come about.

   "Nor does it confuse the judgments of things
and with one observation of its mind
it distinguishes coming things

whether by necessity or not by necessity,
just as when you see at once
a person walk on land and the sun rise in the sky,
even though both are observed at the same time
nevertheless you distinguish them
and decide the former is voluntary and the latter necessary.

"So then divine observation looking through all
does not at all disturb the quality of things
which are present in fact with itself
while future in regard to the arrangement of time.
Thus this may not be opinion
but rather an idea based on truth,
since it understands what is to exist
which the same is not unaware of existing free of necessity.

"At this point if you should say that
what God sees is about to happen cannot not result,
and that what cannot not result occurs out of necessity,
and should bind me to this name of necessity,
I'll admit in fact the matter is of the most solid truth,
but it is one which hardly any explorer has approached
except by the divine.

"For I'll answer that the same future
when it is referred to the divine idea seems necessary,
while when it is weighed in its own nature
it seems absolutely free and so released.

"As a matter of fact there are two necessities,
one single, for instance that all humans must be mortal,
the other conditional,
as when you may know someone is walking
he must be walking.
For what everyone has learned
is unable to be otherwise than what is known,
but the latter condition does not imply
that the other former one is simple.

"For it does not cause this necessity by its own nature
but by the addition of a condition;
for no necessity compels the one stepping by will to march,
although whenever one is stepping
it may be necessary at that time to march.

"Then in the same way, if providence sees what is present,
it must be even though it may have no necessity in nature.
Yet God observes these future things as present
which come out of the freedom of judgment;
then these necessary results arise
according to divine observation
through the arrangement of the divine idea,
while considered through themselves
they do not abandon the absolute freedom of their nature.

"Then beyond doubt all things
which God foreknows to be the future will arise,
but some of them do originate from free judgment,
which although they may come out by existing
nevertheless they do not lose their own nature
in which before they arose they could not even come out.

"To what then does it refer that things are not necessary,
since on account of the arrangement of divine knowledge
by all the means of necessity the appearance comes out?
This of course is why that which I proposed a little before,
the sun rising and the stepping person,
which while arising cannot not arise,
nevertheless one of them was existing by necessity
even before it has arisen, while the other not at all;
so too what God has present beyond doubt exists,
but some of those things in fact result from necessity
while others result from the power of doing.

"Then this we said was not wrong
if they be referred to the divine idea they are necessary,
if they be considered through themselves
they are released from the bonds of necessity,
just as everything which is exposed to the senses
if you should refer to reason is universal,
if to itself you may regard them as individual.

"'But if it is in my power,' you may ask,
'to change the planned situation, I'll avoid providence,
since what that foreknows I shall have bravely changed.'

"I'll answer that you can in fact turn aside your plan,
but since the present truth of providence observes both
that you can and whether or not you may do it or change it

you cannot evade divine foreknowledge,
just as you could not escape observation of a present eye
although by free will you might turn to various actions.

"'What then,' you may ask,
'will divine knowledge be changed from my arrangement,
so that when I may want now this now that
that too may seem to alter
the changing conditions of knowing?'

"Not at all.
For divine observation anticipates every future,
and it turns them back and so recalls them
to the presence of its own knowledge;
it does not alter, as you think,
now this now the other by the alternating of foreknowing,
but remaining in one glance
it comes before and so embraces your changes.

"God is assigned this omnipresence
of comprehending and seeing
not from the result of future things
but from its own singleness.
From this that too is resolved
which you proposed a little before,
that it is unworthy if our future
is said to provide a cause of God's knowledge.

"For this power of knowledge
by an immediate idea embracing all
has itself established the method for all things,
while it owes nothing to posterior things.
Which since they may be so,
the freedom of judgment for mortals remains undefiled,
nor do the laws set forth rewards and penalties unfairly
for wills freed from every necessity.

"Also God remains a foreknowing observer of all from above
and the ever present eternity of its vision
concurs with the future quality of our actions
dispensing rewards to the good and punishments to the bad.
Neither are the hopes nor prayers placed in God in vain,
which when they are right cannot be ineffective.

"Then reject vices, cultivate virtues,
lift up your soul to right hopes,
offer to the heights humble prayers.
Great is the necessity of honesty indicated for you,
if you are not to deceive with appearances,
since you do all before the eyes of a discerning judge."

Introduction to Muhammad
and the *Qur'an*

Muhammad was born at Mecca in 570 CE after his father died; his inheritance included a slave-girl. He was raised in the desert away from the city by a wet nurse for two years. When Muhammad was six, his mother died as they were returning from Medina. His grandfather died two years later in Mecca, and Muhammad joined the family of his uncle Abu Talib. Young Muhammad pastured sheep and goats, and he fought in a local war at the age of twenty. Muhammad began traveling for merchants and gained a reputation as honest and trustworthy. He helped the wealthy widow Khadija double her money; she was 40 and he 25 when they married. On his wedding day Muhammad freed his slave-girl so that she could marry, and he adopted the slave-boy Khadija gave him as his son. During a famine Muhammad adopted Abu Talib's son 'Ali when he was about five. When he was about 35, Muhammad successfully mediated a dispute between tribes at the Ka'ba shrine in Mecca.

Muhammad prayed in seclusion every year during the month of Ramadan. In 610 he began to have visions during his spiritual retreat, and in a cave a voice told him three times to recite. As he was walking down the mountain, the voice identified itself as the angel Gabriel. These recitations were later written down as the *Qur'an*. The first to accept the new religion of Islam were his wife and two sons, and they were called Muslims, which means those who submit to God. Muhammad shared his revelations with those present. He was ordered to pray and established the regular times for prayer. The Quraysh tribe tried to stop his growing following with persecution and boycotts. A group of 82 Muslims migrated to Abyssinia. Muhammad's wife Khadija died in 619. Then when Abu Talib died, the prophet's clan lost some of their protection; Muhammad himself even had to take refuge in an orchard. In spirit Muhammad traveled at night from Mecca to Jerusalem, and Moses urged them to pray fifty times a day; but Muhammad got it reduced to five times a day. Muslims began migrating to Medina. In 622 Muhammad was warned of an assassination plot; he hid and then migrated to Medina.

Muhammad respected the Jews for believing in one God; so they were tolerated, and some became Muslims. Muhammad encouraged the Muslims of Mecca and of Medina to embrace each other as brothers. He proved to the Jews that he accepted the law of stoning adulterers. Muhammad himself had more than one wife and married 'A'isha when she was only nine. In Medina he changed the practice of facing Jerusalem in prayer to facing Mecca. From Medina Muhammad began leading raids himself; as the prophet he received a fifth of the spoils, which he distributed to the poor as needed. Muhammad promised his warriors who died fighting the Quraysh that they would enter paradise, and they charged shouting, "God's victors kill." Conflicts with Jews developed, and Muhammad authorized the killing of Jews.

Twice assassins were sent to Muhammad, but he was able to convert both of them. In a battle between the Muslims of Medina and the Quraysh army from Mecca, Muhammad was wounded. He was angry after the defeat, but a revelation warned him to ban mutilation of prisoners. Some of Muhammad's wives died, and he received a revelation that the prophet was allowed to have more than four wives. Other than 'A'isha, all the women he married were widows. Jews joined the anti-Muslim alliance, and the Muslims were besieged at Medina; but the prophet authorized the use of deception in war, keeping the Qurayza out of the alliance. Then the prophet ordered the Muslims to besiege the Qurayza for breaking their treaty.

Muhammad was able to make an unarmed pilgrimage to Mecca in 628 as he gained a truce for ten years, enabling the Muslim community to more than double in the next two years. Muhammad sent messages to the Persian emperor Khusrau, the Byzantine emperor Heraclius and the patriarch at Alexandria. The Persian viceroy Badhan in Yemen was converted when the prophet's messengers correctly informed him that Khusrau had been killed. Muhammad marched against the Khaybar Jews; though outnumbered, the Muslims were able to overcome the Jews a few at a time. The Jews of Khaybar had to surrender half their crops to the Muslims. After a minor infraction of the truce by two Quraysh, a Muslim army of 10,000 attacked Mecca and took over the city as the idols and icons were destroyed. Other towns were attacked by the large Muslim army, and Muhammad announced that slaves who joined the Muslims would be freed. In 630 he sent a Muslim army of 30,000 that included 10,000 cavalry to attack Byzantine Syria, but he made peace treaties with Christian and Jewish communities along the Gulf of 'Aqabah coast. Muhammad sent officials to collect taxes to support the poor. On his last pilgrimage to Mecca the prophet banned pagans from participating. Muhammad married eleven times and died of illness on June 8, 632.

Qur'an means recital and is the sacred book of Islam. Its literary quality is considered especially remarkable since Muhammad himself was probably illiterate. He recited the verses, and then they were memorized and written down by others. Usually God is speaking to humanity, though occasionally the messengers Gabriel and Muhammad speak. In the longest chapter "The Cow" believers are reminded to pray facing Mecca, give charity to the poor, and fast until sunset during the month of Ramadan. After two of the six Muslims, who had memorized the entire *Qur'an*, were killed, Muhammad's successor Abu Bakr (r. 632-634) ordered the written and oral revelations collected together. *Qur'an* reciters were sent out to teach Islam. The caliph 'Uthman (r. 644-656) had been a secretary of Muhammad, and during his reign the *Qur'an* was edited into its final form. The 114 chapters are ordered mostly by decreasing length. These selections are placed in their approximate chronological order.

Notes to:

30: The Roman empire was greatly diminished by Persian conquest almost to its capital at Constantinople, and Jerusalem was captured in 614. Yet Muhammad correctly predicted that the Byzantine empire would rebound within a few years; their counter-invasion climaxed with the defeat of the Persians at Nineveh in 627.

29: Shuaib has been identified as the Midian priest Jethro, whose daughter Zipporah married Moses.

29 and 17: The northern Nabataean tribe of Thamud was descended from the powerful tribe of Ad, mentioned in an inscription by Sargon II when the Assyrians subjected them in 715 BC.

29: Qarun was a follower of Moses.

29: Haman is probably derived from *Ha-Amen*, meaning priest of Amen, and refers to a chief advisor of the Pharaoh Ramses II (1304-1237 BC), who was encountered by Moses.

31: Luqman was associated in the popular imagination with Aesop. The legendary Luqman was celebrated for his spiritual wisdom in the poetry of Ziyad ibn Mu'awiyah writing under the name Nabighah adh-Dhubyani in the 6th century CE.

17: The temple at Jerusalem was captured by the Babylonians in 586 BC, was rebuilt by Jews in 516 BC, but was captured again by the Romans in 70 CE.

17: Iblis is the personal name of the devil in Islam.

Qur'an

1. The Opening

In the name of God, the gracious, the loving:

Praise God, Lord of the universe, the gracious, the loving,
Master of Judgment Day.
We serve only You; we pray only to You for help.
Guide us on the right path,
the path of those whom You have blessed,
not of those who deserve Your anger
nor of those who have gone astray.

93. Bright Morning

In the name of God, the gracious, the loving:

By the bright morning and the darkening night
your Lord has not forsaken you nor does He hate you,
and truly the hereafter will be better for you than the past.
Soon the Lord will give to you so that you will be content.

Did He not find you an orphan and give you shelter
and find you lost and guide you
and find you in need and supply you?

Therefore do not oppress the orphan
nor repulse those who ask
and proclaim the blessings of your Lord.

103. Passing Time

In the name of God, the gracious, the loving:

By passing time humans surely are losing
except those who believe and do good
and encourage each other to be truthful
and encourage each other to be patient.

106. Quraysh

In the name of God, the gracious, the loving:

For the protection of the Quraysh,
secure during their winter and summer trading
let them serve the Lord of this house

who feeds the hungry and gives them security against fear.

112. Sincerity

In the name of God, the gracious, the loving:
  Say: "God is One.
God is the eternal, prime cause.
God produces but has not been produced,
and nothing can be compared to God."

99. The Earthquake

In the name of God, the gracious, the loving:
  When an earthquake shakes,
and the earth brings forth her burdens,
and man asks, "What has happened to her?"
on that day she will report her news;
for her Lord has inspired her.
  On that day people will come forward
in separate groups to be shown their works,
and whoever has done an atom's weight of good shall see it,
and whoever has done an atom's weight of evil shall see it.

90. The Land

In the name of God, the gracious, the loving:
  No, I swear by this land,
and you are a citizen of this land,
and the parent and the child.
Truly we have created man for struggle.
Does he think that no one has power over him?
He says, "I have squandered much wealth."
Does he think no one sees him?
  Have we not given him two eyes and a tongue and two lips
and guided him on the two highways?
Yet he has not attempted the steep road,
and what will teach you what the steep road is?
The freeing of a slave
or giving food on a day of hunger to an orphaned relative
or to a poor person lying in the dust
will make one a believer and will encourage one another

to be patient and compassionate.

Those are the companions on the right side;
but those who disbelieve our communications
are on the wrong side with fire covering them.

68. The Pen

In the name of God, the gracious, the loving:

By the pen and what they write you are not,
by your Lord's grace, possessed.
You will surely have an unfailing reward,
and surely you are of moral character.
So you will see, and they will see which of you is insane.

Surely the Lord knows best who has strayed from His path,
and He knows best those who follow guidance.

So do not obey the disbelievers.
They want you to compromise so they may compromise,
and do not obey every mean swearer, defamer,
going around slandering, hindering the good,
transgressing limits, sinful, violent, and also ignoble,
because he has wealth and sons.
When our messages are recited to him,
he says, "Fables of ancient times."
We shall brand him on the nose.

We shall try them as we have tried the owners of the garden
when they swore they would certainly cut off the produce
in the morning and did not save a portion.
Then came a visitation from your Lord
while they were sleeping,
and in the morning it was dark and barren.
At dawn they called out to one another,
"Go early to your field if you would pick."

So they went, whispering to each other,
"No poor person shall enter your garden today."

And they went early determined in this purpose;
but when they saw it, they said,
"Surely we have gone astray, for we are made destitute."

The best of them said, "Did I not say to you,
'Why do you not glorify?'"

They said, "Glory be to our Lord; surely we were wrong."
Then they turned against each other in reproach.
They said, "Woe to us! We surely were insolent.
Maybe our Lord will give us instead a better one;
for to our Lord we humbly turn for help."
Such is the punishment,
and surely the punishment of the hereafter is greater,
if they only knew!
Surely for the godly will be gardens of bliss with their Lord.
Shall we then make those who surrender like the guilty?
What is the matter with you? How do you judge?
Or do you have a book that you study
in which you find whatever you want?
Or do you have oaths from us
confirming the day of resurrection
that you will have whatever you demand?
Ask them which of them will guarantee that?
Or do they have associates;
let them bring them if they are truthful.
On the day when the bone is laid bare,
they shall be summoned to make obeisance;
but they will not be able.
Their eyes will be downcast; abasement will overwhelm them;
for they had been summoned to make obeisance
while they were whole.
So leave Me with those who reject this message.
We shall overtake them gradually without their perceiving it,
and I shall bear with them; for my plan is firm.
Or do you ask from them a reward
so that they are burdened with debt?
Or is the unseen in their keeping,
that they are writing it down?
So wait patiently for the judgment of your Lord,
and do not be like the companion of the fish
who cried out in distress.
Had not the grace of his Lord reached him,
he surely would have been cast
onto the barren shore in disgrace.
But his Lord chose him and put him among the just.

The disbelievers might well strike you down with their eyes
when they hear the reminder,
and they say, "Surely he is possessed."
But it is nothing less than a reminder to all humanity.

107. Charity

In the name of God, the gracious, the loving:
   Have you considered the one who denies the moral law?
That is the one who repulses the orphan
and does not encourage feeding the poor.
   So woe to those praying who neglect their prayers,
who act to be seen and withhold charity.

76. Man

In the name of God, the gracious, the loving:
   Has there been a long period of time
when humans were not mentioned?
Surely We have created humans
from a small sperm intermingled for testing,
and we made them hearing and seeing.
Surely We have shown them the way,
whether they are grateful or ungrateful;
for We have prepared for the disbelievers
chains, shackles, and blazing fire.
Surely the just will drink of a cup mixed with camphor,
a fountain from which the servants of God will drink,
making it flow forth abundantly.
They fulfill vows and fear a day, whose evil will spread wide,
and they give food for the love of God
to the poor and the orphan and the prisoner.
We only feed you for God's sake;
we want no recompense nor thanks from you.
We only fear from our Lord a stern and distressing day.
Therefore God will guard them from the evil of that day
and will bestow on them brightness and joy
and will reward them because they are patient
with a garden and silk; reclining there on raised couches,
they will find there neither sun nor bitter cold.
And shade will come down over them,

and its fruits will hang down near.
And passed around for them will be vessels of silver
and crystal goblets of glass made of silver,
measured very precisely.
And they will be given to drink there a cup mixed with ginger,
and a fountain there is named "Seek the Way."
There immortal youths wait on them;
when you see them, you will think them scattered pearls.
When you look there,
you will see blessings and a magnificent realm.
Upon them will be green garments of silk and brocade,
and they will be adorned with bracelets of silver,
and their Lord will give them to drink a pure beverage.
Surely this is a reward for you,
and your effort will be recognized.

We ourselves have revealed the *Qur'an* to you in stages.
So be patient for the command of your Lord
and do not obey among them a sinner or a disbeliever,
and remember the name of your Lord morning and evening
and during part of the night pray
and glorify God during the long night.

Surely these love the fleeting life
and put behind them a grievous day.
We created them and strengthened their joints,
and when We will,
We shall replace them with others like them.

Surely this is a reminder;
so whoever will takes a path to one's Lord.
But you will not unless God wills, for God knows and is wise.
God admits into His grace whomever He will;
but for the unjust He has prepared a painful punishment.

75. The Resurrection

In the name of God, the gracious, the loving:
No, I swear by the day of resurrection.
No, I swear by the self-accusing soul.
Do humans think We shall not gather their bones?
Yes, We are able to restore their very fingers.
But humans want to deny what is ahead.

They question, "When is the day of resurrection?"

But when the sight is dazed, and the moon is eclipsed,
and the sun and the moon are brought together,
on that day humans will say, "Where is the refuge?"
No, there will be no place of safety.
With your Lord alone on that day will be the place of rest.
On that day humans will be informed
of what they sent ahead and put off.
No, humans will testify against themselves
although they will make excuses.

Do not move your tongue with it to hurry it.
It is for us to collect it and recite it.
So when We recite it, follow the recitation;
then We shall explain it.

No, but you love the present life and neglect the hereafter.
Faces on that day will be radiant, looking to their Lord,
and some faces on that day will be gloomy,
knowing that some great calamity will be falling on them.

No, when it reaches the throat,
and it is said, "Who is the magician?"
And he is sure that it is the parting,
and agony is combined with agony;
to your Lord on that day you will be driven.

For he did not accept the truth nor did he pray;
but he denied the truth and turned away.
Then he went to his family in arrogance.

Nearer to you and nearer; again nearer to you and nearer.
Does a person think one is left to wander aimlessly?
Was not one a drop of emitted sperm?
Then one was a clot of blood;
so God created and perfected
and made them of two kinds, male and female.
Is God not able to bring the dead to life?

35. The Angels

In the name of God, the gracious, the loving:

Praise God, the Creator of the heavens and the earth,
who made the angels messengers

with wings two, three, and four;
He adds to creation as He pleases,
for God has power over all things.
Whatever mercy God bestows on humanity
no one can withhold,
and what He withholds no one can release.
God is omnipotent and omniscient.

O humans, remember God's grace toward you.
Is there any creator other than God
who provides for you from the heavens and the earth?
There is no deity but God.
How then are you perverted?

And if they call you a liar,
so messengers before you were called liars.
All things return to God.

O humans, surely the promise of God is true;
so do not let the life of this world delude you
nor let deceptive thoughts about God deceive you.
Surely Satan is your enemy; so treat him as an enemy.
He calls his followers,
that they may be companions of the blazing fire.
Those who disbelieve will suffer severely,
and those who believe and do good
will have forgiveness and a great reward.
Is one's evil conduct made alluring so that one thinks it good?
For God lets go astray one who will and guides one who will.
So do not let your soul expire sighing for them;
for God is well aware of what they do.

God is the One who blows the winds that stir up clouds,
and We drive them to a dead country
and so revive the earth after its death;
such is the resurrection.

If you desire glory, to God belongs all the glory.
To Him ascend the good words,
and He exalts the good deeds;
but those who plot evil deeds will suffer severely,
and their plot will come to nothing.

God created you from dust, then from a drop of sperm;
then He made you in pairs,

and no female conceives or gives birth
but with His knowledge.
Nor is anyone granted a long life nor a diminished life
but it is decreed; for this is easy for God.

   Nor are the two bodies of water alike;
one is fresh, sweet, and pleasant to drink,
and the other salty and bitter.
Yet from each you eat fresh fish and extract gems to wear;
and you see the ships plowing the waves
so that you may seek the bounty of God and may be grateful.
He makes the night grow longer by shortening the day,
and He makes the day grow longer by shortening the night.
He has subjected the sun and the moon,
each running the course of its term.
Such is God, your Lord, and sovereignty is His,
and those you call upon besides Him
do not even have the skin on a date-stone.
If you pray to them, they will not hear your call;
and if they did listen, they could not answer you.
On the day of judgment they will disown your partnership.
None can inform like the One who is aware.

   O humans, you are the ones who need God,
while God alone is self-sufficient and worthy of praise.
If He will, he can wipe you out and bring a new generation.
That is not difficult for God.

   A burdened soul cannot bear the burden of another,
and if one weighed down by a burden cries about the load,
none of it can be carried even by a close relative.
You warn only those
who respect their Lord unseen and pray constantly.
Whoever purifies oneself does so only for one's own soul,
and the goal is God.

   The blind and the seeing are not equal,
nor are darkness and the light, nor the shade and the heat,
nor are the living and the dead equal.
God can make anyone He pleases hear;
but you cannot make hear those who are in graves.
You are nothing but a warner.
Surely we have sent you with the truth

as a bearer of good news,
and there never was a people,
but a warner lived among them.
And if they reject you, so did their predecessors;
their messengers came to them with clear arguments,
books of wisdom, and illuminating revelations.
Then I punished the disbelievers
and how awesome was my disapproval!

Do you not see that God sends down rain from the sky,
and then We produce fruit of various colors;
and the mountains are streaked
with white and red of various hues and intense black?
Also people and beasts and cattle are of diverse hues.
Those of His servants with knowledge truly respect God;
for God is powerful and forgiving.

Those who follow the revelations of God, pray constantly,
and spend what We have provided for them,
secretly and openly, hope for gain that will never fail.
For He will pay them their wages
and give them more from His grace;
for He is forgiving and grateful.
The revelation We have inspired in you is the truth,
confirming what came before;
for surely with respect to His servants
God is aware and observant.
Then We gave the revelation as a heritage
to those whom We chose as Our servants;
but some of them wrong themselves;
some of them are lukewarm;
and some of them excel in good works with God's permission;
that is the highest grace.
Gardens of perpetual bliss will they enter;
there they will be adorned with bracelets of gold and pearls,
and their garments will be of silk.
And they will say, "Praise God,
who has removed sorrow from us;
for our Lord is forgiving and grateful,
who has settled us in a home that will last
where no struggle or weariness can afflict us."

But for the disbelievers will be the fire of hell.
It will not be finished with them entirely
so that they should die
nor will the suffering be lightened for them;
thus We pay back all the ungrateful.
There they will cry for help, "Our Lord, release us,
and we shall do good, not what we used to do."

"Did we not give you a life long enough
in order to be mindful to mind?
Also a warner came to you;
therefore taste it, because the unjust have no helper."

Truly God knows the unseen in the heavens and the earth;
surely He is aware of what is in all hearts.
He is the One who made you rulers on the earth;
so whoever disbelieves, the rejection is against themselves;
their disbelief increases the disbelievers
only in hatred in the sight of God;
their disbelief increases the disbelievers only in loss.
Say: "Have you considered your associates
on whom you call apart from God?
Show me what they have created on the earth,
or do they have a share in the heavens?"
Or have We given them a book from which they get clarity?
No, the unjust promise each other only to deceive.

God sustains the heavens and the earth
so that they do not deviate;
and if they were to deviate,
no one could sustain them anymore.
Truly He is most patient and forgiving.

They swore by God the strongest oaths
that if a warner came to them,
they would be guided better than any of the nations;
but when a warner came to them,
it increased nothing but aversion,
behaving arrogantly in the land and plotting evil;
but the evil plots will not trap any but their devisers.
So do they expect anything except the ways of the ancients?
For you will not find any alteration in God's way
nor will you find any change in God's way.

Have they not traveled in the land
and seen the consequences of those before them,
and they were stronger than these in power?
God is not frustrated by anything whatever
in the heavens or on earth,
for He is omniscient and omnipotent.

If God were to punish people as they deserve,
He would not leave a single creature on its back;
but He gives them a reprieve for a set term;
so when their term expires,
then surely God sees His servants.

67. Sovereignty

In the name of God, the gracious, the loving:

Blessed is the One in whose hand is sovereignty
and who can do all things,
who created death and life
in order to test which of you is best in action,
and God is powerful and forgiving,
who created seven heavens one above another.
You see no imperfection in the creation of the Beneficent.
So look again and again,
and your vision returns to you dazzled and exhausted.
And We have adorned the lower heaven with lamps
as missiles for the devils
and have prepared for them burning punishment.

For those who reject their Lord
is the chastisement of hell, a bad end.
When they are thrown in, they will hear it gasping
as it boils, nearly bursting with rage.
Whenever a group is thrown in,
the wardens ask them, "Did no one come to warn you?"

They will reply, "Yes, indeed,
someone did come to warn us."

But we rejected him and said,
"God has not revealed anything; you are merely in great error."

They will also say, "If we had only listened or understood,
we would not have been living in the flames."
Then they will acknowledge their sins,

but those living in the flames will be far away.

Those who respect their invisible Lord
will be forgiven and have a great reward.

Whether you keep your opinion secret or proclaim it,
God knows all hearts.
Does not the One who created know?
Yes, God is subtle and aware.

This is the One who made the earth serviceable to you;
so travel in its regions and eat of its sustenance,
and to God you shall ascend.

Do you feel secure that the One who is in heaven
will not cause you to be swallowed up in an earthquake?
Do you feel secure that the One who is in heaven
will not loose upon you a sandstorm?
Then you shall know about my warning.

Those who have gone before rejected it
and how awesome was My response!

Have they not seen the birds above them
spreading their wings and drawing them in?
Nothing holds them up except beneficent God.
He truly sees everything.
Or who will be a host for you to help you
besides beneficent God?
The disbelievers are only in delusion.
Or who will provide for you
if He were to withhold His sustenance?
Nevertheless they persist in arrogance and rebellion.

Is the one who gropes prone better guided
than the one who walks upright on a straight path?

Say: "This is the One who has created you
and made for you ears and eyes and hearts;
little thanks you give."

Say: "This is the One who multiplied you on the earth
and into whom you will be gathered."

They ask, "When will this promise occur if you are truthful?"

Say: "The knowledge is with God alone; I only warn clearly."

Yet when they see it near,
the faces of the disbelievers will be grieved,

and it will be said, "This is what you were calling for."

Say: "What do you think?
If God destroyed me and those with me,
or has mercy on us;
then who will protect the disbelievers
from a painful punishment?"

Say: "God is good. We believe in God, and in God we trust.
So you will soon know who is clearly in error."

Say: "What do you think?
If in the morning all your water were to vanish underground,
then who would bring you running water?"

30. The Roman Empire

In the name of God, the gracious, the loving:

The Roman empire has been defeated in a land nearby;
but they after their defeat
will be victorious within a few years.
With God is the decision in the past and the future,
and on that day believers will rejoice in the help of God.
He helps whom He pleases, and He is powerful and merciful.

It is God's promise.
The promise of God will not fail,
but most people do not understand.
They know only the appearance of life in this world,
but of the hereafter they are unaware.
Do they not think within themselves?
God did not create the heavens and the earth
and what is between them without truth and a set term.
But most people disbelieve the meeting with their Lord.
Have they not traveled in the land
and seen the result of those before them?
They were stronger than these in power;
they plowed the earth and populated it more than these.
Messengers came to them with clear evidence.
So God did not wrong them, but they wronged themselves.
Then evil was the end of those who did evil,
because they rejected the communications of God
and ridiculed them.

God originates creation, then reproduces it;
then you will return to Him.
On the day when the hour will come,
the guilty will be in despair.
They will have no intercessor among their deities,
and they will reject their deities.
On the day when the hour will come,
on that day they will be sorted.
Then those who believed and did good will enjoy a garden,
and those who disbelieved
and rejected Our communications and the meeting hereafter
will be brought to suffering.

So glory be to God when you enter the evening hour
and when you rise in the morning.
To God belongs praise in the heavens and on earth,
both in the afternoon and at midday.
He brings forth the living from the dead
and brings forth the dead from the living
and revives the earth after her death;
even so you will be brought forth.

And among His wonders is that He created you from dust,
and look, you are wide-ranging humans.
And among His wonders is that He created mates
for you from among yourselves,
that you may recline with them,
and He ordained between you love and mercy.
Truly these are messages for people who think.
And among His wonders is the creation of the heavens
and the earth and the diversity of your languages and colors;
surely these are messages for those with knowledge.
And among His wonders is your sleeping at night or by day
and your questing for His grace;
truly these are messages for people who listen.
And among His wonders He shows you lightning
for fear and for hope and sends down rain from the sky
and with it gives life to the earth after it is dead;
surely these are messages for people who understand.
And among His wonders is that
the heavens and the earth stand firm by His command;
then when He calls you with one call from the earth,

look, you will emerge.

  To Him belongs whoever is in the heavens and on earth;
all obey His will.
He is the One who originates creation, then reproduces it,
and it is easy for Him.
His are the most exalted attributes
in the heavens and the earth,
for He is omnipotent and omniscient.
He sets forth for you a parable relating to yourselves.
Do you have partners among those
whom your right hands possess
to share as equals in the wealth we have given you?
Do you fear them as you fear each other?
Thus do we explain the messages clearly
for people who understand.
No, those who are unjust
follow their low desires without knowledge;
so who can guide those whom God let stray?
They will have no helpers.

  So set your face steadily toward the faith—
God's nature in which He created humanity.
There is no altering God's creation;
that is the right religion, but most people do not understand.
Turn back to Him and respect Him and be constant in prayer
and be not among those with other deities,
those who divide up their religion among sects,
each rejoicing in what is theirs.

  When trouble afflicts humanity,
they call to their Lord, turning back to Him;
then when He gives them a taste of mercy from Himself,
some of them begin to worship other deities,
showing their ingratitude for what We have given them.
Enjoy yourselves, for soon you will know.
Or have we sent down authority to them
which speaks of them worshipping others besides Us?
When we let people taste mercy, they rejoice in it;
but if an evil afflicts them for what their hands have done,
look, they are in despair.
Do they not see that God makes ample provision

or restricted for whom He will?
Truly these are messages for people who believe.
  So give what is due to the close relative,
the needy, and the wayfarer.
This is best for those who seek the face of God,
and these are the successful.
Whatever you loan out at interest
so that it may increase the people's wealth
will not increase with God;
but what you give in charity in seeking the face of God,
these will get compensation multiplied.
  God is the One who created you, then gave you sustenance;
then He will cause you to die, then brings you to life.
Are there any other deities who can do any of this?
Glory be to God,
and may He be exalted above what they associate.
Corruption has appeared on land and sea
because of what human hands have done,
and so He will let them taste some of what they have done
so that they may return.
  Say: "Travel in the land
and see what happened to those who were before you;
most of them worshipped other deities."
So set your face toward the right religion
before the inevitable day comes from God;
on that day they will be divided.
Whoever disbelieves will be responsible for that disbelief,
while those who do good are providing for their own souls,
that He may reward those
who believe and do good from His grace;
for He does not love the disbelievers.
  And among His wonders is that He sends the winds
as heralds of good news, giving you a taste of His mercy,
that the ships may sail by His command
and that you may seek His grace so that you may be grateful.
  Certainly we sent before you messengers to their people,
and they came to them with clear arguments.
Then we gave the punishment to those who were guilty,
and helping the believers is our incumbent duty.

God is the One who sends the winds
so that they raise clouds;
then he spreads them in the sky as He pleases,
and He breaks them up
so that you see the rain pouring down from inside;
then when He causes it to fall
on whom He pleases of His servants, they are joyful
although before it was sent down on them,
they had been in despair.

Look then at the signs of God's mercy,
how He gives life to earth after her death;
truly He will bring the dead to life and can do all things.
If We send a wind, and they see it turn yellow,
they would remain after that disbelievers.

For surely you cannot make the dead to hear,
nor can you make the deaf hear the call
when they turn back and go away.
Nor can you lead the blind out of their error.
You cannot make anyone hear
but those who believe in Our communications
so that they surrender.

It is God who created you in weakness,
then gave you strength after weakness,
then after strength ordained weakness and gray hair.
He creates what He pleases,
and He is omniscient and omnipotent.

On the day when the hour will come,
the guilty will swear that they did not delay but an hour;
thus do they delude themselves.
But those who are given knowledge and faith will say,
"Certainly you delayed by God's decree
until the day of resurrection.
This is the day of resurrection, but you did not know."
So on that day their excuses will not benefit the unjust,
nor will they be allowed to make amends.

Truly we have set forth for people
all kinds of parables in this *Qur'an*.
Yet if you bring them a message,
the disbelievers are sure to say,

"You do nothing but make false claims."
Thus does God set a seal on the hearts
of those who do not understand.
  So be patient; for surely the promise of God is true,
and do not let those whose faith is uncertain
make you unsteady.

42. Counsel

In the name of God, the gracious, the loving:
  Thus does the omnipotent and omniscient God
reveal to you and to those before you.
His is what is in the heavens and on earth,
and He is the highest and greatest.
The heavens may almost tear apart from above them,
and the angels sing the praise of their Lord
and ask forgiveness for those on earth.
Surely God is forgiving and merciful.
And those who take protectors besides Him,
God watches over them,
and you do not have charge over them.
  Thus We have revealed to you an Arabic *Qur'an,*
that you may warn the mother of cities and those around her
and that you may warn of the day of assembly,
of which there is no doubt;
some will be in the garden and some in the blazing fire.
  If God wished, He could have made them one community;
but He admits whom he will to His mercy,
and the unjust have neither protector nor helper.
Or have they taken protectors besides Him?
But God is the protector,
and He gives life to the dead and has power over all things.
On whatever you may differ, the judgment belongs to God.
Such is God, my Lord, in Him I trust and to Him I turn.
The Creator of the heavens and the earth
has made mates for you among yourselves
and mates among cattle too in order to multiply you.
Nothing is like Him; He is the One hearing and seeing.
His are the keys of the heavens and the earth.
He increases and restricts provisions for whom He will;

He is aware of all things.

He has ordained for you the religion
that he commended to Noah
and that We have revealed to you
and that which We commended
to Abraham and Moses and Jesus,
that you should remain steady in religion and not be divided.
Hard for the disbelievers is that to which you call them;
God chooses for Himself whomever He will
and guides to Himself those who repent.

They did not become divided
until after knowledge had come to them
out of envy among themselves.
Had not a word gone forth from your Lord for a stated term,
it would have been decided between them.
And those who inherited the Bible after them
are truly in disquieting doubt about it.

So then go on inviting and pursue the right course
as you are commanded and do not follow their low desires,
but say: "I believe in whatever *Bible* God has revealed,
and I am commanded to do justice between you.
God is our Lord and your Lord;
we have our deeds, and you have your deeds.
Let there be no contention between us and you.
God will bring us together, and to Him is the homecoming."

But those who dispute about God
after He has been acknowledged,
their arguments are futile in the Lord's sight.
Condemnation falls upon them,
and their suffering will be severe.
God is the One who revealed the *Bible*
with truth and the balance.
What will make you realize that perhaps the hour is near?
Those who do not believe in it ask for it quickly,
while those who believe hold it in awe
and know that it is the truth.
Truly those who dispute obstinately about the hour
make a big mistake.

God is gracious to His servants,
providing for whomever He will,
and He is strong and powerful.

Whoever desires the harvest of the hereafter,
We shall give an increase in his harvest.
Whoever desires the harvest of this world, we give him it;
but in the hereafter he has no portion.
Or do they have associates who have prescribed for them
a religion that God has not approved?
Were it not for the word of judgment,
it would have been decided between them,
and surely the unjust will suffer punishment.

You will see the unjust afraid of what they have earned,
and it must fall back on them;
but those who believe and do good
will be in the meadows of the gardens;
they shall have with their Lord whatever they wish;
that is the great grace.
That is the good news God gives to His servants,
who believe and do good deeds.
Say: "I do not ask of you any reward for this
but love for my family,
and whoever earns good, We give an increase of good for that;
for God is forgiving and grateful."

Or do they say, "He has invented a lie about God."?
But if God wills, He could seal your heart.
And God wipes out the lie and proves the truth by His words;
for He is well aware of what is hidden in hearts.
God is the One who accepts repentance from His servants
and pardons evil deeds; He knows what you do.
If God were to enlarge the provision for His servants,
they would surely revolt on earth;
but He sends it down in due measure as He pleases;
for He is aware of and sees His servants.

God is the One who sends down rain
after they have despaired,
and He unfolds His mercy;
He is the protector worthy of praise.
And among His signs

is the creation of the heavens and the earth
and the living beings He has dispersed in both.
He can also gather them together when He will.

Whatever misfortune happens to you
is because of what your hands have earned,
and He pardons much.
Nor can you escape on earth
nor will you have any guardian or helper besides God.

And among His signs
are the ships that sail like mountains on the sea.
If He wills, He can calm the winds
so that they lie still on its back;
surely in this are signs for everyone
who is patient and grateful.
Or He can make them perish for what they have earned;
but He forgives much.
And let those who dispute Our communications
realize they have no refuge.

So whatever you are given
is only a provision of this world's life,
and what is with God is better and more lasting
for those who believe and trust in their Lord.
Those who respond to their Lord and pray constantly
and take counsel among themselves on their affairs
and spend out of what We have given them,
and who when great wrong afflicts them, defend themselves,
the recompense of injury is an equal injury;
but whoever forgives and amends
will have their reward from God,
who does not love the unjust.

But whoever defends oneself after suffering wrong,
against them there is no cause of blame.
The blame is only against those who oppress people
and transgress beyond the laws of justice on earth;
for these will suffer severely.
But whoever is patient and forgiving,
these truly exercise courage.

Whomever God lets go astray has no guardian at all,
and you will see the unjust when they see the punishment,

say, "Is there any way to return?"
And you will see them brought to that,
humbling themselves because of the disgrace,
looking with a furtive glance.

   And those who believe will say,
"Surely the losers are those who lose themselves
and their followers on the day of judgment."
Truly the wrong-doers will have lasting suffering,
and they will have no friends to help them other than God,
and for anyone God lets go astray there is no way.

   Respond to your Lord before the day comes from God
which cannot be avoided.
You will have no refuge on that day
nor will you be able to deny.

   But if they turn away,
We have not sent you to watch over them;
your duty is only to communicate.

   Truly when we let humans taste mercy from Us,
they rejoice in it;
and if some ill happens to them
because of what their hands have done,
then surely humans are ungrateful.

   God's is the dominion over the heavens and the earth.
He creates what he pleases;
He bestows daughters and sons according to His will.
Or He bestows both males and females,
and He leaves barren whom He will;
for He is omniscient and omnipotent.

   It is not for any mortal that God should speak to them
except by inspiration or from behind a veil
or by sending a messenger to reveal
with God's permission what God wills;
for He is highest and wisest.
Thus We have inspired you by our command;
you did not know what the revelation was nor the faith;
but We made it a Light to guide Our servants as We will,
and truly you do guide to the right way:
the way of God, to whom belongs
whatever is in the heavens and whatever is on earth;

truly all things return to God.

29. The Spider

In the name of God, the gracious, the loving:

Do people think that they will be left alone
to say, "We believe," and that they will not be tested?
We certainly tested those before them;
so God will certainly know those who are true,
and He will surely know the liars.
Or do those who do wrong think that they will escape Us?
Bad is their judgment.
Whoever hopes to meet God, God's term is surely coming,
and He hears and knows.

And whoever strives hard does so for their own souls;
for God is self-sufficient and independent of creation.
Those who believe and do good,
We shall most certainly remit their bad deeds,
and We shall most certainly reward them
for the best of what they did.
We have charged humanity with kindness toward parents;
but if they strive to make you associate with Me
that of which you have no knowledge, do not obey them.
You return to me, and I will tell you what you did.
Those who believe and do good,
surely We shall admit them among the just.

Some people say, "We believe in God;"
but when they are persecuted in God's cause,
they mistake the persecution of people for God's punishment.

Then if help comes from your Lord,
they would say, "Surely we were with you."
Does not God know best what is in the hearts of all?
God certainly knows those who believe,
and certainly He knows the hypocrites.

The disbelievers say to the believers,
"Follow our path, and we shall bear your wrongs."
Yet they cannot bear any of their wrongs; surely they are liars.
Certainly they will bear their own burdens
and other burdens with their own,
and on the day of judgment

they will be questioned about their falsehoods.

We sent Noah to his people,
and he remained among them a thousand years less fifty;
but the flood overwhelmed them because they were unjust.
So We delivered him and those with him in the ark
and made it a sign for all peoples.

And Abraham when he said to his people,
"Serve God and respect Him;
that will be best for you if you understand.
You are worshipping idols instead of God
and invent falsehood;
those you serve besides God are not able to provide for you.
Therefore seek to be sustained by God
and serve Him and be grateful to Him;
to Him you will return.
But if you reject this, so did nations before you,
and the duty of the messenger is only to communicate clearly."
Do they not see how God originates creation,
then reproduces it?
Truly that is easy for God.

Say: "Travel in the land
and see how God originated creation;
then God produces the later growth,
for God has power over all things.
He chastises whom He pleases,
and He has mercy on whom He pleases,
and to Him you will be turned back.
You will not escape on earth nor in heaven
nor have you besides God any protector or helper."
Those who disbelieve the messages of God and His meeting
have no hope of My mercy,
and these will suffer punishment.

So there was no answer of his people
except that they said, "Kill him, or burn him."
But God rescued him from the fire.
Truly in this are signs for people who believe.

He said, "You have only taken idols besides God
because of love between you and the life of this world;
then on the resurrection day you will deny one another,

and you will curse one another,
and your home will be the fire,
and you will have no helpers."

But Lot believed in Him and said, "I am fleeing to my Lord,
for He is omnipotent and omniscient."
And We gave them Isaac and Jacob
and caused the prophethood and the *Bible*
to remain among his progeny,
and We gave him his reward in this world,
and in the hereafter he will be among the just.

And Lot then said to his people,
"You commit such indecency
that no people has ever done before you.
Why do you come to men and cut off the highway
and commit evil deeds in your councils?"

But the only answer of his people was that they said,
"Then bring us God's punishment if you speak the truth."

He said, "Help me against these corrupt people."

When Our messengers came to Abraham with the good news,
they said, "We shall destroy the people of this town,
for its people are unjust."

He said, "But Lot is there."

They said, "We are well aware of who is there.
We shall deliver him and his family,
except his wife, who is one of those staying behind."
And when Our messengers came to Lot,
he was troubled on their account, for he felt powerless;
but they said, "Do not be afraid nor grieve;
we shall deliver you and your family,
except your wife, who is one of those staying behind.
For We are going to bring down on the people of this town
a punishment from heaven, because they transgressed."
And We have left an evident sign for people who understand.

To the Midian their brother Shuaib said, "O my people,
serve God, and expect the last day
and do not act corruptly on earth, making mischief."
But they rejected him;
so a severe earthquake overtook them,
and morning found them prostrate in their homes.

Ad and Thamud are apparent to you from their buildings;
Satan made their deeds seem fair to them
and barred them from the way
although they were endowed with intelligence and skill.
    Qarun, Pharaoh, and Haman also,
Moses came to them with clear arguments;
but they behaved arrogantly on earth,
and they could not escape.
So each We punished for his crime;
against some of them We sent a violent storm,
and some of them were overtaken by a blast,
and some of them We cause to be swallowed up by the earth,
and some of them We drowned.
God would never wrong them; but they wronged themselves.
    The parable of those who take guardians besides God
is like the spider that builds a house;
surely the spider's house is the frailest of houses
if they only knew.
God knows whatever they call upon besides Him,
for He is omnipotent and omniscient.
These examples we set before people,
but no one understands them except the wise.
God created the heavens and the earth in truth;
surely in that is a sign for the believers.
    Recite what has been revealed to you of the scripture
and be constant in prayer;
for prayer restrains shameful and unjust actions,
and remember God is the greatest without doubt,
and God knows what you do.
    And do not argue with the people of the *Bible*
except in a better way
unless it is those of them who act unjustly;
then say, "We believe in what has been revealed to us
and in what has been revealed to you.
Our God and your God are One, and to Him we surrender."
    Thus We have revealed to you the scripture,
and those to whom We gave the *Bible* believe in it,
and some of these believe in it,
and no one denies Our revelations except the disbelievers.

And you did not recite any book before this,
nor did you transcribe one with your right hand;
for then those who follow falsehood would have doubted.
No, these are clear communications
in the hearts of those who are granted knowledge,
and no one denies Our revelations except the unjust.

They say, "Why are not signs
sent down upon him from His Lord?"

Say: "The signs are with God,
and I am only a plain warner."
Is it not enough for them that We have revealed to you
the scripture which is recited to them?
Surely in this is mercy and a reminder for people who believe.

Say: "God is sufficient as a witness between me and you;
He knows what is in the heavens and the earth,
and those who trust in vanity and have no faith in God,
these are the losers.
They ask you to hurry the chastisement,
and if a term had not been set,
the chastisement would certainly have come to them,
and truly it will come to them suddenly
when they are not aware.
They ask you to hurry the chastisement;
but hell will encompass the disbelievers.

On the day when the chastisement will cover them
from above them and from below them,
He will say, "Taste what you did."

O My servants who believe, surely My earth is vast;
therefore Me alone should you serve.
Those who believe and do good,
We shall certainly give them a home in the high places
in gardens under which rivers flow, to live there.
How good the reward of the workers,
who persevere patiently and trust in their Lord!

How many are the creatures
who do not carry their provisions?
God sustains them and you; for He hears and knows.

If you ask them who created the heavens and the earth
and subjected the sun and the moon,

they will reply, "God."
Then how are they perverted?
God increases the means of subsistence
for whom He pleases and restricts it;
for God is aware of everything.

   And if you ask them who sends down rain from the sky
and so gives life to the earth after its death,
they will reply, "God."

   Say: "Praise be to God;"
but most of them do not understand.

   The life of this world is nothing but a sport and play,
but the home in the hereafter is life, if they only knew.

   So when they embark in the ships,
they call upon God in sincere devotion to Him;
but when He brings them safely to land,
then they associate others.
Thus they become ungrateful
for what We have given them in their enjoyment;
but they will soon know.
Do they not see that We have a sanctuary secure
while people are snatched away from all around them?
Will they still believe in vanity and reject the grace of God?
Who is more unjust than one who invents a lie against God
or rejects the truth when it comes to him?
Is there not a home in hell for disbelievers?

   But those who strive hard for Us,
We will certainly guide them in Our ways;
for truly God is with those who do good.

31. Luqman

In the name of God, the gracious, the loving:
   These are the revelations of the wise book
for guidance and mercy to those doing good,
who are constant in prayer and give charity.
These follow guidance from their Lord, and they prosper.

   Among people some buy idle tales
to lead astray from God's path without knowledge
and ridicule it; these will suffer humiliation.

When Our messages are conveyed to such a person,
he turns away arrogantly as if he did not hear them,
as if his ears were deaf;
so announce to him grievous suffering.
Those who believe and do good
will have gardens of bliss to live in.
God's promise is true, and He is omnipotent and omniscient.
He created the heavens without pillars as you can see,
and he placed firm mountains on the earth
lest it shake with you,
and He dispersed on it animals of all kinds,
and We sent down water from the sky
and caused growth of every noble kind.
This is God's creation.
Now show me what those others besides Him have created.
No, the unjust are clearly wrong.

  We gave wisdom to Luqman, saying, "Give thanks to God.
Whoever is grateful does so for his own soul,
and whoever is ungrateful,
then surely God is self-sufficient and worthy of praise."

  And when Luqman said to his son, admonishing him,
"O my son, do not associate others with God,
for false worship is the worst wrong,"
and We have charged man about parents—
his mother bore him in straining and travail,
and his weaning is in two years—
saying, "Be grateful to Me and to your parents;
with Me is the goal.
And if they try to make you associate with Me
something of which you have no knowledge,
do not obey them;
keep them company in this world kindly
and follow the way of the one who turns to Me;
then you will return to Me,
and I shall inform you of all you did.

  "O my son, if it is the weight of a grain of mustard seed,
even in a rock or in the heavens or on the earth,
God will bring it forth;
for God understands the finest mysteries and is aware.

O my son, be constant in prayer and practice justice
and forbid what is wrong
and bear patiently whatever happens to you;
for these require courage.
Do not turn your face away from people in contempt
and do not walk proudly on the earth;
for God does not love an arrogant boaster.
Be modest in your bearing and lower your voice,
for the harshest voice is the braying of an ass."

Do you not see that God has subjected for you
all that is in the heavens and on the earth
and lavished on you His blessings, outward and inward?

Yet there are some people who dispute about God
without knowledge nor guidance
nor an enlightening scripture.
When they are told to follow what God has revealed,
they say, "No, we follow what we found from our fathers."
Why? Even if Satan is inviting them to suffer from the fire?

Whoever submits one's whole self to God while doing good
has grasped truly the firmest handle;
for with God is the end of all affairs.
But whoever disbelieves, do not let his disbelief grieve you;
to Us is their return,
and We shall inform them of what they did.
Surely God is well aware of what is in all hearts.
We grant them their pleasure for a little while;
then We drive them into severe suffering.

If you ask them who created the heavens and the earth,
they would answer, "God."

Say: "Praise be to God."
But most of them do not understand.

To God belongs all that is in the heavens and the earth;
truly God is self-sufficient and worthy of praise.
And if all the trees on earth were pens
and the sea ink with seven more seas to add to it,
the words of God could not be exhausted;
for God is omnipotent and omniscient.

Your creation and your uplifting is like but a single soul;
for God hears and sees.

Do you not see that God
makes the night grow longer by shortening the day
and makes the day grow longer by shortening the night,
and has subjected the sun and the moon,
each running its course in its appointed term
and that God is aware of what you do.
That is because God is the truth
and because whatever else they invoke besides Him is false
and because God is the highest and greatest.
Do you not see that ships sail on the sea by the grace of God,
that He may show you of his wonders?
Surely in this are signs
for everyone patient, enduring, and grateful?
When a wave covers them like a canopy,
they call to God, offering Him sincere devotion;
but when He has delivered them safely to land,
some of them stop half-way.
None reject our signs except every ungrateful traitor.

O humans, be conscious of your Lord and fear the day
when no father will give satisfaction for his child
nor will the child give satisfaction for his father.
Surely the promise of God is true;
so do not let the life of this world delude you
nor let deceptive thoughts about God deceive you.

Surely God is the One with knowledge of the hour.
He sends down the rain,
and He knows what is in the wombs.
No one knows what one will earn tomorrow,
and no one knows in what land one will die.
Truly God knows and is aware.

17. The Night Journey

In the name of God, the gracious, the loving:
Glory to the One who carried His servant on a night journey
from the sacred mosque to the remote temple,
whose precincts are blessed,
so that We might show him some of Our signs;
for He is the One who hears and sees.

We gave Moses the *Bible*
and made it a guide for the children of Israel,
saying, "Take no other protector apart from Me."
O descendants of those We bore with Noah,
surely he was a grateful servant.
And we made known to the children of Israel in the *Bible*,
that twice they would do mischief on earth,
and you will behave with great arrogance.
So when the first of the warnings happened,
We sent against you Our servants of terrible warfare,
who went through your homes,
and the warning was fulfilled.
Then we gave you back your turn against them
and aided you with wealth and children
and made a numerous band.
If you do good, you will do good for your own souls;
if you do wrong, it is against yourselves.
So when the second of the warnings happened,
they ravaged you and entered your temple as they had before
so that they might destroy whatever fell under their power.
It may be that your Lord will have mercy on you,
and if you return again, We shall return also,
and We have made hell a prison for the disbelievers.
   Surely this *Qur'an* guides to the way that is most right
and gives good news to the believers who do good,
that they will have a great reward.
And those who do not believe in the hereafter,
We have prepared for them grievous suffering.
   Humans pray for evil as they pray for good,
for humans are apt to be hasty.
We have made the night and the day two signs;
We have obscured the sign of the night
and made the sign of the day enlightening
so that you may seek grace from your Lord,
and that you might know the numbering of years
and the reckoning;
for We have explained everything distinctly.
We have tied every human's destiny to one's neck,
and We shall bring out for one on the day of judgment
a book, which one will find wide open.

"Read your book;
your own soul is sufficient this day
to make an account against you."
  Whoever is guided is only guided for one's own soul,
and whoever goes astray does so for one's own loss.
Nor can anyone bear the burden of another,
nor do We chastise until we send a messenger.
And when we wish to destroy a town,
We command its people who lead easy lives,
but they transgress there;
thus the word proves true against it;
so We completely destroy it.
How many generations have We destroyed after Noah?
For God is adequate at knowing and seeing
the faults of His servants.

  Whoever desires the transitory things,
We readily grant them what We will to whom We will;
then We assign them to hell,
where they will burn, be despised and be rejected.
Whoever desires the hereafter
and strives for it as one should, having faith,
the striving of these is acceptable.
All do We aid, these as well as those,
from the grace of your Lord,
and the grace of your Lord is not confined.
See how We have made some of them to excel others,
and certainly the hereafter is far superior in excellence.

  Do not associate with God any other deity,
or you will sit despised and neglected.
Your Lord has decreed that you shall not serve any but Him
and to be kind to parents.
Whether one or both of them attains old age with you,
do not scorn them nor chide them
but speak to them graciously
and humble yourself gently to them with compassion
and say, "O my Lord, have mercy on them
as they cherished me in childhood."
Your Lord knows best what is in your hearts;
if you are good, then He is forgiving

to those who turn to Him again and again.
And give your relatives their due rights
and to the needy and to the wayfarer,
but do not squander wastefully.
Surely the spendthrifts are the brothers of Satan,
and Satan is ungrateful to his Lord.
But if you turn from them to seek mercy from your Lord
in your hope, then speak to them gentle words.
Do not keep your hand shackled to your neck
nor stretch it out to the utmost reach
lest you become blamed and destitute.
Surely your Lord provides abundant sustenance
for whom He pleases, and He disciplines;
for He knows and sees all His servants.

  Do not kill your children from fear of poverty.
We shall provide sustenance for them and for you;
surely to kill them is a great wrong.
And do not commit adultery,
for it is shameful and an evil path.
Do not kill anyone whom God has made sacred
except for a just cause.
And if anyone is slain unjustly,
we have given his heir authority;
so let him not exceed the just limits in killing, for he is aided.

  Do not come near the property of an orphan,
except to improve it, until he attains maturity
and fulfills the covenant, for the covenant will be questioned.
Give full measure when you measure
and weigh with a true balance;
this is fair and better in the end.
Do not follow that of which you have no knowledge,
for the hearing and the sight and the heart will be questioned.
Do not walk on the earth arrogantly,
for you cannot cut through the earth
nor reach the mountains in height.
The evil of all this is hateful in the sight of your Lord.

  This is the wisdom your Lord has revealed to you.
Do not associate any other deity with God
lest you be thrown into hell, blamed, and rejected.

Then has your Lord preferred to give you sons
and taken for Himself daughters from among the angels?
Surely you are saying a dreadful thing.
We have repeated in this *Qur'an* so that they may be mindful,
but it only increases their aversion.
Say: "If there were deities with Him as they say,
then certainly they would have been able
to seek a way to the Lord of power.
Glory be to Him! He is exalted high above what they say.
The seven heavens and the earth
and all the beings in them extol His glory,
and there is nothing that does not celebrate His praise;
but you do not understand their glorification;
truly He is ever patient and forgiving."

When you recite the *Qur'an*, We place between you
and those who do not believe in the hereafter a hidden barrier;
and We have placed veils on their hearts
and deafness in their ears lest they understand it.
When you mention your Lord alone in the *Qur'an*,
they turn their backs in aversion.
We know best why they listen when they listen to you,
and when they conspire secretly, the unjust say,
"You are only following a man bewitched."
See what similes they strike for you;
thus have they gone astray and cannot find the way.

They say, "After we have become bones and dust,
shall we really be raised up as a new creation?"

Say: "Become stones or iron
or some other created thing that in your minds is too hard."

Then they will say, "Who will bring us back?"

Say: "The One who created you at first."

Then they will shake their heads at you
and say, "When will it be?"

Say: "Maybe it will be soon.
On the day when He will call you,
then you will answer praising Him,
and you will think that you have delayed but a little while."

Say to My servants that they should speak what is best,
for Satan stirs up discord between them.

Your Lord knows you best;
He will have mercy on you if He pleases,
or He will chastise you if He pleases.
We have not sent you to be their guardian.
And your Lord knows best
all who are in the heavens and on earth.
We have preferred some prophets over others,
and We gave to David the *Psalms*.

  Say: "Call on those whom you assert besides Him;
they have no power to remove your troubles from you
nor to change them."
Those whom they call upon
desire the means to come to their Lord,
even those who are nearest,
and they hope for His mercy and fear His chastisement;
for surely your Lord's chastisement is something to beware of.
There is no town, but We shall destroy it
before the day of judgment or chastise it with severe suffering;
this is written in the decree.

  Nothing could prevent Us from sending the signs
except that the ancient people denied them.
We sent the she-camel to Thamud as a visible portent,
but they treated her wrongly;
We only send the signs to frighten.

  And when We said to you,
"Surely the Lord encompasses humanity,
and We ordained the vision which We showed you
but as a trial for humans as also the cursed tree in the *Qur'an*.
We frighten them, but it only adds to their great insolence."

  And when We said to the angels,
"Make obeisance to Adam."
They made obeisance, except Iblis.

  He said, "Shall I make obeisance to him
whom You created from dust?"

  He said, "Do you see this one
whom You have honored above me?
If you will give me a respite until the day of judgment,
I shall surely master his descendents except a few."

He said, "Go, and whoever follows you,
surely hell will be your recompense, an ample recompense.
Entice whomever you can with your voice;
make assaults on them with your cavalry and your infantry;
share with them wealth and children,
and make promises to them.
Yet Satan makes no promises but to deceive.
As for My servants, you have no authority over them."
Your Lord is sufficient as a protector.

Your Lord is He who speeds the ships for you on the sea,
that you may seek His grace;
for He is ever merciful to you.
When distress afflicts you at sea,
those you call upon besides Him fail;
but when He brings you safely to land, you turn away;
for man is ever ungrateful.
Do you then feel secure
that He will not cause a tract of land to engulf you
or send against you a sandstorm?
Then you will find no protector for yourselves.
Or do you feel secure
that He will not send you back a second time
and send against you a fierce gale to drown you
because of your ingratitude?
Then you will not find any helper against Us.

We have honored the children of Adam,
and We carry them on land and sea
and provide them with good things
and have preferred them over many of those We created.
One day We shall summon all human beings with their leaders;
those who are given their record in their right hand will read it,
and they will not be dealt with in the least unjustly.
Whoever is blind in this world will be blind in the hereafter
and will stray even further from the way.
And their purpose was to tempt you away
from what We have revealed to you,
that you might invent something else against us,
and then they would certainly have accepted you as a friend.
And had We not given you strength,
you would nearly have inclined toward them a little.

Then We certainly would have made you
taste double in this life and double after death;
then you would not have found any helper against Us.
Their purpose was to scare you off the land
in order to expel you;
but in that case they would not have stayed after you
except for a little while.
Such was the way with the messengers We sent before you,
and you will not find a change in Our ways.

  Be constant in prayer from sunset until darkness
and in the recitation at dawn;
for the dawn recitation is witnessed.
And pray during part of the night
an additional prayer for you;
maybe your Lord will raise you to a glorious position.
Say: "My Lord, let me enter in a true and sincere way
and let me go out in a true and sincere way
and grant me from Your grace helpful power."

  And say: "The truth has come, and falsehood has vanished;
for falsehood is bound to vanish."

  We send down in the *Qur'an*
that which is a healing and a mercy to the believers,
while it only adds to the loss of the unjust.
Yet when We bless man,
he turns away and proudly keeps aloof;
but when ill afflicts him, he despairs.
Say: "Everyone acts according to one's disposition;
but your Lord knows best who is best guided on the way."

  They ask you about the soul.
Say: "The soul is at the bidding of my Lord,
and you are given only a little knowledge."
If it were Our will,
We could take away what We have revealed to you;
then you would not find any protector against Us,
except for mercy from your Lord;
for His grace to you is great.

  Say: "If all humans and spirits combine together
to produce the like of this *Qur'an*,
they could not produce anything like it

though they helped each other."
And We have explained for humans in this *Qur'an*
every kind of similitude;
yet most people refuse anything but disbelief.

  They say, "We shall not believe you
until you cause a fountain to gush forth from the earth for us,
or you have a garden of palms and grapes
in which rivers flow abundantly,
or you cause the sky to fall in pieces as you asserted,
or you bring God and the angels face to face,
or you have a house of gold,
or you ascend into heaven,
and we shall not believe in your ascending
until you bring down to us a book we can read."

  Say: "Glory to my Lord!
Am I anything but a mortal messenger?"

  Nothing prevented people from believing
when the guidance came to them except that they said,
"Has God sent a mortal to be a messenger?"

  Say: "If there had been on earth angels walking in peace,
We would have sent down to them from heaven
an angel as a messenger."

  Say: "God is a sufficient witness between me and you;
for He is aware of His servants and sees."

  Whomever God guides, follows the right way,
but for those whom He lets stray
you will not find any protector besides Him.
On the day of judgment We shall gather them together
on their faces, blind and dumb and deaf;
their home will be hell;
whenever it abates, We shall increase the flames.
That is their requital,
because they rejected Our messages
and said, "When we have become bones and dust,
shall we really be raised up in a new creation?"

  Do they not see that God,
who created the heavens and the earth,
is able to create their like,
and He has appointed for them

a term about which there is no doubt?
But the unjust refuse anything but disbelief.
  Say: "If you controlled the treasures of my Lord's mercy,
then you would withhold them from fear of spending;
for humans are ever stingy."
  To Moses we did give nine clear signs;
so ask the children of Israel.
When he came to them, Pharaoh said to him,
"Moses, I think you are a sorcerer."
  He answered, "You know well
that the Lord of the heavens and the earth
has sent down these as clear evidence,
and I consider you, O Pharaoh, to be lost."
  So he resolved to wipe them off the earth;
but We drowned him and those with him all together.
And We said to the children of Israel after him,
"Dwell in the land."
But when the second of the warnings occurred,
We gathered you together from various nations.
  We have revealed the truth, and in truth it has come down;
and We have sent you
only to give the good message and to warn.
The *Qur'an* We have divided
so that you may recite it to people at intervals;
We have revealed it in stages.
Say: "Whether you believe in it or not,
those who were given the knowledge before,
when it is recited to them, fall down on their faces in humility,
saying 'Glory to our God!
Truly the promise of our Lord has been fulfilled.'"
They fall down on their faces in tears,
and it increases their humility.
  Say: "Call upon God or call upon the merciful;
whatever name you call upon, He has the best names.
Do not speak the prayer loudly nor too softly,
but follow a way between these."
  Say: "Praise be to God, who has not taken a son
and who has no partner in the sovereignty
nor has He any protector from humiliation,

and extol his infinite greatness."

64. Loss and Gain

In the name of God, the gracious, the loving:

All that is in the heavens and on earth glorifies God,
Who is sovereign, worthy of praise, and all-powerful.
God created you, disbeliever and believer,
and God sees all you do.
God created the heavens and the earth with truth
and has shaped you well, and God is the final goal.
God knows all that is in the heavens and on earth,
and God knows what you conceal and reveal.
God is aware of what is in your hearts.

Have you not heard the story
of those who disbelieved before?
They tasted the bad results of their actions,
and they will suffer punishment.
That is because
their messengers came to them with clear evidence;
but they said, "Shall mortals be our guides?"
So they disbelieved and turned away,
and God had no need of them,
being self-sufficient and glorious.

The unbelievers think they will never be raised again.
Say, "Yes, my Lord will raise you up again,
and you will be informed of all you did;
that is easy for God."

Therefore believe in God and God's messenger
and in the Light which we have revealed.
God is aware of all you do.

The day when God will gather you for a day of assembly
will be a day of loss and gain.
Whoever believes in God and does good
will have their ills removed,
and He will admit them into gardens under which rivers flow
to live there forever;
that is the supreme achievement.

But those who disbelieve and deny our revelations
will be companions of fire and live there forever, a bad end.
No affliction occurs that is not allowed by God.
Whoever believes in God, their hearts will be guided,
for God knows everything.
   Obey God and obey the messenger;
but if you turn away,
the duty of our messenger is to communicate clearly.
   God—there is no deity but God,
and so let the believers trust in God.
   O believers, among your wives and children
are your enemies;
therefore beware of them.
If you pardon, overlook, and forgive,
surely God is forgiving and merciful.
Your wealth and your children are only a test,
but in God is the greatest reward.
Therefore revere God as best you can;
listen and obey and give charity to benefit your own soul.
Whoever is saved from their own greed will prosper.
If you lend to God a good loan,
God will double it for you and forgive you;
for God is grateful and kind,
knower of the unseen and seen, powerful and wise.

65. Divorce

In the name of God, the gracious, the loving:
   O Prophet! When you divorce women,
divorce them after the prescribed time.
Count the interval and respect God, your Lord.
Do not expel them from their houses
nor shall they leave unless they committed flagrant immorality.
These are God's limits.
Whoever transgresses God's limits
has wronged one's own soul.
You do not know that
God may later bring about a new relationship.
So when they have fulfilled the prescribed time,
either take them back in kindness

or separate from them in kindness,
and call together two people of justice from among you
and give correct testimony before God.
Whoever believes in God and the last day
is admonished to do this.
For whomever respects God, God will find a way out,
and God provides from where one could never imagine.
  Whoever trusts in God finds God to be sufficient.
For God attains His purpose;
God has set a measure for everything.
  For those women who have passed the age of menstruation,
if you are in doubt,
the prescribed time shall be three months,
as it is for those who have not yet had their period.
For pregnant women the prescribed time
is until they deliver their burden.
For those who respect God, God will make this easy.
That is the command of God that God has revealed to you,
and whoever respects God,
God will remove their ills and enlarge their rewards.
Let the women live where you live according to your means
and do not bother them in order to straighten them;
and if they are pregnant,
spend on them until they deliver their burden;
and if they suckle for you, give them compensation
and consult together in order to do good.
But if you find yourselves in difficulties,
let another woman suckle for him.
Let the wealthy person spend from the wealth,
and whosoever means are limited
may spend according to what God has given him.
God puts no burden on any person
beyond what God has given one.
After hardship God will bring about relief.
  How many peoples have rebelled
against the commands of their Lord and God's messengers,
and did we not call them
to severe account with stern chastisement?
Then they tasted the bad results of their actions,

and the consequence of their conduct was loss.
God prepared for them severe chastisement.
Therefore respect God, o people of understanding.

  Believers, God has sent you a reminder, a messenger,
who recites to you clear explanations of God,
that God may bring forth those
who believe and do good deeds from darkness into light.
Whoever believes in God and does what is right
God will admit to the gardens under which rivers flow
to live there forever.
God has given them good sustenance.

  God is the One who created seven heavens
and similarly for the earth.
The decree descends among them
so that you may know that God has power over all things
and that God comprehends all knowledge.

61. The Ranks

In the name of God, the gracious, the loving:

  All the heavens and the earth glorify God,
who is omnipotent and omniscient.
O you who believe, why do you say what you do not do?
It is very hateful to God that you say what you do not do.
Surely God loves those who fight for His cause in ranks
as if they were a solid building.

  And remember Moses said to his people,
"O my people, why do you disappoint me
though you know I am God's messenger to you?"
When they went astray, God made their hearts turn away;
for God does not guide transgressors.

  And remember Jesus, son of Mary, said, "O children of Israel,
I am the messenger of God to you, verifying the previous law
and giving good news of a messenger who will come after me,
whose name will be praised."

  Yet when he came to them with clear evidence,
they said, "This is plain magic."
Who is more unjust than the one who invents lies about God
when one is being called to surrender?
And God does not guide the unjust.

They want to extinguish the Light of God with their mouths;
but God will perfect His Light
though disbelievers may be averse.

O believers, shall I direct you to a bargain
that will save you from a grievous penalty?
You shall believe in God and His messenger
and struggle in God's way
with your property and your persons;
that is better for you, if you only knew.
God will forgive you your faults
and admit you into gardens under which rivers flow
and to beautiful mansions in eternal gardens;
that is the supreme achievement;
and other things you love, help from God and a quick victory;
so give the good news to believers.

O believers, be helpers of God,
as Jesus, son of Mary, asked the disciples,
"Who will be my helpers for God?"

The disciples said, "We are helpers for God."
So some of the children of Israel believed,
and some disbelieved.
Then We strengthened those who believed
against their enemies, and they became masters.

66. Forbidding

In the name of God, the gracious, the loving:

O Prophet! Why do you forbid
what God has made lawful for you,
seeking to please your wives?
God is forgiving and merciful.

God has already sanctioned for you absolution from oaths.
God is your protector, omniscient and wise.

When the Prophet confided a secret to one of his wives,
and she then divulged it, God made it known to him;
he disclosed some of it and passed over some of it.
So when he informed her of it,
she asked, "Who told you this?"

He said, "The wise omniscient one informed me."
If you both turn to God in repentance,
as your hearts are inclined, you will be pardoned;
but if you back up each other against him,
God is his protector, and Gabriel and the good believers,
and the angels too are his helpers.

It may be that if he divorces you,
God will give him in your place better wives than you,
who submit, believe, obey, repent,
and are devout and fasting widows or virgins.

O you believers, save yourselves and your families
from a fire whose fuel is people and stones,
over which are strong and severe angels,
who do not disobey the commands they receive from God.
O you disbelievers, do not make excuses today;
you are only being paid off for what you did.
O you believers, turn to God in sincere repentance.
It may be that your Lord will remove from you your ills
and admit you to gardens under which rivers flow.

On that day God will not shame the Prophet
and those who believe with him.
Their Light will shine before them and on their right hands;
they will say, "Our Lord, perfect our Light for us
and forgive us, You who have power over all things."

O Prophet! Strive hard against the disbelievers
and the hypocrites, and be firm with them.
Their home is hell, a bad refuge.

God has set an example for the disbelievers
in Noah's wife and Lot's wife,
who were under two good servants but betrayed them;
they will be no avail against God,
and it was said, "Enter the fire with those who enter."

God has set an example for the believers in Pharaoh's wife
when she said, "Build for me a house with You in the garden
and deliver me from Pharaoh and his doing
and deliver me from the people doing wrong."
And Mary, the daughter of Imran, guarded her chastity;
so We breathed into her Our Spirit,
and she accepted the truth

of her Lord's words and His books,
and she was one of the devout.

57. Iron

In the name of God, the gracious, the loving:

All the heavens and the earth glorify God,
who is omnipotent and omniscient.
God has dominion over the heavens and the earth;
God gives life and causes death,
and He has power over all things.
God is the first and the last, the outward and the inward,
and He is aware of all.
God is the One who created
the heavens and the earth in six eons,
and He is established in power.
God knows all that enters the earth
and what comes forth out of it
and what descends from heaven and what ascends to it.
And He is with you wherever you are,
and God sees what you do.
His is the dominion over the heavens and the earth,
and all matters return to God.
He makes the night grow longer by shortening the day,
and He makes the day grow longer by shortening the night;
and he is aware of what is in hearts.

Believe in God and His messenger
and spend what He has entrusted to you;
for those who believe and spend will have a great reward.
What reason do you have for not believing in God
since the messenger is calling you to believe in your Lord,
and he has made a covenant with you, if you are believers?
God is the One who sends down
to His servant clear communication
that he may bring you out of darkness into light.
Truly God is kind and merciful to you.
What reason do you have that you do not spend in God's way
since to God belongs the heritage of the heavens and the earth?
Not equal are those who spent and fought before the victory.
They are more exalted

than those who spent and fought afterwards;
but God has promised good to all,
and God is aware of what you do.
Who is there that will lend to God a good loan
so that He will double it for him,
and he will have a generous reward?

On that day you will see the faithful men and women
with their Light shining before them and on their right.
Good news for you this day:
gardens under which rivers flow to live in forever;
that is the supreme achievement.
On that day when the hypocritical men and women
say to the faithful, "Wait for us,
that we may borrow from your Light."

It shall be said, "Return and seek Light."
Then separating them will be a wall with a door;
on the inside of it is mercy,
and on the outside of it is suffering.

They will call out to them, "Were we not with you?"

They will say, "Yes, but you fell into temptation
and hesitated and doubted,
and vain desires deceived you
until the command of God occurred,
and the deceiver deluded you about God.
So today no ransom will be accepted from you
nor from those who disbelieved;
your home is the fire;
that is your friend and your evil refuge."

Is it not time for the hearts of the believers to be humble
in remembering God and the truth which has been revealed?
And that they should not be like those
who were given the *Bible* before,
and their time was so prolonged that their hearts hardened,
and many of them transgressed.
Know that God revives the earth after it was dead.
We have communicated clearly to you
so that you may understand.
Surely the charitable men and women
who gave God a good loan will have it doubled for them,

and they will have a generous reward.
And those who believe in God and His messengers
are the truthful and faithful ones in the sight of their Lord.
They will have their reward and their Light;
but those disbelieving who reject our communications
are the inmates of hell.

Know that the life of this world is only
play and amusement and a show
and boasting among yourselves
and rivalry in wealth and children,
like the rain that causes vegetation to grow,
pleasing the farmers;
then it withers, and you see it turn yellow;
then it dries up and crumbles away.
But in the hereafter is a severe punishment
and forgiveness from God and good pleasure,
while the life of this world is nothing but enjoying delusion.
Vie with one another for forgiveness from your Lord
and for a garden that is as extensive as heaven and earth,
prepared for those who believe in God and His messengers;
that is the grace of God
which He gives to whomever he pleases,
and God is the Lord of abundant grace.

No disaster can happen on earth nor in yourselves
unless it is decreed before We bring it into existence;
that is very easy for God
so that you may not grieve for what escapes you
nor rejoice in what is given you;
for God does not love proud boasters,
such as those who are stingy and encourage avarice in people;
and whoever turns away,
then truly God is self-sufficient and praiseworthy.

Certainly we sent Our messengers with clear arguments
and sent down with them the *Bible*
and the balance so that people may act with justice;
and We have given iron in which is great violence
as well as benefits for humanity,
and so that God may know
who helps Him and His messengers though unseen;

surely God is strong and powerful.
And we sent Noah and Abraham
and established in their line prophecy and revelation
so that some of them are rightly guided,
but many of them are transgressors.

Then We sent Our messengers following in their footsteps,
and afterwards We sent Jesus, son of Mary,
and gave him the good message,
and We put in the hearts of those who followed him
kindness and mercy;
and they invented monasticism,
which We did not prescribe for them,
only seeking God's pleasure;
but they did not observe it as it should be observed.
So we gave to those who believed their reward,
but many of them are transgressors.

O you who believe, remain conscious of God
and trust in His messenger.
He will give you double His grace
and shine a Light where you will walk and forgive you.
God is forgiving and merciful
so that the followers of the *Bible* may know
that they do not control any of the grace of God,
and that grace is in God's hand to give to whom He pleases,
and God is the Lord of abundant grace.

110. Help

In the name of God, the gracious, the loving:

When God's help and victory comes,
and you see people entering the religion of God in crowds,
then celebrate the praise of your Lord and ask His forgiveness;
for He always returns to love.

This *Wisdom Bible* is dedicated to the following propositions:

Every person has the right to know the truth.
The truth can be perceived from many points of view.
No religion is higher than the truth.
Ultimate truth is the spiritual reality often called God.
The truth is imperfectly understood by the mind.
The being, who uses the mind, is the soul.
The soul is one with God and a spark of divine fire.
All souls are eternal beings and return to God.
Only God is infinite and truly wise.
Using the mind, the soul can develop some wisdom.
Wisdom comes from knowing the truth and practicing it.
Everyone loves and pursues what one believes is good.
The wise understand and act for the good of all.
Acting for the good of all is better than acting selfishly.
Wise human relations are based on justice for all.
Peace and loving human relations depend on justice.
Practicing wise action for the good of all takes courage.
Courage is often based on faith in God.
Knowing you are eternal helps remove the fear of death.
Hatred and violence do not defeat hatred and violence.
Love is more powerful than hatred and violence.
Because God exists, ultimately love will triumph.
Humans learn to love by being loved.
Humans are given freedom in order to learn wisdom.
Freedom is enhanced by inner self-mastery.
All experience is education for the soul and its mind.
True philosophy is loving wisely.
True religion is uniting with God and loving God in all.
The best ethic is loving others as you love yourself.
Enlightenment is found in the divine Light of the soul.
There are as many spiritual paths as there are souls.
May all persons realize their oneness in Spirit.
May wisdom, love, and peace increase in humanity.
May God's will be done among humanity with wisdom.

Sanderson Beck
san.beck.org